Constructing Cultures Then and Now

Celebrating Franz Boas and the

Jesup North Pacific Expedition

Vancouver International Airport in Vancouver, B.C., greets passengers with two "Welcome Figures" created by Salish artist Susan Point (1996). Photograph courtesy Bill McLennan.

Constructing Cultures Then and Now

Celebrating Franz Boas and the Jesup North Pacific Expedition

LAUREL KENDALL AND IGOR KRUPNIK, EDITORS

Published by the
Arctic Studies Center
National Museum of Natural History
Smithsonian Institution
Washington, D.C.

ISBN   0-9673429-4-5

Library of Congress Cataloging-in-Publication Data

Constructing cultures then and now : celebrating Franz Boas and the
Jesup North Pacific Expedition / Laurel Kendall and Igor Krupnik,
editors.
    p. cm. — (Contributions to circumpolar anthropology ; 4)
Revisions of papers originally presented at the conference
"Constructing Cultures Then and Now: Celebrating Franz Boas and the
Jesup North Pacific Expedition" held at the American Museum of Natural
History, New York City, in 1997.
Includes bibliographical references.
  ISBN 0-9673429-4-5 (pbk. : alk. paper)
  1. Jesup North Pacific Expedition (1897-1902). 2. Ethnological
expeditions—Russia (Federation)—Siberia—History. 3. Ethnological
expeditions—Northwest Coast of North America—History. 4. Boas, Franz,
1858-1942. 5. Ethnology—Russia (Federation)—Siberia. 6. Indians of
North America—Northwest Coast of North America—Social life and
customs. 7. Siberia (Russia)—Social life and customs. 8. Northwest
Coast of North America—Social life and customs. I. Kendall, Laurel.
II. Krupnik, Igor. III. Arctic Studies Center (National Museum of
Natural History). IV. Series.
  GN635.S5C65 2003
  305.8'00957—dc22
                        2003015439

∞The paper used in this publication meets the minimum requirements of the American National Standard
for Information Sciences—Permanence of Paper for Printed Library Materials.

Technical editor: Kathryn A. Malm
Cover and series design: Anya Vinokour
Production editors: Iris Hahn and Elisabeth Ward
Printed by United Book Press, Inc., Baltimore, MD

This publication is Volume 4 in the Arctic Studies Center series, *Contributions to Circumpolar Anthropology*, produced by the Arctic Studies Center, National Museum of Natural History, Smithsonian Institution.

THIS SERIES IS MADE POSSIBLE IN PART BY THE JAMES W. VANSTONE (1925–2001) ENDOWMENT

Front cover: *Franz Boas posing for exhibit group displaying Canadian Eskimo clothing and harpoon (AMNH 3220)*

Back cover: *An elderly Chukchi lady and her granddaughter in front of the traditional Chukchi skin tent erected for the local festival in the town of Tavaivaam, Chukotka, Russia. Photographer, Igor Krupnik, 1996*

contents

Part One | 100 Years of Jesup: The Intellectual Legacy of the Jesup Expedition

Part Two | Anthropologies and Histories: Jesup Participants Then and Now

Part Three   People, Animals, and Land: A Jesup Theme Revisited

Part Four   Curators, Collectors, and Consumers

contributors

Sergei A. Arutiunov works at the Institute of Ethnology and Anthropology in Moscow as Chair of the Department of the Peoples of the Northern Caucasus. He is a leading Russian expert in ethnology of the Russian North and Far East, as well as a specialist on Japan and South Asia, the archaeology of the Bering Sea region, and Eskimo art. During the 1980s, he was the Russian team leader for the *Crossroads of Continents* exhibit project.

Nora Marks Dauenhauer was born in Juneau, Alaska. She is internationally recognized for her fieldwork, translation and explication of Tlingit oral literature. From 1983 to 1997, she was Principal Researcher in Language and Cultural Studies at Sealaska Heritage Foundation in Juneau. She is married to Richard Dauenhauer, with whom she has co-authored several volumes of Tlingit language and folklore material.

Richard Dauenhauer, born and raised in Syracuse, NY, has lived in Juneau, Alaska since 1969. Much of his professional work has focused on applied folklore and linguistics in the study, materials development, and teacher training in Alaska Native languages and oral literature. From 1983 to 1997, he was Director of Language and Cultural Studies at Sealaska Heritage Foundation, Juneau.

Don E. Dumond is Professor Emeritus of Anthropology and Director Emeritus of the Museum of Natural History at the University of Oregon, Eugene. For more than forty years he has focused on archaeological fieldwork in southwestern Alaska. He has written widely on the prehistory of Alaska.

William W. Fitzhugh is Director of the Arctic Studies Center and Curator at the Department of Anthropology, National Museum of Natural History, Smithsonian Institution, in Washington, DC. His interests include circumpolar prehistory and archaeology, maritime adaptations, and culture contacts. He has organized several special exhibit projects such as *Inua*; *Crossroads of Continents*; *Ainu*; and *Vikings*.

Ruth S. Freed is a Research Associate in the Division of Anthropology at the AMNH in New York. With Stanley A. Freed, she has co-authored papers on the Washoe, Mohave, and Navajo as well as on the Jesup Expedition (also with Laila Williamson). She has taught at New York University and Seton Hall University.

Stanley A. Freed is Curator Emeritus in the Division of Anthropology at the AMNH in New York. A staff member at the AMNH since 1960, he was in charge of North American ethnology. He has helped to create or renovate a number of permanent and temporary exhibitions dealing with the Northwest Coast, the Arctic, the Plains, and the Eastern Woodlands.

Nelson H.H. Graburn is Professor of Anthropology at the University of California, Berkeley and Curator of North America at the Phoebe Hearst Museum. He has published extensively on art and culture in the North, on the anthropology of tourism, and the anthropology of Canada and of Japan.

Robert S. Hoffmann is Curator Emeritus at the National Museum of Natural History, Smithsonian Institution in Washington, DC, and specializes in adaptation and evolutionary biology of northern land mammals. Formerly the

Director of NMNH and Provost of the Smithsonian, he has worked closely with North American, Russian, Mongolian, and Chinese colleagues in the circumpolar and North Pacific regions.

Koichi Inoue is Professor of Ethnology at the Slavic Research Center of Hokkaido University in Sapporo, Japan. He specializes in the ethnology of indigenous peoples of Siberia and of Northern Eurasia, in general. He did extensive fieldwork in the Russian Far East and Siberia. His current research interests include indigenous reindeer economies; theory of ethnos; and the life and work of Bronislaw Pilsudski.

Vladimir Kh. Ivanov-Unarov (1937–2000) was one of the leading Sakha/Yakut scholars of the cultures of northern minority peoples of the Sakha Republic/Yakutia. He was a Department Chair in the Institute of the Problems of the Minority Peoples of the North in Yakutsk, Sakha Republic, Russia. Between 1992–97 he worked on Jochelson's Yakut, Yukagir, and Even collections at the American Museum of Natural History in New York, and he initiated a recent Russian translation of Jochelson's monograph on the Yukagir (1926).

Zinaida I. Ivanova-Unarova is a professor at Yakutsk University in Yakutsk, Sakha Republic, Russia. Originally from a northern Sakha village, she has written extensively on women master artists and on shamanic influences in Siberian Native art. She authored several books on Sakha art and worked with her late husband, Vladimir Ivanov-Unarov, on the Jesup Expedition collections in New York.

Ira Jacknis is Research Anthropologist at the Phoebe Hearst Museum of Anthropology, University of California at Berkeley. His research interests include the art and culture of the Native peoples of Western North America, the history of anthropology, museums, and photography. He is the author of *The Storage Box of Tradition: Kwakiutl Art, Anthropologists, and Museums, 1881-1981* (2002).

Aldona Jonaitis, is Director of the University of Alaska Museum. Prior to her current position, she was Vice President for Public Programs at the American Museum of Natural History. She has taught at the University of Alaska Fairbanks, SUNY at Stony Brook, and Columbia University. She has authored numerous books, papers, and publications and exhibit catalogs on Northwest Coast Native art.

Sergei Kan is Professor of Anthropology and Native American Studies at Dartmouth College in Hanover, NH. Most of his publications deal with Tlingit culture and the history of Russian Orthodox Christianity in southeastern Alaska. Recently he has been writing a book about Russian anthropologist Lev Shternberg discussing Shternberg's relationships with Franz Boas and other members of the Jesup Expedition.

Laurel Kendall is Curator of Asian Ethnographic Collections at the American Museum of Natural History. She is best known for her writing on shamans, ritual life, and gender issues in Korea. Kendall was Project Director for the AMNH Jesup Centenary celebration and co-editor of a catalog of the photographs of the Jesup Expedition, *Drawing Shadows to Stone* (1997), with Barbara Mathé and Thomas Ross Miller.

David Koester is a cultural anthropologist at the University of Alaska Fairbanks and a specialist in the peoples of the circumpolar North. His publications, based on long-term fieldwork in Iceland and Kamchatka, Russia, have focused on the ideological, social and material mechanisms associated with socio-cultural change and continuity.

Michael E. Krauss is the former director of the Alaska Native Language Center, University of Alaska Fairbanks. He is a leading specialist in the preservation and survival of the Native languages of Alaska, Siberia, and the circumpolar area. His latest contributions include a detailed map of Native language areas for the Inuit-Yupik-Aleut Region and a report on the status of indigenous languages of the North for UNESCO.

Igor Krupnik, Arctic Ethnologist at the Arctic Studies Center, Smithsonian Institution in Washington, DC, is currently coordinator of various international projects studying the impacts of global climate change and the preservation of cultural heritage and ecological knowledge of Native peoples. He writes extensively on Arctic peoples, modernization, and minority issues.

Molly Lee holds a joint appointment at the University of Alaska Fairbanks as Curator of Ethnology at the University of Alaska Museum and Professor of Anthropology. She has written extensively on indigenous basketry and art in the North, including most recently *Eskimo Architecture* (2003), with Gregory A. Reinhardt.

Stephen Loring is Museum Anthropologist with the Arctic Studies Center, Smithsonian Institution in Washington, DC. In addition to caring for the Arctic and Sub-arctic collections, he facilitates access to the collections for visiting indigenous researchers and promotes Native community interests. He has conducted archaeological and ethnohistorical research with Innu and Inuit in Labrador, and has worked in the Aleutian Islands, Peru, and Argentina.

Peter P. Schweitzer is Professor of Anthropology at the University of Alaska Fairbanks. Since the mid–1980s, Schweitzer has focused his research activities on the Russian North, conducting fieldwork in Chukotka and the Sakha Republic (Yakutia). His areas of interest include politics, kinship, history, and hunter-gatherer studies. Currently he is writing a book on the history of Siberian anthropology

Theodore G. Schurr is Assistant Professor in the Department of Anthropology, University of Pennsylvania. He has researched the genetic prehistory of Asia and the Americas through studies of mtDNA and Y-chromosome variation in Asian, Siberian and Native American populations. His current projects apply these techniques to modern Aleuts, indigenous peoples of south-central Siberia, and archaeological populations from the Lake Baikal region.

Nikolai Vakhtin, is a professor at the European University at St. Petersburg, Russia. He teaches courses in field linguistics, sociolinguistics, and the cultural anthropology of Siberia. He has done extensive research on Native languages and modern culture change among the minority peoples of northern Russia. He has written several books and articles on the languages and cultures of the northern indigenous peoples of Siberia.

Douglas W. Veltre is Professor of Anthropology at the University of Alaska Anchorage. He has conducted field research in the Aleutian and Pribilof islands since 1971. Much of his work has focused on prehistoric and historical archaeology, but he has also researched contemporary and historical subsistence economies and oral history.

Douglas C. Wallace has conducted studies in human biology for the past 25 years. His pioneering work in mitochondrial DNA genetics and biochemistry has led to numerous important insights into human origins and migrations, including the peopling of Siberia and the Americas. He is currently Director of the Center for Molecular and Mitochondrial Medicine and Genetics at the University of California, Irvine.

Gloria Cranmer Webster was born in Alert Bay, British Columbia, Canada. She is a member of the Nimpkish Band of the Kwakwaka'wakw (Kwakiutl). She founded the U'Mista Cultural Centre at Alert Bay, British Columbia in 1980, where she served as Director and Curator. Her many cultural projects include the production of two documentary films and a series of Kwakwala language books and educational materials for local schools.

Wendy Wickwire is Associate Professor in the Department of History and School of Environmental Studies at the University of Victoria, British Columbia. Her research interests include the oral traditions of the aboriginal peoples of south-central British Columbia and the history of anthropology in British Columbia, most notably the work of James A. Teit.

Laila Williamson is Senior Scientific Assistant for North and South American Ethnology at the AMNH in New York. She is a specialist in North American collections and helped renovate permanent exhibitions of Northwest Coast, Plains and Eastern Woodlands cultures at the AMNH. She has co-authored (with S.A. and R.S. Freed) several papers on the Jesup Expedition.

list of tables

list of figures

abbreviations

AMNH	American Museum of Natural History, New York, NY
AMNH-BTC	American Museum of Natural History, Department of Anthropology Archives, Boas-Teit Correspondence
AMNH-DA	American Museum of Natural History, Department of Anthropology Archives
AFS	American Folklore Society
ANB	Alaska Native Brotherhood
ANCSA	Alaska Native Land Claims Settlement Act, 1971
A/PIA	Aleutian/Pribilof Islands Association
APS-BP	American Philosophical Society, Franz Boas Papers
ARCA	Alaska Russian Church Archives, Manuscript Division (microfilm), Library of Congress, Washnigton, DC
ASC	Arctic Studies Center, Department of Anthropology, Smithsonian Institution
BAAS	British Association for the Advancement of Science
BAE	Bureau of American Ethnology, Washington, DC
BCPA	British Columbia Provincial Archives,Vancouver, British Columbia
BIA	Bureau of Indian Affiars, Department of the Interior, Washington, DC
GNPR	Greater North Pacific Region
IREX	International Research and Exchange Board
JNPE	Jesup North Pacific Expedition, 1897–1902
LC	Library of Congress, Washington, DC
MAE	Peter the Great Museum of Anthropology and Ethnology (Kunstkammer), St. Petersburg, Russia
NAA	National Anthropological Archives, Smithsonian Institution, Washington, DC
NAGPRA	Native American Graves Protection and Repatriation Act, 1990
NEH	National Endowment for the Humanities
NIMA	National Image and Mapping Agency
NMAI	National Museum of the American Indian, Smithsonian Institution, Washington, DC
NMNH	National Museum of Natural History, Smithsonian Institution, Washington, DC
NSF	National Science Foundation
RAC	Russian-American Company
RBCM	Royal British Columbia Museum, Vancouver, Canada
SITES	Smithsonian Institution Traveling Exhibit Service, Washington, DC
UBC	University of British Columbia, Vancouver, Canada
UPM	The University Museum, University of Pennsylvania, Philadelphia

note on Cyrillic transliteration

Two coexisting systems are in use in the United States for transliterating Russian Cyrillic letters into English: that of the Library of Congress (LC), and that of the National Image and Mapping Agency (NIMA, formerly the U.S. Board of Geographic Names). The LC system is used for bibliographic references; the NIMA system applies to geographic names (place names) and to most ethnic names.

All Russian or Siberian geographic names are transliterated here according to the NIMA system, which uses *ya*, *yu*, and *yo* for Cyrillic я, ю, and ё (Yakutsk, Yuzhno-Sakhalinsk, etc.). Throughout this volume, Native Siberian ethnic names are transliterated in accordance with the *Peoples of the Soviet Union* map produced by the National Geographic Society in 1989, which basically adheres to the NIMA system (Yakut, Yukagir, Koryak, Nanay, etc.). Most of these ethnic names are already established in Western anthropological literature—thanks largely to the Jesup Expedition's pioneering publications. This system also results in names reminiscent of several Native American group titles familiar to North American readers: Yurok, Maya, Yup'ik, Eyak, Yokut, Yakutat Tlingit, and so on. Furthermore, the NIMA-based spelling of ethnic and geographic names is similar to the Russian/Cyrillic transliteration system adopted in England and Canada and to the one commonly used by modern Russian authors when writing papers in English. The NIMA-based system is also applied here for transliterating a few Russian or Native Siberian personal names, words, and ethnographic terms in individual papers.

In contrast to the NIMA system, the Library of Congress transliteration system uses *ia*, *iu*, and *io* for the Cyrillic я, ю and ё and an apostrophe for the Russian soft sign (ь). Because today's highly standardized electronic library catalog formats are based on the LC system, names of Russian authors and all titles of items in the bibliographic reference sections in this volume adhere to the LC system. Using two transliteration systems in a single book may be inconvenient, but every effort has been made to adhere strictly to each of these patterns in its designated application in order to establish a high level of consistency for all future Arctic Studies Center publications. For the convenience of readers, an alternative NIMA-based transliteration of Russian authors' names is sometimes provided in parentheses in those cases where such a pattern has been established by earlier publications (for example, the original Jesup Expedition series; *Anthropology of the North: Translations from Russian Sources*). Despite all our efforts, we may not have been able to eliminate all potential cases of confusion or the occasional idiosyncratic usage.

We are grateful to our colleagues Pavel Ilyin (U.S. Holocaust Museum), Michael Krauss (Alaska Native Language Center, University of Alaska), and Marjorie Mandelstam Balzer (editor, *Anthropology and Archeology of Eurasia*) for their advice on transliteration practices for ASC publications.

1/ *Jochelson's team traveling with the expedition collections along the Tos-Khayakhtakh mountain range, East Siberia, winter 1902 (AMNH 1725)*

foreword

This volume marks another important step in the ongoing international effort to explore the legacy of the Jesup North Pacific Expedition of 1897–1902, referred to by its participants as "Jesup 2". This book illustrates, once again, the fruitfulness of broad partnerships when pursuing North Pacific studies, a tradition that began with Franz Boas' pioneering enterprise, and it demonstrates how that has developed over the last 100 years.

If one were to seek for the roots of Jesup 2, it began in 1977, when the U.S.-Soviet ethnographic exhibition, *Crossroads of Continents: Cultures of Alaska and Siberia,* was first proposed. Over the past twenty-six years, these efforts have progressed through a series of exhibits, international conferences, workshops, research exchanges, collection sharing programs, fellowships, and publications. Over time, the balance of these activities gradually shifted from major museums and research hubs in Washington, New York, Moscow, and St. Petersburg to smaller museums and centers in the North Pacific region. This shift also meant increased participation by local North Pacific area scholars and Native cultural activists in bringing objects, photographs, and knowledge recovered by the JNPE back into the homelands where the project originated. Such efforts helped make the Jesup Expedition familiar to hundreds and thousands local residents in Siberia and North America alike.

But the largest effort of Jesup 2, and the inaugural event for this volume, was the Jesup Centenary Conference at the American Museum. I am greatly indebted to Laurel Kendall and the American Museum of Natural History in New York for creating, funding, and hosting so skillfully and graciously this grand international convocation that brought together many North Pacific area scholars and representatives of Native Nations to celebrate the centenary of the Jesup Expedition in 1997. I also wish to thank Igor Krupnik for his perseverance in keeping the spirit of this venture alive by encouraging and heartening its participants over the years.

The appearance of this volume—from the opening of that conference to its appearance under the Arctic Studies Center (ASC) series, *Contributions to Circumpolar Anthropology*—took about the same length of time to complete as it did for Boas to conduct the JNPE fieldwork a century ago. All in all, it was not until the proceeds from the recent Smithsonian exhibit catalog, *Vikings: The North Atlantic Saga*, accumulated that it became possible for the ASC to start a publication series of its own. Here we found a fitting home for this volume, in a series which began with another Jesup 2 conference collection, *Gateways: Exploring the Legacy of the Jesup North Pacific Expedition, 1897-1902*, based on a panel held in 1993 and published in 2001.

Matters 'anthropological' around the North Pacific no longer inhabit the dark recesses of our museum archives and collection cabinets. Newly conserved and stored, they are finding their rightful places both as ideas and as cultural treasures. And with the Jesup 2 effort in its third decade, we are hopefully inching toward that enigmatic "Volume 12" of Boas' original series, the expedition's "Summary and Final Results."

William W. Fitzhugh, Director
Arctic Studies Center

2/ *"Woman's Potlatch" in Fort Rupert, British Columbia, June 1898. Photographer, Harlan I. Smith (AMNH 42992)*

introduction

A Centenary and a Celebration

LAUREL KENDALL
AND IGOR KRUPNIK

This volume examines the living legacy of the American Museum of Natural History's Jesup North Pacific Expedition (1897–1902) and the work of Dr. Franz Boas, the founding father of American anthropology. The Jesup Expedition, as orchestrated by Boas, was a research project of such scientific importance and geographical scope that some regard it as the most ambitious venture in the history of American Anthropology. Named after Morris K. Jesup, then the president of the American Museum of Natural History (AMNH) and the project's key sponsor, the expedition set out to investigate the cultural and biological links between indigenous peoples living in both the Old and the New World—in order to prove that the first Americans had once crossed over to North America from Asia. During a span of more than five years, the expedition field crews studied, recorded, and collected from several Native nations across the Greater North Pacific Region. Their efforts were focused upon a huge area, which extends like a giant arc from the Northwest Coast of North America to the Bering Strait and along the Pacific Coast of Siberia to the cultural borderlands of China, Korea, and Japan. The chapters in this volume began as papers given at a conference held at the American Museum of Natural History in 1997 to mark the Jesup North Pacific Expedition's Centenary. They reflect the enormous scope of the original expedition in both their breadth of geographic coverage and the range of issues they tackle,

Franz Boas (1858–1942), a German-born natural scientist, who became the leading American anthropologist of the early 20th century, was a pioneer in the study of culture, race, and ethnicity. His notion of "culture," as distinct from "race" and "language," is presently taken for granted in contemporary American thinking. Indeed, *culture* has become a core concept of the social sciences and an everyday word frequently invoked in public discourse. While anthropological notions of "culture" have evolved over the intervening century, popular understandings hew to a Boasian notion of culture as the essential configuration of beliefs, social practices, and material and artistic products that define a people.

Today, most anthropologists regard culture as a more mutable construct, anchored within rather than above historical circumstance and mediated by the particular experiences of gender, class, race, and the unfolding of colonial and neo-colonial encounters. But if the old Boasian notion now seems unfashionably "essentialist" and "a-historical," it is worth recalling the historical contingencies of its own construction. The culture concept, which claimed relative worth for every human society, was a radical departure from the supremacist and social-evolutionary thinking of Euro-American science in the late 19th and early 20th centuries where hunters, gatherers, and herders—so-called "primitive people"—were cast on the lowest rungs of an evolutionary hierarchy (Sanjek 1996).

1

Franz Boas saw anthropology as a holistic enterprise and the Jesup Expedition was conceptualized following his founding vision of the comprehensive anthropological survey as an integrated scholarly endeavor (Cole and Long 2001; see also Krupnik and Vakhtin, this volume). A single trained fieldworker, or a small crew of a few professionals, studied social life, folklore, linguistics, prehistory, and biology while also assembling museum collections and documenting significant activities for reproduction as museum exhibits (Miller and Mathé 1997). Boas himself epitomized these multiple endeavors in his own fieldwork as did several other Jesup Expedition participants. Because Jesup scientists encountered many Native peoples who had been badly decimated by epidemics and were under heavy pressure to assimilate to the customs and mores of the Russians or Anglo-Americans, members of the expedition believed that they were recording, collecting, and preserving the last traces of vanishing cultures. Boas enjoined expedition anthropologists to make as comprehensive portraits of the peoples they studied as could possibly be accomplished under local conditions and using the recording technology available to them at that time. Following his instructions, Jesup ethnologists documented local material culture, observed daily life and social rites, reproduced decorative patterns and artistic motifs, and recorded songs, stories, and myths for linguistic and comparative analysis. They took measurements of people, objects, and buildings, and collected artifacts. They also took numerous photographs, literally hundreds of them, in order to preserve an "authentic" image of people they surveyed. This was, in its day, cutting-edge fieldwork for a newly professional anthropology.

Returning from remote regions in Siberia and northern North America (Figs.1 and 2) to the American Museum in New York, expedition anthropologists brought back their written observations as well as tangible objects, visual images, and recordings of Native languages and on this basis, re*constructed* Native cultures for scholarly and popular consumption. They produced

a shelf of ethnographies and folklore collections considered "classics" today. Their collections fill the American Museum's Hall of Northwest Coast Indians and the Siberian section of the Gardner D. Stout Hall of Asian Peoples. Thousands more objects are housed in the Museum's storerooms and are now publicly accessible via the worldwide web. The Jesup Expedition archives include participants' notes and diaries, letters from the field, transcriptions of folklore texts, photographs, wax cylinders, and forms for physical measurements.[1] Through such comprehensive documentation, Boas and his colleagues *constructed* cultures as theory, field sites, configurations of processed data, topical monographs, and museum exhibits aimed at reproducing an idealized pre-contact *then*, spurred on by the mistaken belief that these cultures were rapidly disappearing. With the irony of history, the JNPE fieldworkers preserved invaluable cultural treasures, such that one hundred years later (*now*) the Jesup Expedition's legacy is an unsurpassed resource for scholars as well as for peoples of the North Pacific region who are actively engaged in reconstructing and revitalizing their cultures in a meaningful present tense.

The Centenary: 1897–1997

The Greater North Pacific Region studied by the Jesup Expedition—from northern Japan to the edges of Siberia at the Bering Strait to Alaska to the Northwest Coast—has been a fertile area of cultural development, innovation, and intercontinental exchange for thousands of years. The JNPE teams intended to document the biological and cultural links between northern peoples, and to investigate the ecological and spiritual relationship between these people and their harsh environment as well as religious and artistic traditions which defined them. All these issues are of crucial importance today as the region copes with the outcomes of reckless commercial exploitation of its natural resources and acute environmental degradation during much of the 20th century. Similarly, Native people on both sides of the intercontinental and political divide at the Bering Strait's crossroads are seeking to revitalize their ethnic and spiritual identities after decades of cultural suppression and forced assimilation.

The collections, publications, and archives produced by the Jesup Expedition offer a rich resource to address these and related issues as part of a global scientific and philosophical conversation. The Jesup Expedition team assembled by Dr. Franz Boas mixed educated academic professionals with new recruits, sometimes drawn from the local residents, and by including people of Native and mixed origin, former political exiles, and women. In this, as well as in many other aspects of the Expedition's work, Boas's pioneer design laid the groundwork for the present-day multifaceted "Jesup constituency" that now includes scientists from many disciplines and nations, Native scholars, artists, cultural activists, film-makers, educators, folk-art performers, museum workers, and a large and diverse public audience. Much of this diversity is reflected in the community brought together by the centenary conference and whose work is represented in this volume.

Over the intervening century, all of the sub-fields of anthropology envisioned by Boas as the tools of one single discipline—ethnology, linguistics, archaeology, folklore, biological anthropology, and museum collecting and research—have become highly specialized. They have introduced sophisticated new methods, and, in many instances, have challenged the premises established by Boas, perhaps nowhere more intensely than around the core concept of "culture." New technologies and field techniques now dominate the field of archaeology and physical anthropology. Some, like radiocarbon dating, DNA research, and computer data processing, were not even foreseen in Boas' time. New knowledge, such as the biological anthropologists' use of genetic data, paleoenvironmental research, and the dating of hundreds of excavated prehistoric sites, altered profoundly the way we now study ancient human migrations and construct cultural as

well as biological interactions. In a broader and more philosophical sense, both North American and post-Soviet anthropologists have spent the last several years engaged in a thorough questioning of the many established dogmas in their professional domains; in one instance, reconfiguring a scholarly field once intended to serve the interests of Soviet Marxist doctrines, in the other—under rubrics broadly labeled as "post-modernism"—challenging anthropology's truth claims as a positivistic science. Native scholars and political activists have leveled more fundamental challenges to many core notions and practices of anthropology, in some instances arguing that the non-native observer is incapable of understanding Native culture, in others that such observations are themselves violations of basic human dignity. Disputes over the proper domain of Native cultural properties currently housed in museums have been particularly contentious. For nearly two decades, critiques and soul-searching have reverberated both within and outside the academy. The Jesup Expedition Centenary thus occurs at a particularly pregnant moment in anthropology where a backward glance at who we were and how we have changed might contribute to the larger debate over who we are now and what we might become.

The Jesup Expedition centenary conference and this resulting volume are among the products of a larger initiative named *Jesup 2* in honor of the initial Jesup Expedition and aimed at encouraging coordinated research activities in the Greater North Pacific Region. Its critical goal is in the dissemination of new knowledge, approaches, and perspectives in the study of cultures through scholarly publications, museum exhibits, academic symposia, and public programs. Spearheaded by the Arctic Studies Center at the Smithsonian Institution, these efforts have been carried out since 1992 by an informal consortium of scholars and institutions (Fitzhugh and Krupnik 2001:7–10; see also AAAS 1992; AAA 1993; Fitzhugh 1996; Fitzhugh and Krupnik 1994; IARPC 1995: 22–24; Vakhtin

1993). Like the original expedition, *Jesup 2* is a holistic enterprise, now sustained by a scattered community of international scholars who have come together to address issues of common interest. Unlike the original venture, the new *Jesup 2* program does not have a single sponsor but reflects the combined effort of several institutions. The American Museum of Natural History (AMNH), as the major storehouse of the Jesup Expedition's resources and of Franz Boas's legacy in North Pacific research, has been a critical resource in this effort.

Boas and his colleagues collected about half of the American Museum's 16,755 Northwest Coast artifacts under the auspices of the Jesup Expedition. Although the numbers themselves are noteworthy, it is their diversity, comprehensiveness, and documentation that make the Jesup Expedition acquisitions so valuable. The American Museum's Northwest Coast collection is generally regarded as the world's strongest, holding artifacts from every known group and nation in this culture region. For over 100 years, this collection has been studied by almost every anthropologist, art historian, and historian engaged in research of any magnitude on the Northwest Coast native cultures. As a result of AMNH's first fruitful collaboration with Russian scholars during the original Jesup Expedition, extensive ethnographic collections were also made in Siberia. These are similarly considered among the world's richest, particularly with regard to several groups in northeast Siberia. Their value was subsequently boosted by several key scholarly monographs on Siberian indigenous peoples published in a series of *Jesup Expedition Publications/Memoirs of the American Museum of Natural History* as well as by many other Jesup-based publications promoted by Boas and his colleagues (see Krupnik 2001). These collections and numerous archival materials and photographs now housed at the American Museum of Natural History constitute the single richest stock of museum resources on Native Siberian cultures outside the Russian Federation, if not worldwide.

The role of the Jesup Expedition collections in documenting and preserving the legacy of Native Siberian peoples is particularly noteworthy. For many years—in fact, for almost all of the 20th century—Siberia was closed to American researchers. Thus, for much of the Soviet period, the Jesup Expedition's various collections and publications were the single largest body of anthropological information on Siberian cultures available to Western researchers. While some hesitant contacts with Soviet anthropologists resumed in the late 1950s, it was the Smithsonian Institution's monumental 1980s joint exhibit, *Crossroads of Continents: Cultures of Siberia and Alaska* that finally marked the collapse of the barrier that had separated scholars and Native people on both sides of the North Pacific (Fitzhugh and Crowell 1988; Fitzhugh, this volume). The exhibit, produced by a team of North American and Russian curators, marked a new era of scholarly cooperation and reawakened awareness of the value of the Jesup Expedition's resources, particularly for and among Siberian indigenous people.

Since that time, the American Museum of Natural History, the main depository of the JNPE legacy, has been experiencing an unprecedented call on its collections and archives. On a single memorable day in 1993, Nikolai Vakhtin from St. Petersburg was perusing the Expedition's documented chronicle stored in letters and diaries at the Museum archive. In another room, Stephen Ousley, then from the University of Tennessee, worked with the Jesup Expedition's biological data; a Danish film-maker examined Yukagir materials as background to a film project; and a scholar from Japan researched the Nanay (Gold) and Nivkh (Gilyak) collections from Sakhalin Island and the Amur River. Native Siberian scholars have been prominent among the researchers who have made their way to AMNH, beginning with the Sakha ethnologists, Vladimir and Zinaida Ivanov-Unarov from Yakutsk. Some of the results of these studies are contained in this volume and elsewhere (V. Ivanov-Unarov and Z. Ivanova-Unarova, this volume; Ousley and Jantz 2001; Vakhtin 2001).

The Celebration

Given these developments, it seemed both necessary and appropriate to mark the centenary of the Jesup North Pacific Expedition with a public acknowledgement, assessment, and celebration. In the fall of 1997, the American Museum of Natural History in New York hosted several public events, including an exhibit of expedition photographs, *Drawing Shadows to Stone* curated by Barbara Mathé and Thomas Ross Miller; a program of public lectures; a Greater North Pacific Film Festival; and performances by Native dance troops from both sides of the Bering Strait. A catalog of several dozen historical photographs by the JNPE team members was published (Kendall et al. 1997), followed by many articles in popular and academic journals. But the centerpiece of this celebration, in the spirit of broad scholarly inquiry as embraced by the original expedition, was a five-day international conference, *Constructing Cultures Then and Now: Celebrating Franz Boas and the Jesup North Pacific Expedition*. It brought together an impressive team of over 50 internationally-acclaimed scholars, museum curators, and Native cultural workers who met face-to-face to discuss the history, current prospects, and possible futures of the peoples of the Greater North Pacific Region.

The conference, featuring the legacy of Franz Boas and the Jesup Expedition, was held at the Museum in November 1997, to mark the 100-year anniversary of the Expedition's first printed report from the field, published in the October 1897 issue of the journal *Science* (Boas 1897). The conference built upon *Jesup 2* projects already initiated by the Smithsonian Institution, the American Museum of Natural History, the University of Alaska, the National Science Foundation, and the National Park Service, in collaboration with numerous partners in Russia, Siberia, Canada, Japan, and Europe. Both the conference and related centenary activities were amply covered by the press and hailed by the professional anthropological community (Anonymous 1998; Graburn 1998; Kendall 1997; Lee 1998; Rexer 1997; Shute 1997).

The centenary conference was one product of a joint effort by five anthropologists: Laurel Kendall (American Museum of Natural History), Marjory Mandelstam Balzer (Georgetown University), William Fitzhugh (Arctic Studies Center, Smithsonian Institution), Igor Krupnik (Arctic Studies Center, Smithsonian Institution), and Nikolai Vakhtin (European University, St Petersburg, Russia). The team assembled a broad range of scholars and local cultural experts who specialized in studies of peoples and cultures—both modern and prehistoric—and environments across the Greater North Pacific Region. The diversity of their perspectives is reflected in the twenty conference papers assembled in this volume.

This team of experts was asked to consider a number of issues in light of contemporary scholarship. Are the "cultures" as described and *constructed* by the Jesup Expedition participants relevant to the emerging new identities of Native peoples in the region today? How do modern culturally conscious peoples reconstitute themselves, both politically and spiritually? Are the records of ethnologists, folklorists, and linguists of a century ago a valuable resource in this transformation? Do museums and museum collections have a role to play in this process? How do issues of environmental exploitation play against local sovereignty and local conceptualizations of the land and its resources? These and other taunting issues necessarily include the perspectives of Native people and the voices of Native scholars. Intentionally designed to break through international and interdisciplinary as well as professional and political boundaries, this conference provided one lively forum for dialogues that span the Bering Strait.

Following Boas' founding vision of anthropology as an integrated endeavor, the organizers adopted a similar breadth of vision in defining the conference's framework as well as in inviting topics for individual presentations and focused panel discussions. We were also keenly aware that in the intervening century, many sub-fields once skillfully aligned by Boas have become highly specialized, shifted their boundaries or changed their professional allegiances. The conference presentations (recast as chapters in this volume) suggested how new knowledge—such as the biological anthropologist's use of genetic data, the vastly expanded vision of archaeology and comparative historical linguistics, or the anthropologist's attention to the transcontinental colonial flows of goods, ideas, and people—permitted new insights into questions once posed by the Jesup Expedition. Several speakers revealed how very often the work of newly-recruited disciples in the science of anthropology, like Boas and his counterparts, was dependent upon and consequently enriched by the insights of local residents, who acted as their field partners, knowledge experts, guides, and interpreters. Many papers offered moving illustrations of how scholars worldwide continue to use materials collected by the Jesup Expedition to pose new questions. Of particular significance, scholars commented on the value of the American Museum of Natural History's material and of the Boasian legacy as indigenous peoples of the "Jesup area" engage in projects of cultural revitalization. The full saga of the conference has been described elsewhere (Graburn 1998).

The Volume

The 20 conference papers selected for this volume are directly tied to the historical legacy of the Jesup Expedition, either by way of centennial reevaluation and critique of its scientific premises and results or as a demonstration of how the Jesup Expedition's artifacts and data are used today to new ends. We believe that with the publication of this "centennial" volume—the second volume to be published by the Arctic Studies Center on the *Jesup 2* theme (cf. Krupnik and Fitzhugh 2001) and in conjunction with several other recent monographs, collections, and catalogs featuring the legacy of the JNPE and of Franz Boas (Cole 1999; Fitzhugh and Chaussonnet 1994; Fitzhugh and Crowell 1988; Jacknis 2002; Jonaitis 1988, 1991, 1995, 1999; Kendall et al. 1997; Krupnik 2000; Shternberg 1999,

etc.)—we have raised a significant milestone on the ambitious journey begun by Franz Boas and his team over 100 years ago.

The volume is organized into four thematic sections. Papers in the first section, *One Hundred Years of Jesup: The Intellectual Legacy of the Jesup Expedition Era*, look back over a century to evaluate the Expedition from the perspective of its impact on the anthropology of the late 19th and early 20th century ("*then*") and to re-evaluate its assumptions in light of today's understandings ("*now*"). The Expedition's multi-faceted research agenda offers a stimulating and varied "menu" for such a re-examination. The section opens with the chapter by Igor Krupnik and Nikolai Vakhtin, who examine the saga of the Jesup North Pacific Expedition as if it were a modern scholarly project. Though conceived and executed in a manner consistent with the goals and techniques of anthropological scholarship circa 1900, the Jesup Expedition, according to Krupnik and Vakhtin, meets most of the contemporary criteria of successful interdisciplinary research by virtue of its well thought out scientific design, consistent methodological frame, publication and training agenda, and promotion of international scholarly collaboration.

In a more critical vein, Don Dumond concludes that the post-Jesup century of work in the archaeology of the North Pacific does not, in the main, offer evidence for one of the key pieces of Boas' ethnogenetic theory, the so-called "Eskimo wedge" hypothesis that assumed a late wedge-like intrusion of the Eskimo into the chain of related cultures in the Bering Sea-Bering Strait area. Under a similar revisionist agenda, Peter Schweitzer queries why Boas' preoccupation with diffusion and culture exchange, and his later interest in local history never materialized into a focused ethnohistory of Native peoples residing at the critical junction of trans-Beringian contacts, the Bering Strait area. Molly Lee and Nelson Graburn suggest that for Boas at the time of the Jesup Expedition (*then*), the diffusion of material and non-material cultural traits was as much of an exciting intellectual paradigm as the concept of "transnationalism" is for students of global cultural exchange today (*now*). They argue that Boas' diffusionist agenda erred in excising from his consideration the impact of international commerce on cultural exchanges within the region. Finally, the AMNH team of Stanley and Ruth Fried and Leila Williamson compares the Jesup Expedition's logistics, planning, and research focus to similarly monumental enterprises, such as the Lewis and Clark Expedition (1803–06), the U.S. Exploring Expedition (1838–42), and the Cambridge Anthropological Expedition to the Torres Straits (1898–99).

Part Two, *Anthropologies and Histories: Jesup Members Then and Now*, broadens our understanding of key participants in the Expedition and related fieldwork. Ira Jacknis illuminates an intriguing aspect of Boas' multifaceted personality, his musical skill and deep love of music, which led him to undertake musicological research in the field. Other chapters in this section reveal many instances where the work of Boas and his counterparts was dependent upon and consequently enriched by the insights of local people, both Native and long-term local residents, thus broadening our understanding of such collaborations beyond the well-documented relationship of Boas and George Hunt who is recognized today as an early Native anthropologist (Berman 1996). These papers suggest that today's anthropologists would benefit by more research and soul searching as to how our scholarly predecessors had typically incorporated the work of their local associates into their own academic publications. Wendy Wickwire focuses on one of Boas' longest-standing and most productive local collaborators in Northwest Coast ethnography, James Teit, who—despite his voluminous contributions to the JNPE research and publications—has been commonly regarded as merely Boas' "field assistant." Koichi Inoue examines an uneasy narrative of another contemporary "local" scientist, Bronislaw Pilsudski, an enthusiastic and ethnographically astute Polish exile living on Sakhalin Island whose brief career intersected with the work of three members of the Jesup Expedition team: Boas, Laufer, and Shternberg.

Nora Marks Dauenhauer and Richard Dauenhauer explore the legacy of Louis Shotridge, the first Tlingit, and possibly the first Northwest Coast Native, with training in linguistics and anthropology (primarily from Boas). The first Native Alaskan to become a professional collector and museum curator, Shotridge made invaluable and generally under-recognized contributions to the documentation of the Northwest Coast cultures. Finally, Sergei Kan engages in ethnohistorical detective work to retrieve a pattern of collaboration between the late 19th-century ethnographers and local Native American and "mixed-blood" (Creole, Métis) interpreters, amateur historians, and informants. He draws on his extensive research on Native-outsider interactions in southern Alaska during the late 1800s.

Part Three, *People, Animals, and Land: A Jesup Theme Revisited*, offers a selection of modern perspectives by scholars whose disciplines span the major fields of the Jesup Expedition's activities. Robert Hoffmann describes the biological and natural history work of the JNPE as an early example of the "correlated" multi-disciplinary efforts that would characterize modern scientific expeditions. He offers a sober assessment of biological diversity in the Beringian region today, arguing that such correlated efforts are urgently needed if the region's endangered ecology is to be preserved. Michael Krauss indexes shortcomings in the Expedition's efforts to document North Pacific languages, attributing this to a lack of interest on the part of Expedition scientists in either the documentation of linguistic diversity or the last-minute salvage of dying languages through extensive recording in the interest of comparative linguistics or philological study. As Krauss argues, only Boas appears to have given much priority to that latter task, and even he mostly neglected it during his brief Jesup Expedition fieldwork.

Theodore Schurr and Douglas Wallace describe how modern molecular genetic data obtained from aboriginal populations provide an exciting cross-disciplinary tool to test the old theories of the Jesup Expedition era, a tool which could not have even been imagined by the original JNPE members. They argue that such data can be used successfully to test the original JNPE hypotheses regarding the origins and diversity of Native Siberians and their close evolutionary relationships with Native Americans. The chapter by Sergei Arutiunov records generational transitions within the Russian school of Northeast Siberian prehistoric research; it also offers some new insights on the scenarios of the earliest trans-Beringian interactions based upon methods and approaches that were similarly not even envisioned at the time of the Jesup Expedition (such as the study of prehistoric adaptations; comparative historical linguistics; and analysis of dental features of the prehistoric and modern populations). Finally, David Koester deals with the traumatic consequences of history, unveiling the drama of involuntary relocations and forced separation of indigenous people from their ancestral lands during the "post-Jesup" era. "History" here is not quantifiable molecular or archaeological data, sifted from a perspective of distance, but the stuff of memory and sentiment as revealed in the stories and poetry of the "lost villages" of Kamchatka.

The last section of this volume, *Curators, Collectors, and Consumers*, describes some of the ways in which JNPE and other North Pacific museum resources have become part of local efforts to sustain the cultural heritage of the indigenous peoples of the Greater North Pacific Region. William W. Fitzhugh brings to light many memories, both sweet and sad, as well as the intricacies of a 20 year-long effort in trans-national museum cooperation, publication, and outreach that culminated in the exhibit *Crossroads of Continents: Cultures of Siberia and Alaska* (1988–92) and its follow-up traveling venture, *Crossroads Alaska-Siberia* (1993–97). Stephen Loring and Douglas Veltre share the same vision of the changing role of anthropology (and archaeology, in particular) in protecting and enhancing cultural heritage, describing their own research contributions in the Aleutian Islands.

In the same collaborative spirit, two art historians and ethnographers from Russia's Sakha Republic (Yakutia), Zinaida Ivanova-Unarova and the late Vladimir Ivanov-Unarov (1937–2000) offer a moving account of a personal journey undertaken from the Siberian heartland to work with collections at the American Museum of Natural History in New York and then share the results of their study with Native artisans back home. Their story demonstrates how materials collected by the original Jesup Expedition offer invaluable encouragement to the people engaged in cultural revival and revitalization efforts today. Aldona Jonaitis looks at many intricate aspects of a related process: the reclaiming of a traditional cultural legacy by innovative Native artists, including female artists, who are *constructing* new cultural symbols. She uses the case of a totem pole, the quintessential symbol of the Northwest Coast cultures, and the example of two contemporary female carvers to illustrate how the early anthropological notion of Native art's "timeless traditionalism" has been turned on its head by the creativity of living Native cultures of today. In what could be read as a coda to the entire volume, Kwakwaka'wakw anthropologist and curator Gloria Cranmer Webster writes a highly personal essay as the granddaughter of George Hunt whose collaboration with Franz Boas made an important contribution not only to the ethnographic record, but to the preservation of Kwakwaka'wakw culture. She presents the story of a long friendship between the Boas and Hunt families constructed through Kwakwaka'wakw idioms of name-giving and feasting, an evocation of important "grandfathers" and the inspiration they offer future generations.

Acknowledgments

The Jesup Expedition Centenary Conference of 1997 was supported by The Henry Luce Foundation, Inc., The Ford Foundation, The Rockefeller Foundation, The Trust for Mutual Understanding, Wenner-Gren Foundation for Anthropological Research, and the Chi–Mei Cultural Foundation. Ann Fitzgerald coordinated the complex logistics of an international conference, and AMNH staff, including Ann Wright-Parsons and Alexia Bloch, then with the AMNH Department of Anthropology, ensured that events ran smoothly. We are particularly grateful to the many museum volunteers who offered assistance before and during the conference and to a team of tireless interpreters provided by the Translation Center, Columbia University.

The story of this volume's preparation offers an illuminating lesson that the publishing difficulties the JNPE team encountered 100 years ago still exist today. It was also an example of a successful institutional partnership, quite in the footsteps of the original JNPE venture. Laurel Kendall spearheaded initial editorial work on the volume at AMNH, following the 1997 centennial conference. Kathryn A. Malm helped edit this ambitious bundle of papers into a cohesive manuscript. Eventually, the Arctic Studies Center (ASC) picked up this collection under its recently established publication series, *Contributions to Circumpolar Anthropology*, that had previously featured another *Jesup 2* volume, *Gateways. Exploring the Legacy of the Jesup North Pacific Expedition, 1897–1902* (Krupnik and Fitzhugh 2001). The publication of both volumes was made possible in part by an endowment from the late anthropologist James W. VanStone (1925–2001), who was himself an inspiring symbol of partnership and inter-disciplinary collaboration in Arctic and North Pacific ethnological research.

At the ASC, Igor Krupnik and Iris Hahn carried on the editorial work while Elisabeth Ward supervised the process of layout and printing of the manuscript. Marcia Bakry at the Smithsonian Institution's Department of Anthropology and Tam Thompson offered invaluable assistance with graphic artwork. This collection follows a design pattern created by Anya Vinokour for the ASC *Contributions to Circumpolar Anthropology* series and used for the preceding publications. We would like to commend all our volume contributors for their trust, dedication, as well as for patience during a seemingly interminable editorial process. Special thanks go to Stanley Freed at the AMNH, William Fitzhugh, the ASC Director, and to

Katherine Rusk for their helpful comments and editorial suggestions to many volume papers at this final stage.

This book, as well as the preceding *Jesup 2* volume (ibid), is illustrated with numerous original photographs from the Jesup Expedition era, including many taken by the expedition field crews in Siberia and North America. We are grateful to the expedition's host institution, the American Museum of Natural History, for permission to reproduce the photographs and to Barbara Mathé, Head of Special Collections at the AMNH Library, for her truly heartfelt assistance with the images. Several more illustrations, including historical photographs and images of ethnographic objects, come from other collections, such as that of the Smithsonian Institution's National Anthropological Archives, National Museum of Natural History, National Museum of the American Indian; the University of Pennsylvania Museum, University of Alaska Museum, Alaska State Library, American Philosophical Society, British Columbia Provincial Archives, University of British Columbia Museum of Anthropology, Royal British Columbia Museum, and others (see *List of Illustrations*). We thank all institutions as well as the curators, collection management staff, and archivists who granted us permission and assisted in selecting and securing the illustrations for this second JNPE memorial volume.

Finally, over the years since the initial New York conference of 1997, we have lost one of the most devoted members of the *Jesup 2* team, the Sakha (Yakut) ethnologist and art historian Vladimir Ivanov-Unarov, who passed away in 2000. We regard this volume as a special tribute to Volodya's legacy—which is honored here by Marjorie Mandelstam Balzer—as well as to other colleagues and partners who did not live to see the Jesup Expedition's centenary and to take part in its celebration.

Note

1. The original wax cylinder sound recordings produced during the Jesup Expedition were eventually transferred to the Archives of Traditional Music at the University of Indiana.

References

AAA (American Anthropological Association)
1993   Gateways to Jesup II: Evaluating Archival Resources of the Jesup North Pacific Expedition, 1897–1902. In *American Anthropological Association Annual Meeting, 92, Abstracts.* Pp. 40–1. Washington, DC.

AAAS (American Association for the Advancement of Science)
1992   Arctic Research Repeats History. *Science* 256:163.

Anonymous
1998   The Shadows of a Human Science. *The New York Times,* January 29, p. A–22.

Berman, Judith
1996   "The Culture as it appears to the Indian Himself": Boas, George Hunt, and the Methods of Ethnography. In *Volksgeist as Method and Ethic: Essays on Boasian Ethnography and the German Anthropological Tradition.* George W. Stocking, Jr., ed. Pp. 215–56. History of Anthropology, 8. Madison: University of Wisconsin Press.

Boas, Franz
1897   The Jesup Expedition to the North Pacific Coast. *Science,* n.s., 6(195): 535–38.

Cole, Douglas
1999   *Franz Boas: The Early Years, 1858–1906.* Vancouver: Douglas & McIntyre; Seattle: University of Washington Press.

Cole, Douglas, and Alex Long
2001   The Boasian Anthropological Survey Tradition. The Role of Franz Boas in North American Anthropological Surveys. In *Surveying the Record. North American Scientific Exploration to 1930.* Edward C. Carter II, ed. Pp. 225–49. Memoirs of the American Philosophical Society, 231. Philadelphia: American Philosophical Society.

Fitzhugh, William W.
1996   Jesup 2: Anthropology of the North Pacific. *Northern Notes* 4:41–62. Hanover, N.H.

Fitzhugh, William W., and Valérie Chaussonnet, eds.
1994   *Anthropology of the North Pacific Rim.* Washington, DC: Smithsonian Institution Press.

Fitzhugh, William W., and Aron Crowell, eds.
1988   *Crossroads of Continents: Cultures of Siberia and Alaska.* Washington, DC: Smithsonian Institution Press.

Fitzhugh, William W., and Igor Krupnik
1994   The Jesup II Research Initiative: Anthropological Studies in the North Pacific. *Arctic Studies Center Newsletter.* (Jesup II Newsbrief). Washington, DC: Arctic Studies Center, Smithsonian Institution.
2001   Introduction. In *Gateways. Exploring the Legacy of the Jesup North Pacific Expedition, 1897–1902.* Igor Krupnik and William W. Fitzhugh, eds. Pp. 1–16. Contributions to Circumpolar Anthropology, 1. Washington, DC: Arctic Studies Center.

Graburn, Nelson H. H.
1998   Constructing Cultures Then and Now. *American Anthropologist* 100(4):1009–13.

IARPC (Interagency Arctic Research Policy Committee)
1995   U.S. Arctic Research Plan Biennial Revision: 1996–2000. *Arctic Research of the United States* 9 (Spring).

Jacknis, Ira
2002   *The Storage Box of Tradition: Kwakiutl Art, Anthropologists, and Museums, 1881-1981.* Washington, DC: Smithsonian Institution Press.

Jonaitis, Aldona
1988   *From the Land of the Totem Poles. The Northwest Coast Indian Art Collection at the American Museum of Natural History.* Seattle: University of Washington Press; New York: American Museum of Natural History.
1999   *The Yuquot Whalers' Shrine.* Seattle: University of Washington Press.

Jonaitis, Aldona, ed.
1991   *Chiefly Feasts. The Enduring Kwakiutl Potlach.* Seattle: University of Washington Press; New York: American Museum of Natural History.
1995   *A Wealth of Thought: Franz Boas on Native American Art.* Seattle: University of Washington Press.

Kendall, Laurel
1997   The Jesup North Pacific Expedition. *Rotunda* 22(10):1. New York.

Kendall, Laurell, Barbara Mathé, and Thomas R. Miller, eds.
1997   *Drawing Shadows to Stone: The Photography of the Jesup North Pacific Expedition, 1897–1902.* New York: American Museum of Natural History; Seattle: University of Washington Press.

Krupnik, Igor
2000   Jesup-2: The Precious Legacy and a Centennial Perspective. *European Review of Native American Studies* 14(2), Special Issue.
2001   A Jesup Bibliography: Tracking the Published and Archival Legacy of the Jesup Expedition. In *Gateways. Exploring the Legacy of the Jesup North Pacific Expedition, 1897–1902.* Igor Krupnik and William W. Fitzhugh, eds. Pp. 297–316. Contributions to Circumpolar Anthropology, 1. Washington, DC: Arctic Studies Center.

Krupnik, Igor, and William W. Fizthugh, eds.
2001   *Gateways. Exploring the Legacy of the Jesup North Pacific Expedition, 1897–1902. Contributions to Circumpolar Anthropology,* 1. Washington, DC: Arctic Studies Center, Smithsonian Institution.

Lee, Molly
1998   Exhibition Review: Drawing Shadows to Stone. *American Anthropologist* 100(4):1005–09.

Miller, Thomas Ross, and Barbara Mathé

1997   Drawing Shadows to Stone. In *Drawing Shadows to Stone: The Photography of the Jesup North Pacific Expedition, 1897–1902*. Laurel Kendall, Barbara Mathé, and Thomas Ross Miller, eds. Pp. 19–42. New York: American Museum of Natural History; Seattle: University of Washington Press.

Ousley, Stephen, and Richard Jantz

2001   500 Year Old Questions, 100 Year Old Data, Brand New Computers: Biological Data from the Jesup North Pacific Expedition. In *Gateways. Exploring the Legacy of the Jesup North Pacific Expedition, 1897–1902*. Igor Krupnik and William W. Fitzhugh, eds. Pp.257–78. Contributions to Circumpolar Anthropology, 1. Washington, DC: Arctic Studies Center.

Rexer, Lyle

1997   Doctoring Reality to Document What's True. *The New York Times*, November 9, p.25.

Sanjek, Roger.

1996   Franz Boas. In *Encyclopedia of Social and Cultural Anthropology*. Alan Barnard and Jonathan Spencer, eds. Pp. 71–4. London: Routledge.

Shternberg, Lev,

1999   The Social Organization of the Gilyak. Bruce Grant, ed. *Anthropological Papers of the American Museum of Natural History*, 82. New York: American Museum of Natural History.

Shute, Nancy

1997   Birth of a Science, Rebirth of a People. The Jesup Expedition Turns 100. *U.S. News & World Report*. December 1, p.64.

Vakhtin, Nikolai B.

1993   Jesup-2: Novaia programma sotsial'no-antropologicheskikh issledovanii na Severe (Jesup-2: A New Program of Social and Anthropological Research in the North). *Kunstkamera. Ethnograficheskie tetradi* 1:211–13. St. Petersburg.

2001   Franz Boas and the Shaping of the Jesup Expedition Siberian Research, 1895–1900. In *Gateways. Exploring the Legacy of the Jesup North Pacific Expedition, 1897–1902*. Igor Krupnik and William W. Fitzhugh, eds. Pp.71–89. Contributions to Circumpolar Anthropology, 1. Washington, DC: Arctic Studies Center.

3/ Lev Shternberg, Franz Boas, and Waldemar Bogoras at the 21st International Congress of Americanists, 1924. Courtesy of the Museum Anthropology and Ethnography, St. Petersburg, Russia (original in the MAE collection)

part 1

100 YEARS AFTER JESUP: THE INTELLECTUAL LEGACY
OF THE JESUP EXPEDITION ERA

"The Aim of the Expedition...Has in the Main Been Accomplished"

Words, Deeds, and Legacies of the Jesup North Pacific Expedition

IGOR KRUPNIK
AND NIKOLAI VAKHTIN

The Jesup North Pacific Expedition (JNPE), which took place from 1897 to 1902, was a milestone event for the entire domain of North Pacific/Siberian/North American research. To the field currently known as "Jesup-2 studies" (Fitzhugh and Krupnik 2001) as well as to the expedition's host institution, the American Museum of Natural History (AMNH), the Expedition's recent centennial and the many accompanying events offered a remarkable opportunity to evaluate key components of its legacy, and to review transitions in anthropology and human sciences over the turbulent 20th century.

By modern standards, JNPE was a pioneer scientific venture. It initiated a new pattern of large anthropological/museum surveys, with 17 team members from four countries (the U.S., Russia, Canada, and Germany) working in various combinations over five years on two continents.[1] The expedition's fieldwork was matched by an equally ambitious publication program. A preliminary *Jesup Bibliography* compiled recently (Krupnik 2001) lists about 200 publications produced by JNPE participants over 50 years, including eleven major volumes and dozens of journal articles, and collections of folklore and language materials.

For 100 years following the JNPE, its design, outcomes, and publications have been reviewed many times (Freed et al. 1988; Fitzhugh and Krupnik 2001; Kuz'mina 1994; Vakhtin 1993; Fitzhugh 1996). It has been called "a grandiose, brilliantly conceptualized, and masterfully orchestrated attack on one of the most important problems in American anthropology" (Fitzhugh and Crowell 1988:14), one that initiated "a transvaluation of the entire field of anthropology, and hinted at its development into the most humane of the human sciences" (Jonaitis 1988:213). But the JNPE was also labeled a "remarkable failure," a "disappointment for Morris K. Jesup and for his museum" (Cole 2001:48) or, at least, a "fiasco" in some of its fields of activities, areas surveyed, and/or postulated hypotheses. These conflicting perspectives are illustrated in many papers in this volume.

Many shortcomings of the Jesup Expedition project have been well addressed, since the JNPE team and, particularly, its leader, Franz Boas, neither produced a summary project monograph nor offered any extended outline of cultural history of the North Pacific Region. There are more than ample grounds for critique and revisionism (see chapters by Dumond; Lee and Graburn; Hoffmann; Inoue; Krauss; Schweitzer, this volume; also Ousley 2000; Ousley and Jantz 2001). As a monumental initiative conducted by many strong personalities, the Jesup Expedition can be judged from various perspectives, according to the often conflicting visions of its organizers, sponsors, and individual team members. Some of these visions were openly debated in papers and letters; others have been personal and remained hidden. While certain JNPE initial plans did materialize, many more were abandoned during or after the fieldwork was completed. In addition, the JNPE legacy endured a long period of criticism during the 1920s and

15

1930s, followed by decades of skepticism and abandonment (Krupnik 1998). It was not until recently that the Expedition's legacy underwent a more balanced judgment and a spectacular recovery (see various chapters in Krupnik and Fitzhugh 2001).

This paper introduces a new framework to consider the legacy of the JNPE project by testing it against some basic evaluation criteria commonly applied to large research initiatives in contemporary social science. By no means do we aspire to assume the role of present-day "peer reviewers" for a century-old venture. Rather we would like to illustrate how the Jesup Expedition agenda, its field logistics, and publication plan accomplished *then* can be viewed *now* in a centennial perspective. For this purpose, we have selected five modern evaluation criteria: research integrity; contribution to "basic science"; international cooperation; education and training; and public outreach. These criteria are familiar to every modern social scientist. By applying today's standards to the original JNPE project, we deliberately contemporize its entire context in order to build a new vision of its legacy a century later.

Integrity of the JNPE Design

Despite the expedition's complex design and its numerous achievements, it is clear that the JNPE project put forth a somewhat confusing message from the very start. It seemed to have been "packaged" and presented differently to various constituencies and prospective audiences. In his articles, statements, and letters, Franz Boas, the project leader, delivered at least three different perspectives on the general goals of the JNPE, to say nothing of his many personal objectives revealed through his private correspondence.

The first declared objective of the JNPE was its focus on extensive ethnographic surveys and collecting. Boas advertised it as "[a] systematic exploration of the cultures and languages of the peoples inhabiting the coasts of the North Pacific Ocean between the Amoor River [*sic*] in Asia and Columbia River in America" (Anonymous 1897:455; Boas 1898a:4). This objective

was fulfilled with astounding success (Figs.1-2, 7–10). One can feel the breadth of the JNPE efforts in Bogoras' exuberant report on the outcome of his year-long field work in Siberia (1900–01) as quoted by Boas:

> [T]he results of this work are studies of the ethnography and anthropology of the Chukchee and Asiatic Eskimo, and partly of the Kamchadal and of the Pacific Koryak. These studies are illustrated by extensive collections, embracing five thousand ethnographical objects, thirty-three plaster casts of faces, seventy-five skulls and archaeological specimens from abandoned village sites and from graves. Other materials obtained include three hundred tales and traditions; one hundred-fifty texts in the Chukchee, Koryak, Kamchadal, and Eskimo languages; dictionaries and grammatical sketches of these languages; ninety-five phonographic records, and measurements of eight hundred-sixty individuals [the latter done mainly by Mr. Axelrod in addition to some 770 photographs—I.K., N.V.]. I also made zoological collection and kept a meteorological journal during the whole time of my field-work (Boas 1903:115).

Despite a few gaps in the proposed itinerary and study area, the expedition mostly followed its initial five-year research plan as designed by Boas in 1897. This plan was presented very early in a form of a map, "Field of Proposed Operations of the Jesup North Pacific Expedition." It was enclosed to the Annual Report of the AMNH President Morris Jesup on the activities of the museum during the year 1897 (Fig.4; Jesup 1898; Krupnik and Fitzhugh 2001:xvi). This early blueprint for the JNPE five-year field operation reveals a remarkable agreement with the actual surveys conducted by the expedition's teams between the years 1897 and 1902. The only exception was the fieldwork in western and southern Alaska (that never materialized) and on the Aleutian Islands. The latter was undertaken several years later by Waldemar and Dina Jochelson under a different project, the Ryabushinski Expedition of the Russian Geographical Society in 1909–11. The Alaska Yup'ik and Iñupiat Eskimo as well the Tlingit were dropped from the initial research plan. According to Boas, this was done deliberately, in view of the recently published monographs or the then ongoing studies by Edward W. Nelson, John Murdoch, and George T. Emmons (Boas 1903:77).

However, several later surveys, such as John Swanton's study of the Tlingit in 1904, Harlan Smith's trip to the Columbia River valley in 1903, and the Jochelsons' trip to the Aleutians and Kamchatka in 1909–11, were conducted as direct extensions of the main exped-

scientific achievement, particularly if one considers the distances and communication problems involved. One has to acknowledge, however, that individual JNPE surveys of certain areas and Native groups were quite unequal in terms of the time invested and ethnographic data collected (see critical reviews in chapters by Krauss, Inoue, Schweitzer, and Wickwire, this volume; also Cole 2001; Krupnik 1996).

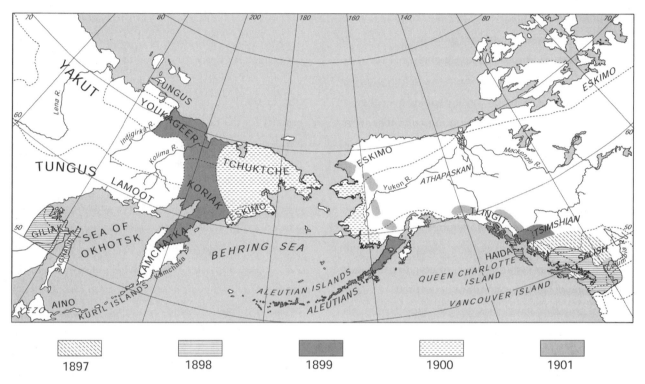

1897	1898	1899	1900	1901

4/ Field of Proposed Operations of the Jesup North Pacific Expedition, 1898 (adapted from American Museum of Natural History, Annual Report of the President for the Year 1897*)*

ition's field operations of 1897–1902. With this, the JNPE team members almost completed their announced objective to cover the area "from the Amoor River in Asia and up to Columbia Valley in North America." Altogether, the expedition field crews surveyed 17 Native nations on the Northwest Coast[2] and 10 nations in Siberia.[3] The task of supervising and coordinating this joint field plan of many individual researchers and field teams over several years was successfully accomplished by Franz Boas, the JNPE's relentless leader. It was and still remains an outstanding logistical and

As a result of these efforts, the map of Native nations of Northeast Siberia and Northwestern North America was significantly amended. The American Museum of Natural History garnered fabulous ethnographic and natural science collections that were quickly put on display in its exhibit halls, which were subsequently redesigned and expanded (Anonymous 1904a, 1904b; Jonaitis 1988; Fig.11). Several ethnographic objects were true masterpieces of Native art, ceremonialism, and ritual practices (Jonaitis 1988, 1991). The JNPE ethnographic and zoological collections (see

Hoffmann, this volume) were matched by the invaluable folklore, linguistic, and anthropometric data as well as by the unique historical photography of Native people and local landscapes of Siberia and Northwestern North America (Kendall et al. 1997; Willey 2001). And finally, albeit not as quickly as originally advertised, the JNPE did produce basic ethnographic monographs and the core folklore and linguistic data for most of the Native nations of the North Pacific. Of those, several Jesup Expedition volumes, like Bogoras' three-part monograph on the Chukchi (Bogoras 1904–9) and Jochelson's study of the Koryak (Jochelson 1908), remained the most complete reference ethnographies and folklore collections on these peoples over the entire 20th century, despite generations of subsequent anthropological research.

The JNPE was far less successful in its second declared objective, "the [s]tudy of the early history of the native races of the North American continent and their relation to the Old World" (Anonymous 1897:456; Boas 1903:91). This, we believe, was more a public-relations statement or an appealing project title, similar to "the origins of the American race" (see Boas 1898a:4–5). Most probably, it was masterminded to attract public interest and to generate funding and institutional support for the JNPE venture. Such a 'public-relations' task was, in fact, splendidly achieved, at least during earlier stages of the project (Vakhtin 2001:74–5). Nonetheless, the issue of the early peopling of the Americas never fully engaged Boas or most other JNPE members. Boas himself disclaimed it quite frankly in some of his private letters (e.g. Boas to McGhee, April 12, 1897), as he was quite skeptical about the utility of archaeological and osteological materials for any large-scale reconstruction of prehistory (cf. Jacknis 1996: 203).

In fact, such an objective was all but impossible to fulfill at that time due to the infancy of contemporary archaeological research and to its very limited technical and analytical capabilities. The time depth of the peopling of the Americas from Northern Asia, as well as the chronological span of the prehistory of the North-west Coast and Siberia, was still primarily guesswork. No reliable chronology had existed for this part of the world by the year 1900, nor was there any technical means available to build such a chronology. William Dall (1877:93–5) argued for a prehistoric crossing on ice at the Bering Strait, presumably during the "Ice Age" period. Several other contemporary scientists favored migration or migrations over a land bridge during an interglacial retreat sometime between 10,000 and 100,000 years ago (cf. Wilmsen 1965:177–8).

To make things worse, comparative archaeological collections from both Siberia and North America were all but missing, and the limited budget and duration of the JNPE was too modest, if not totally inadequate, for the task. Harlan Smith, who almost single-handedly carried out JNPE archaeological surveys on the North American side, found no evidence of distinctive cultures dating to the time of the "original migration" (Thom 2001). His limited work, however, was regarded as "[p]atently inadequate to help to clear the cause of Early Man in America" (Wilmsen 1965:178). A JNPE archaeological survey in the Amur River valley in Siberia provided even fewer results. No doubt, it was declared a "failure" even by the very person, whom Boas put in charge of it (Fowke 1906:297). It came as no surprise that the JNPE field operation produced hardly any legacy for the study of early human migrations from Asia to America and of the prehistory of the "(Native) American race," in particular.

Contribution to "Basic Science"

It was the third stated objective of the JNPE that generated major controversy, and it also contributed to the bulk of later criticism aimed at Boas and the expedition's overall accomplishments. Boas framed this objective as "[exploring] what relations the native tribes on the two sides of the North Pacific bear to each other, and particularly what influence the inhabitants of one continent may have exerted on those of the other...[w]ith a view to discovering as much as possible of their history" (Boas 1903:76).

The JNPE members advanced three basic concepts, in this regard, during and after the expedition fieldwork (see Boas 1903, 1910/2001), in developing the general scenario of the peopling of the Americas from Northeast Asia via the Bering Sea area. All three concepts addressed the issue of similarities between cultures on both sides of the North Pacific. These include:

1. The so-called *"Americanoid theory"* that claimed an American origin of certain Paleoasiatic groups in Northeastern Siberia, such as the Chukchi, Koryak, Kamchadal (Itelmen), and the Yukagir (see reviews in Ousley 2000; Ousley and Jantz 2001)

2. The *"Eskimo Wedge"* theory that suggested a relatively late arrival of the Eskimo to the North Pacific area that subsequently bisected the once unbroken continuum of the Siberian "Americanoid" and Northwest Coast American Indian groups (see review in Dumond, this volume).

3. The idea of a fundamental *cultural and physical gap* between the North Pacific coastal ("saltwater") nations and their inland neighbors, like the Tungus, the Yakut (Sakha), and the Plateau Indian groups (such as Thompson, Shuswap, and others) in Siberia and North America, respectively.

These three paradigms were to become the pillars of the JNPE and Boas' approach to North Pacific cultural (pre)history. In fact, they were advanced very early in the project, well before the entire corpus of the expedition's ethnographic, anthropometric, and linguistic data was processed and published (Anonymous 1897:455; Boas 1898a:4, 1902/1940:526–9, 1903: 115, 1905:98–9; Bogoras 1902:579–80; Jochelson 1904:414,425; Ousley and Jantz 2001:264–5, 275). Later field data and publications notwithstanding, these hypotheses remained basically intact, and they were recycled repeatedly over decades in many post-JNPE papers (cf. Boas 1928, 1933; Jochelson 1926, 1928).

By 1925, the rapidly growing body of new data and theories challenged most of the old Jesup Expedition's scenarios in Arctic/Eskimo/North Pacific prehistory. The main challenge came from the progress in

Eskimo archaeology in the Bering Strait area and in the Canadian Arctic (Krupnik 1998:203). New scenarios for ancient cultural connections in the circumpolar area became popular; they featured circumpolar rather than the Beringian/trans-North Pacific venues of cultural influences and migrations. Renewed interest in more southern lines of cultural exchange between the Northwest Coast and the Amur River area, including Japan, China, and inner Asia has been expressed by younger cohorts of scholars, including students of the original JNPE team (Krupnik 1998:203).

During the 1930s, criticism of the old JNPE paradigms was mounting from many directions. It was, however, the spectacular advance in North Pacific/Arctic archaeology—the field that was the least developed at the time of the JNPE surveys of 1897–1902—that eventually toppled its major theories in North Pacific cultural origins and connections (see Dumond, this volume). But it still gave the work of the expedition approximately twenty to twenty-five years of "theoretical pre-eminence" in the field.

Nevertheless, the core Jesup Expedition vision of the arc of the North Pacific coastland of Siberia and Northwest North America as an integrated culture area has endured for decades. This perspective was used in many later studies of the mid-1900s (e.g., Leroi-Gourhan 1946; Heizer 1943), and it has been revitalized in numerous anthropological, archaeological, and paleoenvironmental projects, publications, and major museum exhibits of the last three decades under such names as *Beringia, The North Pacific Rim, The Greater North Pacific Area*, etc. (Fitzhugh and Crowell 1988; Fitzhugh and Chaussonnet 1994; Fitzhugh 1996; Fitzhugh and Krupnik 2001; Hopkins 1967; Hopkins et al. 1982; Krupnik and Inoue 2003; Michael and VanStone 1983; Turner 1988; West 1981, 1996). Similarly, the cornerstone of the JNPE methodological approach also sustained—matching data on Native customs, folklore, languages, physical types, material objects, and unearthed archaeological remains—to prove the age-old cultural connections.

With its emphasis upon an interdisciplinary approach, the JNPE laid the foundation for the many dominant patterns and paradigms in the Arctic/North Pacific anthropology of the 20th century. Since "Jesup times" it has become a deep conviction that the saga of North Pacific cultural history could be successfully unveiled only by the concerted teamwork of field and museum ethnography, linguistics, physical anthropology, and archaeology. The recent re-evaluation of many of the expedition's outcomes, publications, and collections will, we hope, rejuvenate certain components of the JNPE legacy. Old theories often make a surprising comeback as new research technologies become available to test and challenge earlier studies.

International Cooperation as the JNPE Legacy

One key field in which the JNPE made an unquestioned and lasting contribution was international cooperation in North Pacific fieldwork, academic contacts, museum exchanges, and cultural research. By its very design, the JNPE project pioneered a new format of coordinated and simultaneous cross-boundary anthropological and museum research by the nationals and institutions of the U.S., Russia, Canada, and Germany. It also established for the first time the now common practice of concerted and highly coordinated use of international gatherings as long-term meeting places, presentation, and publication venues. And finally, it produced a model for a publication series of several successive volumes, with former team workers of different origin, country of residence, and affiliation, who delivered their contribution in a prescribed publication format over several years.[4]

The JNPE operation in British Columbia in 1897 was started as a continuation of previous research and it followed a shared program supported by the AMNH and the British Association of the Advancement of Sciences (Boas 1898a:7–8). The five years of fieldwork in Siberia (1898–1902) were carried out with the full cooperation and direct involvement of the Russian Academy of Sciences and of its Permanent Secretary,

Prof. Vasily Radloff. Radloff secured a Siberian travel permit for Berthold Laufer in 1898 (Cole 2001:36; Freed et al. 1988) and he introduced Jochelson and, later, Bogoras to Boas as prospective Siberian team members, who, in turn, introduced Leo Shternberg to Boas as a potential contributor to the JNPE publication series (Kan 2001:225–7; Vakhtin 2001:76–83). The official backing of the JNPE operations in Siberia by the Russian Academy and by Radloff, who also served as the director of the Academy's Museum of Anthropology and Ethnography (MAE) in St. Petersburg, was crucial in many aspects, including permission for traveling in the field, getting support of the local officials, and shipping collections across and out of Siberia (Figs.8–11). For these and several other reasons, Jochelson even insisted that the Siberian team work under some sort of joint sponsorship by the American Museum, the Russian Imperial Geographic Society, and the Russian Academy of Sciences.[5] Whereas Russian Government support of the JNPE proved to be dubious at best (see Freed et al. 1988; Vakhtin 2001:86–7), the Academy's and Radloff's personal backing of the JNPE was absolutely unequivocal.

The Russians also urged that any duplicate specimens from the Jesup Expedition's Siberian collections were to be donated to the MAE in return for their cooperation (Anonymous 1907:68). When the Siberian collections were finally sorted out in New York, Morris Jesup presented approximately 300 specimens as the American Museum's gift to the Tzar's family. These objects were promptly turned over to the MAE collection (Anonymous 1907:68; Mikhailova and Kupina 2002). Boas' interactions with Radloff and the Russian Academy during and after the JNPE began a long tradition of exchanges between the American Museum and the MAE (Kupina n.d.).

The Jesup Expedition team's continuous use of the International Congresses of Americanists as a meeting and promotion venue for the 25 years following the expedition is another illustration of the high value Boas and his Russian partners—Jochelson, Bogoras, and

Shternberg—assigned to international academic contacts. It also showed how strongly they tried to overcome the drawbacks of artificial separation and isolation caused by World War I and the political storms of the 20th century (Kan 2000; 2001). Their professional interactions forged during the preparation and fieldwork of the Jesup Expedition eventually developed into personal ties, as Bogoras and Jochelson stayed for several months in New York in 1903–4 while working on their Siberian collections and preparing their monographs for the JNPE volumes. This, in turn, contributed to more professional cooperation and to the orchestrated international promotion of the JNPE project. In 1904, Boas, Bogoras, Jochelson, and Shternberg delivered four Jesup-related presentations at the 14th International Congress of Americanists in Stuttgart, Germany (Krupnik 1998:205). The JNPE team members continued to use the Americanist Congresses as their main international venue at several successive sessions, including those in Québec in 1906 (Boas and Jochelson), in Vienna in 1908 (Boas), and in London in 1912 (Jochelson and Shternberg; see references in Krupnik 2001:300–7)

Personal contacts among the key Jesup Expedition members, such as Boas, Jochelson, Bogoras, and Shternberg, were rejuvenated at the 21st International Congress of Americanists in 1924 (Fig.3), after a decade-long gap created by World War I, two revolutions, and the Civil War in Russia. It blossomed again at the 23rd Congress of 1928 in New York where Boas, Jochelson, and Bogoras met personally for the last time. Several papers in Arctic/Siberian ethnology were also contributed to the New York Congress of Americanists (1928) by younger Russian students of Bogoras and Shternberg (Bogoras and Leonov 1930; Dyrenkova 1930; Ivanov 1930; Vishnevsky 1930—see Krupnik 1998:206), and by Bruno Oetteking, a Boasian disciple at the American Museum. At this time it appeared that the bonds that were fostered during the JNPE years were about to be transmitted to a second generation of students trained by members of the original Jesup Expedition team.[6] But a new partnership never materialized, because Russian-American academic contacts were severed after the years 1936–38 due to political purges in Russia and Bogoras' death. Soon much of the Pacific Coast of Siberia became enmeshed in barbed wire around GULAG labor camps and military installations, and the region became closed to international research and cooperation for almost 50 years.

However, the JNPE legacy in North Pacific cultural studies made a surprising comeback when academic contacts and exchange visits were gradually reestablished during the 1960s and the 1970s and new joint studies were launched in prehistory, archaeology, ethnology, and museum studies of the North Pacific indigenous peoples (Laughlin 1975, 1985; Michael 1979; Anonymous 1981; Michael and VanStone 1983; Fitzhugh and Crowell 1988). Since that time Russian scholars have often called the Jesup-era partnership "the most productive international venture in Siberian/North Pacific ethnography" (Gurvich 1979; Kuz'mina 1981; Gurvic and Kuzmina 1985). In both the Russian and North American academic tradition, the JNPE has a very special image as a symbol and model of openness and international collaboration (Fitzhugh 1994, 1996, this volume; Fitzhugh and Crowell 1988; Fitzhugh and Krupnik 2001; Kuz'mina 1994; Vakhtin 1993).

This special aura of the Jesup-era partnership in North Pacific cultural research was stressed repeatedly in every new international exchange effort and research cooperation, of which the *Crossroads of Continents* exhibit, the *Mini-Crossroads* exhibit tour in Alaska and Siberia (1993–7), the *Jesup 2* program, and the Jesup Expedition Centenary conference in New York in 1997 were the most successful examples. In fact, the *Crossroads of Continents* project, both as an exhibit and a publication, was promoted in the 1980s as a "delayed summary volume of Franz Boas' Jesup Expedition series" (Fitzhugh and Crowell 1988:15; Fitzhugh, this volume). But more importantly, it was seen as a beginning of a *new* era of cooperation, not a conclusion of the one started by Boas and his team in 1897.

It was surely the charisma of the Jesup Expedition field research and of its voluminous publications that motivated so many Western anthropologists to dream of field studies in Siberia for several decades after the original JNPE surveys of 1897–1902. As soon as the Cold War was over and the Ice Curtain in the Bering Sea disappeared in 1988-90, scores of Western anthropology students flew to Russia to begin the first new series of ethnological studies in Siberia in almost a century. Several of these pioneers—students of students of students of Boas—were among the participants of the Jesup Expedition centenary conference in New York in 1997. Their field studies were often conducted with Russian partners who were similarly trained by students of students of Bogoras and Shternberg or were influenced by JNPE publications. This latter contribution to the lasting JNPE legacy is certainly another of its notable achievements.

Education and Training

Any large research project in the social sciences today is also tested against such "outreach" criteria as dissemination of knowledge, education, and training. The JNPE clearly scores high along these lines. Its outstanding record of approximately 200 publications has been already cited in this regard. What is more important, Boas deliberately targeted certain periodicals, such as *Science, American Anthropologist, The American Museum Journal*, the AMNH *Annual Reports, Proceedings of the International Congresses of Americanists*, and several German scientific journals, to build an extended series of Jesup-generated publications. Other Jesup Expedition team members, particularly Laufer, Smith, Bogoras, and Jochelson followed his lead. For the first time in the history of anthropology, the outcomes of an international research project were printed, edited, translated, and consistently disseminated over several years in three languages—English, German, and Russian—across linguistic and state boundaries. With this, a new pattern in public outreach and concerted dissemination of scientific knowledge was created. Thanks to

the JNPE, this new multilingual format became solidly established in Beringian/North Pacific research, and has been successfully implemented in later efforts, including the most recent "Jesup 2" program (see Fitzhugh and Krupnik 2001).

The success of the JNPE in what is now called education and training is all the more appealing. The original expedition's field team was extremely diverse in terms of its professional and educational background. It included several young people in their early to mid-20s, such as Smith, Dixon, Axelrod, Buxton; freshly-minted Ph.D. graduates, like Laufer and Swanton; it also featured far more seasoned Russians, who were former political exiles with incomplete and aborted educations from decades earlier, such as Jochelson, Bogoras, and Shternberg (and their wives), as well as self-educated local residents, like Hunt and Teit. The only person with an academic status and established publication record in anthropology was Boas himself. Of course, there was also the project's nominal leader, Prof. Frederic W. Putnam, but he never went to the field and there is hardly any evidence that Putnam played an active role in the Expedition after 1898. We know almost nothing about his interaction with the JNPE members, other than Boas and Smith. Hence, it was mainly up to Boas to train his team members and to promote their scientific careers.

With this in mind, the team's post-expedition record in professional achievement is worth acknowledging. Bogoras, Jochelson, Laufer, Smith, Dixon, Swanton, and Shternberg built recognized academic reputations and became world-class anthropologists of their time. Several other Jesup Expedition participants had no less prominent life stories, such as Livingston Farrand, who was later the President of Cornell University and of the American Red Cross, and Dina Jochelson-Brodsky, who became the first trained female North Pacific anthropologist, with a German Ph.D. on the physical anthropology of Native women in Siberia (1906). The outstanding role of local JNPE participants, such as George Hunt and James Teit, was not fully recognized until recently (see Berman 2001; Wickwire, this volume). What *then* had been started as merely an array of enthusiastic students and self-made local experts is *now* unanimously viewed as a team of professional "super-stars."

Over the years following the expedition, the JNPE members also trained students of their own, and some of these students built successful careers in expanding and developing the Jesup Expedition's legacy. The post-Jesup students of Boas—from Kroeber to Goldenweiser to Sapir to de Laguna—eventually became the single most powerful intellectual cohort in the history of North American anthropology (Darnell 2001). Their exposure to, and enrichment by, the Jesup-era experience of their mentor, as well as his influence on the selection of their Ph.D. research, has hardly been explored and remains to be documented.

The educational impact of the Jesup Expedition experience upon the later anthropological research in Siberia was even more striking. Here, the scientific "genealogies" leading from Boas and his JNPE Russian partners have been quite visible (Krupnik 1998:205–6). During the 1920s, the two Russian members of the JNPE project, Waldemar Bogoras and Leo Shternberg, trained dozens of younger Russian anthropology students, who followed the Boasian/Jesup Expedition intellectual paradigm that combined ethnology, linguistics, folklore and museum collecting within small and well-defined research areas. These "post-Jesup" disciples shaped the new face of Siberian ethnography. Many were sent to the field to survey the areas and Native groups once charted by their teachers from the first Jesup generation. Erukhim Kreinovich (1904–84) took up Shternberg's work among the Nivkh on Sakhalin Island; Alexander Forshtein (1904–68) was sent by Bogoras to study the Siberian Yupik in Chukotka; Sergei Stebnitskii (1906–42) worked among the Reindeer Koryak once surveyed by Jochelson; and Nikolai Shnakenburg (1907–41) studied the Chukchi of the northern Chukchi Peninsula, who had not been reached in 1900–1 by Bogoras on his JNPE tour (Krupnik 1998: 207). Others surveyed the arctic and inland portions of Siberia.

Altogether, approximately 70–80 Russian scholars were active in studies of the cultures, languages, and prehistory of Siberian Native populations during the 1930s (Krupnik 1998:207). Almost all of them were born between the years 1895 and 1910; the pattern of anthropological fieldwork and research they followed was inspired, at least in some way, by the Bogoras-Shternberg brand of field and theoretical anthropology (also known as the "Leningrad School" of Siberian ethnography). Though never acknowledged in Russia as a Boasian or a Jesup Expedition legacy, it strongly influenced the field of Russian and Soviet Siberian studies for almost 40 years. Unfortunately, most of these post-Jesup students of Bogoras and Shternberg became World War II military and civilian casualties, as well as victims of the earlier political purges of the 1930s (Krupnik 1998; Reshetov 1994, 1995a, 1995b, 2002).

JNPE as an Archive of Native Cultural Resources

The need to document Native cultures and to collect pieces of this legacy before an anticipated demise under the expanding industrial civilization (later called "salvage anthropology") was clearly on the Jesup Expedition agenda. It was also one of the primary personal concerns of its many individual participants. As Bogoras bluntly put it, even the Chukchi, then the most vibrant Siberian Native nation, could endure "[o]nly if left alone by civilization. As soon as the latter comes too near, the Chukchee must follow in the way of so many other primitive tribes, and die" (Bogoras 1909:733).

The destructive impact of acculturation was reportedly quite obvious to the JNPE researchers on the North American Northwest Coast and in several places in Siberia. By vigorously collecting Native specimens, excavating sites, casting and measuring human faces and bodies, making photographs, and documenting folklore and languages, Boas and other JNPE members espoused the pattern of "salvage anthropology" (see Cole and Long 1999:236–7), which was framed according to the professional standards and positivistic values of the time. Hence, the various artifacts of Native legacies were to be collected, displayed, and preserved first and foremost for the sake of expanding academic knowledge. During the Jesup Expedition era, which was so "obsessed with objects" (cf. Jacknis 1996:194), great museums like the AMNH and the Smithsonian were seen as the main venues for the construction of anthropological knowledge and for its dissemination to the public at large. The latter *then* referred to the urban educated American and European populace. Native people were not considered as potential users of the expedition's voluminous collections and publications; at least we do not see any indications in this regard.

It took almost 100 years for the JNPE collections to undergo a miraculous transition. Before our own eyes, the expedition's various contributions are being transformed from a "corpus of scientific data" into "objects of bright pride" (Wardwell 1978) and finally into a new "cultural resource" for the Native nations of the Jesup area. This transformation has been amply documented by the *Chiefly Feasts* exhibit produced from the Jesup Expedition Northwest Coast collections at the American Museum of Natural History (Jonaitis 1991). It is similarly manifested in two recent catalogs of the traveling *Crossroads Alaska-Siberia* exhibit (Chaussonnet 1995:7) and the AMNH centennial presentation of the Jesup Expedition photography of 1897–1902 (Kendall et al. 1997).

This transformation, in fact, has resulted in an unprecedented (and quite unexpected) increase in the value of the expedition's data, publications, and museum collections. It was as if old papers and photographs, linguistic and folklore texts, archival manuscripts and hundreds of anthropological data sheets acquired additional meaning and found a new constituency. As the JNPE materials become "new resources" inspiring cultural revitalization of the area's Native nations, they do not cease to be objects of anthropological and museum science. Several papers in this volume explore

these new dimensions in the modern use of Jesup-era ethnographic collections (see chapters by Fitzhugh; Ivanov-Unarov and Ivanova-Unarova; Loring and Veltre; and Webster, this volume). They offer an inspiring perspective on how present-day people read early descriptions of their culture; how they enjoy century-old photographs; and how the old folklore records and museum artifacts are used to develop modern art, school curricula, and educate children. This was something the JNPE team members *then* hardly had in mind, but nevertheless, due to their dedicated work, it became possible *now*, 100 years after their enterprise.

Conclusion

As these and other post-JNPE achievements are brought together as parts of a single record, we believe we have solid ground for a centenary celebration. But beyond the list of the Expedition's accomplishments and shortcomings there is a certain lasting charisma to the original JNPE project. It continues to inspire anthropology professionals and local cultural enthusiasts much in the same way it fascinated its prospective members, sponsors, Boas' colleagues, and the public at large, when the expedition blueprint was first unveiled more than 100 years ago (Cole 2001; Vakhtin 2001).

From a modern perspective, one could see the JNPE as a fascinating experiment in scholarly planning and a scientist's once-in-a-lifetime dream. For the first (and in fact, the only) time during his long career, Franz Boas secured ample resources, an excellent team, and the institutional support he needed to carry out a research plan he could design, supervise, and deliver almost exclusively at his discretion.[7] It also offered him a unique opportunity to project his personal vision of anthropology, the "Americanist" tradition, in Regna Darnell's term (Darnell 2001:10–20) on a multi-year research enterprise, and to advertise that vision in the international scientific arena. That was an appeal of tremendous power. Today one can still feel the project's magnetism as palpably as many people did 100 years ago.

However, even the best-designed dreams rarely come true. The JNPE project eventually fell victim to the intellectual battle Boas fought throughout his entire academic career. Since his early professional years, he argued fervently in favor of a clear-cut distinction between two major approaches (or methods) in scientific research—one advocating the search for general laws and the other aimed at scrupulous adherence to facts. In several of his papers Boas repeatedly called this distinction an opposition between the "comparative" and the "historical" method of inquiry (Boas 1896, 1940:271–7), or the one between the "physicists" and the "cosmographers" (Boas 1887, 1940:642–43; Jacknis 1996:186–88; Stocking 1996:5). And he made it clear that he sought his own place firmly in the cosmographers' camp.

This vigorous academic partisanship was quickly challenged by and tested against the very format of the JNPE project. Boas was charged to design what we would call today the "JNPE overall program," including a project justification and fieldwork outline. Toward this end, Boas the physicist offered promises that were tempting to prospective sponsors and public audience, because of the unprecedented general implications of research he suggested (such as to "discover the origin and early history of the native American race"). Ironically, under the same scenario, Boas the cosmographer was assigned to develop a field program and to supervise the process of research, data collecting, and publication down to the minute detail. This worked well for the five years of field surveys and for publication of the expedition's reports and its various collected materials—until the cosmographer was pushed towards his last challenge: project synthesis and historical generalization.

For Boas this must have been a tormenting experience, since he was destined to overstep the very principles he zealously advocated for almost two decades. As he himself urged just one year before the Jesup Expedition began and in citing the very Native cultures of Alaska and Siberia it was supposed to survey, "[o]nly when definite results have been obtained in regard to this area [i.e., small and well-defined individual territories that form the basis of study—I.K., N.V.] is it permissible to extend the horizon beyond its limits; but the greatest care must be taken not to proceed too hastily in this" (Boas 1896, 1940:277). With hindsight, we must conclude that nothing in the expedition's voluminous data rendered any assurance that the results obtained were "definite," that "extensions beyond the horizon" were now permissible, and that any move toward generalization would not be "too hasty."

On the contrary, each Native culture studied and each area covered by the JNPE revealed its never-ending story of cultural complexity and historical depth. It is not surprising that Boas became increasingly reluctant to jump into extensive comparative speculation across the North Pacific area.[8] He did produce several short summaries of the expedition's results and/or some broad overviews of the North Pacific cultural prehistory (Boas 1903, 1905, 1910, 1925, 1928, 1933). But he continuously procrastinated and, as we believe, finally abandoned the idea of a concluding general volume for the *Jesup Expedition* series, which he had promised to Morris Jesup as a key component of the project (Cole 2001:42–3,48).[9] To Boas this was by no means an intellectual failure but rather a deliberate evasion, for he had once again realized that "[t]he solid work is still all before us" (Boas 1896, 1940:280). He simply left the task to those who might possess better data and more extensive knowledge in the future— that is, to us.

Thus, the Jesup Centenary Conference of 1997 and this volume of proceedings marks just one more step in the ongoing re-evaluation of the unique Boasian design of the JNPE project. The very list of the conference participants, which included ethnologists, linguists, physical anthropologists, archaeologists, folklorists, natural scientists, and museum curators; Americans, Canadians, Russians, Japanese, and Europeans; professional academics, Native researchers, cultural workers, and community leaders, was a roster with a distinctly

Boasian outlook. As their papers presented here reveal, there is hardly any present-day inquiry concerning the peoples and cultures of the North Pacific area that does not bear, in one way or another, an imprint of the Jesup Expedition—whether it deals with Native ethnic traditions, physical anthropology, myths, culture transformation, prehistoric relationships, cultural objects, historical photography or museum collections. Indeed, we have good cause to celebrate the centenary of the Boas' Jesup North Pacific Expedition and a memory of the person who introduced such a powerful model to anthropological science.

Acknowledgements

A shorter version of this paper was delivered as the opening address to the Jesup Expedition Centenary conference in 1997. We are grateful to William Fitzhugh, Ira Jacknis, Sergei Kan, Laurel Kendall, Julia Kupina, and William Sturtevant for their critical comments and helpful suggestions. This paper as well as earlier historiographic studies of the Jesup Expedition's legacy is an outgrowth of the *Jesup 2* program initiated in 1992.

Notes

1. The list of contracted (enlisted) participants on the Jesup Expedition includes: Franz Boas (1858–1942), Alexandr Axelrod (1879–1945), Waldemar Bogoras (1865–1936), Norman G. Buxton (1872–?), Roland Dixon (1875–1934), Livingston Farrand (1867–1939), Gerard Fowke (1855–1933), George Hunt (1854–1933), Filipp Jacobsen, Waldemar Jochelson (1855–1937), Berthold Laufer (1873–1934), John Swanton (1873–1958), James Teit (1864–1922). Mrs. Sofia Bogoras and Dina Jochelson-Brodsky (1864–1941) accompanied their husbands in the field and participated in collecting and research activities; Dina Jochelson's contribution was critical for the expedition's success in physical anthropology and photography in Siberia. Oregon C. Hastings, a professional photographer from Victoria, made dozens of photographs for the expedition in 1897; Charles F. Newcombe, another Victoria resident, participated in collecting and coastal surveys in

1897 and 1900. Frederic W. Putnam (1839–1915) officially supervised the project at the AMNH during the years 1897–98. Leo Shternberg (1861–1927) and Bruno Oetteking (1871–1960) joined the JNPE publication program after the completion of fieldwork. Several people—local guides, interpreters, Native informants, recruited dog-team drivers, and local officers—accompanied JNPE team members on their surveys across Siberia and North America, though few are specially acknowledged (see also Kan, this volume).

2. Haida, Tsimshian, Kwakiutl (Kwakwaka'wakw), Heiltsuk, Bella Coola (Nuxalk), Chilkotin, Nootka (Nuu-chah-nulth), Lilooet (Sta'atl'imx), Thompson (Nlaka'pamux), Quileute, Chinook, Chemakum, and Quinault, with the later addition of the Aleut, Tlingit, Shasta, and Maidu.

3. Chukchi, Yupik/Asiatic Eskimo, Koryak, Even (Tungus), Itelmen (Kamchadal), Yukagir, Russian Creole, Nivkh (Gilyak), Nanay (Gold), and Sakha (Yakut), with three more nations, Ainu, Orok (Uilta), and Negidal visited on shorter trips.

4. Co-authored papers and volumes were the only component of modern team work that was missing in the JNPE publications, with the exception of two volumes of Kwakiutl texts that had both Boas' and Hunt's names on the cover, and a few minor pieces by Boas incorporated into contributions by Smith, Teit, and Jochelson. Even the husband-wife field team of Waldemar and Dina Jochelson did not publish anything under their two names.

5. This can be seen from a letterhead printed on several of Jochelson's letters and field reports from Siberia (now at the AMNH): Siberian Department of the Jesup North Pacific Expedition fitted out by the American Museum of Natural History with the assistance of the Russian Imperial Academy of Sciences and the Russian Imperial Geographic Society.

6. The best known example was Julia Averkieva's fieldwork with Boas among the Kwakiutl in 1930–31 (Averkieva and Sherman 1992). Averkieva (1946:102) mentioned five Russian anthropology students who went on exchange fellowships to the U.S. in 1929. At least three American anthropologists and anthropology students—Roy Barton, Emanuel Gonick, a former

student of Kroeber, and Archie Phinney, a Native American student of Boas—were studying or working in Leningrad during the 1930s on international research fellowships arranged by Boas and Bogoras (Krupnik 1998; Willard 2000).

7. Thus, the Jesup Expedition has been rightly credited as one of the stepping stones in what was called "The Boasian Anthropological Survey Tradition" (Cole and Long 1999:234). All postulated tenets of this approach—anti-evolutionism; the tilt toward diffusionist interpretations; the ethics of salvage ethnology; the collection of folklore and linguistic texts; the famous "four-field" focus of fieldwork; and the primary role of trained professionals (ibid:234–6)—were amply displayed in the JNPE organization, fieldwork, and publications.

8. Regna Darnell (2001:43) made a similar point in her evaluation of the general shift in Boas' vision of anthropology that took place around 1905, obviously, or at least partly, as a result of the JNPE experience. "Early in his career, perhaps as a carry-over from his scientific training in physics and geography, Boas emphasized the possibility, albeit at some unspecified future time, of arriving at "laws governing the growth of culture" (Boas 1898b:2). [...]When laws analogous to those of the natural sciences failed to emerge, Boas retreated to a deconstructionist rhetoric of what he considered premature generalizations distorting the increasing body of ethnographic data against which potential "laws" could be tested (see Boas 1906:642).

9. The plan to provide a summary report of the JNPE surveys was first announced by Boas in his paper delivered at the Thirteenth International Congress of Americanists (1902). According to his plan, this would be accomplished as the final volume of the Jesup Expedition series. It was featured several times as "Volume 12. Summary and Final Results" on the cover pages of the subsequent volumes under the Jesup Expedition series published during the 1900s and 1910s. The last time it was mentioned in 1930 as the "forthcoming Pt.3 of Vol. 11" ("Summary and Final Results") on the cover page of Volume 11, Pt. 1 (Oetteking 1930). This summary volume was obviously never produced and probably never even started.

References

Anonymous

1897   Proposed Explorations on the Coasts of the North Pacific Ocean. *Science* 5(116):455–7.

1904a   A General Guide to the American Museum of Natural History. *The American Museum Journal*, Supplement 4(1). New York.

1904b   Primitive Art. A Guide Leaflet to Collections in the American Museum of Natural History. Ibid, 4(3). New York.

1907   Muzei antropologii i etnografii Imperatorskoi Akademii Nauk v period 12-letnego upravleniia V.V.Radlova (1894–1906) [Museum of Anthropology and Ethnography of the Imperial Academy of Sciences during the 12-Year Tenure of V.V. Radloff (1894–1906)]. In: *Ko dniu semidesiatiletiia Vasiliia Vasil'evicha Radlova*. St. Petersburg.

1981   Introduction. In *Traditsionnye kul'tury Severnoi Sibiri i Severnoi Ameriki* (Traditional Cultures of Northern Siberia and North America). Il'ia S. Gurvich, ed. Pp. 3–5. Moscow: Nauka Publishers.

Averkieva, Julia P.

1946   Franz Boas (1858–1942). *Kratkie soobshcheniia Instituta etnografii AN SSSR* 1:101–11. Moscow and Leningrad.

Averkieva, Julia, and Mark A. Sherman

1992   *Kwakiutl String Figures*. Seattle: University of Washington Press and American Museum of Natural History.

Berman, Judith

2001   Unpublished Materials of Franz Boas and George Hunt: A Record of 45 Years of Collaboration. In: *Gateways. Exploring the Legacy of the Jesup North Pacific Expedition, 1897–1902*. Igor Krupnik and William W. Fitzhugh, eds. Pp. 181–213. Contributions to Circumpolar Anthropology, 1. Washington, DC: Arctic Studies Center.

Boas, Franz

1887   The Study of Geography. *Science* 9:137–41 (Reprinted in: *Race, Language, and Culture*. Pp. 639–47. New York: Macmillan. 1940).

1896   The Limitations of the Comparative Method of Anthropology. *Science*, n.s. 4:901–8 (Reprinted in: *Race, Language, and Culture*. Pp. 270–80. New York: Macmillan. 1940).

1898a   The Jesup North Pacific Expedition. *The Jesup North Pacific Expedition*, vol.1, pt.1, pp.1–12. *American Museum of Natural History Memoirs*, 2. New York: G.E. Stechert.

1898b   Introduction. In: Traditions of the Thompson Indians of British Columbia, by James Teit. *Memoirs of the American Folk-Lore Society* 6:3–18. New York.

1902   Some Problems in North American Archaeology. *American Journal of Archaeology* 6:1–6 (Reprinted in: *Race, Language, and Culture.* Pp. 525–9. New York: Macmillan. 1940).

1903   The Jesup North Pacific Expedition. *The American Museum Journal* 3(5):73–119. New York.

1905   The Jesup North Pacific Expedition. In *International Congress of Americanists, 13th Session, Held in New York in 1902.* Pp.91–100. Easton, PA: Eschenbach.

1906   Some Philological Aspects of Anthropological Research. *Sicence* 23:641–45.

1910   Die Resultate der Jesup-Expedition. In: *Internationaler Americanisten-Kongress, 16 Tagung, Wien. 1908. Erste* Hälfte. Pp.3–18. Vienna and Leipzig. Reprinted in 2001 as: The Results of the Jesup Expedition. In: *Gateways. Exploring the Legacy of the Jesup North Pacific Expedition, 1897–1902.* Igor Krupnik and William W. Fitzhugh, eds. Pp. 17–24. Contributions to Circumpolar Anthropology, 1.

1925   America and the Old World. In *Congrès International des Américanists, Compte-rendue de la 21e Session, Deuxième Partie. Tenue au Göteborg en 1924.* Pp.21–8. Göteborg Museum.

1928   Migrations of Asiatic Races and Cultures to North America. *Scientific Monthly.* 28:110–7.

1933   Relations between North-West America and North-East Asia. In *The American Aborigines: Their Origin and Antiquity.* Diamond Jenness, ed. Pp. 357–70. University of Toronto Press. (Reprinted in: *Race, Language, and Culture.* Pp. 344–55. New York: Macmillan. 1940).

Bogoras, Waldemar

1902   Folklore of Northeastern Asia, as Compared with that of Northwestern America. *American Anthropologist,* n.s. 4:577–683.

1904–09 The Chukchee. *The Jesup North Pacific Expedition,* vol. 7, pts. 1–3. *Memoirs of the American Museum of Natural History,* 11. Leiden: E.J. Brill; New York: G.E. Stechert.

1927   Drevnie pereseleniia narodov v Severnoi Azii i v Amerike (Ancient Human Migrations in Northern Asia and in America). *Sbornik Muzeia antropologii i etnografii* 6:37–62. Leningrad.

Bogoras, Waldemar, and Nikolai J. Leonov

1930   Cultural Work among the Lesser Nationalities of the North of the USSR. In *International Congress of Americanists, 23rd Session, New York, 1928.* Pp. 445–50. New York.

Chaussonnet, Valérie, ed.

1995   *Crossroads Alaska. Native Cultures of Alaska and Siberia.* Washington, DC: Arctic Studies Center.

Cole, Douglas

2001   The Greatest Thing Undertaken by Any Museum? Franz Boas, Morris Jesup, and the North Pacific Expedition. In: *Gateways. Exploring the Legacy of the Jesup North Pacific Expedition, 1897–1902.* Igor Krupnik and William W. Fitzhugh, eds. Pp.29–70. Contributions to Circumpolar Anthropology,1. Washington, DC: Arctic Studies Center.

Cole, Douglas, and Alex Long

1999   The Boasian Anthropological Survey Tradition. The Role of Franz Boas in North American Anthropological Surveys. In *Surveying the Record. North American Scientific Exploration to 1930.* Edward C. Carter II, ed. Pp.225–49. Memoirs of the American Philosophical Society, 231. Philadelphia.

Dall, William H.

1877   Tribes of the Extreme Northwest. *Bureau of Ethnology, Contributions to North American Ethnology* 1: 1–121. Washington.

Darnell, Regna

2001   *Invisible Genealogies. A History of Americanist Anthropology.* Lincoln and London: University of Nebraska Press.

Dyrenkova, Nadezhda P.

1930   Bear Worship among the Turkish Tribes of Siberia. In *International Congress of Americanists, 23rd Session, New York, 1928.* Pp. 411–40. New York.

Fitzhugh, William W.

1994   Crossroads of Continents: Review and Prospect. In *Anthropology of the North Pacific Rim.* William W. Fitzhugh and Valerie Chaussonnet, eds. Pp.27–52. Washington and London: Smithsonian Institution Press.

1996   Jesup II: Anthropology of the North Pacific. *Northern Notes* 4:41–62. Hanover, NH.

Fitzhugh, William W., and Valérie Chaussonnet, eds.

1994   *Anthropology of the North Pacific Rim.* Washington and London: Smithsonian Institution Press.

Fitzhugh, William W., and Aron Crowell

1988   Crossroads of Continents: Beringian Oecumene. In: *Crossroads of Continents. Cultures of Siberia and Alaska.* William W. Fitzhugh and Aron Crowell, eds. Pp.9–16. Washington, DC: Smithsonian Institution Press.

Fitzhugh, William W., and Igor Krupnik

2001   Introduction. In: *Gateways. Exploring the Legacy of the Jesup North Pacific Expedition, 1897–1902.* Igor Krupnik and William W. Fitzhugh, eds. Pp. 1–16. Contributions to Circumpolar Anthropology,1. Washington, DC: Arctic Studies Center.

Fowke, Gerard

1906   Exploration of the Lower Amur Valley. *American Anthropologist,* n.s. 8(2): 276–95.

Freed, Stanley A., Freed, Ruth S., and Laila Williamson

1988   Capitalist Philanthropy and Russian Revolutionaries: The Jesup North Pacific Expedition (1897–1902). *American Anthropologist* 90(1):7–23.

Gurvich, Il'ia S.

1979   An Ethnographic Study of Cultural Parallels among the Aboriginal Populations of Northern Asia and Northern North America. *Arctic Anthropology* 16(1):32–8.

Gurvic, Ilya S., and Lyudmila P. Kuzmina

1985   W. Bogoras et W. Jochelson: Deux éminant représentants de l'éthnographie russe. *Inter-Nord* 17: 145–51. Paris.

Heizer, Robert F.

1943   Aconite Poison Whaling in Asia and America. An Aleutian Transfer to the New World. *Bureau of American Ethnology, Bulletin* 133:415–68.

Hopkins, David M., ed.

1967   *The Bering Land Bridge*. Stanford: Stanford University Press.

Hopkins, David M., John V., Matthews, Jr., Charles E. Schwager, and Steven B. Young

1982   *Paleoecology of Beringia*. New York: Academic Press.

Ivanov, Sergei V.

1930   Aleut Hunting Headgear and Its Ornamentation. In *International Congress of Americanists, 23rd Session, New York, 1928*. Pp. 477–504. New York.

Jacknis, Ira

1996   The Ethnographic Object and the Object of Ethnology in the Early Career of Franz Boas. In *Volksgeist as Method and Ethic. Essays on Boasian Ethnography and the German Anthropological Tradition*. George W. Stocking, ed. Pp.185–214. History of Anthropology, 8. Madison: University of Wisconsin Press.

Jesup, Morris K.

1898   *Annual Report of the President for the Year 1897*. New York: American Museum of Natural History.

Jochelson, Waldemar

1904   The Mythology of the Koryak. *American Anthropologist*, n.s. 6(4):413–25.

1908   The Koryak. *The Jesup North Pacific Expedition*, vol. 6, pts. 1–2. *Memoirs of the American Museum of Natural History*, 10. Leiden: E.J. Brill; New York: G.E. Stechert.

1926   The Ethnological Problems of Bering Sea. *The American Museum Journal (Natural History)* 26(1): 90-5.

1928   *Peoples of Asiatic Russia*. New York: American Museum of Natural History.

Jonaitis, Aldona

1988   *From the Land of the Totem Poles. The Northwest Coast Indian Art Collection at the American Museum of Natural History*. Seattle: University of Washington Press; New York: American Museum of Natural History.

1991   Chiefly Feasts: The Creation of an Exhibit. In *Chiefly Feasts. The Enduring Kwakiutl Potlach*. Aldona Jonaitis, ed. Pp. 21–70. Seattle: University of Washington Press; New York: American Museum of Natural History.

Kan, Sergei

2000   The Mystery of the Missing Monograph: Or, Why Shternberg's "Social Organization of the Gilyak" Never Appeared among the Jesup Expedition Publications. *European Review of Native American Studies* 14(2):19–38.

2001   The "Russian Bastian" and Boas: Why Shternberg's "Social Organization of the Gilyak" Never Appeared among the Jesup Expedition Publications. In: *Gateways. Exploring the Legacy of the Jesup North Pacific Expedition, 1897–1902*. Igor Krupnik and William W. Fitzhugh, eds. Pp. 217–55. Contributions to Circumpolar Anthropology,1. Washington, DC: Arctic Studies Center.

Kendall, Laurel, Barbara Mathé, and Thomas R. Miller, eds.

1997   *Drawing Shadows to Stone. The Photography of the Jesup North Pacific Expedition, 1897–1902*. New York: American Museum of Natural History; Seattle: University of Washington Press.

Krupnik, Igor

1996   The 'Bogoras Enigma': Bounds of Cultures and Formats of Anthropologists. In: *Grasping the Changing World. Anthropological Concepts in the Postmodern Era*. Vaclav Hubinger, ed. Pp. 35–52. London: Routledge.

1998   "Jesup Genealogy." Intellectual Partnership and Russian-American Cooperation in Arctic/North Pacific Anthropology. Part 1: From the Jesup Expedition to the Cold War, 1897–1948. *Arctic Anthropology* 35(2):199–225.

2001   A Jesup Bibliography: Tracking the Published and Archival Legacy of the Jesup Expedition. In: *Gateways. Exploring the Legacy of the Jesup North Pacific Expedition, 1897–1902*. Igor Krupnik and William W. Fitzhugh, eds. Pp. 297–316.Contributions to Circumpolar Anthropology, 1. Washington, DC: Arctic Studies Center.

Krupnik, Igor, and Koichi Inoue

2003   The *Raven's Arch* International Symposium. Jesup-2 Program Marches On. *Arctic Studies Center Newsletter* 11 (forthcoming).

Kupina, Julia P.

n.d   Gain or Loss? The History of Collection Exchanges between the Museum of Anthropology and Ethnography of the Russian Academy of Sciences (Kunstkamera) and American Museums. Unpublished paper, 1998 (quoted with author's permission).

Kuz'mina, Liudmila P.

1981   Fol'klor eskimosov (po materialam V.G. Bogoraza) [Folklore of the Eskimo (According to the Data Collected by Waldemar Bogoras)]. In *Traditsionnye kul'tury Severnoi Sibiri i Severnoi*

Ameriki. Il'ia S. Gurvich, ed. Pp. 200–12. Moscow: Nauka Publishers.

1994 The Jesup North Pacific Expedition: A History of Russian-American Cooperation. In: *Anthropology of the North Pacific Rim.* William W. Fitzhugh and Valérie Chaussonnet, eds. Pp. 63-77. Washington and London: Smithsonian Institution Press.

Laughlin, William S.

1975 Aleuts: Ecosystem, Holocene History, and Siberian Origin (Soviet and U.S. Scientists Join in the Study of the Origins of the First Americans). *Science* 189(4202):507–15.

1985 Russian-American Bering Sea Relations: Research and Reciprocity. *American Anthropologist* 87(4):775–92.

Leroi-Gurhan, André

1946 Archéologie du Pacifique-Nord. Matériaux pour l'étude des Relations entre les Peuples Riverains d'Asie et d'Amérique. *Travaux et Mémoires de l'Institut d'Éthnologie* 42. Paris. Institut d'Éthnologie.

Mikhailova, Elena, and Julia P. Kupina

2002 Jesup Collections in Russia (1902–2002): A Life After Jesup. Paper presented at the International Symposium, *The Raven's Arch: Jesup North Pacific Expedition Revisited.* Sapporo, Japan.

Miller, Thomas R., and Barbara Mathé

1997 Drawing Shadows to Stone. In: *Drawing Shadows to Stone. The Photography of the Jesup North Pacific Expedition, 1897–1902.* Laurel Kendall, Barbara Mathé, and Thomas R. Miller, eds. Pp.19–40. New York: American Museum of Natural History; Seattle: University of Washington Press.

Michael, Henry N.

1979 A U.S.-U.S.S.R. Symposium on the Peopling of the New World: Preface. *Arctic Anthropology* 16(1):1.

Michael, Henry N., and James W. VanStone

1983 Introduction. In *Cultures of the Bering Sea Region: Papers from an International Symposium.* Henry P. Michael and James W. VanStone, eds. Pp. 5–6. New York: IREX.

Oetteking, Bruno

1930 Craniology of the North Pacific Coast. *The Jesup North Pacific Expedition,* vol. 11, pt. 1. *Memoirs of the American Museum of Natural History,* 15. Leiden: E.J. Brill; New York: G.E. Stechert.

Ousley, Stephen

2000 Boas, Brinton, and the Jesup North Pacific Expedition: The Return of the Americanoids. *European Review of Native American Studies* 14(2):11–7.

Ousley, Stephen and Richard Jantz

2001 500 Year Old Questions, 100 Year Old Data, Brand New Computers: Biological Data from the Jesup Expedition and the Paradox of the "Americanoid" Theory. In: *Gateways. Exploring the Legacy of the Jesup North Pacific Expedition, 1897–1902.* Igor Krupnik

and William W. Fitzhugh, eds. Pp. 257–77. Contributions to Circumpolar Anthropology, 1. Washington, DC: Arctic Studies Center.

Reshetov, Alexander M.

1994 Repressirovannaia etnografiia: liudi i sud'by (Persecuted Ethnography: People and Their Destiny). *Kunstkamera. Etnograficheskie tetradi* 4:185–221, 5–6:342–68. St. Petersburg

1995a Otdanie dolga. Pamiati sotrudnikov Instituta etnografii AN SSSR pogibshikh v blokadnom Leningrade (Paying the Tribute. In Memory of the Staff Researchers of the Institute of Ethnography of the Academy of Sciences, Who Perished in Besieged Leningrad). *Etnograficheskoe obozrenie* 2:40–62. Moscow.

1995b Otdanie dolga. Pamiati sotrudnikov Instituta etnografii AN SSSR, pogibshikh v boiakh za Rodinu (Paying the Tribute. In Memory of the Staff Researchers of the Institute of Ethnography of the Academy of Sciencess Killed in Action in Defending the Motherland). Ibid 3:3–20; 4:3–24.

2002 Alexander Semenovich Forshtein (1904–1968). Stranitsy biografii repressiorvannogo uchenogo (Alexander S. Forshtein, 1904–1968. Some Biographical Notes about a Purged Scientist). *Dikovskie chteniia* 2:275–9. Magadan

Stocking, George W., Jr.

1996 Introduction: Boasian Ethnography and the German Anthropological Tradition. In *Volksgeist as Method and Ethic. Essays on Boasian Ethnography and the German Anthropological Tradition.* George W. Stocking, Jr., ed. Pp.3–8. History of Anthropology, 8. Madison: University of Wisconsin Press.

Thom, Brian

2001 Harlan I. Smith's Jesup Fieldwork on the Northwest Coast. In: *Gateways. Exploring the Legacy of the Jesup North Pacific Expedition, 1897–1902.* Igor Krupnik and William W. Fitzhugh, eds. Pp.139–80. Contributions to Circumpolar Anthropology,1. Washington, DC: Arctic Studies Center.

Turner, Christy G. II

1988 Ancient Peoples of the North Pacific Rim. In: *Crossroads of Continents. Cultures of Siberia and Alaska.* William W. Fitzhugh and Aron Crowell, eds. Pp. 111–16. Washington and London: Smithsonian Institution Press.

Vakhtin, Nikolai B.

1993 Jesup-2: Novaia programma sotsial'no-anthropologicheskikh issledovanii na Severe (Jesup-2: New blueprint for socio-anthropological research in the North). *Kunstkamera. Etnograficheskie tetradi* 1:211–3. St. Petersburg.

2001 Franz Boas and the Shaping of the Jesup North Pacific Expedition, 1895–1900. In: *Gateways. Exploring the Legacy of the Jesup North Pacific Expedition,*

1897–1902. Igor Krupnik and William W. Fitzhugh, eds. Pp.71–89. Contributions to Circumpolar Anthropology,1. Washington, DC: Arctic Studies Center.

Vishnevsky, Boris N.

1930   Contribution to the Anthropology of Northeast Asiatic Tribes. In *International Congress of Americanists, 23rd Session, New York, 1928*. Pp. 881–94. New York.

Wardwell, Allen

1978   *Objects of Bright Pride. Northwest Coast Indian Art from the American Museum of Natural History.* New York: The American Federation of Arts and University of Washington Press.

West, Frederick H.

1981   *The Archaeology of Beringia*. New York: Columbia University Press.

1996   *American Beginnings. The Prehistory and Palaeoecology of Beringia*. Frederick H. West, ed. Chicago: University of Chicago Press.

Willey, Paula

2001   Photographic Record of the Jesup Expedition: A Review of the AMNH Photo Collection. In: *Gateways. Exploring the Legacy of the Jesup North Pacific Expedition, 1897–1902*. Igor Krupnik and William W. Fitzhugh, eds. Pp.317–26. Contributions to Circumpolar Anthropology,1. Washington, DC: Arctic Studies Center.

Willard, William

2000   American Anthropologists on the Neva: 1930–40. *History of Anthropology Newsletter* XXVII(1):3–8.

Wilmsen, Edwin M.

1965   An Outline of Early Man Studies in the United States. *American Antiquity* 31(2):172–92.

The So-Called "Eskimo Wedge":
A Century after Jesup

DON E. DUMOND

A central accomplishment of the Jesup North Pacific Expedition was the demonstration of systematic cultural similarities among Asian and American peoples around the northern coastline of the Pacific Ocean. Folklore, in particular, suggested a continuity from Northwest Coast Indian groups on the east to Paleo-Asiatic Siberian people such as Chukchi, Itelmen, and Koryak on the west—but a continuity seemingly interrupted by Eskimo in Alaska and around Bering Strait. Bogoras (1902:670) and then Jochelson (1908:359–60) were evidently the first to use the term "wedge" in inferring a late intrusion of these Eskimo people to split apart a formerly unbroken chain of the North Pacific peoples, and both continued in this conception (e.g., Bogoras 1925:225–26; Jochelson 1928:53–4).

Whoever actually originated this vision, Boas (e.g., 1905:98–9) found it to harmonize with his own previously expressed conviction that the Eskimo people had moved to the Bering and Chukchi seas from a place of origin farther east in North America (Boas 1888:39). Thus, he remarked that:

> So far as the available material allows us to judge, it would seem that the similarities between the Eskimo and the North Pacific Coast Indians are unimportant as compared to the similarities between the Koryak and Chukchee and these Indians. We must infer from these facts that the Eskimo are new arrivals on the Pacific side of America, and that they interrupted, at an early period, the communication between the Siberian and Indian tribes (Boas 1905:98–9).

And the theme was set.

Bogoras (1925:224–34) and Jochelson (1908:358–9) were more noncommittal with regard to a point of origin for this "Eskimo wedge." Nevertheless, the custom of arguing over American versus Asian origins of the Eskimo and related Aleut peoples is an old one (see, for example, summaries in Collins 1937:1–13, 1951:423–25) that has continued into recent decades. At the same time, there is a shared opinion that the historic Eskimo possessed the most successful of all aboriginal adaptations to the winter-frozen seas lying between northeast Asia and northwestern North America. Bogoras, the ethnographer, for instance, belittled both Itelmen (Kamchadal) and coastal Koryak when contrasted with Asiatic Eskimo in that regard (Bogoras 1925:217, 226).

The notion of a wedge-like movement of Eskimo to Bering Strait, however, was arrived at by Jesup researchers not only without direct field study of Alaskan Eskimo people, but also in the complete absence of any archaeological information pertaining to the Eskimo region of Siberia and America. To cast light on the development of Eskimo culture and of this postulated "wedge," I examine presently available archaeological evidence both of ancient linkages across the northernmost extension of the Pacific and of the development of that northern maritime adaptation which the Eskimo people so well exemplified.

The Terminal Pleistocene

As is well known, there is no consensus regarding the time and circumstance of the initial peopling of the

New World—generally presumed to have been by way of the Pleistocene-age Beringian land platform that united Asia and America when seas were lower. There is more agreement that by sometime before 10,000 radiocarbon years ago,[1] when the Beringian platform began to flood by rising waters that would form the Bering and Chukchi seas (Elias et al. 1992; Fairbanks 1989), terrestrial hunters of pronouncedly Asian cast were present in what is now Alaska. These chippers of blades, of bladelets ("microblades") pushed from small wedge-shaped cores, and of a few bifaces or spear-point-like implements, have been referred to as the American Paleo-Arctic cultural tradition (Anderson 1968, 1970), and in central Alaska to the Denali complex (e.g., West 1967, 1996:546–7). In Northeast Asia (Fig. 5), the technological analog has been most commonly termed the Diuktai culture, which was well represented in the Lena River drainage a number of millennia before 10,000 years ago (Mochanov 1977; Mochanov and Fedose'eva 1984, 1996), and at partly concurrent times as far east as the territory of Russian coastal Primorye [Far Eastern Maritime Region – ed.] (Larichev et al. 1992), as well as Hokkaido (Aikens and Higuchi 1982), Sakhalin Island (Larichev et al. 1992; Vasil'evskii 1996), Kamchatka Peninsula (Dikov 1977, 1996) and the Chukotka (Chukchi) Peninsula (Dikov 1993).[2]

In both Northeast Asia and Alaska this stage was followed by, or developed into, another stage in which somewhat broader blades were derived from less formally restricted cores, and bifaces were normally lacking (Ackerman 1992; Mochanov 1977; Mochanov and Fedose'eva 1984). In Siberia this Sumnagin culture is dated as early as 10,000 years ago (Mochanov and Fedose'eva 1984). In America the comparable manifestation is present by 8000 years ago, and perhaps some centuries earlier, at which time it would appear that communication with Asia was continuing. People of this stamp and perhaps their microblade-making predecessors were present along the shores of the North Pacific in what is now southeastern Alaska (Ackerman 1992, with many references). Although fau-

nal remains are scarce, one of the sites there has yielded remains of mollusks and of both ocean and freshwater fishes, in levels dated about 8200 years ago (Ackerman et al. 1985).

By this time, also, there were people occupying the Anangula Blade site, located on what is now an islet near the coast of present Umnak Island, one of the two largest of the Fox group of the eastern Aleutians (Aigner 1978; Laughlin 1975). It has been argued that this location was already insular at the time of occupation (Black 1974). Although that view has been challenged (Thorson and Hamilton 1986), the site was clearly positioned at the ocean edge on either an island or a salient peninsula. Again, significant faunal remains are lacking, but the extreme edgewater location alone is enough to suggest subsistence attention to the seacoast.[3]

In Asia, however, sites of the same period appear to have been oriented consistently toward terrestrial resources. Although trade in obsidian from Hokkaido through Sakhalin Island developed to its highest point after the two land masses were separated by the flooding of the strait between them (Vasil'evskii 1996), suggesting an ability to make serious use of watercraft well before 7000 years ago, there is no locational or faunal evidence of any serious focus on marine resources (Yaroslav V. Kuz'min, personal communication, 1997).

Whatever the case for communication between Asia and America in the two or three millennia following the end of the Pleistocene, by about 6000 years ago paths between Alaska and Chukotka (Chukchi Peninsula) were closed by rising seas that established ocean currents in substantially their present pattern through Bering Strait. At this date the earliest Neolithic cultures of Siberia (Mochanov and Fedos-e'eva 1984) show no resemblance to what, in the then deglaciated northwestern America, is called the Northern Archaic tradition (Anderson 1968), or to the Ocean Bay tradition of the north Pacific shore around Kodiak Island (D. Clark 1979).

Nevertheless, at this same time there are clear indications of an improved adaptation to the coast of the North Pacific in Asia as well as in North America. Significantly, in both cases such advances occur south of the region in which sea ice forms in winter. In Northeast Asia, the best information proceeds from the northernmost Japanese island of Hokkaido, where shellmounds that may date as early as 7000 years ago 6000 years ago (David Yesner, personal communication, 1997), although comparable sites are not known to be numerous in the region for another two millennia (Yaroslav V. Kuz'min, personal communication, 1997; see articles in Vostretsov 1998). All of these Asian sites, however, are south of 45° north latitude and more than 3000 km from the nearest point in Asia that was occupied by historically known Eskimo.

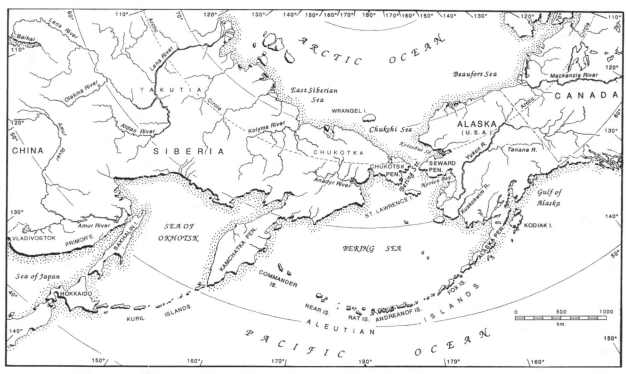

5/ Northeast Asia and the adjacent nothwesternmost section of North America, with major locations mentioned in the text

yield vertebrate fauna including sea lion, fur seal, dolphin, and whale (Nishimoto 1988; Okada 1998). By 6000 years before present some Hokkaido people were deriving as much as 50 percent of their dietary protein from marine sources (Minagawa and Akazawa 1992). The great majority of relevant Hokkaido sites are on coasts open all year, although one or two lie on the northern shore, which is icebound in winter. On the perennially open coast of Primorye [Russian Far Eastern 'Maritime Region' – ed.] near Vladivostok, the site of Boisman 2 (Popov et al. 1995) has yielded a substantial marine fauna possibly dated as much as

In America, the southern limit of icebound coasts lies much farther north. Near Kodiak Island, at latitude 57°, seas are open all winter, and sites dating shortly after 6000 years ago have yielded not only plentiful barbed harpoon heads, but faunal remains of harbor seal, porpoise, sea otter, and Steller sea lion, as well as shorebirds, waterfowl, and albatross, and fishes such as cod, salmon, and halibut (G.H. Clark 1977; Dumond 1998a). By 5500 years ago or shortly thereafter, an analogous complex was present along the open-water seas of the eastern Aleutians, at both Umnak and Unalaska Islands of the Fox Island group, with remains of seal, cod, and halibut at the latter (Davis 2001; Knecht and Davis 2001; Knecht et al. 2001; Yesner and Mack 1998). In contrast to contemporary maritime-related sites in Asia, these are some ten degrees and a thousand kilometers farther north, and both are within the region occupied by Eskimo-Aleut people at the time of first contact with Europeans in the 18th century.

Further, according to evidence now available, the period following those first unmistakable indications of maritime proficiency saw the peopling of the Aleutian Islands west of the Fox Islands group. This is indicated by a substantial body of radiometric dates, including many obtained by the U.S. Bureau of Indian Affairs in the course of investigations pursuant to the Alaska Native Claims Settlement Act. The pattern developed is one of human passage into the island chain from east to west. After dates from the Fox Islands of 5500 years ago and earlier, multiple dates from Amchitka in the Rat group of islands indicate occupation probably well before 4000 radiocarbon years ago, on Agattu and Shemya in the Near Islands by about 2600 years ago (Dumond 2001:301–2).[4] The material culture of all islands sampled is characterized by a variety of sea-hunting artifacts of organic materials including both barbed and toggling harpoons, many with chipped stone insets; it also includes lip ornaments or labrets, oil-burning lamps, and many other implements chipped from stone (e.g., McCartney 1984). In short, this was a culture with unmistakable affinities to that of the ethnographically known Aleut people, as well as with many parallels with the lifeway of Eskimo people farther north. Whatever the case with the earliest inhabitants of the Umnak region 8000 years ago, for at least the past 4500 years the record of continuity in the Aleutian Islands is unmistakable.

In summary, it seems evident that even the Near Islands were reached no less than 2600 radiocarbon years ago, and perhaps considerably earlier. Despite the lack of extensive faunal remains in small collections derived from a number of these tests, such re-

mains from the more extensive investigations, together with the isolated insular character of the western Aleutians, confirm a mature maritime subsistence.

Behind the Ice-Fast Shores of Asia

North of the southern limit of sea ice, however, progress toward full utilization of the seacoast was slower. In Asia, between 5000 and 3000 radiocarbon years ago various Neolithic peoples had begun to move closer to the coasts on Sakhalin Island and around the Sea of Okhotsk, including the lower reaches of the Amur River, and they spread into the interior hinterland of the northwestern coast of the Bering Sea south of the Chukchi Peninsula. These various "Neolithic" peoples, some of whom now used ceramics while others did not, were characterized by subsistence pursuits that emphasized river fishing or the hunting of terrestrial animals. Whereas some of these folk did visit the seacoast, their use of marine resources was evidently seasonal and sporadic, forming no major focus of subsistence effort (Dumond and Bland 1995, with references).

It was several centuries after 3000 years ago that these seasonally ice-bound Asian regions first saw peoples who made more serious use of the ocean shore, establishing permanent settlements by the sea, using implements such as toggling harpoons, and depending significantly on sea mammals and ocean fishes, although in many cases being still seasonally interested in the interior. The newer coastal peoples included those of the Susuia culture of southern Sakhalin Island (Shubin and Shubina 1984; Vasil'evskii 1996), which is seen by some researchers as an initial stage of the maritime Okhotsk culture, by others as a local predecessor; and they included those of the Tokarev culture of the northern Okhotsk Sea (Lebedintsev 1990), and of the Early Lakhtin culture of the Bering Sea coast (Orekhov 1987). The appearance of these cultures was fairly closely contemporary, between about 2700 and 2500 years ago. By 2000 years ago or not long after, they were followed, respectively, by the Ozersk stage of the Okhotsk culture, by the Old Koryak culture, and by the "Paleometal" stage of the Lakhtin culture, all of which involved still more developed adaptations to the coasts that freeze in winter (for tabulations of relevant dates, see Dumond and Bland 1995).

Nevertheless, as with the ethnographic Itelmen and Koryak referred to by Bogoras, even those further developments fell short of the Eskimo adaptation to the icy coasts. For instance, of even the closest Lakhtin-culture neighbors of the Eskimo, Dikov (1979:256) remarked that the bone and ivory technology was not as a rule comparable to that found in early Eskimo sites of the Bering Strait region. And on the coasts of the Chukchi Peninsula later occupied by identifiable Eskimo people, he found no indications of any pre-Eskimo occupations exhibiting a maritime adaptation comparable to those farther south just mentioned (Dikov 1993; see also Dumond and Bland 1995:430–4, with references).[5]

And the Frozen Coasts of America

In America, an analog of the a-ceramic Neolithic cultures of the east Russian interior appeared as the Arctic Small Tool tradition, which by 4000 years ago had spread across northernmost Canada to Greenland. These first people to inhabit the immediate hinterland of the northernmost American coastline made use of river and lake fish and terrestrial animals—especially the caribou—and made seasonal visits to the coast, for example for spring sealing (Maxwell 1985:84–90). Long known by researchers in Alaska as the Denbigh Flint complex dating from times no earlier than 4200 years ago, recent work on the Seward Peninsula has produced apparent Arctic Small Tool occupations dated about 4700 years ago (Harritt 1994:212, 217). The specific place of origin of these newly appearing people is not yet known, but the evidence presently available strongly favors immigration from Asia. Although without ceramics, the stone assemblage of the Denbigh Flint complex includes nothing that is unknown in various northeast Asian Neolithic cultures (see, for instance, Irving 1970), and it has been com-

pared especially to elements of the Bel'kachi Neolithic of the Lena River basin in northeastern Siberia (e.g., Powers and Jordan 1990). At the very least, then, the Arctic Small Tool tradition appears to represent the beginning of a second period in which contact between Asia and America is attested. And this time, with the rise in seas that had covered the former Beringian land bridge, where currents move steadily from south to north at a speed sufficient to disrupt winter ice and render travel across it hazardous, the contact must have been largely through open water.

In regions near the coast, this American culture vanished or was superseded by 3600 years ago in the northwest, 500 years later in the southwest (Anderson 1984; Dumond 1984), although vestiges appear to have persisted for several centuries in some inland Alaskan locations (e.g., Irving 1964; Kunz 1977). It was not long after this disappearance in the north that the first evidence of a people with an unmistakable marine subsistence focus is found in the Kotzebue Sound region. On the beach numbered 53 at Cape Krusenstern on the northern shore of the sound, a single settlement yielding remains of a culture termed "Old Whaling" is dated at about 3200 years ago. Five semi-subterranean houses and five more superficial camp or house traces are interpreted as winter and summer dwellings occupied for a short period, perhaps no more than a single year. Chipped stone implements, stone lamps, two pieces of polished slate, and a single toggling harpoon head occur with seal bones, walrus ivory, and a few bones of caribou. Whale debris is plentiful in the vicinity (Giddings and Anderson 1986, chapter 12); whether the people of the little settlement were themselves whalers or whether the whalebone in and around the houses represents scavenged animals is not certain, but clearly they were deriving the bulk of their subsistence from the sea (see Mason and Gerlach 1995).

The origin of the people represented in this short-term settlement is undetermined. Although their artifacts have been compared by some researchers to the much smaller collection from the site known as

Chertov Ovrag or Devil's Gorge, on Wrangel Island in the Siberian sector of the Chukchi Sea (e.g., Ackerman 1984), which also yielded a single toggling harpoon head and is dated at almost exactly the same time (Dikov 1988; Shilo et al. 1979), no other Asian analog is known. Rather, the only area anywhere in the vicinity of the Bering and Chukchi seas that at this date was demonstrably home to a significant population of humans with specialized dependence on the seacoast is the Aleutian Islands and the adjacent northern Gulf of Alaska. As indicated earlier, by this date the Aleutians were certainly settled as far west as the Rat Islands, and ancestral Aleut people may already have reached the Near Islands. And as noted elsewhere (Dumond 2000), contemporary stone assemblages of the eastern Aleutian Islands and of the Old Whaling settlement are not so dissimilar as to rule out a source of the latter somewhere in these same Aleutians Islands. Of significance here, also, is the conclusion of the linguist Knud Bergsland (1986) that the length of separation between Aleut and Eskimo languages is not more than about 3000 years. In other words, the linguistic separation occurred at approximately the time the Old Whaling settlement appeared.

Three thousand to 2700 years ago also dates the appearance of the Choris culture, again known principally from the region around Kotzebue Sound, but with possible outliers as far east as the Mackenzie River delta in northwest Arctic Canada (Sutherland 1997). The largest site collections include not only plentiful chipped stone implements, but other artifacts strongly reminiscent of open-coastal Alaska to the south: stone lamps, labrets, barbed harpoons, and a modicum of ground slate. A few forms are comparable to those of the Old Whaling predecessors at Cape Krusenstern (Giddings and Anderson 1986, chapters 10, 11). The south Alaskan characteristics of these two earliest of the maritime-focused people of north Alaska, coupled with evidence of continuity in the Aleutians and the Kodiak region and the relationship between the two language families, Aleutian and Eskimoan, seem to argue for a largely American origin for the later Eskimo.

But during this Choris period the first ceramics appeared on the American coast. Impressed on the surface with a paddle wrapped with cords or scored with parallel linear grooves, these are clearly Asian in stimulus and reminiscent of ceramics reported from late Neolithic sites of eastern Chukotka dating after 3000 years ago (Dikov 1993:151–2). Thus, although a clear suggestion of southern Alaskan derivation appears in this successor to the Old Whaling culture, there is evidence at least equally clear of contact across Bering Strait. Meanwhile, as mentioned earlier, aspects of the Arctic Small Tool tradition apparently continued in inland Alaskan regions to the east.

Not long after 2500 years ago, and thus essentially contemporary with the earliest Okhotsk, Tokarev, and Lakhtin cultures of the Asian shore, the Alaskan coast north- and eastward from the Alaska Peninsula at least as far as the present western border of Canada (MacNeish 1956) had become territory of people of Norton culture, who in northwestern Alaska have also been referred to as Near Ipiutak (Larsen and Rainey 1948). These people used linear- or check-stamped ceramics still of northeast Asian type, as well as toggling harpoon heads of bone or antler; stone lamps for burning sea mammal oil, lip ornaments, and polished implements in the plentiful inventory of stone tools are particularly reminiscent of southern Alaska. In all, characteristics of their sites show their strong interest in the seacoast both as a subsistence area and as a location for settlements, while they nevertheless still harvested interior resources such as caribou and freshwater fish (Dumond 1982, 1984). In this, they provide an obvious analog to the contemporary and semi-maritime Tokarev and Lakhtin cultures of the Bering and Okhotsk seas south of the Chukchi Peninsula, but a much less close similarity in settlement and subsistence to those more landlocked contemporary Chukotkans whose sites have been reported thus far from that peninsula itself.

In the Alaskan northwest, not long after 2000 years ago Norton or Near Ipiutak gave way to the Ipiutak culture, of a seasonally coastal people with utilitarian artifacts reminiscent of those of Norton culture, but who did not use either ceramics or oil lamps, and who are known especially for their elaborate art of apparent Asian affinity (Larsen and Rainey 1948). In southwestern Alaska, on the other hand, later stages of Norton culture endured until nearly 1000 years ago (Dumond 1982, 1984). In both north and south, however, a significant proportion of the tool productions of Norton people, like those of the Ipiutak site, have been compared to artifacts included within the Arctic Small Tool tradition. In the north, indeed, Anderson expands the classificatory Arctic Small Tool tradition to include not only the local Denbigh Flint complex, but succeeding Choris, Norton-Near Ipiutak, and Ipiutak as well (e.g., Giddings and Anderson 1986:292–300). Although such expansion has seemed unnecessary in the south, typological continuity there is evident (e.g., Dumond 1981:183). Suffice it to say that the Norton-related cultures in their development drew evidently from the Arctic Small Tool tradition as well as from prototypes on the Alaskan Pacific coast and in Asia. This is what one can reasonably term a continuation and development of the second period of prehistoric contact across Bering Strait.

The Appearance of Eskimo Maritime Culture

It is in this milieu that the heavily sea-mammal-oriented Eskimo culture of the Bering Strait region appeared, and this in turn had a decisive impact on the character of all later Eskimo people. At present date, no direct progenitor is recognized to have been spread throughout the portion of the Bering Strait region that was to come under Eskimo occupation. On the Seward Peninsula of the American side of Bering Strait there is evidence of the one-time presence of bearers of Norton culture (e.g., Giddings and Anderson 1986; Harritt 1994), although no large sites on that peninsula north of Cape Nome (Bockstoce 1979) have been seriously excavated. Nor is there a clear indication there of an actual transition between Norton people and the later maritime Eskimo, despite the designation of Ipiutak and related folk as "Paleo-Eskimo" (e.g., Larsen and Rainey 1948:182-3, using the term "Palae-Eskimo"). Typological continuity between Norton and later sites has been claimed in regions bordering the southern Bering Sea (Dumond 1981:184), and overall continuity and a transition between them is indeed demonstrated with seeming conclusiveness in the low-lying lands between the Kuskokwim and Yukon River mouths (Shaw 1983); but these are well south of Seward Peninsula.

On the eastern Chukchi Peninsula, as well as on the major islands in and near Bering Strait, no sites analogous to those of the semi-maritime Norton have been reported. And yet this is where the maritime-oriented Old Bering Sea and Okvik cultures seem to have appeared full-blown. However, my own recent examination of the material from the original Okvik site on one of the small Punuk Islands located a short distance off the east coast of St. Lawrence Island, showed five of the sixty-three potsherds recovered to be of standard Norton check-stamped type, the remainder plain or bearing the expanded linear-stamp markings characteristic of the Old Bering Sea culture as it is known from St. Lawrence Island. These few Norton potsherds may suggest contact or a one-time Norton presence on the island, although the evidence of either is marginal, to say the least.

With regard to the version of Norton culture that was so plentiful on the Bering Sea coast of Alaska, there is reason to suggest that its early stages were not directly ancestral to the ensuing early Eskimo culture of St. Lawrence Island or, presumably, of that of the nearby Chukotka littoral. Significantly, the decorated ceramics of the early Old Bering Sea and apparently the Okvik cultures, confined to the Bering Strait islands and along the nearby Asian coastal fringe, are stamped with linear impressions somewhat broader than, but reminiscent of, Choris and Near Ipiutak pots, as well as of some early Norton linear-stamped ceramics of the typesite of Norton culture located on the shore of Norton Bay (Giddings 1964; Giddings and Anderson 1986; Larsen and Rainey 1948)—that is, sites generally north of the major Norton heartland of southwest Alaska. Apparently similar also are some ceramics of late Neolithic sites of the Chukchi Peninsula interior (Dikov 1993:151–52). Lip ornaments or labrets, so common in Norton collections from the American coast of the Bering Sea but possibly somewhat less so north of Bering Strait, are lacking entirely in the early Old Bering Sea-Okvik collections, notwithstanding the interpretation of Dikov (1979:170) that some Okvik anthropomorphic carvings illustrate the wearing of labrets in addition to facial tattoos. These characteristics, like evidence for some use of iron in Okvik-Old Bering Sea and Ipiutak collections (Arutiunov and Bronshtein 1993: 67-8; Collins 1937:146; Gusev and Zhilin 2002; Larsen and Rainey 1948:83; Semenov 1964), suggest an axis of connection that ran through Bering Strait between Chukotka and northwestern Alaska, placing the early St. Lawrence Island and some Asian coastal people somewhat closer in material culture to northern than to southern Alaska, despite linguistic classifications that appear to align them more closely to Eskimoan Yupik speakers of the Alaskan south (e.g., Woodbury 1984).

Regarding the chronology of the developed Bering Strait cultures—that is, those to which the term "wedge" has been especially applied—there has been disagreement concerning the temporal relationship of Okvik and early Old Bering Sea, with some researchers assigning temporal priority to Okvik (e.g., Dikov 1979: 175; Giddings 1960), others denying it (e.g., Alekseev et al. 1972; Arutiunov and Sergeev 1990; Rainey and Ralph 1959; but see also Arutiunov and Bronshtein 1993; and Bronshtein and Plumet 1995), in apparent opposition to claims linking Okvik to the Hillside site on St. Lawrence Island and to what Collins (1937) termed the Old Bering Sea I decorative style. My own study of the St. Lawrence Island collections at the Smithsonian National Museum of Natural History and my examination of the sites around Gambell, at the

northwest extremity of St. Lawrence Island, indicate to me that some cultural elements excavated by Collins from two houses at the Hillside site are the oldest of the materials he assigned to Old Bering Sea. In significant part these predate the Mayughwaaq (Collins's Miyowagh) site which produced the largest corpus of his Old Bering Sea material.

This conclusion rests especially on typology of ceramic and stone artifacts, and to some extent on geographic position. The Hillside site near Gambel, St. Lawrence Island, while located on a geomorphically earlier formation than the Mayughwaaq site, is physically so close to it that occupation of the latter would almost surely have deposited material on the former. Understanding of the culture of the Hillside site has been complicated by the course of research there. In 1939, J. L.Giddings excavated a third house, which then became crucial to the conclusion of Rainey (1941) that Hillside was a site of the Okvik culture (then known chiefly from a collection from one of the Punuk Islands); although this third prehistoric house was not then published in detail. In any event, the artifact assemblage from this Hillside House 3 of Giddings, which I analyzed in 1994 and published recently (Dumond 1998b), sets it apart from the bulk of culture represented by the Mayughwaaq site and places it firmly with the Hillside Houses 1 and 2 of Collins, from which it differs only in the uneven survival of decorations on harpoon heads—five heads having been recovered from House 3, virtually none from floor associations of the Collins Houses 1 and 2. One can further assert that the decorative style of House 3 is apart from, and hence possibly earlier than, other elements of the Old Bering Sea style as known from St. Lawrence Island, and that it has at least some (but not total) stylistic affinity to certain artifacts illustrated for the Punuk Island Okvik collection (Rainey 1941). Last of all, excavations at the site in 1973 by Swiss archaeologists evidently cleared one house (designated House 5 in Table 1) that yielded definitively Okvik-style artifacts (Blumer 2002:86–7), though results have not yet been widely disseminated.

The absolute dating of the Hillside site has unfortunately not been without problems. As is generally known, the first application of the radiocarbon method to the Hillside site produced a determination of 2258 ± 230 years before present (C-505), but later re-dating of a sample of the same piece of wood by presumably improved technology in a different laboratory placed it at 1420 ± 230 B.P. (P-70). None of the other Hillside determinations run by that second laboratory were in excess of 1641 ± 65 years ago (Ralph and Ackerman 1961). A few years later, H.-G. Bandi (1969:67) reported having tested a fourth house at the Hillside site, from which he obtained a C-14 age of 1370 ± 60 years; again, no full description of the excavation has been published. His subsequent dating of graves in the Gambell area that he believed on stylistic grounds to be early does not resolve the issue (Bandi 1984; see Table 1). Finally, materials from House 5, which yielded certain Okvik-style harpoon heads, have been dated between about 1800 and 1500 years ago.

In general, determinations from this and other sites yielding material identified as Old Bering Sea have seldom exceeded 1700 years before present. Notable exceptions are dates returned on material subject to the carbon reservoir effect of the seas and thus dating anomalously early—sea-mammal bone or ivory, or human remains that because of heavy dietary dependence on sea mammals are subject to the same skewing factor.[6] And because the Bering Strait region is generally treeless, wood used by humans in either structures or as fuel can be expected to have been obtained as driftwood, and hence to be older than its actual use.

Table 1 shows all Old Bering Sea age determinations of which I am aware that exceed about 1700 years, together with some other newly obtained determinations. The human bone elements of sea-mammal-eating people from the Ekven site (SI-6717, IEMAE-705, SI-6718, Table 1) must stand in need of correction for the reservoir effect for at least 500 years or so. That such a move is reasonable is suggested by the

series of 27 determinations from human bone of the Ekven site listed by Dinesman et. al. (1999, Appendix 2), of which only three are in excess of 2000 radiocarbon years, which when corrected suggest nothing earlier than 1800 years before 1950, and perhaps a century or so later. The only determinations in present Table 1 not evidently suspect because of the reservoir effect and that substantially exceed 1800 B.P. are those shown from two sites on the north Chukchi Peninsula: at Seshan, about 100 km northwest of Cape Dezhnev, and from Cape Dzenretlen, some 200 km northwest of the same point. Whether these two determinations from charcoal actually indicate the presence of Old Bering Sea people on the north shore of the Chukchi Peninsula earlier than elsewhere, or whether additional dates would fall more in line with those from two other sites on the same coast, like the Uten site (MAG-354), 50 km northwest of Cape Dezhnev, or Cape Vankarem (MAG-352, which wants correction for reservoir effect), 350 km northwest of the cape, cannot now be answered. At least I am not aware of any other evidence that would support such an early development along the northern Chukchi Peninsula.

When I analyzed the material from the Giddings House 3 at the Hillside site, I was able to date three uncataloged samples of wood stored with the artifact collection. One problem here is that deficiencies in the documentation prevent one from ascertaining whether these samples came from an integral place in the house itself, from overburden, or even from the exploratory trenching that led to discovery of the house floor (Giddings 1967:170-2). Only one of the three dated older than, or even as old as, 1700 years (Beta-78213, Table 1). At about the same time, Michael Lewis, of the University of Alaska Museum, obtained determinations on two pieces of walrus ivory included in the House 3 (Giddings) collection, as well as on two ivory pieces from the Punuk Island Okvik collection that he identified as bearing Okvik-style decorations (Table 1). Finally, in work with the Collins Hillside site collection at the Smithsonian National Museum of Natural History in

Table 1/ Selected Bering Strait Radiocarbon Ages[a]

SiteMaterial	Age		Lab. Number	Reference
St. Lawrence I.				
Beach burials:				
Burial 26 ('Okvik')	wood	1410 ± 60	B-3205	Bandi 1984:61
	wood	1310 ± 60	B-3206	Bandi 1984:61
Burial 34 ('Okvik')	whale bone*	2450 ± 40	B-2877	Bandi 1984:61
Hillside site:				
1930 excavations:				
House 1	wood	1640 ± 106	P-95	Rainey & Ralph 1959
House 3	wood	2258 ± 230	C-505[b]	Libby 1951
	wood	1420 ± 230	P-70[b]	Ralph & Ackerman 1961
1973 excavations:				
House 5	wood	1460 ± 50	B-2871	Blumer 2002
	wood	1470 ± 80	B-2872	Blumer 2002
	wood	1750 ± 50	B-2867	Blumer 2002
	wood	1810 ± 50	B-2873	Blumer 2002
1994 analysis:				
House 3	willow	1100 ± 70	Beta-78214	Dumond 1998b
	birch/alder	1210 ± 80	Beta-88491	Dumond 1998b
	willow	1800 ± 90	Beta-78213	Dumond 1998b
1995 analyses:				
House 1	grass	1770 ± 40	Beta-93160	Dumond 1998b
	walrus ivory*	2500 ± 50	Beta-113814	Dumond 1998b
	walrus ivory*	2480 ± 50	Beta-113815	Dumond 1998b
House 2	grass	1680 ± 40	Beta-91359	Dumond 1998b
	walrus ivory*	2130 ± 60	Beta-113812	Dumond 1998b
	walrus ivory*	2240 ± 50	Beta-113813	Dumond 1998b
House 3	walrus ivory*	2560 ± 50	Beta-81492	M. A. Lewis, pers. com.
	walrus ivory*	2660 ± 50	Beta-81491	M. A. Lewis, pers. com.
Mayughwaaq site:				
1930 excavations	wood	1630 ± 230	P-71	Ralph & Ackerman 1961
	wood	1700 ± 150	P-93	Ralph & Ackerman 1961
Punuk Islands				
Okvik site:				
1995 analysis	walrus ivory*	2330 ± 60	Beta-81489	M. A. Lewis, pers. com.
	walrus ivory*	2670 ± 60	Beta-81490	M. A. Lewis, pers. com.
Asian Mainland				
Uten	charcoal	1600 ± 100	MAG-417	Shilo et al. 1979
Chini, burial 5	wood, fur	1605 ± 40	MAG-228	Dikov 1977:161
Chini, burial unknown	baleen?*	1670 ± 40	MAG-360	Shilo et al. 1977
Uten, burial 1	wood	1750 ± 100	MAG-354	Dikov 1977:179
Cape Vankarem	baleen*	1840 ± 100	MAG-352	Shilo et al. 1977
Dzhenretlen	charcoal	1990 ± 190	MAG-233	Dikov 1977:194
Ekven, burial 143	human ribs*	1745 ± 75	SI-6717	W. Fitzhugh, pers. com.
Seshan	charcoal	2022 ± 100	MAG-104	Dikov 1977:185
Ekven, burial 121[c]	human bone*	2153 ± 110	IEMAE-705	Bronshtein & Plumet, 1995
Ekven, burial 63	human ribs*	2220 ± 65	SI-6718	W. Fitzhugh, pers. com.

[a] Determinations suggesting a so-called conventional age of 1700 years or more for clearly identified Old Bering Sea or Okvik, plus recently communicated determinations. Omitted are most previously published C-14 determinations suggesting ages of less than 1700 years (6 from the Hillside site, 5 from Mayughwaaq, 4 from the Asian mainland).

* Materials marked with an asterisk are deemed subject to the marine reservoir effect and thus date too early.

[b] Two determinations from a single sample. See text.

[c] Burial number reported by Dinesman (1999, Appendix 2), context by Bronshtein and Plumet (1995).

1995, I identified two samples of grass cataloged as recovered in 1930 from between the floor stones of houses 1 and 2 of the site, which were then dated by the AMS method (Beta-93159, -93160, Table 1). And, as something of an afterthought regarding the magnitude of the marine reservoir effect in the Bering Sea, I later was permitted to date by the same method a pair of samples of walrus ivory from each house floor (Beta-113812 through Beta-113815) that could be compared directly with the results of the determinations on grass from the same excavation units.

Table 1 illustrates the uncertainties that derive from the various factors just mentioned. First of all, I believe that the two determinations on grass, which must be a local product of both the vicinity and time of occupation, are the least ambiguous dates for the Hillside site. Given that House 3 on stylistic grounds stands apart not only from the Mayughwaaq site but to a lesser extent from the two houses of the Hillside site excavated by Collins, from which it varies only slightly in certain frequencies of the more common artifacts, I had come to accept that House 3 and, by extension, at least portions of the collection from the Okvik site of the Punuk Islands, were slightly older than houses 1 and 2. This supposed sequential relationship is supported by the radiocarbon determinations on walrus ivory from houses 1, 2, and 3 of the Hillside site, and by one of the dates from the Okvik site (Table 1). On the other hand, given the magnitude of the reservoir effect suggested by the mixed suites of dates from the floors of houses 1 and 2 (500 to 700 years; see Dumond and Griffin 2002), there seems no reason to suppose that any of the units of these sites exceeds 2000 years in uncorrected radiocarbon age (see also Blumer 2002). This conclusion, of course, provides a relatively young age for the Hillside site and by implication for Old Bering Sea, which has been frequently estimated to be at least as old as 2500 years (e.g., Arutiunov and Bronshtein 1993; Arutiunov and Fitzhugh 1988; Bronshtein and Plumet 1995; Giddings 1960). I note, however, that this later dating accords well with the archaeological sequence from southwestern Alaska as I perceive it.

Concluding Discussion

What, then are the present conclusions as they relate to those of researchers of the Jesup Expedition?

Foremost is the finding that the Eskimo population forming the so-called "wedge"—once postulated by Bogoras and Jochelson—was a fully autochthonous development of the territories adjacent to the Bering Strait region. This population developed linguistically from American progenitors but clearly sharing with Asia important artifacts and cultural practices. So far as archaeology can show, there was no late and intrusive "Eskimo Wedge." In fairness to Boas, however, one must recognize that in later writings, while not repudiating the idea of such a wedge, he did note linguistic evidence that Eskimo and Chukchi had long been neighbors (Boas 1933:369). And long before, even as he expressed his enthusiasm for the notion of a late and intrusive arrival of Eskimo people at Bering Strait, he had accepted the possibility "that a more thorough investigation of the Alaskan Eskimo may correct our present conclusions as to the role that this tribe played in communicating Asiatic culture to America, and American culture to Asia" (1905:99–100). This tentative prediction has proven true, not only as demonstrated by archaeology but through reconsideration of the body of myth, especially Raven myth, on which the ethnographers of the Jesup Expedition relied most heavily, together with the exploration of specifically Alaskan Eskimo conceptions (e.g., Chowning 1962; Meletinskii 1979, 1983). The lack of field study of Alaskan Eskimo societies by researchers of the Jesup Expedition must thus be accounted a serious omission that contributed heavily to their erroneous postulation of a recent wedge-like movement of Eskimo people into the Bering Strait region, a notion that persisted (and confused) well into the mid-twentieth century.

Secondarily, and not in special opposition to Boas, for whom the "late" date of the Eskimo appearance around Bering Strait was relative rather than absolute, but in opposition to later commentators who have ascribed absolute dates to the Eskimo development: the Eskimo way of life developed fully no earlier than 2000 years ago, many centuries later than semi-maritime peoples had appeared on both sides of the Bering Sea. And among these latter, in differing ways and degrees, were the various cultural, genetic, and linguistic ancestors of the historically known Eskimo people.

Acknowledgments

I thank the University of Alaska Museum for the loan of collections from the Hillside site, and the Department of Anthropology of the National Museum of Natural History, Smithsonian Institution, for facilitating study of their collections in 1995 with support of a Smithsonian Senior Research Fellowship. I am grateful to both for agreeing to my requests to allow dating of items of their collections by the radiocarbon method.

Notes

1. Herein I use only uncalibrated radiocarbon ages.

2. I omit consideration of so-called "Alaskan Paleoindian" remains, which appear to date from about 10,000 years ago, appearing somewhat later than traces of the early and apparently Asia-related peoples although in part contemporary with them. These "Paleoindian" sites are characterized both by the absence of microblades and the presence of lanceolate projectile points strongly reminiscent of roughly contemporary artifacts of terrestrially focused peoples of continental America to the south (see pertinent articles in Bever and Kunz 2001). Harking south and east to the American interior, rather than west across Bering Strait, the assemblages appear irrelevant to the present discussion.

3. Sites of similar age and affinity recorded more recently in the Unalaska Bay area of nearby Unalaska Island (also of the Fox group) are thus far known only from elevations of 20 m or more above modern sea level, higher than ocean-edge sites of later date in the region (see Knecht and Davis 2001).

4. A single determination of about 3400 years ago from Shemya, cited previously as a possible indication of occupation by that time in the Near Island (Dumond and Bland 1995, Table 2), has been learned to be from material subject to a marine reservoir effect (see note 5, below) and must be considered younger than the measured age.

5. The coastal site of Naivan, located near the southern tip of the Chukchi Peninsula, has been concluded to represent people who devoted some time to fishing and has been dated to 8000 years or more ago (Gusev 2002)—as have some other sites reported by Dikov (1993) from eastern Chukotka—but displays no evidence of a markedly maritime adaptation.

6. Over the earth as a whole, the surface waters of the ocean preserve older carbon so that organisms inhabiting them yield ^{14}C ages about 400 years greater than terrestrial materials of the same true calendar age, but in certain regions a much greater excess of apparent age is imparted because of upwelling of still more ancient carbon from greater sea depths. This necessitates an additional correction; although a specific additional factor for the Bering Strait region has not yet been announced, data reported from other North Pacific locales entail a further correction of from 100–300 years, for a total of 500–700 years that must be deducted from ^{14}C ages to bring them into line with those from terrestrial samples. See Dumond and Griffin (2002); Stuiver and Braziunas (1993).

References

Ackerman, Robert E.
1984   Prehistory of the Alaskan Eskimo Zone. In *Arctic*. D. Damas, ed. Pp. 106–18. *Handbook of North American Indians*. William C. Sturtevant, gen. ed., Vol. 5. Washington, DC: Smithsonian Institution Press.
1992   Earliest Stone Industries on the North Pacific Coast of North America. *Arctic Anthropologist* 29(1):18–27.
Ackerman, Robert E., K. C. Reid, J. C. Gallison, and M. E. Roe
1985 *Archaeology of Heceta Island*. Washington State University. Center for Northwest Anthropology, Project Report 3. Pullman.

Aigner, Jean S.

1978 The Lithic Remains from Anangula, an 8,500 Year Old Aleut Coastal Village. *Verlag Archaeologica Venatoria, Urgeschichtliche Materialhefte* 3. Tübingen: Institut für Urgeschichte der Universität Tübingen.

Aikens, C. Melvin, and T. Higuchi

1982 *Prehistory of Japan.* New York: Academic Press.

Alekseev, Valerii P., S. A. Arutiunov, and D. A. Sergeev

1972 Results of Historico-Ethnological and Anthropological Studies in the Eastern Chukchee Area. *Inter-Nord* 12:234–43.

Anderson, Douglas D.

1968 A Stone Age Campsite at the Gateway to America. *Scientific American* 188:24–33.

1970 Akmak: An Early Archeological Assemblage from Onion Portage, Northwest Alaska. *Acta Arctica, Fasc.* 16. Copenhagen: Arctic Institute.

1984 Prehistory of North Alaska. In *Arctic.* David Damas, ed. Pp. 80–93. *Handbook of North American Indians.* William C. Sturtevant, gen. ed., Vol. 5. Washington, DC: Smithsonian Institution Press.

Arutiunov, Sergei A., and Mikhail M. Bronshtein

1993 Ethnisch-kulturelle Geschichte der asiatischen Eskimos. In *Arktische Waljäger vor 3000 Jahren: Unbekannte sibirische Kunst.* A.M. Leskov and H. Müller-Beck, eds. Pp 65–72. Mainz: Hase & KOchler Verlag.

Arutiunov, Sergei A., and William W. Fitzhugh

1988 Prehistory of Siberia and the Bering Sea. In *Crossroads of Continents: Cultures of Siberia and Alaska.* William W. Fitzhugh and Aron Crowell, eds. Pp.117–29. Washington, DC: Smithsonian Institution Press.

Arutiunov, Sergei A., and Dorian A. Sergeev

1990 Issues in the Ethnic History of the Bering Sea: The Ekven Burial Ground. *Soviet Anthropology and Archeology* 28(4):50–77.

Bandi, Hans-Georg

1969 Eskimo Prehistory. *Studies of Northern Peoples, 2.* College: University of Alaska Press.

1984 Allgemeine Einführung und Gräberfunde bei Gambell am Nordwestkap der St. Lorenz Insel, Alaska. *St. Lorenz Insel-Studien* 1. Bern: Paul Haupt.

Bergsland, Knut

1986 Comparative Eskimo-Aleut Phonology and Lexicon. *Suomalais-Ugrilaisen Seuran Aikakauskirja/Journal de la Sociète Finno-Ougrienne* 80:65–137.

Bever, Michael R., and Michael L. Kunz, eds.

2001 Between Two Worlds: Late Pleistocene Cultural and Technological Diversity in Eastern Beringia. *Arctic Anthropology* 38(2).

Black, Robert F.

1974 Late-Quaternary Sea Level Changes, Umnak Island, Aleutians—Their Effects on Ancient Aleuts and Their Causes. *Quaternary Research* 4:254–81.

Blumer, Reto

2002 Radiochronological Assessment of Neo-Eskimo Occupations on St. Lawrence Island, Alaska. In *Archaeology in the Bering Strait Region.* Don E. Dumond and Richard L. Bland, eds. Pp. 61–106. *University of Oregon Anthropological Papers* 59. Eugene.

Boas, Franz

1888 The Eskimo. *Proceedings and Transactions of the Royal Society of Canada for the Year 1887*, vol. 5, pt. 2, pp. 35–9.

1905 The Jesup North Pacific Expedition. *International Congress of Americanists, 13th Session, Held in New York in 1902.* Pp. 91–100. Easton, PA: Eschenbach.

1933 Relations Between North-West America and North-East Asia. In *The American Aborigines: Their Origin and Antiquity.* Diamond Jenness, ed. Pp. 355–70. Toronto: University of Toronto Press.

Bockstoce, John

1979 The Archaeology of Cape Nome, Alaska. *University of Pennsylvania, University Museum Monograph* 38. Philadelphia.

Bogoras, Waldemar

1902 The Folklore of Northeastern Asia, as Compared with that of Northwestern America. *American Anthropologist*, n.s. 4(4):577–683.

1925 Early Migrations of the Eskimo between Asia and America. *Congrès International des Américanistes. Compte-Rendue de la 21e Session, Deuxième Partie. Tenue à Göteborg en 1924.* Pp.216–35. Göteborg Museum.

Bronshtein, Mikhail M., and Patrick Plumet

1995 Ekven: l'art préhistorique béringien et l'approche russe de l'origine de la tradition culturelle esquimaude. *Études/Inuit/Studies* 19(2):5–59.

Chowning, Ann

1962 Raven Myths in Northwestern North America and Northeastern Asia. *Arctic Anthropology* 1(1):1–5.

Clark, Donald W.

1979 Ocean Bay: An Early North Pacific Maritime Culture. *Archaeological Survey of Canada Paper* 86. Ottawa: National Museum of Canada.

Clark, Gerald H.

1977 Archaeology on the Alaska Peninsula: The Coast of Shelikof Strait, 1963–1965. *University of Oregon Anthropology Papers* 13. Eugene.

Collins, Henry B., Jr.

1937 Archeology of St. Lawrence Island, Alaska. *Smithsonian Miscellaneous Collections* 96(1).

1951 The Origin and Antiquity of the Eskimo. *Report of the Smithsonian Institution, 1950.* Pp. 423–67. Washington, DC: Smithsonian Institution.

Davis, Brian

2001 Sea Mammal Hunting at the Neoglacial: Environmental Change and Subsistence Technology at Margaret Bay. In *Archaeology in the Aleut Zone of*

Alaska. Don E. Dumond, ed. Pp. 71–86. *University of Oregon Anthropological Papers* 58. Eugene.

Dikov, Nikolai N.

1977 *Arkheologicheskie pamiatniki Kamchatki, Chukotki i Verkhnei Kolymy* (Archaeological Monuments in Kamchatka, Chukotka and the Upper Reaches of the Kolyma River). Moscow: Nauka Publishers

1979 *Drevnie kul'tury Severo-Vostochnoi Azii* (Ancient Cultures of Northeast Asia). Moscow: Nauka Publishers.

1988 The Earliest Sea Mammal Hunters of Wrangel Island. *Arctic Anthropology* 25(1):80–93.

1993 *Aziia na styke s amerikoi v drevnosti (Kamennyi vek Chukotskogo Poluostrova)*. St. Petersburg: Nauka Publishers. (Trans. by Richard L. Bland as *Asia at the Juncture with America in Antiquity*. Anchorage: National Park Service, Beringia Program. 1997).

1996 The Ushki Sites, Kamchatka Peninsula. In *American Beginnings: The Prehistory and Palaeoecology of Beringia*. Frederick H. West, ed. Pp. 244–50. Chicago: University of Chicago Press.

Dinesman, Lev G., N. K. Kiseleva, A. B. Savinetskii, and B. F. Khasanov

1999 *Secular Dynamics of Coastal Zone Ecosystems of the Northeastern Chukchi Peninsula*. Tübingen: Mo Vince Verlag.

Dumond, Don E.

1981 Archaeology on the Alaska Peninsula: The Naknek Region,1960–1975. *University of Oregon Anthropology Papers* 21. Eugene.

1982 Trends and Traditions in Alaskan Prehistory: The Place of Norton culture. *Arctic Anthropology* 19(1):39–52.

1984 Prehistory of the Bering Sea Region. In *Arctic*. David Damas, ed. Pp. 94–105. *Handbook of North American Indians*. William C. Sturtevant, gen. ed. Vol. 5. Washington, DC: Smithsonian Institution Press.

1998a Maritime Adaptation on the Northern Alaska Peninsula. *Arctic Anthropology* 35(1):187–203.

1998b The Hillside Site, St. Lawrence Island, Alaska: an Examination of Collections from the 1930s. *University of Oregon Anthropological Papers* 55. Eugene.

2000 A Southern Origin for Norton Culture? *Anthropological Papers of the University of Alaska* 25(1):87–102.

2001 Toward a (Yet) Newer View of the (Pre)history of the Aleutians. In *Archaeology in the Aleut Zone of Alaska*. Don E. Dumond, ed. Pp.289–309. *University of Oregon Anthropological Papers* 58. Eugene.

Dumond, Don E., and Richard L. Bland

1995 Holocene Prehistory of the Northernmost North Pacific. *Journal of World Prehistory* 9: 401–51.

Dumond, Don E., and Dennis G. Griffin

2002 Measurements of the Marine Reservoir Effect on Radiocarbon Ages in the Eastern Bering Sea. *Arctic* 55(1):77–86.

Elias, S. A., S. K. Short, and R. L. Phillips

1992 Paleoecology of Late-Glacial Peats from the Bering Land Bridge, Chukchi Sea Shelf Region, Northwestern Alaska. *Quaternary Research* 38:371–78.

Fairbanks, R. G.

1989 A 17,000-Year Glacio-Eustatic Sea Level Record: Influence of Glacial Melting Rates on the Younger Dryas Event and Deep-Ocean Circulation. *Nature* 342:637–42.

Giddings, James L.

1960 The Archeology of Bering Strait. *Current Anthropology* 1(1):121–38.

1964 *The Archeology of Cape Denbigh*. Providence: Brown University Press.

1967 *Ancient Men of the Arctic*. New York: Alfred A. Knopf.

Giddings, James L., and Douglas D. Anderson

1986 Beach Ridge Archeology of Cape Krusenstern: Eskimo and pre-Eskimo Settlements around Kotzebue Sound, Alaska. *Publications in Archeology* 20. Washington, DC: National Park Service.

Gusev, Sergei V.

2002 The Early Holocene Site of Naivan: The Earliest Dated Site in Chukotka. In *Archaeology in the Bering Strait Region*, Don E. Dumond and Richard L. Bland, eds. Pp. 111–26. *University of Oregon Anthropological Papers* 59. Eugene.

Gusev, Sergei V., and M. G. Zhilin

2002 The Technology of Bone Working among the Sea Mammal Hunting Cultures of Bering Strait. In *Archaeology in the Bering Strait Region*. Don E. Dumond and Richard L. Bland, eds. Pp. 139–51. *University of Oregon Anthropological Papers* 59. Eugene.

Harritt, Roger K.

1994 Eskimo Prehistory on the Seward Peninsula, Alaska. *U.S. National Park Service, Alaska Region Resources Report*. NPS/ARORCR/CRR-93/21. Anchorage.

Irving, William

1964 *Punyik Point and the Arctic Small Tool tradition*. Ph.D. Dissertation in Anthropolgy, University of Wisconsin, Madison.

1970 The Arctic Small Tool Tradition. *Proceedings of the 8th International Congress of Anthropological and Ethnological Science* 3:340–42. Tokyo and Kyoto.

Jochelson, Waldemar

1908 The Koryak. *The Jesup North Pacific Expedition*, vol 6, pts.1–2. *Memoirs of the American Museum of National History*, 10. Leiden: J.E. Brill; New York: G.E. Stechert.

1928 *Peoples of Asiatic Russia*. New York: American Museum of Natural History.

Knecht, Richard A., and Richard S. Davis

2001 A Prehistoric Sequence for the Eastern Aleutians. In *Archaeology in the Aleut Zone of Alaska*, Don E. Dumond, ed. Pp. 269–88. *University of Oregon Anthropological Papers* 58. Eugene.

Knecht, Richard A., Richard S. Davis and Gary A. Carver

2001 The Margaret Bay Site and Eastern Aleutian Prehistory. In *Archaeology in the Aleut Zone of Alaska*. Don E. Dumond, ed. Pp. 35–69. *University of Oregon Anthropological Papers* 58. Eugene.

Kunz, Michael

1977 Mosquito Lake Site (PSM-049). In *Pipeline Archaeology*. J. P. Cook, ed. Pp. 747–982. Fairbanks: University of Alaska Institute of Arctic Biology.

Larichev, V., U. Khol'ushkin, and I. Laricheva

1992 Northeastern Siberia and the Russian Far East. In *The Upper Paleolithic of Northern Asia: Achievements, Problems, and Perspectives* III. Pp. 441–76. *Journal of World Prehistory* 6.

Larsen, Helge, and Froelich Rainey

1948 Ipiutak and the Arctic Whale Hunting Culture. *Anthropological Papers of the American Museum of Natural History* 42. New York.

Laughlin, William S.

1975 Aleuts: Ecosystem, Holocene History, and Siberian Origin. *Science* 189(4202):507–15.

Lebedintsev, Alexander I.

1990 *Drevnie primorskie kul'tury severo-zapadnogo Priokhotya*. Leningrad: Nauka Publishers. (Trans. by Richard L. Bland as *Early Maritime Cultures of Northwestern Priokhot'e*. Anchorage: National Park Service, Shared Beringian Heritage Program. 2000.)

Libby, W. F.

1951 Radiocarbon Dates II. *Science* 114:291–96.

MacNeish, Richard S.

1956 The Engigstciak Site on the Yukon Arctic Coast. *Anthropology Papers of the University of Alaska* 4(2):91–111.

Mason, Owen K., and S. Craig Gerlach

1995 The Archaeological Imagination, Zooarchaeological Data, the Origins of Whaling in the Western Arctic, and "Old Whaling" and Choris Cultures. In *Hunting the Largest Animals*. Allen P. McCartney, ed. Pp. 1–31. *Studies in Whaling* 3. Alberta: The Canadian Circumpolar Institute.

Maxwell, Moreau S.

1985 *Prehistory of the Eastern Arctic*. Orlando: Academic Press.

McCartney, Allen P.

1984 Prehistory of the Aleutian region. In *Arctic*. David Damas, ed. Pp. 119–35. *Handbook of North American Indians*, Vol. 5. William C. Sturtevant, gen. ed. Washington, DC: Smithsonian Institution Press.

Meletinskii [Meletinsky], Eleazar M.

1979 *Paleoaziatskii mifologicheskii epos* (Paleoasiatic Mythological Epos). Moscow: Nauka Publishers.

1983 The Paleo-Asian Raven Epos and the Relationship between Northeast Asia and Northwest America in Folklore. In *Cultures of the Bering Sea Region: Papers from an International Symposium*. Henry N. Michael and James W. VanStone, eds. Pp. 227–48. New York: IREX.

Minagawa, M., and T. Akazawa

1992 Dietary Patterns of Japanese Jomon Hunter-Gatherers: Stable Nitrogen and Carbon Isotope Analysis of Human Bones. In *Pacific Northeast Asia in Prehistory*. C. M. Aikens and S. N. Rhee, eds. Pp. 59–67. Pullman: WSU Press.

Mochanov, Iurii A.

1977 *Drevneishie etapy zaseleniya chelovekom Severo-Vostochnoi Asii* (The Earliest Stages of Peopling of Northeast Asia). Novosibirsk: Nauka Publishers.

Mochanov, Iurii A., and Svetlana A. Fedose'eva

1984 Main Periods in the Ancient History of North-East Asia. In *Beringia in the Cenozoic Era*. Vitoldas L. Kontrimavichus, ed. Pp. 669–93. New Delhi: Oxonian Press.

1996 Aldansk: Aldan River Valley, Sakha Republic. In *American Beginnings: The Prehistory and Palaeoecology of Beringia*. Frederick H. West, ed. Pp. 157–214. Chicago: University of Chicago Press.

Nishimoto, T.

1988 Maritime Adaptations in Hokkaido Prehistory. *International Symposium on Maritime Adaptations in the North Pacific*, pp. 57–60 (in Japanese). Abashiri, Hokkaido, Japan

Okada, Atsuko

1998 Maritime Adaptations in Hokkaido. *Arctic Anthropology* 35(1):340–49.

Orekhov, Alexander A.

1987 *Drevniaia kul'tura Severo-Zapadnogo Beringomoryia*. Moscow: Nauka Publishers. (Trans. by Richard L. Bland as *An Early Culture of the Northwest Bering Sea*. Anchorage: National Park Service, Shared Beringian Heritage Program. 1999).

Popov, A. N., N. B. Verkhovskaya, and A. S. Kundyshe

1995 The Boysman-II site: The Neolithic Cultures and Paleoenvironment (south of the Russian Far East). In *Archaeology of Northeast Asia and the Pacific Regions: A Festschrift in Honor of Professor Song Nai Rhee*. Pp. 469–90. Seoul: Korean Ancient Historical Society.

Powers, William R., and Richard H. Jordan

1990 Human Biogeography and Climate Change in Siberia and Arctic North America in the Fourth and Fifth millennia BP. *Philosophical Transactions of the Royal Society of London* A. 330:665–70.

Rainey, Froelich G.

1941 Eskimo Prehistory: The Okvik Site on the Punuk Islands. *Anthropological Papers of the American Museum of Natural History* 37(4):453–569.

Rainey, Froelich G., and Elizabeth K. Ralph

1959 Radiocarbon Dating in the Arctic. *American Antiquity* 24(4):365–74.

Ralph, Elizabeth K., and Robert E. Ackerman

1961 University of Pennsylvania Radiocarbon Dates IV. *Radiocarbon* 3: 4–14.

Semenov, Sergei A.

1964 *Prehistoric Technology*. (M. W. Thompson, trans.). Bath: Adams and Dart.

Shaw, Robert D.

1983 *The Archaeology of the Manokinak Site: A Study of the Cultural Transition Between Late Norton Tradition and Historic Eskimo*. Ph.D. Dissertation, Washington State University.

Shilo, Nikolai A., Nikolai N. Dikov, Alexei V. Lozhkin, and A. V. Starikov

1977 Novye radiouglerodinye datirovki arkheologicheskikh pamyatnikov iz verkhnechetvertichnykh otlozhenii Severa Dal'nego Vostoka (New Radiocarbon Dates of Archaeological Objects from Upper Quaternary Deposits in the Soviet Northeast). *Doklady Academii Nauk SSSR* 237(3):688–89.

Shilo, Nikolai A., Nikolai N. Dikov, Alexei V. Lozhkin, Alexander A. Orekhov, and Tasian S. Tein

1979 Novye radiouglerodnye datirovki arkheologicheskikh pamyatnikov Severo-Vostochnoi Azii (New Radiocarbon Datings of Archaeological Monuments in Northeast Asia). In *Novye arkheologicheskie pamyatniki Severa Dal'nego Vostoka*. Pp. 9–11. Magadan: Northeast Interdisciplinary Scientific Research Institute, USSR Academy of Sciences.

Shubin, Valerii O., and Ol'ga A. Shubina

1984 *Novye radiouglerodnye datirovki po arkheologicheskim pamiatnikam Sakhalinskoi oblasti* (New Radiocarbon Datings on the Archaeological Sites of the Sakhalin Province). Yuzhno-Sakhalinsk: Sakhalin Regional Museum, Academy of Science of the USSR, Far East Science Center.

Stuiver, Minze, and Thomas F. Braziunas

1993 Modeling Atmospheric ^{14}C Influences and ^{14}C ages of Marine Samples to 10,000 BC. *Radiocarbon* 35(1):137–89.

Sutherland, Patricia D.

1997 *New Evidence for Links Between Alaska and Arctic Canada: the Satkualuk Site in the Mackenzie Delta*. Unpublished paper presented at the annual meeting of the Alaska Anthropological Association, White Horse.

Thorson, R. M., and T. D. Hamilton

1986 Glacial Geology of the Aleutian Islands. In *Glaciation in Alaska: The Geologic Record*. T. D. Hamilton, K. M. Reed, and R. M. Thorson, eds. Pp. 171–91. Anchorage: Alaska Geological Society.

Vasil'evskii, A. A.

1996 Zametki o do- i protoistorii ostrova Sakhalin (Notes on the Pre- and Protohistory of Sakhalin Island). *Kraevedcheskii Biulleten'* 1:54–79. Yuzhno-Sakhalinsk: Sakhalin Regional Museum.

Vostretsov, Iurii E., ed.

1998 *Pervye rybolovy v zalive Petra Velikogo* (The First Fishers in Peter the Great Bay). Vladivostok: Institute of History, Archaeology and Ethnography of the People of the Far East.

West, Frederick Hadleigh

1967 The Donnelly Ridge Site and the Definition of an Early Core and Blade Complex in Central Alaska. *American Antiquity* 32:360–82.

1996 The Archaeological Evidence. In *American Beginnings: The Prehistory and Palaeoecology of Beringia*. Frederick H. West, ed. Pp. 537–59. Chicago: University of Chicago Press.

Woodbury, Anthony C.

1984 Eskimo and Aleut Languages. In *Arctic*. D. Damas, ed. Pp. 49–63. *Handbook of North American Indians*, Vol. 5. W. C. Sturtevant, gen. ed. Washington, DC: Smithsonian Institution Press.

Yesner, David R., and R. Mack

1998 *Aleut/Eskimo Origins: Margaret Bay Revisited*. Unpublished paper presented at the annual meeting of the Alaska Anthropological Association, Anchorage.

Failing at Bering Strait?
The Jesup North Pacific Expedition and the Study of Culture Contact

PETER P. SCHWEITZER

In 1908, Franz Boas—the organizer of the Jesup North Pacific Expedition (JNPE)—presented an overview of the main results of the expedition, six years after its conclusion (Boas 1908; see Boas 2001:17–24). Despite its unimpressive length of 16 pages, this report—delivered as the Opening Address at the 16th International Congress of Americanists in Vienna—was Boas' final and most extended presentation of what he considered to be the scholarly fruits of a monumental endeavor that lasted for five years (1897–1902), costed at least $100,000, and involved almost 20 researchers. According to Boas, the expedition's goal was to resolve the question of cultural relations between the Old and New World (Boas 1908:4). Bering Strait, the area where the two regions under consideration actually meet and through which most of the supposed movements of people, objects, and ideas must have passed, should thus be considered of prime relevance to the research questions and targets of the JNPE. However, the place name "Bering Strait" was mentioned exactly three times throughout Boas' final JNPE presentation. One of those references was purely locational; the second one referred to Boas' conviction that Eskimo societies were late arrivals at Bering Strait (the so-called "Eskimo Wedge theory"; see Dumond, this volume); and the third was in conjunction with the distribution of reindeer herding in Northern Eurasia (and its absence in the Americas). This last reference is intriguing, since it uses the argument of "lively interaction between Asia and America in the Bering Strait

area" (Boas 1908:17) to argue for the late transition to reindeer herding in northeastern Siberia. Alas, the excited reader does not learn anything more about this "lively interaction" in Boas' final address.

During the years 1993–96, Evgenii Golovko and myself have conducted a multi-site oral history study, entitled "Traveling Between Continents" which was funded by the U.S. National Park Service, Alaska Region. Our primary goal was to document the legacy of inter-continental Native travels between Alaska and Chukotka (Chukchi Peninsula) during the first half of the 20th century (more specifically, until 1948, when all official travel across Bering Strait was halted by Cold War politics). Since our project was situated on the Asiatic and American sides of Bering Strait, we dealt intensively with many Chukchi, Iñupiaq, and Naukan Yupik communities and individuals. Although we were unable to conduct fieldwork on St. Lawrence Island and in the southeastern section of the Chukchi Peninsula, various references to Siberian Yupik societies from these areas are contained in our data. Situated at multiple cultural and linguistic boundaries, "Traveling Between Continents" provided us with ubiquitous instances of culture contact. We learned of social visits, feuds, long-distance economic endeavors, marriage ties, exchanges of personal names and songs, between social units of different cultural and linguistic affiliation. Since we have provided more detailed discussions of our results elsewhere (Schweitzer 1997; Schweitzer and Golovko 1995a, 1995b, 1997a, 2001), I will present here the project's brief summary only, as it pertains to the character of culture contact in the Bering Strait area. This will lead us to the issue of why those very contacts among the North Pacific Native groups have surprisingly eluded the interest of many of the JNPE researchers a century ago.

"Traveling Between Continents" in the Bering Strait Area

Most of the culture contact processes we encountered can be interpreted as exchange transactions. In the first place, the economic realm provides a number of excellent examples: reindeer herders from the interior Chukchi Peninsula exchanged their products for sea-mammal products with coastal communities on the Asiatic and American sides of Bering Strait, whereas transactions between maritime communities on different sides of the strait focused on goods not locally available, some of which were acquired through long-distance trade. Beyond the obvious utilitarian aspect of exchanging goods, there were also instances of transactions that defy a simple supply-and-demand model (for example, wolverine furs were reportedly traded in both directions across Bering Strait). Thus, a major element of "traveling" was the creation and maintenance of social ties. Marriage was a logical vehicle to this end, but so were adoption, formalized partnership, informal friendship, the migration of individuals, and personal naming practices. The social links that were established through these means were a necessary precondition for any kind of visit that was not based purely on negative reciprocity (such as raids and other warfare activities). Since the equivalent of having no recognized ties in a particular community was being considered a stranger and, thus, an enemy, kinship and other links had to be established across community, language, and ethnic boundaries.

The structure of inter-community contacts was in no way arbitrary. Geographic and social proximity determined the frequency of social links between individual communities. Whereas most of these exchange relations were balanced, there were also instances of dominance by one side. This was most clearly expressed in the relations between the reindeer herders and coastal communities, whereby the herders generally considered themselves to be superior. A good example of such unequal relationships was the spread of the Chukchi language among Yupik (and, to a much lesser degree, Iñupiaq) speakers, while there were hardly any instances of Chukchi being able to speak Yupik or Iñupiaq.[1]

After 1920, nation state politics of both Russia and the United States gradually began to exert a domineering influence over these links by encouraging some (those inside the country) and discouraging other ("international") connections. Euro-American group and individual interests were, nothing new to the area under consideration. Ever since the first Russian boats had sailed through Bering Strait in the mid-17th century, the demand for foreign goods had contributed to the structure of economic relations. Until the mid-19th century, the Asian side of Bering Strait was much closer to the supply of Russian goods, which provided its inhabitants with more favorable exchange conditions. Subsequently these conditions were reversed, first by Yankee commercial whalers after 1850 and later by traders operating from Seattle. In the early 20th century, the Alaskan Seward Peninsula (i.e., the town of Nome) became the supply center of imported goods, while the Chukotka residents were primarily contributing raw materials or goods of Native production, such as old ivory, reindeer and fox skins, reindeer fur parkas, and skin-boots.

As we have argued elsewhere (Schweitzer and Golovko 2001), historic warfare in the Bering Strait area was a syncretistic product of traditional social organization (more or less autonomous social units with shifting alliances) and outside pressures (in a nutshell, the encroaching "World-System"). These outside pressures led to competition over access to Euro-American goods and indirectly contributed to the rise of Chukchi reindeer herding, which in itself triggered tremendous changes within the regional network of social relations. However, warfare was as much an expression of the social fabric that linked different communities, as were marriage, economic transactions, or social visits (see Burch 1998). Similarly, the conduct of warfare activities did not exclude those other activities. Since all those forms of culture contact could appear beyond (as well as within) ethnic and linguistic boundaries, "culture change"—that is, the exchange and spread of "culture elements"—was an almost necessary result of "traveling between continents."

One of the most obvious effects of culture contact is in the realm of language. Instances of bi- and multilingualism were quite common throughout the Bering Strait area. As mentioned above, some forms of bilingualism were an expression of one-sided relations; however, in many other cases (e.g., between the Alaskan Iñupiat and Siberian Naukan Yupiit Eskimo) there were approximately equal levels of bilingualism, which reflected more balanced social relationships. In addition, all the languages of the area display a fair number of borrowings in vocabulary and grammar. The existence of previous "trade jargons" is likely, albeit poorly documented (cf. De Reuse 1994). Specific language-related exchanges took place in the realms of the bestowal of personal names and the performance of songs. Iñupiaq and Yupik personal names in the Bering Strait area are "recycled," that is, they are bestowed to a newborn after the death of its previous bearer; in addition, each person can have multiple names, some of which stem from other communities. One specifically interesting aspect of this regional system of naming is the high frequency of Chukchi personal names that is found among the Naukan Yupiit Eskimo (and, to a lesser degree, among the Bering Strait Iñupiat and St. Lawrence Island Yupik people). The preponderance of Chukchi personal names in the Naukan name pool is not the result of Chukchi social dominance, but of the structural properties of Chukchi and Eskimo naming systems, which are distinct but compatible (Schweitzer and Golovko 1997a). Songs and dances in the Bering Strait area are "owned" by the individuals and communities who created them. They are, nevertheless, widely exchanged throughout the region, and songs are generally performed in their original language. In contrast to personal names of "foreign origin," the source of received songs and dances is generally well remembered and usually acknowledged (see also Kingston 2000).

While language-related exchanges and borrowings are easier to detect, those in the realms of social organization, religion, and material culture are often less visible. Nevertheless, there are several well-documented cases in these spheres too. They range from the adoption of reindeer herders' dwellings by the coastal communities of the Chukchi Peninsula and St. Lawrence Island[2] to the disintegrating effect of Iñupiat bilateral kinship organization on the clan system of Naukan Yupiit. Other examples include the adoption of syncretistic religious practices (e.g., a "revitalization movement" in Naukan in the 1920s) and the abandonment of others (e.g., the absence of "messenger feasts" on Little Diomede Island). The above-mentioned forms of culture contact allude to several distinct processes of incorporating "foreign elements." We have argued elsewhere for a preliminary model describing ideal-types of cultural exchanges in the Bering Strait area (Schweitzer and Golovko 1997b). This model proposes to take particular note of whether a certain cultural practice is recognized as borrowed or not. Here it is sufficient to state that even in the early 1990s, after almost 50 years of suspended direct contacts, the effects of culture contact were ubiquitous in the Bering Strait region.

Returning to Boas and the Jesup Expedition, it seems difficult to grasp why a huge joint effort interested in cultural relations between Asia and America had so little to say about the Bering Strait region, a multi-ethnic arena of diverse forms of culture contact and its effects. Most of the forms and effects of culture contact across Bering Strait were at least as visible at the turn of the nineteenth century as they are today (and some of them would then have been much easier to document). The remainder of this paper will shed some light on why the very crossroads between the Old and New World proved to be of marginal interest to the organizer of the JNPE. First, though, it is necessary to break down this general question into at least two components. The first is whether Boas, who never visited the Bering Strait region, slighted the area in his summary reports or whether this deficiency was an unfortunate by-product of the organization and logistics of the JNPE fieldwork in the area during 1900–1. Secondly, what was the relationship between the collected (and published) field data and the interpretations that Boas and other members of the Jesup Expedition drew from them?

For analytical purposes, I will discuss the JNPE fieldwork monographs separately from the interpretations based on them. However, since there has never been (and never will be) a neat demarcation line between data and interpretation, this should not be misunderstood as a naive form of positivism. First, I will briefly review the published monographs that resulted from (and, in one case, preceded) the JNPE. As a second step, I will survey the interpretational tools Boas and his collaborators used to arrive at their conclusions. Finally, I will tackle the title question whether Boas and the JNPE, in general, failed at the task of confronting culture contact in the Bering Strait region.

The Published Field Data

The first thing to be mentioned is that the JNPE teams did not conduct any fieldwork on the Alaskan side of Bering Strait nor hardly anywhere else in Alaska (see Krauss, this volume). Boas justified this circumstance by referring to other available publications for the region, such as those by Nelson (1899), Murdoch (1892), and others (Boas 1908:9).[3] For the Alaskan side of Bering Strait, he certainly had first and foremost Nelson's "The Eskimo About Bering Strait" in mind, which was published in 1899, during the early phase of the JNPE.[4] Thus, I will begin this section with a brief review of the book

that was seemingly considered an adequate substitute for extensive new fieldwork by Boas and his JNPE crew.

Edward William Nelson (1855–1934) was a naturalist who took on a four-year assignment with the U.S. Army Signal Service in St. Michael, Alaska, in 1877. Although his main task was to provide meteorological observations, he agreed to collect ethnological information and specimens for the Smithsonian Institution in exchange for logistical and publication support. Between 1877 and 1881, Nelson was able to travel extensively in the Yukon-Kuskokwim River Delta, the southern part of the Seward Peninsula, and into the Indian country along the Yukon River. In addition, in 1881 he took a trip on the Revenue Cutter *Corwin* to St. Lawrence Island, the Chukchi Peninsula, Wrangel Island, and Northwest Alaska as far as Point Barrow (Fitzhugh and Kaplan 1982:32). Upon his return to Washington, D.C., in the fall of 1881, he began to prepare the publication of his journals and notes; but ill health delayed the process considerably. Finally, in 1899, his monumental monograph, "The Eskimo About Bering Strait" appeared in the Eighteenth Annual Report of the Smithsonian Bureau of American Ethnology for the years 1896–97.

It is not the purpose of this chapter to provide a full analysis of Nelson's anthropological results (see Lantis 1954; Fitzhugh 1983). Instead, I will focus on the issue of culture contact, which Nelson had ample opportunities to experience first-hand. Using just broad linguistic labels of today, he dealt with various Central Alaskan Yup'ik, Siberian Yupik, Naukan Yupik, and Iñupiaq groups and had additional short encounters with Reindeer and Coastal Chukchi in Siberia, as well as with Athapaskan groups in interior Alaska. Using the narrow concept of "traditional societies" (Burch 1980), he had data from more than 20 such groups. His location at St. Michael was ideal for observing real-time culture contact among them; however, that was not what Nelson was interested in. Except for the Athapaskan and the Chukchi, all other Native societies of the region he covered were reduced in his publication to one label, namely the "western Eskimos." While Nelson was aware of some of the linguistic and social boundaries in the region he surveyed (Nelson 1899:24–6), he interpreted them as merely dialect and tribal variations of one ethnic group. Thus, the first chapter of his monograph starts out with the following statement:

> The lives of these people adjacent to the Tinné [Athapaskan - P. S.], as well as those of the Siberian coast who are in constant contact with the Chukchi, have been somewhat modified by their surroundings, although in their language and customs they are still unmistakably Eskimo (Nelson 1899:23).

It is a pity that Nelson did not expand on this mysterious phrase, "have been somewhat modified by their surroundings." These are exactly the forms and results of culture contact we are so interested in. There are, however, a few short sub-chapters, where he provided us with some information about the functional reasons of some forms of culture contact. His three-and-a-half-page account of "Trade and Trading Voyages" (Nelson 1899:228–32) offers a good review of the extent of trade networks throughout the region at the time. Similarly, his short account of "Wars" (Nelson 1899:327–30) is a useful summary of traditional alliances and hostilities in the Bering Strait area. However, neither in those chapters nor in the rest of his book did he try to account for the local cultural differences and their relation to culture contact. Most of the time, his generalizing statements about "western Eskimo" culture mirrors mainly the Central Alaskan Yup'ik area with which he was most familiar.

In the final analysis I have to agree with Margaret Lantis' assessment that "about 250 pages of the [Nelson's] text are essentially an annotated museum catalogue" and that "his presentation of the museum collection of about 10,000 specimens still is unequaled among Alaska Eskimo ones" (Lantis 1954:13). The results of Nelson's sojourn and monograph are strongest in the field of material culture, as in the case of his

fellow Smithsonian affiliate, John Murdoch (1892). Thus, William Fitzhugh's comment that "Nelson's collections. . . can be used for scholarly study of interaction and change across the ethnic, linguistic, and cultural boundary in eastern Norton Sound" (Fitzhugh 1983:34), nevertheless, cannot be fully executed outside the realm of material culture.

The two scholars who conducted fieldwork in northeastern Siberia for the JNPE were Waldemar Jochelson (Vladimir Iokhel'son, in Russian) and Waldemar Bogoras (Vladimir Bogoraz). While Jochelson worked mainly among the Koryak people in northern Kamchatka and among the Even, Yukagir, and Sakha people of the contemporary Republic of Sakha (Yakutia) and the Magadan Province, Bogoras conducted his field surveys mainly in Chukotka, including several locations at Bering Strait. Waldemar Bogoras (1865–1936) was a Russian revolutionary whose first acquaintance with Siberia and its Native people was involuntary: he was exiled to the mouth of the Kolyma River during the years 1890–8. Like several of his fellow *narodniki* exiles, he began collecting ethnographic and folklore material from the Chukchi and other peoples, with whom he was in contact (see more in Vakhtin 2001:78–82). The linguistic competence and ethnographic experience acquired during those years made him an excellent choice for the JNPE Siberian team. In addition, Bogoras had already participated in a large ethnographic expedition to Yakutia, sponsored by the rich gold miner and philanthropist Innokentii Sibiriakov in the years 1895–97.

The fieldtrip for JNPE was conducted by Bogoras and his wife, Sofia Bogoras, over 12 months during the years 1900–1. Unfortunately, Bogoras had to cover an unreasonably broad area. As Igor Krupnik has recently noted , "he [Bogoras – P.S.] was mainly on the move. . . . he surveyed an area from the Bering Strait to Kamchatka Peninsula, over a distance equal to a round trip from London to Sicily" (Krupnik 1996:40). Thus, when Bogoras finally reached the shores of the Bering Strait during the last months of his Siberian sojourn, he was unable to visit all the coastal villages as planned. Especially unfortunate was the fact that he did not make it to the areas closest to the Alaskan mainland, particularly, the villages of Naukan, Uelen, and their surroundings, as he originally proposed to Boas (Vakhtin 2001:83). However, it is worth mentioning that Bogoras

conducted that trip ("traveling half-way between continents") in the "Native way".

The major result of Bogoras' JNPE participation was his three-part monograph *The Chukchee* (Bogoras 1904–9). Despite its mono-ethnic title, the massive work also provides significant information about the Siberian Yupik

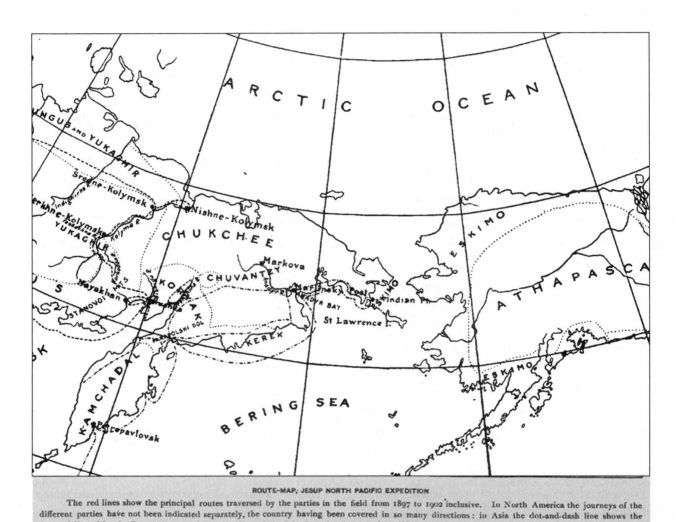

ROUTE-MAP, JESUP NORTH PACIFIC EXPEDITION

The red lines show the principal routes traversed by the parties in the field from 1897 to 1902 inclusive. In North America the journeys of the different parties have not been indicated separately, the country having been covered in so many directions : in Asia the dot-and-dash line shows the course followed by the Bogoras party ; the broken line, that of the Jochelson party ; the solid line, that of the Laufer party.

6/ A segment of the original map of the Jesup Expedition activities, 1897-1902, showing the routes of Bogoras' and Jochelson's parties in the Bering Sea area (Adapted from Boas 1903:72)

was able to reach St. Lawrence Island from the southeastern coast of the Chukchi Peninsula. He traveled by Native skin-boat from Cape Chaplin to Gambell, on St. Lawrence Island in May 1901 and he spent a few days on the island, before coming back by the same boat. That made Bogoras the only early ethnographer who

(whom Bogoras called Asiatic Eskimo) and, to a lesser degree, the Koryak, Yukagir, Even, and Russian Creole. In accordance with other major "base-line ethnographies" of the turn of the century, Bogoras managed to touch upon almost everything anthropologists were supposed to be interested in: from fishing implements to funeral ceremonies, from shamanism to dog-breeding, and from children's games to Native customary law. Unlike his Alaskan predecessors Nelson and Murdoch, he thus succeeded in providing a more holistic portrait of the society he studied and not an account biased primarily towards its material culture. His long-term experience in the area and his fluent knowledge of the Chukchi language surely contributed to the truly impressive scope and quality of his work. In retrospect, one of the few major shortcomings of his monograph was also related to his prolonged stay in western Chukchi territory, among the reindeer herders of the Kolyma River area. Throughout his book, there is a marked preponderance of information about the Reindeer Chukchi, while the Maritime Chukchi (and Siberian Yupik) are generally treated with much less attention. As Krupnik has mentioned, Bogoras continued throughout his career to look at Siberian Native life through a Reindeer Chukchi lens (Krupnik 1996:43). In addition, Krupnik has aptly criticized Bogoras for representing Maritime Chukchi (and Siberian Yupik) social organization as much less structured than it proved to be by later research (Krupnik 1996).

However, recognizing that shortcomings are quite inevitable in a work of the scope of *The Chukchee*, instead, I want to focus on the most notable achievements of the book. To me, those are the already mentioned multi-ethnic focus and the extensive use of historic documents, both of which lend a truly diachronic quality to Bogoras' volume. It should be remembered that the predominant format of ethnographic monographs at the time—including Boas' vision of the JNPE publication series—was to treat a single ethnic group as an isolated phenomenon that could be described without much mention of other groups. *The Chukchee*, to the contrary, was characterized by an unusual amount of historical information. For example, Bogoras' 50-page chapter, "Contact of the Chukchee with the Russians," has few equals in early 20th century ethnographies. Bogoras did not limit his diachronic approach to accounts of "colonial history," but applied it

to a variety of topics, such as the "origin of reindeer breeding" or issues of shamanism.

In addition, Bogoras constantly challenged the narrow confines of single-ethnic monographs. He not only referenced inter-group and inter-ethnic relations in the abstract; but he also contributed hundreds of concrete illustrations of such relationships. For example, in discussing "Mixed Marriages" (Bogoras 1904–9:591–5), he did not merely state that Chukchi men sometimes married Tungus (Even) women. Instead, he provided intricate details about how the problem of distinct marriage presentations (bride-service vs. bride-price) was solved. Similarly, his sections about "Trade" (Bogoras 1904–9:53–69) and "Warfare" (1904–9:645-59) abound in specific details of interethnic conduct. In sum, *The Chukchee* is not only a "world-class monograph" but one that provides ample concrete data about culture contact in areas adjacent to Bering Strait.

Bogoras published several other volumes resulting from his participation in the JNPE. However, these were mainly collections of folklore (Bogoras 1910a, 1913, 1917, 1918) or linguistic sourcebooks (Bogoras 1949). In addition, he wrote a huge assembly of articles; since most of them address specific topical problems and use his JNPE materials mainly as illustrations, they will be discussed in the following section.

Interpretations by Boas and Bogoras

At the turn of the twentieth century, the battle between evolutionists and diffusionists was the defining moment in anthropological debates (see Lee and Graburn, this volume). Boas was among the most vocal and influential critics of evolutionism, which had dominated the generation of scholars preceding him.[5] His article, "The Limitations of the Comparative Method of Anthropology" (1896; abbreviated hereafter as "The Limitations"), remains a textbook example of the "historical method" which dismisses approaches that treat all similar phenomena as the results of the "uniform working of the human mind." Boas was, however, from the beginning a "moderate diffusionist." Already in "The

Limitations" he demanded that the historical method is applied to a "well-defined, small geographical territory" and that "continuity of distribution as one of the essential conditions for proving historical connection" be observed (Boas 1982 [1940]:277). This caveat was directed at more radical diffusionists, many of whom were strongly influenced by the German anthropogeographer Friedrich Ratzel (as was, in fact, Boas himself). At the same time, Boas did not exclude the possibility of "independent invention," nor did he reject the "comparative method" entirely. Instead, he was calling for careful historical investigations before building any sweeping models that rested on evolution or diffusion.

This was very much Boas' mindset during the organization and conduct of the JNPE. The plan for the expedition can be seen as an attempt to apply the historical method, by selecting a well-defined geographical territory and looking for continuities and discontinuities of culture element distribution. As Boas stated after the completion of the expedition, "if we approach the problem of culture parallels from a purely psychological and purely evolutionistic point of view, an investigation or a problem, as the one before the Jesup-expedition, would seem unsolvable" (Boas 1908:5). In other words, the JNPE would have never been designed nor undertaken by an ardent evolutionist.

According to Harris (1968:278–80), around 1910, Boas began to change his general views about the possibilities of finding general laws regarding cultural development. He became more skeptical about the predictability of cultural processes and maintained that there is no necessary correlation between the developmental stages of different aspects of culture. This theoretical development of Boas is important for our purposes. As mentioned above, his final report regarding the results of the JNPE was presented in 1908. However, at that time a significant portion of individual monographs stemming from the expedition was not yet published. It took until 1926 for the final portion of the expedition field data (Jochelson's final delivery of his Yukagir monograph) to appear in one of the last issues under the Jesup Expedition series (whereas Jochelson's JNPE Yakut materials were only published in 1933 and outside of the expedition series). At that point in his career, Boas had entirely abandoned every aspect of the comparative method, devoted himself to "historical particularism," and became more interested in individual rather than in group processes (Harris 1968:280–1).

It is also noteworthy that the final volume of the JNPE series (vol. XII, to be entitled "Summary and Final Results"; Boas 1905:94) was never published. In a sense, the full interpretation of Bogoras' (and Nelson's) results was never accomplished by Boas. It could be argued that Boas' JNPE program reflected primarily his early theoretical preoccupations (as outlined in "The Limitations"). By the time all the results were finally assembled, Boas' interests had significantly changed and, thus, a detailed summary and interpretation of data collected under a "past paradigm" was no longer desirable.

The question remains as to which aspects of the original program might have become obsolete for Boas. Since we have no direct evidence from him on the subject, I cannot make more than informed guesses. By reading through Boas' early reports about the JNPE, I was quite struck by the sheer spatial and temporal scope of the problems he intended to address. Far from staying within the "well-defined geographical territory" of the North Pacific region, Boas addressed questions of culture history ranging from the southern tip of South America to Europe and from the Paleolithic to the recent past. If this is the "historical method," it surely is history on a macro-scale. Boas was dealing with questions such as the when and where of the origin of Eskimo culture; he compared the peoples of the Arctic and Northwestern North America to those of the southern part of North America; he hypothesized about Mesoamerican influences in North America; he tried to assess the relative ages of different culture areas; he classified the languages of northeastern Siberia in relation to North American languages, etc. (Boas 1908).

These questions seemed more appropriate in the writing of an ardent diffusionist rather than of a moderate advocate of the "historical method."

It might well be that the initial program of the JNPE was in reality much more ambitious than Boas' cautionary theoretical prescriptions. Somehow, the strategic location of the JNPE must have tempted Boas to address the "big questions" of culture history, such as the peopling of the Americas. While his JNPE master plan can be said to fit with his theoretical writings of the time, it also made room for much more far-reaching issues. One thing that even Boas' theoretical opponents admit is that he held very high methodological standards (see Harris 1968). It is easy to imagine that Boas realized that, however tempting the "big questions" might be, the JNPE data did not provide more than food for speculation. More in accordance with his (especially, later) views, he eventually abandoned the grand synthesis project. Instead, he went to practice in the field of "historical particularism." However, either because of time constraints or lack of regional interest, he did not work with all the data compiled by the JNPE. In fact, he primarily worked with materials on Northwest coast societies, where he tried to reconstruct detailed historical sequences. The Bering Strait material never received a similar treatment by Boas.

In contrast to Boas, Bogoras was for most of his career an outspoken (although not always conscious) evolutionist. Traces of this approach can easily be found in most of his writings, including "The Chukchee." There, before presenting materials on Chukchi religion, he provides us with his views on the five "developmental stages of primitive religious concepts" (Bogoras 1904–09:277–90). The model suggested by Bogoras displays an eclectic mix of influences ranging from Charles Darwin to Herbert Spencer to Edward B. Tylor. Although those pages contain interesting ethnographic information, its presentation suffers from the straightjacket approach of constructing a unilineal sequence of religious concepts: from animism (a label he rejected) to supernatural beings. In addition, Bogoras provided a short comparative treatment of religious ideas among the Koryak and Itelmen, as compared to the Chukchi (Bogoras 1904–9:290–1). While the similarities between Koryak and Chukchi concepts seem to strengthen Bogoras' evolutionistic argument, his final paragraph of that section indicates an implicit argument for diffusion. He pointed out that Chukchi and Eskimo folklore showed strong resemblances, while Koryak and Itelmen stories were closer to those of the American Northwest coast (Bogoras 1904–9:291).

Other instances of evolutionistic leanings in *The Chukchee* can be found in Bogoras' treatment of social organization. For example, regarding the Chukchi "family group"—a group of kindred families—he suggests that it "may perhaps be called an embryo of a clan" (Bogoras 1904–9:541). However, despite the usage of such terms as "group-marriage," *The Chukchee,* for the most part, stays free of putting Chukchi social organization into an evolutionary framework. Such a framework was to be found in Bogoras' last publications, when Marxist evolutionist line demanded that his views fit into the ruling dogmas such as "pre-clan" and "clan society" (see Bogoras n.d.: 292–6). His views about religion, on the other hand, were consistently phrased in developmental terms (see Bogoras 1906, 1910b).

It has already been indicated that Bogoras was not opposed to explaining the distribution of culture elements through diffusion and migration. This is especially evident from a number of his articles published after the completion of the JNPE. For example, his Russian article "Ancient Migrations of Peoples in Northern Eurasia and America," (Bogoras 1927) reads like a compendium of speculative population movements throughout the northern parts of Eurasia and North America. While Boas and Bogoras seem to meet in this respect, there was a temporal hiatus between their macro-historical contributions. When Bogoras issued his major statements on the subject during the 1920s (e.g., Bogoras 1924, 1927), Boas had already long abandoned the search for the "big picture" of human cultural history.

After reviewing Boas' and Bogoras' general approaches, we still need to look at several specific assumptions that informed their work. One of them is the already-mentioned "Eskimo Wedge theory," which can be called a direct result of the JNPE (Dumond, this volume; Freed et al. 1988:32). According to Boas' view (which was shared by Bogoras), Eskimo cultures originated in Canada and were late arrivals to Alaska, where they "interrupted, at an early period, the communication between the Siberian and Indian tribes" (Boas 1905:98–9).[6] Unfortunately, this view of Bering Strait culture chronology disqualified the various Eskimo societies of the region from being considered an intrinsic part of the regional cultural network. Another specific assumption that informed Boas' (but not Bogoras') approach has at least to be mentioned, being that for Boas "culture contact" was limited to contact among Native societies. He had no interest in the dramatic cultural processes that were taking place before the eyes of the Jesup Expedition members in the field. This aspect of Boas' views —which is so difficult to grasp— has rightly been questioned by several other papers in this volume (see Krauss, this volume; Lee and Graburn, this volume). Here it must suffice to state that Boas' concept of the relationship between science and politics was ambiguous. While he is rightly remembered as a courageous enemy of racism, Boas always considered his "political" views as being entirely "scientific." Thus, there was no room for a moralistic position, which would have been an almost inescapable precondition or consequence of analyzing contemporary Native/non-Native interactions.

Conclusions

Let me now attempt at a preliminary synthesis of the arguments developed above. There is no reason to suggest that Boas' lonely fieldworker on the Russian side of Bering Strait—Waldemar Bogoras—failed the task of documenting culture contacts in the region. On the contrary, his major account of the JNPE-trip, *The Chukchee,* contains many excellent descriptions of such processes. After almost 100 years, this work continues to be a "treasure chest" of information for scholars interested in the subject.

Unfortunately, things were different for the Alaskan section of the region. Nelson's material culture-focused monograph could in no way match Bogoras' lively account. With the possible exception of tracing culture contact through objects of material culture, we are left today with few usable clues. It has to be stated, however, that Nelson's "job description" neither at the time of his Alaskan fieldwork (1877–81) nor during his writing for the Smithsonian (in the 1880s and 1890s) included what we would want to see most in his monograph these days. Thus, to a certain degree, the "blame" should rather be put on Boas who assumed that Nelson's' work in progress could/would become a valid substitute for JNPE fieldwork in Alaska. He seemed to have sensed that after the completion of the Jesup Expedition, when he stated that "unfortunately our knowledge of the Alaskan Eskimo is not thorough enough to permit of a definitive statement in regard to their culture" (Boas 1905:98). However, we at least have to consider the institutional and political pressure Boas was facing while lobbying for "his" expedition (Freed et al. 1988). It might well be that keeping good rapport with the Smithsonian Institution, which had financed Murdoch's and Nelson's report, led him to abandon plans for independent fieldwork in Alaska.[7]

Although Bogoras and Boas are often portrayed as having belonged to mutually exclusive camps of anthropological theory (evolutionism and historical particularism, respectively), most of their synthesizing writings on the subject adopt a strangely similar perspective. Both show a particular interest in "grand culture history," which leaves no room for the study of concrete culture history. In Bogoras' case, his interest in the details of how neighboring groups interact seems to have been satisfied by the completion of his JNPE monographs. Further micro-historical analysis was seemingly not a major concern to him. For Boas, macrohistory held its fascination until around 1908; after that, he devoted much of his energies to local and detailed accounts of historical processes. Unfortunately, the Bering Strait region was never able to attract considerable attention from this outstanding scholar. The "Eskimo Wedge" theory created and defended by Boas, Bogoras, and others, certainly did not contribute to the study of culture contact phenomena in the area under consideration. Since the Eskimo societies around Bering Strait were considered to have "messed up the puzzle" of culture history, instead of being interpreted as an intricate part of it, the heuristic value of the region became negligible. Viewed from their "macro-scale" perspective of history, Bering Strait appeared too "narrow" as to allow a sweeping statement to be applied to the North Pacific Rim.

Finally, Bogoras' detailed descriptions of Native/non-Native interactions in the Bering Strait region did not attract Boas' analytical curiosity, since the latter thought them outside of the anthropologists' goals. Thus, another chance at understanding the mechanisms of culture contact and change was passed over.

The question phrased in the title of this paper—Failing at Bering Strait?—has yet to be addressed. While it is evidently quite easy to point out certain shortcomings some 100 years after the completion of the JNPE, I concede that it would be inappropriate to speak of "failure" regarding the expedition's accomplishments in the Bering Strait region. After all, the research questions and interests of Boas, Bogoras, and the others who contributed to the mega-size endeavor of the JNPE were shaped by the dominant theories and paradigms of their time. Thus, we cannot condemn them for the fact that they did not pose or answer *then* many of our key questions of *today*. In the final analysis, there is nothing more telling than the fact that we are still debating their field data and theoretical positions and will probably continue to do so for at least another 100 years. Few of us can hope for a similar interest by succeeding generations of anthropologists, who will perceive the shortcomings of our approaches all too plainly.

Acknowledgments

This article is a follow-up to a joint paper by Evgenii V. Golovko and myself presented at the conference "Constructing Cultures Then and Now: A Centenary Conference Celebrating Franz Boas and the Jesup North Pacific Expedition, 1897–1997," November 1997, in New York City. I hereby want to acknowledge the input Evgenii Golovko has provided on my anthropological perspectives, especially within the context of our joint research project "Traveling Between Continents." I also want to thank Stacie McIntosh and Igor Krupnik for editorial assistance and advice.

Notes

1. However, in the few villages with a mixed Chukchi and Yupik population, such as Kiwak and Uelen, Chukchi fluent in Yupik were quite common (see Krupnik and Chlenov 1979).

2. To be more specific, coastal residents adopted certain architectural principles of the *yaranga*, the traditional skin-covered dwelling of the Reindeer Chukchi. As its tundra precursor, the coastal *yaranga* was an above-ground structure which featured an inner chamber (*polog*). In contrast to the reindeer herders' dwelling, it was more solid and not designed for frequent moves. This architectural shift only became possible once the coastal residents received a steady supply of reindeer skins (to cover the *polog* and other parts of the *yaranga*) from the tundra (Igor Krupnik, personal communication, November 1998).

3. According to a map of proposed expedition operations published in 1897, fieldwork was also planned in Western Alaska and the Aleutians (see Fitzhugh and Krupnik 2001:xvi; Krupnik and Vakhtin, this volume).

4. In addition, he might have had John Murdoch's "Ethnological Results of the Point Barrow Expedition" (1892) in mind, which was already published by the time JNPE was in the planning stage. However, Murdoch's monograph is not only situated outside of our geographic range of inter-

ests, but has hardly anything to offer on issues of culture contact.

5. Since I am here primarily interested in Boas' treatment of culture change in the Bering Strait area, I cannot provide an in-depth review of Boas' general contributions to anthropology. For recent contributions to this vast body of literature see Baker (1998), Cole (1999), Darnell (1998, 2001), as well as several contributions in Stocking (1996) and Krupnik and Fitzhugh (2001).

6. Frederica de Laguna's statement (1994:12) that Boas' views on the problem were already formulated in his famous early monograph "The Central Eskimo" (1888) can be extended. It could be argued that his general views on the homogeneity of Eskimo culture, formed as they were by his Central Inuit field experience, made him uncritical of Nelson's field data.

7. Boas had a long-standing but complex relationship with the Smithsonian National Museum. In 1887, Boas had a protracted dispute with the museum's Otis Mason about how to properly display museum artifacts (Cole 1995 [1985]:112–8).

References

Baker, Lee D.

1998 *From Savage to Negro: Anthropology and the Construction of Race, 1896–1954*. Berkeley: University of California Press.

Boas, Franz

1888 The Central Eskimo. *Sixth Annual Report of the Bureau of Ethnology*. Washington, DC: Government Printing Office.

1905 The Jesup North Pacific Expedition. In *International Congress of Americanists, 13th Session, Held in New York in 1902*. Pp. 91–100. Easton, PA: Eschenbach.

1908 Die Resultate der Jesup-Expedition. *Verhandlungen des XVI. Amerikanisten-Kongresses in Wien 9. bis 14. September 1908*: 3–18. Reprinted as: The Results of the Jesup Expedition. Opening Address at the 16th International Congress of the Americanists. Translated by Saskia Wrausmann. In *Gateways. Exploring the Legacy of the Jesup North Pacific Expedition, 1897–1902*. Igor Krupnik and William Fitzhugh, eds. Pp. 17–24. Contributions to Circumpolar Anthropology, 1. Washington, DC: Arctic Studies Center.

1982 [1940] *Race, Language and Culture*. Chicago: University of Chicago Press.

Bogoras, Waldemar

1904–9 The Chukchee. *The Jesup North Pacific Expedition*, vol. 7, pts.1–3. *Memoirs of the American Museum of Natural History* 11. Leiden: E. J. Brill; New York: G.E. Stechert.

1906 Religious Ideas of Primitive Man, from Chukchee Material. In *Internationaler Amerikanisten-Kongress, 14. Tagung, Stuttgart 1904. Zweite Hälfte*. Pp. 129–35. Berlin: W. Kohlhammer.

1910a Chukchee Mythology. *The Jesup North Pacific Expedition*, vol.8, pt.1. *Memoirs of the American Museum of Natural History*, 12. Leiden: E. J. Brill; New York: G.E. Stechert.

1910b K psikhologii shamanstva u narodov severovostochnoi Azii (Toward the Psychology of Shamanism among the Native Peoples of Northeastern Asia). *Etnograficheskoe obozrenie* 84–5:1–36.

1913 The Eskimo of Siberia. *The Jesup North Pacific Expedition*, vol.8, pt.3. *Memoirs of the American Museum of Natural History* 12. Leiden: E. J. Brill; New York: G.E. Stechert.

1917 Koryak Texts. *Publications of the American Ethnological Society*, 5. Leiden.

1918 Tales of Yukaghir, Lamut, and Russianized Natives of Eastern Siberia. *Anthropological Papers of the American Museum of Natural History* 20(1):3–148.

1925 Early Migrations of the Eskimo between Asia and America. In *Congrès International des Américanistes. Compte-Rendu de la 21e Session, Deuxieme Partie. Tenue à Göteborg en 1924*. Pp. 216–35. Göteborg Museum.

1927 Drevnie pereseleniia narodov v severnoi Evrazii i v Amerike (Ancient Human Migrations in Northern Asia and in America). *Sbornik Muzeia Antropologii i Etnografii* 6: 37–62. Leningrad.

1949 *Materialy po iazyku aziatskikh eskimosov (Materials Relating to the Language of the Asiatic Eskimo)*. Leningrad: Uchpedgiz.

n.d. *Ocherki kul'tury narodov Severa (Essays in the Cultures of the Peoples of the North)*. Unpublished manuscript, Archives of the Museum of Anthropology and Ethnography (St. Petersburg, Russia); f. K. I, op. 1, No. 29.

Burch, Ernest S., Jr.

1980 Traditional Eskimo Societies in Northwest Alaska. In *Alaska Native Culture and History*. Yoshinobu Kotani and William B. Workman, eds. Pp. 253–304. *Senri Ethnological Studies*, 4. Osaka, Japan: National Museum of Ethnology.

1998 International Affairs. *The Cultural and Natural Heritage of Northwest Alaska*, vol.7. Produced for NANA Museum of the Arctic and U.S. National Park Service, Alaska Region.

Cole, Douglas

1995 [1985] *Captured Heritage: The Scramble for Northwest Coast Artifacts*. Norman: University of Oklahoma Press.

1999 *Franz Boas: The Early Years, 1858–1906*. Seattle: University of Washington Press.

Darnell, Regna

1998 *And Along Came Boas: Continuity and Revolution in Americanist Anthropology.* Amsterdam: John Benjamins.

2001 *Invisible Genealogies: A History of Americanist Anthropology.* Lincoln: University of Nebraska Press.

De Laguna, Frederica

1994 Some Early Circumpolar Studies. In *Circumpolar Religion and Ecology: An Anthropology of the North.* T. Irimoto and T. Yamada, eds. Pp. 7–44. Tokyo: University of Tokyo Press.

De Reuse, Willem J.

1994 *Siberian Yupik Eskimo: The Language and Its Contacts with Chukchi.* Salt Lake City: University of Utah Press.

Fitzhugh, William W.

1983 Introduction. In *Edward W. Nelson, The Eskimo about Bering Strait.* Pp. 5–106. Washington, DC: Smithsonian Institution Press.

Fitzhugh, William W., and Susan A. Kaplan

1982 *Inua: Spirit World of the Bering Sea Eskimo.* Washington, DC: Smithsonian Institution Press.

Fitzhugh, William W., and Igor Krupnik

2001 Introduction. In *Gateways. Exploring the Legacy of the Jesup North Pacific Expedition.* Igor Krupnik and William W. Fitzhugh, eds. Pp. 1–16. Contributions to Circumpolar Anthropology, 1. Washington, DC: Arctic Studies Center.

Freed, Stanley A., Ruth S. Freed, and Laila Williamson

1988 Capitalist Philanthropy and Russian Revolutionaries: The Jesup North Pacific Expedition (1897–1902). *American Anthropologist* 90(1):7–24.

Harris, Marvin

1968 *The Rise of Anthropological Theory: A History of Theories of Culture.* New York: Thomas Y. Crowell.

Kingston, Deanna M.

2000 Siberian Songs and Siberian Kin: Indirect Assertions of King Islander Dominance in the Bering Strait Region. *Arctic Anthropology* 37(2):38–51.

Krupnik, Igor I.

1996 The 'Bogoras Enigma': Bounds of Culture and Formats of Anthropologists. In *Grasping the Changing World: Anthropological Concepts in the Postmodern Era.* V. Hubinger, ed. Pp. 35–52. London: Routledge.

Krupnik, Igor I., and Mikhail A. Chlenov

1979 Dinamika etnolingvisticheskoi situatsii u aziatskikh eskimosov: konets XIX veka-1970-e gg. (Dynamics of the Ethno-linguistic Status of the Asiatic Eskimo: from the late 19th century until the 1970s) . *Sovetskaia Etnografiia* (2):19–29. Moscow.

Krupnik, Igor, and William W. Fitzhugh, eds.

2001 *Gateways: Exploring the Legacy of the Jesup North Pacific Expedition, 1897–1902.* Washington, DC: Arctic Studies Center, National Museum of Natural History, Smithsonian Institution.

Lantis, Margaret

1954 Edward William Nelson. *Anthropological Papers of the University of Alaska* 3(1):5–16.

Murdoch, John

1892. Ethnological Results of the Point Barrow Expedition. *9th Annual Report of the Bureau of Ethnology for the Years 1887–1888.* Washington, DC: Government Printing Office.

Nelson, Edward William

1899 The Eskimo about Bering Strait. *18th Annual Report of the Bureau of American Ethnology for the Years 1896–1897,* pt.1. Washington, DC: Government Printing Office.

Schweitzer, Peter P.

1997 Traveling Between Continents: Native Contacts Across the Bering Strait, 1898–1948. *Arctic Research of the United States* 11: 68–72.

Schweitzer, Peter P., and Evgenii Golovko

1995a Contacts Across Bering Strait, 1898–1948. (Traveling Between Continents, Phases One and Two). Report Prepared for the U.S. National Park Service, Alaska Regional Office.

1995b Traveling Between Continents: The Social Organization of Interethnic Contacts Across Bering Strait. *The Anthropology of East Europe Review* 13(2):50–5.

1997a Local Identities and Traveling Names: Interethnic Aspects of Personal Naming in the Bering Strait Area. *Arctic Anthropology* 34(1):167–80.

1997b *Culture Contact in the Bering Strait Area: Open Questions of Jesup I and Contemporary Approaches.* Paper presented at the conference "Constructing Cultures Then and Now: A Centenary Conference Celebrating Franz Boas and the Jesup North Pacific Expedition, 1897-1997," November 1997, New York.

2001 Pamiat' o voine: konstruirovanie vneshnego konflikta v kul'ture etnicheskikh obshchnostei Beringova proliva (Memory of the War: Constructing Outside Conflict in the Ethnic Cultures of the Bering Strait Region). In *Trudy fakul'teta etnologii Evropeiskogo universiteta v Sankt-Peterburge.* Pp. 26—37. St. Petersburg: Evropeiskii Universitet.

2003 Levels of Inequality in the North Pacific Rim: Cultural Logics and Regional Interaction.. In: *Hunter-Gatherers of the North Pacific Rim.* J. Habu, J.M. Savelle, S. Koyama and H. Hongo, eds. Pp. 83–101. Senri Ethnological Series, 63. Osaka, Japan: National Museum of Ethnology.

Stocking, George W., Jr., ed.

1996 Volksgeist as Method and Ethic: Essays on Boasian Ethnography and the German Anthropological Tradition. *History of Anthropology,* 8. Madison: University of Wisconsin Press.

7/ Jochelson's first expedition camp at the village of Kushka on the Sea of Okhotsk Coast, summer 1900. Dina Jochelson-Brodsky is sitting in the middle; a tall man standing to her left is Norman Buxton (?) (AMNH 4188)

8/ The transport of the JNPE collections near Yakutsk, East Siberia, spring 1902. Photographer, Waldemar Jochelson (AMNH 1755)

9/ Waldemar Bogoras, with the expedition collection freight ready for shipping out of Novo-Mariinsk, summer 1901. Note the label on one of the crates: "Jessup (sic!) Expedition. Jochelson. Vladivostock via Nagasaki." Other crates carry label "Anadyr" (in Cyrillic) and a Russian double-head eagle imperial seal (AMNH 22332)

10/ Jochelson's reindeer team with the JNPE collections, East Siberia, 1901 (?) (AMNH4206)

11/ Jesup Expedition Siberian collections displayed at the AMNH. Photographer, R.E. Dahlgren (AMNH 31003)

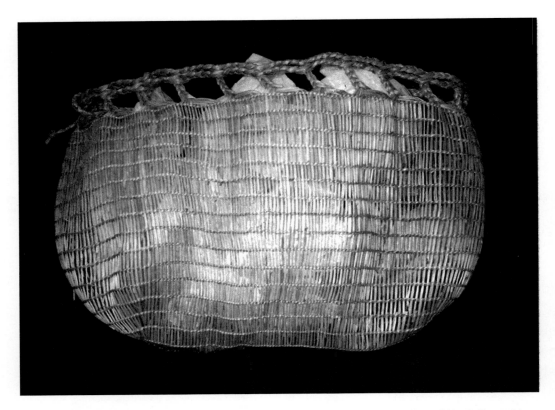

12/ Example of old Eskimo twined basketry (pack sack) issran (Central Yup'ik). Collected by James W. VanStone on Nunivak Island, 1952 (UAM 554-5446)

13/ Coiled willow-root basket. Collected by Edward W. Nelson at Sledge Island, Norton Sound, 1878-81 (NMNH cat. #44234)

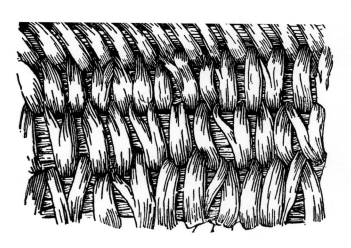

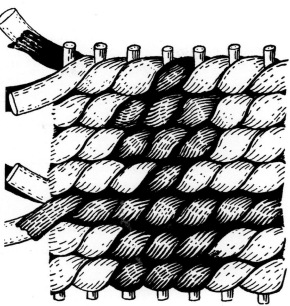

14/ Closeup of grass-coiling technique
(Reprinted from: Otis Mason 1902, Fig.131).

15/ Closeup of twined-grass technique
(Reprinted from: Otis Mason 1902, Fig.152)

16/ Miner Bruce basket
from Kotzebue Sound. Pho-
tographer, Aníbal Rodriguez
(AMNH cat. #60-2324)

17/ Early coiled beach-grass basket. Collected by Lt. G.M. Stoney on Putnam or Kobuk River, northern Alaska, 1887 (NMNH cat. #127891)

18/ Coiled willow-root "tobacco basket", with attached sea-mammal hide bag. Collected by Lt. P. H. Ray at Sidaru (near Pt. Barrow), 1881-83 (NMNH cat. #56564)

70

19/ Eskimo in skin boats (umiaks) *ready to trade with the passing ship. Port Clarence, Alaska, 1899. Harriman Expedition (NMAI P-11078)*

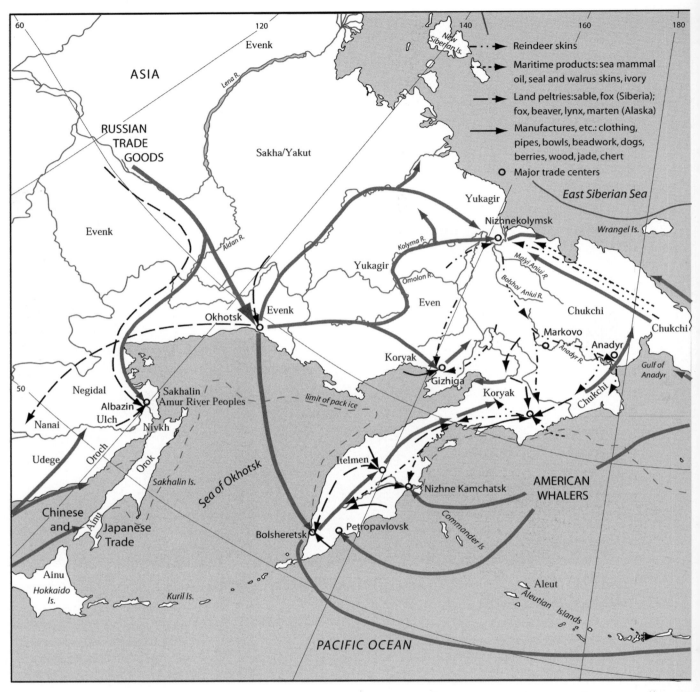

Legend:

- ·-·-·▶ Reindeer skins
- ·-·▶ Maritime products: sea mammal oil, seal and walrus skins, ivory
- ---▶ Land peltries: sable, fox (Siberia); fox, beaver, lynx, marten (Alaska)
- ───▶ Manufactures, etc.: clothing, pipes, bowls, beadwork, dogs, berries, wood, jade, chert
- ○ Major trade centers

20/ *North Pacific–Siberian–Alaskan Trade Systems, ca. 1775–1900. Adapted from Fitzhugh and Crowell 1988:236-37, with revisions.*

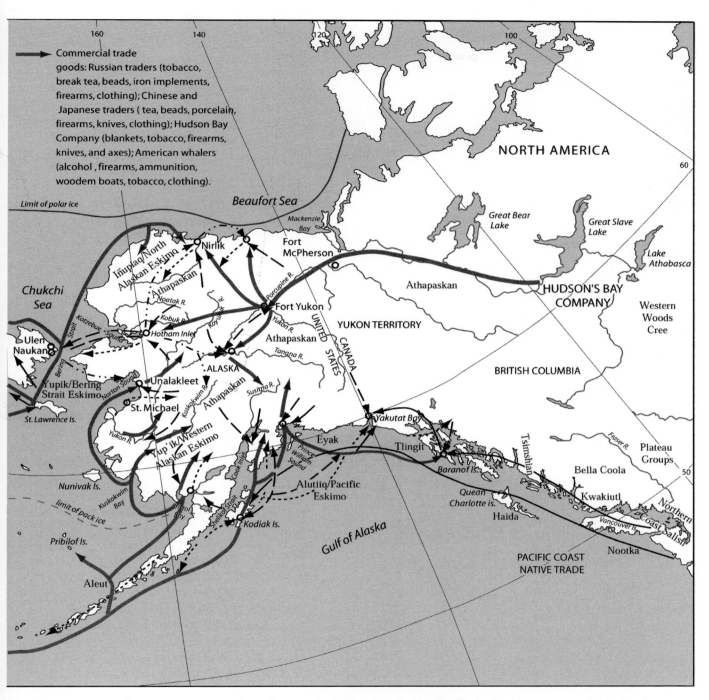

Trade goods moved from east to west, and north to south, creating a crossroads of linked cultures across the Bering Sea area.

7 3

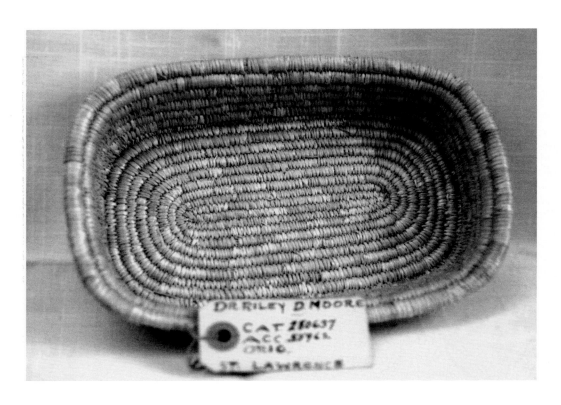

21/ Saint Lawrence Island coiled beach-grass tray. Collected by Dr. Riley D. Moore, 1912 (NMNH cat. #280637)

22/ Chukchi basket. Collected by Waldemar Bogoras, Jesup North Pacific Expedition, 1900-01. Photographer, Aníbal Rodriguez (AMNH cat. #70-7952)

74

23/ Beach at Port Clarence, Alaska, with several whaling ships anchored in the harbor. Photographer, Edward S. Curtis, Harriman Expedition, 1899 (NMAI P-11087)

24/ Koryak coiled grass basket. Collected by Waldemar and Dina Jochelson, Jesup North Pacific Expedition, 1900–01. Photographer, Aníbal Rodriguez (AMNH cat. # 70-3932, 70-3352)

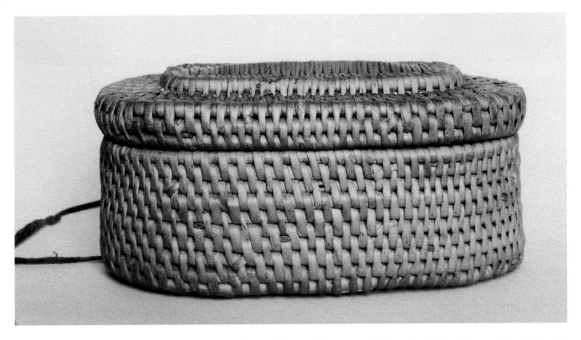

25/ Koryak coiled willow root basket. Collected by Waldemar and Dina Jochelson, Jesup North Pacific Expedition, 1900–01. Photographer, Aníbal Rodriguez (AMNH cat. # 70-3195)

26/ Chinese tea basket, bamboo with porcelain tea cups. Collected by Berthold Laufer, Jesup North Pacific Expedition, 1898–99. Photographer, Aníbal Rodriguez (AMNH cat. # 70-2638)

27/ Ainu basket (tenki). Collected by Bashford Dean, in Hokkaido Shikiu, 1901 (AMNH cat. #70-4091 A&B)

28/ Koryak basket makers at work. Waldemar Jochelson (Dina Jochelson-Brodsky?), photographer, 1900-01 (AMNH 1576)

Diffusion and Colonial Anthropology:
Theories of Change in the Context of Jesup 1

MOLLY LEE
NELSON H. H. GRABURN

The centennial of the Jesup North Pacific Expedition is a fitting occasion on which to reexamine the construct of diffusion, which has lain dormant since the grand theories of the 19th century fell from anthropological grace. Without question, one of Franz Boas' main interests in verifying the Asian origins of North American indigenous cultures was to chart the distribution of cultural elements across Siberia and into Alaska (Boas 1903:73). Nevertheless, Jesup Expedition publications, and those by Boas himself, map the spread of such elements among the Native cultures of Siberia, but are uniformly unenlightening on links across Bering Strait.

The overarching argument of this paper is that diffusion theory never reached its full potential in Jesup Expedition publications because the Boasian model used by its investigators failed to incorporate the agency of World System Theory (Wallerstein 1974). Their perspective ignored hybrid cultural forms emerging from the cross fertilization of the North Pacific indigenous peoples with the world system into which they were linked by the fur trade, the Yankee whaling industry, and the other forms of commerce that escalated across the North at the turn of the 20th century. Whereas Boas and his contemporaries discussed in some detail Native-Native contacts, they bracketed out the trans-Beringian connection, a route largely controlled by Western traders and whalers, because at that time, Native-Western interactions did not fall within the scope of anthropology (see also Schweitzer, this volume). We use a case study of the transmission of two hybrid forms of coiled basketry across Siberia and Alaska through the agency of the world system to illustrate our point.

The World System and the Spread of Coiled Basketry across Siberia and Bering Strait

The hypothetical spread of coiled basketry across Siberia from two different sources, the Chinese border and the Kamchatka Peninsula, underscores the pivotal role of the world system in the diffusion of cultural traits in the areas studied by the Jesup Expedition. It also makes clear the contribution that material culture studies can make to our understanding of culture history. In an era when most branches of anthropology have abandoned the search for relationships between the cultural forms of one group and another, material culture studies and archaeology have retained this approach, not out of any belief that it might lead to the discovery of "Ur-forms," but because the cultural dimensions of material objects can only be understood by charting their variants through time and space. Our research into the spread of coiled basketry across Siberia and into Alaska, for example, illustrates how the failure to take non-Native agency into consideration created an artificially static picture of culture change in the North when the reality was both complex and infinitely protean.

Aboriginally, Alaskan Eskimo people from Bristol Bay to Barrow made basketry and matting in the twined technique (Fig. 12). Between 1878 and 1881, however, Edward W. Nelson collected two types of coiled basketry in the region of Bering Strait (Fig. 13) for which there was no archaeological precedent (Lee 1995:58; Nelson 1899:202–5). Coiling is completely different from twining. Twining involves twisting two flexible weft strands around a set of rigid warp elements. Coiling, by contrast, consists of overwrapping a foundation of one or more fibers with a weft strand and at the same time securing one revolution of the coil to the next (Figs. 14, 15).

Nelson's findings of the newly appearing coiled basketry around Bering Strait were soon joined by those of others, such as Miner Bruce on the northern edge of the Seward Peninsula (Fig. 16) and Murdoch at Point Barrow (Murdoch 1892:326–7; VanStone 1980:50–1). The first type of coiled basketry to appear in Alaska was made of beach grass (Elymus mollis), and spiraled from the center of the base in a technique known as bundle coiling (Fig. 17). The other, made of willow-root, is constructed in the single-rod, non-interlocking coiling technique (Fig. 18; see Mason 1904/1972: 247c). The only ethnic group near the Eskimo people to use any form of coiling was the Athabaskan Indians, who made single-rod willow-root baskets in the same technique as those in the Nelson collection; however, none is known to predate them (Lee 1995:59).

Given the constant flow of traffic, both Native and non-Native, across Bering Strait during the whaling and trading era of the late-nineteenth century (Fig. 19), the next logical place to look for the sources of the two types of Eskimo coiled ware is in Siberia.

Trade Routes between Siberia and Alaska

Establishing a connection between Alaskan Eskimo and Siberian coiled basketry depends on demonstrating technological similarities between them and a possible means of their transmission. In a global sense, Alaska was the final meeting point of the world-encircling capitalist trading system linking Europe and Asia. By 1750, Russian fur traders and commercial hunters had moved across Siberia as far south as Kamchatka,

as far north as Chukotka (the Chukchi Peninsula), and as far east as Alaska (Fisher 1943). At the same time, the North American arm of the fur trade, in the form of the Hudson Bay Company, was approaching Alaska from the East, reaching British Columbia by 1843 and Fort Yukon in the interior Alaskan Arctic by 1847 (Fig. 20).

More immediately, Alaska was directly connected to Siberia by Native and western commerce by the late nineteenth century. As Dorothy J. Ray has put it, the waters of Bering Strait functioned as "an intercontinental highway, its coastal fringes occupied by peoples who had more or less the same way of life" (Ray 1975:10). In the ice-free summer time, both people and commodities moved back and forth by this route in large skin boats known as umiaks. European trade goods had reached the coast of Alaska via Siberia well before the arrival of the first white explorers (Ray 1975:197). Thus the presence of Europeans and the proliferation of imported goods they brought along served to stimulate—but not initiate—a pre-existing practice of tapping into a world system of trade.

Certain groups in the Bering Strait region were central to trans-Beringian trade, notably the Chukchi on the Asian side and in Alaska, the Eskimo people of the coastal settlements along Norton and Kotzebue sounds and the strategically located St. Lawrence, King, Big and Little Diomede, and Sledge islands (Bogojavlensky 1969; VanStone 1980:10). By 1900, furthermore, Siberian Yupik Eskimo and Chukchi, were crossing the strait every summer in skin boats to participate in the trade fairs that had become annual events on Kotzebue Sound, Port Clarence, and at other locations (Burch 1988:234–40; 1998:151–62). Here, as many as 2000 Native people congregated to trade. Though there was exchange of indigenous products such as reindeer and sealskins, the trade also included imported Western goods. At this time, Bering Strait was the locus of both indirect and direct Native-Western trade. After 1848, Yankee whalers also acted as middlemen and took on Eskimo crew members on the Alaskan side before they crossed to Siberia (Bogoras 1904–9:64; Jochelson 1908:808). Sailors from the whaling ships also participated in the Native trade fairs, and later, when the baleen market faltered, many whalers became traders, exchanging western goods for furs on both sides of Bering Strait (Fig. 23; see Bockstoce 1986:180–204). It seems safe to conclude, then, that Natives on both sides of Bering Strait participated in a turn-of-the-century version of a world system and that this system provided a well-established route by which artifacts, including baskets, could have traveled from Siberia to Alaska. (Ray 1975: 97–9; VanStone 1980:9–11).

Coiled Basketry

Both bundle-coiled grass and single-rod coiled willow-root baskets were made by the Siberian Yupik, Chukchi, and Koryak people of this region. These baskets share similarities in shape, decorative designs and other technical features with their Alaskan counterparts.

Bundle-coil grass baskets were commonly made by the Siberian Yupik people of St. Lawrence Island (Moore to Ales Hrdliæka, 21 December 1912, NAA-NMNH 55962; Moore 1923:361), by the reindeer and maritime Chukchi (Bogoras 1904–9:225,228), and the Koryak (Jochelson 1908:636). According to today's St. Lawrence Yupik elders, baskets there were undecorated. The few known examples are made with an evenness of stitch characteristic of trade baskets sold around Bering Strait at the turn of the twentieth century (Fig. 21). Three grass baskets securely documented to the Chukchi are known, all reminiscent of Alaskan Eskimo coiled ware. One, collected by Bogoras, serves as a base for a leather drawstring bag, as do early grass and willow-root baskets on the Alaskan side (Bogoras 1904–9:224–8). The basket is decorated with simple geometric designs also reminiscent of Alaska (Fig. 22). Two later Chukchi grass baskets share ovoid and rounded shapes similar to Alaskan Eskimo examples. Koryak grass baskets are considerably more accomplished. Jochelson (1908:631) reports only

indigenous uses for them; but the repetitive designs and mass-produced quality on fifteen examples in the American Museum of Natural History (AMNH) collection suggests that they were almost certainly made to sell to outsiders, a practice that was already common at that time (Fig. 24).

Sources of Siberian and Alaskan Coiled Basketry

The distribution of the two types of coiled basketry among the Siberian Yupik, the Chukchi, and the Koryak people suggests that these techniques were probably not much older on the eastern side of Bering Strait than on its western shore. Furthermore, the archaeological record of northeastern Siberia parallels that of Alaska: twined ware appears but coiling is absent (Sergei Arutiunov, personal communication to M.L., 1994). What explanations can be found for the sudden appearance of coiling? Certainly, the broadest answer is that the various northeastern Siberian groups were all interlinked through trade. The Chukchi are known to have traded with the Koryak, Yukagir, and Even (Antropova and Kuznetsova 1964:803). Chukchi women apparently had only recently picked up basketmaking from Russianized Natives at trade fairs (Bogoras 1904–9:228). Most northeastern Siberian groups also bartered directly or indirectly with Westerners and others from outside the region (Stepanova et al. 1964:792–3). Assuming that knowledge of these two coiled basketry techniques could have been introduced from elsewhere, the historical record suggests that they may have arrived in Siberia from two different localities to the South. Moreover, the impetus for their appearance is intimately linked to the spread of non-Native goods through trade and commerce.

Willow-Root Basketry and the Culture of Tea

The two known Koryak willow-root baskets with stepped lids and stick starts show strong affinities with lidded willow baskets collected elsewhere in Siberia (Fig. 25). Bogoras collected a basket from Russianized Natives living along the Anadyr River valley, north and east of the maritime Koryak that is strikingly similar to the Koryak willow baskets. Woven in the same single rod, non-interlocking coiling, the lozenge-shaped, stepped-lid was collected with tea-cups and tea paraphernalia inside. Possibly, the Koryak willow-root baskets were also used for this purpose. The Koryak were known to value porcelain teacups, which were "preserved as treasures in special boxes" (Jochelson 1908: 580). Moreover, using similarly shaped and woven baskets for the storage of fragile tea ware seems to have been widespread in Siberia. Among the Khanty people in Western Siberia, for example, single-rod willow baskets were similarly used for storing tea ware (Popov 1955:106, Plate 20).

There is a possible outside source for this practice. During the 19th century the Chinese exported porcelain tea sets in coiled baskets (Fig. 26). That Siberian peoples would have seen the Chinese type, or one deriving from the Chinese type, is certainly possible.

Bundle-coiled Grass Basketry

The coiled grass basketry that appeared in Alaska and northeastern Siberia at the same time as willow-root baskets seems to have a related source. Its closest affinity is with the few known examples of Ainu coiled basketry (Graburn and Lee 1999; Saito 1995). The striking similarities between the twined basketry of the Ainu, the northeastern Siberians, and the Alaskan Eskimo have long been noted (Mason 1904:402; Lawrence Dawson, personal communication to ML and NG, 1986); but a careful analysis of relationships between Ainu and northeastern Siberian coiled grass ware is the subject of future research.

The few examples of Ainu coiled ware that are known closely resemble Koryak baskets in technique, shape, and decoration (Fig. 27). The historical literature attests to frequent contacts between Kurile Ainu and Kamchatka peoples. It documents trade links between Koryak and Kurile Ainu (but not between the Kurile and Hokkaido Ainu), but disagrees on whether coiled basketry might have traveled by this route. In the future we plan to focus on this complex problem.

Discussion: Boasian Models of Change

What, then, does the example of the sporadic spread of coiled basketry across the North Pacific area, from Siberia to Alaska, suggest about Boas's theories of diffusion? Let us step back for a moment to consider theories of culture change as expounded by Franz Boas, the leading anthropological organizer and theoretician of the Jesup Expedition.

Early in his career, Boas was very open to the "principle of the theory of evolution. . . [which] opens the vast field of natural sciences to the historical method" (Boas 1889, in Stocking 1982:67). Thus, he claimed, the understanding of a people not only required knowledge of their history, but of the history of their ancestors, so that there is a "continuity of inventions and ideas from the level of primitive people up to our own time." Furthermore, he asserted at the time, because the histories of any one area are undoubtedly incomplete, any approach to local history would always have to rely on the comparative method, that is, to draw its conclusions with the aid of data from other areas assumed to be at comparable evolutionary levels.

As further ethnological data became available, it grew increasingly difficult to uphold the integrity of these evolutionary levels and their strict placement in a universal evolutionary hierarchy. For instance, Boas' own data on the family system of the Inuit people of Baffin Island (Boas 1888), confirmed the anomalous finding that their kinship-terminology system placed them at the same "level" as Euro-Americans. Thus, in his famous article, "The Limitations of the Comparative Method of Anthropology" (Boas 1896), he rejected as unscientific the possibility of both completing the evolutionary history of mankind and the search for ultimate origins of social customs and technologies. In its place, he privileged historical particularism, stressing detailed knowledge of local ethnological histories, to be gathered from the fast-disappearing Native elders in the rapidly changing milieu of Indian and other tribes under the imperial sway.

While carrying out his own detailed ethnographic fieldwork on the Northwest Coast, and being aware of the equally detailed work of others in the region (Emmons 1903, 1991) and further north (e.g. Murdoch 1892; Nelson 1899), Boas foresaw the possibility of putting together these local histories—these individual pieces of the ethnological jigsaw puzzle—into larger regional histories. In the North Pacific area, Boas planned the Jesup Expedition as such a large-scale research project by choosing those pieces of this geographical puzzle that required fitting in place. In the first volume of the JNPE publications (1898) that is, after only one season of expedition fieldwork, he placed the effort within a larger universal frame by stating, "We must, so far as we can, reconstruct the actual history of mankind, before we can hope to discover the laws underlying that history." (Boas 1898:1). In other words, instead of using the laws of the comparative method to fill in the gaps in reconstructing local histories, it should be the other way round, with the construction of comparative laws being the end point of all human historical research.

As to specific methods for construction of particularistic and regional histories, Boas was unfortunately rather unclear both in defining and assigning the relative importance of migration versus diffusion, and about relating actual field data to either proposition. In this first Jesup Expedition volume, he generalized "In short, historical changes of far-reaching importance took place long before the tribes became known to history. They imply mixture of blood, as well as exchange of cultural achievement" (Boas 1898:6).

In 1903, in his overview article in the *American Museum Journal* about the results of the Jesup Expedition, after the fieldwork had been conducted, Boas essentialy plagiarized himself. Apart from adding descriptions of the later field seasons, the article is otherwise word for word identical with his 1898 introductory piece, with the exception that "Franz Boas" has become "Prof. Franz Boas" or "Professor Boas." (1903:78, 82). His preliminary conclusions, which highlight the importance not of diffusion but of invasive migration and gradual differentiation (akin to linguistic drift?) due to slow spreading migration, are:

> The unity of the race was much greater in former times than it is now; that the invasion [migration] of eastern tribes in America, such as the Eskimo, Athapaskan and Salish, and of the western and southern tribes in Asia, such as Yakut and Tungus, have disturbed the former conditions [i.e. of the contiguity of the Chukchi, Koryak, Yukagir, and the Indians of the American northwest coast]. Nevertheless, enough remains to lead us to think that the tribes of this whole area must be considered as a single race or at least that their culture is a single culture [changed by 'gradual differentiation'?]. Thus the Jesup Expedition seems to have established the close relationship between the peoples of Asia and America (Boas 1903:115).

The following year, in a major address on "The History of Anthropology" (1904), Boas was more explicit. He differentiated between "the historical method, which endeavors to reconstruct the actual history of mankind; and the other, the generalizing method, which attempts to establish laws" (ibid:514). He related how these two had come into conflict, how they are fundamentally opposed, and how "all scientists were equally guilty of premature theories of evolution based on observed homologies and supposed similarities" (ibid:516). He then considered the "psychic causes" of men's propensity to evolve through a fixed evolutionary sequence of stages, as well as "the influence of geographical environment . . . [where] the main stress is laid on the causes which bring about modifications of the fundamental and identical traits" (ibid:517). He contrasted "independent origins [i.e., evolution of the same stages and associations in different places—ML, NG] . . . and transmission from one part of the world to another" while warning readers about Ratzel's claim that "all sameness of cultural traits must be accounted for by transmission." He concluded that "it requires actual investigation into the individual history of such customs to discover the causes of their present distribution" (ibid:519) and that "the grand system of the evolution of culture, that is valid for all humanity, is losing much of its plausibility" (ibid:522).

In later publications touching on the results of the Jesup Expedition, Boas concluded "many of the cultural elements that are widely spread in the Old World have found their way to America" (Boas 1925:22-3). In another paper, he was even more vague: "what is common to the two Americas [in comparison with 'fundamental traits of Old World culture'—ML, NG]," he wrote, "may be due as well to diffusion as to antiquity. Furthermore, most generalized traits of culture may have developed independently in most areas" (Boas 1933:363). Few of Boas' observations on Old and New World connections as we have seen, are closely reasoned enough to see him testing theory against data. Of interest in light of the subject of this paper, Boas declined to consider the distribution of any form of basketry out of the misconception that it was unknown to the Eskimo people: "Less certain," he says, "are the conclusions to be drawn from the distribution of weaving, which is present in all parts of the Old World, but seems to be absent among the Eskimo" (Boas 1925:24).

Boas and his contemporaries did not focus on the actual mechanisms of diffusion. This came up a generation later in anthropological theory, particularly in the acculturation literature (Redfield et al.1934; Schweitzer, this volume). In the North Pacific area, various mechanisms of "pre-capitalist" exchange had been recorded, including "silent trade," armed exchange, begging, and boasting (Burch 1988:234–8). By the beginning of the nineteenth century, trade had become more routinized, with regular trade fairs, units of currency, credit, and so on, all of which were known to the Jesup Expedition researchers. It is probably true that tea drinking, tea sets, coiled baskets for tea sets, and the technique of coiling itself followed these well-worn routes.

At the turn of the twentieth century, it was acceptable in American academic circles to seek explanations, whether diffusionary or evolutionary, only among cultures having "pure" Native culture elements. The assumption was that such cultures were on the edge of extinction; thus it was they who demanded scientific attention. As a result, Boas for the most part studiously ignored evidence of Native-Western trade and of hybrid forms and said little about the hybrid (Creolized) peoples who produced and transmitted them; the one exception was his early interest in the music of urban Indian songs in Vancouver, performed in Chinook jargon (see Jacknis, this volume). In fact, turn-of-the-century American collectors of material culture, for instance, the American Museum of Natural History and the Smithsonian Institution, boasted that they had rejected genres that bore any evidence of contact with the outside world (Graburn 1996:12–3).

We must draw a line, however, between Boas the theorist and organizer, and his seasoned though relatively untrained and politically idealistic Russian exile field workers, Bogoras and Jochelson. These Russians were critical of the Tzar's administrative policies in the area and were well aware of the negative impact of colonialism. Their detailed ethnographies mentioned hybrid cultural forms without placing them in an evolutionary or diffusionary framework; however they did not give too much detail on the multi-cultural communities—Native, white, or mixed—that grew up in the wake of colonization and trade. Bogoras made many references to the Creole/mixed population in the Anadyr River valley, and he described its role in intercultural transmission. In the case of coiled basketry, for example, Bogoras referred to the Chukchi willow root weaving: "One or two of the Chukchee . . . make better baskets of willow-roots, but the style is wholly copied after the work of Russianized natives" (Bogoras 1904–9:228). Jochelson avoided Creole people and mixed cultural traits in his Koryak work (Fig. 28); but in his volume on the Yukagir (1926) he focused on Siberian Native groups whose culture was deeply disrupted by Russian contact, Christianization, language loss, material culture change, and population decline through disease. Boas organized the Jesup Expedition publications so that these "historically contingent" matters were included in the regional reports; but he paid little or no attention to them in his explanatory models of trans-Beringian flows, even though such contacts were evident to all.

It was only decades later that American anthropologists began to study Western-influenced Native material cultures (cf. Graburn 1976). Therefore, it is not surprising to discover that more recent paradigms, such as transnationalism, have considerable relevance to the study of hybrid cultural forms such as the coiled basketry of the Circumpolar North. According to Lavie and Swedenburg (1996:9), for example: "Hybrid products are thus results of a long history of confrontations between unequal cultures and forces. . . . The hybridizations we encounter therefore are not just the product of entirely 'new,' epochal postmodern conditions [but also resemble the old conditions]." This observation could apply equally to the hybrid cultural forms such as the coiled basketry of the North Pacific Rim during the Jesup Expedition era. Indeed, we believe that the so-called *post-colonial* model proposed by Lavie and Swedenburg (1996), Appadurai (1990, 1991), and Inda (1996) is productive for the analysis of *colonial* contexts under discussion here.

Appadurai (1990), for instance, argues that migrating populations impact state and local politics, carrying with them new mechanical and informational technologies, bringing along with them transnational investments and new political ideologies; all of these could characterize Siberia of the mid-nineteenth century. In contrast, the evolutionary and diffusionary paradigms informing Jesup Expedition research were not only inadequate for the colonial context but can be better seen as hypothetical models conceived for imagined but unobservable past.

To return to the title of our paper, we would argue that diffusionism was not a satisfactory model for anthropology of the colonial period, and that the transnationalist model developed for the anthropology of the post-colonial period furnishes a more ad-

equate lens through which to consider the hybridity that defined it.

Acknowledgements

The authors would like to extend their gratitude to the organizers of the Jesup Centennial Conference for their invitation to participate and for the stimulation the occasions and the ensemble of participants presented. They would particularly like to acknowledge the editorial guidance of Igor Krupnik.

References

Antropova, Valentina V., and Vera G. Kuznetsova
1964 The Chukchi. In *Peoples of Siberia.* Maxim G. Levin and Leonid P. Potapov, eds. (trans. Stephen P. Dunn, from Russian original 1956). Pp. 788–98. Chicago: University of Chicago Press.

Appadurai, Arjun
1990 Disjuncture and Difference in the Global Cultural Economy. *Public Culture* 2(2):1–22.
1991 Global Ethnoscapes: Notes and Queries for a Transnational Anthropology. In *Recapturing Anthropology.* Richard Fox, ed. Santa Fe, NM:SAR Press.

Boas, Franz
1888 The Central Eskimo. *6th Annual Report of the Bureau of Ethnology for the Years 1884–1885.* Pp. 399–669. Washington DC: Smithsonian Institution.
1896 The Limitations of the Comparative Method of Anthropology. *Science,* n.s., 4:901–8 (Reprinted in: *Race, Language, and Culture.* Pp. 270–80. New York: Macmillan. 1940).
1898 The Jesup North Pacific Expedition. *The Jesup North Pacific Expedition,* vol.1, pt.1, pp. 1–12. *Memoirs of the American Museum of Natural History,* 2. New York: G.E. Stechert.
1903 The Jesup North Pacific Expedition. *The American Museum Journal* 3(5):72–119.
1904 The History of Anthropology. *Science* 20(511): 513–24.
1925 America and the Old World. In *Congrès International des Américanistes. Compte-Rendu de la 21e Session, Deuxième Partie. Tenue à Göteborg en 1924.* Pp. 21-8. Göteborg Museum.
1933 Relations between North-West America and North-East Asia. In *The American Aborigines: Their Origin and Antiquity.* Diamond Jenness, ed. Pp. 357–70. Toronto: University of Toronto Press.

Bockstoce, John
1986 *Whales, Ice and Men. The History of Whaling in the Western Arctic.* Seattle: University of Washington Press.

Bogojavlensky, Sergei

1969 *Imaangmiut Eskimo Careers: Skinboats in Bering Strait.* Unpublished Ph.D. dissertation. Harvard University, Cambridge, MA.

Bogoras, Waldemar

1904–9 The Chukchee. *The Jesup North Pacific Expedition*, vol.7, pts.1–3. *Memoirs of the American Museum of Natural History*, 11. Leiden: E.J. Brill; New York: G.E. Stechert.

Braudel, Fernand

1982 The Perspective of the World. *Civilization and Capitalism, 15th-18th Century*, vol. 3. (trans. S. Reynolds). New York: Harper & Row.

Burch, Ernest S., Jr.

1988 War and Trade. In *Crossroads of Continents: Cultures of Siberia and Alaska.* William W. Fitzhugh and Aron Crowell, eds. Pp. 227–240. Washington DC: Smithsonian Institution Press.

1998 International Affairs. *The Cultural and Natural Heritage of Northwest Alaska*, vol. 7. Prepared for NANA Museum of the Arctic and U.S. National Park Service, Alaska Region.

Emmons, George T.

1903 The Basketry of the Tlingit. *AMNH Memoirs*, vol.3, pt. 2:229–77.

1991 *The Tlingit Indians.* Frederica de Laguna, ed. Seattle: University of Washington Press; New York: American Museum of Natural History.

Fisher, Raymond H.

1943 The Russian Fur Trade, 1550–1700. In *U.C. Publications in History*, 31. Berkeley: University of California Press.

Graburn, Nelson H. H.

1996 Introduction: the Alaska Company Collection. In *Catalogue Raisonné of the Alaska Company Collection: Phoebe Apperson Hearst Museum of Anthropology.* Nelson H.H. Graburn, Molly Lee and Jean-Loup Rousselot. Pp. 1–18. Berkeley: University of California Press.

Graburn, Nelson H. H., ed.

1976 *Ethnic and Tourist Arts: Cultural Expressions from the Fourth World.* Berkeley: University of California Press.

Graburn, Nelson H. H., and Molly Lee

1999 Saranip and Tenki: Ainu Basketry in the Context of the North Pacific Rim. In *Ainu: Spirit of a Northern People.* William Fitzhugh and Chisato Dubreuil, eds. Pp. 301–8. Washington DC: National Museum of Natural History; Seattle: University of Washington Press.

Graburn, Nelson H. H., Molly Lee, and Jean-Loup Rousselot

1996 *Catalogue Raisonné of the Alaska Company Collection: Phoebe Apperson Hearst Museum of Anthro-* *pology.* Berkeley: University of California Press.

Inda, Xavier

1996 Transnationalism. In *Encyclopedia of Cultural Anthropology.* David Levinson and Melvin Ember, eds. Vol. 4. Pp. 1327–29. New York: Henry Holt.

Jochelson, Waldemar

1908 The Koryak. *The Jesup North Pacific Expedition* vol. 6, pts.1–2. *Memoirs of the American Museum of Natural History*, 10. Leiden: E.J. Brill.

1926 The Yukaghir and the Yukaghirized Tungus. *The Jesup North Pacific Expedition*, vol.9, pts.1–3. *Memoirs of the American Museum of Natural History*, 13. Leiden: E.J. Brill; New York: G.E. Stechert.

Lavie, Smadar, and Ted Swedenburg, eds.

1996 *Displacement, Diaspora and Geographies of Identity.* Durham NC: Duke University Press.

Lee, Molly

1983 *Baleen Basketry of the North Alaska Eskimo.* Barrow, AK: North Slope Borough Planning Department.

1995 Types and Prototypes: Siberian Sources of Alaskan Eskimo Coiled Basketry. *American Indian Art Magazine* 20 (4):56–69.

Lips, Julius

1937 *The Savage Strikes Back.* New Haven: Yale University Press.

Mason, Otis T.

1904 Aboriginal American Basketry: Studies in a Textile Art without Machinery. *Smithsonian Institution Publication*, 128; U.S. National Museum Report for 1902:171–548. Reprinted 1972, Albuquerque: Rio Grande Press.

Moore, Riley D.

1923 Social Life of the Eskimo of St. Lawrence Island. *American Anthropologist* 25(3):339–75.

Murdoch, John

1892 Ethnological Results of the Point Barrow Expedition. In *9th Annual Report of the Bureau of American Ethnology for the Years 1887–1888.* Pp. 19–441. Washington DC: Government Printing Office.

McNeill, William H.

1988 Diffusion in History. In *The Transfer and Transformation of Ideas and Material Culture.* Peter J. Hugill and D. Bruce Dickson, eds. Pp. 75–90. College Station, TX: Texas A & M University Press.

National Museum of Ethnology

1991 *Guide to the National Museum of Ethnology.* Osaka: National Museum of Ethnology.

Nelson, Edward W.

1899 The Eskimo about Bering Strait. In *18th Annual Report, Bureau of American Ethnology for the Years 1896-1897.* Pt 1., pp. 3–518. Washington DC: Government Printing Office.

Popov, Andrei A.

1955 Pletenie i tkachestvo u narodov Sibiri v XIX i

pervoi chetverti XX stoletiia (Wicker Work and Weaving of the Siberian Peoples during the Nineteenthth Century and the First Quarter of the Twenthieth Century). *Sbornik Muzeia Anthropologii i Etnografii* 16:41–146. Moscow and Leningrad: USSR Academy of Sciences.

Ray, Dorothy J.
1975 *The Eskimo of Bering Strait, 1650–1898*. Seattle: University of Washington Press.

Redfield, Robert, Ralph Linton, and Melville Herskovits
1936 Memorandum on the Study of Acculturation. *American Anthropologist* 38(1):149–52.

Saito, Reiko
1995 A Perspective Study on Weaving Plant Fiber on the North Pacific Rim. *Bulletin of the Hokkaido Museum of Northern Peoples* 4: 113–34. Abashiri.

Stepanova, M. V., I. S. Gurvich, and V. V. Khramova
1964 The Yukagirs. In *Peoples of Siberia*. Maxim G. Levin and Leonid P. Potapov, eds. (trans. Stephen P. Dunn, from Russian original 1956). Pp. 788–98. Chicago: University of Chicago Press.

Stocking, George W., Jr.
1974 *The Shaping of American Anthropology, 1883–1911: A Franz Boas Reader*. New York: Basic Books.

Swanton, John R.
1905 The Social Organization of American Tribes. *American Anthropologist*, n.s. 7:663–73.

VanStone, James W.
1980 The Bruce Collection of Eskimo Material Culture from Kotzebue Sound, Alaska. *Fieldiana Anthropology*, n.s. 1.

Wallerstein, Immanuel
1974 *The Modern World System*. N. Y.: Academic Books.

The Jesup Expedition and Its Analogues:
A Comparison

STANLEY A. FREED, RUTH S. FREED,
AND LAILA WILLIAMSON

Several great expeditions of the 19th century have an aura of melodrama about them. They bring to mind hero-explorers operating in rugged country with little logistical support from a distant homeland, overcoming obstacles by ingenuity, courage, and persistence. The men who organized and led their own expeditions were resolute entrepreneurs with a strong interest, often tantamount to an obsession, in some scientific problem. The leaders of expeditions under governmental aegis were frequently military officers. They were experienced commanders, adept at leading small companies of men in difficult, sometimes dangerous circumstances. Leaders of both types of expeditions often carried out some of the expedition's scholarly work; more commonly they acted as the principal scientists of the personally organized expeditions.

Some expeditions of the 19th century have become legendary scientific endeavors, the Jesup North Pacific Expedition (JNPE) among them. What accounts for the enduring fascination of the Jesup Expedition? It was a great adventure story, which is perhaps the chief reason; but it had other less obvious features. They are best seen when the Jesup Expedition is compared to other famous expeditions of the 19th century. We have chosen three well-known expeditions for comparative purposes, the Lewis and Clark Expedition (1803–6), the U. S. Exploring Expedition (1838–42), and the Cambridge Anthropological Expedition to Torres Straits (1898–9). The first two were American, the third one British.

The Jesup North Pacific Expedition (1897–1902)

Franz Boas (1858–1942), a young assistant curator in the Department of Anthropology of the American Museum of Natural History (AMNH), conceived and organized the North Pacific Expedition in 1896–7, to study the relationship between Native peoples of Northeast Asia and North America. Boas was keenly aware that the wealth of the American Museum's trustees and friends could be used to support research and collecting, and he lost no time in joining with Frederic Ward Putnam (1839–1915), the head of the Department of Anthropology, to seek the support of Morris K. Jesup, the AMNH President, for a research project of extraordinary scope and ambition. Putnam and Boas presented Jesup with a six-year project for research on both sides of the Bering Strait.

Putnam's participation was vital, because Boas was a new employee of the Museum, who had yet to prove himself to Jesup. Despite Putnam's role as catalyst and some press reports that Putnam was in charge[1], the expedition was clearly Boas' idea (Vakhtin 2001:74). Jesup liked big projects and important problems. Putnam and Boas played on this aspect of Jesup's personality, arguing that their project would settle the intriguing question of the origin of the first people to enter the New World from Northern Asia. After an unsuccessful effort to raise money from his fellow philanthropists, Jesup vowed to fund the project personally.

The estimated field expenses of the expedition have been variously reported as from $10,000 to $40,000 per year. *The New York Times* (March 12, 1897:12) gave a figure of $60,000 or $10,000 per year. Kennedy (1968:142), citing correspondence between Jesup and Boas, said, "[Jesup] agreed to underwrite the expenses of the expedition for six years, at an estimated cost of $40,000 a year." Boas unsuccessfully suggested a four-year extension of the expedition at a cost of $100,000, which indicates an annual cost of $25,000 (Kennedy 1968:144). There were also later expenses of publication (Cole 2001:39–41). The final cost of the expedition will probably never be known with any precision.

The Jesup Expedition, announced in March 1897, generated considerable interest in the popular press. The origin of the American Indians is "the biggest of the unsolved anthropological and ethical problems" and "alive with human and historic interest," stated *The New York Times* in an editorial of March 14, 1897. *Science*, the bellwether American scientific journal, published a four-page unsigned article [presumably written by Boas—eds.] about the expedition a few months after the departure of the first field party (Anonymous 1897). The following summary of the JNPE activities is based upon our earlier papers (Freed et al. 1988a, 1988b, 1997), as well as upon other review publications that appeared in recent years (Cole 1999, 2001; Vakhtin 2001).

The expedition's research on the Northwest Coast of North America was carried out by young professionals, supplemented by a few local amateurs under Boas' direction and close supervision. Harlan I. Smith (1872–1940), who served at the American Museum until 1911 and eventually became Chief Archaeologist of the National Museum of Canada, excavated sites in British Columbia and Washington State. While Boas was not impressed with him intellectually, he nonetheless considered him to be a reliable person who could be successful with direction. Indeed he was; Smith contributed five volumes to the *Jesup North Pacific Expedition* series, and made important collections.

John R. Swanton (1873–1958), who joined the Bureau of American Ethnology just after receiving his doctorate in 1900, was seconded to the Jesup Expedition for about a year to study the Haida people of the Queen Charlotte Islands. The Bureau paid his salary ($50 per month) and received all the lexical and grammatical material that he collected, whereas the Jesup Expedition paid his traveling and field expenses. All ethnological material, including texts, thus became the property of the American Museum (Boas to W. J. McGee, 1 Oct. 1900, AMNH-DA; Jonaitis 1988:197–201).

Livingston Farrand (1867–1939), then professor of psychology at Columbia University, was a member of Boas' first field party, which left New York in late May 1897 for Spences Bridge, British Columbia. Boas, Farrand, and Smith, the third member of the team, met James Teit, a local resident, who became their field guide and the fourth member of a small party (Wickwire, this volume). The group then left for Bella Coola. Farrand dropped out when the team reached the Chilcotin; there he remained for a disappointing month collecting sparse ethnographic information and trying to measure heads. The next summer, 1898, he worked with indifferent success among the Quileute and Quinault Indians of Washington State. He published only three slim papers in the JNPE series but collected some outstanding artworks (Jonaitis 1988:191).

George Hunt (1854–1933) and James Teit (1864–1922), local residents and amateur ethnographers who straddled Euro-Canadian and Indian cultures, were two of the most important and productive members of Boas' team. Hunt was raised in Fort Rupert, British Columbia as a Kwakwa̱ka'wakw (Kwakiutl), spoke their language fluently, was literate in English, and was a steady and reliable worker. The association of Hunt and Boas began in 1886, during Boas' first trip to the Kwakwa̱ka'wakw. Boas taught Hunt to write the Kwakwa̱ka'wakw language while Hunt was assisting him with his work for the World's Columbian Exposition in 1893. Hunt was truly a remarkable man. Boas recognized his potential, helped him to develop it, and acknowledged his accomplishments by making him collaborator and coauthor of numerous publications. "[T]he Boas-Hunt relationship was one of the most productive and enduring ever to exist between an anthropologist and a member of another culture. [It] was based upon mutual interest, respect, and affection" (Codere 1966:xxviii; see also Berman 2001).

James A. Teit, a Scotsman who lived among the Nlaka'pamux (Thompson) Indians, authored two substantial monographs on the Thompson and another on the Lillooet Indians for the JNPE series; he also collected some exceptionally fine Salish artworks (Wickwire, this volume). After the Expedition, Teit worked on behalf of Indian rights. "The British Columbian natives had immense respect and admiration for, and trust in, this man, whom they asked to accompany them to meetings with government officials. . . .Teit served as translator, sometimes working simultaneously in four or five different languages" (Jonaitis 1988:190).

The Siberian operations of the Jesup Expedition began a year later than the North American research and covered an area many times as large under conditions much more difficult than on the American side. Fieldwork on the Siberian side was an ordeal mainly because of the hostile environment.[2] Climate, terrain, illness, insects, and the vast distances that had to be covered by horse, reindeer sled, dog sled, boat, and raft, or on foot made research a dangerous adventure. It called forth a toughness that is rarely required in the present age of modern transport and communication. Moreover, the Russian government made trouble. The Canadian and American governments took no interest in the activities of Boas and his team, and would help if asked. The Russian government took a definite and hostile interest in the three principal JNPE investigators in Siberia, Berthold Laufer (1874–1934), Waldemar Bogoras (1865–1936), and Waldemar Jochelson (1855–1937). The former happened to be a foreigner and a Jew; the latter two were former Russian political exiles, who spent several years in Siberia for their anti-government activities (Freed et al. 1997:12).

Three teams carried out the Asian fieldwork. Laufer's team surveyed along the Amur River and on Sakhalin Island in the southern section of the Siberian Pacific region, whereas Bogoras' and Jochelson's parties covered northeastern Siberia. The Amur River team of Laufer and amateur archaeologist Gerard Fowke was first into the field. Laufer arrived on Sakhalin Island on July 10, 1898, where he remained until March 21, 1899, studying the Gilyak (Nivkh), Evenk (Tungus), and Ainu. He crossed to the mainland on March 25, and settled in Khabarovsk on the Amur River to study the Nanay (Gold). When navigation opened in late May, he descended the river, visiting Nanay and Gilyak villages on the way. Although he had a taste for fieldwork and for the most part stoically endured its hardships, his endurance was sorely taxed by some frightening illnesses and accidents, among them a two-and-a-half month siege of influenza and pneumonia, and a plunge through weak ice into frigid water that would have been fatal had not his guide saved him.

Laufer's published account in the Jesup North Pacific Expedition series was disappointing, especially when compared to the classic ethnographies produced by Bogoras and Jochelson. His only JNPE volume was a slim, well-illustrated monograph on the art of the Amur River peoples (Laufer 1902). He was especially fascinated by the art of the Nanay and their neighbors, and he collected many of their superb artworks for the American Museum (Kendall 1988:104). After the Jesup Expedition, Laufer joined the Field Museum of Natural History in 1908, where he spent the remainder of his scholarly career. For many years he was easily the outstanding American Sinologist.

Gerard Fowke (1855–1933), Laufer's fleeting and often grudging team partner (Cole 2001:36–7), was a largely self-taught itinerant adventurer who was drawn to archaeology by his love for outdoor life and taste for exotic customs. He worked at various occupations for about 15 years, schoolteacher among them. When he was 30, he abandoned teaching for research in archaeology and geology. For his Siberian research of

1898, he recruited two local companions and set out in a large open boat to explore the Amur River from the village of Verkhne-Tambovsk to the town of Nikolayevsk, about 330 miles downstream at the mouth of the river. From there he traveled out into Tartar Strait, along the coast to the Sea of Okhotsk, and back to Nikolayevsk. They found nothing of any interest; Fowke himself acknowledged that his work was a "dismal fizzle." Boas considered him to have been a mistake and permitted him only one season in Siberia. Undaunted, Fowke continued his archaeological research in the United States well into his seventies.

On the recommendation of Professor Vasily V. Radloff, the Secretary of the Russian Academy of Sciences, Boas entrusted fieldwork in northern Siberia to Waldemar Jochelson and Waldemar Bogoras. Both were already veterans of several years of Siberian field research when they joined the Jesup Expedition team. Friends and colleagues, they were Russian intellectuals and revolutionaries who in their youth were exiled to Siberia where they became ethnographers. The theme of loss through exile and recovery through science gives the lives of Jochelson and Bogoras a special piquancy. A young American, Norman G. Buxton, was charged with zoological collecting of behalf of the AMNH; he was added to the group when Jochelson and Bogoras passed through New York on their way to Siberia (Hoffmann, this volume). Jochelson also engaged Alexander Axelrod, a Russian émigré student from Zurich, as a general assistant, particularly for carrying on geographical work (Boas 1903:101).

The team of Waldemar Bogoras and his wife Sofia (later to be joined by Axelrod) arrived at Mariinsky Post at the mouth of the Anadyr River in July 1900. They spent three months with the local Chukchi. At the end of October 1900, Bogoras went on a long journey to northern Kamchatka for an arranged meeting with Jochelson's team. Traveling mostly by dog sled, he was on the move for the rest of his twelve and a half months in Northeast Asia. He generally remained no more than a few weeks in any location. Terrain and illness made the trip an ordeal. While her husband traveled, Sofia Bogoras stayed in the small local town of Markovo on the Anadyr River and at Mariinsky Post, making collections for the American Museum.

Bogoras published five contributions for the JNPE series, most prominently on the Chukchi. He and Sofia Bogoras collected ethnographic data, linguistic notes and 150 texts, 4,500 ethnographic artifacts, skeletal material, plaster casts of faces, archaeological specimens, 95 phonographic records, and somatological measurements of some 860 individuals. No modern anthropological couple has collected such a diversity of data. After the Expedition, Bogoras had a distinguished career in Russia, engaging in scientific and literary work. In 1932, he established the Museum of the History of Religion of the Russian Academy of Sciences and he was its first director until his death in 1936.

While the Bogorases were occupied with the Chukchi and the Siberian Yupik (Eskimo) in the North, Jochelson, his wife Dina Jochelson-Brodsky, and their associates, Axelrod and Buxton, made another JNPE Siberian team that studied the Koryak and Tungus (Even) along the Sea of Okhotsk, and later, the Yukagir and Sakha (Yakut) of the interior Northeast Siberia. On August 16, 1900, they arrived in Kushka, a small village at the mouth of the Gizhiga River. The Jochelsons then made a difficult journey to the villages of the Maritime Koryak in Penzhina Bay, where they spent the first half of the winter of 1900 living most of the time in native underground dwellings. Conditions were almost intolerable. Lice were the greatest torment. "As long as we remained in these dwellings we could not escape these insects, which we dreaded more than any of the privations of our journey" (Boas 1903:104).

The Jochelsons made comprehensive studies of the Koryak, Even, Yukagir, and Sakha people. They collected about 4,400 ethnographic specimens, 41 face casts, measurements of 900 individuals, 1,200 photographs, phonographic cylinders, skulls and archaeological specimens, and a small zoological collection.

Jochelson published three ethnographic monographs for the American Museum; his wife Dina, who later earned a degree in medicine, handled all the anthropometric work and most of the photography. She published several papers and a Ph.D. thesis on Native women of Northeast Siberia.

After the JNPE, Jochelson led the Aleut-Kamchatka Expedition of the Imperial Russian Geographical Society in 1909–11. Dina Jochelson-Brodsky, again, joined him as a field partner. From 1912 to 1922, he was division curator of the Museum of Anthropology and Ethnography of the Russian Academy of Sciences in St. Petersburg/Petrograd; from 1922 until his death in New York fifteen years later, Jochelson was associated with the American Museum and the Carnegie Institution of Washington.

The Jesup Expedition confirmed the close relationship of the Native populations of northwestern North America and northeastern Asia and strongly supported the view that the ancestors of the American Indians came from Asia. Boas, Jochelson, and Bogoras tried to go beyond these currently accepted points but their analyses have not gained favor. From the data collected by the Jesup Expedition, Boas discerned a close cultural affiliation between eastern Siberia and the region of Southern Alaska and British Columbia, a cultural "break" between the east Siberian tribes and the Eskimo, and a "fundamental break" between the northeast Siberian tribes and the Tungus and Yakut to the west. He wrote, the "Chukchee, Koryak, Kamchadal (Itelmen), and the Yukaghir must be classed with the American race rather than with the Asiatic race." In brief, the JNPE postulated an assumed reverse migration of American Indians to Siberia; Jochelson later gave the name "Americanoids" to the people descended from these hypothetical reverse migrants (Ousley 2000). The Americanoid theory never gained serious attention and is considered today a historical curiosity.

Today, a century after the Jesup Expedition, its published ethnographies and museum collections retain their importance; but the contributions of the Expedition to solving the problem of the origin of the ancient Native Americans have been far superseded by later research. Just before Boas and his party left for the Northwest Coast in 1897, *The New York Times* wrote that the origin of the American Indians is "the biggest of the unsolved anthropological and ethnical problems" and "alive with human and historic interest." That comment is as true today as it was 100 years ago. In those days, the issue was purely scientific, and anthropologists were the only players. There were few theories to be tested and the question lacked the political nuances that it has since acquired. Technology was simple and before the Jesup Expedition data sets were sparse. Today, high technology (like radiocarbon dating and DNA studies) provides the key arguments, whereas ancient and surprising skeletal finds, and newly discovered archaeological sites indicate that the question of the origins of the First Americans is much more complex than imagined a century ago. The next "Jesup Expedition" will probably explore the problem primarily in modern laboratories rather than in the Siberian wilderness.

The Lewis and Clark Expedition (1803–6)

At the beginning of the nineteenth century, President Thomas Jefferson initiated the Lewis and Clark Expedition. Though perhaps the most famous of the great American expeditions, it owes its birth and later fame more to political and historical circumstances than to any enduring scientific legacy. At this point in history, negotiations between France and Spain over the Louisiana Territory were heading in a direction potentially dangerous to the interests of the United States. Fortunately for the Americans, Napoléon was in need of money and he eventually sold the Louisiana Territory to the United States on May 2, 1803. Anticipating the inevitable American occupation of the territory, President Jefferson had initiated preparations for an exploring mission to the region before its purchase. The priority of the expedition enhanced its fame. It was the first overland expedition to the Pacific coast and back (Ambrose 1996:71–3, 101–2).

The Lewis and Clark Expedition has an extraordinary hold on the American imagination. *Time* magazine devoted its cover and a major, 43-page multi-authored article to the Expedition to mark American Independence Day, 2002, and to anticipate the celebration of the Expedition's bicentennial, beginning in January 2003, when the 11 states touched by the explorers plan to commemorate and to re-create the 3-year journey. Trying to explain the American fascination for the Expedition after 200 years, *Time* noted its practical side, "When they launched their wooden boats up the Missouri [River] and into the wilderness, Lewis and Clark were charting the future of America." There had to be a mystical element as well, and *Time* made a stab, "[At that time] the young nation already had a constitution, but it lacked an epic. It had a government but no real identity. Lewis and Clark helped invent one." (Kirn, 2002:38–9)

Captain Meriwether Lewis (1774–1809) and Lieutenant William Clark (1770–1838) led the expedition. Lewis, a confident, strong, and self-reliant member of the Virginia gentry, ran his family's large plantation at the age of eighteen. He and Thomas Jefferson were neighbors. When Jefferson became president he chose Lewis as his secretary and groomed him for leadership of a dangerous exploratory mission to the Pacific. Lewis invited Clark, another Virginian, to share command. Lewis and Clark had served together in the same company and had become friends and mutual admirers. At 33 years of age, Clark was the oldest man on the expedition.

Lewis and Clark selected their men with great care during the summer of 1803. Many men applied, probably for the adventure, but they also were well paid after the expedition. Each man received a land grant and double pay (Ambrose 1996:414–5). The explorers, initially about 40 mostly young unmarried men, were organized as a military unit. Many of the men were from the army and all but 10 were enlisted as privates. All were outdoorsmen and good hunters; specialties critical for a long and enduring journey—from carpentry to gun-smithing to iron-working to boat handling, and translating—were well represented.

President Jefferson instructed Lewis and Clark to explore the Missouri River to its headwaters and from there, the rivers leading to the Pacific to find the most direct and practicable water communication across the continent for purposes of commerce. Prospects for agriculture and settlement were almost as important a motive as commerce, and Jefferson wanted information about plant and animal life, soil, mineral resources, and climate (Ambrose 1996:94–5). Knowledge of Indian tribes was important. As befits an expedition of exploration, they were expected to make detailed maps.

The party traveled the Missouri River in three boats. Lewis and party left Pittsburgh in late summer 1803 and, after wintering near St. Louis, the three boats set out for the upper Missouri in the spring of 1804, reaching the villages of the friendly Mandan Indians in today's North Dakota where they spent the winter of 1804 through early 1805. The next spring, the party continued up the Missouri, crossed the continental divide on horseback, and descended the Columbia River in canoes. They reached its mouth and the Pacific shore in late fall 1805, and passed the winter there. The party arrived back in St. Louis in September 1806, to great excitement.

The journals of Lewis and Clark and shorter diaries by other members of the expedition are interesting narratives of exploration, spiced with accounts of menacing encounters and perilous mishaps: Indian hostilities, accidents, difficult terrain and climate, illness, and dangerous animals. Yet only one encounter with Indians was fatal: Lewis and his men killed two Blackfeet Indians. A member of the expedition died of illness, several were dismissed, and one man was court-martialed and given 100 lashes (Moulton 1986, 2:7–8, 60). The journals contain much important information that was new at the time. "Clark's great map of the west . . . would in itself have justified the expedition" (Moulton 1986, 2:5). However, complete publication of the journals was long delayed, and Lewis and Clark lost some credit for their discoveries (Ambrose 1996:470).

After the Expedition, Lewis and Clark went on to successful careers, not in science, as the members of the Jesup Expedition had done, for they were not scientists, but in politics. Jefferson named Lewis governor of the Louisiana Territory in 1807. It was a difficult role, and his life was complicated by personal financial problems. He also suffered from mental and physical problems—possibly hypochondria and depression, or even from manic-depressive illness (Ambrose 1996:466–7). In less than two years, he committed suicide. Clark later served as superintendent of Indian affairs in Louisiana Territory and as governor of Missouri Territory.

The Lewis and Clark and Jesup Expeditions were so different ventures as to be almost separate species. The purpose of Lewis and Clark was as much political and commercial as scientific. It brought knowledge about a vast new territory and helped open the West to settlement. Politics and the expedition supported one another. By contrast, the Jesup Expedition had no political goal. A purely scientific venture, the JNPE dealt with the most intriguing scholarly issues of the day, such as the problem of American Indian origins and the relations of Native tribes living on both sides of the Bering Strait. Lewis and Clark's mission featured no scientific problem or hypothesis, although the idea of an easy water passage across the continent was still in the air. Lewis and Clark laid that myth to rest.

The two expeditions were also organized very differently. The Lewis and Clark group stayed together. It had a command structure of a military unit with officers and enlisted men. There were further distinctions based on crafts. The Jesup Expedition had almost none of this structure. Expedition personnel were widely dispersed in tiny units. Sometimes even couples were separated; the Bogorases worked separately for most of their time in the field. Technical specialization depended on incidental training and interests. Mrs. Jochelson, a medical student, took care of physical anthropology and photography, particularly of the women; Mrs. Bogoras did most of the couple's ethnographic collecting. Basically, the Jesup Expedition featured investigators working independently and resembled more closely the later style of independent fieldworker than the classic government-sponsored research expedition represented by Lewis and Clark.

The U. S. Exploring Expedition (1838–42)

The U. S. Exploring Expedition dwarfs the other three expeditions in size, scope, drama, and later institutional effects. Yet it had drifted into relative obscurity for almost a century until William Stanton's comprehensive account (1975) and, especially, until the Smithsonian Institution portrayed it ten years later in a major exhibit and book entitled *Magnificent Voyagers* (Viola and Margolis 1985). Coming at a time when the American scientific community was tiny and its resources were minuscule, the "Ex. Ex.," as it is often called, was manna from heaven. There was a rush to win places on the expedition, for scientific reputations were there to be made (Baatz 1986:1020; Stanton 1975:45).

As a large-scale project of science and exploration sponsored by the U. S. Government, the Ex. Ex. set a precedent that continues to the present day and is best compared to today's outer space program. It was the first such project of the U. S. Navy, and served as a model for some fourteen subsequent American naval exploring expeditions before the Civil War. It included a corps of civilian scientists, which was a novelty for the United States. The nine selected expedition's "scientifics" were winnowed from a projected corps of twenty-five. Several of them became giants in their fields. Their scientific qualifications were equal to those of the members of the Jesup Expedition and far exceeded the modest scientific training of Lewis and Clark. "James Dwight Dana, the most gifted of the group . . . became one of America's most distinguished scientific leaders" (Viola 1985:10).

The civilian scientists worked chiefly in geology, botany, zoology, and philology. Most of the physical sciences—geography, hydrography, astronomy, study of terrestrial magnetism, meteorology, and cartography—were assigned exclusively to naval officers. The charter of the Ex. Ex. emphasized the promotion of commerce and navigation, and so the work of the "scientific gentlemen" was seen as less essential to the success of the expedition than the task of exploration and mapping. The scientific character of the expedition was not lessened by the secondary role played by its civilian scientists; in retrospect, their research and collecting turned out to be as scientifically important as the work of the naval officers.

Lieutenant Charles Wilkes commanded the expedition. Born in New York City, he attended various boarding schools, and his well-to-do father had him tutored privately. He was drawn to the sea at the age of 15. After several voyages as a sailor, he received an appointment at the age of 19 as midshipman in the U. S. Navy (Leonhart 1985:189–91). Later he studied surveying, advanced mathematics, triangulation, geomagnetism, and hydrography. After several officers had been given command of the expedition and then were relieved of duty, Wilkes was offered the post and his appointment approved when he was 40. There were forty other naval lieutenants at the time, and thirty-eight had more sea service (Stanton 1975:61). However, Wilkes "respected science" and had scientific qualifications.

Wilkes was an autocrat, much more so than Lewis. He represented the "old navy" where flogging was freely used to maintain discipline. Described as contentious, opinionated, brooding, aloof, arrogant, conceited, rude, a strict disciplinarian, and always fearful of cabals and mutiny, he cultivated the image of a martinet, because it invoked authority and obedience (Stanton 1975:139). Although Wilkes was not loved, he certainly was respected. James Dwight Dana valued Wilkes highly: "I much doubt if, with any other commander . . . we should have fared better or lived together more har-

moniously, and I am confident that the Navy does not contain a more daring or driving officer" (Viola 1985:23).

Six ships set sail from Hampton Roads, Virginia, in August 1838. During the four years of intensive survey of the Pacific Ocean region, the fleet crossed the Pacific three times extending explorations from Tierra del Fuego to Polynesia to Antarctica to New Zealand, Fiji, and to the North Pacific Coast of North America. Two of the smaller ships were lost in rough seas, one with its 15-man crew. The Expedition returned to the United States by way of the Cape of Good Hope. The sailors were young "iron men" in the era of wooden ships; hard work was required and heroics were expected. The Ex. Ex. was the last great circumnavigation of the globe under sail (Kassel 1985:257).

The scientific results of the Ex. Ex. were published in 19 volumes of reports and atlases (originally, 28 were planned). There were also large collections of plants, animals, ethnographic specimens, gems, fossils, and corals. The collections eventually came to the fledgling Smithsonian Institution and helped determine its development toward a museum institution that became the National Museum of the United States, and away from the national research institute that was a real alternative in the 1840s and 1850s (Jackson 1985:450; Viola 1985:9). The publications were probably the expedition's most remarkable achievement. The reports were the grandest scientific production to come out of the U. S. until that time and they had an acknowledged international impact. Much of the survey was still incorporated in nautical charts a century later (Jackson 1985:455). That the work of the Ex. Ex. was mostly published was due to the tireless efforts of Wilkes, who bullied the scientists into completing their reports and battled the Government to ensure publication. Without publication and "Without Wilkes' incredible energy and Byzantine mind, the Expedition's achievements might have been no more lasting than the wake of its ships upon the waters of the world" (Stanton 1975:363).

The Ex. Ex. resembled Lewis and Clark's mission in

its funding and military organization, and the Jesup Expedition in its emphasis on science. All three expeditions operated in difficult and dangerous regions, and the participants were tough men and women. All three had extraordinary leaders, bold, determined men, with enormous energy. However, the exploration of uncharted regions was by far the main purpose of the two military-style expeditions, with additional strong political and commercial motives. The JNPE, lacking both, was an entirely scientific venture.

The Cambridge Anthropological Expedition to Torres Straits, 1898–9

The Torres Straits Expedition, organized by Alfred C. Haddon (1855–1940), was, like the Jesup Expedition, a pure scientific enterprise. Haddon and his team left a lasting mark on British anthropology just as Boas fixed his stamp on American anthropology (Kuklick 1998: 158–9; Rouse 1998:50, 73–6). However, Torres Straits lacked the grimness of the JNPE's grueling fieldwork. Melanesia was no bed of roses—there was one uncomfortable and dangerous voyage of about a week on a crowded small ketch—but it was nothing compared to East Siberia. Writing to Boas from Khabarovsk on the Amur River, Laufer observed, "Nothing is free here except death, which you can have in this country at special bargain rates." By contrast, W. H. R. Rivers decided to join the Torres Straits Expedition because he was feeling run down and "much in need of a holiday," and Charles Myers spoke of his Borneo sojourn as "a delightful way to spend a holiday" (Stocking 1995: 109, 111). Torres Straits was serious business, but it also had the unmistakable air of college boys on a lark.

Haddon came from a family initially in comfortable circumstances: his father owned a printing firm and wanted his son to enter the business (Quiggin 1942:4); but the son's interests, encouraged by his mother, were in science. Clearly not cut out for the business world, he was sent to Cambridge to study physiology and zoology. In 1880, he obtained the chair in zoology at the Royal College of Science in Dublin. Stocking (1995: 99) describes him as gentle and emphatic by nature. He had wide interests, inexhaustible energy, and was deeply religious, impetuous, and devoted to natural science, especially zoology (Quiggin 1942: 10,64).

Haddon and Boas were alike in some ways. They both had backgrounds in the natural sciences, Haddon in zoology and Boas in physics. They both had experience in their areas of interest before organizing their expeditions. Both saw their earlier fieldwork partially in terms of professional advancement. Boas hoped that his multi-year field research in British Columbia on behalf of the British Association for the Advancement of Science (BAAS) would help establish him as an Americanist, thus opening the door to permanent employment and a successful career in the United States. Haddon wanted to escape the dead end of a provincial professorship. He was "perishing for want of research" and opined that "the Department here is played out" (Quiggin 1942:77). In 1888 Haddon went to Torres Straits to study coral reefs and saw opportunities for ethnographic work in the region. Back in England, he turned to anthropology and obtained a post as Lecturer in Physical Anthropology at Cambridge in 1895. In 1897 he decided to return to Torres Straits to gather more information for an ethnography that Cambridge University Press had agreed to publish.

Haddon selected six investigators, his ideal number, by specialization. His concept of anthropology included psychology, for "a successful investigator must have a true insight into the minds of the investigated and understand their reactions and ways of thought" (Quiggin 1942:95). He began with two experimental psychologists, Charles S. Myers and William McDougall, both students of W. H. R. Rivers. When Rivers asked to be included, three of the six investigators on the expedition's team were experimental psychologists who studied such faculties as vision, hearing, smell, touch, and reaction time (Rivers 1901:1–2). Although Haddon felt that the psychological side was rather overweighed, he was pleased to have Rivers. Moreover, Myers was an accomplished musician, thus filling one of Haddon's limitations. The other limitation that Haddon felt keenly was linguistics, and he was fortunate to recruit Sidney H. Ray, the only available English specialist with an excellent knowledge of Melanesian languages. Anthony Wilkins, an undergraduate, joined the group as anthropological trainee and photographer. Charles G. Seligman, a medical pathologist with leanings toward anthropology, was the final addition. Haddon completely neglected archaeology and paid relatively little attention to physical anthropology.

The anthropological work of the Jesup Expedition—compared to the Torres Straits expedition—featured less individual specialization by discipline. Boas selected his two key Siberian investigators (Jochelson and Bogoras) because of their previous work with the tribes he wanted studied. On the other hand, he recognized archaeology as a special field, and he put two archaeologists on his expedition team (Smith and Fowke), in addition to a mammal specialist (Buxton) who collected about 500 mammal specimens. The rest of the personnel, especially on the Siberian side, were expected to take care of everything: ethnography, linguistics, and physical anthropology and a little archaeological and zoological collecting as well. It all worked out very well, mainly because of the competence of the fieldworkers.

Unlike Boas, Haddon pieced together his funding from several sources: Cambridge University, the governments of Britain and Queensland, and several scientific societies. Nonetheless, he did not have enough money, and the six anthropologists had to pay their own way. Unexpectedly, Charles Hose, a district official, on learning of the expedition, persuaded the Rajah of Sarawak to invite the group to Sarawak all expenses paid, which resulted in several additional months of fieldwork on Borneo (Stocking 1995:109).

The group arrived at Thursday Island on April 22, 1898. From there, the seven anthropologists split into two groups and sailed east. Rivers, Myers, and McDougall spent four months on Mer (Murray) Island,

"carrying out the first extended series of psychological and physiological tests ever performed on native populations." (Stocking 1995:109). The other men toured the southeastern coast of New Guinea. Later, part of the group went to Sarawak, and the others toured along the western shore and among the islands of the Gulf of Papua. The last members of the expedition left for England in April 1899.

The veterans of the Torres Straits Expedition, like those of the Jesup Expedition, had distinguished and influential later careers. Haddon did more than any other man to establish anthropology at Cambridge. He had a strong sense of fieldwork and placed it at the heart of what it means to be an ethnographer. He published enormously until the year of his death. Seligman and Rivers, veterans of the Torres Expedition and two of the great anthropologists of the day, are credited with providing the ethnographic core of the "Cambridge School" of anthropology (Stocking 1995:115, 117; Kuklick 1998:158–9). Myers and McDougall became influential in psychology.

Conclusion

Why are these four expeditions famous? First, the timing was favorable. They all were the earliest of their kind, and their scientific work was important at the time. Some of it is still quite valuable today, especially the collections, the ethnographies of the Jesup and the Torres Straits expeditions, and River's development of the "genealogical method," an indispensable tool in ethnography.[3] Second, publication of the scientific results of all the expeditions was massed in a set of volumes rather than dispersed in scattered individual publications, which considerably increased the scientific impact of the work. Boas was certainly aware of this effect. His agreement with his researchers stated that all publications would appear in the museum's series, with certain exceptions but only with museum approval. Coordinated publication is not easily achieved. The leaders of the expeditions had to cajole authors to submit manuscripts and to supervise the process of publication long after the fieldwork was done. On the contrary, neither Lewis nor Clark took the pains to publish the journals of their expedition. Other editors prepared them for publication, the first appearing in 1814.

Thirdly, the investigators—Boas, Jochelson, Bogoras, Laufer, Haddon, Rivers, Seligman, and Dana—were among the greatest scientists of the day. Boas' ideas influenced anthropology in the United States for decades; Haddon built anthropology at Cambridge. There were effects on museums as well as on universities. At the American Museum, the Jesup Expedition was to some extent the model for the next major effort, the study of the Plains Indians, although Clark Wissler did much more theoretically with the Plains project than Boas did with the Jesup Expedition material (Freed and Freed 1983:808–9). The Ex. Ex. was important in the history of the Smithsonian; Baatz (1986:1020) also credits it with catalyzing "the creation of a national scientific association, which appeared a few years later with the genesis of the AAAS [American Association for the Advancement of Science] in 1848." Quiggin (1942:142–3) credits Haddon during his brief curatorship at the Cambridge Museum of Archaeology and Ethnology with arranging related objects to tell a story and thus to make the collections essential factors in ethnographical and geographical work.

A century after two strictly scientific expeditions, Jesup North Pacific and Torres Straits, the people of the regions that were studied recognize the importance of the work done by visiting ethnographers. Although with some reservations, they are thankful that a record of their lives was made before their cultures had irrevocably changed. Kwakwaka'wakw who came to New York for the opening of the *Chiefly Feasts, the Enduring Kwakiutl Potlatch* exhibit at the American Museum in 1991, commented, "Thank God for Hunt and Boas. Without them we would have no culture." The current chief of Thursday Island, Ephraim Bani, on a trip to European museums in 1997, said that when Haddon visited Thursday Island he had found its culture disin-

tegrating and was "on a rescue mission." Chief Bani now found "his culture preserved" in the Cambridge Museum, where Haddon had brought his Torres Strait collections (Merrison and Calvert 1997). In an editorial comment about *Drawing Shadows to Stone*, a photographic exhibition based on the work of the Jesup Expedition on the Northwest Coast and in Siberia, *The New York Times* wrote, "[I]t is impossible to look at these photographs . . . without sensing that their subjects were collaborating with the anthropologists among them to devise a new, and still evolving, form of survival" (*The New York Times*, 29 Jan. 1998:A22). Such collaboration is the key to ethnography that has lasting value.

The chief reason for the fame of the expeditions for the general public is that all four ventures were spellbinding adventure stories. The Ex. Ex., the Jesup Expedition in Siberia, and Lewis and Clark, especially in the Bitterroot Mountains, were dangerous, and full of hairbreadth escapes. Torres Straits was less hazardous, but in those days just being in Melanesia was adventure enough for Europeans. The Ex. Ex. took pride of place with its generous measure of treachery, floggings, hostage taking, shipwreck, and pitched battles. Some 100 lives were lost. All of this would be enough to ensure the enduring fascination of the expeditions.

But there is something else. The expeditions foreshadow major historical trends. Lewis and Clark and the Ex. Ex. are full of optimism and self-confidence, the product of a new strong country fulfilling its "manifest destiny" from ocean to ocean and beyond its borders. Torres Straits was different, as Haddon came face to face with the results of western colonialism. He was not at all sure that its real and alleged benefits were worth the damage it caused to Native peoples.

The Jesup Expedition has a curious foreboding quality. Bogoras and Jochelson were former underground political conspirators who had spent time in prison and lived for years in exile, both abroad and in Siberia. The Russian government maintained a secret surveillance over their field activities during the JNPE mission.

Laufer had considerable trouble obtaining Russian permission even to get to Siberia, because he was Jewish—as were the two other key Siberian investigators (Freed et al. 1988a:12–3). Their lives seemed to herald the murderous political, ethnic, and ideological conflicts that convulsed Europe during the twentieth century. Participants in all four expeditions faced uncomfortable, sometimes dangerous, conditions in the field; but only the JNPE groups working in Siberia had to contend with governmental suspicion if not hostility. In view of this circumstance, Boas wrote to Jesup, "the full success of their investigation deserves the highest praise."

Acknowledgments

Our thanks are due to Laurel Kendall for inviting us to contribute an essay to this volume. We thank Alicia Carmona for research assistance.

Notes

1. *The New York Times* reported, "The expedition will be backed by Mr. Jesup from his private resources. Prof. F. W. Putnam...will conduct the expedition and with him will be the anthropologist Dr. Boas" (12 March 1897:12). In fact, Putnam never went into the field with the expedition, and Boas directed and supervised the whole enterprise.

2. As Bogoras wrote to Lev Shternberg, a fellow political exile, "Kolymsk [in Siberia] is a different planet, even less connected with Earth than the Moon, completely alien to Earth, a block of ice cast out into space and suspended there above the emptiness, where every accidental spark of life freezes down and suffocates" (20 June 1894, quoted in Vakhtin 2001:79).

3. Another methodological innovation that came from the Torres Straits Expedition was a system of recording string figures. Haddon had a longstanding interest in string figures, and, in 1898, he and Rivers invented a method for recording them (Quiggin 1942:128-129; Rivers and Haddon 1902). Although later simplified terminologies have been developed, the precise anatomical nomenclature of Rivers and Haddon is still preferred 100 years later (Averkieva and Sherman, 1992:xxii, xxviii, 5).

References

Ambrose, Stephen E.
1996 *Undaunted Courage. Meriwether Lewis, Thomas Jefferson, and the Opening of the American West.* New York: Simon & Schuster.

Anonymous
1897 Proposed Explorations on the Coasts of the North Pacific Ocean. *Science*, n.s. 5(116):455–57.

Averkieva, Julia P., and Mark. A. Sherman
1992 Kwakiutl String Figures. *Anthropological Papers of the American Museum of Natural History* 71. Seattle: University of Washington Press; New York: American Museum of Natural History.

Baatz, Simon
1986 Magnificient Voyagers. *Science* 232:1020.

Berman, Judith
2001 Unpublished Materials of Franz Boas and George Hunt: A Record of 45 Years of Collaboration. In *Gateways. Exploring the Legacy of the Jesup North Pacific Expedition.* Igor Krupnik and William W. Fitzhugh, eds. Pp.181–213. *Contributions to Circumpolar Anthropology* 1. Washington, DC: Arctic Studies Center.

Boas, Franz
1903 The Jesup North Pacific Expedition. *American Museum Journal* 3(5):72–119.

Codere, Helen, ed.
1966 Franz Boas, *Kwakiutl Ethnography*. Chicago: University of Chicago Press.

Cole, Douglas
1999 *Franz Boas:The Early Years, 1858–1906.* Vancouver/Toronto: Douglas and McIntyre; Seattle and London: University of Washington Press.
2001 The Greatest Thing Undertaken by Any Museum? Franz Boas, Morris Jesup, and the North Pacific Expedition. In *Gateways. Exploring the Legacy of the Jesup North Pacific Expedition.* Igor Krupnik and William W. Fitzhugh, eds. Pp.29–70. *Contributions to Circumpolar Anthropology* 1. Washington, DC: Arctic Studies Center.

Freed, Stanley A., and Ruth S. Freed
1983 Clark Wissler and the Development of Anthropology in the United States. *American Anthropologist* 85(4):800–25.

Freed, Stanley A., Ruth S. Freed, and Laila Williamson
1988a Capitalist Philanthropy and Russian Revolutionaries: The Jesup North Pacific Expedition (1897–1902). *American Anthropologist* 90(1):7–24.
1988b The American Museum's Jesup North Pacific Expedition. In *Crossroads of Continents: Cultures of Siberia and Alaska.* William W. Fitzhugh and Aron Crowell, eds. Pp. 97–103. Washington, DC: Smithsonian Institution Press.

1997 Tough Fieldworkers: History and Personalities of the Jesup Expedition. In *Drawing Shadows to Stone: The Photography of the Jesup North Pacific Expedition, 1897–1902*. Laurel Kendall, Barbara Mathé, and Thomas R. Miller, eds. Pp. 9–17. New York: American Museum of Natural History; Seattle: University of Washington Press.

Jackson, C. Ian

1985 Exploration as Science: Charles Wilkes and the U. S. Exploring Expedition, 1938–42. *American Scientist* 73:450–61.

Jonaitis, Aldona

1988 *From The Land of the Totem Poles. The Northwest Coast Indian Art Collection at the American Museum of Natural History*. New York: American Museum of Natural History; Seattle: University of Washington Press.

Kassel, Bernard M.

1985 Iron Men and Wooden Ships: A Chronology, 1838–1842. In *Magnificent Voyagers: The U. S. Exploring Expedition, 1838–1842*. Herman J. Viola and Carolyn Margolis, eds. Pp. 257–65. Washington, DC: Smithsonian Institution Press.

Kendall, Laurel

1988 Young Laufer on the Amur. In *Crossroads of Continents: Cultures of Siberia and Alaska*. William W. Fitzhugh and Aron Crowell, eds. P.104. Washington, DC: Smithsonian Institution Press.

Kennedy, John Michael

1968 Philanthropy and Science in New York City: the American Museum of Natural History, 1868–1968. Ann Arbor, Michigan: University Microfilms.

Kirn, Walter

2002 Lewis and Clark: The Journey That Changed America Forever. *Time* 162(2), July 8. Pp. 38–41.

Kuklick, Henrika

1998 Fieldworkers and Psychologists. In *Cambridge and the Torres Strait: Centenary Essays on the 1898 Anthropological Expedition*. Anita Herle and Sandra Rouse, eds. Pp. 158–80. Cambridge: Cambridge University Press.

Laufer, Berthold

1902 The Decorative Art of the Amur Tribes. *The Jesup North Pacific Expedition*, vol. 4, pt.1. *Memoirs of the American Museum of Natural History*, 6. Leiden: E.J. Brill; New York: G.E. Stechert.

Leonhart, Joye

1985 Charles Wilkes: a Biography. In *Magnificent Voyagers: The U. S. Exploring Expedition, 1838–1842*. Herman J. Viola and Carolyn Margolis, eds. Pp.189–203. Washington, DC: Smithsonian Institution Press.

Merrison, L., and F. Calvert

1997 *Cracks in the Mask* [a film]. A Talking Pictures Frances Calvert Production.

Moulton, Gary, ed.

1986 *The Journals of the Lewis and Clark Expedition, August 30, 1803-August 24, 1804*. 8 vols. Lincoln: University of Nebraska Press.

Ousley, Stephen D.

2000 Boas, Brinton, and the Jesup North Pacific Expedition: The Return of the Americanoids. *European Review of Native American Studies* 14(2):11–8.

Quiggin, Alison H.

1942 *Haddon, the Head Hunter; A Short Sketch of the Life of A. C. Haddon*. Cambridge: Cambridge University Press.

Rivers, William H. R.

1901 Introduction. In *Reports of the Cambridge Anthropological Expedition to Torres Straits*, vol. 2, pt.1. Alfred C. Haddon, ed. Pp.1–7. Cambridge: Cambridge University Press.

Rivers, William H. R., and Alfred C. Haddon

1902 A Method of Recording String Figures and Tricks. *Man* 2:146–53.

Rouse, Sandra

1998 Expedition and Institution: A. C. Haddon and Anthropology at Cambridge. In *Cambridge and the Torres Strait: Centenary Essays on the 1898 Anthropological Expedition*. Anita Herle and Sandra Rouse, eds. Pp. 50–76. Cambridge: Cambridge University Press.

Stanton, William

1975 *The Great United States Exploring Expedition of 1838–1842*. Berkeley: University California Press.

Stocking, George W., Jr.

1995 *After Tylor: British Social Anthropology, 1888-1951*. Madison: University of Wisconsin Press.

Vakhtin, Nikolai B.

2001 Franz Boas and the Shaping of the Jesup Expedition Siberian Research, 1895–1900. In *Gateways. Exploring the Legacy of the Jesup North Pacific Expedition*. Igor Krupnik and William W. Fitzhugh, eds. Pp.71–89. *Contributions to Circumpolar Anthropology* 1. Washington, DC: Arctic Studies Center.

Viola, Herman J.

1985 The Story of the U. S. Exploring Expedition. In *Magnificent Voyagers: The U. S. Exploring Expedition, 1838–1842*. Herman J. Viola and Carolyn Margolis, eds. Pp.10–23. Washington, DC: Smithsonian Institution Press.

Viola, Herman J., and Carolyn Margolis, eds.

1985 *Magnificent Voyagers: The U. S. Exploring Expedition, 1838–1842*. Washington, DC: Smithsonian Institution Press.

29/ Dina Jochelson-Brodsky steps out of the expedition's winter headquarters at the village of Kamenskoye, 1901. Photographer, Waldemar Jochelson (AMNH 4171-6729)

part 2

ANTHROPOLOGIES AND HISTORIES:
JESUP TEAM MEMBERS THEN AND NOW

Franz Boas and the Music
of the Northwest Coast Indians

IRA JACKNIS

Franz Boas' research strategy for the Jesup Expedition was broad, relying on a wide range of documentation. In addition to casts and measurements of body parts, ethnographic and archaeological artifacts, observers' field notes, linguistic texts in Native languages, and photographs, Boas and his team collected music in the form of notation and sound recordings. A pioneer in so many areas of anthropology, Boas was also a leader in the field of ethnomusicology, generally, and the study of Northwest Coast Indian music, specifically. This essay summarizes and contextualizes Boas' musicological contribution by reviewing his research and writing on the topic during the two decades surrounding the Jesup Expedition, 1886–1906. It also offers a more detailed examination of his most extended Jesup research: his recording of Thompson Indian songs in 1897.[1]

As part of his broad education in mid-nineteenth century Germany, Franz Boas (1858–1942) studied European art and music, and learned to play the piano (Liss 1996:160). According to his biographer, "Music . . . formed an important part of his life. He had begun to learn the piano early, and his enjoyment of Haydn, Mozart, Beethoven, and Bach increased as he grew older" (Cole 1999:32). As Cole makes clear, though, this musical education came informally; that is, Boas acquired it as an avocation. Partly because of the specialization demanded by the German educational system, he never studied music in his secondary or university classes. His older sister Toni was a great

influence, an accomplished pianist with whom he played four-hand piano arrangements (Liss 1996:162). As a student in Bonn, he sang in a choir and formed a trio with two of his friends. Throughout his life Boas made an effort to live with a piano, frequently attended classical concerts, and hung pictures of Mozart and Beethoven in honored places in his home (Cole 1999: 46–7,139). Classical music was often a presence for him on his field trips far from home: He "yearned for Beethoven" during his first fieldwork, among the Baffinland Eskimo in 1883-84 (Liss 1995:122), and on his British Columbia field trips played the piano and organ at the request of local residents (Rohner 1969:67ff, 141–2). While he clearly derived pleasure from this music, the aim of his piano-playing was not so much to be a practiced performer but more to understand the music and the performances of others: "I want to learn only in order to understand and, of course, to listen. I want to learn the playing of music only in so far as it allows me to appreciate" (F. Boas to Toni Boas, 6 October 1876, in Cole 1999:32; cf. Liss 1996:162). This remark makes clear his scholarly or analytic approach to music, and it was these substantial musical abilities that formed the foundation for his subsequent anthropological research on the subject.

From his first field trip to his last, Boas documented Native music. Although his fieldwork among the Baffinland Eskimo (Inuit) of 1883–4 was conducted primarily to determine Native perceptions of the environment, he transcribed folk tales and songs, published in a series of later articles (Boas 1887a, 1889a, 1894a, 1897b) and in his monograph, *The Central Eskimo* (Boas 1888c). His first exposure to Northwest Coast Indian music came in January 1885, when he worked with a troupe of Bella Coola visiting Berlin. Struck by their "unique music," he transcribed four of their songs, which he sent to Carl Stumpf (Cole 1982:119, 117). Stumpf, a German psychologist who was one of the founders of comparative musicology, had studied the songs of the Bella Coola party a few months earlier, when they visited Halle (Stumpf 1886). In the fall of 1886, Boas made his first visit to the Northwest Coast. Here he studied Chinook songs in Victoria and Vancouver, and Kwakiutl song and dance in the villages of northern Vancouver Island.

Music thus lay at the very inception of Boas' Northwest Coast research, and he continued to study the subject in the years leading up to the Jesup Expedition. During the Chicago World's Fair in 1893, he again documented Native music in a displaced setting—this time using the phonograph to record songs of the visiting group of Kwakiutl (Jacknis 1991a: Fig. 30). On his next field trip, he was able to greatly extend his study of the tribe's music in its ceremonial setting, this time over several weeks in the fall of 1894 at Fort Rupert (Fig. 31). The first season of the Jesup Expedition marked an important advancement in Boas' musicological research; for the first time he was able to use the phonograph in the field. In June 1897 he recorded Thompson Indian music with the assistance of James Teit in Spences Bridge, B.C. These sessions also proved to be his most extensive musicological research for the expedition. He was in the field only once more during the Jesup Expedition years; on that second trip of 1900 he focused on Kwakiutl material culture and language, rather than on anything specifically musical.

Although Boas traveled periodically to the Northwest Coast after 1900, he did little musicological fieldwork until his last trip, in 1930-1, when he again worked with the Kwakiutl of Fort Rupert and Alert Bay. This, at the age of 72, was actually his most intensive study of

Native music. He recorded 156 cylinders and exposed about an hour's worth of 16-mm film of dance, crafts, and gesture. On this trip he attempted to gather material that would allow him to delineate tribal, genre, and individual styles, and also to clarify the rhythmic relations of texts and dance movements. Even then he did not stop, recording Kwakiutl Daniel Cranmer on acetate-coated aluminum disks when Cranmer visited Boas in New York in 1941, the year before Boas' death.

Boas' Research and Writing on Music

Franz Boas made important contributions to a number of diverse areas of ethnomusicological research, among them recording and transcription; formal analysis (scales, melody, and rhythm); song genres; song texts and the relations of words and music; performance practice; the social and cultural context of music; organology (the study of musical instruments); areal relations and history; and acculturation; in addition to his support for the institutional structures of scholarship.

Perhaps his most important contributions to the field of ethnomusicology were on the nature of transcription in notation and sound recording (Ellingson 1992:118–25). Boas published over a hundred of his own transcriptions (Fig. 32). At the beginning, he transcribed the music by having the singer repeat the notes until he had written it down in a Western notation style. However, his work with Stumpf and the Bella Coola had made him well aware of the limitations of Western notation for tribal music. In one article, for example, he adopted Stumpf's diacritic of a zero mark placed above a note, to indicate that "the tone is sung a little lower" (Boas 1888a:50; Ellingson 1992:120).

Boas was among the earliest ethnologists to make mechanical sound recordings. The first American anthropologist to use Edison's wax cylinder phonograph in the field was Jesse W. Fewkes, who recorded Passamaquoddy Indian music in Maine in 1890.[2] He followed this test with recordings of the Zuni in 1890 and the Hopi in 1891. Funded by Boston philanthropist Mary Hemenway, this collection was acquired by

Harvard's Peabody Museum in 1894. During the Chicago World's Fair in 1893, Boas worked with musicologist John C. Fillmore to record Kwakiutl songs on 116 wax cylinders. Also at the Chicago Fair, Benjamin Ives Gilman recorded Javanese, Samoan, Turkish, as well as Kwakiutl music (again with Hemenway sponsorship; this collection was also acquired by Harvard). The most important institution for the recording of American Indian music during its first decade was the Smithsonian's Bureau of American Ethnology (BAE). Alice C. Fletcher, a Bureau research associate, had been studying Native American music since the early 1880s, and during the 1890s she recorded the Omaha and many other Plains groups. Other Bureau recordists were Washington Matthews, among the Navajo, and James A. Mooney among the Caddo, Comanche, Arapaho, Kiowa, and Paiute.

Though starting slightly later than the Smithsonian, the American Museum of Natural History under Boas was a leader, especially in quantity and regional range, and it was the first American anthropology museum to collect sound recordings. The history of early American Indian recording remains to be written, but it appears that the American Museum was much more systematic than the BAE in sponsoring recording. Perhaps because of Boas' own interest in the subject, the cylinders were carefully cataloged as soon as they entered the museum. At the Smithsonian, on the other hand, their creation and preservation were left to the interest of individual researchers. Moreover, the American Museum's collection predated the largest European sound archive, the Berlin Phonogramm-Archiv, which began informally in 1900 and officially in 1905 (Reinhard 1971; Simon 2000, cf. Gillis 1984:324). In addition to the 228 cylinders made by the Jesup Expedition, other early American Museum recordings were made among the Blackfoot and other Plains groups by George Bird Grinnell in 1897 and among the Tarahumara and Huichol of northern Mexico by Carl Lumholtz the following year. The American Museum collection, in turn, became the model for others at the University of California and Indiana University.[3]

Although we have no explicit statements from Boas on the ethnographic utility of the phonograph, he must have advocated it for his Jesup Expedition colleagues, as several of the parties used the machine. The first accessioned collection of phonograph recordings in the American Museum is comprised of 139 cylinders from the Koryak, Yukagir, Yakut (Sakha), Tungus (Even), Chukchi, Eskimo (Siberian Yupik), and local Russians made by Waldemar Jochelson and Waldemar Bogoras in Siberia in 1901–2 (Freed, Freed, and Williamson 1988: 101).[4] In addition to Boas' forty-five Thompson Salish cylinders of 1897, Livingston Farrand recorded thirty-four cylinders among the Quinault and another ten of the Quileute of Washington State in 1898. On Sakhalin Island in 1898–9, Berthold Laufer recorded Gilyak (Nivkh) and Tungus (Uilta) songs (Boas 1903:97).[5] On the related Harrington Expedition in 1899, Roland Dixon recorded twenty-one cylinders among the Maidu of northeastern California.[6]

This substantial recording activity is perhaps the greatest ethnomusicological legacy of the Jesup Expedition (Keeling 2001:285–90). The phonograph, although a relatively recent ethnographic medium, was just one part of a multi-media set of tools employed by the Jesup Expedition. Like the extensive photography, primarily of physical types, this activity resulted in the production of a corpus of enduring objects of otherwise ephemeral culture, which could remain the basis for future scholarly research (Jacknis 1984, 1996). Years later, writing to museum founder George Heye in 1927, Boas explained, "I am trying to develop gradually a collection of records of Indian speech and song which, I believe, will be just as important as collections of specimens of their handy craft which are accumulating in museums" (Boas to Heye, 30 November 1927, APS-BP).

Although music was treated in several of the Jesup Expedition publications, it held a relatively minor position. Boas shared some insights into the Thompson (Nlaka'pamux) recording sessions in letters to his wife and parents (Rohner 1969:202–4), but his published remarks on music in the JNPE publications are quite brief. He contributed a chapter on art to Teit's monograph, *The Thompson Indians* (Teit 1900), including several pages on types of songs and a description of musical instruments (Boas 1900:383–85). Boas' report on Bella Coola mythology included notations for four songs, three with texts (Boas 1898:71, 82, 93, 94), with other song texts and translations in passing. The first volume of the *Kwakiutl Texts* contains a section on "Songs" (Boas and Hunt 1905:475–91), with interlinear translations of 32 song texts, including texts for 20 Hamatsa songs and others, plus a description of a winter ceremonial. One reason for this relatively meager output on Boas' part was his conception of his research and publication as an entity. For example, the winter ceremonial description was a more complete version of his earlier account in a report that had been published by the Smithsonian Institution (Boas 1897a). Generally, though, he did not repeat in his JNPE publications the extensive information on music that was contained in that monograph.

While neither Bogoras nor Jochelson supplied any musicological analysis, their JNPE monographs contain good descriptions of music and musical instruments, especially as part of shamanism (Keeling 2001). Both include vivid anecdotes about Native reactions to their recording (Bogoras 1904–7:436; Jochelson 1908:426–7). Bogoras, for example, offered a very sophisticated description of how the Chukchi shaman obscures the source of the music by modifying the sound of his voice with a drum, and another long account of his use of the phonograph to explore the nature of "separate voices" or ritual ventriloquism (Bogoras 1904–7:434, 436). The most extensive publication on music to come out of the Jesup Expedition was John R. Swanton's work. Swanton, a student of Boas then employed by the Smithsonian Bureau of American Ethnology, collected among the Haida in 1900–1 for the American Museum. His JNPE monograph contains a general description of Haida songs and a brief summary of song types (Swanton 1905:212), which he complemented in a longer study of texts and translations for 106 Haida songs collected on the expedition (Swanton 1912). However, he noted only song texts and enclosed a brief description; there were no transcriptions or recordings (cf. Enrico and Stuart 1996). While Farrand, Jochelson, Bogoras, and Laufer recorded music, and Swanton obtained many song texts, only Boas published transcriptions, as he seems to have been the only musically literate person in the team.

Most anthropologists of the time worked with professional musicologists to first transcribe and then analyze their recordings of Native music (Brady 1984:3). Boas was virtually alone (along with Alice Fletcher) as a fieldworker who was able to make recordings in the natural context of musical performance, accompanied with verbal records in the Native language, and then musicologically analyze this material. His training allowed him to investigate technical issues of scales, melody, and rhythm. For example, he was perhaps the first to note complex rhythmical structures in Northwest Coast songs (Ellingson 1992:118; cf. Boas 1888a:51–2). More generally, he also contributed to the first major debate in American ethnomusicology. John C. Fillmore, the collaborator of both Boas and Alice Fletcher, adhered to a widespread notion of the period, that there was a universal harmonic sense, which was realized only imperfectly by tribal music (Filmore 1893, 1895). Reviewing Fletcher's *Study of Omaha Indian Music* (1893), Boas initially accepted Fillmore's theory "that the underlying sense of harmony is the same as ours" (Boas 1894b:171). It is puzzling why Boas supported this position, now regarded as false and ethnocentric. Boas' later research showed how each culture needed to be understood on its own terms. Boas, like Fillmore, may have been influenced by Hermann Helmholtz's theory of a natural musical scale based on Western harmony (Myers 1994:xx), or he may have felt that it actually accorded a degree of cultural respect to Native musical systems. We do know that Boas' early work was marked by evolutionary positions that he later rejected, and that his thought was always caught in intellectual oppositions (Stocking 1974:1–20). In any event, towards the end of his career, Boas did reject Fillmore's theory of latent harmony (Boas 1927:342).

Much of Boas' exploratory writing on Northwest Coast music was an attempt to classify songs into genres. In his early essay on Kwakiutl songs, he noted children's songs, love songs, prayers, and war songs (Boas 1896). His most definitive research on this topic, left unpublished at his death, was his 1930–1 field trip, during which he was able to clarify the distinctions between summer songs, winter songs, gambling songs, love songs, mourning songs, and baby songs (Franz Boas to George Herzog, 18 April 1933, APS-BP).

As a pioneer linguist, Boas naturally focused on the setting and language of song texts. With most of his musical transcriptions, he supplied the words in the Native language and a translation. In his essay on Chinook songs, he noted that "the Tsimshian sing many Haida songs, although they do not understand the meaning of the words" (Boas 1888b:224). From the appended glossary of the Chinook words, he thought it interesting "that not more than seventy-four words occur in the collection of thirty-nine songs" (Boas 1888b:225). In several publications, most notably the Kwakiutl winter ceremonial study, he offered a semantic and cultural explanation of the song texts, identifying, for example, the various mythological characters to which the songs refer.

Franz Boas is known for the contextual ethnographic approach he brought to the study of culture, advocating intensive fieldwork and Native texts over armchair speculation. Naturally, he contributed to the study of the social and performative context of music. For example, he learned from his first Kwakiutl field trip that:

> The songs which are sung during these dances are in part very old, but a considerable number are new, and native poets and composers are continually adding to their stock of songs. As chorus singing is practised [sic] at all festivals by these Indians, and as the rhythms of the songs are very complicated, a good deal of practice is necessary before an artistic effect can be reached. ... Every village has its singing-master, who instructs young and old, and holds regular rehearsals before each festival. (Boas 1888a:51)

Again, his most elaborate study of this type was his monograph on Kwakiutl winter ceremonials, where he specifically describes the seating of the musicians; the roles and duties of the song leader (who acts as composer and music director), his assistant, and the chorus; and the handling of the instruments (Boas 1897a:432, 437); in addition to more general comments on the masked dances to which the music is a vital accompaniment.

Because of his role as artifact collector and museum curator, there was one otherwise minor field of musicology to which Boas made an important contribution—organology, or the study of musical instruments. He himself collected a full range of Northwest Coast rattles, whistles, and drums on his many field trips (Cole 1985; Jacknis 2002:23–6). During the Jesup Expedition, however, he collected relatively little, sharing the responsibility for the Bella Coola and Kwakiutl collections with George Hunt (Jacknis 1991b). An insight into Boas' interest in musical instruments is evident in his instruction to the Jesup collectors. For example, from John Swanton, collecting among the Haida, he requested:

> [R]attles also if fully explained. Please inquire particularly in regard to the significance of the raven rattle with hawk face on its lower side and lying figure on its back. What is the legend of the origin? How are they used and how are they held in dances? What is the difference between these rattles and the round rattles, most of which represent birds or heads? Are they used in different ceremonials? What is the use of the rattle set with puffin-beaks? What is the signficance of the clapper, most of which represent the killer-whale? Specimens of all of these, if fully explained, are desirable. A series of whistels [sic] with explanations would also be good to have. Do you consider the flageolet as an imitation of European patterns or as their own invention? (Boas to John Swanton, 5 June, 1900, acc. 1901–31, AMNH)

Boas described these instruments principally in his study of the Kwakiutl winter ceremonial (Boas 1897a:431–4, 437, 438–40, 445). In addressing the iconography of Hamatsa rattles, for example, he noted the skull motif as a reference to the man-eating theme of the winter ceremonial and the former practice of killing slaves (Boas 1897a:439; cf. Fig. 33). Whistles, he wrote, are considered the voices of spirits (Boas 1897a:447). Perhaps because Northwest Coast instruments are comparatively simple in form, it was these sorts of contextual topics that Boas addressed, as opposed to the more usual musicological concerns of instrument form, construction, and tuning.

One area of research—a major Boasian orientation that underlay the entire Jesup Expedition—was diffusion and history. Boas, however, did little direct writing on this aspect of Native music. Perhaps he felt that it was first necessary to compile an adequate sample and description. This omission is particularly striking in that such issues of areal relations were the ostensible rationale for the expedition's work. In his summary essays, he did cite mythological and artifactual patterns, but nothing from music, most likely because the musical collections were relatively small and because they were not transcribed. Nevertheless, as he often did with his many research topics, Boas suggested this subject to his later students, George Herzog (1930) and Helen H. Roberts (1936).

Franz Boas did, however, make an important contribution to the study of more recent history. It is commonly claimed that he was uninterested in studies of acculturation; but one of his most fascinating musicological essays, "Chinook Songs" (Boas 1888b), was devoted to the music of the urban Indians of Victoria, Vancouver, and New Westminster, B.C. Largely migrant workers, they labored in the saw mills, canneries, and hop fields. Boas published thirty-eight song texts and translations, as well as two melodies in musical transcription. The texts—composed in a complex linguistic creole that combined English, Chinook, and other Native Northwest Coast languages—mostly expressed feelings of loneliness and lost love. For instance, "When the steamboat leaves/ Say good-bye, Jimmy!/ Billy will feel very sad" (Boas 1888b:224), with the words "steamboat" and "good-bye, Jimmy" in English. In his analysis, Boas noted the contexts of performance and transmission.

Throughout his mature career, Boas dedicated himself to creating the institutional structures of scholarship; and ethnomusicology was no exception. Largely as a result of the use of the phonograph, the 1890s was the critical decade for the institutionalization of the field (Lee 1993:21, cf. Densmore 1927). Boas knew and corresponded with the leading students of American Indian music, among them Alice C. Fletcher, James A. Mooney, Washington Matthews, George Bird Grinnell, John C. Fillmore, and Benjamin I. Gilman. In the *Journal of American Folk-Lore*, he favorably reviewed Alice Fletcher's pioneering *A Study of Omaha Indian Music* (Boas 1894b). In December 1898, he invited Fletcher, Matthews, and Carl Lumholtz to join him in demonstrating some of their recordings of Indian songs at the annual meeting of the American Folklore Society (AFS) (e.g., Boas to G. B. Grinnell, 23 December 1898, AMNH-DA; cf. Newell 1899:53–4). This led to the formation of an AFS committee on American folk music, which Boas chaired. As part of this effort, Boas came in contact with leading musicians and composers of his day. He asked his Columbia colleague Edward MacDowell to serve on the committee. Although MacDowell declined, Boas did use another local composer, Frederick R. Burton, to transcribe some of the recorded songs. These composers, along with Arthur Farwell, Charles Wakefield Cadman, and R. Carlos Troyer, were loosely referred to as "the American Indianists" (Pisani 1998). There is no record of Boas' personal opinion on their creative work, but the Native music that he and his colleagues were recording was a vital stimulus to contemporary composers who were attempting to create a genuinely American music.

As a German immigrant, Boas naturally maintained scholarly ties with his homeland. He actively shared his research on Northwest Coast Indian music with two of the founders of the so-called "Berlin school of comparative musicology": Carl Stumpf and his student Erich von Hornbostel (Christensen 1991). Just as Boas had sent his early Bella Coola transcriptions to Stumpf, in 1905 he lent forty-three of the Thompson cylinders to his old colleague, then at the University of Berlin, evidently at his request (cf. Boas to Stumpf, 13 November 1905, AMNH-DA). Von Hornbostel, with his colleague Otto Abraham, used them as the basis for an important early essay in ethnomusicology (Abraham and von Hornbostel 1975 [1906]). Some of these cylinders were reproduced by the Berlin Phonogramm-Archiv and subsequently included in the Archives' Demonstration Collection (Reinhard 1971; Reinhard and List 1963). First produced in the early 1920s, copies of the 120-cylinder set were distributed to archives throughout the world—"the first anthology of traditional music ever issued" (Seeger and Spear 1987:89). Boas continued to teach and encourage growth in the field, training scholars such as George Herzog (who had previously studied under von Hornbostel) and Helen H. Roberts. Through these German connections, Boas infused the study of American Indian music with an international perspective.

Boas' research on music had implications beyond its own sphere of study. As music was the art to which he was most personally attracted, it seems to have become the model for his aesthetic theory, and helps to explain the origins of his rather idiosyncratic theory of primitive art (Boas 1927). Boas suggested that all decorative patterns were derived from a craftsperson's motor patterns (Jacknis 1992:158). Using the word "virtuoso"—a term common in musical criticism—Boas claimed that designs, indeed all formal patterns, were created out of the rhythmical actions necessary to produce the work. In support of this, Boas examined rhythmic patterns in visual, verbal, and musical art forms. Although his theory has it roots in German aesthetics, it must have appealed to someone who was familiar with the nature of artistic (i.e., musical) performance.

As in all his work, Boas' research on music was devoted to the critique of then-popular notions of cultural evolution and to the promotion of cultural equality. In his first essay on Native music, he argued that "the mind of the native enjoys as well the beauties of nature as we do; that he expresses his grief in mournful songs, and appreciates humorous conceptions" (Boas 1887a:383). At the same time, however, Boas' anthropology was committed to appreciating cultures on their own terms. In his now-classic debate with Smithsonian ethnologist Otis T. Mason over the principles of museum classification, he prominently employed a musical example: "From a collection of string instruments, flutes, or drums of 'savage' tribes and the modern orchestra, we cannot derive any conclusion but that similar means have been applied by all peoples to make music. The character of their music, the only object worth studying, which determines the form of the instruments, cannot be understood from the single instrument, but requires a complete collection of the single tribe" (Boas 1887b:62). Note his emphasis, that the character of their music was the only object worth studying. He elaborated this contextual approach in the next response in the debate:

> The rattle, for instance, is not merely the outcome of the idea of making noise, and of the technical methods applied to reach this end: it is, besides this, the outcome of religious conceptions, as any noise may be applied to invoke or drive away spirits; or it may be the outcome of the pleasure children have in noise of any kind; and its form may be characteristic of the art of the people. Thus the same implement belongs to very different departments of a psychological museum. (Boas 1887b:65; see Fig. 33)

Nowhere could one find a better and more succinct example of Boas' approach to the study of culture.[7] It was perhaps not an accident that Boas chose to use musical examples to make a general cultural critique. Such a perspective would come to influence the study of Northwest Coast and other Native musics, as much as it affected anthropology in general. For Franz Boas, music was not a limited or specialized phenomenon, but actually lay at the core of human culture and thus of anthropology.

Recording Thompson Indian Music, 1897

In June 1897, in Spences Bridge, B.C., Boas recorded Thompson Indian music with the assistance of James A. Teit (Rohner 1969:202–4; cf. Wickwire 1988, 2001, this volume). Without doubt, these Thompson sessions were the most important musicological contributions of the entire Jesup Expedition project: first because they involved Boas, the expedition leader; second, because they were the most extensive musical research (as opposed to sheer recording) of the six-year expedition fieldwork; third, because they were Boas' first sound recording in the field; and finally because of their subsequent analysis in a pioneering essay in ethnomusicology (Abraham and von Hornbostel 1975 [1906]). In this section we consider how sound recording, like all ethnographic transcription, can be regarded as the outcome of a social interaction resulting in cultural representations. Like Native-made artifacts, these objects must be understood within their generating context.

The visiting JNPE team—consisting of Boas, Farrand, and Smith—spent about ten days in Spences Bridge (Fig. 34), arriving on the evening of June 3, and leaving the morning of June 14. In addition to sound recording, the party took photographs, plaster casts, and measurements of people, and gathered a small collection of artifacts (see Thom 2001:141–2; Wickwire, this volume). They began recording songs on June 6, documenting ten songs in the first session, with another thirty-five cylinders recorded over the next two days (Wickwire 1993:544). The sessions took place in Teit's house; given the insensitivity of early phonographs, the recording would have been improved by an indoor setting.[8] Earlier cylinder machines were rather large, bulky, and heavy; but by the mid-1890s several companies had introduced home models that were much smaller and lighter (Fig. 35). "About the size and weight of a portable sewing machine today" (Brady 1984:4), such an apparatus could be packed on horseback, as

did Boas and the JNPE team. Although some were or could be driven by an electric motor fitted with a battery, many of the home models were treadle or spring driven and thus were perfect for field recording. And like the modern tape recorder, the same machine could be used for recording and play-back.[9]

Like photography, sound recording is a focused social interaction, minimally involving the ethnographer and the Native performers. In this case, however, a critical player was James Teit (1864–1922). Just as Boas collaborated with George Hunt among the Bella Coola and Kwakiutl, here, too, he relied on a local field assistant (see Wickwire, this volume). For the Jesup Expedition, Boas selected Teit to be the prime researcher for the Plateau tribes of British Columbia. After participating in the 1897 recording session, he went on to do important musicological research under the auspices of the Anthropological Division of the Geological Survey of Canada. With a phonograph acquired in 1912, Teit recorded 250 songs, now preserved in the Canadian Museum of Civilization (Wickwire 1988, 2001:336).

Teit undoubtedly was responsible for selecting the six singers to be recorded. In fact, several of them were his relatives by marriage: Lucy Antko (his wife, Fig. 36), Xwalinek (her sister), and Nsilkapeskit (her sister's son; Wickwire 2001:n.7, 449). Just as Hunt tended to go first to his relatives (Jacknis 1991b:211), Teit must have found it easier to involve people he knew well. This rapport was critical, as Boas encountered some initial resistance to his recording: "Some of the people were bashful, especially the women, who did not want to sing until all the men had left the house" (Rohner 1969: 204). In fact, four of the six singers were female (Wickwire 1993:544). As Wickwire points out, Teit's ethnography was especially sensitive to women's issues, probably because of his marriage to Antko.

Boas indicated that gender was an issue in the performance, but the singers may have also been reluctant to be recorded by a strange contraption. The phonograph was relatively new for everybody, and especially so for Native people. The machines used during the Jesup Expedition were undoubtedly the first that these people had ever experienced, which explained the strong feelings of surprise frequently expressed (cf. Brady 1999:110). [10] Thompson people also had problems with being photographed (Hill-Tout 1978:64). [11] But their initial shyness gave way to pleasure, aided perhaps by the machine's reproductive abilities, as Boas noted that "The singing was a great deal of fun for the villagers" (Rohner 1969:204).

This inter-social encounter produced objects that transcribed or represented aspects of Native cultural "reality" (Jacknis 1996). With his methodological sophistication, Boas spent much of the 1890s attempting to ascertain the strengths and weakness of cylinder recording as an ethnographic medium. On the one hand, a cylinder recording was an indexical representation of actual acoustical phenomena. Within its limitations, it could more accurately record the sonic data apart from the filter of an observer's abilities and knowledge. And it was easier to capture a song by this means than from the repeated singing necessary to produce musical notation. Despite their obvious benefits, Boas was acutely aware of the limitations of the cylinder machines. Early phonographs could not accurately record rhythm, faint notes, or the sounds of choral or instrumental ensembles that were common on the Northwest Coast. Even more critical, many musical performances, among the Thompson as well as the Kwakiutl, lasted several hours, while wax cylinders could record only for short periods (an average of three minutes for a four-inch cylinder, and nine minutes for a six-inch one). [12] During his 1893 Chicago World's Fair session, Boas overcame this limitation by recording a single song across two cylinders; but in Spences Bridge, motivated perhaps by a shortage of cylinders, he was forced to use the machine more as a sampler. The effect of such technological limits was to create the song as a bounded musical object and unit of ethnomusicological study (cf. Shelemay 1991:280).

With his interest in context, Boas clearly realized that there was more to a song performance than the physical sound. While recording the singing of the Thompson, he noted the vivid acting and gestures that accompanied the performance:

"The singers became ecstatic and acted out all their old stories and ceremonies while they sang. One of them sang a prayer. While singing he danced and reached out to the sun with both arms while looking upward. Then he brought them down slowly, looking to the ground. Before that he had crossed his hands in front of his chest with the palms outward, moving them to the left and to the right as if he wanted to embrace the celestial body" (Rohner 1969:203).

To his parents, he added,

"An old woman sang the song into the phonograph which serves to 'cleanse' women who had borne twins. She took bundles of fir branches and hit her shoulders and breast with them while she danced. The song imitates the growl of the grizzly bear because they believe that the children derive from the grizzly bear" (Rohner 1969:204).

Despite noting this detailed description, Boas did not go on to complain about the phonograph's failure to record such gestures, evidently resigning himself to its limitations. On the other hand, perhaps his sensitivity to such failure of transcription led him in 1930–1, at the age of seventy-two, to use a movie camera to document Kwakiutl music and dance.

Returning to New York, Boas had these cylinders cataloged, but he himself was never able to seriously study them. In his musical research, as in all his work, Boas generally devoted more effort to description than analysis. By himself or with colleagues he managed to transcribe most of his recordings, but his musical analyses tended to be partial and expressed in short essays and passages of monographs rather than in longer, specialized works. Although not all his transcriptions were published, Boas undoubtedly felt compelled to publish as many as possible because they were the principal form, at the time, of reproducing the music. In these early years of sound recording, the available technology could produce multiple copies only with great difficulty. When a system of mastering was developed a few years later, there was no commercial market for these cylinders, and thus there was no incentive to reproduce them in quantities. Boas did make copies of his wax cylinders, but they were inevitably distorted from the original, and there was a limit as to how many copies could be made before the original signal was obliterated. Thus transcription was as much a form of reproduction (and preservation) as it was analysis.

As in his linguistic and ethnographic research, Boas was keenly interested in the methodological implications of these alternate forms of transcription. In one of his earliest ethnological essays, "On Alternating Sounds" (Boas 1889b), he had called attention to the role of observer bias in the transcription of exotic languages. In fact, it is hard to tell which was more fundamental for Boas—his approach to musical or linguistic transcription. Moreover, his early training in psychophysics and acoustics, which he applied primarily to linguistics (cf. Mackert 1994), also laid a foundation for his musicological research. After using the phonograph for the first time at the Chicago Fair, he made a careful study of the usefulness of the machine. Working in parallel, Boas transcribed melodies by ear, while Fillmore made his transcriptions from the cylinder recordings. Boas then subjected these to re-analysis during his next field trip in the fall of 1894. His publication of the results (Boas 1896, 1897a) was the first comparative investigation of the transcriptions of the same songs by different transcribers. Although he complained to his wife that Fillmore's music was "not very accurate" (Rohner 1969:178–9), when he published them he claimed that "on the whole" their respective "renderings of the music agree closely" (Boas 1896:1). In any case, for Boas it was necessary to continually confirm his ethnographic transcriptions, so that one could be sure that they represented Native culture and not observer bias.

Boas was not alone in preferring transcription to the actual recording. According to Richard Keeling,

"Early collectors seem to have regarded the machine more as a sampling device or as an aid for producing written transcriptions than as a means of recording actual performance practice. While this approach to field recording partially reflects theoretical presumptions that seem archaic nowadays, the methodology was due in great part to technological limitations of the equipment itself" (Keeling 1991:xiii, cf. Brady 1984:9).

Thus scholars such as Boas and Fillmore played their cylinders over and over again to ensure the accuracy of their transcriptions, in the process drastically degrading the surfaces of the grooves and their ability to preserve the music.

Like Native artifacts, these cylinders were associated with documentation that reflected their creation. Wickwire has noted the differences in Boas' and Teit's field notes from this session.

"Boas made notes of only the cylinder number, the tribal affiliation ('Thompson Indians'), the type of song ('Dancing song, love song, religious song,' etc.), the place of recording ('Spence's Bridge'), and the recorder ('F. Boas'). By way of contrast, Teit made note of the Native names of the singers ('Kaxpítsa', 'Antko', etc.), the Native names of song-types ("s'tläe'êski"-dance song, etc.), and incidental material such as the flexibility of the words used in the songs" (Wickwire 1988:189, cf. 2001).[13]

She also notes that Teit's post-1912 recordings were much better documented, including the Native name of the singer, a reference to photographs, how the singer learned the song, a Native text and translation, and other information such as the age or importance of the song or its ceremonial context. Any analyis would depend on the kind and amount of documentation that accompanied the recorded music. Commenting on the nature of museum documentation, Tom McFeat observed that "*object + data = specimen*, where by 'data' one means notes, measurements, drawings, charts, graphs, photographs, and models" (McFeat 1967:93; italics original). The object alone is not sufficient as a cultural representation. This equation is as true for sound recordings as it is for photographs and artifacts. Unfortunately, such minimal or partial documentation was common in many archives of early sound recordings (Seeger and Spear 1987:11–2).

Boas drew upon this documentation for his brief discussion of music in Teit's JNPE monograph (Teit 1900).[14] However, the principal analysis of these songs was done by his German colleagues Abraham and von Hornbostel (1906). Although Boas would have preferred to have the study published by the American Museum, he felt it was acceptable for it to appear under other auspices as long as proper credit were given (Boas to Carl Stumpf, 13 November 1905, AMNH). The resulting essay was actually published in a *Festschrift* dedicated to Boas. This article was one of the first sophisticated analyses of the musical content of Native American songs, based on recordings of actual performances and the transcriptions of forty-three songs. The essay is divided into two parts: "scales" and "rhythm, tempo, structure, and performance practice." Although Abraham and von Hornbostel analyzed notes and intervals using Western musical terminology (e.g., thirds, tonic, semi-tone), they observed, "But the fact that these concepts, taken from our notions of harmony, cannot be readily applied to Indian music is obvious from the many cases in which the singing departs from pure intonation of the consonant intervals" (1975:303). They had compared the relative tones to measurements of absolute pitch, based on a standard tone. Offering a statistical analysis of the intervals, they confronted Fillmore's argument about "feeling of latent harmony," which Boas had supported. Instead, Abraham and von Hornbostel concluded, tactfully perhaps, that "this delicate psychological question is today not yet ready for discussion" (1975:306).

Turning to a rhythmic analysis, they admitted to encountering "great difficulty in the rhythmic structure and metrical arrangements of many of the melodies" (Abraham and von Hornbostel 1975:302). As Boas had found earlier, they noted the complex rhythms and irregular combinations of beats, and the varying relation of the drumming patterns to the singing (on the thirty-five songs accompanied by percussion). Finally,

they made a few, brief remarks about the quality of the vocal production. Their only contextual comments were that "most of the songs are dance or game songs; others are designated as lyrical, religious, and 'medicine' songs. But a specific musical characterization of the types according to use could not be made" (Abraham and von Hornbostel 1975:309).

Music and Culture/Description and Analysis: The Legacy of the JNPE Recordings

Franz Boas never wrote the concluding volume of the Jesup Expedition reports, summarizing its findings, and it is now the common view that the Expedition's greatest legacy was its numerous accumulated collections (e.g., Krupnik and Vakhtin, this volume). The Thompson Indian recordings were analyzed, although not by Boas himself. That study, however, raises important questions about interpretative modes and disciplinary perspectives.

Citing their "lack of precise knowledge of the culture," Abraham and von Hornbostel admitted that they were necessarily "limited to strictly musical considerations" (1975:301). The implication was that Boas did not share with them any of the contextual information that he and especially Teit had recorded. As Wickwire observes: "Only Boas' information was used in the analysis nor were any of the singers' names mentioned. Only the English names of the song-types were given" (Wickwire 1988:190).[15] She also cites errors the German researchers made because they were not aware of the cultural context. On one song, what Teit called an exhaling sound, indicating blessing or good will, they interpreted as an inhaling sound denoting tension or excitement (Wickwire 2001:444). We have the sound on the cylinders but what does it mean and, more importantly, what does it represent?

Why did Boas not publish information on the cultural context of Thompson songs, as he had for the Kwakiutl? To some extent, these omissions stem from the fact that Thompson ethnography was somewhat marginal to Boas' own research and writing. Over the course of decades, he managed to publish quite a bit about Kwakiutl music; but it took a while and single essays were often limited. From a more fundamental perspective, however, this objectivist perspective characterized all of Boas' ethnography to some extent. Like Abraham and von Hornbostel, Boas often treated cultural elements as if they were discrete and isolable. As I have suggested elsewhere (Jacknis 1996), while Boas moved to a more contextual approach over time, this shift was never complete. Moreover, specific details of his fieldwork were rarely noted in his ethnography, just as he tended to describe cultures in collective rather than individual terms. In this analysis, Boas and von Hornbostel may have been the more sophisticated musicologists, but Teit had the best understanding of the culture. His work, then, was edited largely by Boas.

Perhaps even more important than making available documents of unique performances, recordings also allowed comparison. Just as the invention of photography was necessary to the development of art history, so did sound recording facilitate the creation of (ethno)musicology. A recording makes possible an analysis by scholars—such as Abraham and von Hornbostel—who were not present at the original performance. (Although this is the goal of transcriptions, no system of musical notation can completely capture all important aspects of a performance, a problem made all the more difficult when dealing with non-Western—and frequently non-literate—cultures. Moreover, without recordings even transcriptions were difficult to obtain). As Brady cautions, however, "without personal knowledge of the cultural context in which the recordings were made, many early armchair comparative musicologists reached conclusions and developed theories that were skeptically received even by their contemporaries" (Brady 1984:3). A full analysis of the Thompson songs thus required both formal and contextual information. The contrast between the purely formal analysis of Abraham and Hornbostel compared to the detailed cultural notes of Teit presages a persisting tension in ethnomusicology. As expressed in the 1960s and early 1970s, musicologists such as Mantle Hood (1971) held that it was necessary for scholars to be able to play and technically analyze Native musics, while anthropologists such as Alan Merriam (1964) stressed the importance of investigating their cultural context (cf. Nettl 1991:267).

One hundred years later, what are we to make of these recordings and of Boas' ethnomusicological research? Because of his personal interest in music, and his dual background in science and the humanities, Franz Boas realized the importance of recording and of studying the music of Native peoples. For a public museum, devoted to the display of artifacts, to systematically collect sound recordings was an enlightened policy. Against some opposition on the part of the museum's administration (Jacknis 1985:104–5), Boas was able to argue that the expedition supported by President Jesup needed to return home with as many kinds of records as possible to document these "vanishing cultures." As one of the pioneers of ethnomusicology, Boas encouraged several members of the expedition, who might not otherwise have investigated this topic, to make valuable records and observations. The sound archives that Boas initiated formed the basis for much of the major collections in this country. Over time, these cylinder recordings, like the photographs and all the other collections of the Jesup Expedition, have become historical sources in their own right, as cultures—and especially practices of musical performance—change. Contemporary scholars as well as the descendants of their Native singers can go back and appreciate these objects with keen appreciation. And while we may not know as much as we would like about these recordings, they remain, as Boas intended (Stocking 1974:123): "the foundation of all future researches."

Acknowledgments

For research assistance and valuable discussion of these issues, I am deeply grateful to Wendy C. Wickwire. As the references make clear, I am particularly indebted to her for information on the 1897 Spences Bridge recording session. Thanks also go to Thomas Ross Miller and Richard Keeling for their help and information. I would like to dedicate this essay to my late friend Douglas Cole, who graciously shared his unpublished research on Franz Boas.

Notes

1. For reasons of historical consistency, I use the ethnic names that Boas employed in his writing. The contemporary names for these peoples are as follows: Kwakiutl are the Kwakwaka'wakw, Bella Coola are the Nuxalk, Thompson are the Nlaka'pamux, and Baffinland Eskimo are the Inuit.

2. Thomas Edison patented his phonographic recording machine in 1877, but it did not become commercially available until 1889 (Keeling 1991:xii). For pre-1900 collections of American Indian music, see Gillis 1984; also Densmore 1927; Brady 1984; Seeger and Spear 1987; Lee 1993; Myers 1994:xiii; and Keeling 2001.

3. In addition to the Smithsonian Bureau of American Ethnology (3240 cylinders, ca. 1933), other anthropology museums with music collections were the University of California Museum (2713), National Museum of Canada (1530), Field Museum (1500), and University of Pennsylvania Museum. The American Museum of Natural History had about 2500 cylinders (Inman 1986:3). Undoubtedly, the AMNH was a model for the substantial sound collections in California, directed by Boas' student Alfred Kroeber, beginning in 1901 (Keeling 1991; Jacknis 2003). Indirectly, it was also the basis for the large collection at the Archives of Traditional Music at Indiana University. Much of the American Museum collection was copied for Columbia University by another of Boas' students, George Herzog, between 1936 and 1948, and taken to Indiana in 1948 when Herzog was appointed to the faculty. In 1961 the AMNH deposited its collection—including the recordings from the Jesup Expedition—at the Archives of Traditional Music at Indiana University.

4. Extant documentation attributes the collection to both Jochelson and Bogoras, but as we know that the Bogorases made ninety-five phonographic records, the Jochelsons probably made the remaining forty-four. Furthermore, we know that Jochelson worked with the Koryak, Tungus [Even], Yukagir, and Yakut [Sakha], while Bogoras spent time with the Chukchi and Siberian Eskimo [Yupik]. According to the Indiana University sound archives (Gillis 1984:345), the Siberian cylinder collection comprises: Koryak (18), Yukagir (10), Yakut (6); and Chukchi (28), Russians (45), Tungus (5), Aivan [Yupik] Eskimo (8); for a total of 120 surviving cylinders. On a tribal basis, this would give thirty-nine to Jochelson and eighty-one to Bogoras, which should be roughly correct.

5. Although Berthold Laufer refers to sound recording in his correspondence with Boas, these cylinders have not been located (cf. Keeling 2001:280). The Archives of Traditional Music at Indiana University does have his Chinese music from the American Museum and his Indian and Tibetan collection from the Field Museum. As we know that Laufer worked among the Tungus, those cylinders listed under Bogoras and Jochelson's name may be his, but Jochelson also worked with the Yukagirized Tungus.

6. Again, the dating of the Maidu collection is uncertain. The Archives of Traditional Music, Indiana University, indicates a 1910 date for this (Seeger and Spear 1987:40), which would be unlikely from what we know of Dixon's Maidu fieldwork; in one 1903 letter Dixon refers to recording "last year" (Dixon to Boas, 26 March 1903, AMNH-DA).

7. From a more technical perspective, such a critique was directly addressed to the evolutionary displays in which all the musical instruments of the world were grouped according to technical attributes (i.e., production of sound from vibrating strings, membranes, or columns of air in a tube), popular in institutions such as Oxford's Pitt-Rivers Museum and the Smithsonian. The Berlin school of "comparative musicology" developed just such a universal system of classification for musical instruments (Hornbostel and Sachs 1961 [1914]; cf. Kartomi 1990:167–74), one which has

become the basis for most subsequent analysis. Despite his ties to German scholarship, Boas seems to have had little interest in such approaches. Instead, almost all of his musicological research and writing came in the context of specific cultures and regions.

8. Although Boas writes of going "down to the village" to collect melodies (Rohner 1969:202), Teit's catalogue of the song sessions states that the songs were "recorded on Phonograph by Dr. Boas (at Teit's house), June 1897" (Archives of Traditional Music, Indiana University, cf. Wickwire 2001:432, 434, 437). Furthermore, Boas refers to the singing occurring in "the house" (Rohner 1969:204).

9. After the stay in Spences Bridge, there is no further mention of the phonograph. At the end of July, however, Harlan Smith complained to a clerk at the American Museum that the phonograph cylinders and photographic plates that the museum had sent to Victoria in May were missing. Consequently, he had to "do without the phonograph cylinders" (Smith to John Winser, 30 July 1897, AMNH, cited in Mathé and Miller 2001:110). After leaving Spences Bridge, Smith had gone to Kamloops, which was Shuswap (Secwepemc) territory, and Lytton, Thompson territory, where he focused on archaeology and physical anthropology (Thom 2001:142–3). Perhaps he was not able to make projected recordings because of these missing cylinders. Wickwire (personal communication 1998) suggests that the Jesup team left the machine with Teit, who continued to record songs, or Farrand might have used it the following year in Washington State. In any case, it is clear that the American Museum had several phonographs.

10. Several members of the Jesup Expedition noted the impression that sound recording made among Native people. Both Jochelson (among the Koryak) and Laufer (among the Gilyak) reported similar Native beliefs that there had to be a little man inside the machine with an amazing ability to learn songs (Jochelson 1908:426–7; Laufer to Boas, 4 March 1899, in Boas 1903:97). Negative reactions to this mimetic ability were also expressed. Jochelson wrote: "Older people [of Kamenskoye] stop the younger ones from singing into the phonograph saying [that] 'the old one' as they call the phonograph will take their voices and they'll die" (Jochelson to Boas, 3 December 1900, in Kendall, Mathé, Miller 1997:39). Because of such feelings, performances were sometimes modified: "In Siberia, some shamans forbade the phonograph recording of actual ceremonies, instead performing special demonstrations in front of the machine. Besides the possibility that the recordings might be used for evil purposes, they were concerned that spirits would fly into the recording horn and be trapped irretrievably inside the phonograph box" (op. cit., pp. 36–7).

11. Somewhat similar to the reactions to the phonograph were Native responses to cameras, which were much more familiar, especially on the Northwest Coast (Blackman 1982; Rohner 1969:189; Kendall, Mathé, Miller 1997:33). Unlike that tool, however, the recording could be played back immediately for the subjects.

12. Probably because of their lack of sonic sensitivity, Boas found cylinder machines to be of little use for recording speech: "I have used the phonograph quite a good deal for certain purposes, and particularly for recording Indian music. I find that it is absolutely without any value for recording Indian languages" (Boas to D. P. Penhallow, 10 February 1899, AMNH-DA)

13. The respective field notes are: Franz Boas, 1897, unpublished note, copy from Archives of Traditional Music, Indiana University; James Teit, 1897, unpublished notes on songs, Salish Ethnographic Notes, APS.

14. There are a few tantalizing clues that Harlan Smith was to have analyzed the Thompson music. Writing in Spences Bridge in 1897, Boas casually noted, "the other night when he [Smith] took down the songs . . ." (Rohner 1969:205). See note 9 on the possibility of Smith's use of the phonograph. On one list of potential Jesup Expedition publications, Smith was listed as the author of "Songs of the Thompson Indians" (cf. F. W. Putnam to Boas, 12 August [?] 1903, AMNH-DA).

15. Of the texts for the Thompson River songs, Boas wrote years later, "If I remember correctly I sent the words to Hornbostel, but I am not sure" (Boas to George Herzog, 18 April 1933, APS-BP).

References

Abraham, Otto, and Erich M. von Hornbostel

1906   Phonographierte Indianermelodien aus Britisch-Columbia. In *Boas Anniversary Volume: Anthropological Papers Written in Honor of Franz Boas . . . Presented to Him on the Twenty-fifth Anniversary of His Doctorate.* Pp. 447–74. New York: Stechert. Translated as Nettl, Bruno. Indian Melodies from British Columbia Recorded on the Phonograph. In *Hornbostel Opera Omnia*, 1. Klaus P. Wachsmann, Dieter Christensen, and Peter Reinecke, eds. Pp. 299–322. The Hague: Martinus Nijhoff, 1975.

Blackman, Margaret B.

1982   "Copying People": Northwest Coast Native Response to Early Photography. In *The Past in Focus: Photography and British Columbia, 1858–1914.* Joan M. Schwartz, ed. *BC Studies* (52):86–112.

Boas, Franz

1887a   Poetry and Music of some North American Tribes. *Science* 9:383–5.

1887b   The Occurrence of Similar Inventions in Areas Widely Apart: Museums of Ethnology and Their Classification. *Science* 9:485–6; 587–9. Reprinted in *The Shaping of American Anthropology, 1883-1911: a Franz Boas Reader.* George W. Stocking, ed. Pp. 61–7. New York: Basic Books, 1974.

1888a   On Certain Songs and Dances of the Kwakiutl of British Columbia. *Journal of American Folk-Lore* 1(1):49–64.

1888b   Chinook Songs. *Journal of American Folk-Lore* 1(3):220–6.

1888c   The Central Eskimo. *6th Annual Report of the Bureau of Ethnology for 1884–85.* Pp. 399–669. Washington, DC: Smithsonian Institution.

1889a   Eskimo Tales and Songs (with Hinrich J. Rink). *Journal of American Folk-Lore* 2(2):123–31.

1889b   On Alternating Sounds. *American Anthropologist* 2(1):47–52.

1894a   Eskimo Tales and Songs. *Journal of American Folk-Lore* 7(1):45–50.

1894b   Review. A Study of Omaha Indian Music, by Alice C. Fletcher. *Journal of American Folk-Lore* 7(2):169–71.

1896   Songs of the Kwakiutl Indians. *Internationales Archiv für Ethnographie* 9:1-9.

1897a   The Social Organization and Secret Societies of the Kwakiutl Indians. *Report of the U.S. National Museum for 1895*, Pp. 311–738.

1897b   Eskimo Tales and Songs. *Journal of American Folk-Lore* 10:109–15.

1898   The Mythology of the Bella Coola Indians. *The Jesup North Pacific Expedition*, vol.1, pt. 2, pp. 25–127. *Memoirs of the American Museum of Natural History*, 2. New York: G. E. Stechert.

1900   Art. In *The Thompson Indians of British Columbia.* James A. Teit. *The Jesup North Pacific Expedition*, vol. 1, pt. 4, Pp. 376–86. *Memoirs of the American Museum of Natural History*, 2. New York: G. E. Stechert.

1903   The Jesup North Pacific Expedition. *American Museum Journal* 3(5):73–119.

1927   Primitive Art. *Instituttet for Sammenlignende Kulturforskning*, ser. B, 8. Oslo/Cambridge, Mass.: H. Aschehoug/Harvard University Press.

Boas, Franz, and George Hunt

1905   Kwakiutl Texts. *The Jesup North Pacific Expedition*, vol. 3. *Memoirs of the American Museum of Natural History*, 5. Leiden: E. J. Brill; New York: G. E. Stechert.

Bogoras, Waldemar

1904–9 The Chuckchee. *The Jesup North Pacific Expedition*, vol. 7, pts.1–3. *Memoirs of the American Museum of Natural History* 11. Leiden: E. J. Brill; New York: G. E. Stechert.

Brady, Erika

1999   *A Spiral Way: How the Phonograph Changed Ethnography.* Jackson: University Press of Mississippi.

Brady, Erika, et al.

1984   Introduction and Inventory. In *The Federal Cylinder Project: a Guide to Field Cylinder Collections in Federal Agencies*, vol. 1. Washington, DC: American Folklife Center, Library of Congress.

Christensen, Dieter

1991   Erich M. von Hornbostel, Carl Stumpf, and the Institutionalization of Comparative Musicology. In *Comparative Musicology and Anthropology of Music: Essays on the History of Ethnomusicology.* Bruno Nettl and Philip V. Bohlman, eds. Pp. 201–9. Chicago: University of Chicago Press.

Cole, Douglas L.

1982   Franz Boas and the Bella Coola in Berlin. *Northwest Anthropological Research Notes* 16(2):115–24.

1985   *Captured Heritage: The Scramble for Northwest Coast Artifacts.* Seattle: University of Washington Press.

1999   *Franz Boas: The Early Years, 1858–1906.* Vancouver/Toronto: Douglas & McIntyre; Seattle and London: University of Washington Press.

Densmore, Frances

1927   The Study of Indian Music in the Nineteenth Century. *American Anthropologist* 29(1):77–86.

Ellingson, Ter

1992   Transcription. In *Ethnomusicology: an Introduction.* Helen Myers, ed. Pp. 110–52. New York: W. W. Norton.

Enrico, John, and Wendy Bross Stuart

1996   *Northern Haida Songs.* Lincoln: University of Nebraska Press.

Fillmore, John C.
1893   A Woman's Song of the Kwakiutl Indians. *Journal of American Folk-Lore* 6:285–90.
1895   What Do Indians Mean to Do When They Sing, and How Far Do They Succeed? *Journal of American Folk-Lore* 8:138–42.

Fletcher, Alice C.
1893 [1994]   A Study of Omaha Indian Music. Aided by Francis La Flesche. *Archaeological and Ethnological Papers of the Peabody Museum*, vol. 1, no. 5. Cambridge, Mass.: Peabody Museum of American Archaeology and Ethnology, Harvard University. Reprinted, with a new introduction by Helen Myers. Lincoln: University of Nebraska Press.

Freed, Stanley A., Ruth S. Freed, and Laila Williamson
1988   The American Museum's Jesup North Pacific Expedition. In *Crossroads of Continents: Cultures of Siberia and Alaska*. William W. Fitzhugh and Aron Crowell, eds. Pp. 97–103. Washington, DC: Smithsonian Institution Press.

Gillis, Frank J.
1984   The Incunabula of Instantaneous Ethnomusicological Sound Recordings, 1890–1910: A Preliminary List. In *Problems and Solutions: Occasional Essays in Musicology Presented to Alice M. Moyle.* Jamie C. Kassler and Jill Stubington, eds. Pp. 323–55. Sydney: Hale and Iremonger.

Herzog, George
1930   Musical Styles in North America. *International Congress of Americanists, 23rd Session, New York, 1928.* Pp. 455–8. New York.

Hill-Tout, Charles
1978 [1900]   Notes on the N'tlaka'pamuq of British Columbia, a Branch of the Great Salish Stock of North America. *69th Annual Report of the British Association for the Advancement of Science for 1899*, pp. 500–84. London. Reprint, In *The Salish People: The Local Contributions of Charles Hill-Tout*. Ralph Maud, ed. Vol. 1. The Thompson and the Okanagan. Pp. 41–129. Vancouver: Talonbooks.

Hood, Mantle
1971   *The Ethnomusicologist.* New York: McGraw-Hill.

Hornbostel, Erich M. von, and Curt Sachs
1961 [1914]   Systematik der Musikinstrumente: Ein Versuch. *Zeitschrift für Ethnologie* 45:3–90, 553-90. Translated as: A Classification of Musical Instruments, by Anthony Baines and Klaus P. Wachsmann. *The Galpin Society Journal* 14:3–29.

Inman, Carol F.
1986   George Herzog: Struggles of a Sound Archivist. *Resound, a Quarterly of the Archives of Traditional Music* 5(1):1–5.

Jacknis, Ira
1984   Franz Boas and Photography. *Studies in Visual Communication* 10(1):2–60.
1991a   Northwest Coast Indian Culture and the World's Columbian Exposition. In *Columbian Consequences, vol. 3: the Spanish Borderlands in Pan-American Perspective.* David Hurst Thomas, ed. Pp. 91–118. Washington, DC: Smithsonian Institution Press.
1991b   George Hunt, Collector of Indian Specimens. In *Chiefly Feasts: the Enduring Kwakiutl Potlatch.* Aldona Jonaitis, ed. Pp. 177–224. New York: American Museum of Natural History; Seattle: University of Washington Press.
1992   'The Artist Himself': the Salish Basketry Monograph and the Beginnings of a Boasian Paradigm. In *The Early Years of Native American Art History: the Politics of Scholarship and Collecting.* Janet Catherine Berlo, ed. Pp. 134–61. Seattle: University of Washington Press.
1996   The Ethnographic Object and the Object of Ethnology in the Early Career of Franz Boas. In *Volksgeist as Method and Ethic: Essays on Boasian Ethnography and the German Anthropological Tradition.* George W. Stocking, ed. Pp. 185–214. History of Anthropology, vol. 8. Madison: University of Wisconsin Press.
2002   *The Storage Box of Tradition: Kwakiutl Art, Anthropologists, and Museums, 1881–1981.* Washington, DC: Smithsonian Institution Press.
2003   Yahi Culture in the Wax Museum: Ishi's Sound Recordings. In *Ishi In Three Centuries.* Clifton B. Kroeber and Karl Kroeber, eds. Lincoln: University of Nebraska Press.

Jochelson, Waldemar
1908   The Koryak. *The Jesup North Pacific Expedition*, vol. 6. *Memoirs of the American Museum of Natural History*, 10. Leiden: E. J. Brill; New York: G. E. Stechert.

Kartomi, Margaret J.
1990   *On Concepts and Classifications of Musical Instruments.* Chicago: University of Chicago Press.

Keeling, Richard
1991   *A Guide to Early Field Recordings (1900–1949) at the Lowie Museum of Anthropology.* Berkeley: University of California Press.
2001   Voices from Siberia: Ethnomusicology of the Jesup Expedition. In *Gateways. Exploring the Legacy of the Jesup North Pacific Expedition, 1897–1902.* Igor Krupnik and William W. Fitzhugh, eds. Pp. 279–96. *Contributions to Circumpolar Anthropology*, 1. Washington, DC: Arctic Studies Center.

Kendall, Laurel, Barbara Mathé, and Thomas Ross Miller, eds.
1997   *Drawing Shadows to Stone: the Photography of the Jesup North Pacific Expedition, 1897–1902.* New York: American Museum of Natural History; Seattle: University of Washington Press.

Lee, Dorothy Sara

1993 Native American. In *Ethnomusicology: Historical and Regional Studies*. Helen Myers, ed. Pp. 19–36. New York: W. W. Norton.

Liss, Julia E.

1995 Patterns of Strangeness: Franz Boas, Modernism, and the Origin of Anthropology. In *Prehistories of the Future: The Primitivist Project and the Culture of Modernism*. Elazar Barkan and Ronald Bush, eds. Pp. 114–30. Stanford: Stanford University Press.

1996 German Culture and German Science in the *Bildung* of Franz Boas. In *Volksgeist as Method and Ethic: Essays on Boasian Ethnography and the German Anthropological Tradition*. George W. Stocking, ed. Pp. 155–84. History of Anthropology, vol. 8. Madison: University of Wisconsin Press.

Mathé, Barbara, and Thomas R. Miller

2001 Kwazi'nik's Eyes: Vision and Symbol in Boasian Representation. In *Gateways. Exploring the Legacy of the Jesup North Pacific Expedition, 1897–1902*. Igor Krupnik and William W. Fitzhugh, eds. Pp. 107–38. *Contributions to Circumpolar Anthropology*, 1. Washington, DC: Arctic Studies Center.

Mackert, Michael

1994 Franz Boas' Theory of Phonetics. *Historiographia Linguistica* 21(3):351–86.

McFeat, Tom F. S.

1967 [1965] The Object of Research in Museums. *National Museum of Canada Bulletin 204*, Anthropological Series 70, Contributions to Ethnology 5:91–99.

Merriam, Alan P.

1964 *The Anthropology of Music*. Evanston: Northwestern University Press.

Myers, Helen

1994 Introduction. In *A Study of Omaha Indian Music*. Alice C. Fletcher. Pp. vii–xxix. Lincoln: University of Nebraska Press.

Nettl, Bruno

1991 The Dual Nature of Ethnomusicology in North America: the Contributions of Charles Seeger and George Herzog. In *Comparative Musicology and Anthropology of Music: Essays on the History of Ethnomusicology*. Bruno Nettl and Philip V. Bohlman, eds. Pp. 266–74. Chicago: University of Chicago Press.

Newell, William Wells

1899 The Tenth Annual Meeting of the American Folk-Lore Society. *Journal of American Folk-Lore* 12(1):51–4.

Pisani, Michael V.

1998 "I'm an Indian Too": Creating Native American Identities in Nineteenth- and Early Twentieth-Century Music. In *The Exotic in Western Music*, Jonathan Bellman, ed. Pp. 218–57. Boston: Northeastern University Press.

Reinhard, Kurt

1971 [1962] The Berlin Phonogramm-Archiv. In *Readings in Ethnomusicology*. David P. McAllester, ed. Pp. 17–23. Reprinted from *The Folklore and Folk Music Archivist* 5(2):1–4. New York: Johnson Reprint Corp.

Reinhard, Kurt, and George List

1963 *The Demonstration Collection of E. M. von Hornbostel and the Berlin Phonogramm-Archiv*. New York: Ethnic Folkways Library [Smithsonian Institution]. FE 4175. LP recording.

Roberts, Helen H.

1936 Musical Areas in Aboriginal North America. *Yale University Publications in Anthropology* 12.

Rohner, Ronald P., ed.

1969 *Letters and Diaries of Franz Boas Written on the Northwest Coast from 1886 to 1931*. Chicago: University of Chicago Press.

Seeger, Anthony, and Louise S. Spear

1987 Ethnographic Cylinder Recordings: an Introduction. In *Early Field Recordings: a Catalogue of Cylinder Collections at the Indiana University Archives of Traditional Music*. Anthony Seeger and Louise S. Spear, eds. Pp. 1–14. Bloomington: Indiana University Press.

Shelemay, Kay Kaufman

1991 Recording Technology, the Record Industry, and Ethnomusicological Scholarship. In *Comparative Musicology and Anthropology of Music: Essays on the History of Ethnomusicology*. Bruno Nettl and Philip V. Bohlman, eds. Pp. 277–92. Chicago: University of Chicago Press.

Simon, Artur, ed.

2000 *Das Berliner Phonogramm-Archiv 1900–2000: Sammlung der traditionellen Musik der Welt* [*The Berlin Phonogramm-Archiv, 1900–2000: Collections of Traditional Music of the World*]. Bilingual (German/English) edition. Berlin: Verlag für Wissenschaft und Bildung.

Stocking, George W., Jr., ed.

1974 *The Shaping of American Anthropology, 1883–1911: a Franz Boas Reader*. New York: Basic Books.

Swanton, John R.

1905 Contributions to the Ethnology of the Haida. *The Jesup North Pacific Expedition*, vol. 5, pt.1, pp. 1–300. *Memoirs of the American Museum of Natural History*, 8(1). Leiden: E. J. Brill; New York: G. E. Stechert.

1912 Haida Songs. *Publications of the American Ethnological Society* 3:1–63.

Stumpf, Carl

1886 Lieder der Bellakula-Indianer. *Vierteljahrschrift für Musikwissenschaft*, II:405–26.

Teit, James A.

1900 The Thompson Indians of British Columbia. *The Jesup North Pacific Expedition*, vol. 1, pt.4, pp.

163–392. *Memoirs of the American Museum of Natural History*, 2. New York: G. E. Stechert.

Thom, Brian

2001   Harlan I. Smith's Jesup Fieldwork on the Northwest Coast. In *Gateways. Exploring the Legacy of the Jesup North Pacific Expedition, 1897–1902.* Igor Krupnik and William W. Fitzhugh, eds. Pp. 139–180. *Contributions to Circumpolar Anthropology*, 1. Washington DC: Arctic Studies Center.

Wickwire, Wendy C.

1988   James A. Teit: His Contribution to Canadian Ethnomusicology. *The Canadian Journal of Native Studies* 8(2):183–204.

1993   Women in Ethnography: the Research of James A. Teit. *Ethnohistory* 40(4):539–62.

2001   The Grizzly Bear Gave Them Song: James Teit and Franz Boas Interpret Twin Ritual in Aboriginal British Columbia, 1897–1920. *American Indian Quarterly* 25(3):431–52.

Beyond Boas? Reassessing the Contribution of "Informant" and "Research Assistant": James A. Teit

WENDY WICKWIRE

Few of the many early anthropologists who worked in the Pacific Northwest were more productive than James A. Teit (1864–1922). For the Plateau region, Teit generated a rich ethnographic record of over 2,000 pages in forty-two published sources, and another 5,000 pages in thirty-four unpublished sources (Sprague 1991:103). He also collected artifacts, took photographs, made sketches, collected plant specimens, and recorded songs on wax cylinders. Much of this work was undertaken under the direction of Franz Boas and the Jesup North Pacific Expedition (JNPE), an arrangement in which Teit is often seen as an "assistant" and "informant to Boas."[1] Yet, given the prodigious, independent, and high quality of his output, it is time to re-evaluate Teit as an anthropologist in his own right.[2]

Teit's role in the JNPE was to document the *interior* regions of British Columbia and, in so doing, fill a noticeable gap in the ethnographic record. Boas devoted much of his own time and attention to the central coastal region, partly because this is where he had good contacts, and also because his few ethnographic field trips inland had not gone well. In fact, without Teit's assistance, Boas' JNPE output would have been substantially smaller. When one looks closely at Teit's on-the-ground work for the JNPE, it could be argued that his contribution not only stands on its own, but in many ways goes beyond that of Boas.

A Timely Meeting in 1894

James Alexander Teit was the eldest of 12 children born into a merchant family in the town of Lerwick in the Shetland Islands (Fig. 37). In 1884, two years after finishing secondary school in Lerwick, Teit travelled to Canada to join his Uncle John Murray at Spences Bridge on the Thompson River in south central British Columbia (Fig. 38)[3]. Murray owned a popular trading outlet in the village (Figs. 39, 40). As his uncle's employee, Teit came into regular contact with the local Nlaka'pamux people who lived in the region (Fig. 41).[4] He obviously established immediate rapport with the latter, for within three years, he had taken up residence with Susannah Lucy Antko, a member of the Spences Bridge Band (Fig. 42). When not working in the store, Teit undertook whatever jobs were available, for example, ranching, fruit farming, hunting, and ferry work.[5]

Teit's life took an unusual turn in September 1894 when he encountered Franz Boas who was in the region to complete work for his sixth and second-to-last field season for the Committee of the British Association for the Advancement of Science (BAAS) for the Study of Northwestern Tribes of Canada in British Columbia. En route by train from the Okanagan Valley to the coast, Boas had decided to spend a night at Spences Bridge. On hearing of a local man, a "Scotsman" who was married to "an Indian woman [who knew] . . . a great deal about the Indians and was especially kind," Boas immediately tracked him down

123

at his small ranch across the river from his hotel (F. Boas to M. Boas, 21 September 1894, Rohner 1969:140). Seeing him so at ease with his wife and her relatives and quite fluent in their language, Boas employed him on the spot (Figs. 43, 44). As he explained it to his wife in a letter: "The young man is a treasure [who] knows a great deal about Indian tribes. I engaged him right away" (F. Boas to M. Boas, 21 September 1894, Rohner 1969:139). With Teit's assistance, Boas instantly gained access to a cultural region that hitherto was not well represented on his ethnographic map.

A Link to the Interior

The demands of the BAAS survey on Boas were great. Horatio Hale, an American philologist who had retired to Ontario, was charged with directing Boas' fieldwork in the Pacific Northwest. Hale's instructions to Boas were to "give an ethnological description of the whole region [of British Columbia], from north to south, without omitting any stock" (Rohner 1969:81). Hale, who had worked in Oregon as a member of the Wilkes Expedition of 1832–42, wanted a comprehensive survey of everything, from languages and tribal divisions to the physical characteristics of the peoples of the various regions. Boas was often impatient with his superior's demands, describing him as an "old man [who] knows nothing about general ethnology" (Cole 1973:41).

Boas found ethnographic fieldwork in areas beyond the coast a challenge. He had recorded the stories of a small group of Nlaka'pamux gathered at an Anglican church at Lytton at the end of his second field season in the Northwest Coast (his first for the BAAS) in July 1888. But he was not satisfied with these due to the heavy influence of Christian missionaries. After Lytton, he headed east to Windemere, just west of the Rocky Mountains where he encountered what he referred to as his first "real Indians" on account of their "red skin, eagle noses, the famous blanket, moccasins, rabbit [?] apron, and deerskin jacket, with hair hanging loose or

braided, more than six feet long" (F. Boas to M. Boas, 18 July 1888, Rohner 1969:102). Here too he expressed disappointment. Although he collected a fair number of stories and vocabularies there, he found it difficult to find suitable "informants." He also found little common ground with his coastal work. As he explained to his wife: "I am not so very much interested in these tribes, because they have very little relation to all my former work. . . . The language is very unfamiliar to me and the interpreter does not understand well enough to make it worthwhile to stay another week" (F. Boas to M. Boas, 18 July 1888, Rohner 1969:102).

Boas tried again the following summer of 1889 to work with peoples of the interior, but this proved to be even more disappointing than his earlier efforts. As he noted in a letter to his wife, "The last two weeks were not very fruitful. To my great distress a Lillooet Indian who had promised me the evenings has gone again and I had wanted to learn something about their language" (F. Boas to M. Boas, 14 September 1889, Rohner 1969:114). His lack of success with these forays into the interior regions of the province may account for his decision to spend the entire 1890 and 1891 field seasons on the coast.

It was not until his sixth field trip in September 1894, that Boas ventured again into the interior region. This time he decided to focus on the Okanagan region, with stops also at Glacier, Enderby, Sicamous and Kamloops. Again, his results were meager. "My Okanagan trip was a great failure," he complained to his wife in a letter dated September 16, 1894:

> Friday I went with an Indian to Lake Okanagan in pouring rain to measure Indians. Unfortunately he took me to the chief first instead of letting me go from house to house. We had to parley a lot, and then the chief told me to wait, that he was going to talk it over in the evening. From the way he acted I could tell that the good chief was afraid and that I wouldn't get what I wanted. When all the Indians had scattered in all directions in the evening, I left, arriving in Enderby very late and very angry. I was so cold that I could not move my fingers. . . . Well, there was nothing I could do about it. . . . Yesterday

I got five people in Enderby. I met a missionary there who had come from the Lake. I greeted him politely, he asked me what I was doing, and I explained everything to him as well as I could. He answered very politely (he is French), 'That seems very foolish. What do you want to do such nonsense for?' The Indians ask his advice, which he freely gives. And that is the reason for my lack of success in Enderby. I will be glad when I am back on the coast again! (F. Boas to M. Boas, 16 September 1894, Rohner 1969:136).

Not surprisingly, when Boas arrived at Spences Bridge two days later, he was beginning to lose faith in his abilities as a fieldworker. Teit's willingness to assist him did much to lift his spirits. On the first day of their meeting, Teit convinced his relatives and friends to submit themselves to Boas' anthropometric measurements; on the second day Teit saddled two horses and took Boas to visit numerous aboriginal settlements in the vicinity of Spences Bridge.

Immediately Boas' attitude to his fieldwork changed. "The disagreeable feeling I had that I don't get along with the Indians is slowly wearing off now," he wrote to his wife, "and I am hopeful that I will have good results" (F. Boas to M. Boas, 21 September 1894, Rohner 1969:139). By the end of the visit, he noted, "I am slowly getting into the mood of 'fieldwork' again" (F. Boas to M. Boas, 23 September 1894, Rohner 1969:142).

Before departing for New York in December, Boas made a return trip to Spences Bridge to continue his work with Teit who had arranged a trip to a number of outlying aboriginal communities: Lytton, Stain [Stein], and North Bend. Boas was pleased, especially with his success at measuring "one hundred and twenty-three Indians" in just three days (F. Boas to M. Boas, 15 December 1894, Rohner 1969:195).

There were many rich ethnographic experiences on this trip, such as one at Stain, at the confluence of the Thompson and Fraser Rivers where a chief regaled Boas and Teit with speeches in the company of numerous onlookers (F. Boas to M. Boas, 15 December 1894, Rohner 1969:196). Boas was particularly pleased

to find that Teit was already well along on an ethnographic report on the Nlaka'pamux that he had proposed the previous September (F. Boas to M. Boas, 15 December 1894, Rohner 1969:196).

A Year of Continuous Work

During the first year of their collaboration, Teit proved to be an ideal ethnographic assistant for Boas. He worked diligently to answer the latter's queries about the languages and traditions of the interior cultures. By early spring 1895, he had completed a 216-page report on the Nlaka'pamux, noting that this did not in any way exhaust his knowledge of the topic: "There is no subject which [sic] I have taken up in the paper, but what I could have treated more fully if I had wanted to, especially as this [is] the case with beliefs and customs, many of which I have never made mention [of] at all in the paper" (Teit to Boas, 22 February 1895, AMNH-BTC).

One of Boas' early requests of Teit was to find out what existed about the "Stuwixamux," an Athapaskan-speaking group that was once resident in the Nicola Valley. Teit tracked down three elderly men knowledgeable about this little-known group and wrote an account, which Boas included in his "Report of the 65th Meeting of the British Association for the Advancement of Science" (Boas 1895). By the spring of 1895, Teit had also assembled a large collection of "articles of ethnological value" (buckskin leggings, a shirt, moccasins, beaver-teeth dice, gambling sticks, a stone axe, a tent mat, two root-diggers, a fire drill, and a stone hammer), which he mailed to Boas in New York (Teit to Boas, 12 March 1895, AMNH-BTC).

By August 1895, Teit felt sufficiently comfortable with Boas to begin offering the latter critical feedback. "I thank you very much for the copy [of the Sixth Report on the Northwest Tribes of Canada] you sent," wrote Teit to Boas, "and have looked over it with much pleasure and profit. You have made a few slight mistakes in your vocabulary of the Ntlakyapamux. I will send you a list sometime of these when I have more time and also the words and compound forms which you seem to have been unable to obtain" (Teit to Boas, 12 August 1895, AMNH-BTC). Teit also challenged Boas on some of his conclusions regarding interior people:

> I consider it very surprising that you should find four, I might say five, such remarkably different types of Indian [sic] in the rather small area of BC. If you investigate the Lillooet next summer you will I am sure find that they are different from the NLakyapamuxôe and the NkamtcinEmux perhaps resembling the Harrison Lake type, or perhaps somewhat different. You will also find if you go into that field that the average Carrier and average Chilcotin are not alike at least in countenance or features and in stature. The only mistakes which I notice in looking over your sheets of measurements are on sheet 10 (Teit to Boas, 22 October 1895, AMNH-BTC).

Teit's Role in the Jesup North Pacific Expedition

In June 1897, Boas returned to British Columbia to finish his work for the BAAS and to initiate the first phase of his own field project funded by Morris K. Jesup, President of the Board of Trustees of the American Museum of Natural History. The goal of the Jesup North Pacific Expedition was to conduct a systematic ethnological and archaeological investigation of the relations among the indigenous peoples of the North Pacific Rim—Northwestern America and Northeastern Asia. Field parties would work in stages over a five-year period on the American west coast, along the coast of the Sea of Okhotsk, and in the northern portion of the Bering Sea. Boas saw this project as an opportunity to pursue a more historical approach. In his words: "A detailed study of customs in their relation to the total culture of the tribe practicing them, in connection with an investigation of their geographical distribution among neighboring tribes, affords us almost always a means of determining with considerable accuracy the historical causes that led to the formation of the customs in question and to the psychological processes that were at work

in their development" (Boas 1896, quoted in Cole 2001:32–3).

Boas sought out primary materials of all sorts, but especially texts recorded in the Native languages (retellings of myths, dreams, ideas, etc.), which he considered to be the best source of accurate and authentic ethnographic data (Berman 1996:220). Since few First Nation peoples in the Pacific Northwest were fluent in English at this time, however, such texts were difficult to elicit by non-linguists. Boas' fine ear for languages enabled him to proceed quickly. But he could not undertake the task of such large-scale ethnographic and linguistic recording and mapping alone. He therefore organized his Jesup Expedition around teams of ethnographers. For its first field season in the Pacific Northwest, he appointed Harlan I. Smith, assistant curator of the archaeology collections at the American Museum of Natural History, to undertake the archaeological component of the project. Boas also brought along Livingston Farrand, a colleague in psychology from Columbia University, to assist with the general ethnographic field research. The only problem here was that neither Smith nor Farrand had had any previous field experience in this region. In fact, Farrand was a complete novice, having had no previous ethnographic field experience in Aboriginal North America. He had joined this expedition at his own expense, in order to gain some field experience under Boas' tutelage.

To overcome the linguistic and cultural limitations of his co-workers, Boas appointed Teit. The latter's fluency in the Nlaka'pamux language and two years of field research under his close supervision qualified him well to work on the JNPE project. As Boas explained in his first Jesup Expedition report, Teit had begun his Jesup research even before the arrival of the expedition team in British Columbia (Boas 1898a). Boas also designated Spences Bridge to be the initial site for his Jesup research in North America. He had outlined in letters how he wanted Teit to prepare for his visit. Teit had responded accordingly: "I have been preparing the Indians here for your taking their pictures. If you bring a camera I think you will have no trouble getting a lot of both men and women" (Teit to Boas, 10 March 1897, AMNH-BTC). Teit also prepared his friends and neighbors for the plaster casting process that Boas planned to use to document human facial features. He noted that without such preparation most would be reluctant to participate (Thom 2001:141).

Boas' goal was to travel by way of the Cariboo Wagon Road from Spences Bridge to Bella Coola. A seasoned horse-packer, Teit planned this trip carefully, even advising Boas that he and his colleagues would need to bring little with them: "Regarding the camping outfit required," wrote Teit in April 1897, "you will not need to buy any of it. I will furnish it all. All you have to bring will be your blankets and any other thing you may wish in that line. Also anything you think best as a protection against mosquitoes and flies which are bad in some parts of the country through which we will pass" (Teit to Boas, 29 April 1897, AMNH-BTC; Fig. 45). Due to Teit's careful planning, the New York-based research team was able to launch into its work immediately on arriving at Spences Bridge. As Boas noted after measuring and photographing people and collecting ethnographic objects: "It was not much effort . . . Teit had prepared everything for us very well. The Indians were ready for us promptly yesterday afternoon, and we could not work quickly enough to finish with all of them" (F. Boas to M. Boas, 5 June 1897, Rohner 1969:202).

The party of four worked incessantly on a variety of projects, from plaster casting, photography and recording songs: "We can be satisfied with the results of our first two days here. If it only will continue this way!" (F. Boas to M. Boas, 5 June 1897, Rohner 1969:202). And it did continue. At the end of the third day, Boas wrote to his wife:

> We seem to be finished here with the castings. I let Farrand and Smith make the casts ready for shipping. This afternoon Jimmy Teit and I went down to the village

and collected melodies. The phonograph works very well, and we got ten good songs.... I can really be satisfied with my first few days here. We got eleven casts and many photos, a few measurements and three songs (Franz Boas, 5 June 1897, Rohner 1969:202).

Boas also noted that he had obtained explanations of the various designs on woven baskets, jewelry, and masks (F. Boas to M. Boas, 14 June 1897, Rohner 1969:205). In addition to helping Boas and Farrand, Teit also made time to acquaint Smith with some of the archaeological sites along the banks of the Thompson River. Boas could not have wished for a more productive beginning to his Jesup Expedition.

On June 14, Boas, Farrand, and Teit headed north to the central interior, leaving Smith behind to continue his archaeological work at Spences Bridge, Kamloops, and Lytton. Because Teit had organized everything, including four riding horses, five pack horses, and three guides, who traveled behind on foot, Boas and Farrand had little to do but to follow Teit. The travel was slow, however, and Boas expressed frustration in his letters about the monotony of the trip. He was particularly concerned about the time required to pack and unpack the horses. He was also disappointed to find most of the aboriginal villages along the way to be completely deserted. He commented repeatedly that people had "scattered" in all directions. This was late spring, a time when women traveled to their favorite berry-picking and root-digging areas. Men may have accompanied them to catch fresh fish or meat. "I will be very glad when we finally reach the coast," he wrote to his wife. "I am fed up with these trips into the wilderness" (F. Boas to M. Boas, 6 July 1897, Rohner 1969:208). At Puntzi Lake, on the Chilcotin plateau, the party dropped Farrand to undertake a month-long field study of language and oral narrative traditions. Meanwhile Boas continued with Teit onto Bella Coola where he had arranged to work with George Hunt. The son of an English Hudson's Bay Company employee and a high-ranking Tlingit woman, Hunt had grown up among, and married into, the Fort Rupert

Kwakwa̱ka'wakw. Boas met him in 1886. Later he comissioned him to mount an artifact exhibit and organize a performing group for the World's Columbian Exposition in Chicago in 1893 (Cole 1985: 122–40; Berman 1996).

After seven weeks of slow horse travel, Boas and his party arrived at Bella Coola on 20 July 1897. Teit and the guides remained there for three days before beginning the return trip to Spences Bridge. They carried with them the plaster casts and artifacts the group had collected on the trip north. While Boas worked with Hunt at Bella Coola and later at Rivers Inlet, and with Charles Edenshaw at Port Essington, Teit continued the ethnographic work in the more southerly regions that he had been doing prior to Boas' arrival: collecting myths, working on the language, and revising his Nlaka'pamux ethnographic report.

Boas returned to New York in late September 1897 and wasted no time booking Teit for further ethnographic fieldwork. With the Upper Nlaka'pamux research well underway, Boas was eager for Teit to begin documenting adjacent groups—the Lower Thompson and the Lillooet. Teit agreed to do this, reporting to Boas by April 1898 that he had completed two weeks of field research at Spuzzum, which included collecting thirty-one myths and a range of artifacts: a stone pipe, two stone hammers, and a copper *spek* (Teit to Boas, 6 April 1898, AMNH-BTC). By September 1898, Teit had completed another two months of fieldwork among the Lillooet (Teit to Boas, 28 August 1898, AMNH-BTC). Although this was his first field research beyond his home community, it went well: "I found the Lillooets to be a very fine people—the most tractable and kindest I was ever amongst. I had no difficulty with them in any way. The Pemberton people especially were very good" (Teit to Boas, 8 October 1898, AMNH-BTC). "My notes on customs alone," he wrote to Boas, "fill 122 pages and I have also gathered many stories." He brought home about 110 artifacts, the majority of which were baskets, and a large collection of myths. After spending the fall writing up his Lower Thompson report (Teit to Boas, 11 November 1898, AMNH, BTC), Teit returned to Lillooet country again, reporting to Boas in July 1899 that this field research had also gone well (Teit to Boas, 12 July 1899, AMNH-BTC). In addition to seventeen artifacts, including some very fine baskets, he had collected more oral narratives, bringing his total number of Lillooet stories to sixty (Teit to Boas, 19 July 1899, AMNH-BTC).

Early in the year 1900, with *The Thompson Indians* in press (Teit 1900), Boas urged Teit to write up his Lillooet field notes: "What are you doing with your Lillooet material? Do you expect to find time soon to send me your notes?" (Boas to Teit, 7 February 1900, AMNH-BTC). Teit replied a week later that he would send him "some (perhaps all) this spring" (Teit to Boas, 16 February 1900, AMNH-BTC). Boas was now so delighted with Teit that he proposed a five-year research plan:

> I should like to suggest to you to commence systematic work in this line by writing down texts in the Indian language with interlinear translation, and putting down at the same time material for a dictionary. It is best to select for the texts, on the one hand traditional material, such as myths, and on the other hand material in the form of conversations or speeches, because the grammatical forms that occur in the latter are, on the whole quite different from those found in the former. I hope you will be willing to undertake this work, and I believe I shall be able to set aside a certain amount of money to compensate you for the time that you devote to this matter. I think if you could continue work of this kind for four or five years, we shall be able to obtain a very full dictionary and grammar of the Thompson language (Boas to Teit, 27 January 1900, AMNH-BTC).

In July 1900, Boas made his second and final field trip to the Northwest Coast under the auspices of the Jesup Expedition. As he had done in 1897, Boas started out at Spences Bridge where he spent a week working with Teit prior to heading to Alert Bay to work with William Brotchie, George Hunt, and others.

After Boas' departure, Teit undertook two months of field research in August and September 1900 among the Shuswap and Chilcotin: "I have now interviewed old men belonging to High Bar, Big Bar, Canoe Creek, Dog Creek, and Alkali Lake," he wrote to Boas (Teit to Boas, 20 September 1900, AMNH-BTC). "I had one man living with me for three weeks under wages, and pumped him until he got tired." Teit was pleased with his results: "I think I have obtained the great majority or nearly all the stories remembered by the Fraser River Shuswap" (Teit to Boas, 21 October 1900, AMNH-BTC). By November, he had crated and mailed to Boas some seventy items gathered during this trip (Teit to Boas, 15 November 1900, AMNH-BTC). Meanwhile, he continued his work on his Lillooet report for the JNPE series noting that, "I am writing the whole out in chapters in the same way as you grouped my paper on the Thompsons." He worked hard on this: "As I am writing steady every night I expect to be able to send you the whole paper before very long. As soon as I have finished it, I will commence to write out the Shuswap myths" (Teit to Boas, 23 November 1900, AMNH-BTC). Teit hoped to get to the more westerly bands of the Shuswap the following summer: "I think it will be a wise thing if you can see your way clear to send me as early as possible next summer to the Shuswaps of Canim Lake, Upper North Thompson and Shuswap Lake. . . . If this were done I would be able to write out a paper on the whole Shuswap tribe in the same way as the Lillooet and Thompsons have been dealt with" (Teit to Boas, 23 November 1900, AMNH-BTC). Finally, early in the year 1901, Teit sent Boas the last chapters of his Lillooet report (Teit to Boas, 26 February 1901, AMNH-BTC).

After a six month trip to the Shetlands in 1902, Teit resumed his work for Boas: "I am going up Nicola on the fourteenth to collect myths there," he wrote to Boas in July 1902, "and I expect it will take me until the end of the month" (Teit to Boas, 12 July 1902, AMNH-BTC). Later, he noted that he would be willing to go to the coast to work among the Lower Fraser people. "Please give me full directions for the carrying out of same" (Teit to Boas, 19 November 1902, AMNH-BTC).

By mid-March 1903, Teit had completed this work.

Perhaps due to the success of the field research undertaken by Teit and Hunt, Boas decided against a field trip in 1903. As he explained to Teit: "I am sorry to say that I shall not be able to go out West this summer. I have not had time so far to work out the material that I collected three years ago, and so I think it better to stay here and finish that work. I shall send $400 for your Shuswap work within a few days. I am looking forward to your next shipment" (Boas to Teit, 1 April 1903, AMNH-BTC). Just one month later, Boas outlined to Teit a five-year research plan:

> I wish you would take the time before you start to think over the further development of your work on the Shuswap, and also the extension of your work on the Okanogon [sic] and the Salish tribes of Washington. I should like very much to be able to continue your work in the whole region, which you know so well, and to push it a little more rapidly than we have been doing these last few years. Could you not make some estimate, say, for a period of about five years, including in such an estimate the expenses for fieldwork during such period and a salary for yourself. I should like to see included in this work also the recording of texts in the Thompson language about which we have so often spoken. My idea would be that you should begin to write these texts down, and that after you have made a considerable collection, I should come out, and that we should spend together some time with the Indians, getting really thorough information on the grammar of the language (Boas to Teit, 5 May 1903, AMNH-BTC).

Teit responded that he needed financial compensation to do this: "I am quite willing to devote more of my own time to it (the southern tribes), if you could manage and afford to give me sufficient remuneration so I could be able to give up some other lines of work I at present partly depend on" (Teit to Boas, 14 June 1903, AMNH-BTC). Teit estimated that he would need $850 to cover five years of research at eight months per year.

By the end of the summer of 1903, Teit reported to Boas that he had "visited all the Shuswaps and their villages excepting the Spallumcheen and, of course, the Kootenai band. I got some additional information and cleared up some points, but on the whole I did not add much to the information I obtained from the Fraser River Shuswaps two or three years ago" (Teit to Boas, 24 August 1903, AMNH-BTC).

With his Shuswap report well under way by the following spring, Teit began to make plans for further work among the Okanagan. "Personally I feel much interested in the work," he wrote to Boas, "and will try to take an elderly man with me from this region, who is well acquainted with the Southern dialects, and interested in old things" (Teit to Boas, 25 May 1904, AMNH-BTC). "I think I will make a trip there this summer leaving in about two weeks time, and making the Okanagan River my objective point for this year. Going, I will pass through Similkameen where I will probably stay a short time, and returning I will visit Okanagan Lake. I am not sure yet if I will cross the Boundary Line with the pack train as there may be bother with the customs" (Teit to Boas, 13 May 1904, AMNH-BTC). By the middle of August, he had completed six weeks of work among the Okanagan (Teit to Boas, 12 August 1904, AMNH-BTC).

Meanwhile Boas, by 1904, had spent only five months in the field during the Jesup Expedition. His productive ethnographic exchange by mail with both Teit and Hunt, and his faith in both field researchers to work largely on their own for months at a time had eliminated the need for Boas to be on site. Smith and Farrand were similarly dependent on their mail correspondence with Teit to finalize their Jesup Expedition reports (Teit to Smith, 4 December 1899, AMNH-BTC).

Boas had not been pleased with his own fieldwork during the first Jesup season in 1897, mainly due to slow and awkward travel through the inland regions. And Farrand's month at Puntzi Lake had resulted in very sparse results. Meanwhile, Teit, who dealt with slow and awkward travel on a daily basis, had generated a rich ethnographic database. He had also become a sensitive and sophisticated fieldworker

who could negotiate easily between the world of his interviewees and that of his distant employers. For example, on the basis of unacceptable protocol, he refused to comply with the AMNH's request for signed receipts from aboriginal interviewees:

> To them 'touching the pen' is a very serious and solemn matter requiring much deliberation, and explanation, as for instance when they make an argument with the Government, or with some big *tyhee* about some important matter. It is also very unhandy for example in open camps, in all kinds of weather (raining or blowing) or perhaps pested with mosquitoes, or blinded with smoke, to get the Indian to mark a voucher for some little specimen I have purchased from him. Understanding the Indian mind about the thing as I do, it seems to me in the nature of a joke. I know it is business, but up to date New York City methods do not always work out in the wilds of B. C. Any way it is no check on me, for it would be easy for me to put crosses and Indian names on any amount of them, and no one would know whether they are genuine or not. Signatures are different, but not one Indian in 200 can sign his name. Even amongst the Whites it is not the style here (in small matters) when say you get a meal (as I may sometimes do when on a trip) to ask the waitress to sign a voucher for it (Teit to Boas, 10 March 1904, AMNH-BTC).

Teit's Place in the Publication Record of the Jesup North Pacific Expedition

Of the twenty-seven publications under the AMNH Jesup North Pacific Expedition series, Teit authored four: *The Thompson Indians* (1900), *The Lillooet* (1906), *The Shuswap* (1909), and *Mythology of the Thompson Indians* (1912). He was a major contributor to four others, acting as a field assistant (identifying sites, collecting artifacts) and consultant to Harlan Smith for the latter's *Archaeology of Lytton* (1899) and *Archaeology of the Thompson River* (1900a); facilitating the photographic work that formed the core of the Expedition's *Ethnographical Album of the North Pacific Coasts of America and Asia* (Boas 1900); and providing the bulk of the primary data featured in Livingston Farrand's *Basketry Designs of the Salish Indians* (1900). In comparison, Boas' written contributions were substantially smaller, consisting of five JNPE publications, of which three (Boas and Hunt 1905, 1906; Boas 1909) drew heavily on the research of George Hunt, and two (Boas 1898b, 1898c) drew on data provided by Charles Edenshaw, a Haida artist at Port Essington, and an unidentified storyteller at Bella Coola. Teit's monographs on the Thompson, Lillooet, and Shuswap, were also the only full ethnographic overviews ("basic ethnographies") of the individual aboriginal groups completed for the Northwest Coast segment of the JNPE and published under the Expedition's series.

Conclusion

The Jesup North Pacific Expedition was one of the great expeditions of American anthropology (Fitzhugh and Crowell 1988:14). Historian Douglas Cole described it as "the most cherished" of Boas' museum projects. It was, he notes, "the showpiece of Boas' association with the American Museum of Natural History" (Cole 2001:29). For Boas it was also important for establishing American anthropology as a field-based discipline. It is ironic, therefore, that other than two short field trips to the Northwest Coast in 1897 and 1900, the JNPE marked the end of Boas' longterm fieldtrips. After the JNPE, his fieldwork consisted of a small archaeological study in the American Southwest, followed by two short trips to British Columbia in 1914 and 1923 and a longer one in 1930. In fact, the JNPE helped establish Boas as a supervisor of distant teams of resident fieldworkers. The key members of the British Columbia field team were Teit and Hunt, who submitted their results regularly to Boas by mail. Boas' decision to move away from on-site field research may be a consequence of the problems he encountered during his 1897 field season, especially the inconvenience and expense of cumbersome travel through the inland areas of British Columbia. Shortly after the JNPE, he concluded that ethnography produced by observers who had command of the language and who were friends with the Native peoples was of a higher quality

than that of the scholarly types "who had to work through an interpreter" (Jacknis 1996:221).

Clearly Boas had Teit and Hunt in mind when he made this statement, as by the end of the Jesup Expedition, he had secured both as long-term, dedicated assistants. In the case of Hunt and the ethnography of the Coastal region, Boas could claim some credit as a co-fieldworker. But Teit's case was different. Although Boas had tried to do fieldwork in the Interior regions, he never managed to accomplish anything close to what he had accomplished on the Coast. Indeed, without Teit, the JNPE ethnographic record for the interior regions would have been weak. For this reason, Teit deserves to be recognized today as more than a "JNPE informant" or a "Boas' research assistant," but rather as a full and productive JNPE team-member who made a lasting contribution to the anthropology of aboriginal North America.

Acknowledgements

First, I would like to thank Igor Krupnik and Laurel Kendall for planning this special volume and working so diligently with us to bring it to completion. I am especially grateful to Sigurd Teit, who supported my work on his father with such enthusiasm and generosity over the years. In particular, I would like to thank Sigurd for donating the photographs of his father, James Teit, and of the historical Spences Bridge community that appear in this essay. Special thanks to my workstudy student assistant, Quinn Dupont for his work on the photographs that appear in this essay. I also extend my thanks to the British Columbia Provincial Archives in Victoria, BC, the Kamloops Museum, Kamloops, BC, and the American Museum of Natural History in New York for allowing me to reproduce photographs from their collections.

Notes

1. Anthropologist Ronald Rohner's reference to Teit as "one of Boas' principal informants" (Rohner 1966:183) is typical.

2. Anthropologist Roderick Sprague has argued similarly that Teit's contribution to the study of Plateau ethnology, folklore, linguistics, and ethnographic analogy in archaeology has often been "overlooked by researchers in that culture area" (Sprague 1991:103).

3. James changed his surname from Tait to Teit on arriving in Canada (Sigurd Teit, personal communication).

4. Many names have been applied to the "Interior Salishan" peoples who occupy the south central interior of British Columbia. In the early published ethnographic record, they were called the "Thompson," the "Okanagan," the "Shuswap," and the "Lillooet." In recent years, these anglicized names have been replaced by the indigenous names, spelled variously: "Nlaka'pamux," "Secwepemc," and "Sta'atl'imx." "Okanagan" has remained the same. Throughout this paper the terms are used interchangeably.

5. For fuller biographical details on Teit, see Pat Lean and Sigurd Teit (1995:3–60) and Wickwire (1993, 1998, 2002). There is some difference of opinion regarding Teit's early residency in British Columbia. According to Peter Campbell (1994:38), Teit spent time from 1887 until 1892 in Nanaimo working in the coal mines. Teit's son, Sigurd Teit, however, reports that his father spent only two weeks in the Nanaimo coal mines (Sigurd Teit, personal communication 1989).

References

Berman, Judith
1996   "The Culture as It Appears to the Indian Himself": Boas, George Hunt, and the Methods of Ethnography. In *Volksgeist as Method and Ethic: Essays on Boasian Ethnography and the German Anthropological Tradition*. George W. Stocking, Jr., ed. Pp. 215–56. History of Anthropology, 8. Madison: University of Wisconsin Press.

Boas, Franz
1895   The Tinneh Tribes of Nicola Valley. In *The North-Western Tribes of Canada—10th Report of the Committee*. Report of the Sixty-Fifth Meeting of the British Association for the Advancement of Science, vol. 8, pp. 295–7.
1896   The Limitations of the Comparative Method of Anthropology. *Science*, n.s. 4:901–08.
1898a   The Jesup North Pacific Expedition. *The Jesup North Pacific Expedition*, vol.1, pt.1, pp.1–12. *Memoirs of the American Museum of Natural History*, vol. 2. New York: G.E. Stechert.
1898b   Facial Paintings of the Indians of Northern British Columbia. *The Jesup North Pacific Expedition*, vol.1, pt. 2, pp. 13–24. *Memoirs of the American Museum of Natural History*, vol. 2. New York: G.E. Stechert.
1898c   The Mythology of the Bella Coola Indians. *The Jesup North Pacific Expedition*, vol.1, pt. 2, pp. 25–127. *Memoirs of the American Museum of Natural History*, vol. 2. New York: G. E. Stechert.
1900   *Ethnographical Album of the North Pacific Coasts of America and Asia: Jesup North Pacific Expedition*. New York: American Museum of Natural History.
1909   The Kwakiutl of Vancouver Island. *The Jesup North Pacific Expedition*, vol. 5, pt. 2, pp. 301–522. *Memoirs of the American Museum of Natural History* 8. Leiden: E.J. Brill; New York: G.E. Stechert.

Boas, Franz, and George Hunt
1905   Kwakiutl Texts. *The Jesup North Pacific Expedition*, vol. 3. *Memoirs of the American Museum of Natural History* 5. Leiden: E.J. Brill; New York: G.E. Stechert.
1906   Kwakiutl Texts (Second Series). *The Jesup North Pacific Expedition*, vol. 10, pt. 1, pp. 1–269. *Memoirs of the American Museum of Natural History* 14. Leiden: E.J. Brill; New York: G.E. Stechert.

Campbell, Peter
1994   Not as a Whiteman, not as a Sojourner: James A. Teit and the Fight for Native Rights in British Columbia, 1884–1922. *Left History* 2(2):37–57.

Cole, Douglas
1973   The Origins of Canadian Anthropology. *Journal of Canadian Studies* 7(1):33–45.
1985   *Captured Heritage: The Scramble for Northwest Coast Artifacts*. Vancouver: Douglas and McIntyre.
2001   "The Greatest Thing Undertaken by any Museum": Franz Boas, Morris Jesup, and the North Pacific Expedition. In *Gateways. Exploring the Legacy of the Jesup North Pacific Expedition*. Igor Krupnik and William W. Fitzhugh, eds. Pp. 29–70. Contributions to Circumpolar Anthropology 1. Washington, DC: Arctic Studies Center.

Farrand, Livingston
1900   Basketry Designs of the Salish Indians. *The Jesup North Pacific Expedition*, vol.1, pt.5, Pp.393–99. *Memoirs of the American Museum of Natural History*, 2. New York: G.E. Stechert.

Farrand, Livingston, and W.S. Kahnweiler
1902   Traditions of the Quinault Indians. *The Jesup North Pacific Expedition*, vol.1, pt.3, pp.77–132. *Memoirs of the American Museum of Natural History* 2. New York: G.E. Stechert.

Fitzhugh, William, and Aron Crowell, eds.
1988   *Crossroads of Continents: Cultures of Siberia and Alaska*. Washington, DC: Smithsonian Institution.

Jacknis, Ira

1996   The Ethnographic Object and the Object of Ethnology in the Early Career of Franz Boas. In *Volksgeist as Method and Ethic: Essays on Boasian Ethnography and the German Anthropological Tradition.* George W. Stocking, Jr., ed. Pp.185–214. History of Anthropology, 8. Madison: University of Wisconsin Press.

Lean, Pat, and Sigurd Teit

1995   Introduction. In *Teit Times* 1 (Summer):3–5.

Rohner, Ronald

1966   Franz Boas: Ethnographer on the Northwest Coast. In *Pioneers of American Anthropology.* June Helm, ed. Pp. 149–222. Monograph of the American Ethnological Society 43. Seattle: University of Washington Press.

Rohner, Ronald, ed.

1969   *The Ethnography of Franz Boas: Letters and Diaries of Franz Boas Written on the Northwest Coast from 1886 to 1931.* Chicago: University of Chicago Press.

Smith, Harlan I.

1899   Archaeology of Lytton, British Columbia. *The Jesup North Pacific Expedition*, vol.1, pt.3, pp. 129–61. *Memoirs of the American Museum of Natural History*, 2. New York: G.E Stechert.

1900a   Archaeology of the Thompson River Region, British Columbia. *The Jesup North Pacific Expedition*, vol.1, pt. 6, pp. 401–42. *Memoirs of the American Museum of Natural History*, 2. New York: G. E. Stechert.

Sprague, Roderick

1991   A Bibliography of James A. Teit. *Northwest Anthropological Research Notes* 21(1):103–15.

Teit, James A.

1900   The Thompson Indians of British Columbia. *The Jesup North Pacific Expedition*, vol.1, pt. 4, pp. 163–392. *Memoirs of the American Museum of Natural History*, 2. New York: G.E. Stechert.

1906   The Lillooet Indians. *The Jesup North Pacific Expedition*, vol. 2, pt.5, pp. 192–300. *Memoirs of the American Museum of Natural History*, 4. New York: G.E. Stechert.

1909   The Shuswap. *The Jesup North Pacific Expedition*, vol.2, pt. 7, pp. 443–813. *Memoirs of the American Museum of Natural History*, 4. E.J. Brill: Leiden; New York: G.E. Stechert.

1912   Mythology of the Thompson Indians. *The Jesup North Pacific Expedition*, vol.8, pt. 2, pp. 199–416. *Memoirs of the American Museum of Natural History*, 12. E.J. Brill: Leiden; New York: G.E. Stechert.

The Shetland Times

1904   Obituary: Death of Mr. John Tait, Merchant, Lerwick. *The Shetland Times*, 24 December.

Thom, Brian

2001   Harlan I. Smith's Jesup Fieldwork on the Northwest Coast. In *Gateways. Exploring the Legacy of the Jesup North Pacific Expedition, 1897–1902.* Igor Krupnik and William W. Fitzhugh, eds. Pp. 139–81. Contributions to Circumpolar Anthropology 1. Washington, DC: Arctic Studies Center.

Wickwire, Wendy

1993   Women in Ethnography: The Research of James A. Teit. *Ethnohistory* 40(4):539–62.

1998   We Shall Drink from the Stream and So Shall You: James A. Teit and Native Resistance in British Columbia, 1908–22. *Canadian Historical Review* 79(2):199–236.

2002   "The Grizzly Gave Them the Song:" James Teit and Franz Boas Interpret Twin Ritual in Aboriginal British Columbia, 1897–1920. *American Indian Quarterly* 25 (3):431–52.

Franz Boas and an "Unfinished Jesup" on Sakhalin Island: Shedding New Light on Berthold Laufer and Bronislaw Pilsudski

KOICHI INOUE

Sakhalin Island, which was inhabited by three groups of the North Pacific indigenous people—the Paleo-Asiatic Nivkh (Gilyak), Tungusic Uilta (Orok), and the Ainu—was included in the original fieldwork and operational plan of the Jesup North Pacific Expedition (JNPE) at a very early stage (cf. Boas 1905:92,99). However, none of the Sakhalin Native nations were represented in the subsequent JNPE publications, except for the Nivkh featured in a special monograph contributed by Lev (Leo) Shternberg. His monograph entitled "The Social Organization of the Gilyak," however, was not published with other volumes under the main JNPE publication series nor in any related contemporary proceedings. For several reasons, it remained in a manuscript form for several decades, until its recent publication by the American Museum of Natural History in 1999 (Shternberg 1999; Grant 1999; Kan 2001).

The first section of this paper reviews and assesses the "unfinished" fieldwork conducted on Sakhalin Island within the framework of JNPE in 1898–9. The second section deals with Franz Boas' presumed concerns about the quality of the JNPE Sakhalin data and his desire to expand the study of Sakhalin indigenous people. The latter was clearly demonstrated through Boas' post-JNPE relationship with two Sakhalin-focused scholars: Leo (Lev) Shternberg and Bronislaw Pilsudski.

Laufer's JNPE Fieldwork on Sakhalin

Berthold Laufer (1874–1934), a German orientalist, was appointed by Boas in 1897 as the first participant in the JNPE Siberian operations (Boas 1903; Kendall 1988; see also Cole 2001:36–7; Vakhtin 2001:75–6). Having just received his doctorate from the University of Leipzig with a thesis on Tibetan texts, Laufer arrived in Sakhalin via San Francisco, Vladivostok and Khabarovsk on July 10, 1898. This started his field survey of the Sakhalin Island and its Native people that lasted eight months—until March 21, 1899.[1] During his eight-month stay in Sakhalin, Laufer studied three local Native languages, the Nivkh, Tungusic [Orok?], and Ainu, and visited the northern, central, and southern sections of the island (Freed *et al.* 1988a:12–3; Kendall 1988:104).

From a preliminary published account of his fieldwork (Laufer 1900a), it appears that Laufer began his Sakhalin survey with visits to the Nivkh (Gilyak) villages near the mouths of the Tym and Nabyl Rivers and along the shore of the Sea of Okhotsk, in the present-day Nogliki District (*rayon*). These were the residences of the so-called "Tro-Gilyak" whose main villages were *Milk-vo, Nabyl-vo, Lun'-vo, Tyrmits, Nyi-vo, Chay-vo*, and *Kaekr-vo* (Laufer 1900a:315). Laufer laconically writes: "I visited them [i.e., seven above mentioned villages—K.I.] in the summer of 1898" (ibid).

It was probably on this first survey that Laufer also paid a brief visit to "the village of Wal" (today's Val—K.I.) and its vicinity, in expanding his ethnographic exploration to the "Olcha" people. These were actually not the Olcha/Ulchi (who reside on the Siberian mainland, along the Amur River) but the Orok/Uilta, who still comprise the core of the present-day residents of the village of Val, about 50 km north of the eastern Sakhalin district center, the town of Nogliki. Laufer collected a number of valuable ethnographical specimens (see his brief description of amulets in: Laufer 1900a:326–7). He also observed a series of traditional Orok funeral rites and ceremonies. In his brief published account (Laufer 1900a:327–9), he presented a fairly short, though detailed information on certain Orok funeral practices, such as placing coffins on trees or on high wooden frames, and, in particular, about the funeral of a drowned hunter. By September 1898, Laufer sent the following field report to Boas:

> I have taken about [a] hundred [anthropometrical] measurements and carried on investigations on the physical types and the culture of those tribes [i.e. the Nivkh and Orok (Tungus)—K.I.], particularly regarding their decorative art, of that I have obtained interesting specimens together with good explanations, daily life, fishing and hunting, social organization, shamanism, medicine and so on; as to their healing methods, I got a very important collection of amulets...[for protection] from diseases and representing the figures of various animals [quoted from: Kendall 1988:104].

Laufer also recorded songs and folktales on wax cylinders by making use of the Edison phonograph. In March 1899, he even requested from Boas "a small instant camera" with the aim to secure visual documentation of what he observed in the field. In response, Boas recommended that he hire a professional for field photography. Laufer followed his recommendation promptly.[2]

Judging from the aforementioned field reports, we may assume that Laufer was, or at least tried to be, faithful to the initial fieldwork instructions given to him by Boas in 1897, to write a "rounded" ethnography of the Sakhalin Native people. Meanwhile, Laufer's specific and keen interest in the patterns of Native decorative art was already clearly manifested in his reports.

In early September 1898, Laufer fell seriously ill with influenza and was obliged to attend to his health for two-and-a-half months (Laufer 1899b:733).[3]

This two-and-a-half month time roughly corresponds to a period from September to mid-November, when, upon recovery from the influenza (and also pneumonia contracted among the Gilyak—see Freed et al., 1988a:13), Laufer resumed his field survey. He stopped first for five days at the village of Rykovskoye [now called Kirovskoye] where he observed a Nivkh bear festival, and then proceeded southward on horseback, and reached the valley of the Poronay River (Laufer 1899b:733). Here he arrived at the southern portion of the territory occupied by Uilta (Orok) people in Sakhalin. Laufer summarized his trip as follows:

> I visited the whole valley of the Poronai [Poronay River] as far as the mouth of the river on a reindeer sledge, and stayed for some time in the large Tungus village Muiko,[4] where I had the great pleasure of obtaining additional information in regard to the texts which I had recorded during the preceding summer. I have measured almost the whole population of this area and collected statistical information. . . . In December I reached Tikhmenevsk [present-day city of Poronaysk—K.I.], which is called Siska by the natives. . . . On the following day I started on an excursion eastward, in which I was particularly fortunate and successful. I obtained many specimens and much information on the Shamanistic rites and the ceremonials of the natives (Laufer 1899b:733).

With regard to Laufer's Orok survey, we should pay special attention to the fact that he not only collected museum specimens, but also recorded sound information on wax cylinders and made ethnographic notes. Laufer's Sakhalin wax cylinders and field notes deserve serious investigation, if they can be found (see Keeling 2001:280). Since we have Pilsudski's contemporary comparable ethnographic and phonographic materials on the Orok (Pilsudski 1985, 1987, 1989), it would be desirable to make a comparative analysis between the two sets of documentation.

Although Laufer wrote: "There are a great many errors in Schrenck's descriptions of the tribes of Saghalin"[5] (Laufer 1899b:733), it was Laufer himself who made an error when he said: "The Orok tribe, to which he [i.e., Schrenk—K.I.] refers, does not exist" [cf. Laufer 1901:36], since the "Tungus", the "Olcha", or the "Olcha Tungus" in Laufer's denomination were nothing but the Orok (Uilta) (cf. Demidova 1978:119).

The area of Taraika through which the Poronay River flows was also inhabited by the so-called Taraika Ainu. Laufer first met them on his visit to the villages of Tarankotan and Taraika (present-day town of Ust'ye) located across the river. He later visited the Orok villages of "[U]nu, Muiko and Walit, having passed the famous lake of Taraika"[6] (Laufer 1899b:734).

On December 31, Laufer returned to Siska and on January 2, 1899, he

> "[s]tarted by dog-sledge for Naiero [present-day town of Gastello—K.I.], where I had the best results in my work with the Ainu. Then I visited all the settlements on the [east] coast as far as Naibuchi,[7] which is 260 versts from Siska. This journey was exceedingly difficult, and sometimes even dangerous" [ibid].

In fact, Laufer encountered numerous difficulties during his fieldwork among the Ainu. First, a winter dog-sled trip along the coast-line was physically very trying, and Laufer experienced a near drowning in icy water when his sledge broke through the thin ice (Laufer 1899b:734; Kendall 1988:104). Second, he suffered from the lack of an operational language, since Russian was entirely unknown among the Ainu. Laufer was forced to make full use of his knowledge of the Japanese language, with which, however, the Sakhalin Ainu were barely familiar at that time (Laufer 1899b:732). Third, and probably the most serious, gaps in communication and shortage of time (even though he spent almost a month on that trip), resulted in Laufer's inability to gain the confidence of the local Ainu. That was obvious from his very poor data on physical anthropology, since he did not succeed in obtaining any anthropometrical measurements among the Ainu, except for a single "man of imposing stature" in Korsakov. Laufer attributed his failure to the extreme superstitions of the Ainu (Laufer 1899b:733).

Some comments to Laufer's trouble and methods he used were noted in a letter to Leo (Lev) Shternberg written in 1903 by Bronislaw Pilsudski:

> Several days ago I heard that he [i.e., Laufer—K.I.] had taken measurements of eight Ainu people in Korsakov and paid to each one by ten bottles of spirits. I don't intend, of course, to give either spirits or such amount of money that may be equal to the [price of] spirits, and the question is, whether I will be able to obtain those [Ainu] who are willing to be measured (Pilsudski 1996:212–3, Letter no. 59).[8]

Laufer summarized his evaluation of the field survey on the Ainu in the following manner:

> I succeeded in obtaining a great deal of ethnological material and information, traditions, and a large amount of grammatical and lexicographical material, although a short time only was available for this purpose. . . . I am well satisfied with the results of my ethnographical researches among these people. I have obtained full explanations of their decorative designs (Laufer 1899b:733–4).

I am of the opinion that Laufer did *not* record Ainu texts on wax cylinders. Despite the fact that he widely informed others about his success in recording Gilyak and Orok songs by the phonograph (Laufer 1899a:36), no other mention is found with regard to his Ainu recordings. On the contrary, an additional message runs as follows: "The only difficulty is that the instrument cannot be used in the winter, owing to the effect of severe cold" (Laufer 1899b:732). As we know, his Ainu survey was conducted exactly in the mid-winter, through the month of January.

Toward the end of January, Laufer arrived on horseback in Korsakov, the southernmost town of the Sakhalin Island. Although he intended to return from there northward along the west coast of the island, this idea proved to be impossible, due to the lack of any reliable means of communication in winter. Hence, he was obliged to return following the same track he used before, and proceeded "[a]s rapidly as possible in order to reach Nikolaievsk[9] in time", i.e., by the end of March. Thus in the morning of March 4, 1899, he returned to the starting point of his Sakhalin journey (Laufer 1899b:734), most probably the town of Aleksandrovsk, the Russian military post and sea-port situated on the Northwest coast of Sakhalin Island. Here, he finished writing his field report cited above.

Was Laufer's Sakhalin expedition successful? As far as his own accounts are concerned, it appears that Laufer was fully confident that he had fulfilled the whole task assigned to him by Boas, and that the data he collected would enable him to write a "rounded" ethnography of the Sakhalin people, i.e., the Gilyak, the Orok, and the Ainu. In addition to those field reports quoted above (Laufer 1899a, 1899b, 1900a), Laufer published a few other pieces with some data gathered during his Sakhalin trip. These include his short monograph on the decorative art of the Amur River people (Laufer 1902); two short articles on rock-paintings (Laufer 1899c, 1901); an article dealing with the issue of the "Koropokguru" and "Tonchi" [prehistoric people on Sakhalin Island—K.I.] (Laufer 1900b); a single linguistic paper on Ainu numerals and phonology (1917a); and a fairly long paper on the origin of reindeer breeding in Siberia, in which he covered the Orok reindeer economy extensively (Laufer 1917b).

Laufer's ethnography of the Nanay (Gold) people of the Amur River was once announced on the list of forthcoming JNPE publications as its Volume IV, Part II, entitled *The Gold* (Boas 1905:94). However, this monograph was never published and, moreover, as Sergei Kan recently pointed out, was "probably never written" (Kan 2001:232). Besides, the Nanay are not among the Sakhalin indigenous people, as they reside along the Amur River on the mainland.

Then, why did Laufer never publish his advertised monograph on the Gold (Nanay) nor those on the Gilyak, Orok, and Ainu? Since I was unable to look through the voluminous personal correspondence between Laufer and Boas at the American Philosophical Society in Philadelphia, I can only speculate in trying to find a reasonable explanation. Even taking into account the various

other collections made by Laufer on his Sakhalin trip, including the ethnographic specimens now at the AMNH, the wax cylinders, his field notes, and manuscripts, it is beyond my present focus to evaluate Laufer's legacy as a whole, that of a great scholar who produced more than 200 scientific publications (Anonymous 1934:352–62; Hummel 1936:103–11). Laufer's further career was different from his early fieldwork on Sakhalin Island, as he "stood out primarily as an ethnologist, and perhaps his chief contribution was the application of the principles of ethnology to historic civilizations" (Kent 1934:349; Gale 1935:137). Therefore I am eager to confine my role here simply to a very general evaluation of what Laufer could (as well as what he could not) achieve during his eight-month-long Sakhalin fieldwork.

As to the former, Laufer's contribution regarding his collection of ethnographic specimens has been already examined by several modern curators. Here one may refer to Laurel Kendall's unpublished review of Laufer's collection from the Amur River area (Kendall 1986), as well as to the most recent evaluation of Laufer's ethnographic collections from the entire Sakhalin-Amur River region (Roon 2000). As far as Laufer's Ainu collection at the AMNH is concerned, it was carefully examined recently by Prof. Y. Kotani from Nagoya University and his team (Kotani *et al.* 1993). According to their report, 418 Ainu items are preserved at the AMNH altogether, of which Laufer collected thirty-eight items in 1898–1900. Although only nine items are registered as obtained on the east coast of Sakhalin, we may safely conclude that the whole set of thirty-eight specimens was collected on Sakhalin, including three pieces of nettle robe, six "moustache lifters," and other utensils for everyday use (Kotani et al. 1993:118–20). This Ainu collection, though not numerous, well represents the Sakhalin Ainu culture at the turn of the twentieth century, at a time when the Ainu barely retained many traditional forms of their culture. In this sense, Laufer's collecting was a successful enterprise, and we may well call him a successful field collector not only of Ainu, but probably also of Orok and Nivkh (Gilyak) specimens. It would be desirable for the Orok and Nivkh items obtained by Laufer to be also re-examined and re-assessed in the same way.[10]

With regard to what Laufer could not have achieved during his Sakhalin journey, I cite another quote from Pilsudski's letter to Shternberg written at Rykovskoye on September 4, 1898:

> Oh yes, I have forgotten about a main issue. Young Doctor Laufer from Berlin, who is a member of an American expedition, has already been here. He heard of me still in Vladivostok and wanted to drop in Aleksandrovsk, but he didn't come. Then, I left for Rykovskoye. Hence, it was just here where we got acquainted with each other. He called upon me with another German, i.e., an engineer.[11] . . . Laufer has remained at Natro. He has with him an interpreter, i.e., a German deportee. Laufer himself does not understand even a word in Russian, and it is interesting to see what will come out. He is going to stay the whole winter. Although I did not say anything definite, I was and am ready to give advice, but he showed very little interest, and more often kept silent during his visit. Despite my proposal that I would answer him whatever he might be eager to ask about, he appeared the second time not at the appointed hour, and the following day he departed. I do not know what will occur further. I did not give him my own notes, but I shall not refuse him in any advice and guidance (Pilsudski 1996:161–2, Letter no. 46).

Pilsudski's depiction of Laufer and his circumstances on Sakhalin—however subjective and personal it might be—is the sole source so far that may disclose Laufer's real posture and behavior in the field. What was particularly disappointing to me was Laufer's invariable reluctance to ask for Pilsudski's insight and advice, notwithstanding the latter's repeated offers. No further communication between the two ever took place after the expedition. I deeply regret this situation, since it was Laufer who could have benefited from Pilsudski's consultation and help. Pilsudski was then the only person on Sakhalin Island who was engaged in the study

of its Native people, the Nivkh, the Orok, and the Ainu. Therefore, he was an invaluable resource and the only available consultant at the very beginning of Laufer's fieldwork. Besides, no language barrier existed between the two, since Pilsudski was fully proficient in German.

With regard to Laufer's language competence, Pilsudski referred that "Laufer himself does not understand even a word in Russian." Although this was an exaggeration (since Laufer had mastered Russian in his student years), often a foreigner who is competent in reading Russian, hardly understands the speech of Russian village people, let alone the Russian speech of indigenous people in Siberia. I encountered this exact situation during my early fieldwork in Siberia. I wonder if Laufer, when placed in a similar situation, might not have become fully dependent upon his local interpreter, "a German deportee." While Laufer used Russian as his operational language in the Nivkh and Orok surveys, he was unable to while among the Ainu, as mentioned above. It was great loss that Laufer did not resort to asking for Pilsudski's help, since the latter was by that time already proficient in Sakhalin Ainu to a certain extent.[12]

It has to be taken into consideration that Laufer was rushed into his Sakhalin fieldwork very shortly after his doctorate course in philology, presumably with little if any training and preparation for field research (Cole 2001:36). The Sakhalin Island trip for the JNPE was his first experience conducting an ethnological survey in this distant and inhospitable terrain, meaning that he was obliged to educate himself in the field. In addition, he spent two-and-a-half months of his Sakhalin journey recuperating from infectious diseases he had contracted there. Eventually, he finished an ethnological survey of the Sakhalin Island Nivkh, Orok, and Ainu within five-and-a-half months.

And yet, as seen from his field reports and early publications, Laufer was confident that he had fulfilled the whole task assigned to him by Boas and that Laufer was well satisfied with the results, even from his less successful Ainu survey. Are we then to call Laufer's

Sakhalin expedition a "success"? I wish to refrain from any final judgment for the time being, since many of Laufer's Sakhalin materials are still missing and no full account of his Sakhalin survey has been found. Some of his manuscripts may still be discovered, as happened recently with Pilsudski's unpublished work and other materials (Pilsudski 1996, 1998a, 1998b; Inoue, 1997b). But, it may also be possible that Laufer was too proud and too rigorous of himself to produce a substantial ethnographic monograph with a level of preparation that he came to consider as insufficient. Or else, he simply did not like the idea of writing the "rounded" ethnography he was assigned to produce.

In the meantime, Pilsudski maintained a keen interest in Laufer's achievements and continued to ask Shternberg for information regarding Laufer's publications. The references are numerous during the following years: "What has Laufer written on the Gilyak? Where is it published?" (Pilsudski 1996:178, Letter no. 51 written in 1902); "Did Laufer publish anything? I should like to have his works not only on the Gilyak but also the Ainu as the result of his trip on Sakhalin" (ibid, p. 212, Letter no. 59 written in 1903); "Did Laufer write, didn't he?" (ibid, p. 259, Letter no. 81 written in 1910). If Laufer ever knew of Pilsudski's persistent interest in his work, would that have helped to change his mind and initiate some contact between the two scholars if not *during* than *after* Laufer's JNPE Sakhalin-Amur survey of 1898–9?

And lastly, I refer to a statement made by Boas in 1902, two years after Laufer's return from his JNPE fieldwork, when his Siberian collections were already processed at the AMNH and most of his Sakhalin contributions were already published and/or written down. In his summary paper on the Jesup Expedition presented at the International Congress of Americanists in New York, Boas asserted that : "[A]t the present time we are unable to state definitely what the relations of the Gilyak and Ainu to the other isolated Siberian tribes[13] may have been. ... It remains for future researches to show whether these tribes may definitely be classed

with the Northeast Siberian tribes" (Boas 1905:99). This may be a signal of Boas' growing dissatisfaction with what Laufer achieved during his Sakhalin survey. I assume that this might have prompted Boas to contact Shternberg for additional data on the Nivkh (Gilyak) and to try to enlist Pilsudski to conduct new Ainu studies several years after the completion of the JNPE.

Pilsudski's "Second Expedition" to Sakhalin: A Non-Journey?

"I hear from a friend of mine, Mr. L. Sternberg that you are interested in Aino-folklore" (Inoue 1999a:115). This was the opening sentence of Bronislaw Pilsudski's first letter to Franz Boas, written on December 19, 1907, in Zakopane, a resort Polish town in western Galicia, then under the Austrian rule. Thus started Pilsudski's relationship with Franz Boas through the introduction of Leo (Lev) Shternberg.

Bronislaw Pilsudski (1866–1918), a Polish Siberian anthropologist was born in the manor of Zulow (present-day Zalavas) in Wilna province (today's Lithuania), which had been annexed to the Russian Empire.[14] In 1887, when he was 19 years old, Pilsudski, a freshman at St. Petersburg University, was arrested on the charge that he had been involved in an abortive conspiracy to assassinate the Russian Czar, Alexander III. Pilsudski was sentenced to penal servitude for 15 years and exiled to the Sakhalin Island. He remained in the Russian Far East for 19 years (Fig. 46), first as a "state criminal" in Sakhalin (1887–97) and later as a "deported peasant" (1897–1906). After the Russian-Japanese War of 1904–5, he managed to return—via Japan, the U.S., and Western Europe—to the Polish province of Galicia, then under Austrian rule. He died in Paris on May 17, 1918. Pilsud-ski's death, often referred to as a suicide, occurred just six months before the Polish statehood was resurrected owing to the efforts of his younger brother, the future Polish military dictator, Jozef Pilsudski (1867–1935).

In 1899, Pilsudski was able to leave Sakhalin Island for Vladivostok, the main Russian port city on the mainland, where he found a job as a custodian at the Museum of the Society for the Study of the Amur Region. But, as early as 1901, he fell into depression and apathy. His old friend, correspondent, and a Sakhalin co-exile, Lev Shternberg tried to help him by organizing new fieldwork for Pilsudski through the Imperial Academy of Sciences. "Knowing that the sole medicine for him is the work, and understanding that nobody can carry it out better than Pilsudski," Shternberg organized a trip to Sakhalin for Pilsudski (Latyshev 1996:395). Thus, in July 1902, Pilsudski commenced his new fieldwork among the Ainu on Sakhalin Island where he had previously spent twelve years as a political prisoner. This was Pilsudski's "first Sakhalin expedition," which was extended for two more years (1904–5) at Pilsudski's own request in 1903 under the sponsorship of the newly founded Russian Committee for the Study of Central and East Asia[15] (Inoue 1985:8).

Pilsudski's fieldwork in Sakhalin (1902–5) was highly successful despite the interruption of the Russian-Japanese War of 1904–5. Shortly before the war broke out, Pilsudski took part in an unsuccessful Russian expedition[16] (1903) to the Hokkaido Ainu, headed by a Polish ethnographer and writer, Waclaw Sieroszewski[17] (Inoue 2003). Pilsudski collected valuable ethnographic specimens, recorded folklore texts—especially on wax cylinders[18]—and took numerous photos of the Ainu, Uilta (Orok), Nivkh (Gilyak), and Nanay (Gold) (Figs. 47–49; see also Latyshev 1998).

Six letters sent by Pilsudski to Boas between 1907–16 are preserved at the Franz Boas' Collection at the Archives of the American Philosophical Society in Philadelphia (APS-BP), of which I reproduced the five then available in an earlier Japanese publication (Inoue 1990:309–18). Upon re-reading Pilsudski's six letters to Boas[19] at the APS as well as his numerous letters to Shternberg (cf. Pilsudski 1996), I have come to the conclusion that Boas had helped Pilsudski a great deal between the years 1908 and 1918. Boas answered all Pilsudski's letters promptly[20]; he published Pilsudski's article on the Ainu in the *Journal of American Folk-lore*

(Pilsudski 1912a); and he most probably acted as a go-between in the sale of Pilsudski's photos to various American museums (Figs. 46–49)[21]. He also persisted in encouraging Pilsudski to continue his scientific work. However, Pilsudski's biggest morale boost came, I believe, when he was asked by Boas to go on a new Sakhalin expedition in 1909. Although this trip never materialized, the fact remained that Boas—one of the leading anthropologists of the time—regarded Pilsudski as a first-ranking expert on the Sakhalin Ainu.

Presumably, in the beginning of 1909, Pilsudski wrote to Shternberg:

> Several days ago, I received also a letter from Boas, who wrote [to] me to send a proposal to Chicago Museum, which might probably dispatch me to collect ethnographical specimens among the Ainu. Boas considers that Sakhalin Ainu artifacts are more preferable to the Hokkaido ones, although the Hokkaido Ainu might be more interesting for me. He thinks that the whole expense may be 6000 dollars (Pilsudski 1996:240, Letter no. 68).

And later he informed Shternberg about his progress in this task in another letter (stamped as March 8, 1909), saying: "I have sent my proposal to Chicago, asking for 2000 dollars for my work and living during 9–10 months" (Pilsudski 1996:243, Letter no. 71). In the next letter to Shternberg (no. 72), however, Pilsudski reported that "From Chicago I have received no answer, even though I asked to let me know by telegram about the decision, so as to prepare for my departure as early as possible. Now I want to write again, asking for the answer. I had better write to Boas himself" (Pilsudski 1996:245; the date is missing). Presumably, Pilsudski wrote a new letter to Chicago, and on May 10, 1909, he informed Boas that:

> [I] have received the answer from Dr. Dorsey, who writes me [that] Chicago Field Museum wishes [to] send me to the Ainu and will take steps to secure the sum of 6000.00$ and request You to ascertain what I might undertake to the journey (APS-BP, no. 470; Inoue 1999a:123).

On October 10, 1909, Pilsudski wrote the first letter to Shternberg from Paris:

> Not the slightest answer from either Dorsey or Boas. I asked Boas to give me instructions, as to what I should pay attention to. I would agree to go to Sakhalin, if he considered it indispensable, even if I myself had planned a trip to Northern Hokkaido. Boas wrote in reply that he didn't write to me, since he had heard nothing from Dorsey. Here [i.e., in Paris—K.I.] Prof. Manuorte[22] told me that Dorsey worked in a very large museum, and that I should turn up the heat, but how and in what way? I understand myself that this is the only way-out for me. But, how to break through? I wrote to Hawes[23] who was currently professor at Madison, but I have received no reply. I want to ask Kennan[24] who once promised me help, if it was necessary (Pilsudski 1996:248, Letter no. 75).

And, on November 7, 1909, Pilsudski again wrote to Shternberg from Paris:

> I got a letter from Dr. Dorsey, who was already in Europe and six weeks afterwards was planning to come to me in Lwow. I answered that I was at the moment in Paris and preferred to see him here. And, in case he could not come, I would try to appear wherever he asks (Pilsudski 1996:250, Letter no. 76).

Pilsudski's next letter to Shternberg (the date is missing but the letter was most probably sent in November 1909) includes the following direct quotation from Dorsey's letter, which runs:

> I thank you for the references you gave me in Cracow and will be glad to call upon your friends. I shall probably not reach Galicia for two or three months yet. I am sorry there has been this delay in our getting together, but I will warn you that you cannot in any sense consider yourself as employed by the Field Museum until I have taken the matter up formally with my Director and secured his permission, and before this can be brought about, it is necessary that I should talk the situation over with you. I say this, feeling lest you might be disappointed (Pilsudski 1996:252, Letter no. 77).

Pilsudski's letter to Shternberg (no. 76) goes on:

> I'm writing the same to Boas, who will be surprised at the fact that Dorsey has not seen me yet, since he promised Boas to do so on leaving the US. I want to propose Dorsey two plans: one is that I remain here for a year in order to learn more English, to work on what could be done by treating the materials at hand, to look up more literature, and to obtain practical training both in photography and anthropometry. The other plan is to start a field trip this winter, if he is in a hurry and doesn't want to postpone it. And anyway, if there were something for me to receive in St. Petersburg, I should secure it (Pilsudski 1996:250–1).

Meanwhile, commenting bitterly on Dorsey's letter, Pilsudski writes to Shternberg:

> Consequently, it delays, he writes to me nothing of when we shall meet, obviously three months later and not earlier, and he will still return to America and have a talk with the director, although in his first letter he said that he was going to discuss with the director. No doubt, there cannot be any trip in 1910. There can be a better development, too. But, I'm afraid that nothing will come of it and it will be necessary for me to do something, without any expectation (Pilsudski 1996:252, Letter no. 77).

It seems to me that Pilsudski never met with Dorsey, since I have found no reference to this meeting in his letters to either Shternberg or Boas. And, consequently, his second Sakhalin expedition did not take place at all—not only in 1910 but also later, as Pilsudski had anticipated. The reason(s) and the cause(s) of why the idea was eventually dropped remain unknown. My guess is that too many personal motives were involved.

George Amos Dorsey (1868–1931), an American anthropologist, held the position of curator in charge of Anthropology at the Field Columbian Museum of Natural History in Chicago from 1898 to 1915. He took a three-year leave (1909–12) from his museum work and traveled abroad as a foreign correspondent for *The Chicago Tribune* (Calhoun 1991:153–4). Therefore, although he arrived in Europe in 1909, he was surely too busy to meet Pilsudski even in Paris. In Europe, Dorsey was acting not as a Field Museum curator but primarily as a journalist. Besides, I wonder if the well-documented personal hostility between

30/ Kwakiutl Indians dancing at the Chicago Worlds Fair. Photographer, John H. Grabill, 1893 (AMNH 337217).

31/ Franz Boas, with George Hunt and his family, Fort Rupert, B.C. Photographer, Oregon C. Hastings, November 1894 (APS neg. # 466)

[To page 464.]

SONG OF HA'MSHAMTSES.

1. Hamasa'yā'lag·ilā haisai yē hamāmamai.
   Trying to look for food all around   yē   hamāmamai.
   the world
2. Bā'bakuayā'lag·ila haisai yē hamāmamai.
   Looking for men all around the   yē   hamāmamai.
   world
3. Q'ula' mEnsāyag·ila haisai yē hamāmamai.
   Life   swallowing all around the   yē   hamāmamai.
   world
4. Xa'xauquayā'lag·ila haisai yē hamāmamai.
   Looking for heads all around the   yē   hamāmamai.
   world

TUNE, RECORDED BY F. BOAS.

32/ Musical notation by Franz Boas: Song of Ha'mshamtses. Reprinted from: Franz Boas, The Social Organization and Secret Societies of the Kwakiutl Indians, Report of the U.S. National Museum for 1895. 1897, p.697

145

33/ Hamatsa skull rattle (Kwakiutl). Collected by George Hunt in Quatsino, B.C., 1899. Photo by Lynton Gardiner, (AMNH Cat. #16/6897, neg. 2A 19017)

34/ Pit house, Spences Bridge, B.C. Photographer, Harlan Smith, 1897 (AMNH 42776)

35/ Wax cylinder machine: Edison Standard Phonograph with horn, ca. 1900. Photo by Carl Fleischhauer. Library of Congress, American Folklife Center

36/ Lucy Antko, wife of James Teit, one of the six singers recorded by Franz Boas at Spences Bridge, B.C., 1897. Photographer, Harlan Smith, 1897 (AMNH 22695)

37/ James Teit and two friends in Lerwick, Scotland, prior to his departure to Canada. Courtesy of Sigurd Teit

38/ James Teit's uncle John Murray in British Columbia, circa 1888. Courtesy of Sigurd Teit

39/ Spences Bridge, 1887. Note John Murray's white cottage is visible on the left. His store is the large building in the center of the photograph. Courtesy of the Kamloops Archives (Kamloops, BC)

40/ Spences Bridge, circa 1890. This photo shows Spences Bridge on both sides of the Thompson River. Courtesy of Sigurd Teit

41/ Drying salmon on the beach on the north side of the Thompson River, just below John Murray's store. Courtesy of Sigurd Teit.

42/ James Teit and his wife Lucy Antko, 1897 (AMNH 11686)

43/ James Teit in his cabin at Tswall Creek. Courtesy of Sigurd Teit

44/ James Teit and George Tomaxkain on the banks of the Thompson River, 1890. Courtesy of Sigurd Teit

45/ James A. Teit and Harlan I. Smith's pack train, Spences Bridge. Courtesy of the British Columbia Provincial Archives, Vancouver.

46/ Bronislaw Pilsudski, three "Oltchi" (Ulchi) men, and a local settler. Studio photo. Original hand-written caption by Pilsudski: "Oltchi (Mangun) from Amur River. Three standing men are Oltchi (the middle is son of a Chinese man and Oltchi woman), the sitting I am (the left) and a Jew (the right)." (SI-NAA 041253.00)

47/ Sakhalin's Ainu bear festival. Photographer, Bronislaw Pilsudski. Original handwritten caption by Pilsudski: "Ainu of Saghalien. The bear-fest. The bear is wounded." (SI-NAA 047396.00)

48/ Sakhalin Ainu women. Photographer, Bronislaw Pilsudski. Original Pilsudski's caption: "Ainu of Saghalien. Women scraping the fiber of the great nettle." (SI-NAA 047380.00)

49/ Sakhalin Ainu bear festival. Photographer, Bronislaw Pilsudski. Original caption by Pilsudski: "Ainu of Saghalien. The bear-feast. The feast about the killed bear." (SI-NAA 047398.00)

Dorsey and Boas (cf. Freed *et al.* 1988b:97–8) might have contributed to the collapse of the planned new Sakhalin affair.

In the meantime, Boas was eager to help Pilsudski in the venues he controlled. In 1908, Boas tried to publish Pilsudski's abundant Ainu folklore material in the U.S.[25] Boas advanced this possibility to an AMNH patron, Arthur Curtis James, by asking him a direct question: "Would you be sufficiently interested in this matter to let me look over the material in detail and give you a more definite report regarding the value and the status of his manuscripts?" (Franz Boas to A. C. James, June 6, 1908, APS). Although this proposal failed, it is evident that Boas was seriously interested in Pilsudski's Ainu material and regarded it very highly. At the end of his letter to A. C. James, Boas presented his evaluation: "I am reasonably certain from what I know about it that it is exceedingly unlikely that material of this kind could ever be duplicated" (ibid.).[26]

In Lieu of a Conclusion

Notwithstanding his passion and endeavor, Boas could not succeed in either obtaining the desired publications from Laufer's Sakhalin survey nor in incorporating Shternberg's as well as Pilsudski's contributions into the JNPE proceedings. Hence, the Jesup Expedition program on Sakhalin Island remained "unfinished" for several decades to come. Sakhalin Island, or more properly the larger Sakhalin-Amur River area, was of critical importance to Boas. This portion of the trans-Pacific "Jesup region," from the Amur River in Northern Asia to the Columbia River in North America presented a unique cultural area, where the deeply rooted cultural impact from, and connections with, the ancient agricultural civilizations of China, Korea, and Japan met with the hunter-gathering cultures of the North Pacific indigenous people. This was why, in my view, Boas tried very hard to organize a multidisciplinary study of this area under the JNPE program. He asked Laufer and Fowke, an archaeologist, to do the same job that he had assigned to Bogoras and Jochelson in more

northerly areas in Northeast Siberia as well as to Smith, Swanton, and others (but first and foremost to himself) on the Northwest Coast of North America. However, neither Laufer nor Fowke were in any way comparable to Bogoras, Jochelson, or to Boas himself, as field researchers.

Due to repeated failures of Boas' several attempts to document the culture, the Sakhalin-Amur area remained one of the least studied sections under the JNPE program and for years afterwards. The initial effort was not completed until almost ninety years later. In 1998, the Mouton de Gruyter Publishers started the publication of *The Collected Works of Bronislaw Pilsudski* in seven volumes. The first two volumes are already printed (Pilsudski 1998a, Pilsudski 1998b). The first volume, entitled *The Aborigines of Sakhalin,* contains twenty of Pilsudski's articles on the Ainu, Nivkh (Gilyak), and Uilta (Orok), which had been published previously in various languages (Russian, Polish, Japanese, etc.), and have been translated into English by the volume's editor, Prof. Alfred F. Majewicz from Poznan. The second volume is a modern reprint of Pilsudski's only Ainu monograph published in his lifetime (Pilsudski 1912b), with the addition of *An Ainu English Index Dictionary to B. Pilsudski's Materials*, compiled by Alfred and Elzbieta Majewicz (Pilsudski 1998b). Subsequent volumes include Nivkh/Gilyak folklore texts, the Orok grammar and dictionary, vocabularies of the Nanay and Olcha languages, and other contributions by Pilsudski, which were discovered recently as unpublished manuscripts. These works were mainly the products of Pilsudski's first Sakhalin expedition of 1902–5.

As *The Collected Works of Bronislaw Pilsudski* will be finally available to scholars eighty years after the death of their author, it is safe to say that Pilsudski was one of the critical figures in the ethnography of the Sakhalin-Amur region. He was a contemporary of the Jesup Expedition efforts and was in contact with some of its key participants, like Boas, Laufer, and Shternberg. Therefore, we have but to regret that Pilsudski's expertise was never used by Laufer during his field work on Sakhalin. Nor was Franz Boas fortunate in the following years in strengthening his cooperation with Pilsudski—either through American publication of his folklore materials in 1907–8 (Inoue 1999a:115–20) or in arranging Pilsudski's "second Sakhalin expedition" of 1909–10 that never materialized.

Acknowledgements

This paper is a substantially revised version of the original presentation delivered at the Franz Boas' Centenary Conference in New York (November 13–17, 1997; Inoue 1999b). In the present paper, the original sections that dealt with the relationship between Shternberg and Pilsudski are omitted, and a new section focused on Berthold Laufer's work on Sakhalin Island was added, thanks to the suggestion of Igor Krupnik. My thanks are due, first of all, to Igor Krupnik, for his persistent encouragement and support; to Prof. Jiro Ikegami, Hokkaido University; and to my colleagues at the Slavic Research Center, Hokkaido University, for their valuable comments to the earlier draft of this text. I am also grateful to Paula Fleming from the National Anthropological Archives (NAA), Smithsonian Institution and to the NAA staff for assistance and permission to use four of Pilsudski's original Sakhalin photographs as illustrations to this paper.

Notes

1. This is confirmed by one of Laufer's earliest reports published in *Globus*, which says that "[D]r. Laufer left New York in May 1898 and traveled to Sakhalin Island via Japan and Vladivostok where he lived among the various local races from Summer 1898 until March of 1899." (Laufer 1899a:36).

2. See one of the studio portraits of the Amur River people that Laufer ordered to be taken (Fitzhugh and Crowell 1988:25).

3. The place where Laufer fell ill was most probably the village of *Natro* (Pilsudski 1996:161).

4. Without doubt, this was not a Tungus (i.e., Evenk) but the Uilta (Orok) village, since *Muiko* was known as an Orok summer campsite on the Poronay River (Oral communication by Prof. Jiro Ikegami).

5. The book referred to here is by Leopold von Schrenck (1881–95).

6. Lake Nevskoye on present-day maps.

7. A contemporary Russian name is Ust'-Dolinki.

8. All quotations from Pilsudski's letters that have been published in Russian (see Pilsudski 1996) were translated into English by myself.

9. The town of Nikolayevsk-na-Amure, the main Russian administrative center located on the continent, is at the mouth of the Amur River, across the Mamiya/Tatar Strait from the Sakhalin Island.

10. This task was recently fulfilled by Tatyana P. Roon from the Sakhalin Regional Museum (Roon 2000). For over nine months, between December 1998 and September 1999, she conducted an extensive survey of the Amur and Sakhalin ethnographic collections preserved at the various American museums.

11. Friedrich Kleie, an oil prospector. Cf. Pilsudski 1996:309, Note 99.

12. A testimony thereto was given by John Batchelor who met Pilsudski in Hokkaido in 1903. Batchelor writes: "I met this gentleman [i.e., Pilsudski—K.I.] in Sapporo several years ago and the only language we could properly converse in was Ainu! He in Saghalien Ainu and I in Yezo." (Batchelor 1938:3).

13. Evidently, the Chukchi, Koryak, Even, and the Yukagir, surveyed by other JNPE Siberian teams.

14. Main biographical sources on Bronislaw Pilsudski in English are: Inoue 1985; Sawada 1985; Kowalski 1995; Majewicz 1998.

15. The Chairman of the Committee was Prof. Vasily V. Radloff, then Director of the Russian Imperial Museum of Anthropology and Ethnography (Kunstkamera). Shternberg was appointed as the Committee's executive secretary. Concerning the Committee, see Inoue 1999b:146.

16. The expedition was organized by the Russian Imperial Geographical Society and the Russian Academy of Sciences. Being invited as the only Ainu expert in Russia, Pilsudski joined the team directly from Sakhalin. It was on this occasion that he met John Batchelor in Sapporo (see above note 11 and also Inoue 2003)

17. Waclaw Sieroszewski (1858–1945), a Polish revolutionary exile to Siberia, was an author of the basic ethnography on the Sakha

(Yakut) people (Seroshevskii 1896). From his trip to Hokkaido, he published two small pieces of travelogue entitled *"Wsrod kosmatych ludzi"* (Among the Hairy People) in1926 and *"Volcano Bay"* (1903). Both were included in Sieroszewski's *Collected Works*, vol.18 (1961).

18. It appears that Pilsudski followed Laufer's example of making use of the Edison phonograph in recording Native language and folklore. In 1981, some eighty years afterwards, more than eighty original phonographic cylinders on which Pilsudski had recorded Ainu folklore texts and which were preserved at A. Mickiewicz University in Poznan, Poland, gave birth to the so-called ICRAP (the International Committee for the Restoration and Assessment of Bronislaw Pilsudski's Work). ICRAP has been engaging in editing and publishing *The Collected Works of B. Pilsudski*, in seven volumes, under the editorship of Prof. Alfred F. Majewicz of A. Mickiewicz University in Poznan.

19. They are registered as "Franz Boas Papers, nos. 1169; 414; 470; 607; 472" (APS-BP), and a letter without any catalog number (Inoue 1999a).

20. Unfortunately Boas' letters to Pilsudski are not preserved at the APS, except for one carbon copy (APS-BP, no. 524a), which is reproduced in: Inoue 1999a:130-1. Nevertheless, there are signs of Boas' answers, as indicated by handwritten messages found on a letter sheet: "F.B./ Ordered July 7, 1914" and "Answered July 7th" (APS-BP, no. 472; Inoue, 1999a:127-8).

21. APS-BP, no.607; Inoue 1999a:125.

22. Latyshev's reading for this name notwithstanding, it was in fact French physical anthropologist Louis Pierre Manouvrier (1850–1927), that Pilsudski had referred to here. For this clarification, I want to thank Aleksandr M. Reshetov of the Museum of Anthropology and Ethnography (MAE) in St. Petersburg, who has kindly confirmed its Cyrillic spelling as "Manuvriye," looking up the original hand-written letter.

23. Charles H. Hawes, a British traveler, who published a book on the Russian Far East entitled *In the Uttermost East* (1903).

24. George Kennan, an American journalist, who published several books, including an excellent essay, *Siberia and the Exile System* (1891).

25. On Dec.19, 1907, in his first letter to Boas, Pilsudski made a proposal to deliver a complete set of Ainu folklore texts (240 tales and120 riddles) to be published in America, if he were guaranteed a monthly income of $120 for eight months (APS-BP, no.1169; Inoue, 1999a:117).

26. Pilsudski's Ainu folklore material was partially published by Boas in a short article (Pilsudski 1912a). Most probably, however, Boas meant here the whole material that Pilsudski had offered to Boas for publication (cf. note 25). It was printed in Poland as a more extended collection (Pilsudski 1912b). That was Pilsudski's only monograph published during his lifetime.

Reference

Anonymous
1934   On Laufer. Bibliography of Berthold Laufer, 1895–1934. *Journal of the American Oriental Society* 54:352–62.

Batchelor, John
1938   *An Ainu-English-Japanese Dictionary*. Tokyo: Iwanami-Syoten.

Boas, Franz
1905   The Jesup North Pacific Expedition. In *International Congress of Americanists, 13th Session, Held in New York in 1902*. Pp.91–100. Easton, PA: Eschenbach.

Calhoun, Michele
1991   Dorsey, George A. In *International Dictionary of Anthropologists*. Christopher Winters, ed. Pp.153–4. New York and London: Garland Publishing.

Cole, Douglas
2001   The Greatest Thing Undertaken by Any Museum? Franz Boas, Morris Jesup, and the North Pacific Expedition. In *Gateways. Exploring the Legacy of the Jesup North Pacific Expedition, 1897–1902*. Igor Krupnik and William W. Fitzhugh, eds. Pp. 29–70. *Contributions to Circumpolar Anthropology*, 1. Washington, DC: Arctic Studies Center.

Demidova, Ye. G.
1978   Issledovaniia Bertol'da Laufera na Sakhaline [Berthold Laufer's Research on Sakhalin Island]. In *Kul'tura Narodov Dal'nego Vostoka SSSR, XIX–XX vv.* L. I. and Yu. A. Sem, and L. Ye. Fetisova, eds. Pp. 116–22. Vladivostok: Akademiia Nauk SSSR.

Fitzhugh, William W., and Aron Crowell, eds.
1988   *Crossroads of Continents: Cultures of Siberia and Alaska*. Washington, DC: Smithsonian Institution Press.

Freed, Stanley A., Ruth S. Freed, and Laila Williamson
1988a   Capitalist Philanthropy and Russian Revolutionaries: the Jesup North Pacific Expedition (1897–1902). *American Anthropologist* 90(1):7–24.

1988b The American Museum's Jesup North Pacific Expedition. In *Crossroads of Continents: Cultures of Siberia and Alaska*. William W. Fitzhugh and Aron Crowell, eds. Pp. 97–103. Washington, DC: Smithsonian Institution Press.

Gale, Esson M.
1935 Berthold Laufer. *Journal of the North China Branch of the Royal Asiatic Society* 66:136–7. Shanghai.

Grant, Bruce
1999 Foreword. In Lev Shternberg. *The Social Organization of the Gilyak*. Bruce Grant, ed. Pp. xxiii–lvi. *Anthropological Papers of the American Museum of Natural History*, 82. New York.

Hummel, Arthur W.
1936 Berthold Laufer: 1874–1934. *American Anthropologist* 38(1):101–11. Bibliography prepared by Paul S. Martin, pp.103–11.

Inoue, Koichi
1985 A Brief Sketch of Br. Pilsudski: Until his Exodus from Sakhalin. In *Proceedings of the International Symposium on B. Pilsudski's Phonographic Records and the Ainu Culture*. Pp.1–9. Sapporo: Hokkaido University.
1990 B. Pilsudski's Letters to Franz Boas. In *Comparative Studies in Northern Cultures*. Yoshinobu Kotani, ed. Pp.309–26. Nagoya: Nagoya University.
1999a Bronislaw Pilsudski's Letters to Franz Boas. In *"Dear Father!": A Collection of B. Pilsudski's Letters, et alii*. Koichi Inoue, ed. Pp.115–31. *Pilsudskiana de Sapporo* 1. Sapporo: Hokkaido University.
1999b L. Shternberg and B. Pilsudski: Their Scientific and Personal Encounters. In *"Dear Father!": A Collection of B. Pilsudski's Letters, et alii*. Koichi Inoue, ed. Pp.133–55. Pilsudskiana de Sapporo 1. Sapporo: Hokkaido University.
2002a *B. Pilsudski in the Russian Far East: From the State Historical Archive of Vladivostok*. Koichi Inoue, ed. *Pilsudskiana de Sapporo* 2. Sapporo: Hokkaido University.
2002b *Sakhalin Ainu Folk Craft*. Vladislav M. Latyshev and Koichi Inoue, eds. Sapporo: Hokkaido Publication Planning Center.
2003 B. Piusutsuki to Hokkaido: 1903 nen-no Ainu chosa-wo tsuiseki-suru [*B. Pilsudski and Hokkaido: Tracing the Ainu Expedition of 1903*], In *Quest for an Entire Picture of B. Pilsudski's Far Eastern Indigenous Studies*. Koichi Inoue, ed. Pp. 11–31, Sapporo: Hokkaido University.

Kan, Sergei
2001 The "Russian Bastian" and Boas. Why Boas Shternberg's "The Social Organization of the Gilyak" Never Appeared Among the Jesup North Pacific Expedition Publications. In *Gateways. Exploring the Legacy of the Jesup North Pacific Expedition, 1897–1902*. Igor Krupnik and William W. Fitzhugh, eds. Pp.

217–56. *Contributions to Circumpolar Anthropology*, 1. Washington, DC: Arctic Studies Center.

Keeling, Richard
2001 Voices from Siberia: Ethnomusicology of the Jesup Expedition. In *Gateways. Exploring the Legacy of the Jesup North Pacific Expedition, 1897–1902*. Igor Krupnik and William W. Fitzhugh, eds. Pp. 279–96. *Contributions to Circumpolar Anthropology* ,1. Washington, DC: Arctic Studies Center.

Kendall, Laurel
1986 *Berthold Laufer and the Amur Collection at the American Museum of Natural History*. Unpublished manuscript preserved in AMNH.
1988 Young Laufer on the Amur. In *Crossroads of Continents: Cultures of Siberia and Alaska*. William W. Fitzhugh and Aron Crowell, eds. P. 104. Washington, DC: Smithsonian Institution Press.

Kent, Roland G.
1934 Berthold Laufer, 1874–1934. *Journal of the American Oriental Society* 54:349–51.

Kotani, Yoshinobu, T. Irimoto, T. Sasaki, H. Kirikae, K. Deriha, T. Ikeda, and H.-D. Oelschleger
1993 Hokubei no Shuyo Ainu Korekushon Ichiran [Lists of Main Ainu Collections at Various North American Museums]. In *Ethnological Study of Ainu Materials in North American Museums*. Yoshinobu Kotani, ed. Pp. 89–170. Nagoya: Nagoya University.

Kowalski, Witold
1995 The European Calendarium (Bronislaw Ginet-Pilsudski in Europe, 1906–18). *Linguistic and Oriental Studies from Poznan* 2:7–19. Poznan: Adam Mickiewicz University.

Latyshev, Vladislav M.
1996 Predvaritel'nyi otchet Bronislawa Pilsudskogo [A preliminary Report of Bronislaw Pilsudski]. *Vestnik Sakhalinskogo Muzeia* 3:394–7, Yuzhno-Sakhalinsk: Sakhalin Regional Museum.
1998 Nauchnoe nasledie Bronislawa Pilsudskogo v muzeiakh i arkhivakh Rossii [Scientific Legacy of Bronislaw Pilsudski preserved at Russian Museums and Archives]. *Izvestia Instituta nasledia Bronislawa Pilsudskogo* 1: 4–20. Yuzhno-Sakhalinsk: Sakhalin Regional Museum.

Laufer, Berthold
1899a Laufer's ethnologische Forschungen auf der Insel Sachalin. *Globus*, Bd.LXXVI:36. Braunschweig
1899b Ethnological Work on the Island of Saghalin. *Science*, n.s. 9(230):732–4.
1899c Petroglyphs on the Amoor. *American Anthropologist*, n.s. 1:746–50.
1900a Preliminary Notes on Explorations among the Amoor Tribes. *American Anthropologist*, n.s. 2: 297–339.
1900b Die angeblichen Urvoelker von Yezo und

Sachalin. *Centralblatt fuer Anthropologie, Ethnologie und Urgeschichte* 5(6):321–30. Jena.

1901　Felszeichnungen vom Ussuri. *Globus*, Bd.LXXIX (5):69–72, Braunschweig.

1902　The Decorative Art of the Amur Tribes. *The Jesup North Pacific Expedition*, vol. 4, pt. 1. *Memoirs of the American Museum of Natural History* 7. Pp.1–79. New York: G. E. Stechert.

1917a　The Vigesimal and Decimal Systems in the Ainu Numerals, with Some Remarks on Ainu Phonology. *Journal of the American Oriental Society* 37: 192–208.

1917b　The Reindeer and its Domestication. *Memoirs of the American Anthropological Association* 4(2):91–147.

Majewicz, Alfred F.

1998　The Scholarly Profile of Bronislaw Pilsudski. In *The Collected Works of Bronislaw Pilsudski*. Alfred F. Majewicz, ed. Pp.14–36. Berlin and New York: Mouton de Gruyter.

Pilsudski, Bronislaw

1912a　Ainu folklore. *Journal of American Folk-Lore* 25 (95):72–86.

1912b　*Materials for the Study of the Ainu Language and Folklore.* Cracow: Polska Akademia Umiejetnosci.

1985　Materials for the Study of the Orok (Uilta) Language and Folklore, I. *Working Paper of the Institute of Linguistics*, 16. Alfred F. Majewicz, ed. Poznan: Adam Mickiewicz University.

1987　Materials for the Study of the Orok (Uilta) Language and Folklore, II. *Working Paper of the Institute of Linguistics*, 17. Alfred F. Majewicz, ed. Poznan: Adam Mickiewicz University.

1989　*I z poyezdki k orokam o. Sakhalina v 1904 g.* [*From a Trip to the Orok on Sakhalin Island in 1904*]. Vladislav M. Latyshev, ed. Yuzhno-Sakhalinsk: Sakhalin Regional Museum.

1996　*"Dorogoi Lev Iakovlevich…" (Pis'ma L. Ia. Shternbergu. 1893–1917 gg.)* [*"Dear Lev Yakovlevich…" (Letters to L. Ya. Shternberg. 1893–1917)*]. Compiled, introduced, and annotated by Vladislav M. Latyshev. Yuzhno-Sakhalinsk: Sakhalin Regional Museum.

1998a　The Aborigines of Sakhalin. In *The Collected Works of Bronislaw Pilsudski*, vol.1. Alfred F. Majewicz, ed. Berlin and New York: Mouton de Gruyter.

1998b　Ainu Language and Folklore Materials. In *The Collected Works of Bronislaw Pilsudski*, vol. 2. Alfred F. Majewicz, ed. Berlin and New York: Mouton de Gruyter.

Roon, Tatiana

2000　Kollektsii narodov Amuro-Sakhalinskogo regiona v muzeiakh SShA (Ethnology Collections on the Peoples of the Amur and Sakhalin Regions in American Museums). *Izvestia Instituta naslediya Bronislawa Pilsudskogo* 4:139–57. Yuzhno-Sakhalinsk: Sakhalin Regional Museum.

Sawada, Kazuhiko

1985　B. Pilsudski in Japan. In *Proceedings of the International Symposium on B. Pilsudski's Phonographic Records and the Ainu Culture.* Pp.20–3, Sapporo: Hokkaido University.

Schrenck, Leopold von

1881–95　*Die Voelker des Amur-Landes.* In *Reisen und Forschungen im Amur-Lande in den Jahren 1854–6 im Auftrage der Kaiserl. Akademie der Wissenschaften zu St. Petersburg.* Bd. III. Pts.1–3. St. Petersburg: Eggers.

Seroshevskii, Vatslav (Sieroszewski, Waclaw)

1896　Yakuty: opyt etnograficheskogo issledovania (The Yakut. An Ethnographic Study). St. Petersburg: Izdanie Imperatorskogo Geograficheskogo Obshchestva.

1961a　Volcano Bay. In *Varia: Szkice podroznicze i wspomnienia.* Waclaw Sieroszewski, *Dziela*. Tom XVIII. Pp.201–8. Krakow: Wydawnictwo Literackie.

1961b　Wsrod kosmatych ludzi. In *Varia: Szkice podroznicze i wspomnienia.* Waclaw Sieroszewski, *Dziela.* Tom XVIII. Pp.219–74. Krakow: Wydawnictwo Literackie.

Shternberg, Lev

1999　The Social Organization of the Gilyak. Bruce Grant, ed. *Anthropological Papers of the American Museum of Natural History*, 82. New York.

Vakhtin, Nikolai B.

2001　Franz Boas and the Shaping of the Jesup Expedition Siberian Research, 1895–1900. In *Gateways. Exploring the Legacy of the Jesup North Pacific Expedition, 1897–1902.* Igor Krupnik and William W. Fitzhugh, eds. Pp. 71–89. *Contributions to Circumpolar Anthropology*, 1. Washington, DC: Arctic Studies Center.

Louis Shotridge and Indigenous Tlingit Ethnography: Then and Now

NORA MARKS DAUENHAUER
AND RICHARD DAUENHAUER

One of the lasting features of Franz Boas' work during and after the years of the Jesup Expedition was his collaboration with indigenous writers and intellectuals such as George Hunt for Kwakiutl, Henry Tate for Tsimshian, and Louis Shotridge for Tlingit. As far as we can tell, these relationships were productive and mutually beneficial, and resulted in scholarship of enduring quality and value. Details of how Boas' working relationships actually shaped the texts are only more recently attracting critical attention (Rohner 1969; Hymes 1985; Maud 1993, n.d.). In Tlingit, for example, Boas, working with Louis Shotridge, a Tlingit Indian from Klukwan, was able to document Tlingit phonology accurately for the first time (Boas 1917). This analysis has been confirmed by subsequent generations of linguists. For his part, Shotridge attended Boas' lectures at Columbia University, and he benefited greatly from Boas' training in phonetics and current anthropological theory and methods. Shotridge became the first Tlingit, and possibly the first Northwest Coast Native, with professional training in linguistics and anthropology. He led expeditions to the Northwest Coast, and between 1913 and 1929 he published several articles in the *University of Pennsylvania Museum Journal*, one of which is the subject of this chapter.

Louis Shotridge and the Jesup Expedition Connection

Although not a part or project of the Jesup Expedition per se, Shotridge's work belongs to the spirit of the Jesup Expedition era and is intimately linked to one of its major figures, Franz Boas. The beginning of their collaboration falls within the wider timeframe of the period, and, along with the work of John Swanton, it forms one of the cornerstones of Tlingit research and publication. His work with Boas seems to have been a pivotal event in shaping Shotridge's career. This chapter covers the biographical and historical background of the relationship and examines the mutual influence of Boas and Shotridge on each other's work. Focus is on the scholarly publications of language and folklore by Louis Shotridge, especially his 1920 article, "Ghost of Courageous Adventurer," and his role in the 1917 grammar of Tlingit by Boas.

The chapter examines and evaluates Louis Shotridge as a Tlingit intellectual in the western, academic sense of the term; as the first indigenous transcriber and translator of Tlingit oral literature; and as a stylist in English. He deliberately used archaic English and "poetic diction" in an attempt to retain the integrity of the original Tlingit style. The result is a highly crafted translation, but one that is awkward by modern standards and difficult for or even unintelligible in places to the average contemporary reader. Parallels between the stilted English and everyday Tlingit become clear when the English is back-translated into Tlingit (a work in progress by Nora Marks Dauenhauer, not included here). The heart of the paper is Nora Marks Dauenhauer's new English editing of Shotridge's 1920 translation.

Biographical Background and Early Career of Louis Shotridge

Louis Shotridge was born in 1882 in the Chilkat village of Klukwan, in southeast Alaska. He died in Sitka in 1937. He was the son and grandson of prestigious Tlingit leaders. His paternal grandfather, L Shaaduxísht (ca. 1819–1889) from whose Tlingit name the anglicized form "Shotridge" derives, was a leader of the Kaagwaantaan (Eagle moiety) Finned House (Keet Gooshi Hít), an off-shoot of the Kaagwaantaan Killer Whale House, and was one of the leaders of the 1852 Tlingit raid on the Hudson Bay trading post at Ft. Selkirk at the confluence of the Pelly and Yukon Rivers. His father was George Shotridge (1852–1917), whose Tlingit name was Yeilgooxú, and who was leader of the prestigious and famous Whale House (Yaay Hít) of the (Raven moiety) Gaanaxteidí. George was a friend of Lt. George Emmons, the famous ethnographer and collector among the Tlingit (see Kan, this volume), and both Louis' father and grandfather are well documented in historical writings and photographs. Shotridge's mother was Kudeit.sáakw of the Finned House Kaagwaantaan. Thus Louis belonged to the same house group as his paternal grandfather.

Louis Shotridge was no stranger to the English-speaking world. His family had a long history of interaction with Euro-Americans, and he was educated in the Presbyterian mission school. Louis' marriage to his first wife Florence was arranged by their families at birth, but their relationship blossomed at mission school. She was Susie F. Scundoo (c. 1882–1917), of the Mountain House Lukaax.ádi, whose Tlingit name was Kaatxwaantséx. Photographs show her to be a stunning beauty, and by all accounts she was a talented and charming woman. They were married on December 25, 1902, in Klukwan.

In 1905, Florence Shotridge was invited to demonstrate Chilkat weaving at the Portland International Exposition, and Louis accompanied her. There he met and impressed Dr. George Gordon of the University of Pennsylvania Museum, who a decade later hired Louis as an agent and to document the museum's Northwest Coast collection.

Milburn (1997) traces and examines a number of phenomena that converged in the lives of Louis and Florence Shotridge. The rise of tourism and the "curio" trade paralleled the start of museum collecting. At some point, Louis decided to become involved in the curio and collecting trade. He was no stranger to this activity, the Chilkat area being influenced by earlier museum collectors, such as the Krause brothers, Emmons, and various Presbyterian missionaries. The latter encouraged Native carving as crafts to generate revenue, while Sheldon Jackson was collecting traditional artifacts for his museum in Sitka (the future Sheldon Jackson Museum). Milburn observes that Shotridge's pursuit of an entrepreneurial career through his interaction with American society was consistent with the activities of his father and grandfather, and she suggests that this may be seen as an attempt to maintain his prestige within a rapidly changing Tlingit society (1997:103). Despite the high level of schooling in Southeast Alaska, only a small percentage of Natives succeeded in breaking into Euro-American professions. The "civilizing" rhetoric of Protestant missionaries was aimed at creating an indigenous laboring class. Perhaps Louis and Florence saw the curio market as a stepping-stone to become involved in professional, intellectual work.

The years from 1907 to 1911 were highly productive for the young couple. They hired tutors to teach them English and music. Florence was an accomplished pianist, and Louis is remembered for his outstanding baritone voice. They performed duets and toured with an Indian Grand Opera Company. From the time when Florence was first asked to demonstrate Chilkat weaving through their years of participation in Indian fairs and the Opera, the Shotridges functioned as what Milburn calls "cultural" entrepreneurs, re-inventing their "authentic" and "exotic" selves as the circumstances dictated (Milburn 1997:117). It is difficult to evaluate this phase of their careers, which seems embarrassing and stereotyped today. To some extent, Louis and

Florence may have "bought into" this style of presentation as the prevailing model, but even if they found it offensive and demeaning, living up to the popular stereotype may have been the only vehicle available to them at the time. As his later career demonstrates, Louis Shotridge constantly fought against the trivialization of Indian culture by the white establishment.

In 1910, Louis was offered a temporary position at the University of Pennsylvania Museum in Philadelphia. He was essentially a "show and tell," dressing in Plains Indian style to meet public expectation. Florence was the "Indian Princess." George Emmons urged the museum officials to hire Shotridge full time. Edward Sapir also wanted to hire him for the Canadian National Museum in Ottawa, but Louis decided to stay in Philadelphia. In 1912 he was admitted to the Wharton School of Finance and Economics, where he studied for two years. Through talent, ambition, and hard work, the Shotridges had achieved the educational and social refinements that were necessary to participate in the middle-class worlds of academe, museum patronage, and business administration (Milburn 1997:122). In 1913, Florence authored an article for the University of Pennsylvania Museum Journal (Shotridge 1913).

George Gordon, Franz Boas, and Shotridge's Flourishing Career

In the meantime, George Gordon had been busily developing an Anthropology Department at the University of Pennsylvania Museum (UPM). In the winter of 1914, he set up a meeting at Columbia University between Louis Shotridge and Franz Boas. For two months the two men worked together every morning recording Tlingit songs and phonetics. Some of the excitement of their working out the phonetics of Tlingit is recorded in Shotridge's letters of November 4 and 17, 1914, to Gordon (Milburn 1997:123–4,143). This research resulted in the publication of the first reliable Tlingit grammar (Boas 1917). While in New York,

Shotridge also attended Boas' General Anthropology classes at Columbia University and participated in weekly anthropological discussions with a group of peers. Although he did not receive a formal degree, Shotridge was the first academically trained Native American ethnographer from the Northwest Coast. This achievement earned him the authority to work unsupervised within the Euro-American art/culture system. In 1915, Gordon offered Shotridge full-time employment as Assistant Curator in the UPM North American Section. He worked for the museum for the next seventeen years, the first Native American from the Northwest Coast to be employed full-time within a museum context (Milburn 1997:124).

Growing interest in collecting texts in the indigenous languages positioned Native ethnographers such as Hunt and Shotridge in the forefront of scientific ethnography. Milburn's fascinating study of the evolution of anthropological thought during this period is beyond our scope here, and we only note the developing conflict between two personal and professional influences on Shotridge's life: the clash between Boas (and other "scientific professionals") and George T. Emmons, the amateur entrepreneurial pragmatist. Shotridge had great potential as a cultural insider with outside professional training. However, his circumstances were very complex, and ultimately he continued to be tokenized and stereotyped by the establishment. But still, Shotridge managed to use the system and to exploit it to his own professional agenda, which, as Milburn demonstrates, was congruent with the widely accepted progressive Tlingit societal goals of the era.

In 1915, Shotridge led the Wanamaker Expedition (1914–8) to Alaska (named after its sponsor, John Wanamaker, department store magnate and member of the UPM's Board of Managers; Milburn 1986:64–5), the first anthropological expedition led by an Alaska Native. Much has been written about Shotridge as a collector, and most of that has been rather negative (cf. Mason 1960; Carpenter 1975; Cole 1985; Price

1998). Milburn reviews and refutes this anti-Shotridge line of argument (Milburn 1997), and we agree with her. Shotridge's detractors have grossly oversimplified; much of their evidence is hearsay and is not borne out in reality. The situation in southeast Alaska was complex and times were changing rapidly. Shotridge had two major agendas: to show the greatness of Tlingit culture through the clan art; and to find an institutional sanctuary for Native art objects that were then being seen as obsolete, negative, or contested in a Tlingit society that was advocating assimilation to western norms, patrilineal inheritance, and Christianity. In particular, his collecting goals were then fully compatible with the "progressive" (modernist) cultural agenda of the Alaska Native Brotherhood, founded in 1912, of which Shotridge was elected Grand President in 1930. It seems unlikely that Shotridge would have been elected to the office of Grand President if his personal life and professional philosophy were not in keeping with the mainstream or majority of the membership.

Thus, in his collecting practices, Shotridge subscribed to a "salvage paradigm." Rather than being in conflict, the acquisition goals of the University Museum and the Tlingit assimilationists' goals of removing traditional art objects from the community were complementary with each other and with Shotridge's personal and professional goals. Milburn sees this as a synthesis of Native Tlingit and institutional Euro-American attitudes and desires (1997:268). Shotridge worked to preserve what he considered to be the strengths of his heritage without compromising Native American ability to achieve civil equality. In this regard Shotridge exemplified the Native American struggle of the early 1900s for recognition within the dominant society and he was personally impacted by the ambivalent, often contradictory worlds within which he operated. He evidently achieved support from the Alaska Native Brotherhood (ANB) membership because he wanted to preserve and display objects as texts on the history of Tlingit society and as monuments to Tlingit greatness (Milburn 1986:203–4).

Personal tragedy entered Shotridge's life in 1917. His wife Florence had tuberculosis; her health deteriorated and she died on June 12, 1917. One wonders what her achievements would have been had she lived another twenty years or more, and shared the decades during which Louis' research and writing came to fruition. Louis remarried in 1919, and returned to Philadelphia. His employment with the museum was secure; Gordon, the Anthropology Department's head, encouraged and promoted Shotridge as a professional ethnographer, and the next ten years were highly productive. During these years, Shotridge continued to build and document the collection, and he published eight articles in the *University Museum Journal*, one of which is the subject of this chapter (Shotridge 1920). Of his assigned activities, Shotridge did not care for writing, but preferred fieldwork and collecting.

It was Shotridge's grand strategy to collect those objects of clan art that best represent Tlingit societal history and show Tlingit social structure in a microcosm. His agenda was to show the greatness of Tlingit art and culture, but to do it in a clan-specific way. His attention to clan identity is reflected in his collecting and in his publications such as "Ghost of Courageous Adventurer" (Shotridge 1920) As noted previously, these items were becoming increasingly controversial in the Tlingit community because of the conversion to Protestant Christianity (which was much more intrusive on Tlingit lifestyle than Russian Orthodoxy, and which also had the full backing of the American secular authorities) and because of increasing conflict between Native matrilineal and Euro-American patrilineal systems of inheritance. Although recognition of clan ownership was "notarized" through the traditional protocol of reciprocity at potlatches, Shotridge felt that this was only temporary, because people forget, and times change. In contrast, a museum would provide a permanent record of glory. This would be an honorable alternative.

Shotridge also sensed a growing shift away from the clan system and toward the community as the unit of identity and political action. He saw future political and social strength coming from a collective approach. In retrospect, we can see even more clearly that Shotridge perceived correctly that clan-centered identity and political power were already on the wane and were being replaced by western forms and concepts. The ANB and other Pan-Indian movements were (and are) community-based rather than clan-based. The pattern becomes increasingly evident in the subsequent history of the ANB and later Native organizations, such as Tlingit and Haida Central Council, and Alaska Federation of Natives, culminating in the Alaska Native Claims Settlement Act of 1971 and the creation of regional, for-profit corporations; the latter (in 1921) had no precedent or parallel in traditional Tlingit social structure. Shotridge saw this coming, and made a special effort to collect and document Tlingit cultural achievement on a clan-by-clan basis, from a Tlingit point of view, in contrast to the more generic and western-based approaches of others.

Museum management, however, was then characterized by a conflict of priority between catering to public display and public expectation, and pursuing the advancement of science. Shotridge collected what the Tlingit considered significant, sometimes disagreeing with museum management on this. As noted previously, Shotridge wanted to represent the historical greatness of the Tlingit clans. In doing so, his work goes far beyond formal classificatory analysis or collection of texts. Shotridge goes into the social and historical context of the art objects. He treated myth and legend as events that situated the various Tlingit clans in time and place, within history and geography. For Shotridge, the agents by which groups were distinguished and by which social structure was defined were visually articulated in crest objects. We will return to this shortly.

The End of Louis Shotridge's Career

By the end of the 1920s, Shotridge's career at the UPM was winding down. George Gordon died in January 1928, and in August, Louis' second wife, Elizabeth, died of tuberculosis. With the stock market crash of 1929 and the Great Depression, funding became a problem, and new management had interests in areas other than Native America. In 1932, after twenty years of service, Shotridge was dropped from the UPM staff.

Sometime between 1931 and 1932, Shotridge married for the third time. His last years were financially troubled, and in 1935 he was hired as a stream guard to police fishing. In July 1937 he apparently fell from a roof. He was discovered and taken to the hospital in Sitka, where he died ten days later, on August 6, 1937. He was survived by his third wife and four children. Milburn emphasizes that the factual record sharply contradicts the sensationalized accounts of Shotridge's death published in the 1960s and 1970s (Milburn 1997:321; Cole 1985:266). These stories also circulate in oral tradition. We, too, have heard the oral accounts cited by Cole (1985:266) but have preferred not to discuss them. As much as they may be fascinating folklore, they may not be accurate.

Shotridge's Concern with Context

Shotridge's insistence on the social and historical context of art objects raises an interesting and important theoretical debate. This is covered fully by Milburn (1997: chapter 7, esp. 271ff) but it is also necessary to touch on it briefly here. Major experts in Tlingit ethnography of Shotridge's time, such as Emmons, John Swanton, and Boas differed in their approaches to objects and their meanings. Emmons was probably closest to Shotridge in his interest in obtaining detailed Native interpretations of objects. Swanton explicitly discounted the association of myth, oral history, and the imagery found on crest objects (Swanton 1908:395), and Boas advocated a formalist approach, arguing that designs could be interpreted outside the social context of clan and personal history (see especially Boas 1907:386–7, which is contained within Emmons 1907 and discussed by Milburn 1997:272–3; see also Jonaitis 1995:306–35). Milburn concluded that "The tightly knit Tlingit relationship between social structure, personal and clan histories, myths, and objects was obscured when Boas opted to rely exclusively on a formal, decontextualized analysis of design systems" (1997:273). Quoting Marjorie Halpin (1994: 13), Milburn continues, "By separating art from its stories, Boas and his followers separated art from the community context which gave it meaning and life, and, finally, obscured the vital connection between art and the land which, whether intentional or not, was part of the colonial enterprise of separating Natives from their lands" (1997:274). For anthropological museums it was essential to recontextualize ownership of Native American objects within a Western patrimony because there was no value in an exchange that continued to perpetuate concepts of Native ownership and the historic associations they represented. In this regard, Shotridge's emphasis on the particulars of collective ownership was at odds with the anthropological configuration of objects within a Western system of acquisition and display (Milburn 1997:274–5).

Milburn describes how Shotridge's emphasis on the accurate representation of Tlingit society and history became even more of a focus after Gordon's death. Shotridge then had sole discretionary responsibility for composing and framing the collection. In the final years of Shotridge's employment, his work was essentially neglected by the UPM officials, enabling him to base his purchasing decisions almost exclusively on his own agenda rather than on more generalized visual or interpretative considerations. In the final analysis, his combined oral history and photographic record places objects in the Shotridge collection at UPM among the best documented of Northwest Coast objects in any non-Native institution (Milburn 1997:271–2, 275).

The Knife and the Story as Text and Context

In 1920, Shotridge published "Ghost of Courageous Adventurer" in the *University Museum Journal* (Shotridge 1920). This article provides an excellent example of Shotridge's philosophy as described previously. It documents the history and social context of a single artifact in the collection—one that, in fact, might easily be overlooked by the casual museum visitor. The Tlingit knife named "Ghost of Courageous Adventurer" (Fig. 50) was acquired by Louis Shotridge in Sitka in 1918 and was soon mentioned as being on display (Shotridge 1920:11). In his article, Shotridge shows how stories illuminate the complex relations between objects, oral history, and social structure. It is a powerful story and an excellent example of Shotridge's concern with keeping objects in their cultural contexts of clan ownership and history—his emphasis on clan ownership and historical presentation, in contrast to timeless and decontextualized, generic display (Fig. 51). As Milburn explains, "Shotridge's histories were intimately related to particular crest objects and the clans that owned them. Because of their detailed oral histories the objects constituted a metonym for the existing fabric of Tlingit society" (Milburn 1997:345). This will become evident in his story and its frame.

In his opening paragraph, Shotridge explained that his purpose was to illustrate how a selected object of Tlingit visual art represented its mythic prototypes, how "prototypes of animals of land, air, and water, and the denizens of the unseen world are represented". In what was to be recognized as the hallmark of Shotridge's style, he described in detail the object and how he acquired it:

> To illustrate these arts, I have chosen, for this article, a war knife. This specimen, although not among the most conspicuous of the many important objects exhibited in the Northwest Coast Hall of the University Museum, has its own story and has in fact a special importance. The knife itself, its name, the material in which it is wrought and everything connected with it have many sentimental associations for the Tlingit.
>
> The blade and guard are made of iron and the pommel of ivory. The grip has an iron core covered with mesh made from the hair of the wild goat. Both the iron and the ivory are said to be the same pieces mentioned in the legend given in the following pages. The ivory pommel is carved like a human skull

which represents a ghost, the cavities being inlaid with blue iridescent abalone shell that glows with soft hues. The blade is well hardened metal with sharp edges on both sides, wrought out in one piece with one end reduced like a stem or tang which is driven into the ivory pommel. A separate piece of the iron is shaped to fit the handle end to form a guard. The length of the weapon, from tip to the top of the handle, is fifteen and one-half inches.

I obtained this old knife from the last of Thunderbird House group of the Shungukeidí

G̲aayshaayí, who is called in the story by the English translation of his name, Eagle Head. Shotridge explains:

There is no accurate geographical information to be offered to indicate the exact location of the regions referred to in the account of the journey, and we can only guess at localities by computing the time it took to walk from the starting point. The legend shows that after crossing the desert of ice, the party went along the Pacific coast all the way to what is now known as Copper River. This journey on foot, which is said to

50/ The "Ghost of a Courageous Adventurer" knife, with sheath, both of which are associated with the story. UPM Coll #NA 8488 (knife 38.6cm long)

51/ Yendaayank', the last direct descendant of Tlingit chief Eagle Head, who headed the party described in the story, as photographed in Sitka, 1908.

clan of Chilkat. It was the only object which carried with it to the present day a record of the important part which the clan took in establishing a trade connection between the northern Tlingit and the alien tribes of the Interior. It was the last link with the past and therefore the last thing with which the clan was willing to part (Shotridge 1920:11–12).

The knife alludes to or recalls an expedition by the Chilkat Tlingit from Klukwan over what is now known as the St. Elias Range to the Copper River. The trek was led by a man of the Shangukeidí clan named

have taken all of the favorable season, proved a difficult one. Even at the present time with maps and modern equipment, one is often puzzled as to a safe course over the deserts of ice along the way.

When the explorers returned to Klukwan, the old Native town on the Chilkat River where I was born, only very few of the men survived to receive the honors of discovery and the prospect of acquiring riches. Some lost their lives while crossing the ice and others died of starvation. The survivors on their return told their story and made known the inhabited regions of the west coast. They also brought back iron and ivory, articles previously unknown to the Tlingit people (Shotridge 1920:12–4).

The aspect of Shotridge's work that we focus on in this chapter is his English version of the history that the knife recalls. The pattern of the text and context of the story is typical in Tlingit folklife and oral tradition. An important narrative genre consists of accounts of how clans acquired the right to claim and use certain areas, objects, or crest designs, called in Tlingit *at.óow*, literally meaning "an owned or purchased object." As in the case of the knife, the purchase was through the lives of clan ancestors, whose experience gives subsequent generations the right to claim and use the crest or object. As Shotridge articulates in an editorial comment in the story, "Only through sacrifice does man acquire something of value. It was at the cost of brave lives that we now have in our hands those objects that constitute our pride." For more on this, see Nora Dauenhauer (1986, 1995) and Dauenhauer and Dauenhauer (1987, 1990, 1994).

The Style of the Story

Shotridge's style in the story itself is quite different from his style in the introduction cited above. The biggest problem the modern reader immediately faces in the story is Shotridge's use of archaic English. This was a deliberate choice. He explains: "In rewriting the account of the journey I have preserved the original form as far as translation from Tlingit to English permits. The language in which these legends are told is what might be called poetic in form and often archaic. It is a form of diction that will sometimes yield in translation to obsolete forms of English" (Shotridge 1920:14).

This raises a point of translation theory on which we disagree with Shotridge. Is it correct to use deliberately archaic and obsolete forms in translation if the style of the original is not really archaic or obsolete? Shotridge chose archaic English in an attempt to convey a sense of the Tlingit. He also used unnatural English word order to convey a sense of Tlingit syntax.

On one hand, he brilliantly succeeds. Upon reading his text, Nora Marks Dauenhauer's first reaction was, "I could hear the Tlingit on the back side of what he was saying." In fact, this gave her the idea of back-translating the English into Tlingit, a work currently in progress but far from completion. She found this relatively easy to do, because the Tlingit grammar was so transparent in Shotridge's English text. We are not suggesting that there was ever a written Tlingit "Ur-text" from which Shotridge translated. Although Shotridge was a good speller of Tlingit and there are many examples of his linguistic transcriptions of names and terms extant, it is unlikely that he ever transcribed or wrote a version of the story down in Tlingit. It would be an archivist's delight if there were. But there is no extant text of the story in Tlingit written by Shotridge, and we have no reason to assume that he ever did write it out in Tlingit. His written version composed in English is based on Tlingit oral accounts. He probably called to mind oral traditions that he had heard in Tlingit, and translated them into written English.

Shotridge undeniably succeeded in conveying a sense of Tlingit in his English. The down side of this success is that his translation is difficult and even unintelligible to the average reader of English. It uses the full set of archaic English locationals and directionals:

here	there	where
hither	thither	whither
hence	thence	whence

These are not obsolete in Tlingit, and in fact match quite well. Most educated readers would be able to follow these. But some vocabulary sends even educated readers, unless they are educated in Middle English, to the dictionary, like:

whilom = formerly

I trow = I think

Shotridge's impression and description of Tlingit as "poetic in form and often archaic" is true only relative to his English translation. The style of Tlingit narratives such as this tends to be formal and conservative in Tlingit, but not alien or archaic. Unlike Tlingit oratory with its rich metaphor and simile that people consider bewildering and often call "old time Tlingit," the prose narrative of crest stories is relatively straightforward. Therefore, one could argue that the level of style called for in English should be also formal and conservative, but not archaic or confusing. This is the balance we have tried to strike in the revised translation: it is intended to be formal, but natural (see below). Thus, we debated many of Shotridge's vocabulary choices. For Shotridge's "comrades," the word "buddies" was too conversational. Likewise, the leader's taunt to his despondent trekkers, "Did you come here for pleasure?" sounds a bit stiff, but "Did you come here for a good time?" is too colloquial.

While the planned obsolescence of Shotridge's translation succeeds in conveying a sense of Tlingit structure, it creates unnecessary barriers for all readers, even the most educated, and therefore it fails to communicate the power of the story as fully as it might. His effort to preserve the letter of the original fails to preserve the spirit; it does not convey the emotional power and function of the original because it fails to communicate even literally to the modern reader.

Our Editorial Procedures

The balance of this paper is our edited version of the Shotridge's English composition. Here are some of the general procedures we have followed in the revision:

1. We have kept the gems of "poetic diction" wherever they are "poetic" but not obscure. For example "foliage moon." We like this so much that we have added a few of our own, such as the buds "puckering," which conveys the theme of the Tlingit verb.

2. Most of Shotridge's parenthetical notes are incorporated into the main text, especially where they explain the "poetic diction"; for example "the month of May" in the opening line. Some of his comments are relegated to notes, and we have added some notes of our own.

3. All archaic English nouns, directionals, and locationals are replaced with modern English.

Thus "girdle" becomes "belt," and all the hithers, thithers, and whences are dropped. The "drift log with spurs of queer genus," which borders on bombast, becomes "a drift log with an unusual kind of spur." It sounds more pedestrian, but clear.

4. Where the word order is unnatural or unclear, it is changed. "To follow that river big" becomes "to follow that big river."

5. Anything that creates linguistic confusion is edited and in extreme cases paraphrased.

6. Generally translators do not translate personal names such as Eagle Head, but Shotridge did, and we have left them as is. Shotridge also plays with ethnonyms: Tlingit, meaning "human," and Gunanaa, meaning Athapaskan but literally "other," or "alien," which now conveys all kinds of sci-fi associations. Technically, "alien" as an English word comes from the Latin for "other."

Here is an example of a passage we edited: "Carefully that man looked and felt, then to the camp and to comrades he told. Right away with him they went thither." This becomes: "Carefully the man looked at it and felt it. Then he returned to camp to tell the rest of them. Right away they went back there with him."

This review of examples illustrates Eugene Nida's idea of levels of "transfer" (Nida 1964:184–92). He identifies literal transfer, minimal transfer, and literary transfer. "Literal transfer" is word-for-word, whereas "minimal transfer" is whatever is necessary to make acceptable sense in the target language: for example, adding "a" or "the" in English when translating from languages that have no articles, such as Russian or Tlingit. In Nida's context, it seems that Shotridge confused the literal and minimal transfers. His style is optional and operates at the level of literary transfer; his grammar is not optional and exemplifies the minimal transfer.

We should note that the division of the narrative into sub-sections with titles is not in the Shotridge original, but is a preferred publishing convention today, and one that we hope will be of help to readers in following the story and possibly tracing its route.

"Ghost of Courageous Adventurer,"

[Translated from Tlingit oral tradition by Louis Shotridge (1920), edited by Nora Marks Dauenhauer (1997)]

Opening Frame

It was May, the foliage moon, the month when buds are puckering on trees, when the Shangukeidí laid their packs in canoes and poled away to lands unknown. They weren't many. Maybe they numbered twenty men. Among them was Eagle Head. They steered their canoes toward Tleheeni, a branch of the Chilkat River. A traveler never took this stream too far inland because a glacier grew there, shutting off their passage.

From Sea Level to Timberline

The canoes of cottonwood moved on and on. Now they pole and now they tow. Through ice water wade the bare feet of those brave men of long ago. The common cold was unknown in those days. Where did the man of today come from to be so soft? Regardless of all protection he catches cold.

One camp ahead they reached Trout Creek, across from where the town of Porcupine now is. Here the canoes were beached, turned upside down, and wrapped with underbrush. "Maybe we'll be lucky and make our return through here." Though the trail of the sun was still long, they didn't go any farther that day, for as always on such a journey, little things must be fitted together, retying packs so they lay better on backs. Staffs, too, were always made to fit the hands. Thus, they always made camp there at the canoe landing.

As the sky turned gray at dawn, faces passed through loops of pack straps. Those packs of food were heavy. Trout Creek Mountain was steep. The journey moved in that direction, without eating breakfast, because the tongue was still coated. How different is the man of today. Eat first and work next. But with the man of long ago it was work first, and with sunrise comes time for breakfast. Food eaten before the tongue is cleared, they say, was unwholesome to the stom-

ach. It was when the sun was sliding down that the journey climbed to the timberline. Their guess was right. The next trees were far away from here, so the journey made camp.

Chilkat Summit; O'Connor and Tatshenshini Rivers

Then from that place, while it was still dark, they mounted the journey again. When the sunbeams lowered their feet to the base of the mountain, the expedition had reached the summit. They made a fire for their lunch stop. When they had finished eating, the group continued, following the short cut called Despondent Man's Trail, that ran from the prairie to Chilkat Pass. The expedition moved on and on. At times the new trail was good, and sometimes bad. In hollows the old snow was melting slowly and retarded their travel without snowshoes.

After two camps in that direction, no more trees were seen, only a low growth of willows here and there. From the summit of Chilkat Pass there is a stretch of rolling land of about forty miles, a divide between the timber line of the Tlingit forest and the interior.

Maybe six camps from home, the group came to a big river. Now people call it Alsek (Tatshenshini).[1] From there they moved downriver along the shore. Two camps in that direction, they thought they might be too far down. From piles of driftwood they dragged logs and right away they lashed together a raft. This is how they gained the far side of the river. From there the group went westward.

Following the Ice Field to Yakutat

One camp from the river, the group came to the face of a glacier. Looking north and south, they couldn't see the end. Their guess was right: that growth of ice was wide. Where should the journey go? To the ocean, one would think. It was from there that a traveler had formerly come. The expedition had wandered onto the route that strangers had taken home.[2] The group stopped to camp at the timber line of the glacier. That evening the men agreed on a certain course.

When the Big Dipper [Yaxté; Great Bear] was turning over to daybreak, they were already walking on the glacier. In the cool of dawn, it was firm underfoot. But as the sun rose higher, the firm surface began to melt, and fear crept in. But ready was the rope of the man of long ago. It was strong, made from the hind quarter of mountain goat. It was tied to the leader's waist and stretched through the hands of all the men.

Far ahead of them, side by side, stood two mountains, (Seattle and Ruhamah). In between them looked good. They kept their faces moving that direction. Eagle Head was in the lead. It was slow going, they say, because of many crevices. Even though the mountains looked quite near, when night fell they still were far ahead. At night, it was like a tanned skin underfoot, with less precaution needed for each step. Twilight lay over the icefield and it was clear to the men where the danger lay. No one had making camp to rest in mind, and the line moved on throughout the night.

Those travelers of long ago stood in the haze of dawn. They looked up to the face of the mountain on the north side, and then up to the face of the mountain on the south. It was Chaan Yuká, Midway of the Ice Field called Chaan. From that time on this name, given by those men of long ago, was fixed in our language. No one knows what language the name is borrowed from. [Probably the Athabaskan name had been applied to these mountains in more ancient time, and the name made more widely recognized only since the Tlingit discovery—NMD].

On went the journey till the mountains with the night were left behind.[3] The sun was falling into its slide when the sound of a great drum reached the men's ears. The wind was down, and through the still air louder and louder came that thunder-like drumming as they traveled on. It was the ocean, the great salt water, beating its arms against the shore in waves. When they recognized the sound, relief swept through their heart and limbs, and their pace increased. The sun had taken its last steep slide when the group came to camp among the first timber. There was no courage

left in anyone to go farther; sleep had overpowered courage.

How much sleep had they taken when each man squatted into his pack straps and rushed off to follow the first to leave camp? Maybe joy was what they felt. What did each expect from where the sound was reaching their ears? It's always this way: a little change in a hard experience brings a feeling like berries to the mouth—for a while it's good, but soon the taste melts away. The sun was half way along its trail when the group came to a lake. Where is this? They thought it was a lake, but it was really Yakutat Bay. Until the tide went out, they had no idea they had come to the shore of the ocean. The sun had sunk behind a mountain when the group arrived at the lip of the waves. Against the shoreline, up and down, the great salt water moved its arms. But there was no sign of human habitation. Where were those feelings of joy now? Like spruce pitch from a tree, slowly, they melted away.

Malaspina Glacier

After this, their feet, just like their feelings, became heavy, too. They camped one night. With pointed words, they disagreed. What kind of a man was strong willed enough to continue? So one speech went against another. It is said that Eagle Head, that real man, while humming a little tune to himself, pushed and drew an awl through his moccasin patch. They say that Eagle Head's little humming was an omen of the anger in his heart. Speaking slowly, he said, "You sound to me like homesick children. Did you come here for fun? Turn in your tracks now if you choose, before it gets any harder. As for me, my feeling is not to turn my face homeward empty handed." It was then the men realized their shame and how they were discouraged and disheartened. Once more courage pierced their weak hearts. But in camp on the edge of another glacier (probably the Malaspina Glacier) this talk continued. There are few men with courage enough to blame them. Maybe they too, even these courageous few, would have weakened had they stood there face to face with this glacier with its end unknown.[4] Toward dawn the expedition moved along on the glacier. They say this was even more dangerous, since the crevices were many and bigger. On and on slowly, the expedition moved. Had two young men taken more care, no grief would have come to the travelers. Maybe their minds wandered away from thoughts of caution. From this, the first two deaths occurred among them. They fell into ice crevices. This is the way it always is: a man may take much care, but his time to die ignores that care.

Who was to blame for these lost lives? No one dared to say the way he felt about what happened. They feared the words of Eagle Head. The travelers sat in meditation. Maybe some minds vacillated and decided now one way and then the other, but no one there was strong enough to turn back. While the travelers sat with troubled hearts, Eagle Head snatched his pack strap and said, "Let's keep going. Is it something new to you that a man should die?" With this remark he started to walk. One by one the men slowly moved after the leader. There was trouble underfoot, but in spite of everything, the heart of Eagle Head never yielded. How strong the heart of that man must have been. Maybe it was like European steel from people beyond the horizon; it never bent. It took them two days and one night to reach the other side of the glacier. From there, once again the expedition moved along the wave-lip shoreline.

Following the Shoreline; the Discovery of Iron

After making camp, one of the men was walking along the shore. Unless there was something that needed to be done, the traveler of long ago never kept still or sat around in camp. What was he looking for? It was to drive away the tiredness that created such a habit. He was walking not too far from camp. There, across his path, lay a drift log with an unusual kind of spur. The man had never seen such spurs. From his belt, that man of long ago drew out his adze. What could be harder than this green stone?[5] Therefore, little did that

man of long ago take care. He struck the unusual growth with all his strength. "Dummm" the sound came out. What was it that had such a sound, and what did it mean? The edge of that hard, green-stone adze had broken off, with only a bright spot where it had slipped on the spur. "My adze—so much depended on you," he said in amazement. For a moment, trouble pierced his mind, but the thought of the unusual log was stronger.

Maybe then came to mind for the man of long ago that something lay at hand superior to his green-stone. For some moments the man contemplated the unusual log. Then he rolled it over. More of the spurs were sticking out. Carefully the man looked at it and felt it. Then he returned to camp to tell the rest of them. Right away they went back there with him. They carried the log to camp. First they pounded on it with rocks. No, these unusual spurs only bent. "What will fire do to it?" They laid the unusual log on the fire, and on it lay all eyes. Behold! Before their eyes the log burned, but what they thought were spurs only turned like red-hot coals. Thus, through a drift log, iron was carried to the hands of the Tlingit.

To the Copper River

In late summer, when the Coho salmon were swimming, one by one, in streams to shore, the expedition reached the bank of a large river. Maybe it's the one now called the Copper. Here their minds vacillated, deciding now to cross the river and continue on along the ocean shore, and now to follow the river upstream. Camping at the same place one night after another, Eagle Head slept through all those days. Never were his feelings heard from his lips. Maybe now his strong heart and courage were bending a little. No one can say what luck will favor any man's effort.

They don't say how many days it was that they'd been camping in this one place when smoke was sighted toward away upriver. "Aliens. Gunanáa," someone said.[6] They wanted to make certain, but no one said anything. Whoever happened to be near his pack squatted to put it on, and with one accord they made a run toward the smoke. The smoke appeared close, but in spite of their haste, night fell before they reached it. But it was not too dark, and they could see the way ahead clearly. Where did the depression go? Excitement overwhelmed it, and onward rushed the hurried feet.

Up the Copper River: Encountering the Athapaskans

The travelers came out from behind a point, and right before their eyes lay many fires. It looked like a long row of houses, maybe a sizeable town. Maybe they never scented all that smoke because the breeze was blowing away from them. The travelers were still some distance away when the dogs began to bark at them. On the opposite side of the stream from the town, the travelers quietly halted. From out of the village came forth a voice. Maybe it meant, "Who are you?" No one was there to tell them what the strange language had said. "We are human—Tlingit—and we seek your presence." Likewise, they failed to understand the person from another place. While they hesitated to wade across, the fires were all extinguished. Alien people, always, like wild animals, are shy. Above the swishing sound of the running stream they could hear talking at night. Infants in cradles were crying. There was nothing else the travelers could do but to wait for daylight. The people they had searched out were afraid of them.

Gradually night faded away, and dawn opened on a large camp with a long row of brush houses. Presently, one by one, smoke rose from within each dwelling. It was Eagle Head who came out to the stream edge. He gestured to the people across, and one by one those new people assembled. In front of them stood their headman, who likewise talked by gestures to the travelers. He only exchanged a few words, and when he was finished, they talked among each other. They all seemed happy. Then the travelers were summoned to come over.

Trading with the Athapaskans

The Tlingit waded across and walked among the alien tribe. To this day we still walk toward a place in the same manner. The travelers were surrounded in the open, and strange eyes were on them. Maybe they were curious to those eyes. From among the crowd, their leader emerged. Likewise Eagle Head stepped forward to meet him, and face-to-face stood the Tlingit and the man of the alien tribe. Gesturing, they acknowledged each other. Presently, from his pouch, the Tlingit brought out his *dáadzi* for him to see (a fire-making apparatus of flint and pyrites – NMD). With it was some tinder of shredded cedar root. Before the eyes of the alien people a fire began to blaze from a spark. For a moment there was silence, and then confusion of voices. The alien people were amazed. After demonstrating his *dáadzi,* Eagle Head placed it in its pouch and then offered it to the alien man. "I brought this for you, my friend." With these words he placed the fire-making set in the hands of the alien man. Those inland people used a wooden drill to make fire. In return, the leader lifted his quiver of arrows from his shoulder, and with his bow gave it to Eagle Head. This is how the greetings of the Tlingit and the alien were expressed with gifts.

No longer was there a feeling of suspicion. Before feasting there, those alien people lined up to dance for the travelers, according to their custom. They greet friendship with dance. Do they put on special make-up for dance, as we do? Not at all. Those nomads— whoever happens to be near, some maybe with packs of infants—move, just as they are, into dancing the moment a song is started. Happy are they, these inland people. Though all the dangers of man were known to them, life among them was peaceful. Why do the Tlingit not learn this good life? How bad it must have been on our ancestor for his offspring only to be the antagonist to another man. Maybe we were bothered first, and then we struck back hard at the other man.[7]

It is not told how long they camped with the alien people. All through their stay, of course, they went on exchanging things. Everything the travelers had went as gifts in return for the many things the alien people gave them. It was at that time that walrus tusk ivory was given to the Tlingit, which, up to that time, like the iron, was unknown to them.

The people the travelers met in that camp pointed to still other people, (probably Eskimo – NMD) living further to the west, and told them that this was the meeting and trading point.[8] Maybe it was at that time the Tlingit came to know of copper, but we don't know. It was from that region, in later years, that we acquired copper.

Returning to Klukwan

It was autumn, when the cottonwood trees had turned yellow, when a warning cry of the return approach of the Chaan Yuká travelers was heard in Klukwan. Their canoes drifted in front of the town. When the canoes came ashore there, only a very few of those men came home. The missing had fallen along the way. To some person a son, to another a husband, or perhaps a father, too, was missing. That was a moment of sorrow. From the different parts of the village, only cries of grief were heard.

In his canoe stood Eagle Head. Never before in his manhood did his voice tremble. Maybe sorrow entered his strong heart from above, when he called out those names, one by one, of the brave men who fell along the way. From the beginning it was this way. Only through sacrifice does man acquire something of value. It was at the cost of brave lives that we now have in our hands those objects that constitute our pride.

Forging of the Dagger from the Iron; Ceremonial Debut of the Dagger; Oratory; Naming and Passing of the Dagger

It is not known how long after that they had this piece of iron. Until Kaa.ushtí, a war leader of the Kaagwaantaan rose in his maternal uncle's stead, it was

never brought into view. During his possession it was first formed like a war knife. When first completed, it was not as you see it now. Only after we came to have grindstones was its rough surface made smooth. The ivory head, however, was never changed. It's just the way it was first made.

It was during a Kaagwaantaan encounter with T'ikanaa, a Tlingit division occupying the southwest coast of Prince of Wales Island, that the knife was finished.[9] The man of long ago always did a thing like this at the right time. Thus it was in wartime this knife was awarded. One day a messenger went from house to house, announcing "Kaa.ushtí is calling all his clansmen to the Finned House."

When all were seated in his clan house, that great warrior stood before the people. "You men of Nees.ádi, Shangukeidí, and Kaagwaantaan, I desire your support. Without you, what can I accomplish? At this moment I call on you to confirm the desires of those men in whose place I stand before you. From the moment it was told to me, not once did the deed performed in confirmation of the noblest claim by those men who gave their lives in the Chaan Yuká journey ever leave my mind. My heart feels good that it has fallen to me to bring out the object of concern on the minds of those men whom I have succeeded." When their minds were set at ease, Eagle Head stood up and spoke, "Only our ghosts have returned to you, you children of Shangukeidí." From that time on, people never forgot his remark.

At the end of his speech, that great warrior drew forth from its sheath this knife, called "Denizen of Unseen World."[10] It was Kaa.ushtí who pronounced the name. With outstretched hand he lifted it and called him, saying, "Eagle Head, take it. In your hands shall rest the memories of those brave men." Eagle Head came forward from the group. He was all bent over, his eyesight, too, was very short; old age had overcome him. "Kaagwaantaan! I can only offer acceptance in this old age. Only in my dream will it be my post. If only this moment had come while I was young! I take this knife only to pass it through these old hands, I think, to hands of greater power." In this way the knife passed to the Shangukeidí.

Thus it was the remark made by the courageous adventurer that inspired the artist who made an image of the name[11] as the pommel of the war knife, and as nearly as the Tlingit idea can be interpreted in English, the name of the knife is The Ghost of Courageous Adventurer.

Conclusion

We hope that this newly edited translation is faithful to Shotridge's intention to show the greatness of Tlingit, and will in fact help convey it by removing his meaningful work of almost 80 years ago from relative obscurity and placing it in the linguistic mainstream for a new generation of readers.

The example of his style shows us how language changes. The example of his life's work shows us how attitudes can change as well. Milburn summarizes, "To Shotridge and others of his era, preservation and representation were key factors in seeking institutional sanctuary for objects, while today, control over representation and possession are the issues that dominate Native American peoples' concerns. ...What emerges from this discussion is a realization of the historically contingent and politically charged nature of possession and interpretation and its long and complex history among the Northwest Coast peoples" (Milburn 1997:347).

We are all part of that history, and as we judge those who have gone before us, so will we be judged by those who will come after us. We are dealing with the same issues as Louis Shotridge, but almost a century later. His concern was recording the greatness of the Tlingit clans through their visual art documented in the fullest context possible. Our concerns are more for recording the Tlingit language and the classics of Tlingit oral literature composed and published orally in that literature. It is perhaps indicative that we focus on Shotridge's writing here, as an example of his success.

We believe that Milburn is correct in her conclusion that Northwest Coast art has always been contextualized politically, and that the context changes from generation to generation. Back in Shotridge's time ("*Then*"), it was politically correct to assimilate to Western culture, and to remove traditional art from the community. Now it is seemingly "politically correct" to demand that art back, with the demands often couched in confrontational terms. Then, the Tlingit language was not in danger; now it is, with fewer than 600 speakers remaining today, most of whom are above the age of fifty. It is similarly politically correct these days to demand "the language" back, as if it were an object kept in a vault or in a display case, rather than a living process and relationship. Languages are not like objects of art, and the dynamics of loss and restoration are far more complex.

We would like to conclude with two quotations from the letters of Louis Shotridge, in some small way to link our work in general and this paper in particular to his legacy. In 1923, Shotridge wrote, "It is now clear that unless someone goes to work to record these old things as evidence, the noble idea of our forefathers shall be entirely lost" (Louis Shotridge to George Gordon, January 27, 1923; Milburn 1997:345). We subscribe to this, even today, and especially today. In this spirit, we also edit Shotridge's composition of 1920, which has now joined its place among the "old things." In 1932, in his farewell words to the University of Pennsylvania Museum, Shotridge wrote, "I hope that in the future the old Tlingit objects will always have a fair chance in representing their former masters" (Louis Shotridge to Horace Jayne, January 18, 1932; Milburn 1997:346). We hope that our small editorial effort will help to keep this fair chance going.

Acknowledgments

We express our debt to Maureen Milburn, who has been researching and writing about Louis Shotridge for over 15 years (Milburn 1986, 1994, 1997). We have relied heavily on her unpublished Ph.D. dissertation

(Milburn 1997) for historical and archival information on Shotridge. This is the most definitive study on this issue, and it is indispensable for anyone interested in Shotridge's life and work. We also thank Judith Berman for her comments and support, and the staff of the University of Pennsylvania Museum in Philadelphia for their assistance in securing illustrations.

Notes

1. What some older travel accounts call the Alsek River is now called the Tatshenshini River. Sometime since the turn of the twentieth century, the major river names used in the early travel accounts have all "rotated" one position counter-clockwise to the northwest on modern maps. The name "Alsek" no longer refers to the Tatshenshini, but now refers to both to the Upper Alsek River, which requires a helicopter portage to navigate, and to the Lower Alsek River which flows into the Pacific at Dry Bay. The Shotridge reference to Alsek is now called the Tatshenshini, which flows into the Alsek and continues to the coast as the Lower Alsek River. What was formerly called the Tatshenshini is now called the Blanchard River, and is a tributary of the Tatshenshini River joining it shortly above the usual put-in spot for rafters at Dalton Post, Shawshë in Southern Tutchone. One possible route for the journey Shotridge is describing was for the group to follow the drainage of what is now called the O'Connor River and to cross the Tatshen-shini River below the confluence. On the famous Kohklux map drawn in 1852 (Davidson 1901:76; de Laguna 1972:88; Kohklux 1995:15) there is a dotted line labeled "reported trail" connecting the headwaters of the Tklaheenae (Tleheeni) River and "Sticks Village," an Athapaskan village on the east bank of the All-Segh (Alsek = Tatshenshini) River, north of the confluence of the O'Connor River. The travelers head down river on foot. There are several points in this section of the river where they could have crossed to the west bank and to the ice fields. They probably went westward on the ice from this section of the river and not after the confluence with the Alsek, which would be more than a two-day hike. The trekkers presumably crossed the Alsek River over an ice bridge. Glaciers and ice fields covered rivers in places, and there are songs and stories in Tlingit oral tradition about people coming down rivers under the ice. Alternatively, their route could have been over what is the Novatak glacier on modern maps, below the confluence of the Alsek and Tatshenshini Rivers. This is now the inland side of the Alaskan Glacier Bay National Park, and a region of dramatic ice movement. All of these glaciers are part of the same larger ice field, and however the hikers ascended, they eventually used Mt. Ruhamah as a bearing. This mountain is also on the Kohklux map and modern maps. It is near Russell Fjord, an area of spectacular glacial advance in recent years.

2. Other travel. Shotridge noted: "It is evident it was this bit of vague information, which occasionally, had been heard in Chilkat as passed on from no known authority, that convinced these men to be all the more determined in their purpose to penetrate into the unknown country" (Shotridge 1920:17). By the time of Russian contact in the late 1700s, there was established travel between Chilkat and Yakutat. Traveling in 1788, Izmailov and Bocharov noted that they met people in Yakutat who were from Chilkat (Shelikov 1981:94); but it is unclear if they traveled between Chilkat and Yakutat by land or sea. River travel between Dalton Post and Dry Bay was well established (de Laguna 1972:85–90). The present story treats the legendary time of first exploration of the route, but suggests that even these early travelers suspected they were not the first to use the route.

3. Light. It is now approaching midsummer, and the trekkers are facing the land of the midnight sun; the sun is gradually moving to the north, where the sky will appear red all night, and night is literally in the south, behind them.

4. Malaspina Glacier, of today's map. The original is ambiguous here: literally "at this moment." We take the reference as not to the men at this moment in the story, but to Shotridge's audience of readers in the present time frame. Possibly he meant both. Who among us is to say that he or she wouldn't weaken at the thought of continuing when faced with the awesome sight of the Malaspina Glacier. This glacier is larger than the entire state of Rhode Island. There are historical accounts from the Russian period by an officer named Tarkhanov who accompanied the Yakutat Tlingit over that glacier to the Copper River.

5. Green Stone (probably jade). The pre-contact adze or axe was made of stone. According to Tlingit traditional accounts (including this story) the first metal was found in driftwood from European ships. After contact, steel axes replaced stone, and the technology of Northwest coast wood carving was revolutionized. The Tlingit obtained native copper from the interior, notably from the Copper River, and indigenous techniques evolved for working it.

6. Athapaskan Indians. The Tlingit term is Gunanáa, meaning "alien" or "other tribe." The original is: "Gunanah" [alien tribe] man said. In the next paragraph, the original is: "Tlingit [human] we are, it is thy presence we seek." As with many other ethnonyms around the world, the Tlingit word for themselves is Lingít, meaning "human."

7. "Happy Athapaskans". Shotridge seems to be indulging in some romantic stereotyping here about the idyllic life of primitive people in contrast to the warlike tendencies of the sophisticated people of the coast.

8. The reference here is most probably to the Chugach or Pacific Eskimo, also called Alutiiq or Sugpiaq. This passage is ambiguous and we are guessing and paraphrasing that the aliens are not telling the Tlingit of yet another separate place where they can meet and trade with the Eskimo, but rather that this is the same trading spot where the Tlingit found the Athapaskan. Shotridge's original is, "The people found in that camp pointed to still other people [probably Eskimo] living farther on [westward], and meeting point it was where they were found" (Shotridge 1920:25—brackets are Shotridge's). The "aliens" were probably either Eyak or Ahtna. Presumably, this is their trading spot. The reference to brush houses indicates a temporary camp rather than a permanent village.

9. Precise clan identification of the T'ikanaa is unclear. The term is unique here, and means "the tribe on the outer or seaward side of the island," from t'iká (outer, seaward) and naa (tribe). The Nees.ádi, Shangukeidí, and Kaagwaantaan are clans of the Eagle moiety. The host, Kaa.ushtí, makes a speech alluding to the departed leaders of his clan. At the end of the passage, Eagle Head responds and addresses "Children of Shangukeidí." This term is normally used when a person of one moiety is addressing people of the opposite moiety whose fathers are of the speaker's clan. Thus, this phrase makes sense only if members of the Raven moiety were present as witnesses to the passing of the knife by Kaa.ushtí of the Kaagwaantaan to the Shangukeidí. The Finned House is also the house group of Louis Shotridge, so listeners and readers know that his clan and house passed the dagger on to the Shangukeidí. It is important to note here that the story does not end with adventure and the return of the explorers, but with the creation, history, and social contextualization of the art object that alludes to that adventure. This part of the narrative structure is very important in Tlingit oral tradition and to Shotridge's efforts at contextualization.

10. "The Denizen of Unseen World" is presumably a spirit or a ghost, an inhabitant of the spirit world. We have not heard the orginal name of the dagger in Tlingit, but Shotridge calls it "Denizen of Unseen World" or "as near as Tlingit idea can be interpreted in English, the "Ghost of Courageous Adventurer" (Shotridge 1920:21) Passing the knife to Eagle Head, a participant of the original journey, also identifies it with him and his spirit.

11. We added the word "image" to Shotridge's translation—cf. his original text, "artist who fashioned the name of the war knife on the Pommel" (Shotridge 1920:26). We take this not as written inscription, but use of the artistic image and design of the death's head—the spirit or ghost. The story illustrates how an art object becomes at.óow, an object purchased with the lives of ancestors, in this case the courageous adventurers who died on the expedition. The object is made, brought out ceremonially, and passed on to new stewards. Along with the memories and spirits of the original men who lost their lives and all the previous stewards of the object, Eagle Head, who survived the journey but who will die and join the spirit world, becomes included among those whose spirits are remembered by the object, and who are typically recalled in ceremonial oratory, for examples of such traditional oratories connecting and contextualizing individuals and the art objects (see Dauenhauer and Dauenhauer 1990:229–323).

References

Boas, Franz
1907 *Notes on the Blanket Designs*, to Emmons 1907:351–400. Reprinted in: Jonaitis 1995:188–247.
1917 *Grammatical Notes on the Language of the Tlingit Indians*. Philadelphia: University of Pennsylvania Museum.

Carpenter, Edmund
1975 Collecting Northwest Coast Art. In *American Indian Art of the Northwest Coast: A Dialog on Craftmanship and Aesthetics*. Bill Holm and Bill Reid, eds. Pp. 9–27. Seattle: University of Washington Press.

Cole, Douglas
1985 *Captured Heritage: the Scramble for Northwest Coast Artifacts*. Seattle: University of Washington Press.

Dauenhauer, Nora Marks
1986 Context and Display in Northwest Coast Art. Voices of First America: Text and Contest in the New World. *Special Issue of New Scholar* 10:419–32.
1995 Tlingit At.óow: Tradition and Concepts. In *The Spirit Within: Northwest Coast Native Art from the John H. Hauberg Collection*. Abbott, Brown, Price, and Thurman, eds. Seattle: Seattle Art Museum.

Dauenhauer, Nora Marks, and Richard Dauenhauer
1987 *Haa Shuká, our Ancestors: Tlingit oral Narratives*. Seattle: University of Washington Press.
1990 *Haa Tuwunáagu Yís, for Healing our Spirit: Tlingit Oratory*. Seattle: University of Washington Press.
1994 *Haa Kusteeyí, Our Culture: Tlingit Life Stories*. Seattle: University of Washington Press.

Davidson, George
1901 Explanation of an Indian Map of the Rivers, Lakes, Trails and Mountains from the Chilkaht to the Yukon drawn by the Chilkaht Chief, Kohklux, in 1869. *Mazama* 2(2):75–82.

De Laguna, Frederica
1972 Under Mount Saint Elias. The History and Culture of the Yakutat Tlingit. *Smithsonian Contributions to Anthropology*, vol. 7, pts.1-3. Washington, DC: Smithsonian Institution Press.

Emmons, George T.
1907 The Chilkat Blanket. *Memoirs of the American Museum of Natural History*, vol. 3, pt. 4, pp. 329–350.

Halpin, Marjorie Myers
1994 A Critique of the Boasian Paradigm for Northwest Coast Art. *Culture* XIV (1):5–16.

Hymes, Dell
1985 Language, Memory, and Selective Performance: Cultee's Kathlamet Sun's Myth as Twice-Told to Boas. *Journal of American Folklore* 98(390):391–434.

Jonaitis, Aldona, ed.
1995 *A Wealth of Thought. Franz Boas on Native American Art*. Seattle and London: University of Washington Press. Vancouver and Toronto: Couglas and McIntyre.

Kohklux Map
1995 *The Kohklux Map*. Whitehorse: Yukon Historical and Museums Association.

Mason, J. Alden
1960 Louis Shotridge. *Expedition* 2:10–16.

Maud, Ralph
1993 *The Porcupine Hunter and other Stories. The Original Tsimshian Texts of Henry Tate*. Vancouver: Talonbooks.
n.d. *"The War of the Ghosts:" Two Tellings by Charles Cultee to Franz Boas, 1891 and 1894*. Manuscript in a yet-untiteld and unpublished collection of papers on Northwest Coast literature edited by Richard and Nora Dauenhauer.

Milburn, Maureen
1986 Louis Shotridge and the Objects of Everlasting Esteem. In *Raven's Journey*. Susan Kaplan and Kristin Barsness, eds. Pp. 54–90. Philadelphia: University of Pennsylvania Press.
1994 Weaving the 'Tina' Blanket: the Journey of Florence and Louis Shotridge. In *Haa Kusteeyí, Our Culture: Tlingit Life Stories*. Nora Marks Dauenhauer and Richard Dauenhauer. Pp. 549–64. Seattle: University of Washington Press.
1997 *Politics of Possession: Louis Shotridge and the Tlingit Collections of the University Museum*. Unpublished Ph.D. Thesis in Anthropology. University of British Columbia, Vancouver, B. C. The edition cited in this paper is Draft 4, February 16, 1997.

Nida, Eugene A.
1964 *Toward a Science of Translating*. Leiden: E. J. Brill.

Price, Sally
1989 *Primitive Art in Civilized Places*. Chicago: The University if Chicago Press.

Rohner, Ronald P., ed.
1969 *The Ethnography of Franz Boas. Letters and Diaries of Franz Boas written on the Northwest Coast from 1886 to 1931*. Chicago: University of Chicago Press.

Shelikov, Georgii
1981[1791] *A Voyage to America 17683–1786*. Translated by M. Ramsey. Ed. by Richard Pierce. Kingston, Ontario: The Limestone Press.

Shotridge, Florence

1913 The Life of a Chilkat Indian Girl. *The Museum Journal.* University of Pennsylvania Museum 4:101-3.

Shotridge, Louis

1920 Ghost of Courageous Adventurer. *The Museum Journal.* University of Pennsylvania Museum 11(1):11–26.

Swanton, John R.

1908 Social Conditions, Beliefs, and Linguistic Relationship of the Tlingit Indians. *Twenty-Sixth Annual Report of the Bureau of American Ethnology for the Years 1904–1905*, pp. 391–512. Washington, DC: Government Printing Office.

Bilingual/Bicultural Interpreters and Informants of the Jesup Expedition Era

SERGEI KAN

Much of the writing on the Jesup North Pacific Expedition (JNPE) (e.g., Freed et. al. 1988, 1997; Jonaitis 1988; Krupnik and Fitzhugh 2001) as well as a number of the essays in this volume which celebrates the expedition's centennial, inevitably focus on its organizers and sponsors and, especially, on its field ethnographers. After all, they are the ones who collected the data sought by Boas and whose names appear in the JNPE publications. Our research on the lives and scholarly contributions of these ethnographers is obviously made easier by the availability of substantial biographical materials, published and archival (see Al'kor 1935; Codere 1959; Cole 1999; Rohner 1969; Kan 1992, 2000, 2001a; Krupnik 1996; Shavrov 1935; Stocking 1974, 1996; Vakhtin 2001; Vdovin 1991; Wickwire 1993).

However, as the present paper as well as several other essays in this volume demonstrate, we could achieve a much better understanding of the expedition's contribution to circumpolar ethnology by paying serious attention to these ethnographers' local informants, interpreters, research assistants, and collaborators (see chapters by Dauenhauer and Dauenhauer, and by Wickwire, this volume).

At the turn of the twentieth century, when the JNPE volumes were being put together, most anthropologists did not bother to include much information on their local interpreters and Native as well as non-Native consultants, considering it to be irrelevant to scholarship. In the context of the JNPE, the only exceptions to this rule were, of course, James Teit (see Wickwire,

this volume) and Boas' long-term collaborator and colleague, the great Kwakwa̱ka'wakw ethnographer, George Hunt (Cannizzo 1983; Jacknis 1991; Berman 1996, 2001; Webster this volume), whose name appears next to Boas' as the co-author of the *Kwakiutl Texts* (Boas and Hunt 1905, 1906). While Hunt's role as the JNPE's key Native participant is unique, a number of other Native American and "mixed-blood" (Creole, Métis) interpreters, amateur ethnographers, and informants played a major role in collecting and making sense of this and related expeditions' voluminous data (see Wickwire 1993; cf. Milburn 1986; Dauenhauer and Dauenhauer 1994, this volume).[1]

In recent decades many practicing cultural anthropologists as well as historians of anthropology have become interested in the interaction and the relationship between the ethnographer and his or her informant as the context within which "ethnographic data" is not only collected but, to some extent, constructed (see Buckley 1989; Kan 2001b). A number of scholars have been referring to this interaction as a "dialogue" (Dwyer 1977; Tedlock 1979). As Clifford and Marcus (1986:15) have pointed out, "In this view, 'culture' is always relational, an inscription of communicative processes that exist, historically, *between* subjects in relations of power."

Like many other ethnographers of their time, JNPE expedition fieldworkers, with the exception of Bogoras among the Chukchi (Bogoras 1904–9); Jochelson among the Sakha (Yakut) (but not among the Koryak, cf. Jochelson 1908, 1926); Hunt (Boas and Hunt 1905, 1906) and Teit (1900), were not fluent in the local Native languages. Therefore, they had to rely on bilingual interpreters and informants who could speak at least some English or Russian.[2] Such interpreters or cultural brokers, as Karttunen (1994:xi) has suggested, "functioned as conduits through which information flowed between worlds in collision, translating more than just words and bringing comprehensibility to otherwise meaningless static".

I believe that by examining the biographies and the ethnic/cultural background of these *local* participants in JNPE we would not only gain a much deeper and more nuanced understanding of the nature and the quality of the ethnography bequeathed to us by Boas and his colleagues but would also assign these unnamed (or barely mentioned) men and women to their proper place in the JNPE's annals.[3]

Jesup Expedition Ethnographers

Even a cursory examination of the ethnographic monographs included in the JNPE series reveals how uneven their quality really was. Some, like Bogoras' *The Chukchee* (1904–9) or Teit's *The Thompson Indians* (1900), were true classics of early twentieth century ethnology, covering many of the major aspects of Native material, social, and spiritual culture. Other, such as Farrand's collection of Chilcotin myths (Farrand 1900) or Laufer's brief ethnography of the Amur River people (Laufer 1900), were rather disappointing.

The reasons for this disparity are quite obvious. On the one hand, we are dealing with very experienced field workers, like Waldemar Bogoras, a Russian ethnographer who, prior to JNPE, had spent years living among the Chukchi and spoke their language (Kan 1992; Krupnik 1996), or James Teit, a British expatriate who had settled among the Thompson Indians (Nlaka'pamux), married a Native woman and became fluent in Nlaka'pamux (Wickwire 1993, this volume). Both of these men had already conducted some ethnographic research before they joined Boas' team.

On the other hand, there were some JNPE team members who were like Livingston Farrand. He was not an anthropologist by training, had ever conducted any fieldwork, nor had even visited American Indians prior to his trip to the Northwest Coast in 1897. To make matters worse, he seemed to have trouble establishing good rapport with the "Indians." Here, for example, is what he said about his research among the Chilcotin: "The conditions were not particularly favorable for the work, for the Indians were by no means cordial at the outset, and good interpreters were not to be found. That great resource of ethnological work in the Northwest, the Chinook jargon, was also not available in this tribe" (1900:3–4).[4] Farrand did not fare much better among the Quinault whom he visited during the summer, when most people had already left for their salmon fishing camps. In addition, many of those remaining behind had converted to Shakerism a few years prior to his visit and considered the old religious traditions to be evil and not worth discussing. Luckily, Farrand located an elderly man who had refused to become a Shaker and was willing to talk about the old culture. This man, Bob Pope, who was dying of TB, became Farrand's main informant (Farrand and Kahnweiler 1902:79; Jonatis 1988:191).

I would argue that if we could obtain biographical information on this Quinault man, on Teit's Shuswap informant Sixwilexken, or Swanton's Haida informants and interpreters, such as Henry Edenshaw (Blackman 1982), Mary Ridley, Walter McGregor and "Abraham,"[5] the ethnographic texts produced by these JNPE participants might tell us a lot more than they currently do.[6] Similarly our understanding and appreciation of Bogoras' ethnography of the Chukchi and Jochelson's monograph on the Koryak—JNPE's classic publications—could be enhanced if researchers ever manage to figure out who their local informants and interpreters were.[7]

To illustrate this argument I devote the rest of this paper to the discussion of a relatively short but rich account of certain key aspects of the nineteenth century Tlingit culture given in the 1880s to George T. Emmons, the great "amateur" ethnographer of the Tlingit, by his bilingual Russian/Tlingit informant, Ivan Zhukov.

George T. Emmons, Sergei I. Kostromitinov, and Ivan Zhukov

Although George T. Emmons (1852–1945), one of the characters in my story, was not a participant in the JNPE, his outstanding and voluminous ethnography of the Tlingit, both published and unpublished (see de Laguna 1991; Emmons 1991)[8] clearly complemented the new information being collected by Boas and his associates. In fact, because of Boas' familiarity with Emmons' research in southeastern Alaska, this region was not the focus of the expedition's activities (Boas 1903:77). This would also explain why Swanton's monumental ethnography of the Haida (Swanton 1905) did appear as part of the JNPE publication series while his two important works on the Tlingit did not (Swanton 1908, 1909).

Like Bogoras and Teit, Emmons spent years interacting with the Native people, learning their language and studying their ways. Having come to southeastern Alaska in the early 1880s to serve on a Navy ship that policed the area, he eventually became the major authority on Tlingit culture and the main collector of Tlingit artifacts (de Laguna 1991; Low 1991). He developed good rapport with a number of Tlingit families, including that of Shaaduxícht (ca. 1819–89), the head of the Finned House of the Kaagwaantaan clan and a powerful Chilkat leader; he was also the maternal grandfather of Louis Shotridge (Dauenhauer and Dauenhauer 1994:549–51, this volume). The latter may have been the one to adopt the Navy officer into his lineage and clan. As Emmons himself put it, "I have visited all of their villages. . . . I have made a study of their history and I have lived with them on the most intimate terms, until they have given me one of the their family names and look upon me as one of themselves" (de Laguna 1991:xvii).[9]

Emmons' most important work on the Tlingit, a monograph entitled *The Tlingit Indians*, which he began working on in the late 1880s, was never completed and languished in the AMNH archives until it was finally published in 1991, after having been painstakingly edited by Frederica de Laguna.[10] While putting together this manuscript, Emmons not only relied on his own observations and interviews but used a unique ethnographic account, entitled *A Glance at the First Customs of the Tlingit or Kolosh as the Russians Found Them at Sitka*.[11] According to Emmons' notes, this text was written in Tlingit by "Shukoff," a half Russian and half Tlingit, and given to a Russian interpreter who translated it into English in 1887 or 1888.[12]

The English version of the sketch is about twenty typewritten pages long and contains a variety of interesting data, from myths of the Raven cycle to descriptions of memorial ceremonies (potlatches) and shamanism. By the time this text was written and translated only two other detailed ethnographies of the Tlingit had appeared in print. The first one was Ivan Veniaminov's pioneering account, based on his sojourn as a Russian Orthodox missionary in Sitka in the late 1830s and published in Russia in 1840 (Veniaminov 1984). The second was Aurel Krause's monograph based on his trip to southeastern Alaska in 1881–2 and published in Germany in 1885 (Krause 1956). The latter account relied heavily on the former, particularly when it came to mythology and spiritual culture. Compared to those two works, *A Glance at the First Customs of the Tlingit* was less detailed and was not written as a scholarly work, but as a rendition of an oral presentation. However, it did contain some unique pieces of information that were more likely to have come from a speaker of Tlingit and a partial insider, like "Shukoff," than from outsiders, like Veniaminov and Krause.

In order to better evaluate this text, we must establish the identity of "Shukoff" and that of his translator. The former task is fairly easy, since Emmons tells us that the man was educated by the Russian Church in Sitka and in the early 1880s was employed by the U.S. Naval Commander and later by the civil authorities as a native policeman in Sitka. He died in the mid-1880s at the age of sixty.

The only individual who fit this profile was Ivan Zhukov, who was born in about 1825 at a Russian-American Company (RAC) post on the Nushagak River to a Tlingit mother and a Russian father, a Baranov-era *promyshlennik* (colonial hunter and trader).[13] As a young man in 1841, Zhukov served as an apprentice (*iunga*) on the Company ships. He later studied at the Novo-Arkhangelsk (Sitka) seminary to become a priest for the Tlingit but was expelled for some "disgusting deed." However, due to a significant increase in the number of Tlingit converts in Sitka, the Church decided to appoint him as its interpreter in 1844. A letter to the local RAC office by the local Orthodox priest, Fr. Misail, in which this reassignment of a young Tlingit Creole[14] was requested, stated that Zhukov could also work as a teacher, instructing Tlingit children in the Russian language and teaching the Tlingit language to the non-Tlingit seminarians. The Company agreed to honor the Consistory's request, bringing Zhukov back to Novo-Arkhangelsk and appointing him the official *tolmach* (interpreter) of the Alaska Consistory, with a salary of fifteen rubles a month, plus five rubles a month for teaching the "Kolosh" (Tlingit) language.

Zhukov must have been a gifted interpreter and teacher: in 1845 Bishop Innokentii (Ivan Veniaminov) instructed the Consistory to award him 85 rubles for his diligent two years of service as a church interpreter, and especially for his work on translating the Gospel into Tlingit. In 1849–50 he received a large monetary award for translating several new chapters of the New Testament as well as other religious texts into his mother's native tongue. However, a letter from a member of the Consistory to the RAC Governor, Michail Teben'kov, dated August 1850, pointed out that, while Zhukov had been an excellent interpreter and did not drink,

His behavior in other respects has become so unclean in the last few years, that only a dire need forced us [the Consistory] to continue employing him. However, lately, despite all of our measures aimed at making him improve his conduct, it has become even worse, thus damaging the cause of Christianizing the Kolosh. Consequently he must be removed from the Church's service . . . and sent away from Novo-Arkhangelsk to some other Company post; in the meantime, he should at least be sent away from the town, so that he would no longer be in contact with the Kolosh.

One wonders whether Zhukov had been involved in some sexual misconduct (as he seems to have been in the post-1867 era) or whether he was obtaining illicit benefits from his special position as a powerful intermediary between the Church and the local Tlingit community with which he was still connected through his maternal kin. In any event, he appeared to have been a real survivor. While transferred to Kodiak by Teben'kov in 1850, he must have been needed by the Novo-Arkhangelsk parish and was brought back there by Voevodskii, since he continued to work for the Consistory until 1852–3 when he was finally fired from his job at the Seminary and as the Church's main interpreter, having been given his final monetary reward for good work.

In the mid-1860s, Zhukov reappeared in the church records as the RAC interpreter assigned to the Novo-Arkhangelsk port, whom the current missionaries relied on for information about the Tlingit population of Sitka and whom they wished to rehire as a church interpreter. In 1866, having been frustrated by his own lack of command of the Tlingit language and having examined Tlingit translations available in Novo-Arkhangelsk and found them inadequate, Fr. Nikolai Kovrigin, assigned to serve as a missionary to the "Kolosh," decided to ask Zhukov if he had done more and better translations and to give him Tlingit lessons (ARCA, D 316). Zhukov replied that he had no additional translations in his possession and that he would not mind teaching Kovrigin some Tlingit for a nominal fee. When the priest asked him to take part in his visits to Tlingit homes, the interpreter replied that he was too busy working in the port but, if offered a salary, he would be willing to help the priest not only to speak to the Natives but to work on translating Orthodox prayers.[15] Despite Zhukov's bad reputation among the local clergy, Kovrigin, desperate to have a Tlingit-speaking assistant, hired him to help compile a census of Sitka's Native population. Before leaving Novo-Arkhangelsk, Fr. Nikolai recommended that the Church hired a full time Tlingit interpreter, "even a man like Zhukov." However, because of Zhukov's dubious reputation, the local bishop vigorously objected to this proposal.

We know almost nothing about Zhukov's mother and her family, except that she must have been a high-ranking woman, since missionary records mention her sister being married to one of the Sitka lineage heads (ARCA, D 316). Zhukov must have learned to speak fluent Tlingit from his mother and other Tlingit relatives and it is very likely that he maintained close ties with them, listening to their stories and taking part in their ceremonies or at least observing them, since he seemed to know a great deal about them (see below). After all, their houses were just outside the walls of Novo-Arkhangelsk where he lived during the 1840s to the 1860s. At the same time, the tone of his ethnographic sketch suggests that he identified more with the Russians.[16]

When Alaska was sold by Russia to the United States in 1867, Zhukov, like many other Creoles, did not take advantage of an opportunity to return to his father's country. But neither did he try to obtain American citizenship.[17] However, like other "Russians" who remained in Sitka after its purchase by the U.S., he must have had a difficult time trying to make ends meet, since his name appeared on an 1874 list of 123 local Russian and Creole inhabitants requesting financial assistance from the Russian government to cover the cost of moving to Russia.[18] This request was not granted and Zhukov continued to reside in Sitka. Although, like most other local Russians and Creoles, he

remained listed in the parish records, he must not have been devout, since the record-keepers referred to him as a "doubtful" (*somnitel'nyi*) Christian (ARCA, D 405; D 414).

A real survivor, Ivan Zhukov continued to use his linguistic skills as well as his ability to act as an intermediary between his mother's people and the newcomers. Thus we know that the local American officials relied on him to spy on the restless members of the Kiks.ádi clan during the so-called 1879 "Tlingit unrest" (ARCA, D 434; *The Alaskan* 2/6/1886, p. 3; Kan 1999:198–201, n.d.). Soon thereafter, as I have already mentioned, he was hired by the U.S. Naval commander, in charge of maintaining law and order in Alaska, to serve as an interpreter and an Indian policeman.[19] Zhukov served in that capacity until his death (caused by syphilis and a wound which led to gangrene) on February 2, 1886.[20]

Before discussing Zhukov's ethnography, a word must be said about his sketch's translator, referred to by Emmons only as "George." I believe that he was none other than Sitka's most prominent Russian resident, Sergei Ionavich Kostromitinov, known to the Americans as George Kostrometinoff. A son of a RAC employee and a Creole (Russian-Aleut) woman, he was born in Sitka in 1854 and educated at the local Russian colonial and later American schools.[21] Having grown up in Sitka, Kostromitinov must have had plenty of opportunities to interact with the local Tlingit. It was also rumored that he had a Tlingit mistress (Stepan Ushin's Diary, ARCA D 434).[22] From these contacts, he must have learned to speak fluent Tlingit. Using that knowledge as well as his fluency in Russian and English,[23] Kostromitinov served for twenty years as an official interpreter for court and civil officials in Sitka and traveled throughout the region in that capacity.[24] As a Deputy U.S. Marshal, he frequently took Native and non-Native prisoners south to Seattle and Portland. A respectable and fairly well-to-do Sitka citizen, he belonged to the town's upper crust and was the darling of the Russian clergy and American officials alike, who called upon him for information on Sitka's pre-1867 history and Tlingit culture. Sergei Ionavich often wrote articles on these subjects for the Sitka newspaper and was among the founders of the Alaska Society of Natural History and Ethnology established in Sitka in 1887. In 1893 he was appointed Lieutenant Colonel of the organized militia of the District of Alaska and he continued to be referred to as the "colonel" for the rest of his life. A staunch Russian patriot, he also served as the warden (*starosta*) of Sitka's St. Michael's Russian Orthodox cathedral from 1886 until the early 1910s, when he decided to become an Orthodox priest. Ordained in 1912, he became one of the Sitka parish's most popular pastors, well liked by its Creole and Tlingit parishioners alike. For his work for the Orthodox Church, Kostromitinov received two awards from the

52/ Sergei Ionavich Kostromitinov, ca. 1901 in Sitka. Photographer, Elbridge W. Merrill. Alaska State Library, Vinokouroff Collection, PCA 243-1-27.

Russian government: a St. Daniel's cross in 1900 (Fig. 52) and a silver goblet in 1906 (Ziorov 1893, passim; *The Alaskan* 1/5/1901, p.2; 12/29/1906, p.2; *Russian Orthodox American Messenger* 1912, vol. 16:305–7). When "Fr. Sergei" died in 1915, the Church honored him by burying his body underneath the cathedral floor. Thus, like Zhukov, Kostromitinov was a bicultural and multilingual cultural broker who found a new niche for himself on the new post-1867 Alaska frontier.

While it is impossible to establish how much of Kostromitinov's own knowledge of Tlingit culture is reflected in his translation of Zhukov's ethnographic sketch, I suspect that he did modify the text; in fact,

there is a parenthetical note by Emmons which says that "George" had added some information on a "would-be shaman."

Zhukov's Ethnography

Zhukov's ethnographic sketch is an interesting document. While its author was a semi-educated amateur, he was trying to offer Emmons a description of "traditional" Tlingit culture of an earlier era while offering occasional comments on the changes that had taken place in it during his lifetime.[25] Thus his brief and rather naively worded ethnography has a *temporal* dimension, something lacking in the accounts of indigenous cultures produced by Boas himself and most of Boasian ethnographers of the JNPE era. For example, Swanton (1908)—whose early works are archetypically Boasian—portrayed the Tlingit culture as a timeless entity. To a lesser extent, so did Emmons (1991) in his monumental work, even though the latter does contain a significant number of references to important historical events involving the Tlingit.

In contrast to Swanton, Zhukov sprinkled his text with such statements as, "I am writing about ancestors of present race. The present race are far from their ancestors, although they are trying to follow in steps of ancestors but not with same force" (p. 2). His rich account of the killing of slaves at a ritual for dedicating a new lineage-owned house (pp. 4–8) ends with the following comment, "Now [they] tear blankets [and? or?] cotton instead of killing slaves" (p. 8).

Zhukov's biculturalism can be felt in the two voices with which he speaks about his mother's people. On the one hand, one can hear some nostalgia, or at least regret, in a passage which tells us that the ancestors of the present-day Tlingit were healthier and physically stronger, since they did not drink.[26] On the other hand, as a son of a Russian father who identified himself with the Russians and who spent his entire life working for them and later for the Americans, he gave his Tlingit contemporaries credit for being "very industrious" and earning money by fishing, hunting, cutting wood, etc. (ibid).

At the same time, some of Zhukov's observations are written in a non-judgmental, neutral tone, more typical for ethnographers than missionaries or government officials. For example, immediately after describing traditional magical practices and formulae, he states that the modern-day Natives' use Christian prayer as a way of bringing luck in hunting as well as gambling, something of which neither Russian nor American clergy would approve (p. 4).

On the whole, Zhukov's account offers a lot more information on Tlingit religion and mythology (much of which he describes in a section entitled "Superstitions

of [the] Tlingit," thus switching from his more neutral "ethnographic" voice to that of an outsider and long-time interpreter for the Orthodox Church) than on social organization or material culture. This might be a reflection of his experience as a missionary interpreter who had to translate theological concepts from one language into another. Not surprisingly, Veniaminov's ethnography has the same quality (Kan 1990, 1999). Of course, some of the things Zhukov says about Tlingit mythology (especially the episodes of the Raven myth cycle), religious beliefs, and ritual practices can also be found in Veniaminov's and Krause's works as well as in the subsequent ethnographies by Kamenskii (1906/1985), Swanton (1908, 1909) and Emmons (1991).

Zhukov's account, nevertheless, is valuable in some of its minor but unique ethnographic details[27] as well as in its use of direct quotations from ceremonial speeches and magical formulae. Zhukov's ethnographic sketch is also sprinkled with Tlingit terms, some of which would be familiar to most modern-day speakers of this language as well as to specialists in Tlingit linguistics and ethnology, while others appear to be archaic and would require careful scholarly examination (something I am not ready to do at this point). Thus in his description of the magical observances involved in halibut fishing, Zhukov quotes an actual utterance made by the fisherman addressing the fish, "Look out, you will tear your mouth [if you struggle]. Your bones were in the fire long ago!" (pp. 3–4). The last sentence meant that this particular halibut was a reincarnation of its ancestor whose bones had been burned in a ritually correct manner (cf. Emmons 1991:145).

Another example of the richness of Zhukov's account is his description of a special ritual involved in the potlatch host's greeting of his out-of-town guests, which took place just before they landed in front of his village. According to the Creole ethnographer, having been asked by the host where they had come from, the guests (standing in their canoes) replied, "We came here by the road . . . of the sun." Since the sun-wise direction was a ritually positive one, this reply meant that, as Zhukov himself explained, "they came with good faith; they came to have a joyous time" (p. 7). Prior to the guests' landing, the chief host ordered some slaves to be sacrificed, so as "to kill the trail" about to be followed by the guests from the beach to his house (ibid). Although Zhukov does not explain the meaning of this expression, I have argued that this is another illustration of the central notion of the entire cycle of Tlingit memorial feasts, i.e., that the guests, who were members of the moiety opposite to that of the hosts, served as the link between the latter and their departed matrilineal kin (see Kan 1989).[28]

My final example is from Zhukov's description of a smoking feast, which was a major component of a series of rituals following a high-ranking aristocrat's death. According to Zhukov, at the conclusion of smoking and an exchange of speeches between the hosts and the guests, the chief host addressed the spirit of his deceased predecessor, in whose honor the ceremony was being given, with the following words, "Stand on one side and let your fathers go by." As the author himself explains in parenthesis, this meant that the spirit of the deceased was present in the house until his body was cremated (p. 17). While other ethnographers mentioned the existence of such a belief among the Tlingit, Zhukov offers us an actual ritual utterance confirming it.

Conclusion

Compared to Emmons' monumental ethnography of the Tlingit, Zhukov's sketch is not long at all. Nonetheless, a careful review of the former demonstrates that Emmons did learn a lot from this Sitka Creole and incorporated bits and pieces from Zhukov's account into his own text. Hence, *A Glance at the First Customs of the Tlingit or Kolosh as the Russians Found Them at Sitka* not only adds some rather significant details to our knowledge of the nineteenth century Tlingit culture

(presented from the point of view of a partial insider fluent in the local Native language) but helps us better understand the material presented in Emmons' own oeuvre. How much more this classic work could have told us about the Tlingit people of the pre-JNPE era if we had similar information on Emmons' other Native sources of data and the specific circumstances of his fieldwork.[29]

This brief review of Zhukov's ethnography and its relationship to that of Emmons, Swanton, Veniaminov, and other fieldworkers who recorded information on Tlingit culture is an attempt to suggest ways in which we could try to transform the old monographs of the JNPE-era from monolithic and monological texts to more polyphonic or dialogical ones. The same can be said about several other papers appearing in this volume. In its own unique way, each of them demonstrates how much work still remains to be done on the JNPE legacy, despite a century that separates us from it and the frustrating silence of many of its professional ethnographers about their bilingual/bicultural interpreters, informants, research assistants, and collaborators.

Acknowledgements

I would like to thank all of the organizers of the Jesup Expedition Centenary Conference, and especially Laurel Kendall and Igor Krupnik, for inviting me to present a paper at this important scholarly gathering and then to transform it into the present piece. Krupnik's suggestions and comments on the essay's first draft were very helpful in my work on its final version. Over the years, my understanding of George Emmons' contribution to Tlingit ethnography has benefited greatly from conversations and correspondence with Frederica de Laguna as well as Richard and Nora Dauenhauer. As always, a special "thank you" (*gunalchéesh*) goes to my Tlingit friends, adopted relatives, and teachers who shared with me some valuable inside information on both Emmons and Kostromitinov.

Notes

1. Cf. Anderson and Halpin's discussion (2000) of the recently published field notes of William Bynon, a talented ethnographer of mixed Tsimshian-Welsh descent.

2. This was true of Boas himself whose command of Kwakwaka'wakw was limited and who relied heavily on English as well as the Chinook jargon in his research on the Northwest Coast and the adjacent areas (Berman 1996; Rohner 1969).

3. Thus Judith Berman's (1996, 2001) rethinking of George Hunt's role in Boas' Kwakwaka'wakw research, including her detailed linguistic analysis of the Boast/Hunt texts, has given us a very different understanding of their nature and quality.

4. I suspect that the reason for the Chilcotin unfriendliness towards the visiting anthropologist was the mistreatment they had suffered from gold rush packers and prospectors in the 1860s, which eventually precipitated a violent confrontation, mislabeled in the annals of British Columbia history as the "Chilcotin War" (Lane 1981:411).

5. More information is currently available on some of Swanton's Tlingit informants and interpreters during his later fieldwork of 1904. Thus, his principal Wrangell informant, Katishan, was a well-known local leader, prominent in his clan (the Kaasxagweidí) and the Presbyterian Church (see Swanton 1909:1; Young 1927). Don Cameron, his main Sitka interpreter and a source of some of the ethnographic data, was also an active member of the Presbyterian Church. Since some of his descendants still live in Sitka, his biography could be reconstructed (Kan 1979–97). At the same time, we know nothing about Dekináak'w, "an old man of the Box House," the source of many of the texts recorded by Swanton in Sitka in English and Tlingit (ibid.).

6. For an interesting and thoughtful discussion of Native American ethnographers and anthropologists' informants outside the JNPE context see, for example, several essays in Casagrande (1960), Liberty (1978), and especially the more recent and more theoretically-sophisticated works by Buckley (1989) and Brown (1989).

7. Like Bogoras, Jochelson did mention some of his Native assistants in the introduction to his works. Thus we know that his two main Yukagir interpreters and informants were Aleksei Dolganov and Ivan Spiridonov, while a Russianized Koryak, Nikolai Vilkhin ("the only tolerably good interpreter in the Gishiga district") assisted him in recording and translating Koryak myths (Jochelson 1908:15).

8 Emmons' most important publications on Tlingit culture include a monograph on basketry (1903), the Chilkat blanket (1907), and the Whale House of the Chilkat (1916). The only other Native American culture that he studied was that of the Athapaskan-speaking Tahltan of the British Columbia interior (1911).

9. Clear evidence of Emmons' being accepted by the Tlingit is the fact that he was invited to various feasts and potlatches (e.g., Emmons 1991:391). In addition several of my Tlingit consultants and friends told me that for years Emmons was involved in an intimate relationship with a Tlingit woman (Kan 1979–1997).

10. A related manuscript by Emmons, entitled *History of Tlingit Tribes and Clans*, still remains unpublished, although material from it has been incorporated by de Laguna into Emmons' (1991) monograph and used by Hope (2000) in his ongoing research on traditional Tlingit tribes, clans, and clan houses.

11. This document has been deposited in the Anthropology Archive of the American Museum of Natural History (AMNH-DA), together with Emmons' *The Tlingit Indians*.

12. While the title page of this sketch lists 1882 as the date of its translation into English, a parenthetical remark within the text itself indicates that in 1887 the interpreter himself added some information to Shukoff's (Zhukov's) account of shamanism. Hence I cannot agree with de Laguna's (1991:xi) dating of this translation as 1884.

13. Biographical information on Zhukov could be found in the Alaska Russian Church Archives (ARCA, D 347; D 434). Some of the material presented in this paper appeared in my earlier monograph on the history of Russian Orthodox Christianity among the Tlingit (Kan 1999:131–3,167–8).

14. "Creole" was a standard term used by the Russian-American Company to refer to the offspring of a mixed Russian-Native Alaskan union.

15. From Zhukov's other comments, it appears that he was trying to get a higher price for his services, portraying the study of Tlingit language as a very difficult task.

16. Thus Zhukov never referred to the Tlingit as "my people," calling them "the natives" instead.

17. Church records dating back to the early 1870s list him as a "Creole" rather than an "American citizen," a category which included the more respectable segment of the local "Russian" community whose members did not or claimed not to have any Native Alaskan blood.

18. Fr. Nikolai Mitropol'skii's file (ARCA, B 20).

19. Thus, in 1880 Zhukov traveled on board of the U.S.S. *Jamestown* to various coastal villages in order to interpret for the Navy officers in their deliberations with the Tlingit (Stepan Ushin's Diary, ARCA, D 434).

20. Zhukov's Tlingit fellow-policemen carried his coffin to the cemetery and were followed by uniformed sailors and soldiers. As his body was lowered into the ground, guns were fired (Stepan Ushin's Diary, ARCA D 434).

21. For biographical data on Sergei I. Kostromitinov, see ARCA (B 14), Kostrometinoff (1876–1908), Pierce (1990:262–3), and Kan (1999, passim).

22. According to Tlingit sources (Kan 1979–97), a number of his descendants still reside in several Tlingit communities.

23. Kostromitinov might have also had the command of Aleut.

24. The Russian Church also took advantage of Kostromitinov's knowledge of Tlingit, assigning him the task of translating Veniaminov's famous sermon, *Guide to the Heavenly Kingdom*, into that language. The translation was published in Sitka in 1901.

25. It is actually not entirely clear whether Zhukov wrote his sketch specifically for Emmons.

26. Zhukov's sketch begins with am interesting page-long description of the physical characteristics and bodily adornment of the "old-time" Tlingit men and women (Pp.1–2).

27. Thus, for example, his description of the practices involved in the preservation and ceremonial use of enemies' scalps (2) is more detailed than Emmons' (1991:335).

28. Cf. an expression "killing the money," used to refer to the potlatch hosts' distribution of money among the guests (Kan 1979–97).

29. To Emmons' credit, he did occasionally mention the name of a Tlingit person who had given him a particular piece of information; he also often indicated whether he had personally attended a native ceremony he was describing (see Emmons 1991).

References

Al'kor, Ian P.

1935   V.G. Bogoraz-Tan. *Sovetskaia Etnografiia* 4–5:5–31.

Anderson, Margaret, and Marjorie Halpin

2000   Introduction. In *Potlatch in Gitsegukla: William Beynon's 1945 Field Notebooks.* Margaret Anderson and Marjorie Halpin, eds. Pp. 3–52. Vancouver: University of British Columbia Press.

Berman, Judith

1996   "The Culture as It Appears to the Indian Himself": Boas, George Hunt, and the Methods of Ethnography. In *Volksgeist as Method and Ethic: Essays on Boasian Ethnography and the German Anthropological Tradition.* George W. Stocking, Jr., ed. Pp. 215–56. History of Anthropology, 8. Madison: University of Wisconsin Press.

2001   Unpublished Materials of Franz Boas and George Hunt: A Record of 45 Years of Collaboration. In *Gateways: Exploring the Legacy of the Jesup North Pacific Expedition, 1897-1902.* Igor Krupnik and William W. Fitzhugh, eds. Pp. 181–213. Contributions to Circumpolar Anthropology, 1. Washington, DC: Arctic Studies Center.

Blackman, Margaret B.

1982   *During My Time: Florence Edenshaw Davidson, a Haida Woman.* Seattle: University of Washington Press.

Boas, Franz

1903   The Jesup North Pacific Expedition. *American Museum Journal* 3(5):73–119.

Boas, Franz, and George Hunt

1905   Kwakiutl Texts. *The Jesup North Pacific Expedition,* vol.3. *Memoirs of the American Museum of Natural History,* 5. Leiden: E.J. Brill; New York: G.E. Stechert.

1906   Kwakiutl Texts (Second Series). *The Jesup North Pacific Expedition,* vol. 10, pt.1, pp.1–269. *Memoirs of the American Museum of Natural History,* 10. Leiden: E.J. Brill; New York: G.E. Stechert.

Bogoras, Waldemar

1904–9 The Chukchee. *The Jesup North Pacific Expedition,* vol. 7, pt. 1–3. *Memoirs of the American Museum of Natural History,* 11. Leiden: E.J. Brill; New York: G.E. Stechert.

Brown, Jennifer S. H.
1989   "A Place in Your Mind for Them All": Chief William Berens. In *Being and Becoming Indian*. James Clifton, ed. Pp. 204–25. Chicago: Dorsey.

Buckley, Thomas
1989   Suffering and the Cultural Construction of Others: Robert Spott and A. L. Kroeber. *American Indian Quaterly* 13:437–45.

Cannizzo, Jeanne
1983   George Hunt and the Invention of Kwakiutl Culture. *Canadian Review of Sociology and Anthropology* 20(1):44–58.

Casagrande, Joseph B., ed.
1960   *In the Company of Man: Twenty Portraits by Anthropologists*. New York: Harper and Brothers.

Clifford, James, and George E. Marcus, eds.
1986   *Writing Culture: the Poetics and Politics of Ethnography*. Berkeley: University of California Press.

Codere, Helen
1959   The Understanding of the Kwakiutl. In *The Anthropology of Franz Boas*. Walter Goldschmidt, ed. Pp. 61–75. *Memoir of the American Anthropological Association*, 89. *American Anthropologist* 61(5), pt. 2.

Cole, Douglas
1999   *Franz Boas. The Early Years, 1858–1906*. Vancouver and Toronto: Douglas & McIntyre; Seattle and London: University of Washington Press.

2001   The Greatest Thing Undertaken by Any Museum? Franz Boas, Morris Jesup, and the North Pacific Expedition. In *Gateways: Exploring the Legacy of the Jesup North Pacific Expedition, 1897–1902*. Igor Krupnik and William W. Fitzhugh, eds. Pp. 29–70. Contributions to Circumpolar Anthropology, 1. Washington, DC: Arctic Studies Center.

Dauenhauer, Nora Marks, and Richard Dauenhauer
1994   Louis Shotridge/Florence Shotridge. In *Haa Kusteeyí, Our Culture: Tlingit Life Stories*. Nora Marks Dauenhauer and Richard Dauenhauer, eds. Pp. 548–64. Seattle: University of Washington Press.

n.d.   Collisions in Tlingit America: Tlingit Interpreters for the Russian-American Company. In *Worlds in Collision: Critically Reflections on Aboriginal and European Contact Narratives*. John Lutz, ed. Vancouver: University of British Columbia Press (in preparation).

De Laguna, Frederica
1991   Editor's Introduction: George Thornton Emmons as Ethnographer. In George T. Emmons. *The Tlingit Indians*. Frederica de Laguna, ed. Pp. xvii–xxv. Seattle: University of Washington Press.

Dwyer, Kevin
1977   The Dialogic in Anthropology. *Dialectical Anthropology* 2:143–51.

Emmons, George T.
1903   The Basketry of the Tlingit. *Memoirs of the American Museum of Natural History*, vol. 3, pt. 2:229–77.

1907   The Chilkat Blanket. *Ibid*, vol.3, pt. 4:329–401.

1911   The Tahltan Indians. *University Museum Anthropological Publications* 4(1):5–120.

1916   The Whale House of the Chilkat. *Anthropological Papers of the American Museum of Natural History* 19(1):1–33.

1991   *The Tlingit Indians*. Frederica de Laguna, ed. Seattle: University of Washington Press; New York: American Museum of Natural History.

Farrand, Livingston
1900   Traditions of the Chilcotin Indians. *The Jesup North Pacific Expedition*, vol.2, pt.1, pp. 1–54. *Memoirs of the American Museum of Natural History*, 4. New York: G.E. Stechert.

Farrand, Livingstone and W. S. Kahnweiler
1902   Traditions of the Quinault Indians. *The Jesup North Pacific Expedition*, vol.2, pt.3, pp. 77–132. *Memoirs of the American Museum of Natural History*, 4. New York: G.E. Stechert.

Freed, Stanley A., Ruth S. Freed, and Laila Williamson
1988   Capitalist Philanthropy and Russian Revolutionaries: the Jesup North Pacific Expedition. *American Anthropologist* 90(1):7–24.

1997   Tough Fieldworkers: History and Personalities of the Jesup Expedition. In *Drawing Shadows to Stone: The Photography of the Jesup North Pacific Expedition, 1897–1902*. Laurel Kendall, Barbara Mathé, Thomas R. Miller, eds. Pp. 9–17. New York: American Museum of Natural History; Seattle: University of Washington Press.

Hope, Andrew, III
2000   Appendix. In *Will the Time Ever Come? A Tlingit Source Book*. Andrew Hope, III and Thomas F. Thornton, eds. Pp. 127–59. Fairbanks: University of Alaska Press.

Jacknis, Ira
1991   George Hunt, Collector of Indian Specimens. In *Chiefly Feasts: The Enduring Kwakiutl Potlatch*. A. Jonaitis, ed. Pp. 177–224. Seattle: University of Washington Press; New York: American Museum of Natural History.

Jochelson, Waldemar
1908   The Koryak. *The Jesup North Pacific Expedition*, vol.6, pts.1–2. *Memoirs of the American Museum of Natural History*, 10. Leiden: E.J. Brill.

1926   The Yukaghir and the Yukaghirized Tungus. *The Jesup North Pacific Expedition*, vol. 9, pts.1–3. *Memoirs of the American Museum of Natural History*, 13. Leiden: E.J. Brill; New York: G.E. Stechert.

Jonaitis, Aldona

1988   *From the Land of the Totem Poles: The North-west Coast Collection of the American Museum of Natural History.* Seattle: University of Washington Press; New York: American Museum of Natural History.

Kamenskii, Anatolii

1985 [1906]   *Tlingit Indians of Alaska.* Translated by Sergei Kan. Fairbanks: University of Alaska Press.

Kan, Sergei

1979–97   Unpublished Notes on Tlingit History and Culture in Author's Possession.

1989   *Symbolic Immortality: Tlingit Potlatch of the Nineteenth Century.* Washington, DC: Smithsonian Institution Press.

1990   Recording Native Culture and Christianizing the Natives—Russian Orthodox Missionaries in Southeastern Alaska. In *Russian in North America. Proceedings of the 2nd International Conference on Russian America.* Richard Pierce, ed. Pp. 298–313. Kingston, Ontario: The Limestone Press. Fairbanks: University of Alaska Press.

1992   Boas' Research Agenda and the Russian Participants in the Jesup Expedition. Unpublished paper presented at the First International Congress of Arctic Social Sciences, Ste-Foy, Quebec.

1999   *Memory Eternal: Tlingit Culture and Russian Orthodox Christianity Through Two Centuries.* Seattle: University of Washington Press.

2000   The Mystery of the Missing Monograph or Why Shternberg's "The Social Organization of the Gilyak" Never Appeared among the Jesup Expedition Publications. *European Review of Native American Studies* 14(2):19–38.

2001a   The "Russian Bastian and Boas": Why Shternberg's "The Social Organization of the Gilyak" Never Appeared among the Jesup Expedition Publications. In *Gateways: Exploring the Legacy of the Jesup North Pacific Expedition, 1897–1902.* Igor Krupnik and William W. Fitzhugh, eds. Pp.217–56. Contributions to Circumpolar Anthropology, 1. Washington, DC: Arctic Studies Center.

2001b   *Strangers to Relatives: The Adoption and Naming of Anthropologists in Native North America.* Sergei Kan, ed. Lincoln, Nebraska: University of Nebraska Press.

n.d.   Events and Nonevents on the Tlingit/Russian/American Colonial Frontier. In *New Perspectives on Native North America: Cultures, Histories, and Representations.* Sergei Kan and Pauline Turner Strong, eds. Lincoln: University of Nebraska Press (in press).

Karttunen, Frances

1994   *Between Worlds: Interpreters, Guides, and Survivors.* New Brunswick: Rutgers University Press.

Kostrometinoff, George [Kostromitinov, Sergei I.]

1876–1908   Scrapbook. Unpublished Manuscript. Alaska State Library. Juneau.

Krause, Aurel

1956 [1885]   *The Tlingit Indians.* Translated by Erna Gunther. Seattle: University of Washington Press.

Krupnik, Igor

1996   The "Bogoras Enigma": Bounds of Culture and Formats of Anthropologists. In *Grasping the Changing World: Anthropological Concepts in the Postmodern Era.* Václav Hubinger, ed. Pp. 35–52. London: Routledge.

Krupnik, Igor, and William W. Fitzhugh, eds.

2001   Gateways: Exploring the Legacy of the Jesup North Pacific Expedition, 1897–1902. *Contributions to Circumpolar Anthropology*, 1. Washington, DC: Arctic Studies Center. Smithsonian Institution.

Lane, Robert B.

1981   Chilcotin. In *Handbook of North American Indians.* Vol. 6. Subarctic. June Helm, ed. Pp. 402–12. Washington, DC: Smithsonian Institution.

Laufer, Berthold

1900   Preliminary Notes on Explorations among the Amoor Tribes. *American Anthropologist*, n.s., 2:297–338.

Liberty, Margot, ed

1978   *American Indian Intellectuals.* St. Paul: West Publishing Co.

Low, Jean

1991   Lieutenant George Thornton Emmons, USN, 1852–1945. In George T. Emmons. *The Tlingit Indians.* Frederica de Laguna, ed. Pp. xxvii–xl. Seattle: University of Washington Press

Milburn, Maureen

1986   Louis Shotridge and the Objects of Everlasting Esteem. In *Raven's Journey. The World of Alaska's Native People.* Susan Kaplan and Kristin J. Barsness, eds. Pp.54–77. Philadelphia: The University Museum, University of Pennsylvania.

Pierce, Richard A.

1990   *Russian America: a Biographical Dictionary.* Kingston, Ontario and Fairbanks, Alaska: The Limestone Press.

Rohner, Ronald P., ed.

1969   *The Ethnography of Franz Boas: Letters and Diaries of Franz Boas Written on the Northwest Coast from 1886 to 1931.* Chicago: University of Chicago Press.

Shavrov, K. B.

1935   V.I. Iokhel'son. *Sovetskaia Etnografiia* 2:3–13. Leningrad.

Stocking, George W., Jr.

1974   Introduction: The Basic Assumptions of Boasian Anthropology. In *The Shaping of American Anthro-*

pology, 1883–1911: A Franz Boas Reader. George W. Stocking, Jr., ed. Pp. 1–20. New York: Basic Books.

1996 Boasian Ethnography and the German Anthropological Tradition. In *Volksgeist as Method and Ethic: Essays on Boasian Ethnography and the German Anthropological Tradition*. George W. Stocking, Jr., ed. Pp. 3–8. History of Anthropology, 8. Madison: University of Wisconsin Press.

Swanton John R.

1905 Contributions to the Ethnology of the Haida. *The Jesup North Pacific Expedition*, vol.5, pt.1, pp. 1–300. *Memoirs of the American Museum of Natural History*, 8. Leiden: E.J. Brill; New York: G.E. Stechert.

1908 Social Conditions, Beliefs, and Linguistic Relationship of the Tlingit Indians. In *26th Annual Report of the Bureau of American Ethnology*. Pp. 391–486. Washington, DC: Government Printing Office.

1909 Tlingit Myths and Texts. *Bureau of American Ethnology Bulletin* 39. Washington, DC.

Tedlock, Dennis

1979 The Analogical Tradition and the Emergence of a Dialogical Anthropology. *Journal of Anthropological Research* 35:387–400.

Teit, James A.

1900 The Thompson Indians of British Columbia. *The Jesup North Pacific Expedition*, vol. 1, pt.4, pp.16–392. *Memoirs of the American Museum of Natural History*, 2. New York: G.E. Stechert.

Vakhtin, Nikolai

200 Franz Boas and the Shaping of the Jesup Expedition Siberian research, 1895–1900. In *Gateways: Exploring the Legacy of the Jesup North Pacific Expedition, 1897–1902*. Igor Krupnik and William W. Fitzhugh, eds. Pp. 71–89. Contributions to Circumpolar Anthropology, 1. Washington, DC: Arctic Studies Center.

Vdovin, Innokentii S.

1991 V. G. Bogoraz-Tan—uchionyi, pisatel', obshchestvennyi deiatel' (V. G. Bogoras-Tan: Scholar, Fiction Writer, Public Figure). *Sovetskaia Etnografiia* 2:82–92. Moscow.

Veniaminov, Ivan

1984 [1840] *Notes on the Islands of the Unalashka District*. Translated by Lydia T. Black and R. H. Geoghegan. Richard Pierce, ed. Kingston, Ontario and Fairbanks, Alaska: The Limestone Press.

Wickwire, Wendy

1993 Women in Ethnography: the Research of James A. Teit. *Ethnohistory* 40(4):538–62.

Young, S. Hall

1927 *Hall Young of Alaska*. New York: Fleming H. Revell Company.

Ziorov, Bishop Nikolai

1893 *Iz moego dnevnika* (From My Diary). St. Petersburg: Tserkovnye Vedomosti.

53/ A group of the "forest" Yukagir on the Yassachnaya River, fall 1901. Photographer, Waldemar Jochelson (AMNH 11013)

part3

PEOPLE, ANIMALS, AND LAND: A JESUP THEME REVISITED

The Jesup Expedition and the Modernization of North Pacific Natural History

ROBERT S. HOFFMANN

At the turn of the last century, the Jesup North Pacific Expedition of the American Museum of Natural History (1897–1902) established a new paradigm for the "field sciences"—those scientific endeavors that explore the natural world and the role of humans and their cultures within that world. Disciplines such as geology, geography, botany, zoology, and anthropology were at that time, and to a significant extent remain, based primarily on data collected directly from the natural world ("the field"), through observation, measurement, and collection of specimens. While in the Western scientific tradition such fieldwork had been carried on for at least four centuries, it was given strong impetus by the worldwide growth of European colonial empires in the eighteenth and nineteenth centuries, which allowed Western scientists freer access to the more remote and less studied parts of the globe. This access was primarily used to accumulate specimens in the narrow field of the individual scientist's area of interest (for example, mammals), which were placed in museums in Western, or in some cases, colonial capitals.

The significant difference in the Jesup North Pacific Expedition and the later (1916–1930) Asiatic expedition of the American Museum of Natural History lay in deliberate combining of scientists from different disciplines into a single field team ("the method of correlated work"; see Andrews 1932). Similarly, the Jesup Expedition Centennial—with its arrays of papers, symposia, and historiographic research—brought together anthropologists, linguists, geneticists, and evolutionary and environmental biologists (note the changing disciplinary nomenclature) to examine changes that have occurred in our knowledge and understanding of both human cultures and biotas of the North Pacific, including Beringia.

The Jesup Expedition as a "Natural History" Venture

This "correlated work", which made the Jesup Expedition such a breakthrough, is effective only if the several specialists staffing a complex expedition are willing to spend at least some of their time working outside of their own specialties. That this was true of the JNPE pattern of fieldwork can be seen by the results of its mammal collecting (Allen 1903). Altogether, about 500 specimens of twenty-nine species were obtained from seven different localities throughout eastern Siberia. These were, from south to north:

(1) Vladivostok (43°09' N, 131°53' E);

(2) "lower Amoor" (Amur River, near Nikolaevsk-na-Amure, at 53°10' N, 140°44' E);

(3) "Gichiga, on the west coast of the Sea of Okhotsk" (the town of Gizhiga, actually, at the extreme northeast corner of that sea, at the head of Shelikov Gulf and mouth of the Gizhiga River, 62°00' N, 160°34' E);

(4) "Marcova, on the middle Anadyr River, 600 miles north of Gichiga" (the town of Markovo, actually, about 330 miles northeast of Gizhiga);

(5) "near the mouth of the Anadyr River" (near or at the site of the present-day city of Anadyr, 64°50' N, 176°00' E);

6) "Indian Point, on the extreme northeastern coast of Siberia" (Cape Chaplin, actually, the southeastern tip of the Chukchi Peninsula, at 64°24' N, 172°10' E); and

(7) "Verkhne Kolimsk, on the middle Kolyma River" (the town of Verkhne-Kolymsk on the upper Kolyma River, at 65°38', N 150°40' E).

Most specimens were, to be sure, collected and prepared by Norman Buxton, the Jesup Expedition's designated zoologist (Figs.54–56); but a significant number were captured by several of the expedition's anthropologists—Bogoras, Jochelson, and Laufer (Allen 1903:101–2).

The collection, now at the American Museum, includes what were then considered to be twelve new species, two of them named by their describer, J. A. Allen, in honor of Norman Buxton. In addition, Buxton obtained 800 birds representing 125 species, published subsequently by Allen (1905), including a new species of lark, *Alauda buxtoni*; he was also commissioned to collect other vertebrates.

Norman Geer Buxton (1872–??), the only trained biologist on the JNPE staff, remains a shadowy figure in the expedition. His only written material appears to be section of J. A. Allen's report titled "Itinerary and General Description of the Country" (Buxton 1903; see also Figs. 57-61). He was from Johnstown, Ohio, and had served earlier as a collector for Edward Avery McIlhenny's expedition to Point Barrow, Alaska, for the Philadelphia Academy of Natural Sciences in 1897–8 (Allen 1903; Stone W. 1900).[1] The only other source of information about that expedition may be found in a popular article written by McIlhenny (1904). Although it does not mention Buxton, it gives some hint of what he experienced in Alaska on that trip.

None of the new species from Siberia named by Allen has retained its identity up to the present, all now being considered synonyms of earlier names. This was due to the way in which post-Jesup systematists altered their views of evolution and speciation in the ensuing century, discussion of which makes up the remainder of this essay.

Franz Boas, the lead scientist for the Jesup Expedition, was a pivotal figure in this changing course of Western science. Formally educated in mathematics and physics as well as geography, Boas was fascinated by what he saw as a fundamental dichotomy between "physics" and "cosmography." Today we use different words—inductive science versus deductive, observational or field sciences (see above) that can be grouped under the rubric of natural history (Boas 1887). It was his lifelong goal to produce a synthesis of these two modes of science, which probably led him to staff the Jesup Expedition with a variety of specialists.

The "natural history" aspect of the Jesup Expedition was thus quite broad. However, in contrast to the anthropological team whose fieldwork was undertaken by seasoned ethnographers (like Bogoras, Jochelson, and Boas himself) or professionally trained young graduates (like Laufer), the fieldwork of the biology team was undertaken by hired collectors, such as Buxton in Siberia, and A. J. Stone for the collecting in Alaska and northwestern Canada supported by the American Museum at about the same time. Whereas the anthropologists published their own scientific reports, the natural history reports of the JNPE were written by other people, such as J. A. Allen, Curator of Birds and Mammals at the American Museum, who was no longer physically capable of field work under the strenuous conditions encountered in Siberia or Alaska (Allen 1903, 1905). It was, however, common in the natural history tradition for museum curators to remain with their collections, while they employed collectors to obtain the material necessary for their research. Perhaps the best known such team was the British Museum's Oldfield Thomas and his collectors, among them Malcolm Anderson and Douglas Carruthers.

Andrew J. Stone was from Missoula, Montana, but no more is known of him than is of Buxton. He was engaged by Allen to collect in Alaska, Yukon, and Northwest Territories from 1896 to 1903, funded mainly by J. M. Constable, Trustee and First Vice President of the American Museum. Logically, this might have been considered the New World portion of the Jesup Expedition, since the area surveyed was the counterpart of northeastern Siberia east of the Bering Strait. However, it was not so designated, nor was it called the "Constable Expedition" after its funder, but was named after the hired collector. Stone published only one paper from his trip (Stone 1900), covering his itinerary and geographical notes, observations of the larger mammals, and a few comments on Native inhabitants for 1896–8 —the same type of material that Buxton wrote for Allen— while the scientific results were published by Allen in a series of twelve papers between 1897 and 1905. Why Allen (and Boas) should have downplayed the museum's fieldwork in eastern Beringia, while publicizing it on the other side of the Bering Strait, is unclear. It may be related to the fact that the U. S. National Museum in Washington already had a headstart in this area through the activities of W. H. Dall, R. Kennicott, E. W. Nelson, W. H. Osgood, E. A. Preble, and others.

Collections and the Changing View of the Species

At the close of the nineteenth century, the term "biological diversity" had not been coined, and ecology was in its infancy. Species of organisms, and for that matter, human populations ("races"), were defined typologically, on the basis of their morphology, and while Darwinian evolution was generally accepted by the scientific community, an understanding of the basis— the genetics of individuals and populations—was just developing. It is interesting to compare the number of species recognized by systematists of the Jesup Expedition era with those later in the century. I will restrict myself to Beringian mammals, since that is my specialty, but similar trends are evident in most other groups, and in the wider North Pacific region.

Table 2/ Total Number of Recognized Land Mammal Species in Beringia at the End of the Nineteenth Century

West Beringia only (Northeast Siberia)	Holarctic	East Beringia only (Alaska and Yukon)
10 shrews		10 shrews
2 lagomorphs		3 lagomorphs
1 marmot		1 marmot
1 ground squirrel		4 ground squirrels
1 red-backed vole	1 red-backed vole	3 red-backed voles
3 lemmings		4 lemmings
4 gray voles		12 gray voles
14 carnivores		24 carnivores
	2 carnivores	
5 ungulates		4 ungulates
subtotal: 41	3	65
TOTAL 44		68

Around 1900, a total of 109 species of terrestrial mammals had been named as inhabiting Beringia, forty-four in eastern Siberia, and sixty-eight in the Alaskan-Yukon region (Table 2). But of these, only three were considered Holarctic species; that is, found both in Eurasia and North America. These were the northern redbacked vole, *Evotomys* (=*Clethrionomys*) *rutilus*, arctic fox, *Vulpes* (=*Alopex*) *lagopus*, and polar bear *Thalarctos* (=*Ursus*) *maritimus*. A fourth species, musk-ox *Ovibos moschatus*, had a historically Holarctic distribution, but was extinct in both western and eastern Beringia at that time; subsequently it was successfully reestablished on both sides of the Bering Strait. That more than 100 species of mammals were to be found in the northern North Pacific at the time of the Jesup Expedition suggests a degree of species richness that we now believe was almost a two-fold overestimate. However, the application of systematics and taxonomy in the study of biodiversity does not always lead to exaggeration of species richness. I will illustrate its ups and downs in the twentieth century by focusing on a few major groups of Beringian mammals with which I am most familiar.

In 1900, there were thought to be ten species of red-toothed shrews (genus *Sorex*) in east Beringia, and nine in west, none shared, for a total of nineteen species. Of the ground squirrels and marmots, there were two in west Beringia and five in east Beringia, again, none shared. Of the gray voles (genus *Microtus*), there were four in the west and twelve in the east, none of which were Holarctic (Table 3).

A pattern of more described species in east Beringia (Alaska-Yukon) is evident, both in total mammals, and in the selected groups, caused for the most part by the tendency of North American mammalogists to "over-split" taxonomic units. In its extreme form, this was exemplified by the taxonomy of the North American brown bears, or grizzlies, published by Merriam (1918) in which he recognized seventy-six species of bears, allocated among fifteen groups, in North America alone. This for a species now regarded as a single entity, with fewer than ten subspecies at most.

Genetics and the Biological Species Concept

Shortly thereafter, a reaction against such taxon splitting began to set in, culminating in the work of Julian Huxley (1940, 1942) and Ernst Mayr (1942) of the American Museum and supported by the work of the expatriate Russian geneticist and natural historian, T. Dobzhansky of Columbia University (1941). They introduced the important new ideas of "polytypic species" and the "biological species concept." Mayr (1942:146) commented that "new investigation . . . show[s] that many of the previously recognized species are nothing but subspecies of widespread polytypic species. The acceptance of the modern biological concept . . . resulted in an extraordinary simplification of the system."

The shift from a monotypic, typological species concept to a polytypic, biological one was important, but the emergence of statistical applications and numerical systematics also contributed to "simplification," (i.e., the "lumping" of two or more taxa previously considered distinct species into a single, presumably polytypic one. This paradigmatic shift also had an impact on anthropologist's views of what constituted

Table 3/ Numbers of Shrews, Marmots, Ground Squirrels, and Gray Voles Recognized in Beringia, End of Nineteenth Century

West Beringia only	Holarctic	East Beringia only
Shrews (*Sorex*)		
Sorex macropygmaeus		*Sorex personatus*
araneus		pribilofensis
ultimus		arcticus
sibiriensis		tundrensis
sanguinidens		richardsoni
tomensis		sphagnicola
vir		glacialis
gracillimus		hoyi
tscherskii		hydrodromus
		palustris
subtotal: 9	0	10
Marmots (*Marmota*) and Ground Squirrels (*Spermophilus*)		
Arctomys kamtschatica		*Arctomys pruinosus*
Citellus undulatus		*Spermophilus empetra*
		beringianus
		osgoodi
		barrowensis
subtotal: 2	0	5
Gray Voles (*Microtus*)		
Arvicola slowzovii		*Microtus miurus*
buturlini		abbreviatus
tshuktshorum		operarius
Aschizomys lemminus		unalascensis
		macfarlani
		sitkensis
		kodiacensis
		innuitus
		drummondii
		xanthognathus
		pennsylvanicus
subtotal: 4	0	12
TOTAL: 13	0	27

human species and subspecies ("races"), particularly by emphasizing the importance of gene flow between populations. The shift resulted in an apparent decline in mammal species richness in Beringia; in the 1950s and early 1960s, the number in west Beringia was thirty-two, and in east Beringia, also thirty-two, equal on both sides of the Bering Strait. But of these, twenty-five had Holarctic distributions, so the total number of species recognized fell to thirty-nine (Table 4), slightly more than a third of the number recognized in 1900. Of the nineteen species of *Sorex* that had been named by the early 1900s (see Table 3), only six were recognized at mid-century, two of which were Holarctic. One marmot (instead of two) was recognized, but it was Holarctic, as was a single Holarctic ground squirrel. Five species of gray voles, instead of sixteen, were recognized, three of which were Holarctic (Table 5).

Cladistics and the Evolutionary Species Concept

The next, and current, phase of systematic analysis began in the mid-1960s with the widespread adoption of the concepts and principles of cladistic analysis of systematic relationships, or phylogenetic systematics, which have, in this period, produced a revolution in evolutionary studies, including the evolutionary species concept. The concept was pioneered by G. G. Simpson, who held joint tenure at both the American Museum and Columbia University. It is a "lineage" or "clade" concept of the species, "a single lineage of ancestor-descendant populations which maintains its identity from other such lineages, and which has its own evolutionary tendencies and historical fate" (modified from Simpson 1961; quoted in Wiley 1981:25).

Additionally, development of several new techniques—comparative studies of chromosomes, protein electrophoresis, and multivariate statistics—were followed by DNA studies (restriction site analysis, base pair sequencing, etc.) and sophisticated modeling of phylogenetic topology and significance testing. The combination of new data generated by different techniques, and their analysis through the principles of phylogenetic systematics, has resulted in an increase once more in the number of species recognized, as those previously thought to be polytypic species have been shown to consist of two or more distinct species. Species richness in Beringia now stands at forty species in west (Siberia), and forty-two in east Beringia (Alaska and Yukon), of which eighteen are Holarctic in distribution, for a total of sixty-four species in Beringia as a whole (Table 6), more than one and one-half times the number admitted during the period of indiscriminant lumping under the polytypic species rubric.

The Future:
Gene Sequencing and Phylogeography

The new techniques mentioned above have led to more robust hypotheses of phylogenetic relationships based

Table 4/ Total Number of Recognized Land Mammal Species in Beringia, Mid-twentieth Century

West Beringia only (Northeast Siberia)	Holarctic	East Beringia only (Alaska and Yukon)
3 shrews	2 shrews	1 shrew
1 lagomorph	1 lagomorph	2 lagomorphs
	1 marmot	
	1 ground squirrel	
1 red-backed vole	1 red-backed vole	
1 lemming	2 lemmings	1 lemming
1 gray vole	3 gray vole	1 gray vole
	10 carnivores	2 carnivores
	4 ungulates	
Subtotal: 7	25	7
Total:	**32**	**32**

on cladistic analysis of larger and more diverse sets of characters. Examples of such hypotheses can be illustrated by the shrews, marmotines, and voles I have been emphasizing. George (1988) based her analysis on electrophoretic data from twenty-six species of the genus *Sorex*, including ten from the North Pacific region. She found that they clustered into three major clades; a primitive North American one; then a Eurasian group that included, in addition, two North American species (*S. arcticus, S. tundrensis*); and, finally, a larger group of North American *Sorex* belonging to the subgenus *Otisorex*. Only one small clade, consisting of *S. araneus* (Eurasia), *S. arcticus* (North American), and *S. tundrensis* (Beringian) displayed an Holarctic distribution. Recently, Dokuchaev (1997) described a new allospecies, *Sorex yukonensis*, which with *S. minutissimus* forms an Holarctic superspecies.

With respect to the ground squirrels and marmots (tribe Marmotini), ongoing work in molecular phylogeny of the *Spermophilini* by an international research group[2] clearly demonstrates several novel points:

(1) ground squirrels are paraphyletic, with at least five distinct clades (Harrison et al., n.d.);

(2) marmots, instead of being ancestral to ground squirrels, fall within the ground squirrel clades;

(3) both ground squirrels and marmots have distinct North American and Eurasian species groups, with only one species, the arctic ground squirrel, having an Holarctic distribution. These

preliminary conclusions are based on complete sequencing of the mitochondrial cytochrome *b* gene, and sampling of all species level taxa in the two groups, a total of sixty-three, plus five outgroup taxa (Harrison et al., n.d.).

Gray voles of the genus

Table 5/ Number of Shrews, Marmotines, and Gray Voles Recognized in Beringia, Mid-twentieth Century

West Beringia only	Holarctic	East Beringia only
Sorex minutus hawkeri	*Sorex caecutiens araneus*	*Sorex vagrans*
	Marmota marmota	
	Spermophilus undulatus	
Eothenomys lemminus	*Microtus agrestis · gregalis economus*	*Microtus xanthognathus*
Total: 3	7	2

Microtus (*sensu lato*) are widely agreed to be among the most difficult mammals systematically. A new hypothesis based on fairly complete chromosomal studies at the species level, less complete electrophoresis, and DNA comparisons of a few species, have been synthesized into a new taxonomic scheme with relevance for the North Pacific and Beringia. What was previously regarded as a single genus, *Microtus*, a very large and heterogeneous taxon, has now been subdivided into twenty genera or subgenera, of which several have Holarctic distributions (Zagorodnyuk 1990; Musser and Carleton 1992). In this scheme, there are four major clades of gray voles, one restricted to the Palearctic, two to the Nearctic, and one in the Holarctic, which contains Beringian species and species groups. This pattern is similar to what we have already seen in the Beringian shrews and marmotines, and suggests the possibility of chronological and evolutionary concordance across the Bering land bridge in the Pleistocene.

The groups I have focused on are small to medium-size mammals, and the general patterns I have described tend to hold for these size classes. However, Beringian ungulates and carnivores are mostly large to very large in size, and a greater proportion of them show Holarctic distributions. Note, however, that the smallest carnivores—the ermine and weasel—are also Holarctic. This correlation of distributional pattern with body size and ecological niche probably results from the fact that such mammals have larger home ranges and greater dispersal ability compared to small mam-

mals, and are thus more likely to have established amphiberingian ranges at sometime during the Pleistocene (Hoffmann 1984).

The most recent trend is what has been termed "phylogeography" (Avise 1998), the "historical aspects of the contemporary spatial distributions of gene lineages." Most phylogeographic studies have been based on sequence data from maternally inherited mitochondrial genes, but other gene markers are rapidly being developed. At a recent international mammal congress held in Spain in July 1998, over forty papers employing the phylogeographic approach were given (Reig 1998), a considerable number of them being devoted to mammals of the Beringian region, both large and small. Thus, this newest application will lead to explicit hypotheses of animal migrations, and has been applied to human migrations across Beringia as well (Schurr and Wallace, this volume).

And the Sea Between

Beringian marine mammals, all large to very large, require comment at this point. Thirty-one species currently occur in the cold-temperate to arctic waters of the North Pacific and Arctic Oceans, linked by the Bering Sea. Of these, one is the coastal sea otter (*Enhydris lutris*); seven are coastal to pelagic seals and sea lions (including northern fur seal); and twenty-three are whales, including eight baleen and fifteen toothed whales. In sharp contrast to the nomenclatural instability described above for Beringian terrestrial mammals, the marine mammal species limits and recog-

Table 6/ Total Number of Recognized Land Mammal Species in Beringia, End of Twentieth Century

West Beringia only	Holarctic	East Beringia only
9 shrews	2 shrews	6 shrews
1 lagomorph	1 lagomorph	2 lagomorphs
1 marmot	1 ground squirrel	2 marmots
1 red-backed vole	1 red-backed vole	
4 lemmings	1 lemming	5 lemmings
3 gray voles	1 gray vole	4 gray voles
2 carnivores	8 carnivores	4 carnivores
1 ungulate	3 ungulates	1 ungulate
subtotal: 22	18	24
Total:	40	42

nized names have changed very little in the past century. Only one new species of whale has been described from this region in the last 100 years; *Mesoplodon carlhubbsi* in 1963, from the southern edge of the area in question. Similarly, only one additional seal, *Phoca largha*, was recognized in 1977 as a distinct species, having formerly been considered a subspecies of the common harbor seal, *Phoca vitullina*.

All of these marine mammals have Holarctic ranges, not surprising given the virtually continuous coastal and pelagic habitats spanning the rim of the North Pacific. Only one now extinct Beringian species was not known to be Holarctic—the Steller seacow, *Hydrodamalis gigas*—whose only known range encompassed the Commander Islands off the eastern coast of the Kamchatka Peninsula. Discovered in 1741 and exterminated in 1768, it was strictly coastal in habitat. Its closest living relative is the dugong of the Indian and Western Pacific Oceans, but more closely related fossil forms are known from the North Pacific. The extinction of this unique species through indiscriminant harvest for meat by hunters was a severe loss to the biological diversity of the Beringian region, since it represented the end of a specialized, highly adapted lineage.

Conserving North Pacific Biological Diversity

Other Beringian species nearly suffered the same fate. Sea otter populations shrank back from the southern ends of their large original range, and no longer occur in northern Japan, southern California, and northern Mexico. Elsewhere, the population was severely reduced and fragmented, surviving only in small areas of central California, the outer Aleutian Islands, and the Kurile Islands. Under protection, the species has now recovered some of its range, with help from reintroduction, and is now fairly regular in Kamchatka, the Commander Islands, central and southern Alaska, and parts of British Columbia.

Many of the baleen whales suffered a similar fate, and their numbers are still depressed, especially the Eurasian population of gray whale, and all populations of blue, right, and bowhead whales. There has also been a recent serious decline in the Steller sea lion population of unknown origin; it is speculated that heavy fishing pressure in the North Pacific and Bering Sea may be at least part of the cause, by reducing the sea lion's food base.

Terrestrial mammals have fared better. Populations of many of the large mammals have been reduced, and local extinctions are widespread, but overall, species populations are not endangered. Small and medium-size mammals are still widespread and often common, but no accurate assessments of population status exist for most places.

Due to some degree of protection (hunting regulations, preserves, captive breeding, reintroductions, etc.), the status of some species has improved. In addition to the sea otter, the musk-ox has benefited from protection and reintroduction, and is now reestablished both in Alaska and eastern Siberia. The sable, seriously over-harvested in the past, has also increased in both numbers and distribution.

In most, if not all, cases, reduction of biodiversity in Beringia and the North Pacific, both historically and up to the present, has been caused by direct human exploitation. The future challenge is not only to gain sufficient knowledge of these ecosystems so that human use of biotic resources can be placed on a sustainable basis; but also, it is to conserve enough of the natural world to ensure that these ecosystems, both terrestrial and marine, will remain viable. Four major formations encompass terrestrial ecosystems of the lands bordered by the North Pacific between about 35° and 75° North latitude. These are arctic and mountain tundra, taiga (boreal forest), and mixed coniferous/broad-leafed forest, with patches of steppe inland along the southern margins.

The most threatened of these formations is the mixed forest. In the United States and Canada, this formation, sometimes called a "temperate rainforest," is the focus of an ongoing controversy over what level of logging is sustainable in these forests, and what proportion of the old-growth "ancient forests" should be protected. On the Eurasian side, a parallel controversy focuses on the mixed forest of the Russian Far East, particularly in the drainages of the Amur and Ussuri River basins, which also includes a significant part of northeastern China (former Manchuria), and the appended Korean Peninsula. Another country in this region is Japan, in particular, its two northern islands, Hokkaido and Honshu. Along the southern margins of the region, on both sides of the Pacific, much of this unique forest is already cut over. However, the opportunity to manage the mixed forests of Alaska, western Canada, and the Russian Far East still exists, and with it the opportunity to preserve their rich biodiversity, with many unique species. A small sampling includes Siberian tiger, Amur leopard, Lake Evoron vole, three or four species of tree voles, mountain beaver, shrew-moles, Chinese soft-shelled turtle, giant salamander, Steller's sea eagle, and northern spotted owl.

With a few conspicuous exceptions, these species have little or no commercial value. On the other hand, trees, when reduced to logs, have an immediate commercial value to the people who cut them down, even though the forest ecosystem from which the trees came had an even greater global economic value in terms of photosynthesis (carbon dioxide absorption from,

oxygen release to, the atmosphere), watershed protection (runoff, erosion control), soil building, and other ecosystem services.

Past history demonstrates that when individuals or corporations have the opportunity for short-term profit by exploiting natural resources (be they sea otters or redwoods), they will usually act to do so. This is especially true if the exploiter does not reside in the ecosystem or community that is exploited.

The two keys to sustained utilization of natural resources from ecosystems are: (1) sufficient knowledge of composition and function of the ecosystem to make informed decisions concerning exploitation; and (2) policies controlling exploitation determined by people residing within the ecosystem, who have a vital stake in prudent policy-making (of course, good policy is only as good as its implementation and enforcement). Here is a vital problem, the solution to which both natural historians and anthropologists could contribute more effectively if they worked together rather than separately. It is time to revive "the method of correlated work" to conduct research on a wide variety of topics by international teams of scientists in the spirit of the Boasian synthesis.

That the broad view of field research espoused by Boas remains alive is seen in the scope of "planetary biology", a newly coined name for the combined disciplines of biology (both molecular and whole organism) with palaeontology and geology. One can only wonder what those industrious but almost unknown field collectors, Buxton and Stone, would make of that.

Notes

1. We are grateful to Mr. Donald Cunningham for the information on Buxton's year of birth as well as his first and second name.

2. N. N. Vorontsov, E. A. Lyapunova, Institute of Developmental Biology, Moscow; R.G. Harrison, P. W. Sherman, Cornell University, Ithaca, New York, E. Yensen, Albertson College, Idaho and R. S. Hoffmann, Smithsonian Institution.

References

Allen, Joel A.

1903   Report on the Mammals Collected in Northeastern Siberia by the Jesup North Pacific Expedition, with Itinerary and Field Notes, by N. G.Buxton. *Bulletin of the American Museum of Natural History* 19:101–84.

1905   Report on the Birds Collected in Northeastern Siberia by the Jesup North Pacific Expedition, with Field Notes by the Collector. *Ibid* 21:219–57.

Andrews, Roy C.

1932   The New Conquest of Central Asia. *Natural History of Central Asia*, vol. 1. New York: AMNH.

Avise, John C.

1998   The History and Purview of Phylogeography; a Personal Reflection. *Molecular Ecology* 7:371–79.

Boas, Franz

1887   The Study of Geography. In *Volksgeist as Method and Ethics: Essays on Boasian Ethnography and the German Anthropological Tradition*. George W. Stocking, Jr., ed. Pp. 9–16. History of Anthropology, 8. Madison: University of Wisconsin Press.

Buxton, Norman G.

1903   Itinerary and General Description of the Country. In *Report on the Mammals Collected in Northeastern Siberia by the Jesup North Pacific Expedition*. By A.J. Allen. *Bulletin of the American Museum of Natural History* 19:104–19.

Dobzhansky, Theodore

1941   *Genetics and the Origin of Species*. 2nd ed. New York: Columbia University Press.

Dokuchaev, Nikolai E.

1997   A New Species of Shrew (*Soricidae, Insectivora*) from Alaska. *Journal of Mammalogy* 78:811–17.

George, Sarah B.

1988   Systematics, Historical Biogeography, and Evolution of the Genus *Sorex*. *Journal of Mammalogy* 69:443–61.

Harrison, R. G., Steven M. Bogdanowicz, Robert S. Hoffmann, Eric Yenson, and Paul W. Sherman

n.d.   Evolutionary Relationships in the Ground Squirrels (*Rodentia, Marmotinae*). (in revision).

Hoffmann, Robert S.

1984   An Ecological and Zoogeographical Analysis of Animal Migration across the Bering Land Bridge in the Cenozoic. In *Beringia in the Cenozoic*. V.L. Kontrimaviuchus, ed. Pp. 464–81. Washington, DC: U. S. Department of the Interior and the National Science Foundation.

Huxley, Julian S., ed.

1940   *The New Systematics*. London: Oxford University Press.

1943   *Evolution, the Modern Synthesis*. New York: Harper and Brothers.

Mayr, Ernst

1942   *Systematics and the Origin of Species*. New York: Columbia University Press.

McIlhenny, Edward A.

1904   The Nelicatar of Arctic Alaska. The Great Feast of the Whale. *Century Magazine* 68: 701–5. New York.

Merriam, C. Hart

1918   Review of the Grizzly and Big Brown Bears of North America (Genus *Ursus*) with Description of a New Genus, *Vetularctos*. In *North American Fauna*, vol. 41. Washington, DC: Gov. Printing Office.

Musser, Guy G., and Michael D. Carleton

1992   Family *Muridae*. In *Mammal Species of the World*, 2nd Edition. D.E. Wilson and D.M. Reeder, eds. Pp. 501-755. Washington, DC: Smithsonian Institution Press.

Reig, Santiago, ed.

1998   *Abstracts. Euro-American Mammal Congress*. Universidade de Santiago de Compostela.

Stone, Andrew J.

1900   Some Results of a Natural History Journey to Northern British Columbia, Alaska, and the Northwest Territory, in the Interest of the American Museum of Natural History. *Bulletin of the American Museum of Natural History* 13:31–62.

Stone, Witmer

1900   Report on the Birds and Mammals Collected by the McIlhenny Expedition to Pt. Barrow, Alaska. *Proceedings of the Academy of Natural Sciences* 52:4–49. Philadelphia.

Wiley, Edward O.

1981   *Phylogenetics. The Theory and Practice of Phylogenetic Systematics*. New York: John Wiley and Sons, Inc.

Zagorodnyuk, Igor V.

1990   Kariotipicheskaia izmenchivost' i sistematika serykh polevok (Rodentia, Arvicolini). Soobshchenie 1. Vidovoi sostav i khromosomnye chisla (Karyotypic Variation and Systematics of Gray Voles. Communication 1. Species Composition and Chromosome Numbers). *Vestnik Zoologii* 2:26–37. Moscow.

The Languages of the North Pacific Rim, 1897–1997, and the Jesup Expedition

MICHAEL E. KRAUSS

Throughout most of our historical perspective the connection between the "Old World" and the new has been the Atlantic European expansion westward since 1492. This movement has by now almost completely obliterated the aboriginal connection, culminating in the control of the North Pacific area by distant Moscow and Washington, and a Cold War which utterly sealed off that connection for the lifetime of most of us now living. This period also minimized contact between scientists on both sides, and greatly intensified the processes that have been destroying what remains of the indigenous cultures and languages along that entire North Pacific arc.

The understanding of the relationship between the two hemispheres and its history that the Jesup Expedition promised only reached its beginning stages. Except for the Russian Ryabushinski Expedition of 1909–11 across the Aleutian-Kamchatkan arc, the JNPE remained unique; and all further work was severely limited by the political situation of 1917–90. After this tragic lapse, the scientific and social issues surrounding the Jesup Expedition remain, and even have developed new importance, including the question of survival of these cultures and languages and their role in the society of the future.

This paper lists the eighty languages of the North Pacific rim; describes the texture of that diversity; summarizes their status from robust viability to extinction during the century 1897–1997; the causes of that situation, including American and Russian politics,

often in contrast; the role of Jesup Expedition fieldworkers in documenting the diversity; and the issues of the social responsibility of the scientist. It also deals with the critically endangered state of most of these languages today (with twenty already extinct, and all the rest, except for around three to five, with speakers of the older generation only), as part of the global crisis of impending mass language extinction.

Definitions: Jesup Area Languages

I shall here first present my definition of the Jesup Expedition area for language purposes, as a framework for a quick survey and statistical overview of the indigenous languages in the North Pacific arc, and of their viability status then and now. For these purposes, I shall consider the languages along the coast, on salt water, from the Columbia River on the American side to the Ussuri River on the Asian—Astoria to Vladivostok—and secondarily also the first tier inland (up to about 500 kilometers).[1]

As we well know, counting languages as opposed to dialects is often arbitrary and artificial, but in terms of the mutual intelligibility criterion and according to the best current statements,[2] from the Columbia to the Ussuri in 1897 there was up to eighty different Native languages spoken, or, at least still remembered, on the coast and first tier inland.

I shall not detail the considerations defining the languages listed here, but only shall note that my definition of languages is somewhat finer, especially on the Asian side, than that established in the Russian literature.[3] For example, Ainu is (or was) two languages (Kurile including Hokkaido, and Sakhalin); Nivkh is two; Yukagir is (or was) perhaps four; Asiatic Eskimo is (was) three; Kerek-Koryak-Alyutor is three; Itelmen is (was) three; and Arman Tungusic is counted separately. On the other hand, I have been perhaps overgenerous in retaining the established (Russian) count for Primorski Tungusic languages, with Negidal, Ulch and Oroch treated as separate from Evenk and Nanay (following Doerfer 1978), though Kili is not counted here because it is further inland than Nanay. By some counts, then, the Asian languages could be a lot fewer; but I am making a special effort to differentiate evenhandedly for both sides—a difficult task, where I hope I am not overcompensating for under-differentiation on the Russian side.

Diversity

Though the arc as defined is almost symmetrical (actually, Vladivostok is about 300 kilometers further south than Astoria) and the Asian side, at least grossly viewed, (including Kamchatka and Sakhalin) appears to have much more coastline than the American, there are significantly more languages and greater diversity on the American side than on the Asian. Fifty-three of the eighty area languages are American, and only twenty-seven are Asian (Tables 7 and 8), even with the fineness or generosity just allowed for the Asian. (Overlap is eliminated by calling St. Lawrence Island part of Asia, and by including the Aleut of the Commander Islands with American Aleut, and Big Diomede Iñupiaq with Little Diomede.) The diversity is, at most, only slightly greater on the American side, however, in terms of different genetic language families represented—a much deeper measure of diversity: eight families on the American side (Chinookan, Salishan, Chemakuan, Wakashan, Tsimshianic, Haida, Athabaskan-Eyak-Tlingit, and Eskimo-Aleut), and six on the Asian (Eskimo-Aleut—due to the presence of three Siberian Yupik languages—also Chukotko-Kamchatkan, Yukagiric,

Tungusic, Nivkh and Ainu). That could, in fact, be made seven and seven, since it is arguable that Kamchatkan and Chukotkan are genetically different,[4] and that Tsimshianic is genetically related to Chinookan.[5] I think also that in a global perspective, the density of diversity here is below average for pre-agrarian parts of the world in terms of area, but not per capita, and the diversity is greater on both sides in the more southerly latitudes.

The diversity is greater along the coast than on the first inland tier: of the eighty total, fifty-eight are coastal, and only twenty-two are first tier inland. Most diverse is the American coast, with thirty-six, followed by the Asian coast, with twenty-two; then the American inland with seventeen; and last the Asian inland, with only five (and that by counting Yukagiric in 1897 as four languages).

Viability Status 1897

We now come to the issue of viability status and fate of these North Pacific languages. By viability I mean, most essentially, that the language is being transmitted by the traditional natural method of speaking it to the children as their first language.[6] Sheer numbers is a major factor in language power and language survival; but the language of 100 people, including all the children, will probably remain alive longer than the language of 100,000, including no children.

In 1897, most of the eighty North Pacific languages were still viable, learned as a first language by all or most children. (This we can judge from the subsequent and current situation, by projecting backwards; the accounts of the time seldom make mention of viabilty.) On the Asian side the main exceptions were South Itelmen[7], already very nearly extinct, replaced by Russian; also probably Omok and Chuvan Yukagiric, if not already extinct,[8] replaced by Russian or Chukchi; and on the American side, two widely separate Athabaskan languages mainly by near extinction of the group, Tsetsaut[9] and Kwalhioqua,[10] and probably also Chemakum.[11] These six languages must all have been extinct by about 1935.

Of the remaining seventy-four, about eight more were by then reduced to such small numbers, and/or were being learned by so few or no children, that they would have been rather moribund in 1897: Kurile Ainu confined on Shikotan Island and languishing;[12] Arman Tungusic on Siberian mainland;[13] probably also Pentlatch, Nooksack and Twana Salishan; and Lower and Cathlamet Chinook in North America.[14] All of these became extinct during the last half of the last century. Northeast Kamchadal probably belongs in this category, but reports are contradictory, and it could conceivably belong in the next category.[15]

By 1897, at least eleven more languages were entering a precarious state: Kerek[16] in dwindling numbers; Sirenikski Eskimo[17] assimilating to Chaplinski; Tagish Athabaskan[18] assimilating to Inland Tlingit; Eyak[19] first assimilating to Tlingit and by 1897 overwhelmed by American canneries; and Southern Tsimshian assimilating to Coast Tsimshian. With the death of Valentina Wye, the last speaker, in February 1997, Sirenikski Eskimo was the sixteenth of the eighty to become extinct, now leaving sixty-four languages still with us; Eyak and Tagish each have one remaining speaker, while Kerek and Southern Tsimshian[20] reportedly each have two. The last children taught Ainu on Sakhalin were born about 1905 (those on Hokkaido not much later); Sakhalin Ainu is now extinct (Hokkaido very nearly so). Furthermore in Washington state Lower and Upper Chehalis, Cowlitz, Quinault, and Quileute were not much longer to be learned by any children, and all have from two to five speakers at present.

In 1897, the other fifty-five may still have appeared fairly robust, with all or most of the children being raised speaking them. Here, however, we come to a sharp contrast in conditions on the American side as opposed to the Russian.[21]

Indigenous Language Policy and Results, 1997

On the American side (Table 7), heavy Euro-American settlement and development was already advanced,
especially in Washington State and British Columbia, and generally more advanced than the Russian on the Asian side. However, the federal Indian language policy for the school system, a rigid policy already well established along the entire American coast in both the United States and Canada, still had more impact on the viability of the languages themselves. The policy called for strict speaking of English only; children were punished for speaking a Native language. Though there was still missionary support for using Native languages (by Russian Orthodox, Moravian, Anglican-Episcopal, Roman Catholic Oblates and Jesuits), including in written form and printed books, the pro-language mission policy was rapidly losing out to the mainstream Protestant-led federal policy.[22] The rigid English-only policy was powerfully reinforced, incidentally, by the assimilationism so urgently needed to deal with vast hordes of "barely white" immigrants who now poured in not from Northern or Western Europe, but from Southern and Eastern Europe.

In contrast, Russian demographic pressure was minimal on the Asian side, and hardly increasing. It was so far behind the American that Chukotka, for example, was more American than Russian;[23] the schools were generally far fewer if present at all, and were not motivated by any deliberate policy to eliminate indigenous languages. Ironically, even the influence of the Russian Orthodox Church was far stronger in Alaska than in Russia. Orthodox support for Alaskan languages, even printing materials in four of them and nothing in the Asian languages, provided some significant opposition to the American policy,[24] while on the Asian side there was no policy to oppose. Such was the contrasting context on the two sides for the Jesup Expedition era. We shall return to this after a brief account of development since then.

The American anti-Native language policy reigned supreme for about sixty years, from 1910 to 1970, until generally there were no more Native-speaking schoolchildren to punish. By 1970, along the Pacific coast from California to the Aleutians the only elementary schools where young children could speak any of these languages were at Atka (Aleut) and English Bay (Chugach Alutiiq). Further North, the youngest Native speakers on the American side are for the central part of Central Yup'ik, seventeen of sixty-seven villages, and St. Lawrence Island Yupik, in two villages. Liberalization of the policy began only in the 1970s, too late to help in most cases in the United States or Canada.[25]

On the Russian side, the Revolutionary regime took over the Russian Far East in the 1920s and established schools for indigenous communities, reaching most by the 1930s, with a policy that was basically favorable for indigenous languages, for populist-idealistic or cynical reasons, or perhaps both. Languages were more or less officially recognized and defined, with literary standards for some, often disregarding divergent dialect or even language-level differences, for practical reasons (e.g., Sakhalin Nivkh, Naukan Yupik).[26] Several languages, or at least parts thereof, were relatively well served in the printing of school literature from the 1930s through the 1950s; such as Siberian Yupik Eskimo (with over 100 titles for 1,200 total population, best per capita, but in Chaplinski Yupik only), or Chukchi (460 titles for 12,000 people), Nanay (217 titles, 10,000 people), Evenk (25,000 people, 400 titles, probably one dialect only), Even (12,000, 190 titles), Koryak (7,100, 117 titles, Chavchuven dialect only). However, far less well served were Nivkh (4,000 people, 20 titles, Amur dialect only?).[27] (West) Itelmen (1,200 people) got only the bare beginnings (1932 primer and arithmetic), and for 300 Commander Island Aleut a primer and dictionary were drafted but not published (in Bering Atkan language). Several other recognized languages still spoken by schoolchildren at the time, but with populations under 1,000, got no books: Yukagir, Ulch, Oroch, Negidal, and Orok. Also, the degree to which the books were properly distributed or really used is inconsistent and questionable. In any case, the policy and practice were favorable enough that the Soviet-side languages remained quite generally viable through the period 1930–60,[28] the same period when American parents, now bilingual in English, switched to speaking English with their children, as instructed.

The Soviet literatures in indigenous languages first adapted the Latin alphabet of International Communism, but were Cyrillicized already in 1937. World War II, the Great Patriotic War, increased Russian activity and development in the Far East, along with Russian nationalism. Finally, and most devastatingly, in about 1957 came *ukrupnenie* ("village consolidation") with the destruction of the many smaller villages, and above all *internaty* (boarding schools) in the consolidated villages, severely restricting children's contact with their parents and following a *de facto* policy of Russification,[29] in some cases even making a point of burning the native-language books.[30] The result of this abrupt and disastrous change in the 1960s and 1970s, ironically at the same time that American policy began to liberalize, is that now only Chukchi may have a significant proportion of children speakers in some less settled groups. Evenk probably also has some young speakers in the Amur-Chita region; Koryak and Even perhaps also in some pockets; Nanay perhaps a few children somewhere. But for all other Russian-side languages the youngest speakers are now in their thirties or older.[31]

There are ironic contrasts in the timing; replacement by English occurred mostly 1930–1960 while the Russian policy was liberal, then the replacement by Russian occurred while American policy liberalized.

The result is that of the fifty-five languages that might have appeared robust in 1897 (thirty-six on the American side, nineteen on the Russian), only two may still be viable or partly so on the American side (Central Alaskan Yup'ik and St. Lawrence Island Siberian Yupik; Table 7), only three or four on the Russian have any children speakers (Chukchi, Evenk, Koryak, perhaps also Even), and the status of even these most-favored languages is extremely endangered (Table 8). The less endangered Native languages of the North are all quite distant from the «Jesup arc»: almost all Greenlandic and East Canadian Inuit; Tundra Nenets, Northern and Eastern Khanty in Russia; Northern Saami in Scandinavia;

and Dogrib or South Slavey in Canada. These are not to be compared with Sakha (Yakut), which has three or four times as many speakers as all other Northern languages combined, placing it in an entirely different class of languages in this respect.[32]

Social Responsibility of the Scientist, and the Global Language Extinction Issue

What did Boas, Jochelson, Bogoras, and their collegues think, if anything, about the future of these languages in 1897? First though, I take 1897 and the Jesup Expedition merely as symbolic of the larger effort and careers of these men, in the field from the 1880s to the 1920s, right while the fate of the American Native languages (but not yet that of the Russian) was being sealed, or prepared. The extent or intensity of their linguistic fieldwork hardly even peaked during the Jesup Expedition time; they may have done more before and/or after it than on it. Second, I need to emphasize that they did not document all of the eighty languages during their longer career period, and far fewer still during JNPE surveys, which skipped Alaska altogether, a huge "keystone" of the North Pacific arc. In fact, coverage was much spottier on the American side, where two-thirds of the languages are located.

How much solid survey-like knowledge the JNPE team members had of what languages and dialects were in the area in 1897 or 1902 is quite unclear. Whether they were or were not interested in a regional overview, such an overview was in any case rather impossible with the transportation facilities of the time (some of their travel was quite heroic, to achieve what they did under those circumstances), with limited resources, and with Boas' strict rule over the plans. As for last-minute salvage of dying languages for linguistic science, in the interest of comparative linguistics or philology, only Boas appears to have given much priority to that, and during the JNPE even Boas disregarded that priority, as his interest clearly centered on documenting indigenous life in its oldest "purest" form, while languages were still alive and fully functioning.

Finally, insofar as the JNPE funding was through a museum, with a natural priority on collecting material objects, it is indeed remarkable that so much language work got done, thanks to the interest, linguistic skill, and hard work of these men.

I now come to the question of the social responsibility of the scientist, as a humanist and human being, then and now. Taking only the central examples I know of best—Boas, Jochelson, and Bogoras—I am struck, even shocked, that as revolutionaries, discoverers of cultural relativism, they wrote so little in their JNPE contributions to protest or even express regret about the then very active colonial suppression of the languages and cultures. They hardly said and did anything to oppose the decline of the languages and cultures they were documenting. Perhaps it was "scientific detachment" above all, or assumption that the disappearance of those languages and cultures was inevitable, or that there was nothing they themselves could do about it anyway, especially as transient outsiders and foreigners. Or perhaps it was some combination of the above. I have myself noted little or no trace of regret: Bogoras did not have much exposure to American suppression, but Jochelson certainly did, in the Aleutians 1909–10, but there is not a word about it even in his correspondence. Boas, likewise, left no written word that I have seen—except perhaps to his wife about the banning of the Kwakiutl potlatch, or late in life a general thought about culture loss—about language suppression or loss. Jochelson had converted fully, from revolutionary to scientist, never to return. His old friend Bogoras, on the other hand, was ever the revolutionary and activist, and, instead of fleeing Russia after the October Revolution of 1917, he became, among other things, founding director of the Leningrad Institute for the development of Northern minority languages in education (Institut Narodov Severa).

On the American side, one thing that Boas and his colleagues could realistically have done was to have helped resident pro-language missionaries to develop

Table 7/ North American Languages Current Status, Sequenced from the Columbia River toward the Bering Strait

Coastal Languages	Fam.	Status	Speakers	Total Pop.
Lower Chinook		e 1930	0	--
Lower Chehalis	S	>d	<5	200
Quinault	S	>d	<6	1,500
Lushootseed	S	<d	60	2,000
Twana	S	e 1980	0	350
Clallam	S	d	<20	3,000?
Quileute	Chm	>d	3	784
Chemakum	Chm	e>1928	0	0
Makah	W	c	50?	1,000
Nitinaht	W	>c	20	500?
Nootka	W	c	500?	5,000?
Northern Straits	S	<d	<30	3,000
Nooksack	S	e 1958	0	350
Halkomelem	S	<d/>c ?	50?	7,000
Squamish	S	d	<20	2,300
Pentlatch	S	e 1940	0	55
Sechelt	S	>c	40	700
Comox	S	<c	300	1,000
Bella Coola	S	>c	50	700
Kwakiutl	W	C	400?	4,000?
Heiltsuk-Oowekyala	W	C	300	1,500
Haisla	W	C	100	1,000
Southern Tsimshian		>d	2	--
Coast Tsimshian		b-d	500	4,500
Nass-Gitksan Tsimshian		b-d	1,000	5,500
Tsetsuat	AET	e 1934	0	10
Southern Haida		D	10	500
Northern Haida		<d	40	1,700
Tlingit	AET	c-d	575	11,000
Eyak	AET	>d	1	--
Alutiiq	EA	b-c	400	3,000
Tanaina	AET	b-d	75	900
Central Alaskan Yup'ik	EA	a-c	10,000	21,000
Aleut	EA	b-d	300	2,200
Inupiaq	EA	c	500	3,200[1]

Inland Languages	Fam.	Status	Speakers	Total Pop.
Kwalhioqua	AET	e>1923	0	0
Cathlamet Chinook		e 1930	0	--
Cowlitz	S	>d	2	200
Upper Chehalis	S	>d	2	200
Columbian	S	C	75	500
Thompson	S	c	<500	3,000
Lillooet	S	c	300	2,800
Chilcotin	AET	>b	1,000	2,000
Carrier	AET	a-c	2,400	5,000
Babine	AET	B?	200–300?	2,000?
Sekani	AET	C	100	500
Tahltan	AET	>c	40	1,200
Tagish		>d	1	--
Southern Tutchone	AET	c	200	1,400
Ahtna	AET	c	80	500
Upper Kuskokwim	AET	>b	40	160
Koyukon	AET	c	300	2,300

Coastal Languages	Fam.	Status	Speakers	Total Pop.
Naukan Yupik	EA	c	60	400
Central Siberian Yupik	EA	a-c	1,300	2,300
Sirenik Yupik	EA	e 1997	0	--
Chukchi	ChK	a-b	10,000	15,000
Kerek	ChK	>d	2	400
Koryak	ChK	a-c	2,500	7,000
Alyutor	ChK	c	200	2,000
Even	T	a-c	<7,500	17,000
Arman Tungus	T	e 1960	0	--
Northeast Itelmen	ChK	e? 1950	0[3]	--
South Itelmen	ChK	e 1910	0	--
West Itelmen	ChK	e 1986	70	1,500
Amur Nivkh		c-d	100	2,000
Sakhalin Nivkh		c	300	2,700
Negidal	T	c	<100	500
Ulch	T	c	<500	3,200
Oroch	T	c	100	900
Orok	T	c	35	300
Udegey	T	c-d	100	1,600[3]
Kurile Ainu		e 1960	0	0
Hokkaido-Sakhalin Ainu		e 1986	0	3[4]

Inland Languages	Fam.	Status	Speakers	Total Pop.
Chuvan Yukagir		e<1900	0	"1,300"
Omok Yukagir		e<1900	0	--
Tundra Yukagir		c-d	50	600
Kolyma Yukagir		d	20	300
Evenk	T	a-c	9,000	30,000
Nanay	T	c	<2,000–12,000[3]	<2,000–12,000[3]

Abbreviations used in Tables 7 and 8:

Status:

a	all generations including children
b	parental generation and up
c	grandparental generation and up
d	small number of very old speakers
e	extinct, with approximate date of extinction
<	in a situation approaching a particular status
>	beyond the situation described for a particular status
X-Y	Communities within the language area range in status from one status to another.

Language families:

AET	Athabaskan-Eyak-Tlingit
EA	Eskimo-Aleut
ChK	Chukotka-Kamchatkan
Chm	Chemakuan
S	Salishan
T	Tungusic
W	Wakashan

Footnotes for Tables 7 and 8:

[1] Seward Peninsula only; Northern Alaska, Canada and Greenland not counted
[2] Russia only, China and Mongolia not counted
[3] Russia only, China not counted
[4] Sakhalin only, Hokkaido not counted

better orthographies. But Boas evidently had little use for missionaries of any kind, and they consequently for him—a lost opportunity.

As for a conclusion, I can only offer my personal view, which has motivated my whole career. It would be a tragedy if these Native minority languages disappear, not just for linguistics, or ethnohistory, or for science, or for human rights, or for these peoples themselves; but their loss would be a tragedy, I claim, for humanity at large. We have come to understand biologically that our physical survival depends utterly on a certain condition of the biosphere, the ecosystem biodiversity, that we need desperately to learn to preserve and not to destroy. I believe it is the same with human cultural, linguistic, and intellectual diversity. Diversity itself also constitutes a system of its own, which I call our "logosphere," the web of intellectual life that is our very humanity. We obviously have the power now to destroy that too, and are doing so at an explosive rate, globally.[33] We must learn to control the growth of English-, Spanish-, Chinese-, Russian-, even Yakut-speaking culture, and see it as a supplement, a merely practical enrichment to the minority indigenous ones. We must prevent this unnecessary destruction of all other languages in the path of that development, or we destroy the complex and beautifully diverse system upon which our survival as human beings depends. That is my claim.

Therefore, for us here now, it is our job to document and preserve, but also to protest where still necessary, to intervene, and to help support efforts to maintain or revitalize this heritage, and to make the work of Jesup Expedition researchers on North Pacific languages a lasting contribution to that.

Notes

1. Compare the maps in Jesup 1897; Boas 1903, with Krauss 1988 (reprinted, with some corrections in Chaussonnet 1995:109, 1996:108). Coastal is defined as having territory on salt water, or so by default (no other indigenous group intervening, e.g., Udegey).

2. See especially Goddard 1996 for the Northwest Coast to Alaska, and Krauss 1997 for Alaska and the Asian side; also *Krasnaia kniga iazykov narodov Rossii* 1994.

3. See Krauss 1997; Vakhtin 1992:13; Al'kor 1932 (especially pp. 48–51, 54 ff., 84–7, 102–3); Gurvich 1985:184; Vdovin 1959:288–91; *Mladopis'mennye iazyki narodov* SSSR 1959:12; Isaev 1977:246–53.

4. See Volodin 1976:17–9, 1997:12–14.

5. See Tarpent 1996.

6. I have been estimating the number of speakers of Alaskan since 1961 and, later, Siberian languages; results were published first in Krauss 1973a, 1973b, but only for Alaska (and border languages, including USSR Eskimo and Aleut), likewise Krauss 1974, 1982 (map); the whole arc map and table see Krauss 1988 (also Chaussonnet 1995, 1996) and especially Krauss 1997.

7. Patkanov (1912 III: 915, 920) shows that according to the 1897 census, one man in the village of Apacha spoke Kamchadal, which, if he was not displaced, would have been Southern Kamchadal. Jochelson in 1910 (1911:139) reports of Southern Kamchadal that "the last old woman still remembering that dialect, died shortly before [my] arrival" (no location given). Obviously there was no careful investigation, but it does seem probable that speakers of Southern Kamchadal surviving in 1897–1910 were few and scattered. See below for the status of Northeastern Kamchadal, which may well have been quite different.

8. G.N. Kurilov, personal conversation 1997; see also Jochelson 1934:150 for Chuvan and Jochelson 1926:57 for Omok.

9. See Boas and Goddard 1924:1; Krauss 1973a:916–7. The last speaker, Jane Dangeli, died in approximately 1934.

10. See Krauss 1973a:917–8, 1990:531–2. One speaker, Tonamal (Melissa or Blizzy Moxlah or Moxley), was still alive in 1923.

11. See Boas 1892:37, who reported three speakers in 1890, one of whom, his informant Louise Webster, was still alive in 1928 (Elmendorf 1990:440).

12. Torii 1919:3–5, 15–9; Bergman 1933: 211–7; Murasaki 1963. Murasaki in 1962 checked on seven possible speakers, most of whom probably knew nothing of Kurile Ainu, but general

extreme stigma, shame, and reluctance added to the uncertainty.

13. Doerfer 1978:55; Novikova 1960:20, 1968:107, and Sunik 1959:338–9; also Juha Janhunen personal communication 1993.

14. Thompson and Kinkade 1990:37, 41, also Kinkade p.c. ca. 1995. The last speaker, Charles Cultee, died in the 1930s.

15. Patkanov (1912 III:914, 920) shows that according to the 1897 census, 207 of 696 Kamchadals in twelve villages in the Kamchatka River drainage still spoke (Northeastern) Kamchadal. More precisely, in seven of those twelve villages no Kamchadals spoke Kamchadal, in two more 5% and 6%, while in the rest, most or all (76%, 84%, 100%) did, in no clear geographical pattern. The Jesup Expedition did not visit the area. Moreover, since Kamchadal was surely low-prestige, and a choice between Kamchadal and Russian was forced in the 1897 census, it is probable that the actual 1897 figure was well above 207. It seems that no one really investigated, and I consider it conceivable that someone might still remember Northeastern Kamchadal even today.

16. See Leont'iev 1983:12–9; Kibrik (1991:263) names three speakers, two at Meynypil'gyn, for 1989.

17. See Menovshchikov 1964:7–10, and especially Krupnik 1991, which carefully describes the whole decline and extinction process, far better than I have seen for any other language in the area, or perhaps in the world.

18. Krauss, 1997: 9. Angela Sidney died in the 1990s, leaving only Lucy Wren (John Ritter, personal communication).

19. Krauss 1997:11-12; Krauss 1982:11–8; de Laguna, 1990:195-196. The one remaining speaker, Marie Smith Jones, 80, was still alive in 1998.

20. Marie-Lucie Tarpent 1997. Southern Tsimshian is probably the last "language" in the Jesup area to be "discovered" by John Dunn around 1975; see Dunn 1979:62–3.

21. For the Russian side in 1897, see especially Patkanov 1912, a remarkable and important source.

22. See, for example, Krauss 1980:18–24, 94–6; also Alton 1998, a dissertation that extensively documents U. S. Federal and Alaska Native language policy and its effects, for Alaska; and Levine and Cooper 1976 for British Columbia, an important source.

23. See, for example Hunt 1975; Krauss 1994:366; Vdovin 1965:258–62.

24. See, for example Krauss 1980:15–7, 1990:206–11, for Alaska; and Vdovin 1965:258–62 for failure of missions to the Chukchi.

25. Krauss 1980:21–4, 95–7; 1997:5–19, 23–34; Thompson and Kinkade 1990.

26. Vakhtin 1992:13–4; Al'kor 1932, especially pp. 48–9, 56–7, 102–3.

27. These counts were done in large part by myself, in 1990, with kind permission from Galina Sergeevna Mishchenko to enter the stacks at the Leningrad Public Library annex at Kupchino for ethnic literatures, an official depository for all such publications, where I simply counted the items for each language present.

28. See e.g., Savoskul 1978, especially pp. 145–8; Avrorin 1970; Chichlo 1985:80.

29. Vakhtin 1992:17-23; Krauss 1980:47–9.

30. G. A. Menovshchikov, L. Aynana, and others, personal communications 1985, 1990; see also Chichlo 1990: 55.

31. Krauss 1997:13–9, 27–34; *Krasnaia kniga iazykov narodov Rossii* 1994:69, 32, 70, 37, and especially personal communications of Toshiro Tsumagari, Viktor Atknin 1994.

32. For circumpolar overview and viability status of all Northern languages, see Krauss 1997.

33. I have written a number of articles about the impending global collapse of linguistic diversity, e.g., Krauss 1992, 1996.

References

Al'kor, Yan P.

1932 *Materialy k vserossiiskoi konferentsii po razvitiiu iazykov i pis'mennosti narodov Severa* (Materials to the All-Russian Conference on the Development of Languages and Literacy among the Peoples of the North). Leningrad: Uchpedgiz.

Avrorin, Valentin A.

1970 Opyt izucheniia funktsional'nogo vzaimodeist-viia iazykov u narodov Sibiri (A Study in Functional Interaction of Languages among the Peoples of Siberia). *Voprosy iazykoznaniia* 1:33–43. Moscow.

Bergman, Sten

1933 *Sport and Exploration in the Far East: a Naturalist's Experiences in and around the Kurile*

Islands. Translated by Frederic Whyte. London: Methuen & Co., Ltd.

Boas, Franz
1892. Notes on the Chemakum Language. *American Anthropologist* 5(1):37–44.
1903 The Jesup North Pacific Expedition. *The American Museum Journal* 3(5):73–119.

Boas, Franz, and Pliny E. Goddard
1924 Ts'ets'aut, an Athapascan Language from Portland Canal, British Columbia. *International Journal of American Linguistics* 3(1):1–35.

Chaussonnet, Valérie, ed.
1995 *Crossroads Alaska: Native Cultures of Alaska and Siberia*. Washington, DC: Arctic Studies Center, National Musuem of Natural History, Smithsonian Institution.

Chichlo, Boris
1985 *L'Anthropologie Soviétique et les Problèmes de la Culture Sibérienne.* Unpublished Ph. D. Dissertation. Paris: Université de Paris-Sorbonne.
1990 La première victoire des 'petits peuples.' *Quéstions Sibériennes* 1: 44–56. Paris.

Comrie, Bernard
1981 *The Languages of the Soviet Union.* Cambridge: Cambridge University Press.

De Laguna, Frederica
1990 Eyak. In *Northwest Coast*. Wayne Suttles, ed. *Handbook of North American Indians*, vol. 7. Pp. 189–96. Washington, D.C.: Smithsonian Institution.

Doerfer, Gerhard
1978 Classification Problems of Tungusic. *Beiträge zur nordasiatischen Kulturgeschichte (Tungusica 1)*. Wiesbaden: Otto Harassowitz.

Dunn, John
1979 Tsimshian Internal Relations Reconsidered: Southern Tsimshian. In *The Victoria Conference on Northwestern Languages 1976*. British Columbia Provincial Museum Heritage Record, 4:62–82. Victoria, B.C.

Elmendorf, William W.
1990 Chemakum. In *Northwest Coast*. Wayne Suttles, ed. *Handbook of North American Indians*, vol. 7. Pp.438–40. Washington, DC: Smithsonian Institution.

Goddard, Ives, ed.
1996 Languages. *Handbook of North American Indians*, vol.17. Washington, DC: Smithsonian Institution.

Gurvich, Il'ia S.
1966 Etnicheskaia istoriia severo-vostoka Sibiri (Ethnic History of Northeastern Siberia). *Trudy Instituta etnografii AN SSSR*, 89. Moscow.

Gurvich, Il'ia S., ed.
1985 *Narody Dal'nego Vostoka SSSR v XVII–XX vv.* (Peoples of the Far East of the USSR From the 17th to the 20th Century). Moscow: Nauka Publishers.

Hunt, William R.
1975 *Arctic Passage: The Turbulent History of the Land and Peoples of the Bering Sea, 1697–1975.* New York: Scribner.

Iazyki narodov SSSR
1968 *Iazyki narodov SSSR* (Languages of the Peoples of the USSR). Vol. 5: Mongolian, Tungus-Manchu, and Paleoasiatic Languages. Leningrad: Nauka Publishers.

Isaev, Magomed I.
1977 *National Languages in the USSR: Problems and Solutions.* Moscow: Progress Publishers.

Jesup, Morris K.
1897 *Annual Report of the President for the Year 1896.* New York: American Museum of Natural History.

Jochelson, Waldemar
1911 Ekspeditsiia V. I. Iokhel'sona na Aleutskie ostrova i Kamchatku (The Jochelson's Expedition to the Aleutian Islands and to Kamchatka). *Zemlevedenie* 4:136–9.
1926 The Yukaghir and the Yukaghirized Tungus. *The Jesup North Pacific Expedition*, vol. 9, pts.1–3. *Memoirs of the American Museum of Natural History*, 13. Leiden: E.J. Brill; New York: G.E. Stechert.
1934 Odul'skii (Yukagirskii) iazyk. In *Iazyki i pis'mennost' narodov Severa*, 3. Ya P. Al'kor, ed. Pp. 149–89. Leningrad: Uchpedgiz.

Krasnaia kniga
1994 *Krasnaia kniga iazykov narodov Rossii* (The Red Book of the Languages of Russia). V.P. Neroznak, ed. Moscow: Institut iazykov narodov Rossii.

Krauss, Michael
1973 Na-Dene. *Current Trends in Linguistics* 10(2):903–78. The Hague: Mouton.
1973b Eskimo-Aleut. *Current Trends in Linguistics* 10(2):796–902. The Hague: Mouton.
1974 *Native Peoples and Languages of Alaska.* Map. Fairbanks: Alaska Native Language Center. (2nd ed., 1984).
1980 Alaska Native Languages: Past, Present, and Future. *ANLC Research Papers* 4. Fairbanks: Alaska Native Language Center.
1982 *In Honor of Eyak.* Fairbanks: Alaska Native Language Center.
1988 Many Tongues—Ancient Tales. In *Crossroads of Continents: Cultures of Siberia and Alaska*. William W. Fitzhugh and Aron Crowell, eds. Pp. 144–50.Washington, DC: Smithsonian Institution.
1990 Kwalhioqua and Clatskanie. In *Northwest Coast*. Wayne Suttles, ed. *Handbook of North American Indians*, vol. 7. Pp. 530–2. Washington, DC: Smithsonian Institution.

1992 The World's Languages in Crisis. *Languages* 68(1):4–10.

1996 Linguistics and Biology: Threatened Linguistic and Biological Diversity Compared. *CLS (Chicago Linguistic Society)* 32:69–75.

1997 The Indigenous Languages of the North: a Report on Their Present State. In *Northern Minority Languages: Problems of Survival*. Hiroshi Shoji and Juha Janhunen, ed. Senri Ethnological Studies 44:1–34. Osaka, Japan: National Museum of Ethnology.

Krupnik, Igor

1991 Extinction of the Sirenikski Eskimo Language: 1895–1960. *Études/Inuit/Studies* 15(2):3–22.

Leont'ev, Vladilen V.

1983 *Etnografiia i fol'klor kerekov* (The Kerek: Their Ethnography and Folklore). Magadan: Magadanskoe knizhnoe izdatel'tsvo.

Levine, Robert, and Freda Cooper

1976 The Suppression of British Columbian Languages: Filling in the Gaps in the Documentary Record. *Sound Heritage* 4(3–4):43–75. Victoria, B.C.

Mladopis'mennye iazyki

1959 *Mladopis' mennye iazyki narodov SSSR*. Leningrad: Institut iazykoznaniia AN SSSR.

Murasaki, Kyoko

1963 Report on the Extinction of the Kurile-Ainu Language. *Minzokugaku-Kenkyu* 27(4):51–4 (in Japanese).

Novikova, Klavdia A.

1960 *Ocherki dialektov evenskogo iazyka* (Essays on the Dialects of the Even Language). Moscow: Nauka Publishers.

1968 Evenskii iazyk (The Even Language). *Iazyki narodov SSSR*, 5:88–108. Leningrad: Nauka Publishers.

Patkanov, Serafim K.

1912 Staticheskie dannye pokazyvaiushchie plemennoi sostav naseleniia Sibiri, iazyk i rody inorodtsev (na osnovanii dannykh spetsial'noi razrabotki ma-teriala perepisi 1897 g.) (Statistical Data on the Tribal Composition of the Siberian Natives, Their Languages, and Clans, Based Upon the Records of the 1897 Census). Vol.3. *Zapiski imperatorskogo russkogo geograficheskogo obshchestva* 11(3). St. Petersburg.

Savoskul', Sergei S.

1978 Social and Cultural Dynamics of the Peoples of the Soviet North. *Polar Record* 19(119):128–52.

Sunik, O. P.

1959 Tunguso-man'chzhurskie iazyki (The Tungus-Manchu Languages). In: *Mladopis'mennye iazyki narodov SSSR*. Pp. 318–51. Leningrad: AN SSSR.

Tarpent, Marie-Lucie

1996 Reattaching Tsimshianic to Penutian. In: *Proceedings of the Hokan-Penutian Workshop*. Survey of California and Other Indian Languages, 9.

Thompson, Laurence C., and Dale Kinkade

1990 Languages. In: *Northwest Coast*. Wayne Suttles, ed. *Handbook of North American Indians*, vol. 7. Pp. 30–51. Washington, DC: Smithsonian Institution.

Torii, Ryuzo

1919 Les Ainou des Iles Kouriles. *Journal of the College of Science, Tokyo Imperial University* 42:1–337, plates.

Vakhtin, Nikolai B.

1992 *Native Peoples of the Russian Far North*. London: Minority Rights Group.

Vdovin, Innokentii S.

1959 Obshchie svedeniia o sozdanii pis'mennosti na iazykakh narodov Severa (The Creation of Literacy for the Minority Languages of the Peoples of the North: General Review). In: *Mladopis'mennye iazyki narodov SSSR*. Pp. 284–99. Leningrad: AN SSSR.

1965 *Ocherki istorii i ètnografii Chukchei* (Essays in the History and Ethnography of the Chukchi). Leningrad: Nauka Publishers.

Volodin, Aleksandr P.

1976 *Itel'menskii iazyk* (The Itelmen Language). Leningrad: Nauka Publishers.

1997 Chukotsko-kamchatskie iazyki mira (The Chukchi-Kamchatka Languages). In *Paleoaziatskie iazyki*. Pp.12–22. Moscow: Indrik.

Worth, Dean Stoddard

1960 Russian Borrowing in Kamchadal. *Orbis* 9(1):83–109.

54/ *Waldemar Jochelson, Norman Buxton, and Waldemar Bogoras in San Francisco before their departure for Siberia, spring 1900. Studio photo (AMNH 38343)*

55/ Norman G. Buxton in Gizhiga, Siberia, flanked by the local Russian officer and his secretary, Spring 1901 (AMNH 22089)

56/ Buxton's cabin in Gizhiga, Siberia, 1901. Norman Buxton, photographer (AMNH 22050)

57/ Shestakova, a Koryak winter settlement at Penzhina Bay, Siberia, winter 1901. Norman Buxton, photographer (AMNH 22065)

58/ Native dog-teams in Markovo, Anadyr River valley, winter 1901. Norman Buxton, photographer (AMNH 22053)

59/ The town of Markovo, Anadyr River valley, winter 1901. Norman Buxton, photographer (AMNH 22051)

60/ Mr. Nikolai Sokolnikov, commanding officer of the Anadyr District, with Native
children. Markovo, winter 1901. Norman Buxton, photographer (AMNH 22054)

61/ Dried salmon on the sled, used for both human and dog food. Markovo, winter 1901.
Norman Buxton, photographer (AMNH 22065; AMNH 22055)

62/ A group of Yakut (Sakha) children, 1902. Photographer, Waldemar Jochelson (AMNH 11015)

63/ A group of Maritime Koryak children, 1900. Photographer, Waldemar Jochelson (AMNH 4121)

64/ Itelmen poet Anatoly Levkovsky, with his wife Tatiana and son Nikolai. Photographer, Nelson Hancock

65/ Respected Itelmen elder and educator, Tatiana Petrovna Lukashkina was born in the village of Sopochnoe. She remembered fondly growing up there under the tutelage of her blind grandmother, Maria Vasil'evna Pavlutskaia. Photographer, Nelson Hancock

66/ The village of Kovran in 1994 from across the Kovran River. Photographer, Ingrid Summers

67/ Store closed, Verkhne Khairiuzovo, February, 1994. This became an increasingly frequent occurrence. It was some-times rumored that the store was closed during usual opening hours because of the drunkenness of the storekeeper. But it also began to be closed simply because there was nothing to sell. This store owned by the Fishing Cooperative went entirely out of business. Photographer, David Koester

68/ The remains of the Kovran clubhouse (dom kul'tury). Photographer, David Koester

69/ The village of Verkhne Khairiuzovo, summer of 1992. Photographer, David Koester

70/ Itelmen elder Tatiana Petrovna Lukashkina speaks to a group of children at a cultural revival event in 1995. Photographer, David Koester

71/ Itelmen elders Anastasia (Nadia) Pritchina, Aleksandra Krasnoiarova and Polina Popova from Kovran, at an Itelmen gathering in 1995. Photographer, Nelson Hancock

72/ The site of the now closed village of Moroshechnoe as it appeared in 1996. Photographer, Nelson Hancock

73/ The village of Kirganik, on the Kamchatka River in central Kamchatka, is another site that indigenous peoples are re-inhabiting. Closed in the 1960s, Kirganik is now a summer home to a small number of indigenous Kamchadals, such as Aleksandr Tolman, shown here in the summer of 2001. As the regional economy continues to worsen, some people are choosing to move permanently to Kirganik, as it provides better access to fish and game. Photographer, Nelson Hancock

74/ Afanasii Reshetnikov, another of Kirganik's elderly resettlers, in front of his house. 1997. Photographer, Nelson Hancock

7166
1754

75/ *Family of the Chief of the Tundra Yukagir band, winter 1902. Photographer, Waldemar Jochelson (AMNH 1754).*

Genetic Prehistory of Paleoasiatic-speaking Populations of Northeastern Siberia and their Relationships to Native Americans

THEODORE G. SCHURR
AND DOUGLAS C. WALLACE

Franz Boas initiated the first systematic exploration of the population relationships across Bering Strait with the launch of the Jesup North Pacific Expeditions (JNPE) of 1897–1902. Assuming that the ancestral home of the American Indians was Asia, Boas was eager to establish the links between aboriginal groups residing in Siberia and the New World, and to elucidate the processes by which these relationships developed. To this end, the JNPE collected an enormous amount of cultural and linguistic data from populations inhabiting the northern regions of both sides of the North Pacific, including folk tales, grammars, songs, artifacts, masks, boats, dwellings, and clothing (Crowell 1988; Fitzhugh 1988; Gurvich 1988; Krupnik 1988; Rousselot et al. 1988). The similarities in folklore, shamanistic practices, cultural traditions, types of dwellings, decorative motifs, and languages across Bering Strait convinced Boas (1903, 1905), Bogoras (1902), and Jochelson (1908, 1926) that northeastern Siberians were much closer to American Indians than to other Asian/ Siberian peoples.

Furthermore, Boas believed that the physical differences between populations would reveal their relationships in the present, which, in turn, would reflect their origins and relationships in the past (Boas 1912, 1928). To test these ideas, Boas and his colleagues took measurements of body and facial features of thousands of individuals from dozens of ethnic populations within a 10-year span (Boas 1905; Jantz et al. 1992; Ousley and Jantz 2001). From these data, they concluded that populations of the North Pacific constituted a single racial type which originated from a common cultural and linguistic tradition that was formerly more widespread than at present, encompassing Northeast Asia, Alaska, and the Northwest Coast of North America (Boas 1905, 1912, 1928; Jochelson 1926). However, the exact links between Siberian and Northwest Coast populations and the Eskimo were less clear, with the Aleut falling somewhere in the middle of the two geographic extremes.

Based on these findings, Boas proposed that ancient Asians initially migrated across a land bridge to America, and were subsequently cut off for a long period of time by glaciers, thereby allowing the differentiation of the distinctive and heterogeneous American physical types. Later, when the glaciers retreated, the land bridge was opened up again and Americans flowed back into Asia until they met "Mongoloid" populations migrating from the south and west, a concept which became known as the "Americanoid" theory (Bogoras 1902; Jochelson 1908; Boas 1912, 1928). In this model, the back migration of American cultures from east to west across the North Pacific produced the Chukchi, Koryak, Kamchadal, Yukagir and Nivkh (Gilyak) (Boas 1905). The peoples on either side of the North Pacific were then separated at Bering Strait by the intrusion of the Eskimo, a people who were culturally and morphologically distinct and purportedly originated in Central Canada (Boas 1905, 1912), with further diffusion between northern populations being prevented by this "Eskimo wedge" (Collins 1937; Dumond, this volume).

Table 9/ Siberian Populations Analyzed for Genetic Variation

Population	N	n	Field Collection Site(s)	Collection Date(s)	Sample Collection	Ref
Siberian Yupik	79	79	Anadyr, Providenya, & Sireniki; Chukchi Autonomous District, Magadan Region	1994-5	Sukernik	1
Siberian Yupik	>102	70	New Chaplino, Uelen, & Sireniki; Chukchi Autonomous District, Magadan Region	1979-82	Sukernik et al.	2, 3
Coast Chukchi	66	66	Anadyr, Providenya, & Sireniki; Chukchi Autonomous District, Magadan Region	1994-5	Sukernik	1
Reindeer Chukchi	515	70	Rytkuchi & Amguyema; Chukchi Autonomous District, Magadan Region; Middle Pakhachi & Achayvayam; Koryak Autonomous District, Kamchatka Region	1977-9	Sukernik et al.	3, 4
Koryak	104	104	Tymlat, Ossora, & Karaga; Koryak Autonomous District, Kamchatka Region	1993	Schurr and Sukernik	5
Koryak	51	51	Voyampolka & Kovran; Koryak Autonomous District, Kamchatka Region	1996	Schurr, Sukernik & Starikovskaya,	5
Itel'men	47	47	Voyampolka & Kovran; Koryak Autonomous District, Kamchatka Region	1996	Schurr, Sukernik & Starikovskaya,	5
Nivkh	57	57	Nekrasovka & Rybnovsk; Sakhalin Region	1991	Sukernik and Starikovskaya	3
Udegey	45	45	Gvaysugi; Primor'ye Region	1992	Sukernik and Starikovskaya	3
Ulchi/Nanay	87	87	Old and New Bulava; Khabarovsk Region	1997	Sukernik and Starikovskaya	6
Negidal	14	14	Old Bulava, Vladimirovka; Khabarovsk Region	1996	Sukernik and Starikovskaya	6
Yukagir	68	27	Andryushkino & Nelemnoye; Yakut-Sakha Republic	1986-7	Sukernik et al.	3
Even	375	43	Sebyan-Kujhal & Beryozovka; Yakut-Sakha Republic	1990	Sukernik et al.	3, 7
Nganasan	700	49	Novaya, Ust-Avam, & Volochanka; Taymyr Autonomous District, Krasnoyarsk Region	1974-5, 1984	Sukernik et al.	3, 8, 9
Evenk	250	51	Suringa & Polygus; Evenk Autonomous District, Krasnoyarsk Region	1991-2	Sukernik et al.	3
Northern Altai	30	28	Suronash, Tuloi, & Artybash; Gorno-Altai Republic	1994	Sukernik and Starikovskaya	10
Ket	23	23	Sulamai; Evenk Autonomous District, Krasnoyarsk Region	1992	Sukernik et al.	10
Selkup	50	20	Farkovo; Krasnoyarsk Oblast	1990	Sukernik et al.	3, 11
TOTALS	**2,663**	**931**				

Note: 'N' = original number of samples taken during the initial period of field research, and 'n' = number of samples analyzed for mtDNA variation. The 'Field Collection Site(s)' are indicated by village then administrative district and region. 'Ref' = References: 1 = Starikovskaya et al. (1998); 2 = Sukernik and Osipova (1982); 3 = Sukernik et al. (1981); 4 = Torroni et al. (1993b); 5 = Schurr et al. (1999); 6 = Schurr et al. (2000); 7 = Posukh et al. (1990); 8 = Karaphet et al. (1981); 9 = Osipova and Sukernik (1983); 10 = Sukernik et al. (1996); 11 = Sukernik et al. (1992).

Although not confirmed through systematic statistical analyses until recently, these preliminary findings of the JNPE posed a series of hypotheses about Siberian and Native American origins and affinities that have formed the basis of subsequent studies of population relationships in this region. What all of these later analyses have attempted to explicate are the number of migrations or population expansions which entered the New World and gave rise to Paleoindians; the timing of these migrations, i.e., how early the Americas were colonized; and from where in Asia or Siberia the progenitors of these aboriginal peoples originated. In what follows, we describe how the modern molecular genetic data obtained from aboriginal populations of Siberia, in particular, those from Chukotka and Kamchatka, may be used to test the hypotheses about the origins and diversity of eastern Siberians and their evolutionary relationships with Native Americans that were raised in the JNPE investigations (Figs. 62, 63). Although there is a burgeoning literature on Y-chromosome variation in indigenous Siberians and Native Americans, we focus here on mitochondrial DNA (mtDNA) diversity in these populations.

The body of data brought to bear on these questions derives from a large number of anthropological genetic studies conducted among various aboriginal Siberian populations by Dr. Rem I. Sukernik, his colleagues at the Institute of Cytology and Genetics, Novosibirsk, and his collaborators, over the past twenty years, including us from Emory University (Table 9). All of the recent molecular data that are the focus of this paper were obtained from these samples in the laboratory of Dr. Douglas C. Wallace, Center for Molecular Medicine, Emory University. These samples represent over a dozen different ethnic groups that occupy a wide geographic expanse of northern Asia, with a strong eastern Siberian emphasis. As such, this data set permits the direct comparison of molecular genetic information with the craniometric and anthropometric data that were collected from many of these same populations by members of the JNPE.

Table 10/ Haplogroups in Native Siberian and East Asian Populations

Haplogroups	Polymorphic Restriction Sites
A	+663e
B	COII-tRNA^{Lys} intergenic 9-bp deletion, +16517e
C	+10394c, +10397a,-13259o/ +13262a, +16517e
D	-5176a, +10394c, +10397a
F	-12406h/-12406o (-9052n/ -9053f), +16517e
G	+4830n/+4831f, +10394c, +10397a, +16517e
H	-7025a
Y	+7933j, -8391e, +10394c, +16517e
Z	+10394c, +10397a, +11074c, +16517e

Note: The polymorphic restriction sites are numbered from the first nucleotide of the recognition sequence according to the published sequence (Anderson et al. 1981). The restriction enzymes used in the analysis are designated by the following single-letter code: a, AluI; c, DdeI; e, HaeIII; f, HhaI; g, HinfI; h, HpaI; j, MboI; n, HaeII; o, HincII. Sites separated by a diagonal line indicate either simultaneous site gains or site losses for two different enzymes, or a site gain for one enzyme and a site loss for another because of a single common nucleotide substitution.

Mitochondrial DNA Variation in Paleoasiatic-speaking Populations

Among Paleoasiatic-speaking populations, six distinct haplogroups have been identified[1]. These include three of the five haplogroups observed in Native Americans (A, C, and D), and three additional mtDNA lineages (G, Y, and Z) which are present in Asian populations (Table 10)[2]. Each of these haplogroups is defined by both restriction fragment length polymorphisms (RFLPs) and control region (CR) sequence polymorphisms (Table 11), with several different CR sublineages usually present within each haplogroup. The haplogroups and their constituent haplotypes, as well as their associated CR sublineages, have specific distributions in Native Siberian and Native American populations that suggest genetic relationships between them.

Chukotkan Populations

The majority of Chukchi and Siberian Yupik (Eskimo) haplotypes belong to haplogroups A and D (Tables

Table 11/ CR Sequence Sublineages in Siberian and Native American Populations

Haplo-group	CR Sub-lineage	Polymorphic Nucleotides
A	I	16111T, 16192T, 16223T, 16290T, 16319A, 16362C
	II	16111T, 16223T, 16265G, 16290T, 16319A, 16362C
	III	16223T, 16290T, 16319A, 16362C
	IV	16111T, 16223T, 16290T, 16319A, 16362C
C	I	16223T, 16298C, 16327T, 16519C
	II	16124C, 16223T, 16298C, 16327T, 16519C
	III	16093C, 16189C, 16223C, 16261T, 16288C, 16298C, 16519C
	IV	16223T, 16298C, 16325C, 16327T, 16519C
D	I	16223T, 16362C
	II	16093C, 16173T, 16223T, 16319A, 16362C
	III	16129A, 16223T, 16271T, 16362C
	IV	16223T, 16325C, 16362C
G	I	16017C, 16093C, 16129A, 16223T, 16519C
Y	I	16126C, 16189C, 16231C, 16266T, 16519C
Z	I	16129A, 16185T, 16223T, 16224C, 16260T, 16298C, 16519C

Note: *The polymorphic nucleotides are reported as nucleotide changes relative to the published reference sequence (Anderson et al. 1981).*

12, 13). In both Chukotkan populations, the frequencies of haplogroup A haplotypes are found to be consistent with those observed in the Yupik people from St. Lawrence Island and southern Alaska, and are similar to the frequency of this mtDNA lineage in Na-Dené Indians (Haida, Dogrib) and Amerindians from the Northwest Coast of North America (Bella Coola, Nuu-Chah-Nulth). Conversely, the Aleut differ from the Siberian Yupik and Alaskan Alutiiq and Yup'ik in exhibiting haplogroup D mtDNAs at the highest frequency (Merriwether et al. 1995; Rubicz et al. 2001, in press; Derbeneva et al. 2002). In addition, the Chukchi have haplogroup C, G and Y mtDNAs (Derenko et al. 1997, 1998; Starikovskaya et al. 1998; Schurr et al. 2001), which are also present in the Koryak and Itelmen. Based on what is known of Eskimo family histories, the low frequency of haplogroup C mtDNAs in Siberian Yupik could have been obtained through gene flow from the Chukchi. However, haplogroup C mtDNAs

are also observed in Alaskan Eskimo populations (Merriwether et al. 1995), making it possible that these haplotypes were part of the genetic stock of ancestral Eskimo, albeit present in low frequencies.

Kamchatkan Populations

Haplogroup A, C, and D encompass around forty-two percent of Koryak mtDNAs but only twenty percent of Itelmen mtDNAs, with the remainder belonging to haplogroups G, Y, and Z (Derenko et al. 1997; 1998; Schurr et al. 1999) (Table 12). Although the Koryak and Itelmen are more genetically similar to each other than to any other Siberian population, and share founding haplotypes from haplogroups C, G, Y, and Z, they also exhibit statistically significant differences in haplogroup frequencies and haplotype distribution, implying some degree of genetic differentiation between them (Schurr et al. 1999). The CR sequence data also reveal recent gene flow between the two Paleoasiatic-speaking populations (Schurr et al. 1999), confirming previous observations of population contact between them (Antropova 1964a, 1964b; Krasheninnikov 1972; Arutiunov 1988a; Krushanov 1993). These results support linguistic and culture evidence which indicates that Itelmen and Koryak populations arose from temporally distinct expansions into the Kamchatka Peninsula (Vasil'evskii 1971; Arutiunov 1988a; Arutiunov and Sergeev 1990; Dikov 1990).

In contrast, the Reindeer and Coastal Chukchi gropus show much higher frequencies of haplogroup A, C, and D mtDNAs (Table 13; Torroni et al. 1993b; Starikovskaya et al. 1998; Schurr 1998). Based on these data, the three studied Chukchi populations resemble each other more than any of them do to the Koryak or Itelmen. Furthermore, the intermediate frequencies of haplogroup A, C, and D mtDNAs in the Reindeer Chukchi groups relative to the Koryak and the Coastal Chukchi is consistent with the known historical expansion of Reindeer Chukchi south across the Koryak Mountain Range, during which local Koryak tribes were at least partially absorbed (Bogoras 1904;

Jochelson 1908), as well as documented gene flow between the Coast Chukchi and Siberian Yupik (Sukernik and Osipova 1982).

Mitochondrial DNA Variation in Eastern Siberian Populations

Among other Native Siberian groups, mtDNAs belonging to haplogroup G are found primarily in eastern populations, specifically the Even, Yukagir, and Nganasan (Table 13). These results, along with the higher frequencies of haplogroup G mtDNAs in the Chukchi, Koryak, and Itelmen, imply a considerable degree of genetic contact between eastern Siberian and Paleoasiatic-speaking groups from Kamchatka and Chukotka. This interpretation is supported by ethnographic evidence of contact, trade, and conflict among eastern Siberian populations (Jochelson 1908, Antropova 1964a; Krushanov 1993). By contrast, haplogroup Y mtDNAs are absent in most eastern Siberian populations, but occurred at a high frequency in the Nivkh and were present at polymorphic frequencies in the Udegey, Nanay, Ulchi, Negidal, Korean, Ainu, and Japanese (Torroni et al. 1993b; Horai et al. 1996; Schurr et al. 1999, 2000).

The remaining "Other" mtDNAs in the Chukchi and eastern Siberian groups probably belong to haplogroup Z, with the highest frequency of these mtDNAs occurring in the Even and the Chukchi of the Pakhachi River group. This interpretation is supported by CR sequence data from another Even population (Derenko et al. 1997, 1998). Because these mtDNAs are also present at low frequencies in the Nganasan and Yukagir, they could have originated in Tungusic-speaking populations and then spread to other ethnic groups through contact in the past several millennia. If correct, this interpretation would be supported by ethnographic

Table 12 / Haplogroup Frequencies in Eastern Pacific Rim Populations

POPULATION	n	A	B	C	D	G	Other	Ref
		Frequency (%)						
Paleoasiatic:								
Chukchi	66	68.2	—	10.6	12.1	9.1	—	1
Eskimo-Aleut:								
Siberian Yupik	79	77.2	—	2.5	20.3	—	—	1
Savoonga Yupik	49	93.9	—	—	2.0	—	4.1	2
Gambell Yupik	50	58.0	—	14.0	26.0	—	2.0	2
Old Harbor Alutiiq	115	61.7	3.5	—	34.8	—	—	2
Ouzinkie Alutiiq	41	73.2	—	4.9	14.6	—	7.3	2
Pribilof Is. Aleut	72	25.0	—	1.4	66.7	—	6.9	2
Na-Dene:								
Dogrib	154	90.9	—	2.0	—	—	7.1	2
Haida	38	92.1	—	7.9	—	—	—	3
Haida	25	96.0	—	—	4.0	—	—	4
Amerindians:								
Bella Coola	32	78.1	6.3	9.4	6.3	—	—	3
Bella Coola	25	60.0	8.0	8.0	20.0	—	4.0	4
Nuu-chah-nulth	63	44.4	3.2	19.0	22.2	—	11.1	5
Nuu-chah-nulth	15	40.0	6.7	13.3	26.7	—	13.3	4

Note: 'Ref' = References: 1 = Starikovskaya et al. (1998); 2 = Merriwether et al. (1995); 3 = Ward et al. (1993); 4 = Torroni et al. (1993a); 5 = Ward et al. (1991). Other = Other haplotypes, i.e., those which do not belong to the haplogroups identified in the table but may have different lineal affiliations

evidence indicating considerable assimilation of Yukagir populations by the Even (Arutiunov 1988c), and cultural and genetic contacts between Even and Koryak along the northern Sea of Okhotsk coast, due to the expansion of the Even into that region during the seventeenth and eighteenth centuries (Jochelson 1908; Antropova 1964a; Arutiunov 1988c).

In this regard, we now know that haplogroup Z occurs in populations spanning the entire breadth of northern Eurasia. It is observed as far west as the Saami of Finland (Sajantila et al., 1995), also occurs among the Udmurt, Tatar, Bashkir, and Mari of the Volga-Uralic region (Meinila et al., 2001; Bermisheva et al., 2002), and in seen in a number of eastern Siberian populations (Table 13). Based on its distribution, haplogroup Z could possibly have accompanied the expansion of Neolithic herding cultures throughout Eurasia.

Another trend seen in these data is that central Siberian populations exhibit genetic profiles that are quite different from those of eastern Siberian groups. Although haplogroup A-D mtDNAs are present at varying frequencies in the Mansi, Ket, Selkup, and Northern

Table 13/ Haplogroup Distribution in West Pacific Rim and Siberian Populations

Population	n	A	B	C	D	F	G	H	J	M	Y	T	U	Z	Oth	Ref
						Haplogroup Frequencies (%)										
Coastal Chukchi	66	68.2	—	10.6	12.1	—	9.1	—	—	—	—	—	—	—	—	1
Reindeer Chukchi	70	28.6	—	21.4	12.6	—	7.0	—	—	—	1.4	—	—	25.7	—	2
Amguema Chukchi	24	37.5	—	20.8	16.7	—	8.3	—	—	—	—	—	—	16.7	—	2
Pakhachi Chukchi	46	23.9	—	21.7	10.9	—	10.9	—	—	—	2.2	—	—	30.4	—	2
Koryak*	155	5.2	—	36.1	1.3	—	41.3	—	—	—	9.7	—	—	5.8	—	3
Reindeer Koryak	89	5.6	—	31.5	1.1	—	43.8	—	—	—	7.9	—	—	10.1	—	3
Maritime Koryak	54	5.6	—	40.7	1.9	—	37.0	—	—	—	14.8	—	—	—	—	3
Itelmen	47	6.4	—	14.9	—	—	68.1	—	—	—	4.3	—	—	6.4	—	3
Nivkh	57	—	—	—	28.1	—	5.3	—	—	—	64.9	—	—	—	1.8	2
Udegey	45	—	—	17.8	—	—	—	—	—	—	8.9	—	—	—	73.3	2
Nanay	14	—	—	14.3	42.9	7.1	14.3	—	—	—	21.4	—	—	—	—	
Ulchi	37	5.4	—	21.6	10.8	—	10.8	—	—	—	37.8	—	—	—	13.5	
Negidal	13	—	23.1	7.7	23.1	—	15.4	7.7	15.4	—	7.7	—	—	—	—	
Even	43	—	—	58.1	7.0	—	2.3	—	—	—	—	—	—	—	32.6	2, 3
Yukagir	27	—	—	59.3	33.3	—	3.7	—	—	—	—	—	—	—	3.7	2, 3
Nganasan	49	2.0	—	38.8	36.7	—	4.1	—	—	2.0	—	2.0	12.2	—	2.0	2, 3
Evenk	51	3.9	—	84.3	9.8	2.0	—	—	—	—	—	—	—	—	—	2
Tofalar	27	—	7.4	59.3	—	11.1	—	—	—	22.2	—	—	—	—	—	
Tuvan	43	—	7.0	47.6	23.3	—	—	2.3	2.3	11.6	—	—	—	—	2.4	
Buryat	24	—	—	45.8	9.1	—	—	—	4.2	25.0	—	—	2.3	—	2.3	
Northern Altai	28	3.6	3.6	35.7	14.3	3.6	—	10.7	—	7.1	—	—	21.4	—	—	3, 5
Ket	23	4.3	—	17.4	—	34.8	—	4.3	—	—	—	—	17.4	—	60.9	3, 5
Selkup	20	—	—	35.0	—	—	—	30.0	—	—	—	—	35.0	—	—	2, 3
Korean	13	7.7	7.7	—	23.1	15.4	23.1	—	—	—	7.7	—	—	—	15.4	6
Taiwanese Han	20	10.0	20.0	5.0	5.0	10.0	—	—	—	—	—	—	—	—	45.0	6

Note: n = sample size, and Oth = 'Other' haplotypes, i.e., those which do not belong to the haplogroups identified in the table but may have different lineal affiliations. The asterisk (*) indicates that 12 individuals were not certain of their ethnicity in terms of Maritime versus Reindeer Koryak, but included in the totals for all Koryaks. 'Ref' = 'Reference': 1 = Starikovskaya et al. (1998); 2 = Torroni et al. (1993b); 3 = Schurr (1998); 4 = Schurr et al. (1999); 4 = Sukernik et al. (1996); 5 = Ballinger et al. (1992).

Altayan, the majority of their haplotypes belong to other mtDNA lineages (Torroni et al. 1993b; Sukernik et al. 1996; Derbeneva et al. 2002a; Schurr et al. 2003). These populations also largely lack mtDNAs belonging to haplogroups G, Y, and Z (Torroni et al. 1993b; Sukernik et al. 1996; Derbeneva et al. 2002a; Schurr et al. 2003). In fact, based on their RFLP composition, most of these haplotypes appear not to be of East Asian origin (Table 13). Instead, all of the central Siberian populations exhibit mtDNAs from West Eurasian haplogroups H and U (Schurr 1998; Derbeneva et al. 2002a; Schurr et al. 2003), with the remaining haplotypes belonging to other West Eurasian haplo-groups. These results clearly indicate that western/central Siberian populations are distinctive from eastern Siberian populations, and appear to have mtDNAs of both ancient Eurasian and Asian origin as part of their overall genetic composition.

When these differences in haplogroup composition among Native Siberian populations were statistically analyzed, several distinct population groupings reflecting the regional differences amongst them were observed (Fig. 76). These included branches leading to Chukotkan groups, Kamchatkan groups, Uralic-Tungusic groups, and central Siberian groups. The closeness of the Yukagir to Tungusic-speaking groups probably reflected the recent assimilation of the former populations by the Even (Arutiunov 1988c), with the Nganasan showing intermediate position between the Uralic-Tungusic and central Siberian clusters due to having haplotypes in common with each set of populations. Interestingly, the Nivkh were positioned away from the rest of the eastern Siberians, and clustered with the Koreans, who also had haplogroup D, G, and Y haplotypes (Ballinger et al. 1992; Horai et al. 1996). Similarly, the Udegey were something of an outlier relative to other Siberian populations, and clustered with the Taiwanese Han, who also had significant frequencies of "other" mtDNAs with similar mutational characteristics as those present in the Udegey, although not belonging to the same exact haplogroups, since most of those present in the Udegey belong to haplogroup M (Torroni et al. 1993b).

Genetic Discontinuity of Paleoasiatic-speakers and Native Americans

Given the overall pattern of genetic divergence in Siberia, it was not surprising that a comparison of the haplotypic diversity of Paleoasiatic-speaking and Native American groups revealed a striking discontinuity between these populations.

Table 14/ Sequence Divergence of Siberian and Native American Haplogroups

Haplogroup	Geographic Region	n	N	Sequence Divergence (%)	Divergence Time (YBP)
A	Siberia	10	119	0.0280	12,714 – 9,645
	America	46	189	0.0789	35,550 – 26,969
B	America	30	99	0.0391	15,205 – 11,534
C	Siberia	14	123	0.0433	19,686 – 14,934
	America	31	72	0.1223	54,009 – 40,972
D	Siberia	13	47	0.1115	50,664 – 38,434
	America	16	62	0.0565	25,682 – 19,483
G	Siberia	11	106	0.0239	10,855 – 8,234
Y	Siberia	7	58	0.0138	6,864 – 5,207
Z	Siberia	4	12	0.0209	9,495 – 7,203

Note: n = number of haplotypes, and N = number of individual mtDNAs, for each haplogroup. The sequence divergence estimates were weighted by the number of individuals within each haplogroup. Divergence times were calculated by multiplying the haplogroup sequence divergences by the mtDNA evolutionary rate of 2.2-2.9% per MYR (Torroni et al. 1994a).

Haplogroup Distribution

Although having a number of haplogroup A, C, and D haplotypes, the Chukchi, Koryak, and Itelmen, as well as the Siberian Yupik, are not closely genetically related to Native American populations. In fact, they actually share only the founding haplotypes from haplogroups A and C with Amerindian groups, and, based on CR sequence data, these do not appear to be identical to comparable mtDNAs from Native American populations. Otherwise, Paleoasiatic-speaking and North Pacific Rim groups exhibit a number of population- or region-specific haplotypes in each of these haplogroups, which apparently arose in their ancestral populations independent of those occurring in Paleoindian groups (Ward et al. 1991, 1993; Torroni et al. 1992, 1993b; Shields et al. 1993; Starikovskaya et al. 1998; Schurr et al. 1999). Therefore, the majority of these mtDNAs cannot be the same as the founding haplotype in New World populations, and instead, must have arisen after the colonization of the New World.

This degree of genetic differentiation of Siberian and Native American populations provides evidence for at least two major expansions of ancient Beringian populations into northern North America before and after the last major period of glaciation, the timing of which are mirrored by the different divergence values for haplogroup A in Siberia and the Americas (Table 14). The estimated sequence divergence for this haplogroup in Siberia is 0.028 percent, a value considerably less than that for the Americas, 0.079 percent. These values give correspondingly different divergence times for Siberia (13,000–10,000 years before present (YBP)) and the Americas (36,000–27,000 YBP). This apparent discrepancy is largely attributable to almost exclusively Chukotkan haplotypes being present in the haplogroup A estimate for Native Siberians. In fact, the three estimates of the genetic divergence of haplogroup A in Siberian and Native American populations, one for Chukotkan groups (0.029 percent; 12,727–9,655 YBP), Na-Dené Indians (0.021 percent; 9,545–7,241 YBP), and Amerindians (0.079percent; 35,909–27,241 YBP) (Torroni et al. 1992; Starikovskaya et al. 1998; Schurr et al. 1999), show very clearly the extent of diversity which has developed between them, not just within the haplogroup itself. Thus, while these divergence estimates do not give exact times for the ages of specific ethnic groups, they provide a temporal framework in which to view the emergence of the ancestral populations for the three major Native American linguistic divisions.

In addition, haplogroup B mtDNAs are absent in the Koryak and Itelmen, as well as in the Chukchi and Siberian Yupik (Torroni et al. 1993b; Starikovskaya et al. 1998; Schurr et al. 1999). In fact, haplogroup B is absent in almost all eastern Siberian populations (Shields et al. 1992; Petrishchev et al. 1993; Torroni et al. 1993b), excepting those inhabiting the southern margin of Siberia adjacent to Mongolia and northern China, where low frequencies of deletion haplotypes appear (Petrishchev et al. 1993; Kolman et al. 1996; Sukernik et al. 1996). Conversely, this mtDNA lineage is present in almost all Amerindian populations at low to moderate frequencies (Schurr et al. 1990; Ward et al. 1991, 1993; Torroni et al. 1992, 1993a, 1994a; Merriwether et al. 1995; Lorenz and Smith 1994). These results suggest that haplogroup B was never part of the ancestral gene pool for Paleoasiatic-speaking populations, and that these groups played no role in the

dispersal of this mtDNA lineage into the New World. Furthermore, the virtual absence of haplogroup B mtDNAs in modern Eskimo, Aleut, and northern Na-Dené Indian populations (Table 11), which represent more recent expansions into North America, implies that haplogroup B mtDNAs were not present in the Beringian region after 10,000 YBP, when these populations were likely founded.

Regarding the other mtDNA lineages present in northeastern Siberians, haplogroup G, Y, and Z mtDNAs have not been observed in either ancient or modern Native American groups (Schurr et al. 1990; Torroni et al. 1992, 1993a, 1994a, b; Stone and Stoneking 1998; Lorenz and Smith 1996, 1997). Therefore, populations bearing these haplotypes must have spread in northeast Asia after the initial populating of the New World. Consistent with this hypothesis, the divergence times of haplogroups G, Y, and Z are shallower than those of haplogroups A-D in Siberia and the Americas (Table 13). Of these Siberian mtDNA lineages, haplogroup G is the oldest and most diverse, a result paralleled by its broader distribution within Asia itself (Horai et al. 1996; Ballinger et al. 1992; Torroni et al. 1993b; Schurr 1998; Starikovskaya et al. 1998; Schurr et al. 1999, 2001; Bermisheva et al. 2001; Derbeneva et al. 2002a).

CR Sublineage Distribution

The distribution of CR sublineages in Siberian and Native Americans further highlights the genetic discontinuities between these populations. To begin with, the primary sublineages within haplogroups A, C, and D present in northeastern Siberians differ from those in Native Americans (Table 15). In general, Paleoasiatic-speakers and North Pacific Rim populations share more of these sublineages than either did with eastern Siberian or Native American populations. Within haplogroup A, almost every CR sequence from these populations has the 16111T mutation that delineates "American" from "Asian" haplotypes from this mtDNA lineage. Since the founding CR sequence for this haplogroup is the only mtDNA shared between the Chukchi, Siberian

Table 15/ Distribution of haplogroup A, C and D Sublineages in Siberian and Native American Populations

Haplogroup	CR Sequence Sublineage	Eastern Siberians	Paleo-Asiatics	N. Pacific Rim Populations	Amerindians
A	I		X	X	
	II			X	
	III	X	X		
	IV			X?	X
C	I	X			
	II		X		
	III		X		
	IV				X
D	I	X			
	II		X	X	
	III			X	
	IV				X

Note: 'Eastern Siberians' include Nivkh, Udegey, and Evenk; 'Paleoasiatics' include Itelmen, Koryak, and Chukchi; 'North Pacific Rim Populations' include Siberian and Alaskan Yupik, Alaskan Inuit, and Na-Dené Indians; and 'Amerindians' include NW Coast and all other Amerindian populations

Yupik, Alaskan Alutiiq and Yup'ik, Na-Dené Indians, and Amerindians (Ward et al. 1991, 1993; Shields et al. 1993; Starikovskaya et al. 1998), it clearly demarcates the occurrence of the 16111T mutation in haplogroup A mtDNAs, hence, the initial population expansion which brought them to the New World.

Several other polymorphic nucleotides identify specific sublineages of haplogroup A. The 16192T mutation distinguishes a set of mtDNAs that are found only in the Koryak, Chukchi, Siberian Yupik, Alaskan Alutiiq and Yup'ik, Aleut, and Na-Dené Indians (Table 14), and, hence, delineates a "North Pacific Rim" branch of this haplogroup. These sublineage I mtDNAs comprise sixty percent of the Chukchi and Siberian Yupik mtDNAs (Starikovskaya et al. 1998), as well as the majority of CR sequences in Alaskan Athapaskans, Alaskan Alutiiq and Yup'ik (Shields et al. 1993) and Aleut (Rubicz et al. 2001, In Press). Such a distribution implies that these haplogroup A mtDNAs evolved in isolation from similar haplotypes in the Na-Dené Indians and Amerindians living in the NW Coast, and that they are part of the common genetic stock that gave rise to the Chukchi, Eskimo-Aleut, and Alaskan Athapaskans.

Within sublineage I, a Na-Dené-specific sub-branch is also present. This sub-branch is characterized by

the np 16233G and np 16331G transitions, the latter also causing the RsaI np 16329 site loss which has been observed in Na-Dené-specific RFLP haplotypes (Torroni et al. 1992, 1993a). Haplotypes with this mutation occur in the Dogrib and Tlingit of Canada, and are also present in the Navajo and Apache of the United States Southwest (Torroni et al. 1992, 1993), populations that descended from Northern Athapaskans (Haskell 1987). Based on these data, it appears that this sub-branch of sublineage I arose early in the differentiation of Athapaskan populations prior to their dispersal into Alaska and North America, and was spread to neighboring Amerindian populations through gene flow.

In addition, all of the CR lineages having the 16265G transition form a distinct cluster that contain exclusively Eskimoan sequences (Table 14). In fact, every Eskimo population analyzed for CR sequence variation exhibits mtDNAs from sublineage II (Shields et al. 1993; Starikovskaya et al. 1998; Saillard et al. 2000). As a consequence, these mtDNAs appear to have arisen in ancestral Eskimoan populations, and spread to various circum-arctic regions during the expansion of the ancestors of today's Yupik and Inuit people during the last several thousand years. In contrast, the third sublineage (III) lacks the 16111T mutation altogether. These CR sequences appear largely in East Asian and eastern Siberian populations. Because they lack the 16111T mutation, sublineage III mtDNAs likely represent the ancestral state for this mtDNA lineage (Table 11). Among Paleoasiatic-speakers, the Koryak and Itelmen have haplogroup A CR sequences from sublineages I and III, whereas the Chukchi and Siberian Yupik lack them altogether.

Recent studies of Aleut populations also indicate that they have unique haplogroup A sequences (Rubicz

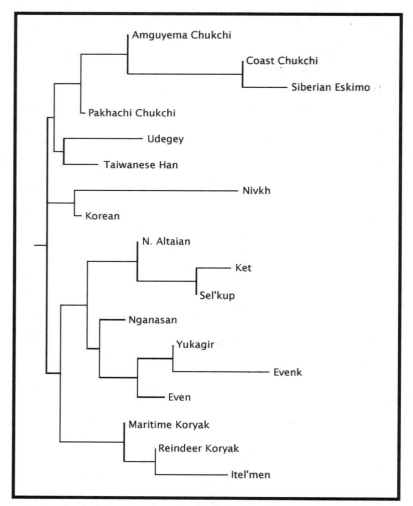

76/ Neighbor-joining Tree for Aboriginal Siberian and East Asian Populations

The genetic distances used to generate this tree were estimated from RFLP haplotype data (modified after Schurr et al. 1999, Fig. 5).

of Haida, Nuu-Chah-Nulth, and Bella Coola CR sequences, and, within this cluster, a subgroup consisting of only Nuu-Chah-Nulth mtDNAs is seen (Shields et al 1993; Starikovskaya et al. 1998). Another cluster defined by the 16355T transition contained only Haida and Bella Coola mtDNAs (Ward et al. 1991, 1993; Starikovskaya et al. 1998). The uniqueness of these Haida haplogroup A CR sequences, and the lack of mtDNAs having the Na-Dené–specific 16331G transition, explains in large part the genetic differences previously observed between the Haida and other Na-Dené Indian populations (Torroni et al. 1992, 1993b; Shields et al. 1993). Overall, these population-specific CR sublineages may reflect the isolation and re-emergence of remnant populations occupying biogeographic refugia in Beringia and southern Alaska, which existed until the end of the last glacial maximum (Rogers et al. 1991). Moreover, these findings imply that Amerindian populations have become genetically differentiated from groups residing in Arctic and Subarctic regions, and that considerable gene flow has taken place among NW Coast populations.

Similar trends were observed for the CR sequences of haplogroups C and D. Two sublineages in haplogroup C bear a close resemblance to haplogroup C mtDNAs present in Native American populations (sublineage IV) by having the 16223T–16298C–16327T sequence motif characteristic of this mtDNA lineage (Tables 11, 15). Sub-lineage I occurs predominantly in East Asian and eastern Siberian populations, whereas the other (II), having the additional 16124C and 16318T

et al. 2001, In Press). The majority of these sequences derive from sublineage I, with two distinct subsets also having the 16212A—G (16212G) and 16234C—T (16234T) transitions, both of which appear to be Aleut-specific. However, none of the Aleut sequences have the Eskimo-specific 16265G transition (Shields et al. 1993; Starikovskaya et al. 1998; Saillard et al. 2000), or the Athapaskan-specific 16331G transition (Shields et al. 1993; Torroni et al. 1993a).

mtDNAs belonging to a fourth sublineage (IV) of haplogroup A occur exclusively in Native American populations (Table 15). Within this sublineage, the 16129A mutation defines a largely North Amerindian cluster of haplogroup A mtDNAs which is comprised mutations, occurs only in Paleoasiatic groups (II). Amerindian sub-lineage IV differs from these Siberian sublineages by the presence of the 16325C mutation. The only populations found to have similar mtDNAs are Mongolians and Amur River populations (Kolman et al. 1996; Schurr et al. 2001), suggesting these regions as possible source areas for ancestral Native Americans. By contrast, the third Siberian sublineage (III) has a quite different sequence motif than the others, and appears only in Paleoasiatic groups, possibly reflecting its origins amongst them.

Likewise, haplogroup D has several sublineages within it (Table 14). The first (I) occurs at very low frequencies among Paleoasiatic-speaking groups and Siberian Yupik, and represented the only haplogroup D mtDNA in the Koryak (SIB40; Starikovskaya et al. 1998). The second sublineage (II) occurs exclusively among Chukotkan populations, as no similar types are seen among Native American groups with high frequencies of haplogroup D (Ward et al. 1991, 1993; Shields et al. 1993). The remaining mtDNAs from East Asian and eastern Siberian populations formed a sublineage (III) that had a sequence motif most similar to haplogroup D haplotypes in Native American populations (sub-lineage IV), indicating that sublineage III probably represents the ancestral state for this mtDNA lineage in Asia and the Americas. Amerindian sublineage IV mtDNAs were distinguished from similar Asian haplotypes by the 16325C mutation. Interestingly, the only Asian populations that were found to possess haplogroup D mtDNAs with the 16325C mutation are Japanese and Koreans (Horai et al. 1996) and Amur River groups (Schurr et al. 2001). These findings suggest that East Asia could be a possible source area for these haplotypes in New World populations.

Aleut populations also have unique haplogroup D sequences (Rubicz et al. 2001, In Press; Derbeneva et al. 2002b). These sequences have the 16129A and 16271C transitions defining the D2 subtype described by Forster et al. (1996), which is defined by the 16223T–16271C–16362C motif. The D2 subtype has previously been detected in the Chukchi and Siberian Eskimo (Starikovskaya et al. 1998), as well as a single Alaskan Athapaskan Indian (Shields et al. 1993), but is absent from Greenland Eskimos and Kamchatkan populations (Saillard et al. 2000, Schurr et al. 1999). This pattern suggests that D2 haplotypes arose in ancestral Aleut and were disseminated to surrounding groups through gene flow.

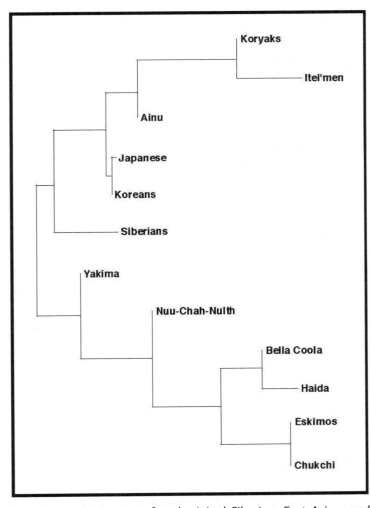

77/Neighbor-joining tree for aboriginal Siberian, East Asian, and Amerindian populations. The genetic distances used to generate this tree were estimated from CR sequence data (Schurr et al. 1999, Fig.8).

The phylogenetic analysis of CR sequence variation in eastern Siberian, East Asian, and Native American populations revealed sets of relationships which were consistent with this assessment (Fig. 77). First, there was an obvious split between the Paleoasiatic-speaking groups from Chukotka and Kamchatka. The Koryak and Itelmen showed much closer genetic ties to the Ainu and East Asian populations, whereas the Chukchi were much closer to the Siberian Yupik, Haida, and Northwest Coast Amerindian populations. In addition, the contemporary Korean and Japanese populations showed close genetic affinities, and the Ainu had genetic similarities to both groups, as seen in Horai et al. (1996). The latter association was probably attributable to recent admixture between the Ainu and Japanese, rather than these groups having an ancient shared ancestry.

Certain affinities among Native American populations were also evident in this analysis. All Northwest Coast Amerindian populations clustered together, and the Bella Coola and the Haida showed a particularly close relationship. This close relationship seemed to imply that the Haida were an Amerindian population that was linguistically influenced by Na-Dené Indians, rather than being a Na-Dené Indian group that was genetically influenced by Amerindians. However, further comparisons of genetic diversity in the Haida, Alaskan Athapaskans, and Northwest Coast Amerindian groups will be necessary to confirm this hypothesis.

Furthermore, eastern Siberians and the Yakima of Washington state show some degree of similarity to each other. This similarity largely results from the fact that eastern Siberians contained a number of different haplotypes from haplogroups A, C, and D, and these had CR sequences that were more similar to those in Amerindian populations than those in Chukotkan and Kamchatkan populations. As a result, eastern Siberians and Amerindian populations were positioned fairly close to each other (Fig. 77). In other words, populations located some distance away from the North Pacific Rim on either side of Bering Strait tended to have more similar CR sequences than those occupying the former Beringian region. However, it should be noted that all of the Siberian haplotypes differed from comparable Native American haplotypes at the RFLP level. Hence, both eastern Siberians and Amerindians appear to have arisen from common ancestral populations, rather than from those that expanded in this region more recently, such as Paleoasiatic groups, Eskimo-Aleut, and Na-Dené Indians. Concomitantly, those populations whose ancestors last occupied the former Beringian region have become genetically differentiated from Siberian and Amerindian groups, and now resemble each other more closely than to their putative sister groups in northern Asia and the New World.

When additional CR sequences from other Native Siberian populations are used to assess the genetic affinities of these populations, some of these same patterns are observed (Fig. 78). Paleoasiatic populations are split into Chukotkan and Kamchatkan groups, while the Reindeer Koryak show similarities to the Even, who probably influenced them culturally and genetically. The Koryak and Itelmen also show similarities to Amur River groups, who have significant frequencies of haplogroup G and Y mtDNAs, and this may reflect the common origins of these populations. While forming a distinct branch separate from the easternmost populations, the Tofalar, Evenk, Buryat and Tuvan clustered together within a larger grouping that included all eastern Siberian peoples. By contrast, the Yakut, Northern Altayan, Ket, and Selkup clustered at some distance from eastern Siberian populations, most likely because of the sizeable portion of Western Eurasian haplotypes in their mtDNA gene pool (Table 10).

Comparison of Genetic and Anthropometric Data for North Pacific Rim Populations

The results of these studies allowed a direct comparison of the patterns of biological variation among North Pacific Rim populations based on mtDNA, nuclear DNA, anthropometric, and craniometric data. The first notable difference between these sets of analyses was the relationship between the Koryak and Itelmen. Based on mtDNA data, these two populations show close genetic affinities (Schurr et al. 1999), while the principal components (PC) analysis of JNPE anthropometric data shows the Kamchadal (Itelmen) to be distantly related to other eastern Siberian groups, including the Koryak (Comuzzie et al. 1995). In all likelihood, this discrepancy reflects the significant level of admixture between Itelmen and Russians since the turn of the eighteenth century (Antropova 1964b; Murashko 1994), and mostly that mediated through non-Native male gene flow, since the mtDNA data clearly show the Itelmen to have only aboriginal genotypes amongst them.

There were also shifting patterns of association amongst the Paleoasiatic-speaking populations of Chukotka and Kamchatka. Aside from the Koryak-Itelmen closeness, the mtDNA data show the Koryak to have some affinities with Chukchi populations, but stronger links with populations from the Lower Amur River/ Sea of Okhotsk region farther south (Nivkh, Udegey, Nanay, Ulchi, Negidal, Ainu). The PC analysis of JNPE anthropometric data also reveal affinities between the Koryak and the Even and Yukagir (Comuzzie et al. 1995; Ousley 1995), associations that are reflected in the genetic distance estimates based on mtDNA haplogroup and frequencies and CR sequence variation in Siberian groups (Figs. 76 and 78).

Third, the relationship of the Nivkh to other eastern Siberian and circumpolar Arctic populations differs depending on the type of analysis being conducted. mtDNA studies indicate that the Nivkh are an outlier relative to most eastern Siberian groups, but do have links to both Lower Amur River, Sea of Okhotsk, and Kamchatkan populations. By contrast, the PC analysis

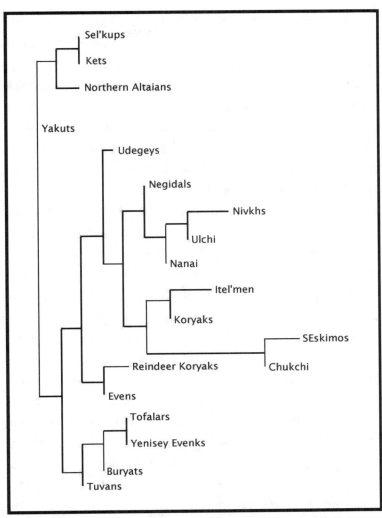

78/ Neighbor-joining tree for Native Siberian and East Asian Populations.
The genetic distances used to generate this tree were based on CR sequence data from these populations (Shields et al. 1993; Derenko et al. 1997, 1998; Starikov-skaya et al. 1998; Schurr et al. 1999, 2000, 2001, 2003)

of JNPE anthropometric data position the Nivkh close to both the Chukchi and Aleut (Comuzzie et al. 1995), or to the Alaskan Athapaskans (Ousley 1995). Although having a high frequency of haplogroup D, none of these Nivkh haplotypes are closely related to those appearing in Paleoasiatic-speaking populations. These differences may, thus, reflect the convergence of physical features in the Nivkh and other North Pacific populations, rather than being the consequence of substantial contact and gene flow amongst them.

Fourth, the clustering of Eskimo populations varies according to the type of data being used in the analysis. One PC analysis of JNPE anthropometric data (Ousley

1995) suggested a link between the Labrador, MacKenzie Delta, and Siberian Yupik, and affinities between the other Alaskan Yup'ik with Aleut and Amerindians, whereas another showed the Siberian Yupik to be intermediate between the Koryak and Chukchi (Comuzzie et al. 1995). Nuclear genetic data reveal a different pattern, with most Eskimo populations clustering together, and the Aleut diverging from Eskimo groups (Harper 1980; Crawford et al. 1981). The mtDNA data also highlight the genetic similarity among Eskimo populations, both Siberian and Alaskan, and the relative closeness of Eskimo groups and Alaskan Athapaskans, as well as the strong ties between Siberian Yupik and Chukchi (Starikovskaya et al. 1998). These differences imply that regional interactions with eastern Siberian, Aleut, or Athapaskan populations may have influenced the distribution of physical features in Eskimo groups.

Fifth, the Aleut also show varying degrees of similarity to North Pacific Rim populations, depending on the type of data being analyzed. Based on limited mtDNA data for this population, the Aleut appear to be part of the genetic stock which emerged after the initial peopling of the New World, although exhibiting haplogroup A and D frequencies which distinguished them from other Eskimoan populations. On the other hand, PC analysis of JNPE anthropometric data has identified affinities between the Aleut and Alaskan Yup'ik (Ousley 1995), or between them and Athapaskans and Northwest Coast Amerindians (Comuzzie et al. 1995). Therefore, the Aleut appear to have biological characteristics that are intermediate between those of a number of populations from the North Pacific Rim, perhaps as a consequence of their geographic isolation and later contact with various ethnic groups.

Finally, unlike the Aleut, the Haida show rather consistent patterns of similarity to North Pacific Rim populations, irrespective of the type of data being analyzed. The mtDNA data reveal the Haida to have affinities with both Athapaskan and NW Coast Amerindian populations, although tending to be closer to the latter groups. The same pattern is observed in the PC analysis of JNPE anthropometric data (Ousley 1995) and previous nuclear genetic data (Field et al. 1988), as well as linguistic evidence for this group (Krauss 1988). Thus, to a degree not seen for other Arctic populations, all biological anthropological data for the Haida are generally concordant in revealing mixed Athapaskan-Amerindian genetic and cultural influences on the formation of this tribal group, as well as certain unique features that may have arisen as a consequence of its geographic isolation.

Overall, these analyses confirm that single locus genetic systems such as the mtDNA are informative for delineating the origins and affinities of human populations, in this case, Paleoasiatic-speaking and other eastern Siberian groups. In addition, they have shown that certain populations cluster together on the basis of shared maternally-inherited genetic lineages and their constituent haplotypes, probably due to their common origins and subsequent regional differentiation. These studies have further demonstrated how the genetic substructure within these groups can be used to piece together the population history of northeast Siberia and northern North America. However, the uncertain relationships among some North Pacific Rim populations revealed by the comparison of mtDNA data with those from anthropometric, craniometric, and nuclear genetic studies indicate that data from bi-parentally inherited genetic systems, as well as the uniparentally inherited Y-chromosome, are needed to more fully characterize the process of population differentiation in these regions, and hence, test previous hypothesizes about the genetic prehistory of aboriginal Siberian groups.

Revisiting JNPE Conclusions About Northeastern Siberian Origins

Based on these molecular data, it is possible to make a number of conclusions about the associations between eastern Siberian and Native American populations, and to determine how well these findings relate to the models proposed by Boas and his colleagues at the turn of the century. First, from a genetic standpoint, Paleoasiatic-speakers do not appear to be closely related to Native American populations. Although having haplogroups A, C, and D in common, Paleoasiatic-speaking and Amerindian populations share few, if any, haplotypes from these mtDNA lineages. Such differences probably reflect the fact that the former populations expanded into northeastern Siberia following the last glacial maximum, whereas ancestral Amerindians had entered the New World well before this time. Thus, from a molecular perspective, Paleoasiatic-speakers cannot be considered "Americanoids."

Second, the genetic data reveal a dichotomy between Paleoasiatic-speakers from Chukotka and those from Kamchatka. Based on mtDNA data, the Chukchi and Siberian Yupik have strong genetic ties with populations located across the Bering Strait from them, such as Alaskan Eskimo and Na-Dené Indians, as well as affinities with some northern Amerindian groups. By contrast, the Koryak and Itelmen have stronger genetic connections with ethnic groups originating in the Lower Amur River/Sea of Okhotsk region, such as the Nivkh, Udegey, Nanay, Ulchi, Negidal, and Ainu. These associations suggest that Kamchatkan and Lower Amur River populations emerged from a common gene pool some 5000–8000 years ago, or perhaps that the emerging northern Okhotsk cultures that gave rise to the Koryak and Itelmen subsequently influenced those evolving from southern Okhotsk cultures.

Along the same lines, the molecular data do not reveal the presence of an "Eskimo wedge" among northeastern Siberians and Native American groups (see also Dumond, this volume). In general, Eskimo groups have mtDNA haplotypes that are similar to those appearing in Na-Dené Indians and Chukchi, and hence, appear to have emerged from the last inhabitants of ancient Beringia before the flooding of the land bridge. The mtDNA data may also suggest that Eskimo populations evolved in the Bering Sea region, perhaps in southwest Alaska, rather than north-central Canada,

as suggested by the "Eskimo wedge" model. On the other hand, the Chukchi, Eskimo, Aleut, and Na-Dené Indians all tend to be genetically distinctive from each other, implying some degree of geographic isolation amongst them since the occupation of their respective homelands.

Fourth, the molecular data show both the genetic distinctiveness of Tungusic-speaking groups, and their genetic influence on the Yukagir, Chukchi, and Koryak. These findings are consistent with both ethnographic evidence from northeastern Siberian groups, and the analyses of the anthropometric data collected in this region during the JNPE. In addition, central Siberian groups, such as the Northern Altayan, Selkup, and Ket, are not closely linked to eastern Siberian populations, and instead show a distinct genetic profile that includes both West Eurasian and East Asian genotypes. These regional differences support previous assertions by Boas and members of the JNPE that northeastern Siberian populations had origins and affinities distinct from those groups located in the interior of northern Asia, such as the Mongolian, Buryat, Tungusic-speakers, and Yakut (Sakha), the later two sets of populations having entered this region in relatively recent prehistory.

Finally, the mtDNA data have provided a number of insights into the process of the peopling of the World. To begin with, they suggest a pre-glacial maximum date (>18,000 cal BP) for the emergence and expansion of ancestral Paleoindians into the New World (Table 13), as also proposed by Boas (1905). They also suggest the occurrence of multiple population movements across the Bering Strait during this early period of settlement (between 35,000-15,000 cal BP), possibly using both interior and coastal routes (Torroni et al. 1993a, b; Starikovskaya et al. 1998; Schurr et al. 1999; Schurr and Wallace 1999). Furthermore, as noted above, these data are generally consistent with the glacial barrier model of Rogers et al. (1991). According to this model, once ancestral Amerindian populations began settling in the New World, glacial coalescence cut them off from related groups living farther north on the Beringian land mass. The resulting ice barriers in Beringia and North American isolated in glacial refugia the populations that would eventually develop into the Eskimo-Aleut, Na-Dené Indians, and Amerindian populations. Similar refugia were created within eastern Siberia, with the concomitant population isolation leading to the linguistic and biological differentiation of the ancestral groups that gave rise to Chukotko-Kamchatkan-, Yukagir-, Altaic-, and Uralic-speaking, populations. On a larger scale, these glacial refugia may also have permitted the divergence of "caucasoid" and "mongoloid" populations, thereby influencing the pattern of genetic variation throughout all of Eurasia.

Acknowledgments

The authors thank Drs. Rem I. Sukernik and Elena B. Starikovskaya for their participation in a larger study of Siberian and Native American origins, from which this paper is contributed. Thanks also to Lorri Griffin and the Clinical Research Center of the Emory University School of Medicine for their assistance in the processing of blood samples, and Drs. Andy Kogelnik and Sandro Bonatto for their assistance with the statistical analysis of the mtDNA data. Many thanks are also due to the hospital staff and doctors in the villages of Ossora, Karaga, Tymlat, Voyampolka, and Kovran in Kamchatka, Russia for their assistance with this project; the Koryak and Itelmen people from these villages for their participation in this research and hospitality during our fieldwork in Kamchatka in 1993 and 1996; Dr. Vladimir V. Slavinskiy of the Providenya hospital for his generous help and assistance with sample collection in the Chukchi Autonomous Area; and the Chukchi and Siberian Yupik people for their participation in this research during fieldwork in Chukotka in 1994. This research was supported by the International Science Foundation, the J. Worley Brown Fellowship Fund, the Leakey Foundation, the National Institutes of Health, the National Science Foundation, the Russian Fund for Basic Research, Sigma Xi, and The Wenner-Gren Foundation for Anthropological Research.

Notes

1. A "haplotype" is an individual mtDNA defined by a specific set of polymorphisms, whereas a "haplotype group," or "haplogroup" is a set of related haplotypes that share the same set of identifying mutations. The term "mtDNA lineage" is used interchangeably with "haplogroup" in the text, since both denote the same genealogical associations among mtDNAs.

2. For a description of the methods used to characterize mtDNA variation in Siberian and Native American populations, please refer to the publications cited in the text and tables.

References

Anderson, S., A. T. Bankier, B. G. Barrell, M. H. L. de Bruijn, A. R. Coulson, J. Drouin, I. C. Eperon, D. P. Nierlich, B. A. Rose, F. Sanger, P. H. Schreier, A. J. H. Smith, R. Staden, and I. G. Young
1981   Sequence and Organization of the Human Mitochondrial Genome. *Nature* 290(5806):457–65.

Antropova, Valentina V.
1964a   The Koryaks. In *The Peoples of Siberia*. Maxim G. Levin and Leonid P. Potapov, eds. Pp. 851–75. Chicago, IL: University of Chicago Press.
1964b   The Itelmens. In *The Peoples of Siberia*. Maxim G. Levin and Leonid P. Potapov, eds. Pp. 876–83. Chicago, IL: University of Chicago Press.

Arutiunov, Sergei A.
1988a   Koryak and Itel'men: Dwellers of the Smoking Coast. In *Crossroads of Continents. Cultures of Siberia and Alaska*. William W. Fitzhugh and Aron Crowell, eds. Pp. 31–5. Washington, DC: Smithsonian Institution Press.
1988b   Even: Reindeer Herders of Eastern Siberia. In *Crossroads of Continents. Cultures of Siberia and Alaska*. William W. Fitzhugh and Aron Crowell, eds. Pp. 35–8. Washington, DC: Smithsonian Institution Press.

Arutiunov, Sergei A., and Dorian A. Sergeev
1990   Issues of the Ethnic History of the Bering Sea: The Ekven Burial Ground. Chapter 1: Problems in the Study of the Ethnic History of the Northwestern Coastline of the Pacific Ocean. *Soviet Anthropology and Archeology* 28(4):50–61.

Ballinger, S. W., T. G. Schurr, A. Torroni, Yik-Yuen Gan, J. H. Hodge, K. Hassan, Kwang-Ho Chen, and D. C. Wallace
1992   Southeast Asian Mitochondrial DNA Analysis Reveals Genetic Continuity of Ancient Mongoloid Migrations. *Genetics* 130(1):139–52.

Bermisheva, M.A., T.V. Viktorova, O. Beliaeva, S.A. Limborskaia, and E.K. Khusnutdinova

2001 Polimorfizm gipervariabel'nogo segmenta i mitokhondrial'no' DNK v trekh etnicheskikh gruppakh Volgo-Ural'skogo regiona (Polymorphism of hypervariable segment and of mitochondrial DNA in three ethnic groups of the Volga-Ural region).*Genetika.* 37(8):1118–24.

Boas, Franz
1903 The Jesup North Pacific Expedition. *American Museum Journal* 3(5):73–119.
1905 The Jesup North Pacific Expedition. In *International Congress of Americanists, 13th Session, Held in New York in 1902.* Pp. 91–100. Easton, PA: Eschenbach Printing.
1912 The History of the American Race. *Annals of the American Academy of Sciences* 21:177–83.
1928 Migrations of Asiatic Races and Cultures to North America. *Scienctific Monthly* 28:110–17.

Bogoras, Waldemar
1902 Folklore of Northeastern Asia as Compared with that of Northwestern America. *American Anthropologist*, n.s. 4(4):577–683.
1904–9 The Chukchee. *The Jesup North Pacific Expedition*, vol 7, pts. 1–3. *Memoirs of the American Museum of Natural History*, 11. Leiden: E.J. Brill; New York: G.E. Stechert.

Collins, Henry B.
1937 Culture Migrations and Contacts in the Bering Sea Region. *American Anthropologist* 39(3):375–84.

Comuzzie, Anthony G., Ravi Duggirala, William R. Leonard, and Michael H. Crawford
1995 Population Relationships Among Historical and Modern Indigenous Siberians Based on Anthropometric Characters. *Human Biology* 67(3):459–75.

Crawford, Michael H., James H. Mielke Eric J. Devor, Dale D Dykes, and Herbert F. Polesky
1981 Population Structure of Alaskan and Siberian Indigenous Communities. *American Journal of Physical Anthropology* 55(2):167–85.

Crowell, Aron
1988 Dwellings, Settlements, and Domestic Life. In *Crossroads of Continents. Cultures of Siberia and Alaska.* William W. Fitzhugh and Aron Crowell, eds. Pp. 17–21. Washington, DC: Smithsonian Institution Press.

Derbeneva, Olga A., Elena B. Starikovskaya, Douglas C. Wallace, and Rem I. Sukernik
2002 Traces of Early Eurasians in the Mansi of Northwest Siberia Revealed by Mitochondrial DNA Analysis. *American Journal of Human Genetics* 70:1009–14.

Derbeneva, O. A., R. I. Sukernik, N. V. Volodko, S. H. Hosseini, M. T. Lott, and D. C. Wallace
2002 Analysis of Mitochondrial DNA Diversity in the Aleuts of the Commander Islands and Its Implications for the Genetic History of Beringia. *American Journal of Human Genetics* 71(2):415–21.

Derenko, Miroslava V., and Gerald F. Shields
1997 Raznoobrazie nukleotidnykh posledovatel'nostei mitokhondrial'noi DNK v trekh gruppakh korennogo naseleniia severno' Azii (Mitochondrial DNA sequence diversity in three north Asian aboriginal populations). *Molekulyarnaya Biologiya* 31(5):784–789.

Derenko, Miroslava V., and G.F. Shields
1998 Izmenchivosti mitokhondrial'noi DNK v trekh gruppakh korennogo naseleniia severno' Azii (Variability of mitochondrial DNA in three groups of indigenous inhabitants of Northern Asia). *Genetika* 34(5):676–81.

Dikov, Nikolai N.
1990 The Origin of the Aboriginal Populations of America: The Role of Ancient Northeastern Asiatic Cultures in the Formation of the Paleoindian Population of America. *Soviet Anthropology and Archeology* 28(4):12–29.

Felsenstein, Joseph
1995 *PHYLIP Phylogeny Inference Package, version 3.573c.* Distributed by author. Seattle, WA: University of Washington (http://evolution.genetics.washington.edu/phylip.html).

Field, L. L., J. P. Gofton, and D. Kinsella
1988 Immunoglobulin Gm and Km Allotypes and Relation to Population History in Native Peoples of British Columbia: Haida and Bella Coola. *American Journal of Physical Anthropology* 76(2):155–63.

Fitzhugh, William W.
1988 Comparative Art of the North Pacific Rim. In *Crossroads of Continents. Cultures of Siberia and Alaska.* William W. Fitzhugh and Aron Crowell, eds. Pp. 294–312. Washington, DC: Smithsonian Institution Press.

Forster, Peter, Rosalind Harding, Antonio Torroni, and Hans-Jürgen Bandelt
1996 Origin and Evolution of Native American mtDNA Variation: A Reappraisal. *American Journal of Human Genetics* 59:935–45.

Gurvich, Il'ia S.
1988 Ethnic Connections across Bering Strait. In *Crossroads of Continents. Cultures of Siberia and Alaska.* William W. Fitzhugh and A. Crowell, eds. Pp. 17–21. Washington, DC: Smithsonian Institution Press,

Harper, Albert B.
1980 Origins and Divergence of Aleuts, Eskimos and American Indians. *Annals of Human Biology* 7(6):547–54.

Haskell, J. Loring
1987 *Southern Athapaskan Migration A.D. 200–1750.* Tsaile, NM: Navajo Community College Press.

Horai, S., K. Murayama, K. Hayasaka, S. Matsubayashi, Y. Hattori, G. Fucharoen, S. Harihara, K. Sook Park, K. Omoto, and I. Pan
1996 mtDNA Polymorphism in East Asian Populations, with Special Reference to the Peopling of

Japan. *American Journal of Human Genetics* 59(3):579–90.

Jantz, Richard L., David R. Hunt, Anthony B. Falsetti, and Patrick J. Key
1992   Variation among North Amerindians: Analysis of Boas' Anthropometric Data. *Human Biology* 64(3):431–65.

Jochelson, Waldemar
1908   The Koryak. *The Jesup North Pacific Expedition*, vol. 6, pts. 1–2. *Memoirs of the American Museum of Natural History*, 10. Leiden: E.J. Brill; New York: G.E. Stechert.
1926   The Ethnological Problems of Bering Sea. *Natural History* 26(1):90–5.

Karaphet, Tatiana M., Rem I. Sukernik, Ludmilla P. Osipova, and Yurii B. Simchenko
1981   Blood Groups, Serum Proteins, and Red Cell Enzymes in the Nganasans (Tavghi)—Reindeer Hunters from the Taimir Peninsula. *American Journal of Physical Anthropology* 56(2):139–45.

Kolman Connie J., Nyamkhishig Sambuughin, and Eldridge Bermingham
1996   Mitochondrial DNA Analysis of Mongolian Populations and Implications for the Origins of New World founders. *Genetics* 142(4):1321–34.

Krasheninnikov, Stepan
1972 [1755]   *A Description of the Land of Kamchatka, 1735–1741*, 2 vols. ed. trans. E.A.P. Crownhart-Vaughn. Portland, OR: Oregon Historical Society.

Krauss, Michael E.
1988   Many Tongues—Ancient Tales. In *Crossroads of Continents. Cultures of Siberia and Alaska*. William W. Fitzhugh and A. Crowell, eds. Pp. 145–50. Washington, DC: Smithsonian Institution Press.

Krupnik, Igor I.
1988   Economic Patterns in Northeastern Siberia. In *Crossroads of Continents. Cultures of Siberia and Alaska*. William W. Fitzhugh and A. Crowell, eds. Pp. 183–90. Washington, DC: Smithsonian Institution Press

Krushanov, A. I., ed.
1993   *Istoriia i kul'tura koriakov* (The History and Culture of the Koryak). St. Petersburg: Nauka Publishers.

Lorenz, Joseph G., and David G. Smith
1994   Distribution of the 9-bp Mitochondrial DNA Region V deletion among North American Indians. *Human Biology* 66(4):777–88.
1996   Distribution of Four Founding mtDNA Haplogroups among Native North Americans. *American Journal of Physical Anthropology* 101(3):307–23.
1997   Distribution of Sequence Variation in the mtDNA Control Region of Native North Americans. *Human Biology* 69(6):749–76.

Meinila, M., S. Finnila, and K. Majamaa
2001   Evidence for mtDNA Admixture between the Finns and the Saami. *Human Heredity* 52:160–70.

Merriwether, D, F. Rothhammer, and R. Ferrell
1995   Distribution of the Four Founding Lineage Haplotypes in Native Americans Suggests a Single Wave of Migration for the New World. *American Journal of Physical Anthropology* 98(4):411–30.

Nei, Masatoshi, and Li Jin
1989   Variances of the Average Number of Nucleotide Substitutions Within and Between Populations. *Molecular Biology and Evolution* 6(3):290-300.

Osipova, Ludmilla P., and Rem I. Sukernik
1983   Immunoglobulin Allotypes in Aboriginal Populations of the Taimir Peninsula. *Journal of Immunogenetics* 10(1):11–16.

Ousley, Stephen D.
1995   Relationships between Eskimos, Amerindians and Aleuts: Old Data, New Perspectives. *Human Biology* 67(3):427–58.

Ousley, Stephen D., and Richard L. Jantz
2001   500 Year Old Questions, 100 Year Old Data, Brand New Computers. Biological Data from the Jesup Expedition. In *Gateways. Exploring the Legacy of the Jesup North Pacific Expedition, 1897–1902*. Igor Krupnik and William W. Fitzhugh, eds. Pp. 257–77. Contributions to Circumpolar Anthropology, 1. Washington, DC: Arctic Studies Center.

Petrishchev, V. N., A. B. Kutueva, and Y. G. Rychkov
1993   Deletsionno-insertsionni' polimorfizm v V-oblasti mtDNK v desiati mongoloidnykh populiatsiiakh Sibiri: chastota deletsii korreliruet s geograficheskimi koordinatami mestnosti (Deletion-Insertion Polymorphisms in Region V in Ten Mongoloid Populations of Siberia: Frequency of Deletion Correlates with the Geographical Coordinates of the Area). *Genetika* 29(7):1196–1204.

Posukh, O. L., V. P. Wiebe, R. I. Sukernik, L. P. Osipova, T. M. Karaphet, and M. S. Schanfield
1990   Genetic Studies of the Evens, an Ancient Human Population of Eastern Siberia. *Human Biology* 62(4):457–65.

Reynolds, J. B., B. S. Weir, and C. C. Cockerham
1983   Estimation of the Coancestry Coefficient: Basis for a Short-Term Genetic Distance. *Genetics* 105:767–79.

Rogers, R. A., L. A. Rogers, R. S. Hoffman, and L. D. Martin
1991   Native American Biological Diversity and the Biogeographic Influence of Ice Age Refugia. *Journal of Biogeography* 18:623–30.

Rousselot, Jean-Loup, William W. Fitzhugh, and Aron Crowell
1988   Maritime Economies of the North Pacific Rim. In *Crossroads of Continents. Cultures of Siberia and Alaska*. William W. Fitzhugh and A. Crowell, eds. Pp. 151–72. Washington, DC: Smithsonian Institution Press.

Rubicz, Rohina, Theodore G. Schurr, Paul Babb, and Michael H. Crawford

In Press Mitochondrial DNA Diversity in Modern Aleuts and Their Genetic Relationship with Other Circum-arctic Populations. *Human Biology*

Rubicz, Rohina, Theodore G. Schurr, and Michael H. Crawford

2001 Mitochondrial DNA Diversity in Modern Aleut Populations. *American Journal of human Biology* 13(1):139.

Saitou, Naruya, and Masatoshi Nei

1987 The Neighbor-Joining Method: A New Method for Reconstructing Phylogenetic Trees. *Molecular Biology and Evolution* 4(4):406–25.

Sajantila, A., P. Lahermo, T. Anttinen, M. Lukka, P. Sistonen, Marja-Liisa Savontaus, P. Aula, L. Beckman, L. Tranebjaerg, T. Gedde-Dahl, L. Issel-Tarver, A. DiRienzo, and S. Pääbo

1995 Genes and Languages in Europe: An Analysis of Mitochondrial Lineages. *Genome Research* 5(1):42–52.

Schurr, Theodore G., Rem I. Sukernik, Yelena B. Starikovskaya, and Douglas C. Wallace

2003 mtDNA Variation in Central Siberians Identifies West Eurasian and East Asian Components of Their Gene Pool. *American Journal of Physical Anthropology Supplement* 34(4):186–87.

Schurr, Theodore G., Yelena B. Starikovskaya, Rem I. Sukernik, and Douglas C. Wallace

2001 A mitochondrial DNA Perspective on Asian and Native American Population Relationships. *American Journal of Physical Anthropology Supplement* 32:134.

Schurr, Theodore G., Yelena B. Starikovskaya, Rem I. Sukernik, Antonio Torroni, and Douglas C. Wallace

2000 Mitochondrial DNA Diversity in Lower Amur River Populations, and Its Implications for the Genetic History of the North Pacific and the New World. *American Journal of Physical Anthropology Supplement* 30(4):274–75.

Schurr, Theodore G., and Douglas C. Wallace

1999 mtDNA Variation in Native Americans and Siberians and its Implications for the Peopling of the New World. In *Who Were the First Americans: Proceedings of the 58th Annual Biology Colloquium, Oregon State University*, Robson Bonnichsen, ed. Pp. 41–77. Corvallis, OR: Center for the Study of the First Americans.

Schurr, Theodore G., Rem I. Sukernik, Yelena B. Starikovskaya, and Douglas C. Wallace

1999 Mitochondrial DNA Diversity in Koryaks and Itel'men: Population Replacement in the Okhotsk-Bering Sea Region during the Neolithic. *American Journal of Physical Anthropology*. 108(1):1-40.

Schurr, T. G., S. W. Ballinger, Y.-Y. Gan, J. A. Hodge, D. A. Merriwether, D. N. Lawrence, W. C.

Knowler, K. M. Weiss, and D. C. Wallace

1990 Amerindian Mitochondrial DNAs Have Rare Asian Variants at High Frequencies, Suggesting They Derived from Four Primary Maternal Lineages. *American Journal of Human Genetics* 46(3):613–23.

Shields, G. F., A. M. Schmiechen, B. L. Frazier, A. Redd, M. I. Voevoda, J. K. Reed, and R. H. Ward

1993 mtDNA Sequences Suggest a Recent Evolutionary Divergence for Beringian and Northern North American Populations. *American Journal of Human Genetics* 53(3):549–62.

Shields, Gerald F., Kristen Hecker, Mikhail I. Voevoda, and Judy K. Reed

1992 Absence of the Asian-specific Region V Mitochondrial Marker in Native Beringians. *American Journal of Human Genetics* 50(4):758–65.

Soong, Deok Lee, Ho Shin Chang, Beom Kim Ki, Seong Lee Yoon, and Bin Lee Jung

1997 Sequence Variation of Mitochondrial Control Region in Koreans. *Forensic Science International* 87(2):99–116.

Starikovskaya, Yelena B., Rem I. Sukernik, Theodore G. Schurr, and Douglas C. Wallace

1998 Mitochondrial DNA Diversity in Chukchi and Siberian Eskimos: Implications for the Genetic Prehistory of Ancient Beringia. *American Journal of Human Genetics* 63(5):1473–91.

Stone, Anne C., and Mark Stoneking

1998 mtDNA Analysis of a Prehistoric Oneota Population: Implications for the Peopling of the New World. *American Journal of Human Genetics* 62(5):1153–70.

Sukernik, Rem I., and Ludmilla P. Osipova

1982 Gm and Km Immunoglobulin Allotypes in Reindeer Chukchi and Siberian Eskimos. *Human Genetics* 61(2):148–53.

Sukernik, Rem I., Ludmilla P. Osipova, and Moses S. Schanfield

1992 Distribution of GM Allotypes and deleted IGHG1 Haplotypes in the Sel'kups in comparison to the Forest Nentsi of northwestern Siberia. *Experimental and Clinical Immunogenetics* 9(1):15–23.

Sukernik, Rem I., Sergei V. Lemza, Tatiana M. Karaphet, and Ludmilla P. Osipova

1981 Reindeer Chukchi and Siberian Eskimos: Studies on Blood groups, Serum Proteins, and Red Cell Enzymes with Regard to Genetic Heterogeneity. *American Journal of Physical Anthropology* 55(1):121–28.

Sukernik, Rem I., Theodore G. Schurr, Elena B. Starikovskaya, and Douglas C. Wallace

1996 Izmenchivosti mitokhondrial'nykh DNK u korennykh zhitelei Sibiri v sviazi s rekonstruktsiei evoliutsionnoi istorii amerikanskikh indeitsev (Mitochondrial DNA Variation in Native Siberians, with Special Reference to the Evolutionary History of American Indians. Studies on Restriction Polymorphism). *Genetika* 32(3):432-39.

Torroni, Antonio, James V. Neel, Ramiro Barrantes, Theodore G. Schurr, and Douglas C. Wallace

1994a   A Mitochondrial DNA 'Clock' for the Amerinds and Its Implications for Timing Their Entry into North America. *Proceedings of the National Academy of Sciences* 91(3):1158–62.

Torroni, A., K. Huoponen, P. Francalacci, M. Petrozzi, L. Morelli, R. Scozzari, D. Obinu, Marja-Liisa Savontaus, and D.C. Wallace.

1996   Classification of European mtDNAs from an Analysis of three European Populations. *Genetics* 144(4):1835–50.

Torroni, Antonio, Marie T. Lott, Margaret F. Cabell, Yu-Sheng Chen, Leo Lavergne, and Douglas C. Wallace

1994c   mtDNA and the Origin of Caucasians: Identification of Ancient Caucasian-specific Haplogroups, One of Which is Prone to a Recurrent Somatic Duplication in the D-loop Region. *American Journal of Human Genetics* 55(4):760–76.

Torroni, A., R. I. Sukernik, T. G. Schurr, Y. B. Starikovskaya, M. A. Cabell, M. H. Crawford, A. G. Comuzzie, and D. C. Wallace

1993b   mtDNA Variation of Aboriginal Siberians Reveals Distinct Genetic Affinities with Native Americans. *American Journal of Human Genetics* 53(3):591–608.

Torroni, A., T. G. Schurr, Chi-Chuan Yang, E. Szathmary, R. C. Williams, M. S. Schanfield, G. A. Troup, W. C. Knowler, D. N. Lawrence, K. M. Weiss, and D. C. Wallace

1992   Native American Mitochondrial DNA Analysis Indicates that the Amerind and the Na-Dené Populations were Founded by Two Independent Migrations. *Genetics* 130(1):153–62.

Torroni, A., T. G. Schurr, M. F. Cabell, M. D. Brown, J. V. Neel, M. Larsen, D. G. Smith, C. M. Vullo, and D. C. Wallace

1993a   Asian Affinities and Continental Radiation of the Four Founding Native American Mitochondrial DNAs. *American Journal of Human Genetics* 53(3):563–90.

Vasil'evskii, Ruslan S.

1971   *Proiskhozhdenie i dreviaia kul'tura koriakov* (The Origins and Ancient Culture of the Koryak). Novosibirsk: Nauka Publishers.

Ward, R. H., A. Redd, D. Valencia, B. Frazier, and S. Pääbo

1993   Genetic and Linguistic Differentiation in the Americas. *Proceedings of the National Academy of Sciences,* 90(22):10663–67.

Ward, Ryk H., Barbara L. Frazier, Kerry Dew-Jager, and Svante Pääbo

1991   Extensive Mitochondrial Diversity within a Single Amerindian Tribe. *Proceedings of the National Academy of Sciences,* 88(19):8720–24.

The Post-Jesup Century of Research on the Prehistory of Northeast Siberia

SERGEI ARUTIUNOV

The contributions of the Jesup North Pacific Expedition (1897–1902) marked a giant leap in the accumulation of knowledge about the cultures and peoples of Northeast Siberia. To the Russian participants of the Expedition, their JNPE fieldwork and subsequent publication efforts were formative experiences. It also helped transform them into professional anthropologists and key figures in the emerging field of the Russian Siberian/North Pacific/Circumpolar research. It was thus not surprising that some twenty years later, the former JNPE members, particularly Waldemar Bogoras (Vladimir Bogoraz) and Lev Shternberg, became key players in the development of northern anthropological research in the former Soviet Union in the 1920s and in the early 1930s. Many other Russian Siberian anthropologists who did not participate directly in the JNPE efforts were, nevertheless, well informed about this venture and its scientific results, and were deeply influenced by them (see Krupnik 1998).

The impact of the ideas generated by Franz Boas, the intellectual and organizational leader of the Jesup Expedition, on this early development of Soviet/Russian Siberian anthropology was decisive. The subsequent Stalinist purges and the obnoxious ideological control by the Communist Party over all kinds of humanitarian studies in the former Soviet Union stalled and obscured this impact over almost fifty years. However, the attempts to discredit this influence

as a manifestation of "bourgeois" ideas were reflected in propaganda statements only. The core of Siberian anthropological research during the entire Soviet era remained primarily evolutionist in spirit and generally Boasian in its focus and content. In was not until recently that popular though superficial post-modernist approaches were established among a portion of Russian anthropologists during the most-recent post-Soviet years.

Three Generations of Researchers

There were several successive cohorts, or generations, of Russian (Soviet) scholars who were active in the study of Northeast Asia and the Russian Far East [the Pacific Coast of Russia—ed.] following Bogoras, Shternberg, and Jochelson. The first cohort consisted of people born in the early 1900s, like Maxim G. Levin, Georgii F. Debetz, Nikolai N. Cheboksarov, abd Alexei P. Okladnikov. The second cohort consisted primarily of the students of this first generation, including Valerii P. Alekseev, Dorian A. Sergeev, Rudolf F. Its, Nikolai N. Dikov, Yurii P. Mochanov, Anatolii P. Derev-ianko, and many others, myself included. Our cohort became active in Russian Siberian/Far East research in the early to mid-1950s. In the 1970s, the third cohort entered the scholarly forum, and its members are currently most active in Russian Siberian research in anthropology and prehistory.

These three cohorts, or generations, are distinct groups of people. They can be singled out not only in the studies of Northeast Asia, and not only in the history of Russian anthropology, in general, but perhaps in the overall history of Soviet (as well as post-Soviet) science. Many people, who were born between 1910 and 1926 and who were still young in the 1940s, were decimated during World War II. The birth rates at the peak of the Stalinist terror and in the subsequent war years (i.e., between 1937 and 1945) were relatively low compared to both the preceding and the following decades. Therefore, the first generation consisted mostly of people born between 1900 and 1913; the second generation—of those born between 1925 and 1937; and the third generation—of those born in the late 1940s and during the 1950s, that is, well after World War II. Perhaps, we can now identify the fourth cohort that consists of scholars born during the 1960s and 1970s. As a very promising current trend, a growing number of young anthropologists have been trained from among representatives of Native Siberian people, including a fairly high percentage of women. In absolute numbers they are still few, but the total number of Native people across Eastern Siberia and the Russian Far East does not exceed 50,000 [excluding the Sakha/Yakut people—ed.].

In general, there was a high degree of continuity between these distinctive generations of scholars in Siberian anthropology. The general framework of scholarly approach, laid down by Boas, is highly visible in publications of the key JNPE participants, such as Waldemar Bogoras, Waldemar Jochelson, and Lev Shternberg, although the latter was not a direct JNPE team member. It is still articulated in the subsequent contributions by Levin, Debetz, Cheboksarov, and others who either attended classes of some of the "seniors" of the "Jesup Generation" [mostly courses taught by Bogoras in Leningrad in the 1920s—ed.] or at least were influenced by their writings. Apart from the influence of Franz Boas in the field of cultural anthropology, important intellectual beacons

for all the Russian students in Siberian anthropology had been A. Hrdliæka in the field of physical anthropology and V. Gordon Childe in the area of archaeology.

All the 'senior' scholars have greatly influenced the next generation of Russian Siberian anthropologists. The impact was spread not only via theoretical approach, which can be generally characterized as broadly evolutionist rather than strictly Marxist, but also by sharing the experience and practices of fieldwork conducted between the late 1920s and the 1950s in various areas of Siberia. Among other scholars of the same "post-Bogoras" generation, who were not directly affiliated with the tradition transmitted by Bogoras and Shternberg, was Boris O. Dolgikh. Dolgikh was even more deeply immersed in long-term field studies in Siberia and thus, in a certain sense, he continued the pattern of fieldwork once determined by the participants of the Jesup Expedition. Dolgikh's field experience and methods greatly influenced the endeavors of his disciples of the following (World War II) generation, such as Vladimir I. Vasil'iev, Yurii B. Simchenko, Vladilen A. Tugolukov, and others.

The joint efforts of three post-Jesup generations of Russian Siberian scholars have elevated the status of our knowledge about physical and cultural anthropology as well as the prehistory of Northern Eurasia to a qualitatively new and higher level compared to that of the turn of the twentieth century. The general background of this knowledge made it possible also to advance new scenarios of events that have happened across Siberia and the Northeastern tip of Asia adjacent to North America in the course of the last three or four millennia. These events resulted in the formation of the current ethnic and cultural mosaics of the area, mainly of the Chukotka and Kamchatka Peninsulas, and the Kolyma River Basin in the interior portion of the present-day Magadan Province (*oblast*). The academic efforts and their results over some seventy years after the publication of the main JNPE Siberian volumes were quite impressive. Nevertheless, many questions still remain unresolved and many more new issues have arisen in the course of research and studies that could not be proposed in the time of the Jesup Expedition a century ago.

Basic Milestones in Research in the Siberian Northeast

One of the basic questions in cultural (pre)history of Northeast Asia is the transition from a mainland (interior) adaptation to a maritime one, that is, when and how the shift occurred in Arctic subsistence from hunting of inland big-game mammals to the pursuit of the pinnipeds and the cetaceans on and off shore. So far we can trace only the more or less late stages of maritime adaptation, which undoubtedly had to be preceded by a long initial evolution.

On the Russian side, archaeological studies across the northeast section of Siberia (adjacent to Alaska and the Bering Strait) began in 1945 by Sergei I. Rudenko. History repeats itself. At the turn of the century, in the time of the Jesup Expedition, the basic anthropological research in Siberia was conducted by many progressive-minded social activists (often, dedicated revolutionaries), who were exiled to this remote area by the repressive Czarist government. In the Soviet time, a still more oppressive Stalinist regime once again exiled hundreds and thousands of liberal-minded intellectuals and scholars to Siberia. Sergei Rudenko was one of those exiles. Among the hardships of exile, he found enough energy to prepare for and to design a trip around the shores of the Chukchi Peninsula, which he would realize when released from his exile. In 1945, Rudenko finally was able to undertake a long and not too safe journey, largely in wooden and skin-boats, with Native crews around the coasts of the Chukchi Peninsula. All the difficulties notwithstanding, he managed to conduct a broad archaeological reconnaissance survey and also to undertake critical excavations at some sites. The results of his excavations were published in his well-known Russian monograph and were later translated into English by the

Arctic Institute of North America (Rudenko 1947, 1961).

In the mid-1950s, Maxim G. Levin, Dorian A. Sergeev, and Nikolai N. Dikov began organizing numerous Russian expeditions to this area. They contributed a large amount of archaeological and paleoanthropological (osteological) materials that were derived from ancient populations of the Bering Strait area and the adjacent regions along the shores of the Chukchi Peninsula. This work is now continued by the members of the next cohort of scholars, such as Mikhail M. Bronstein, Kirill A. Dneporvskii, and others.[1] These materials can be matched by the data gathered by American and Western European archaeologists in Alaska and Northern Canada, and viewed against a broader background of recently accumulated knowledge on the origins and distribution patterns of prehistoric human populations in the Northern part of Asia. They have enabled us to formulate some tentative new hypotheses about the formation of ancient Eskimo culture(s) in the Bering Strait area and about its impact on populations of the adjacent territories (cf. summaries in Fitzhugh and Crowell 1988; Leskov and Müller-Beck 1993).

The Most Important Archaeological Sites and Cultures of Northeast Asia

A good compendium of prehistoric sites and cultures of Northeast Siberia (Northeast Asia) was produced in two volumes by Nikolai Dikov and published more than twenty years ago (Dikov 1977, 1979). One should also consult the monograph of Ruslan Vasilievskii (1973), and those of Yurii Mochanov (1977) and Svetlana Fedoseeva (1980) for the adjacent inland regions, basically in Yakutia (Sakha Republic). As the basic ancient cultures and their most representative sites across the northeast (Pacific) section of Siberia are concerned, the complex of sites excavated by Nikolai Dikov at the Ushki Lake on Kamchatka Peninsula should be ranked among the most important discoveries. Numerous cultural layers at the Ushki sites are safely separated by stripes of volcanic ashes. This provides reliable absolute and relative dates for a series of Upper Paleolithic and Neolithic cultures, which tentatively can be compared to, and connected with, some ancestors of Amerindian, Eskaleut, and modern Paleoasiatic populations of this part of Northern Asia and the adjacent regions in North America.

The discovery by Nikolai Dikov of the Chortov Ovrag (Devil's Gorge) site on Wrangel Island in the Chukchi Sea is evidence of an early maritime adaptation in the northernmost regions of Siberia at the beginning of the 2nd Millennium BC. The excavations at the Chortov Ovrag site produced a rough but efficient harpoon head for hunting marine mammals. Sites of the Ust-Belsk culture in the interior of the Chukchi Peninsula show definite connections to the ancient residents of the Lena River Basin. The Ust-Belsk sites also indicate an early penetration of bronze tools into the Siberian Arctic, which were incorporated into the more or less unchanged pedestrian hunting economy typical of the preceding cultural stages.

Numerous ancient archaeological sites have been discovered along the Russian (Siberian) side of the Bering Strait and in adjacent coastal areas. Of those the most critical are the Uelen and Ekven cemeteries, excavated by the Russian teams of Maxim G. Levin, Dorian A. Sergeev, Sergei A. Arutiunov, and recently by an international group led by Mikhail Bronstein and Kirill Dneprovskii. These two ancient Eskimo sites provide infinitely rich material on the evolution of the Okvik, Old Bering Sea, Punuk, Birnirk, and Thule variations of the ancient Neo-Eskimo culture (see Arutjunov and Bronshtein 1993; Bronshtein 1993; Dumond and Bland 2002).

Non-Archaeological Evidence and Considerations

According to the hypothesis of Christy Turner (1985, 1988), which was based on dental features of the American aboriginal populations, there have been three major waves of migrations from Asia to (North) America. One migration took place probably not later than 13,000 BP and is responsible for the ancestry

of the majority of the American Indian populations (Amerinds), with the exception of the members of the Na-Dené linguistic family (and some related groups). The second wave represented the ancestors of Na-Dené and can be tentatively dated to around 9000 or 8000 BP. The third wave gave birth to the Eskimo-Aleut (Eskaleut) populations; it may be dated approximately by 4000 or even 6000 BP.

From the most general viewpoint, the linguistic composition of the huge Eurasian continent, with the exception of its southeastern portion of mainly southern China and Indochina, can be reduced to only two major linguistic (super-)phyla. This classification is based upon the most radical current perspectives and concepts in historical comparative linguistics that are advocated by such modern linguists as H. Fleming, Aron Dolgopolskii, and Sergei Starostin. Those theories literally "lump" several major language families into groups or phyla, in this case—even in super-phyla. One of these phyla is known as 'Nostratic' (as named by Illich-Svitych 1971), and the other as 'Sino-Dagestanic' (named by Starostin 1989). The latter includes North-Caucasian languages; Burushaski language of the Hindukush Mountains, Sino-Tibetan; Yenisseic (Ket); and possibly Na-Dené language families (the position of the Basque language remains unclear). The former includes all other languages of Northern, Central, and Western Eurasia; its Eastern "sub-phylum" consists of the Dravidic and Uralo-Altaic. There is some evidence in favor of a hypothesis that all of the so-called Paleo-Asiatic languages of Siberia and the North Pacific, including the Yukagir, the Nivkh, Chukchi-Koryak, Itelmen, and also Eskaleut, and the Ainu, can be placed in a remote connection with this "Eastern sub-phylum" (Fleming 1987).

To date, the first Amerinds, who supposedly crossed more than 13,000 years ago from Asia to America by the Bering Land Bridge, could not be traced with any certainty in any archaeological sites in Siberia. Some of the analogies that are often proposed—for example, by Russian archaeologist Yurii Mochanov (1969) and others—between American and Siberian Paleolithic industries can seem spectacular. But the actual gap in most cases is too big, both in time and space. Most probably the archaeological traces of the early migrants from Siberia may now all be buried deep under the waters of the Bering Sea. Therefore, although there can be no doubt that the ancestors of the Amerinds once lived in Asia, so far attempts to find material indications of their Asiatic habitat and connections have been futile.

After the first wave of Amerind ancestors' migrated to North America, the Bering Land Bridge had given its place to the Bering Sea. It can be assumed that the kinsmen of the Amerinds (if any), who might have remained in Asia, have been assimilated by another wave of migrants. The newcomers were probably from the stock of the Sino-Caucasian speakers. In eastern and northeastern sections of Asia these were the ancestors of the present Sino-Tibetan, Yenisseic (Ket), and Na-Dené linguistic families, and, possibly, also bearers of some intermediate linking languages, which are now completely extinct.

Amerind ancestors were in all probability strongly oriented towards large inland game hunting, since nothing seems to indicate that there was any trend towards a maritime adaptation among them. On the other hand, the second migration wave, that is, the ancestors of the Na-Dené people, could not use the land bridge and they had to cross the Bering Strait in some type of sea-going vessels. Therefore, these people had to be maritime adapted, to some extent. Most of their present westernmost descendants like the Eyak, Haida, and the Tlingit are among the most specialized maritime-adapted populations in North America. The Ket people in Siberia, the only remaining present-day group of the Yenisseic speakers, also are predominantly fishing-oriented, although they live thousands of miles away in the inland boreal forest zone of Central Siberia.

It can be assumed that fishing specialization has deep roots in the Final Upper Paleolithic and Mesolithic cultures of Northern and Eastern Siberia. Hence, the present-day fishing Siberian populations belonging to the Nostratic phylum, such as the Khanty of the Ob River Basin or the Nivkh of the Lower Amur River and Sakhalin Island, might have acquired some initial fishing skills from the preceding Sino-Caucasians—the Yenisseic and Proto-Na-Dené (and other related extinct groups) "substratum"—ancient inhabitants of the Beringian zone. Nikolai Dikov argued more than thirty years ago (Dikov 1967) that there were obvious cultural parallels between Paleolithic cultures of Kamchatka (as illustrated by the Ushki sites) and some prehistoric cultures of North America. The latter include Palisades, British Mountain, and Anangula. In Dikov's opinion, beyond the obvious parallels in stone tools, the shell beads, red ocher used in burial rituals, and other cultural traits are strong indicators of close cultural similarities between the two prehistoric stocks.

If these analogies are correct, then we can assume that the early sites in Kamchatka (dated from somewhere about 13,000 BP to approximately 10,000 BP or later) preceded or could well be correlated with the alleged dates of the Na-Dené migration to North America. Therefore, not only the linguistic affiliation of the Ushki site inhabitants can be quite possibly Na-Dené linked; the creators of the earliest known maritime cultures in Alaska and the Aleutians, including the Anangula site, are believed to have been early Na-Dené speakers as well, rather than the Eskaleut, as is often claimed.

The migration of the Na-Dené speakers across the Bering Strait could have been at least partially caused by the growing pressure of the later Nostratic migrants to Siberia. We can logically suppose that this pressure must have been particularly strong between 7000 and 6000 BC, or between 9000 and 8000 BP. This is the time of the earliest agricultural sites in the Northwestern portion of the Indostan sub-continent, which mark the hypothetical Nostratic (Dravidian) intrusion into the continental (northern) portion of South Asia. The movement of the early agriculturalists might have been paralleled by a similar intrusion of other Eastern Nostratic

(Old Uralic) populations from farther north into the central section of Northern Eurasia. The latter were not agriculturalists but could still have been technologically well-advanced. A simultaneous start of these two population shifts can be corroborated by an alleged greater proximity between proto-Dravidic and proto-Uralic languages, than with any other Nostratic proto-languages (Illich-Svitych 1971).

The subsequent millennia, that is 7000 to 4000 BP (5000–2000 BC) in Northern Eurasia, was the era of the "Neolithic evolution" and of the formation of the many local Neolithic cultures in Siberia. These were created by the distinct though distantly related ethnic groups of Nostratic origins, such as the Yukagir, the proto-Tungus, and the ancestors of the Northeastern Paleoasiatic populations (such as Chukchi-Koryak-Itelmen, Nivkh, etc.). They were gradually assimilating, replacing, and/or ousting out of Asia, across the Bering Strait, the remains of the preceding Sino-Caucasian (Yenisseic, Proto-Na-Dené) stock.

This earlier Sino-Caucasian substratum, while being assimilated, might have been a significant factor in ethnic and linguistic diversification of the incoming Nostratic migrants. Even more important must have been their racial (i.e., physical anthropological) impact. Many physical traits of these new populations, including typically Mongoloid features, began to prevail due to earlier processes of climatic biological adaptation.

Let us now consider the question of the position of the Eskaleut ethno-linguistic group in this complex formation of the modern native populations of Northeast Siberia. The exact data that can help answer this question are rather scarce, and any speculations on this subject can only be tentative and hypothetical. Still, an attempt at a broad integrating hypothesis can be made, according to the data of physical anthropology (cf. Alexeev 1993). On the one hand, the Eskimo as well as the Aleut and the Chukchi demonstrate definite features of the Arctic local race. This reflects their millennia-long adaptation to the extreme climatic conditions of the Arctic. On the other hand, their relatively dark pigmentation suggests that they belong to the Pacific branch of the Mongoloid race and that initially they were formed in more southern latitudes than their current habitat. While Asiatic Eskimo display certain evidences of recent admixture of Central Siberian populations, the Aleut show some "Europeoid" (Caucasoid) deviations from the basic Mongoloid type which cannot be reduced to the late European (mostly Russian) admixture only.

There are also important archaic ethnographic parallels between ancient Eskimo and Nivkh (Gilyak) cultures (Arutiunov et al. 1972) as well as between the Nivkh and the Aleut. There is also some evidence of an early and even historical Eskaleut habitation in Kamchatka (cf. Vdovin 1972). Finally, Nikolai Dikov, who insisted upon some obvious Amerind parallels in one of the Ushki sites in Kamchatka, argued that there were definite Eskaleut (Eskimo) parallels at another, later Ushki site.

The Cultural Peak of the North Pacific Maritime Adaptation in Siberia

The cultures that can be considered the highest achievements of the Arctic maritime adaptation in Northeast Siberia were the classic forms of the Old Bering Sea and Punuk cultures of the Bering Strait area. Surprisingly, their basic cultural features first appeared in sites of almost three millennia ago in a practically ready-made form. From its known beginnings, these cultures demonstrate an astonishingly high number of features which are almost identical to the modern stage of cultural development identified by the ethnographic data. The features that differentiate the modern culture from the culture of nearly three millennia ago are rather less important and minor. Probably, nowhere in the world can we observe such a high degree of cultural continuity, with so little change in the course of millennia.

This may signify that the sea animal hunting adaptation of the Bering Strait Eskimo people has reached the maximum level of its possible development in a pre-industrial context. We may speculate that this highly sophisticated culture was not imported to the Bering Strait area from some other territories in a ready-made form. Rather, it was assembled and developed to its utmost perfection here from a number of mutually adjusted cultural "details." Many of those "details" might have been introduced from some other areas in which they had originally developed.

We may hypothetically single out two main directions of such cultural diffusions. One venue of critical cultural influence came from the shores of the Arctic Ocean, from the mouths of the great Siberian rivers. The other input came most probably from the south, from the Sea of Okhotsk shores, mainly from the areas to the north of the Amur River. Here it received some important influences from the more southerly regions. The first stream clearly can be traced via ancient traditions of Eskimo decorative ornamentation. It introduced the exquisite technique of engraved straight and punctuated lines, points and circles that are visible already in the bone industry of the Burulgino site of the para-Ymyyakhtakh cultural affiliation in the present-day Yakutia (Sakha Republic). The second stream, probably having its origins somewhere near the Sea of Japan, brought with it the rich curvilinear designs, *t'ao-t'ieh*-like images, and fantastic faces. The harpoon technology was most probably developed independently in both of these two cultural traditions. It reached its high level of perfection in the Bering Strait area.

The late Old Bering Sea and the subsequent Punuk cultural traditions seem to have been the peak of artistic, social, and food-obtaining efficiency of the maritime-adapted cultures at the Bering Strait "Crossroads." It was probably the Little Ice Age of AD 1500–1700 that brought about a relative deterioration of the environmental abundance. Consequently, the relative artistic, social, and cultural impoverishment of the coastal population occurred. This same environmental trend, however, triggered the rise of a Native reindeer-breeding economy in the interior regions of Siberia (Krupnik 1993). Thus, around AD 1500–1700, a critical

and partly regressive transition took place, with a significant portion of the formerly sedentary coastal population moving inland and becoming nomadic. Its results are well observed in the historically documented diversity of Native cultures and economies in Northeast Siberia (cf. Krupnik 1988).

Conclusion

The current destiny and the future of the sea-mammal hunting culture of Northeast Asia are currently even less clear than its remote past. The Native maritime hunting economy in Siberia has been able somehow to endure, although in a very deformed and distorted condition, under the artificial paternalism of the Soviet system. Now, under the stress of transition to a market economy, the prospects for its continuity are very dim. On the other hand, the beauty and sophistication of technical and artistic achievements of the ancient Eskimo and their Siberian neighbors may become and, in fact, is currently emerging as a new source of inspiration, pride, and cultural reassertion of identity for their modern descendants

Acknowledgements

The author expresses his gratitude to the Kennan Institute for Advanced Russian Studies in Washington, DC, which partly sponsored his work on this paper.

Notes

1. See the most recent summary of the current Russian archaeological research on the Chukchi Peninsula and in the adjacent areas of the North Pacific in several papers published in Dumond and Bland 2002

References

Alexeev, Valerii P., and Tatiana I. Alexeeva
1993   Die heutige und die prähistorische Bevölkerung des Beringstrassengebietes. In *Arktische Waljäger vor 3000 Jahren*. A. Leskov and H. Müller-Beck, eds. Pp. 7–18. Mainz-Munich: Hase & Koehler Verlag.
Alexeev, Valeri P., Sergei A. Aroutiounov, and Dorian A. Sergeev
1972   Results of Historico-Ethnological and Anthro-

pological Studies in the Eastern Chukchee Area. *Inter-Nord.* 12: 305–11.

Arutjunov, Sergei A., and Mikhail M. Bronshtein

1993 Ethnisch-kulturelle Geschichte der asiatischen Eskimos. In *Arktische Waljäger vor 3000 Jahren.* A.Leskov and H. Müller-Beck, eds. Pp. 65–72. Mainz-Munich: Hase & Koehler Verlag.

Arutiunov, Sergei A., and Dorian A.Sergeev

1975 Problemy etnicheskoi istorii Beringomoria (Ekvenskii mogilnik) (Issues in Ethnic History of the Bering Sea Region: The Ekven Cemetery). Moscow: Nauka.

Arutiunov, Sergei A., Dorian A. Sergeev, and Chuner M. Taksami

1972 Etnokulturnye sviazi narodov Pribrezhnoi Severo-Vostochnoi Azii (Ethno-cultural Connections of the Peoples of Coastal Northeast Asia). In *Etnicheskaia istoriia narodov Azii.* R. Its, ed. Moscow: Nauka.

Bergsland, Knud

1959 The Eskimo-Uralic Hypothesis. *Journal de la Société Finno-Ougrienne* 61–2. Helsinki.

Bogoraz, Vladimir G. (Waldemar)

1949 Materialy po izucheniiu iazyka aziatskikh eskimosov (Materials for the Study of the Asiatic Eskimo Language). Leningrad: Uchpedgiz.

Bonnerijea, R.

1971 Is there any Relation Between Eskimo-Aleut and Uralo-Altaic? *Acta Linguistica* 21(3–4). Budapest.

1975 Some Probable Phonological Connections Between Uralo-Altaic and Eskimo-Aleut. *Orbis* 24 (Pt.1), 28 (Pt.2; 1979). Louvain.

1978 A Comparison Between Eskimo-Aleut and Uralo-Altaic Demonstrative Elements, Numerals, and Other Related Semantic Problems. *Journal of American Linguistics* 44(1).

Bronshtein, Mikahil M.

1993 Ekven—einzigartige archäologische Fundstelle in Nordostasien. In *Arktische Waljäger vor 3000 Jahren.* A.Leskov and H.Müller-Beck, eds. Pp. 73–82. Mainz-Munich: Hase & Koehler Verlag.

Dikov, Nikolai N.

1967 Otkrytie paleolita na Kamchatke i problema pervonachalnogo zaselenia Ameriki (The Discovery of the Paleolithic (Sites) in Kamchatka and the Problem of the Original Peopling of America). *Trudy Severo-Vostochnogo Kompleksnogo Instituta* 17: 16–31. Moscow.

1977 *Arkheologicheskie pamiatniki Kamchatki, Chukotki i Verkhnei Kolymy. Aziia na styke s Amerikoi v drevnosti* (Archeological Sites of Kamchatka, Chukotka, and the Upper Kolyma Area. Asia Joining America in Prehistory). Moscow: Nauka.

1979 *Drevnie kultury Severo-Vostochnoi Azii. Aziia na styke s Amerikoi v drevnosti* (Ancient Cultures of North-east Asia. Asia Joining America in Prehistory). Moscow: Nauka.

Dumond, Don E., and Richard L. Bland, eds.

2002 Archaeology in the Bering Strait Region. *University of Oregon Anthropological Papers* 59. Eugene.

Fedoseeva, Svetlana A.

1979 Ymyyakhtakhskaia Kultura Severo-Vostochnoi Azii (The Ymyyakhtakh Culture of Northeast Asia). Novosibirsk: Nauka.

Fitzhugh, William W., and Aron Crowell, eds.

1988 *Crossroads of Continents: Cultures of Siberia and Alaska.* Washington, DC: Smithsonian Institution Press.

Fleming, H. C.

1987 Toward a Definitive Classification of the World Languages. *International Journal for Historical Linguistics* 4: 155–223.

Illich-Svitych, V. M.

1971 Opyt sravneniia nostraticheskikh iazykov (Attempt at Comparative Study of the Nostratic Languages). Moscow.

Krupnik, Igor I.

1988 Economic Patterns in Northeastern Siberia. In *Crossroads of Continents: Cultures of Siberia and Alaska.* William W. Fitzhugh and Aron Crowell, eds. Pp. 183–191. Washington, DC: Smithsonian Institution.

1993 *Arctic Adaptations. Native Whalers and Reindeer Herders of Northern Eurasia.* Hanover: University Press of New England.

1998 "Jesup Genealogy." Intellectual Partnership and Russian-American Cooperation in Arctic/North Pacific Anthropology. Part 1: From the Jesup Expedition to the Cold War, 1897–1948. *Arctic Anthropology* 35(2):199–225.

Leskov, Aleksandr M., and Hans Müller-Beck, eds.

1993 *Arktische Waljäger vor 3000 Jahren. Unbekannte sibirische Kunst.* Mainz-München: Hase & Koehler.

Mochanov, Yurii A.

1969 Drevneishie etapy zaselenia Severo-Vostochnoi Azii i Alaski (Ancient Stages in Human Peopling of Northeast Asia and Alaska). *Sovetskaia etnografia* 1: 79–87.

1977 *Drevneishie etapy zaselenia chelovekom Severo-Vostochnoi Azii* (Ancient Stages of Human Peopling of Northeast Asia). Novosibirsk: Nauka.

Mudrak, Oleg A.

1984 K voprosu o vneshnikh sviaziakh eskimosskikh iazykov (To the Issue of External Connections of the Eskimo Languages). In *Lingvisticheskaia rekonsruktsiia i drevneishaia istoria Vostoka.* 1: 64–8. Moscow.

Okladnikov, Alexei P., ed.

1975 Yukagiry:istoriko-etnograficheskii ocherk (The

Yukagir: Historical and Cultural Synopsis). Novosibirsk: Nauka.

Rudenko, Sergei I.

1947   *Drevniaia kultura Beringova moria i eski-mosskaia problema.* Moscow and Leningrad: Glavsevmorput'. Translated as: The Ancient Culture of the Bering Sea and the Eskimo Problem. *Arctic Institute of North America Translation from Russian Sources* 1. Toronto: University of Toronto Press, 1961.

Shternberg, Lev Ya.

1933   *Gilyaki, orochi, gol'dy, negidal'tsy, ainy* (The Gilyak, Orich, Negidal, and the Ainu). Khabarovsk.

Simchenko, Yuri B.

1976   *Kultura okhotnikov na olenei Severnoi Evrazii* [The Culture of Reindeer (Caribou) Hunters in Northern Asia]. Moscow: Nauka.

Starostin, Sergei A.

1989   Sravnitel'no-istoricheskoe iazykoznanie i leksiko-statistika (Comparative-Historical Linguistics and Lexico-Statistics). In *Lingvisticheskaia rekonstruktsiia i drevneishaia istoriia Vostoka* 1: 1–39. Moscow.

Swadesh, Morris

1962   Linguistic Relations across Bering Strait. *American Anthropologist* 64(6): 1262–91.

Turner, Christy G. II

1985   The Dental Search for Native American Origins. In *Out of Asia: Peopling the Americas and the Pacific.* Robert Kirk and Emöke Szathmary, eds. Pp. 31–78. Canberra: Australian National University.

1988   Ancient Peoples of the North Pacific Rim. In *Crossroads of Continents: Cultures of Siberia and Alaska.* William W. Fitzhugh and Aron Crowell, eds. Pp. 111–6. Washington, DC: Smithsonian Institution Press.

Tyler, S. A.

1968   Dravidian and Uralian: The Lexical Evidence. *Language* 44 (4). Baltimore.

Uesson, A. M.

1970   *On Linguistic Affinity. The Indo-Uralic Problem.* Malmo.

Vasiliev, Vladimir I.

1971   Siirtia- legenda ili real'nost (*Siirtia* – Legend or Reality). *Sovetskaia Etnografia* 1: 151–7.

1979   *Problemy formirovaniia severo-samodiiskikh narodnostei* (Issues in the Formation of the Northern Samoyedic Peoples). Moscow: Nauka.

Vasilievskii, Ruslan S.

1972   *Drevnie kultury Tikhookeanskogo Severa* (Ancient Cultures of the North Pacific). Novosibirsk: Nauka.

Vdovin, Innokenti S.

1972   Sledy aleutsko-eskimosskoi kul'tury na tikhookeanskom poberezh'e Kamchatki (The Traces of an Aleut-Eskimo Culture on the Kamchatka Pacific Shore). *Strany I narody Vostoka* 13: 41–51. Moscow: Nauka.

Life in Lost Villages: Home, Land, Memory and the Senses of Loss in Post-Jesup Kamchatka

DAVID KOESTER

This paper is about social absence, that is, about the absence of irreducibly social aspects of experience. It is about the contemporary significance of closed and dying Native villages in Kamchatka, in the Russian Far East. To suggest a metaphor for my strategy here, one might think of the following analysis as an inquiry into what would happen to the fabric of social life if some force were to snip threads throughout the weave, leaving behind a set of connections that seem random without their previous supports. This is not to ask what would happen if certain roles were not filled or specific reciprocal obligations were not met; such occurs regularly when individuals in a community leave or die. Rather, it is about what happens when, for example, the possibilities for maintaining obligations, fulfilling plans and expectations have disappeared, when a rupture has occurred in the continuing process of re-establishing familial ties through the daily experience of places where memories are generated or when the skills and understandings one has learned no longer contribute to one's relationships in one's community.

In examining social relations and loss, I will not present a culturological vision of society in which all components of the socio-cultural system fit together in a functioning whole, only to point out the subsequent gaps. My aim is, rather, to examine the nature and formation of durable interconnections in social life. My argument is that specific features of the social understanding of loss help to make sense of the rela-

tive success and failure at current efforts in cultural revitalization among the Native peoples in Siberia whose ancestors were surveyed by the teams of the Jesup Expedition one hundred years ago.

The phenomena of social absence that I will describe are familiar to anthropologists. An historical example, well known in the North Pacific, is the banning of the potlatch on the Canadian Northwest Coast, against which Franz Boas and others protested vigorously (Stocking 1974:307; Boas 1974[1899]:106; Cole and Chaikin 1990:130–1). Boas had argued that the potlatch was part of the Indian economic system, a public paying of debts that was at the same time an investment in one's future. It obligated recipients to repay at a later time and thereby encouraged the giver to give freely so as to have more to receive:

> The sudden abolition of this system. . . destroys therefore all the accumulated capital of the Indians. It undoes the carefully planned life-work of the present generation, exposes them to need in their old age, and leaves the orphans unprovided for (Boas 1974[1899]:106).

Boas' argument implied that even with performances banned, the social effectiveness, the obligations still existed as long as people remembered them and remembered the status that went along with giving and receiving. He remarked, in his polemic to protect the tradition, that we should not be surprised that abolition was resisted by what he called "the best class" of Indians, "only the lazy should support it, because it relieves them of the duty of paying their debts" (Boas 1974[1899]:106). Political goals aside, Boas's point was that the silencing of the practice opened a gap in the set of relations by which people interacted and lived.

The rapid decline of indigenous populations and the curtailing of traditionally held practices by external cultural and economic influences and governmental authorities led anthropologists to undertake major salvage operations. The Jesup Expedition, with its variety of salvage activities, became a founding and exemplary model. The aims of salvage ethnology and linguistics in the U.S. were to establish an account of how Native American cultures varied geographically and to inscribe in a durable representative form as much as possible of languages, customs, practices and general information concerning the lives the various peoples led and the stories they would tell before those ways of life and stories passed away. This recording was done, as Bernard Cohn has pointed out, by stripping away the obvious signs of White influence and focusing on features that seemed peculiarly Native (Cohn 1968). The task was to record as much as possible, before the last generation that could tell of the prior way of life disappeared.

Today's cultural revival movements across the North Pacific, with their attention on preserving language and tradition, sometimes resemble salvage anthropology. For the most part, however, they are much more attuned to specific sentiments of loss and contemporary needs of economic development (e.g., Abryutina 1996; Stroganova 1997; Fondahl 1998: 89–131).[1] I focus here not on the practical issues of cultural restoration or the salvaging act of preserving in writing and other media that which was passed down through emulation, imitation and teaching. Instead, I examine the meaning of the loss of that which was taken away or displaced by government policy.

To explain what it means to lose one's village, I present here descriptions of three senses of the idea of life in a "lost village." These descriptions are based on published texts, songs, poetry and narratives I recorded during fieldwork in indigenous communities in Kamchatka during the early-mid 1990s. The first sense is a past-oriented sentiment toward life in the villages lost when resettlement was forced by Soviet economic policies of the 1950s and 1960s.[2] These closed villages still today constitute "original homelands," places of personal and familial identification. Many people, including young people, say that they are descendant from Utkholok or descendant from Sopochnoe, villages that no longer exist. These settlements were "closed" (that is, abandoned under government pressure) some thirty or even fifty years ago. The youngest who claim to be descendant from them may never even have seen them. An important second sense of loss is that people now feel that, because of the post-Soviet rupture in communication, funding, and delivery of social services they are living in villages that are "lost" to the outside world. They recognize that the governmental responsibility that once supported rural Soviet village life has disintegrated and feel that no one cares about their plight. Contemporary life for them now is life in a "lost village." And finally, a third sense of life in lost villages is the attempt of various groups of people to live in villages once closed, to actually establish, or reestablish, life in these lost villages.[3]

Village Ties Expressed in Poetry

In a general discussion of the experience of place Keith Basso has written that, "Relationships to places may. . . find expression through the agencies of myth, prayer, music, dance, art, architecture, and in many communities, recurrent forms of religious and political ritual" (Basso 1996:57). The various ways for place to be experienced and articulated includes the meaning of village life as it is and has been expressed in poetry, both written and in song. The four poems examined here issue from differing points of view. All of indigenous Kamchatkan origin, two of the authors still live in the villages of which they write and the other two live in Kamchatka's capital city, Petropavlovsk. For one of them her natal village no longer exists.

The first example is a song by a young Itelmen composer Anatoly Levkovsky (Levkovskii), born in 1962 (Fig. 64). It was his first song and he composed it while he was in Moscow, missing his home village of Kovran on the western shore of Kamchatka.[4] It is entitled simply, "My Village" and the melody is simple and straightforward as are the ideas. In the following translation I have cut out repetitions, in part melodically motivated, that emphasize that he loves and will never leave his village.

> My little village is set out by the sea,
> My beloved native home.
> I'll never leave it behind,
> it's dear to me.
> Our people are unpretentious,
> I'll never leave it behind,
> indeed they are talented craftspeople
> My family lives here and my many relatives.
> We all love you village.
> There is no limit to our love.[5]

(Levkovsky 1997)

For Levkovsky, his family, his relatives, his people share the affection they feel toward the village and that shared affection is his affection. He loves Kovran as his home, as the place of his people. His appreciation for the village also derives from the practical way in which people make their lives there.[6]

Levkovsky is director of cultural activities for the village of Kovran and he still lives there, in the place of his birth.

Tatiana Evstropovna Gutorova, a published author —renowned for her singing voice—was also born in Kovran. She now lives with her children and grandchildren in the city of Petropavlovsk. In 1994, at a gathering of Itelmens and Kamchadals[7] in the hot spring area of Upper Paratunka, she sang a song in Itelmen that she had composed specially for the occasion. Addressed to her sister, her song was a doleful lament, performed in the style of the Itelmen traditional *khodila*[8] and composed about the village and the relatives whom she misses. It echoes the same theme of love for the village associated with its inhabitants.

> Swans took flight at dawn
> Their cries resounded
> as if they were weeping
> At once my heart yearned
> they're flying past Kovran
> My village, my Kovran
> I cannot forget
> As if some evil demon is holding me
> I cannot break loose
> The geese are going to fly over Kovran
> They will circle over my village
> I send warm greetings
> I miss my fellow Kovraners
> God give me wings
> I will fly to my village
> My soul will be calmed among my kin
> I'll walk throughout the village

(Recorded by the author, 3 July 1994, in Itelmen)[9]

Tatiana Evstropovna herself explained in Russian the meaning of the poem to me from which the translation here. With the village of her birth still in existence her song evokes ties to the village through kin and through the experience of its topography. In the images of circling over and walking throughout the village (particularly in contrast to being held, unable to break loose) her feeling of loss and of attachment to the place is expressed as memory and desire. The poem sets in opposition the far away distance to the village, marked by flight and the grounded contact of walking through the village.

These two songs about ties to Kovran through its landscape and people can be contrasted with a poetic cycle of verses about the town of Milkovo, the hometown of Kamchadal poet, Nina Berezhkova-Porotova. Milkovo, in central Kamchatka, is much larger than Kovran and its present-day population is predominantly of Russian origin. Many of its indigenous Kamchadals have been active in local cultural revitalization and have established a Kamchadal Club. Less tied to people-in-the-place, the opening lines and much of the remaining ten verses of Berezhkova-Porotova's poem extol natural beauty, the permanent features of the landscape, dramatic changes of season and the familiar, relatively unchanging characteristics of plant and animal life. Rather than writing of people in the environment, she humanizes the landscape:

> Milkovo in a valley cradle
>
> Was hidden under a down-coat of snow
> . . .
> The mountains put on a snowy *malakhai* [hood in Itelmen]
>
> they hid a grey tress in ravines

(Berezhkova-Porotova 1993:11–2)

As in the two songs above, Berezhkova-Porotova's sentiments toward the place are linked to an elder relative. The title verse, "I've been panged by Milkovo since childhood" reflects on the tale of the author's grandmother, who sought to defend the village church when Soviet officials came to take away its bell. Other verses recall childhood, and give vignettes of traditional life, sprinkled with Itelmen words (Berezhkova-Porotova 1993:7–15). This poem, about a relatively urbanized village, contrasts with the two about rural, predominantly Itelmen Kovran in its greater emphasis on the aesthetic features of the natural environment and more specific focus on a single close relative in relation to a single historical event.[10] Her tie to a relative-in-the-place is less participatory than that ex-

pressed by Levkovsky or Gutorova, yet is nevertheless an important aspect of her nostalgia.

Itelmen poet Nelia Suzdalova (born in 1937) similarly included a poem about her native village Sopochnoe in a prominent place in her first published poetic collection (1993). It followed the opening poem "Dog Teams" from which the entire collection gets its name, "Those dog teams sped away." The image of a dog team disappearing in the distance metonymically and symbolically refers to the loss of traditional cultural life. Soviet government-enforced resettlements of Itelmen villagers for the purposes of consolidating the labor force and economizing on delivery of services began in 1956 (Starkova 1976:32). The next poem in the collection, entitled simply, "Sopochnoe" reflects the feelings from that period and Suzdalova's sense of loss with the closing of her village.

> We have grown up and died on our land
> And expected always to live here...
> At the whispers of the forest,
> we stood still in happiness,
> There was no time to grieve.
> But the time arrived—bad news,
> The river became a mere legend,
> In a foreign region, in a cold place
> Centuries came to a halt.
> Farewell warmth, goodbye, mountains,
> And you too, moon, above our homeland,
> An evil alien pushed a button,
> And the strand broke.

(Suzdalova 1993:3–4)

Suzdalova emphasizes the continuity of ancestry at her homeland, affirmed by life and death on the land. The warmth and happiness associated with this continuity contrast with the mechanical coldness that replaced them and, as in Gutorova's song, an arbitrary, unhindered power has caused their loss.

PEOPLE, ANIMALS, AND LAND/ LOST VILLAGES

In all of these odes to villages the tie to the home-land is through people and relationships to those people, especially ancestral. Such sentiments seen and heard expressed in these examples of published and performed poetry, were also echoed in remembrances that I recorded on various occasions. A respected Itelmen elder, teacher and cultural expert, Yakov Lvovich Zhirkov, for example, also spoke of life in the village of Sopochnoe at a presentation for children. He spoke on the occasion of Itelmen language week in the village school:

> In childhood I lived with my grandfathers (*dedy* – male elders). There were many elders there, grandmothers (*babushki* – female elders), my parents. And I had to live in the forest and out fishing. They brought me everywhere with them, when it turned spring. When I was little they took me fishing, hunting, though I never really hunted and did not become a hunter. I walked and wandered but did not hunt. Everything around me gave me pleasure. I looked at this nature, at the richness that we had. Now there is no village (Zhirkov 1994).

It is important to note in this statement how the relations with his elders tied him to the natural environment. His memory, the lost experience that he sought to convey to today's children, was that of living and working in the forest and on the tundra with kin and fellow villagers. Another elder from Sopochnoe, Tatiana Petrovna Lukashkina (born in 1918; Fig. 65), who lost her parents in the Stalinist repressions, has similarly focused much of her reminiscence of childhood on the elder who raised her, her blind grandmother. Both Tatiana Petrovna and Yakov Lvovich placed value not on just the relative alone or just the place, but primarily on their experiences of and with their relatives in the village and its environs. The focus on recollections of family and village life tied to the land is reminiscent of sentiments about places recorded in other parts of the world. Writing of Wamirans in Papua New Guinea, Kahn notes that for them, places in the landscape "resonate . . . deeply about the importance

of social relations and obligations based on feeding, sharing and caring for one another" (1996:176; cf. also Rosaldo 1980).

Lost Villages I: Living in the Past

With Suzdalova's poem and the recountings by Zhirkov and Lukashkina we have come to sentiments about a village closed several decades ago by a Soviet policy decision. As we move to consideration of the significance of such closed villages it is important to keep in mind that people's recollections represent complex images overlain by the profound effects of Soviet economic and cultural programs. Attuned to effecting a change of consciousness, much of the former Soviet policy sought specifically to patch and replace elements of the social-economic fabric it was destroying. For Itelmen in Kamchatka, increasingly year-round settlements replaced summer/winter seasonal habitation and state-run boarding schools (*internaty*) replaced local schools. State-supported and managed clubhouse ("house of culture") activities, including the celebration of holidays, came to replace both church attendance and festivities associated with winter visiting. Brigade work (organized production teams) replaced family-, friendship- and need-determined cooperative production, and so on (Starkova 1976). In the wake of these transformations, what seems consistent in recollections and laments about the past is the sense of loss of community tied to a place and associated with practical activity over time.

Despite socially engineered, "progressive" replacements for various aspects of social life, most people remember the closing of the villages as a devastating blow.[11] Over and over again, elders have said to me that life was hard in earlier days, but it was better; we "lived amicably" (*zhili druzhno*), they say. They acknowledge that their fond memories are somewhat gilded by the flow of time.[12] They speak of how laborious subsistence was, that they did not have readily available flour, bread and tea as appeared later. Yet they nevertheless maintain that this time was happy, and they associate this lost happier life with the move from the villages.

Bruce Grant found loss of Native villages on Sakhalin Island (another area covered by the Jesup Expedition) to be comparably significant. The primary difference was that the village closings in Sakhalin during the 1950s and 1960s took place on a much larger scale there than in Kamchatka. He writes that Soviet intentions to improve economic prospects in villages by consolidating labor in efficient administrative centers proved vain hopes:

> Rather than strengthening and internationalizing, the resettlements produced a spirit of absence felt on economic, social, and personal levels. Rather than moving forward, they generated a retrospective force that pulled many back (Grant 1993:244).

The closed villages came to represent a longed-for, lost way of life in Sakhalin, as they did in Kamchatka. Moreover, Grant found that the lost way of life has been understood to be traditional. It is in part because of this understood traditionality that the closed villages have become an object of interest for cultural revivalists. Grant cites the example of the lone brigadier who, having refused to leave when the resettlements

79/ Location of Lost Villages on Kamchatka Peninsula, Russia, discussed in the paper

took place, now stands as symbol and metonymic sign of traditional life (Grant 1995:134).

Itelmen people who today live in the villages of Kovran, Verkhne Khairiuzovo, Tigil, Sedanka and even in the city of Petropavlovsk (Fig. 79) still inhabit these lost villages in their memories. Experiences on a daily basis ranging from negative ones such as family tension, drunkenness, and economic hardship to more positive ones of family celebration, collective singing

and dancing all evoke memories of contrasting and comparable experiences in the old villages. Elders commonly remark, for example, that there was no drunkenness in their childhood villages. People drank, they acknowledge, and enjoyed doing so, but the alcoholic kind of public drunkenness now common was, they say, unknown.

The experiences of entering new village life after forced resettlement contributed greatly to the memories that create today's sense of loss. Soviet planners' aim was not, in the initial move, to create (or recreate) a village, but to provide a place for workers to live. When resettled villagers arrived in Kovran in 1960, they found that promised housing was not yet constructed and they were placed in temporary housing (barracks). Life was, from all descriptions, difficult. Local administrators moved quickly to establish work as the basis for social relations in the relocated community. Strategically, their mission was to replace older village social values with the value of work for the greater society. The effectiveness of this effort is articulated in the first memories that resettled villagers recount— self-worth and status among peers were to be linked to diligent labor and productivity.[13]

Prestige was granted to those who worked hard, achievements in production were recognized on a public honor roll and prizes were awarded. Several Itelmen elders recounted to me the thrill of a family member receiving a "premium"—sometimes extra rations of flour, and sugar and in one case I heard of, a new rifle. But, although there were individual rewards, the differentiation that took place is now also remembered in intergroup terms. One woman told me repeatedly, when

PEOPLE, ANIMALS, AND LAND/ LOST VILLAGES

recollecting her resettlement to Kovran, that the people from her native village of Sopochnoe knew how to work. She also said, however, that they had unfairly been accused by Kovraners of being slackers. Neither an ideology nor merely a command, this shaping of relations by means of instilling a competitive work ethic was given added moral weight, founded in praxis, when internally segmented others were perceived in comparative, competitive terms. Public support was given to intergroup competition by the publication of village, *kolkhoz* (common Russian abbreviation for 'collective farm'–ed.) and brigade production rankings.

This value of competitive work continues today even in non-wage labor contexts. When I joined groups of people traveling with *kolkhoz* tractors (the *kolkhoz* was defunct but still alive in name) out to gather the local "wild garlic," *cheremsha*, on what seemed in many respects to be a community outing, some families talked distinctly in productive terms. For these families much of the conversation focused on how much they could gather and how quickly. The emphasis on productivity, whether constructed as competition among siblings or among members of a work brigade, refers back in time to the larger Soviet social economic project in which rationalized, quantifiable production aims were the goal. This focus on time-intensified production contrasts starkly with the image of life in Sopochnoe portrayed by Yakov Lvovich Zhirkov, however nostalgically embellished. His description of wandering and working in the forests, composing songs in response to the beauty of nature, lacked any sense of urgency or competitiveness.

It would not, however, be right to say that the work ethic was introduced with the forced migrations in the 1950s and 1960s. Collectivization in Kamchatka, including in remote Native communities, had already occurred in the 1930s (Starkova 1976:30) and many elders' recollections of productive activities rehearse quantitative competitive notions. Moreover, the instilling of competition did not constitute the introduction of the idea, or the valuing, of hard work. Tatiana Petrovna Lukashkina, who participated actively in the Soviet project to modernize the lives of the Native peoples of Kamchatka, has written that the Itelmen were always a work-loving people (*trudoliubivye*).

Whether before or after resettlement, the social relation created in the Soviet-inspired world of work was not to the community but to the productive apparatus. Though it would be too hasty to conclude that social valuation by competitive work was entirely introduced by the Soviet government, this value, nevertheless, contrasts with the image given by Yakov Lvovich Zhirkov. In his remembrance of a young boy being dragged along to work in the forests and on the river, "work" created ties to people he deeply respected, the memories of whom tie him to his homeland. The competitive work relations, in contrast, while giving many a sense of self-worth, divided people and provided no sense of ties to a place.

When elders say that they lived more amicably in the past it reflects this difference in productive relations. Whereas in the past subsistence activity tied people to places through collective efforts with elders, after resettlement, productive effort was purposefully generated by prestige stratification. Status was conferred individually and collectively and articulated in recollections as inter- and intra-village group difference. The social absence mentioned in the introduction is sensed, I would suggest, largely in this transition from affective relations created through cooperative work to social differentiation created in state-controlled labor.

Lost Villages II: Lost in Today's World

The second sense of loss emerges from the collapse of support for Soviet village infrastructure during the 1990s, especially between 1991 and 1997. Many of the factors of loss present in Itelmen villages in Kamchatka have been discussed in the literature on more general economic and social problems facing Siberian indigenous people in post-Soviet Russia (Pika and Grant 1999; Ryvkina et al. 1996; Zaidfudim et al.

1994). Kamchatka was spared the worst of the catastrophic environmental damage that took place during the Soviet period in Siberia, such as that which occurred in the West Siberian oil and gas fields, devastating landscapes and curtailing subsistence based on natural resources (Trumbull 1995; Wiget and Balalaeva 1997; Feshbach and Friendly 1992:137–8). On the other hand, significant environmental degradation due to industrialization and localized overpopulation has taken place in Kamchatka. These days, people need to make day-long trips to gather berries, firewood is increasingly difficult to obtain and fewer and fewer salmon are coming up river. Thus, it is important to enumerate some of the consequences of withdrawal of governmental support.

During the 1950s and 1960s, the Soviet government orchestrated the construction of new villages for Native people in Kamchatka consisting of small wooden houses that required firewood for heating or larger apartment buildings that required coal in the winter. As electrification came, in the form of fuel-dependent diesel generator stations, all households became equipped with stoves and utensils for cooking with electricity. Radio was brought in by cable and telephone along with it. Stores were supplied with basic foodstuffs, including flour, pasta, tea, sugar, cereal grains, and pickled and canned fruits and vegetables. The village of Kovran (Fig. 66) had its own dairy, bakery, public bathhouse, post office and clubhouse where movies were shown and people came to meet. Helicopters regularly flew from village to village and it was often possible for villagers to hitchhike for travel to school, work or even just to visit relatives. Ground transportation from the nearby airport in Ust-Khairiuzovo was organized by the *kolkhoz* to meet scheduled flights from Petropavlovsk. The end of the Soviet Union meant that collapse of these government services. In the five-year period from 1992–7, except for the houses, and occasional and unreliable service from the telephones, the bathhouse and the post office, virtually everything I have listed has fallen away.

Village electricity was cut to three hours a day, the bakery died fitfully from shortages of firewood, the dairy's cows either died or were sold for meat or private use, the clubhouse which burned down just before this period was not to be restored (Fig. 68) and the store, by 1996, sold little more than tea, confections and vodka (Fig. 67). Travel became very difficult as helicopters began to fly only commercial and emergency traffic, allowing fewer and eventually no hitchhikers, and the regular "bus" from Ust-Khairiuzovo became increasingly unreliable and eventually ceased to run altogether. All of this would clearly give anyone a sense of material loss.[14]

The social sense of loss that I want to describe is, however, a deeper feeling of isolation and helplessness. I have written elsewhere about villagers' decision in 1993 to write a letter to the U.N. to ask for assistance (Koester n.d.). The letter came out of a meeting of school teachers with Itelmen Cultural Restoration Council[15] leaders to discuss the annual festival *Alkhalalalai*. The topic of conversation constantly turned from the festival to problems in the village. As village leaders described their futile attempts to get help from both the regional and the district administrations, those attending the meeting increasingly began to talk about being forgotten. They complained of the difficulties of reaching ever-absent bureaucrats over correspondingly unreliable phone lines, and the impossible expense and time required to fly to the regional capital town of Palana, some 270 km to the north. Finally, as the idea to write to the U.N. emerged one person said, "Our government has no use for us." This summarized the collective sentiment and much of the sense of lostness.

Kovran, like so many other Native Siberian communities (Fig. 69), was for decades economically dependent on supplies from outside and along with this, after many years of hearing of "the proud feeling of belonging in the one great Soviet Homeland" (Moiseev 1989:16), the sentiment developed that relationships and reciprocal obligations built up in the construction of these Soviet villages were to the country and to the government. Thus, the villagers did not just feel cut off, they felt cast aside; their effort in living and working in the village no longer brought reciprocation from the state and no longer contributed to a "feeling of belonging" to the country as a whole.

Lost Villages III: Living in Closed Villages

From the time of the founding in 1989 of the first Native organization in Kamchatka, the Itelmen Cultural Restoration Council *Tkhsanom*, the longing for home villages that I described in Part I played a significant role in plans for restoration. People had persistent dreams of re-establishing their lives on the sites of the closed villages. The village of Sopochnoe figured prominently in these plans. It was the southernmost village in which the Itelmen language was spoken when Waldemar Jochelson visited the west coast of Kamchatka in 1910 (Jochelson n.d.:2). It consisted of about fourteen households in the 1930s and remained predominantly Itelmen speaking. A school was created in Sopochnoe in 1924 when virtually no one in the village spoke Russian. Then, in the 1930s, school policy was changed from encouraging Native languages to banning of them on school grounds and at that point the changeover took place very rapidly. Sopochnoe is of particular significance because its descendants have played such a prominent role in Native cultural life in Kamchatka of the twentieth century. Tatiana Petrovna Lukashkina, who was born in Sopochnoe, was the first Itelmen woman to receive a higher education (1934–8) and she was involved in the transformation of Kamchatkan dance to forms appropriate for performance on stage (Lukashkina 1991:53–4). After her return from the Institute of Peoples of the North in Leningrad in 1938, she spent the rest of her life as an educator in outposts and small villages of the Kamchatkan north (Fig. 70). Sopochnoe was also the home village of the first president of the Restoration Council, Klavdia Nikolaevna Khaloimova (born in 1934) and of others who were active in the beginnings of the cul-

tural restoration movement, including Boris Zhirkov (born in 1946), a noted dancer and local folklorist.

At the third annual Itelmen cultural revival conference in 1989 a decision was taken to support resettlement at Sopochnoe. In March of 1991 a Native fishing *artel* (cooperative) named "Itelmen" was officially registered with the regional administration. They received a fishing quota and began work at the former village site of Sopochnoe in the summer. The fishing went well by most accounts but the whole venture ended badly. The *artel* got a low price for its fish in Petropavlovsk so that there was very little return for the workers. In the meantime, they had alienated the local fish processing factory, whose fishing limit they had usurped, by sending the fish to Petropavlovsk rather than to it. And while the workers received very little for their efforts, the director of the *artel*, brother of the new Cultural Restoration Council head, received a new snowmobile. This failure to pay the workers and the new snowmobile was bannered in the local papers as a sign of corruption or at least greed, and with considerable innuendo, the Council head was blamed (Kravchuk 1992). There were hard feelings in the village, but the bad press was worse. The newspaper coverage posed restoration as a ruse, a means by which one Itelmen family could acquire access to resources and this slant proved a deft move in interethnic politicking. The articles were written as exposés, and supported and generated anti-restoration sentiment and exacerbated divisions within the Itelmen community.[16] Fondahl has written that similar reports describing ethnically based mismanagement had been published in a newspaper concerning an Even Native association with similar results (Fondahl 1995).

Despite the failure of the *artel*, some families lasted there for a while. The most valiant effort in this early attempt was probably that of the son and daughter-in-law of a revitalization activist. They built a home in Sopochnoe and with two young children moved from Kovran to live there on a full-time, and potentially permanent basis. The difficulties were tremendous. It was not simply that there was no electricity, radio or other conveniences of village life. Sopochnoe is over 100 kilometers—a minimum four days walk—from the nearest village. Though most food, building materials and firewood could be obtained in the area, any other necessities had to be hauled and planned for well in advance. It was particularly hard on the mother of the household, who, for the children, felt the necessity of maintaining a home on roughly a village standard of living. After almost a year, and with relatively few regrets, they gave up and moved back to Kovran. In comparison to the past, life in the village was too isolated. It was not a village with others on whom one might depend for assistance and comradery (Fig. 71). And despite the existence of modern transport, there was less interchange between the village site and other places. The nearest neighboring village Moroshechnoe was also closed, meaning that the density of people in the area was so light that even with shorter travel times made possible by mechanized transport, the value of making the trip was too slight. Thus, all families eventually left.[17]

For the purpose of this analysis, what is striking in the story of this failed attempt to revive village life in Sopochnoe is the Soviet nature of the original organizational plan. The villagers began by creating a work brigade for the purpose of producing a certain amount of fish that would then be delivered to a centralized processing unit. Instead of returning to the village with an understanding of living as they had in the past, their return was predicated on industrially modeled production that, they thought, would allow them to survive in today's world market. High hopes for the resettlement were dashed on the shoals of the commercial fisheries business.

Much greater success has been obtained in the reinhabiting of the area associated with another "closed" Itelmen village, Moroshechnoe, located sixty kilometers north of Sopochnoe (Fig. 72). Yuri [a pseudonym] was born in the village of Sopochnoe and spoke Russian as his first language. At a very young age,

however, he moved with his family to Moroshechnoe where the entire community was Itelmen speaking. The village then consisted of about nineteen households strung along a sharp bend in the Moroshechnaya River, over fifty kilometers upstream from the Sea of Okhotsk. Like Sopochnoe, Moroshechnoe has produced a number of people active in trying to revitalize Itelmen cultural life in the 1990s. Yuri was not, however, particularly active in this movement. He and his wife spent most of their working lives in a central Kamchatkan village where they had moved to alleviate their young son's extreme case of asthma. Yuri worked as a professional hunter, working mostly with Russian hunters from the area. During his years there he often dreamed of having his own hunting cabin in the woods, back where he had grown up. It was not, however, his intention to try to rebuild his lost village.

His father had been a brigadier, in charge of the fishing brigade of Moroshechnoe's old *kolkhoz* "International." The fishing brigade worked at a fishing encampment twelve kilometers upstream from the village of Moroshechnoe itself. Yuri spent his summers there, playing, working and swimming when young and gradually taking on more responsibilities as he got older. Not long after he learned to write he took on the job of recording the *kolkhoz*'s catch and eventually keeping the fish camp's books. He became good at math and was eventually offered the possibility to study in Moscow. One summer in the 1940s, however, while they were stationed at the fishing site, his father became ill and died. This, of course, had a profound impact on the family, and each member, that is, all of Yuri's siblings, have told me about the suddenness of their father's death at this place (e.g., in Petrasheva and Koester 1997:10). One of the implications was that Yuri decided to stay behind to work with his family rather than go to the Russian West for further education.

Several years ago, during the winter, Yuri was hunting with his son, Volodya, and they stopped their snowmobiles near this fishing site. He recognized it as the place where they used to fish during the summer and the place where his father had died. There is a small spring there that never freezes over and it is thus a good source of fresh water; they decided to camp for the night. During the night Yuri dreamt that his father came to him. When he awoke he remembered the night's vision and decided that he would realize his lifetime dream and have his hunting cabin at this site. With the help of the Cultural Restoration Council, he obtained rights to hunting territory in the vicinity and built a small cabin. As conditions worsened in his home village of Kovran, he and his family began to see the site as more than a hunting cabin and actually an economically viable refuge. They built another structure to be their home, converted the original cabin into a steam bathhouse (*banya*) and constructed a storage shed (*ambar*) and greenhouse as well. They now have a garden and an ordinary outhouse in convenient proximity. The hunting territory and the river make possible a reasonable living at the site. With three horses to take care of, they now have someone living there—Yuri or one or more of his younger male descendants or relatives— all year. This is necessary both to take care of the horses and garden and to prevent theft from the storehouse and household.

In its fifth year (at the writing of this text) this relative success story was in part made possible by the abysmal conditions in the village of Kovran. The loss of infrastructure there, including electricity, regular telephone service, pay for employment, etc. has meant that life at an extremely isolated encampment, two days walk from the nearest village, can be better than in their home village. Socially this means that the infrastructural relations founded on institutionalized wage-labor and monetary consumption, collective activity in the village clubhouse and home life that was increasingly centered around entertainment by electronic media have, for this extended family, been replaced. Much stronger familial connections and ties have reemerged through the use and sharing of local

natural resources. One of the connections that has been "revitalized" with this return settlement is the tie to the place of predecessors; loss is being replaced by reconnection to a place where elder relatives had lived. For Yuri and all of his siblings it is very important that he has come to live in this place where his father died.

In late July, 1994 I returned to Kovran from visiting my friends at this settlement in Moroshechnoe. Kovraners were of course curious about my impressions but their overwhelming reaction was to reminisce about their own villages. I came across one group of women standing on the stoop to their apartment building. Each in turn reflected on her own former village. One asked me if I had been to her village of Belogolovoe (closed in 1972), upstream from Moroschechnoe. I had and she looked up rapturously and said "Oh how I would like to see it again . . . to go there." She asked if I thought it was beautiful. I said I thought it was.

Conclusion

In setting out to discuss the three different perspectives on life in lost villages that I have presented, it was not my initial intention to try to bring them all together with a final unifying conclusion. It seemed to me sufficient to describe the sensibilities people have toward villages long closed, toward the villages in which they live, and toward villages in which they have tried once again to live. It has become clear to me, however, that there is a connection among these differing feelings of loss and sensibilities of absence. The Itelmen people with whom I have talked have articulated a strong sense of being connected to places through the past and continuing inhabitance of elder kin and fellow villagers in those places. Their feelings for villages and the natural environs that surround them are intimately tied to elder relatives and friends with whom they walked, hunted, fished, gathered berries, sang, danced, loved and laughed. All three components—people, engaging in activities with those people, and the landscape—are interlinked in creating social, material bonds to homelands. The connections were riven by the resettlements in the 1950s and 1960s. As the Soviet government encouraged and forced people to reorient their productive relations from kin and fellow villagers to the *kolkhoz*, village and national (Soviet) effort, one of the primary means by which villagers felt attachment to their natural surroundings as homeland was pushed aside. Soviet forms of social life organized on the basis of dedication to work and productivity did not, however, come to replace these sentiments. The attachments have been maintained, rather, in both the memories of elders and practiced in weekend outings by small family groups. Village restoration seems to be succeeding on a small scale where ties to family history have been realized (Figs. 73, 74).

I want to end with a song by Itelmen composer Anatoly Levkovsky, a lullaby for his son, that explains all of these ideas of ties to people in places and of ties to the land through the experience of living and producing in it with kin.

Lullaby

Sleep my son,

sleep dear boy,

Lying comfortably on your cradleboard,

sleep gives strength.

Then you'll see, my boy,

you'll see your homeland

Where we were born along with you,

where you will live.

All our grandfathers and fathers

lived here from time immemorial,

Caught fish for food

and hunted sea animals.

And you, son, when you grow,

you'll learn these things.

You'll take this all in hand

and know how to use it.

Indeed, though our homeland is rich,

there are still limits to everything.

Your father will tell you where and how,

so that you can pass it on

for your grandchildren

Sleep quickly my son,

sleep quickly my dear boy

Lying comfortably on your cradleboard,

sleep gives strength.

(Levkovsky 1997)

Acknowledgments

I would like to thank the people of the villages of Kovran, Verkhne-Khairiuzovo and Ust-Khairiuzovo for their hospitality and kind assistance, and especially the people mentioned in this paper (pseudonymously and otherwise) and especially Elena D'iakonova, Nina Tolman and Georgi Zaporotsky. I would also like to thank Viktoria Petrasheva for a long collaboration and kind friendship and her Institute, the Pacific Ocean Division of the Department of Geography of the Russian Academy of Sciences (formerly the Kamchatka Institute of Ecology and Nature Management), Robert Moiseev, Director.

Notes

1. This paper was written for the Jesup Expedition's centennial conference in 1997. Since that time, numerous ethnographic accounts of post-Soviet life that report relevant comparable and contrasting experiences in the Russian Far East have appeared in print or been completed as dissertations. Because of space limitations I cannot expand this paper to include reference to them all.

2. Referring to the destruction in people's lives that took place, Petra Rethmann (1997) has noted the euphemistic quality of this notion of merely "closing" villages.

3. The fieldwork on which this article is based was conducted primarily in the villages of Kovran, Verkhne-Khairiuzovo, Ust-Khairiuzovo and the city of Petropavlovsk, with subsequent work in the

villages of Tigil, Tilichiki, and short visits to other places in Kamchatka.

4. The population of Kovran has declined over the past decade from nearly 500 in 1993 to less than 400 in 2002.

5.Unless otherwise noted, the texts quoted here are my translations from Russian.

6. Literally, the song says that the people of Kovran have "golden hands" (*zolotye ruki*) which means more than just crafts, as I have translated. They can do what needs to be done to make a living and do it well.

7. The terms "Itelmen" and "Kamchadal" are overlapping ethnic designations for indigenous peoples of Kamchatka. "Kamchadal" was the term used historically by Russians for the Native inhabitants of Kamchatka. The term "Itelmen" was eventually formally recognized by the Soviet government as the Native self-designation of the people(s) who occupied the central part of Kamchatka in 1927 (Murashko 1997:181). "Kamchadal" has gradually come to be used specifically to mean indigenous Kamchatkans of mixed Native and Russian (that is, Slavic Russian, including Cossack, Ukrainian, etc.) ancestry. Some of today's "Itelmen" are happy to be called "Kamchadal" and some "Kamchadals" from village of Tigil and the city of Petropavlovsk find "Itelmen" acceptable. A detailed analysis of the history and use of the terms can be found in: Murashko 1996, 1997.

8. The Itelmen *khodila* is a kind of chanting song, usually mournful in tone, sometimes with meaningless syllables in the place of lyrics. Communities were known to have their own particular styles (melodic and rhythmic). *Khodily* were sung while along traveling, hunting, gathering and walking in the woods or composed to be performed for others at gatherings. They often expressed the emotional state of the singer in relation to observations of nature (there is an example in Steller 1996 [1774]:234). The *khodily* (pl.) I recorded in 1993–1996 sounded remarkably like *khodily* recorded by Jochelson on the Ryabushinski Expedition in 1910. There are no more than four or five Itelmen today who still know, and even fewer who perform, these songs.

9. Tatiana Evstropovna herself explained in Russian the meaning of the poem to me from which the translation here.

10. Close ties to nature have often been noted as features of nostalgic remembrances in modern society (Frykman 1986; Burgos 1996) and would make an interesting point of comparison more generally to remembrances of Soviet modernity (Creuziger 1996).

11. Boris Chichlo tells similarly of the devastating affects of Asiatic Eskimo (Yupik) village closings (Chichlo 1981).

12. Interpreting this period and these recollections is also complicated by Russian idealizations of childhood that pervade pedagogical and popular literature and local understandings (Creuziger 1996; Wachtel 1990).

13. An intensive dedication to work was characteristic of many of the public personas involved in the development of the Soviet North. Writing in the 1930s after travels through the Soviet Arctic Ruth Gruber described the energy of local party leaders who in the pursuit of their duties regularly went with only four hours' sleep per night (Gruber 1939).

14. Since 1997 there has been improvement in some area and loss in others. Lack of fuel has caused villagers to tear down uninhabited housing to burn in their stoves. Electricity was restored for a time with the connecting of a high power inter-tie from the village of Ust-Khairiuzovo, but that quickly fell into disrepair. The most significant bright spot has been the phenomenal development and popularity of the village's dance troupe Elvel. They have performed in Berlin, Paris, Moscow, San Francisco and numerous other places as well as around much of Russia and Kamchatka. Though they make relatively little money for their performances, their travel and small income have had a significant economic impact in the village as a whole.

15. "Sovet Vozrozhdeniia Itelmenskoi Kultury" (*Council for Revival of the Itelmen Culture*) was founded in 1989. It was at the time a government-sanctioned organization. It has since become the primary representative organization of the Itelmen people and is affiliated with the Russian Association of Indigenous Peoples of the North (RAIPON).

16. Fondahl has written that similar reports describing ethnically based mismanagement had been published in a newspaper concerning an Even native association with similar results (Fondahl 1995).

17. Since that attempt however, with the house

built, Klavdia N. Khaloimova has returned to the village site for extended periods and was once accompanied by her elder aunt, Tatiana P. Lukashkina. Additionally, one man originally from the village, has taken up more or less year-round residence alone, with visiting relatives to help out.

References

Abryutina, Larisa I.
1996   The Rights of the Indigenous Peoples of Chukotka and the Reality. In *Anxious North: Indigenous Peoples in Soviet and Post-Soviet Russia.* A. Pika, J. Dahl, and I. Larsen, eds. Pp. 233–9. IWGIA Document, 81. Copenhagen: IWGIA.

Basso, Keith H.
1996   Wisdom Sits in Places: Notes on a Western Apache Landscape. In *Senses of Place.* S. Feld and K.H. Basso, eds. Pp. 53–90. Santa Fe: School of American Research Press.

Berezhkova-Porotova, Nina
1993   *Ia s detstva Mil'kovom bol'na* (I've Been Panged by Milkovo Since Childhood). Petropavlovsk-Kamchatskii: Dal'nevostochnoe   knizhnoe izdatel'stvo.

Burgos, Martine
1996   The Child and the Bee: Nature and Nurture in Four Life Stories. In *Imagined Childhoods.* M. Gullestad, ed. Pp. 119–35. Oslo: Scandinavian University Press.

Cole, Douglas, and Ira Chaikin
1990   *An Iron Hand upon the People: the Law against the Potlatch on the Northwest Coast.* Vancouver: Douglas & McIntyre; Seattle: University of Washington Press.

Chichlo, Boris
1981   Les Nevuqaghmiit ou la fin d'une ethnie. *Etudes/Inuit/Studies* 5(2):29–47.

Cohn, Bernard S.
1968   Ethnohistory. In *International Encyclopedia of the Social Sciences.* Vol. 6. D. L. Sills, ed. Pp. 440–8. New York: Macmillan.

Creuziger, Clementine G. K.
1996   *Childhood in Russia: Representation and Reality.* Lanham, Maryland: University Press of America.

Feshbach, Murray, and Alfred Friendly, Jr.
1992   *Ecocide in the USSR: Health and Nature Under Siege.* New York: BasicBooks.

Fondahl, Gail
1995   The Status of Indigenous Peoples in the Russian North. *Post-Soviet Geography* 36(4):215–24.
1998   *Gaining Ground? Evenkis, Land, and Reform in Southeastern Siberia.* Boston: Allyn and Bacon.

Frykman, Jonas, and Orvar Löfgren
1986   *Culture Builders.* New Brunswick: Rutgers University Press.

Grant, Bruce
1993   Siberia Hot and Cold: Reconstructing the Image of Siberian Indigenous Peoples. In *Between Heaven and Hell: the Myth of Siberia in Russian Culture.* G. Diment and Y. Slezkine, eds. Pp. 227–53. New York: St. Martin's Press.
1995   *In the Soviet House of Culture. A Century of Perestroikas.* Princeton: Princeton University Press.

Gruber, Ruth
1939   *I Went to the Soviet Arctic.* New York: Simon and Schuster.

Jochelson, Waldemar
n.d.   *The Kamchadals.* Unpubl.manuscript. New York: New York Public Library, Manuscript Division.

Kahn, Miriam
1996   Sharing Emotional Landscapes in Wamira, Papua New Guinea. In *Senses of Place.* S. Feld and K.H. Basso, eds. Pp. 167–96. Santa Fe: School of American Research Press.

Petrasheva, Viktoria V., and David Koester, eds.
1997   *Khraniteli Rodovykh Ochagov - Vospominaniia i rasskazy.* New York - Petropavlovsk: Desktop publication.

Koester, David
n.d.   Globalization in Local Discourses of Justice and Need: the Itelmens of Kamchatka Write to the U.N. In review, typescript .

Kravchuk, I.
1992   Kto zhe razgadaet kommercheskie tainy? (Who Can Guess the Business Secrets?) In *Panorama.* Pp. 3. Palana.

Lukashkina, Tatiana P.
1991   *Skazki babushki Petrovny* (Tales of Grandmother Petrovna). Petropavlovsk-Kamchatskii: Kamshat.

Moiseev, Robert S.
1989   *Sotsial'no-ekonomicheskie problemy razvitiia narodnostei Severa* (Social-Economic Problems of the Development of Peoples of the North). Petropavlovsk: Dal'nevostochnoe knizhnoe isdatel'stvo.

Murashko, Olga A.
1996   Itel'meny i kamchadaly: metamorfozy etnicheskoy identichnosti (Itelmens and Kamchadals. The Metamorphoses of Ethnic Identity). In *Gumanitarnaia nauka v Rossii: Sorosovskie laureaty. Istoriia. Arkheologiia. Kul'turnaia Antropologiia i Etnografiia.* Pp. 358–77. Moscow: Mezhdunarodnyi nauchnyi fond Sorosa.
1997   Itelmens and Kamchadals: Marriage Patterns and Ethnic History. *Arctic Anthropology* 34(1):181–93.

Pika, Alexander, and Bruce Grant, eds.
1999   *Neotraditionalism in the Russian North: Indigenous Peoples and the Legacy of Perestroika.* Edmonton: Canadian Circumpolar Institute; Seattle: University of

Washington Press [Original Russian edition: Pika, Aleksandr I., and Boris B. Prokhorov, eds. *Neotraditsionalizm na Rossiiskom Severe*. 1994. Moscow: Institut narodno-khoziaistvennogo prognozirovanniia.

Rethmann, Petra
1997   Chto Delat'? Ethnography in the Post-Soviet Cultural Context. *American Anthropologist* 99(4):770–4.

Rosaldo, Renato
1980   *Ilongot Headhunting 1883–1974: A Study in Society and History*. Stanford: Stanford University Press.

Ryvkina, R. V., L. Ya. Kosals, and K. A. Kovalinka
1996   The Small Peoples of the Soviet North: Life in the Soviet Empire and Future Prospects. In *Anxious North*. A. Pika, J. Dahl, and I. Larsen, eds. Pp. 249–61. IWGIA Document, vol. 81. Copenhagen: IWGIA.

Starkova, Nadezhda K.
1976   *Itel'meny: Material'naia kul'tura XVIII v.—60-e gody XX v* (Itelmens: Material culture—18th century to the 1960s). Moscow: Nauka.

Steller, Georg Wilhelm
1996   [1774] *Beschreibung von dem Lande Kamtschatka*. Bonn: Holos Verlag.

Stroganova, E. A.
1997   Natsional'no-kul'turnoe vozrozhdenie v Buriatii: vzgliad iznutri sela (National and Cultural Revival in Buryatia: A View from Within the Rural Community). *Etnograficheskoe obozrenie* (1):86-99.

Suzdalova, Nelia
1993   *"Te sobach'i upriazhki umchalis'..."* (Those Dog Teams Sped off...). Petropavlovsk-Kamchatskii: Dal'nevostochnoe knizhnoe izdatel'stvo.

Trumbull, Nathaniel
1995   Komi's Patchwork Pipeline: The Crudest Method of Damage Control. *Surviving Together* 13(3):18–9.

Wachtel, Andrew Baruch
1990   *The Battle for Childhood: The Creation of a Russian Myth*. Stanford: Stanford University Press.

Wiget, Andrew, and Olga Balalaeva
1997   Saving Siberia's Khanty From Oil Development. *Surviving Together* 15(1):22–5.

Zaidfudim, P. Kh., et al.
1994   *Sotsial'naia reabilitatsiia naseleniia Severa Rossii* (Social Rehabilitation of the Population of the Russian North). Moskva: IVTs Marketing.

Zhirkov, Yakov Lvovich
1994   *Vospominaniia*. Kovran: Shkolnyi Muzei (recorded in 1993).

81/ King Island Iñupiat dancers perform in the Rotunda of the Smithsonian National Museum of Natural History at the opening of the "Crossroads of Continents" exhibit, September 1988. Photographer, Jeffrey Tinsley

part 4

CURATORS, COLLECTORS, AND CONSUMERS

81/ The Russian-American "Crossroads of Continents" exhibit team examines the Northwest Coast collections at the Museum of Anthropology and Ethnography in St. Petersburg (then Leningrad), Russia. Left to right: William Sturtevant (Smithsonian Institution), an unidentified Russian curator, Sergei Serov (1940–1992, Institute of Ethnography, Moscow), James VanStone (1925–2001, Field Museum), and Bill Holm (Burke Museum). Photographer, Jean-Loup Rousellot (ASC collection).

Heritage Anthropology in the "Jesup-2" Era:
Exploring North Pacific Cultures through Cooperative Research

WILLIAM W. FITZHUGH

In the late 1970s the Smithsonian's National Museum of Natural History and the Russian (then Soviet) Academy of Science's Institute of Ethnography began discussions that would lead to a new type of scholarly collaboration between anthropologists and museum researchers from the United States and the Soviet Union. This new approach followed decades of stagnant scholarly exchange and the first partially-successful re-start of Russian-American cooperation pioneered by field exchanges led by Alexei P. Okladnikov and William S. Laughlin in the Aleutian Islands in 1974 and in 1975 at Lake Baikal (Laughlin 1985). Focused on the politically sensitive lands on either side of Bering Strait, these discussions sought to advance Soviet-American scholarship on and knowledge of cultures and history, not only of the Beringian area, but of the larger relationships and cultural patterns of the entire Greater North Pacific Region (GNPR), the circum-North Pacific Rim, extending from the Island of Hokkaido in Asia to the Columbia River in North America.

Although the years preceding our efforts of the late 1970s had produced advances in anthropological knowledge of this region as a result of scholarly exchanges sponsored by the International Research and Exchange Board (IREX) (see Michael 1979; Michael and VanStone 1983), political difficulties with access to field opportunities and research collections required another venue if cooperation was to continue. The decision to proceed with studies of museum collections, whose trans-Beringian histories themselves required collaborative Soviet, Canadian, and American

scholarship, eventually lead to a major exhibition, *Crossroads of Continents: Cultures of Siberia and Alaska* (1988–92), and a series of related publications. It also offered a plausible option for the political stalemate that had developed in the 1970s during this final phase of the Cold War era over access for American researchers to field locations in northeastern Siberia, and for Soviet researchers in North America.

In the twenty years that followed the birth of the *Crossroads of Continents* project, a number of institutional and international initiatives were undertaken that provided momentum toward the Jesup Expedition Centennial years of 1997–2002. In addition to strengthening the exchange of information and researchers, and conducting joint projects of the sort pioneered by Franz Boas, these initiatives included museum collection study, traveling exhibits, media programs, and museum training. Perhaps even more important than scholarly development and public education needed for a strategically and economically important part of the world that was remarkably poorly known, was the engagement of Native peoples themselves in the research and public programs. By the end of the twentieth century it had become clear that Native involvement at all levels of the new cycle of research, collecting, archiving of cultural resources, and education was the essential new dimension of the Jesup Centennial era.

Very early in the project we envisioned the *Crossroads of Continents* exhibit and catalog as an effort to partially answer the scholarly need for the final "summary" volume of the Jesup Expedition publication series—a volume that Boas and his colleagues never produced (cf. Fitzhugh and Crowell 1988:15). The exhibit was also planned as a platform for a new cycle of comparative cultural studies and public programs that emerged from the *Crossroads* project to become the new *Jesup 2* program announced by the Arctic Studies Center in 1992 (Fitzhugh and Krupnik 1993, 1994, 2001; Fitzhugh 1996). In addition to new research and publications, *Jesup 2* called for making museum ethnographic collections and other cultural resources more widely available in Alaska (and, where possible, also in Siberia and the Russian Far East). It also advocated promoting traveling exhibits and Native participation in museum-based research and education through workshops and training programs.

The prospects and circumstances of *Jesup 2* are vastly different from those originally proposed for the original Jesup Expedition (or *Jesup 1*) venture. The primary goal of the JNPE was to build museum collections and conduct research on the origins and relationships of North Pacific peoples and cultures. While these goals are still important, an additional target for the next century must be the preservation of and shared access to cultural and linguistic heritage. As in the *Jesup*-era, museums must have a prominent role in this work, and values other than strictly academic ones must be promoted. It is for this reason that the focus of this paper is the past and future role of museums as trustees of the North Pacific heritage and cultural legacies. Museums whose roles have been confined previously to research and being trustees of cultural treasures must also become pro-active agents in the re-connection of "lost cultural treasures" with Native peoples in their homelands.

The Jesup North Pacific Expedition

The century since the Jesup North Pacific Expedition (1897–2002) has seen profound change to the cultures and peoples of the North Pacific region. On both sides of Bering Strait political, economic, and technological change has transformed Native lives, brought massive influxes of outsiders into previously autonomous ethnic territories, and imposed alien national structures on a diverse group of traditional societies. By the middle of the twentieth century, schools, hospitals, industrialization, militarism, and new ideologies had affected every Native person along the North Pacific Rim, from the Columbia River to Bering Strait to Hokkaido.

North Pacific peoples had much to lose in this encounter, which arrived in an overwhelming onslaught. On the Asian side, Native groups had been in contact with Europeans, directly or indirectly, since the early 1600s and with complex East Asian societies for many hundreds of years earlier. On the American side, contact with Europeans began abruptly in the mid-eighteenth century. Yet by 1900, peoples in both regions had undergone massive transformations that reached into almost every aspect of their cultures, from technology to ideology.

The discovery of these cultures and rich new lands amazed early explorers and propelled naturalists and anthropologists to seek answers about the origins and relationships between Alaskan and Siberian animals and peoples. The idea of studying Beringian relationships was not new to natural science. Biologists had expressed interest in the similarities and differences between American and Asian biota, and these questions had been a principal stimulus of the surveys organized by the Smithsonian's Spencer Baird in northwestern Canada and Alaska between 1857 and 1887 (Rivinus and Youssef 1992:81–97). Boas' paradigm of cross-field regional survey and synthesis marked a major advance over the descriptive science that had characterized research in this area previously (Fitzhugh 1982, 1994; Krupnik and Vakhtin, this volume). Although JNPE results failed to attain the theoretical goals of Boas' grand design, it produced masses of information about a crucial, previously unknown region, and its museum collections were a priceless benchmark and treasure-house for understanding GNPR cultures and heritage.

The Boasian paradigm laid the foundation for the development of anthropological science in North America and remains important today. Implicit was the belief that cultures could be *understood* by trained observers, and that their components (ethnology, language, archaeology, folklore, and human biology), separately and together, could be analyzed to produce an objective representation of cultures, history, and relationships. Although this view is still seen as the basis for much modern anthropology, post-modernist anthropology views this paradigm as partly flawed by Western-observer bias and adherence to a unified theory of culture. Today's anthropology, while anchored in empirical science, has been strengthened by multi-dimensional theory, Native science, and participation of indigenous peoples.

Boas and the Post-Jesup Research Agenda

The scholarly output of the JNPE appeared as a series of volumes and research papers for over four decades between 1898–1940 (see reviews in Krupnik and Fitzhugh 2001; Krupnik 1998, 2001). The principal and most substantive results were descriptive ethnographies and linguistic works. These volumes soon became the primary research documents on the cultures they described. For the non-Russian reading scholars of many Native Siberian groups they remained the only detailed scientific reports available on these peoples throughout most of the twentieth century. Even in North America, the reports produced under the Jesup Expedition banner by Boas, Teit, Swanton, and others remain the primary ethnographies for these Northwest Coast groups to this day. However, when one examines the origins of the JNPE venture, one confronts a clear disconnect between the theoretical problem focus of Boas' JNPE plan and its scholarly antecedents. The questions of trans-Beringian origins and relationships raised by Boas were not to be found in the descriptive earlier works of the 1800s, such as that of Veniaminov, Zagoskin,

and Edward Nelson in Alaska, and they are barely detectable in the less anthropological but nevertheless significant monographs by Krasheninnikov, Steller, and other naturalists and explorers of Siberia of the 1700s. While this is not the place for a detailed critique of the Jesup Expedition's accomplishments, it is worth noting that the genius of the *Jesup* program was in its conception as a research plan, in its detailed ethnography, and in its field collecting program, as reported elsewhere in this volume.

However, as an anthropological synthesis, JNPE also had serious shortcomings. For instance, by neglecting to incorporate results from the extensive earlier or contemporary research in Alaska that was conducted by Edward W. Nelson, Lucien Turner, George T. Emmons, John Murdoch, and others working for the Smithsonian, the cursory and relatively unsubstantiated attempts made by Boas to synthesize Jesup Expedition's results (Boas 1903, 1905, 1933) produced some glaring deficiencies. The most prominent was the re-affirmation of Boas' earlier pre-Jesup idea that Eskimo had been late arrivals on the North Pacific cultural scene from the Central Canadian Arctic (the so-called "Eskimo wedge" hypothesis – see Dumond, this volume).

Even though Boas and his collaborators failed to fulfill the interpretive potential of their project, the results of the JNPE stimulated further research on the North Pacific Native cultures and had a huge positive effect on the development of the twin fields of "Eskimology" and circumpolar studies. Throughout most of the twentieth century anthropologists and folklorists used JNPE data for studies of North Pacific, circumpolar, and hemispheric culture relationships. "Jesup cultures" were an important source of data for Hatt's (1914) studies of circumpolar clothing styles. Folklorists such as Hallowell (1926), Hatt (1949), and others utilized JNPE data for studies of comparative religion, mythology, and folklore. Jesup Expedition experiences and personal contacts encouraged Waldemar Jochelson to undertake later field research in the Aleutian Islands and Kamchatka (Jochelson 1925,1928,1933). It led another Jesup team-member, Waldemar Bogoras (1929) to write an important paper on circumpolar culture theory; and it led eventually to studies such as Sergei V. Ivanov's (1954) on Siberian representational art and Tamara Mitlyanskaya's (1996) on Chukchi folk art traditions.

From the archaeological perspective, it triggered a host of comparative archaeological work (Quimby 1947; de Laguna 1932, 1940) on Beringian prehistory, culminating with Leroi-Gourhan's (1946) ambitious study of North Pacific technology. The latter attempted to advance JNPE historical goals by a synthesis of ethnographic and archaeological evidence but only succeeded in demonstrating the inadequacy of un-controlled archaeological data. During this period more productive results in archaeology were being made by Collins (1937), Gjessing (1944), Spaulding (1946), Heizer (1956), Rudenko (1947/1961), Arutiunov and Sergeev (1969, 1975), and others who used detailed excavation techniques. It was here that real progress on the goals of Jesup Expedition were achieved, even though the results were painfully slow, due in part to the nature of archaeological research but primarily because of increasing political differences.

Fortunately, the other major legacy of the JNPE, the collections of objects, photographs, sound recordings, and ethnographic notes of the expedition, were being carefully maintained, primarily by the American Museum of Natural History in New York. Smaller "duplicate" collections of the materials that were gathered by Jochelson and Borogas were also shared with the Museum of Anthropology and Ethnology (MAE) in St. Petersburg, which already had a North Pacific collection of its own, with special strength in Russian America.

Exhibiting North Pacific Cultures

In Paris, Berlin, and Copenhagen, North Pacific eth-nographic materials had been displayed to the public for nearly two hundred years prior to the JNPE, but the resources were thin and documentation was poor.

More substantial North Pacific collections existed in St. Petersburg at the MAE (Dzeniskevich and Pavlinskaya 1988). Among these were the collections from Russian America made by Lavrentii Zagoskin and Il'ia Voznesenskii in the mid-1800s. The latter was of special value because a museum scientist who was attentive to careful documentation secured it. Arctic cultures had been displayed at the Smithsonian since the 1870s; but it was not until the 1890s that they began to be presented in depth (Fitzhugh 1997). The American Museum of Natural History (AMNH) in New York had few Northwest Coast or Alaskan collections and no large Siberian materials before 1890. The arrival of huge JNPE collections gave the American Museum a truly comprehensive resource for exhibiting North Pacific cultures (Kendall et al. 1997).

Unfortunately, like Boas' JNPE science plan, the Jesup Expedition collections never found a comprehensive exhibit outlet at the American Museum. Boas oversaw the installation of his famous "Northwest Coast Hall," but he and his successors never attempted to produce the exhibit of North Pacific peoples that should have been the logical outcome of the AMNH-financed JNPE program. The AMNH exhibition program remained locked into the schema of museum science that called for cultures to be displayed in their traditional hemispheric blocks: the Chukchi and Koryak were "Asian" peoples and were therefore exhibited with the Asian groups; while the Eskimo and Northwest Coast Indians were matched with other North American groups even though, in many ways, they were more 'Asian' than 'American.' Despite Boas' interest in trans-Beringian comparisons, Bering Strait remained the dividing point rather than the hinge for cultures of Asia and the Americas, conforming to the pre-existing geographi-cally-based classification system of anthropological museums. Of course, Boas' departure from the American Museum in 1905 to take a position at Columbia University made his contribution to these matters moot at best.

Science, Natives, and the American Public

Throughout most of the twentieth century, museum science followed the Boasian tradition. As personnel and financial support grew, Russian and North American researchers returned to the unfinished work of the JNPE, attempting to clarify the history of North Pacific cultures through archaeological, linguistic, and ethnohistorical studies. In this effort Native peoples became informants, field team-members, guides and navigators, and in a few cases joined the ranks of researchers or curators. During this period a culture of academic and museum science prevailed in northern research that divided Native communities in Siberia and North America from pursuit of cultural research in their own countries. Until the 1960s, scholars rarely consulted communities about research projects to be undertaken. Similarly, they rarely presented their results to local sponsors or made any special efforts to disseminate project materials among local audiences in ways that made it possible for Native people to study or use anthropological data that was collected by scientists. Research occurred mostly apart from community interests, and scientists rarely addressed local media and school or community meetings as venues for outreach, information sharing, and community participation.

In some cases alienation resulted from the growing commercial trade in antiquities. Archaeologists who had once purchased prize specimens from local collectors began to condemn "pot-hunting" and commercial digging, even after Native claim settlements had given Native people legal title to these resources. During the 1970s through 1990s, St. Lawrence Island became a prime location for the commercial market in artifacts, but other locations in the Beringian region also participated in the antiquities trade. Many sites were damaged or destroyed; those in Gambell, St Lawrence Island, were so devastated that they eventually were removed from the U.S. National Register of Historic Sites. Social damage was also caused by drugs and alcohol that came with the ivory and artifact trade. And with a relaxation of border control after 1990, digging for profit became a new quasi-condoned economy in Chukotka, and the lucrative Japanese and Euro-American art market resulted in smuggling through Nome and Gambell.

On the American side, the alienation of Native and non-Native northerners was rooted in a long tradition of top-down government policy-making. Examples abound: the BIA schooling system which denied Native language and culture; Aleut removal from Aleutian homelands in World War II; the 'near miss' of a "peaceful" atomic blast at Cape Thompson near Point Hope in northern Alaska in 1959 (O'Neil 1994); nuclear detonations on Amchitka Island in the late 1960s and early 1970s; loss of lands and resources to state and federal land-taking, etc. The passage of the Alaska Native Claims Settlement Act (ANCSA) in 1971 provided a measure of local control; but it was not until the 1980s and 1990s that legal mechanisms, government decentralization, and co-management strategies began to turn the tide, and scholars adopted formal ethical standards for social science research.

Culture offered one possible avenue for Native self-determination, but in anthropology and museum studies the system continued to be strongly stacked against Native interests. In Alaska, the collection of objects that had begun during the period of early exploring expeditions accelerated rapidly when Smithsonian Institution's naturalists began to take up residence after 1867. By the 1880s European collectors like Adrian Holmberg and James Lowther (Earl Lonsdale) were complaining that all of the choice material had already been collected and what remained was of poor quality and not fit for museums. The "rush" for the Northwest Coast collections has been well documented (Cole 1985). By 1900 most of the old objects from Alaska and the Northwest Coast were no longer in Native hands but in museum collections in Washington, New York, Chicago, Victoria, or in Europe. But there were some notable exceptions. Reverend

Sheldon Jackson built a local collection of Alaska artifacts during the decades after 1900 in Sitka, and a good regional collection grew following the establishment of the College (later, University of Alaska) in Fairbanks in the 1920s.

The situation was roughly similar in eastern Siberia, where systematic collecting began a bit later than in Alaska, during the 1890s, when Nikolai Gondatti made an excellent collection for the MAE from the Chukchi (Dzeniskevich and Pavlinskaya 1988). Only in a few instances were regional collections gathered and kept locally, for instance, by Vladimir K. Arseniev in the 1910s, in Khabarovsk and Vladivostok. However, most ethnographic and archaeological objects were sent back west to scientific centers far from their home territories. It was not until the 1970s that local voices began to be heard calling for the retention or return of cultural properties and the creation of local museums and culture centers. Of course, throughout much of the twentieth century both in Siberia and northwestern North America it was not the loss of collections that was the principal concern of Native peoples. Rather it was the loss of language, traditional religion, and economic and political independence that was the more direct threat to the existence of ethnic nationalities. In both cases these losses were different and had different causes and effects.

Soviet Cultural Policy

Many of these problems also existed in the Soviet Far East where, after the Russian Revolution in 1917, Native cultural policy was more codified (Slezkine 1994) than in the laissez-faire North American political and economic system. For the early Soviet social planners, which included Waldemar Bogoras, who became a powerful leader of the "Committee for the North," the preservation of culture, which was believed to be an essential element of ethnic nationality, was a high priority of the Socialist state. However, Native culture was far more often condemned as "primitive"

and illiterate—something to be exploited and replaced by modern social progress. For instance, incentives were put in place to encourage vegetable farming in Native communities in the 1930s and fox farming during the 1950s. Cultural education was taken on as a socialist task conducted through the so-called "Red Yaranga" system [a traveling educational and political team, using a Native skin-tent, *yaranga*, as its mobile headquaters—ed.].

As the Soviet system transformed itself into a more rigid authoritarian regime, Native cultural heritage became a state-defined and state-managed commodity, and its roots in local societies were severed. Small Native groups lost all hope of preserving their cultural traditions (Arutiunov and Vasiliev 1994; Sokolova 1994). Here, unlike in Alaska, language, culture, and history were offered in schools, but content was planned to support state-determined goals concerning the nature and content of new "socialist culture." Native dance companies were instructed to present traditional themes with formulaic Soviet music and choreography; Native writers whose work expressed Soviet political goals were promoted, and Native mythology was reduced to the quaint "fairy-tales" familiar in Russian literature.

Shamanism and other Native religions were officially repressed, considered being as socially dangerous as private ownership of reindeer by big herd-owners (*kulaks*). But in marked contrast to the theoretically "freer" political atmosphere in Alaska, which was, in fact, deadly to Native religious traditions; under the Soviet system, which was repressive to religion in general, traditional Native religious beliefs continued either underground or as a folk genre. Whereas Alaskan and Northwest Coast Native culture and religion were actively stamped out by entrepreneurial capitalism and the missionizing frenzy of the 1870s–90s in an effort to recast ethnic peoples into a Euro-American mold, Siberian Native "culture" was elevated in an attempt to create Soviet nationalities out of some tribal groups. This stands as one of the defining distinctions between the two political systems in their relations with their respective ethnic populations.

Full Circle: *Crossroads* at the "Crossroads"

My personal journey to the Beringian crossroads began in the mid-1970s, when my studies of culture history and prehistoric human-environmental interactions in Labrador broadened into cross-cultural work on northern maritime cultures. As organizer of a symposium on "Prehistoric Maritime Adaptations of the Circumpolar Zone" for the 9th International Congress of Anthropological and Ethnological Sciences in Chicago in 1973, and editor of the ensuing volume (Fitzhugh 1975), I met some of the Russian archaeologists working in the North Pacific, including Sergei Arutiunov, Valerii Alexeev, and Ruslan Vasil'evskii, as well as many American scholars working in Alaska, including Don Dumond, Christy Turner, Robert Ackerman, Allen McCartney, and others. Shortly afterwards, as Arctic curator at the National Museum of Natural History, I became intrigued by the potential of the Smithsonian's large, under-utilized Arctic ethnographic collections for research and public education. Working with Susan Kaplan, then on a post-doctoral position at the Smithsonian, I explored the phenomenal collections from Western Alaska acquired by Edward W. Nelson in 1877–81. This resulted in our joint exhibit and catalog, *Inua: Spirit World of the Bering Sea Eskimo* (Fitzhugh and Kaplan 1982), for which Ron Senungetuk, an Iñupiat artist from Wales, Alaska, provided assistance. Later, to reach the rural audience in Alaska, I also assembled a smaller ('mini-Inua') traveling version which traveled to villages in Alaska, Canada, and Greenland in 1983–87 (Fitzhugh and Kaplan 1983). Susan Rowley later organized an USIA-sponsored version of this exhibit ('Euro-Inua') which toured to Eastern and Northern Europe in 1988. The experience with these projects revealed a strong and growing interest among Alaskans to be reconnected with their "lost heritage" that had been squirreled away in the Smithsonian's attic for more than a century. It was obvious that more

was needed than simply re-issuing modern reprints of Edward Nelson's and John Murdoch's old ethnographies (Nelson 1983; Murdoch 1988); Native communities were looking for a more palpable connection with the material and archival remains of their ancestors.

An opportunity to expand this program of 'heritage re-connection' appeared most unexpectedly when William C. Sturtevant and I began to take part in cultural exchanges between American and Russian anthropologists being organized by the International Research and Exchanges Board (IREX) during the 1970s. Initially these exchanges had been planned to familiarize scholars with research data resulting from a generation of anthropological studies on both sides of Bering Strait. Some of these projects had produced revolutionary results, especially in archaeology (Arutiunov and Sergeev 1969, 1975; Collins 1937, 1951; Larsen and Rainey 1948; Giddings 1967; Rudenko 1961). Intense interest also existed in areas of physical anthropology, linguistics, ethnology, and folklore. After a few years during which several symposia were arranged by IREX (Michael 1979; Michael and VanStone 1983), frustration had begun to grow due to the lack of progress on the one goal that eluded researchers from both sides: inability to gain permission to visit field sites and Native-populated regions across what had by this time become a heavily militarized frontier. The only positive results had been a series of exchanges led by A. P. Okladnikov and W. S. Laughlin that unfortunately were extremely limited in scope (Laughlin 1985).

In 1978 the author and William C. Sturtevant proposed a new approach to the late Julian Bromley, then Director of the Soviet Institute of Ethnography. Why not develop, we suggested to the Russians, a type of Beringia-focused collaboration that would not be so politically sensitive? Such a program might foster joint studies of ethnographic and cultural materials that would have institutional goals that were broader than the scholarly objectives of individual anthropologists. Why not design and produce a major joint

Soviet-American museum exhibition featuring traditional cultures of the Native peoples on both sides of the North Pacific? Such a study would incorporate the interests of Soviet and American scholars in gaining access to previously unstudied collections with a specific, highly visible outcome. The Russians, who were then eager for travel and research opportunities in North America, could study the early collections of Siberian peoples gathered by the Jesup Expedition and housed in the American Museum of Natural History in New York. The Americans, in return, could gain experience with Soviet anthropology and study the large collections of Alaskan and Russian–American objects that dated several decades earlier than any other systematic collections available from these regions in Western museums. After the many deadlocked disputes over field access, the Russians found this idea a most welcome shift of focus.

For the next nine years (1978–87), teams of Soviet and American scholars met periodically under the auspices of IREX to plan a project that in the best meaning of cultural exchange accomplished much more than create an exhibition. In reality, "Crossroads of Continents" proved to be an effective research and education venture that served as an ideal bridge during the difficult transitional period in Soviet-American relations in the last phase of the Cold War, from the late 1970s to 1990. In addition to providing for the continuation of scholarly exchanges, it highlighted the achievements and shared history of Native cultures in portions of North America and Eurasia that had been engaged in contacts and exchanges for thousands of years, beginning with the peopling of the New World. It also happened that the project content had a highly symbolic political message as our respective countries were groping toward rapprochement.

For this reason, although we were careful to keep the exhibition from straying into dangerous political waters, the planning of the exhibition nevertheless was a political process, including the acceptance of its title. From the North American side, Americans and

Canadians immediately accepted "Crossroads" as the central theme. On the Soviet side, however, there was some concern that the use of a title that implied open borders until the twentieth century would only accentuate the darker realities of the Soviet period.

A further concern of Soviet officialdom was the desire of American and Canadian curators to include the Ainu people of Sakhalin, the Kuriles, and Hokkaido to the list of Native cultures of the North Pacific to be exhibited. Yes, all parties agreed that the Ainu were to be considered as culturally affiliated to North Pacific indigenous peoples; nevertheless the Russian side refused to condone their inclusion as this would lead to "political problems" connected with the Soviet expulsion of the Ainu from Sakhalin in 1946 and the taking of the southern Kurile Islands from Japan in 1945. As the Soviet side expressed it, the Ainu were "barely touched" by the Jesup Expedition, and since the JNPE had become the historical bedrock for Crossroads, it was not appropriate to include the Ainu. Faced with adamant opposition, we retreated, realizing also that our officially bilateral project, though operationally trilateral due to Canadian collaboration, could not accommodate further organizational complexity with the inclusion of Japanese partners. As it happened, we were able to fill the cultural gap in our coverage of North Pacific peoples in "Crossroads" several years later by organizing a special Ainu exhibition and catalog (Fitzhugh and Dubreuil 1999).

With these hurdles crossed, in 1979 William Sturtevant and I prepared a proposal that outlined the exhibition project and themes. Initially, the plan was received positively by the Russian Academy of Science, but in 1980, discussions broke off for a year during the period of the Soviet invasion of Afghanistan. New proposals were submitted in 1981 and in the fall of 1982 a delegation of ethnologists from the Institute of Ethnography including Sergei Arutiunov, Vladimir Vasil'ev, and Ilya Gurvich came to inspect Siberian collections at the Smithsonian and the Jesup

Expedition collections and archives at the American Museum of Natural History. This was followed in 1983 by a reciprocal visit of North American curators including William Sturtevant, Bill Holm, George and Joan MacDonald, William Fitzhugh, and James VanStone (Figs. 81, 82, and 87), to study collections in Moscow and Leningrad. It was at this time that George MacDonald, then Director of the Canadian Museum of Civilization in Ottawa, suggested we title the exhibition "Crossroads of Continents."

The Russian team made two more visits to the States in 1984 and during the second meeting in December 1984 made a careful evaluation of the AMNH Siberian collections. This institution turned out to be steadfast partner as these exchanges unfolded. The legacy of the Jesup Expedition could not have been more unstintingly fulfilled by the AMNH administration, curators, collections, and archival staff (and eventually, their exhibition and educational programs) as we began the hard work of resurrecting the Jesup collections from storage and presenting them for research and to the public.[1]

During the Crossroads project these exchanges, on both sides, were funded for the duration of the project by IREX and were managed by Dr. Wesley Fisher and his staff. We also began to receive grants from the Smithsonian's Special Exhibition Fund and in 1986 a formal protocol agreement was signed by both sides that stipulated that the Smithsonian's National Museum of Natural History would mount the show and the Smithsonian's Traveling Exhibition Service (SITES) would travel it to five venues in North America. April 1986 found the exhibition team and conservator Vera Espinola in the Soviet Union to make the final selections of objects, all of which were to come from the collections at the Museum of Anthropology and Ethnography (Kunstkamera) in Leningrad, then the part of the Academy of Sciences' Institute of Ethnography structure. Aron Crowell and Valérie Chaussonnet joined the American curatorial team, and the late Russian Americanist, Sergei Serov (1940–92), was designated Crossroads project coordinator for the Soviet side (Fig. 86). Sergei Arutiunov and I were the respective project directors for the Soviet and North American teams.

In the fall of 1986 the Soviet group returned to the United States to make the selection of objects from the Siberian collections at AMNH. The final hurdle in securing Soviet permission so that their artifacts could come to North America was a serious disagreement that developed over the issue of reciprocity. During the project's development it had always been understood that the exhibit would be produced in Washington and after the North American tour would travel to the Soviet Union. However, at the last minute Soviet authorities disavowed this understanding and declared that there could be no Soviet tour because the Russian Ministry of Culture, whose museums were the only possible sites for exhibiting *Crossroads*, had not participated in the project's development, and resented the opportunities garnered by the Russian Academy of Sciences in this process. At the last minute, in mid-1987 the impasse was bridged by high-level American diplomacy with the-then Soviet chief leader Mikhail Gorbachev, that required the Soviet Ministry of Culture and Russian Academy of Sciences to come to an agreement on budgets, space, and scholarly travel. With these hurdles cleared—at least on paper—the production of a catalog began, the MAE collections were sent to the Smithsonian, and plans were made for a major scholarly symposium to take place at the time of the opening.

Crossroads of Continents: Cultures of Siberia and Alaska opened on September 18th, 1988, at the Smithsonian's National Museum of Natural History in Washington, DC (Fig. 80). Emphasizing cultural diversity but also featuring historical trends and comparisons, the exhibition succeeded in demonstrating the long history and complex developments across this continental divide. It educated North Americans about the Native peoples of a part of the world that was hardly known to them, and it demonstrated both the shared history of its peoples and the need for scientific collaboration in its modern anthropological study. It also conveyed the message that the political barriers that had been erected at Bering Strait during the twentieth century were anomalous in the longer history of cultural contacts across this crossroads region. After the Smithsonian venue, the exhibition traveled for four years to the American Museum of Natural History in New York City, the Seattle Center, the Anchorage Museum of History and Art, the Eideljorg Museum in Indianapolis, the Roy Rogers Museum in Los Angeles, and the Canadian Museum of Civilization in Ottawa, ending in 1992 (Fig. 85). Hundreds of thousands of visitors saw the exhibition, and more than 100,000 catalogs were distributed.

During the course of the tour, a large number of Russian scholars visited the United States and Canada where they lectured, instructed docents, and conducted research. Many of these venues organized scholarly symposia, which were attended by Russians and American scientists. Although the exhibit had been developed primarily by ethnologists from the Institute of Ethnography's Moscow headquarters, a number of curators from the venerable Museum of Anthropology and Ethnology (Peter the Great Museum, or Kunstkamera) in St. Petersburg were able to visit North America. Many Americans met the first Russians they ever knew through these exchanges and formed new impressions about Russians that were quite different from the image of the Cold War Soviets derived from the American Government and media.

"Big" ("*Bolshoi*") Crossroads was a product of the central institutes and museums, and their scholars and curators. Sergei Arutiunov and Sergei Serov (Fig. 86) from the Institute of Ethnography directed the Soviet component from Moscow. The St. Petersburg (then Leningrad) MAE supplied collections but took a smaller role in planning although its curators participated in the catalog and the North American tour. For many unfortunate reasons (timing, place, poli-

tics, etc.), Native participation in the curatorial work and exchanges on both sides was almost nil.

When the Soviet system collapsed in 1991–2, our plan for a reciprocal tour in Russia met the same fate as the Soviet government. The administration of the Institute of Ethnography and its parent Academy of Sciences had no financial resources for supporting the tour, especially given the uncooperative attitude of the Ministry of Culture. Not having benefited from the planning phase and the U.S. tour, the new Russian Ministry of Culture (the heir of the former Soviet Ministry) had no interest in providing an internal platform in Russia for an exhibit organized by a bureaucratic rival, the Academy of Sciences. Corporate sponsors were nowhere to be found, and costs of transport and security within the new Russia had become prohibitive. SITES and the Smithsonian concluded that the exhibition could not be sent to Russia. IREX was unwilling to honor the agreements we had signed with the old Soviet authorities, and the reciprocal opportunities for research and scholarly exchange that Americans had hoped to reap from the reciprocal tour of the exhibition in Russia were irrevocably lost . Although this was a painful development, most people agreed that the benefits of the North American tour had been considerable and that much good had come from the extensive contacts with Russian scholars in America. The project officially ended in 1992 and the Russian objects were shipped back to Russia after the exhibit's last venue in Ottawa.

"Mini-*Crossroads*" in Alaska and Siberia

The collapse of the Russian tour made it impossible for us to gain national exposure for our joint efforts in Russia. But it did not diminish our interest in having the 'Crossroads' message heard there, especially in the Russian Far East. Our previous experience touring a small version of the *Inua* exhibit in Alaska during the 1980s suggested that a "mini-Crossroads" exhibit might also be feasible in the Russian Far East. For this project we intended to rectify two glaring omissions of the

"Big Crossroads" project: failure to involve Native collaborators and to have the show presented in local museums in Native North Pacific homelands.

Crossroads Siberia/Alaska (or 'Mini-Crossroads,' as we generally called this new project) was launched for the special purpose of presenting "Crossroads" themes of cultural interactions and mutual influences across the North Pacific to local audiences in Alaska and the Russian Far East. As such, it carried forward the project begun by Boas and the Jesup North Pacific Expedition, bringing Jesup and subsequent results on North Pacific cultural heritage back to the peoples of this region. Unfortunately, the task of bringing Native people into the dialog about preservation, origins, and enhancement of their cultures had never been on the original expedition's agenda, framed as it was under the paradigms of "salvage museum anthropology" of the late 1800s. In keeping with this declared goal of the new project, several Alaskan scholars and Native cultural experts were invited to write sections of a new exhibit catalog featuring Alaska Native cultures (see Chaussonnet 1995). The list of contributors included Jana Harcharek from Barrow, Rachael Craig from Kotzebue, Larry Kairaiuak and Darlene Orr from Nome, Gordon Pullar and Richard Knecht from Kodiak and Anchorage, Barbara Svarny Carlson from the Aleutians, Melinda Chase, Miranda Wright, and Bernice Joseph from interior Alaska, and Nora Marks Dauenhauer and Richard Dauenhauer from Juneau. In addition to objects selected from the Smithsonian, we also chose collections from local Alaskan museums. Incorporation of Russian Far East materials and curators was more complex and was accomplished by a tour of regional museums in the Russian Far East during March of 1990, funded by the Smithsonian, the Alaska Humanities Forum, and the Alaska State Council on the Arts. The research team that visited the Russian Far East included Valérie Chaussonnet, William Fitzhugh, the late Richard Jordan, James Dixon, Roger Powers, and Darlene Orr (Fitzhugh 1995:6–7; Fig. 89).

This amazing trip from the Bering Strait to Vladivostok took place during a time of *glasnost* and *perestroika* during the last years of the old Soviet Union and was organized by Valerii Shubin of the Sakhalin Regional Museum in Yuzhno-Sakhalinsk. Much of its cost was borne by that institution and others along our route. The tour gave us a first-hand look at regional museums and their collections in Provideniya, Anadyr, Khabarovsk, Vladivostok, Yuzhno-Sakhalinsk, Novosibirsk, and Magadan. We were the first Western anthropologists to visit some of these museums, and Vladivostok was then still a closed city to outsiders. Typically, we met curators, cultural experts, and local officials, but few Native people. We found every institution willing to loan objects and expertise and willing to take part in the 'mini-Crossroads' Far Eastern tour. Valerii Shubin and his museum's Director, Vladislav M. Latyshev, offered to coordinate the planning and assemble Siberian collections.

In the end, Provideniya, Anadyr, and Novosibirsk were unable to participate in the mini-Crossroads' project; but collections were assembled from local museums in Magadan, Petropavlovsk, Khabarovsk, Vladivostok, and Yuzhno-Sakhalinsk. Two years later the late Nikolai N. Dikov of the Magadan Northeast Research Institute brought these materials to Alaska., in his hand luggage, considering it prudent—indeed, 'customary' by Russian standards—not to inform U.S. Customs. The American collections were assembled from the University of Alaska Museum in Fairbanks, the Kodiak Area Native Association in Kodiak, and the Smithsonian's National Museum of Natural History and National Museum of the American Indian. The Smithsonian, NSF, NEH, National Park Service, and other organizations financed the traveling exhibition.

The exhibit was curated magnificently by Valérie Chaussonnet in 1994 and toured to fifteen regional museums and culture centers in Alaska under the guidance of local organizer Jean Flanagan Carlo between 1994–6. These museums included almost every regional center in Alaska, such as Barrow, Nome, Bethel, Sitka,

Kodiak, Juneau, Fairbanks, Anchorage, Homer, Ketchikan, and others. A beautiful catalog was also issued (Chaussonnet 1995). The exhibit itself had a huge impact on Native Alaska. During various phases of production and the Alaskan tour we hosted several Russian colleagues in Washington and in Alaska.

The lessons of *Crossroads Alaska* were evident in the tremendous response given to this exhibit as it traveled from town to town in Alaska. In the decade since the 'mini-Inua' tour of the 1980s we had learned more about how to package small traveling shows, especially about the need for curricula development, school tours, tours for children given by elders, education resource kits, and the importance of visual resources like photographic albums and videos. The energy of a local tour coordinator was crucial for raising local and national funding for education components and for local coordination. Terry Dickey, Wanda Chin, Leonard Kammerling, and other staff of the University of Alaska Museum in Fairbanks assisted us masterfully in these areas.

We also learned that small exhibits (if one can call twenty-five large bright purple crates a small exhibit package!) could safely be shipped around Alaska in any season if the artifacts are selected for this task, are permanently installed in climatically-buffered cases, and are given careful conservation monitoring). There is no reason why such traveling exhibits cannot safely be presented in any place in the North. Given careful planning, issues of object security can be met even under rigorous conditions of northern environments. Unfortunately we also discovered that touring small exhibits in this manner is also very expensive: *Crossroads Alaska/Siberia* cost more than $500,000 to produce and circulate in Alaska alone. Reports of this tour are found in various issues of the *Arctic Studies Center Newsletter* for the years 1994 to 1997.

With this experience in Alaska the Arctic Studies Center organized the next 'mini-Crossroads' tour—this time in the Russian Far East, in 1996–7. This project was undertaken by Igor Krupnik, who began the planning effort with the Russian Institute for the Cultural and Natural Heritage in Moscow through the generous assistance of its Director, Yurii Vedenin, and Assistance Director, Pavel Shulgin. However, following a highly successful planning meeting of regional museum directors in early 1997 in Khabarovsk, hosted by Nikolai Ruban, Director of the Khabarovsk Regional Museum, the tour quickly became an Arctic Studies Center-Russian Far East enterprise, with venues planned at Khabarovsk, Blagoveshchensk, Vladivostok, and Yuzhno-Sakhalinsk. Krupnik directed the primary organizing group with assistance from Deborah Hull-Walski and Greta Hansen of the Smithsonian's Anthropology collection staff, and the Arctic Studies Center's Anne Stone. The primary collaborators on the Russian Far East side included Nikolai Ruban (assisted by Dr. Anna Ponomareva, Khabarovsk Museum chief Ethnography Curator) and Vladislav Latyshev, Director of the Yuzhno-Sakhalinsk Regional Museum. Olga Shubina, of this latter museum, took on the extremely important and difficult role of Russian tour coordinator, and performed miracles to ensure the safety of the collections. This project, which to my knowledge was the first traveling exhibition to tour in the Russian Far East, quickly revealed the great potential as well as the pitfalls of a regional approach to exhibition sharing and museum-based education in this region. The problems were many. Besides the obvious lack of funds, there was a critical shortage of Native participation and 'Native voice' in the Russian tour planning and in public education and museum programs. A Native-based cultural agenda was much less important in the local museums' agendas than appealing to the general Russian public, and the exhibit was often presented with only token involvement of local Native cultural leaders, limited to the opening public ceremonies. Whereas our local Russian partners were not always able to match the full scale of educational programming plan we had mounted in Alaska, the 'mini-Crossroads' experience implanted models for future development of these concepts. Perhaps most importantly, the exhibition familiarized Russian museum curators with conservation requirements, installation technology, and educational programming that will be useful in future efforts (Figs. 90, 91). Our Russian partners did a masterful job protecting and traveling the exhibit and, not the least, raising local funds for its transport and care. Other than the crucial payment of the exhibition's insurance bill by the Russian Ministry of Culture, the entire tour was locally supported.

Our part, to get the exhibition cases and objects to Russia and to get the North American collections home cost a mere $50,000! Igor Krupnik deserves great credit for editing the Russian language version of the catalog (Krupnik 1996), for courting the support of the Russian Ministry of Culture, for successfully arranging for the catalog's printing by the United States Information Agency, and for managing the entire tour process by phone and fax. Among Krupnik's contributions was his success in securing Russian Native authors for the Russian language catalog, including Vladimir Etylen and Tatyana Achirgina-Arsyak from Anadyr, Valentina Dedyk-Ivkavav from Palana, Tasyan Tein from Magadan, Lyudmila Ainana from Provideniya, Anatoly Alexeev from Yakutsk, Nadezhda Laigun from Yuzhno-Sakhalinsk, Nadezhda Kimonko, Antonina Kile, Valentina Samar, and Valentina Fedorova-Diatala from Khabarovsk and the Amur River region. This was the first time—at least, to my knowledge—that Native people from both sides of the North Pacific were able to present their respective cultures under one cover and with a similar format. Looking back one can truly say that accomplishing the Russian Far East tour was a minor miracle, to the great credit of Olga Shubina and her colleagues, Igor Krupnik, and the Smithsonian staff.

Siberian Museums and Native Peoples

In addition to its role in regional cultural education, *Crossroads Alaska/Siberia* provided curators from Siberia and Alaska with opportunities to exchange visits, meet Native groups, study collections, and learn each others' museums. As mentioned above, the process started in 1990 when a team of American curators was able to visit several Russian Siberian museums from Provideniya to Vladivostok to Novosibirsk. This trip gave us a glimpse of provincial Russian museums at an historic turning point in Soviet/Russian history, and we found them, like the rest of Russia at that time, in the midst of self-examination and renewal. Most of the old system and institutional architecture prevailed, but curators and directors were searching for new directions. All were interested in collaborating with a traveling version of *Crossroads* even though few people in these areas of Russia had ever heard of the larger Crossroads show or seen its catalog.

Most important, the regional museum system at that time was still part of the bigger cultural program of the Soviet State. Unlike Alaska and the Northwest Coast, where museums functioned in more diverse, informal, entrepreneurial ways, Soviet regional museums received state support and were seen as important educational institutions that purveyed state-sanctioned knowledge. Budgets were modest but assured, and directors and curators concentrated on collecting and archiving cultural materials, conducting research, and producing exhibits, local publications, and education pamphlets. Regional museums always had three internal departments with three corresponding exhibit sections: natural science, pre-Soviet history, and Soviet history. Since ethnography and archaeology were always relegated to the "pre-Soviet" history, Native culture, as far as museums were concerned, officially was not a part of modern life or of its museum displays. Russian Far East regional museums sponsored substantial archaeological and ethnographic research in their local areas and were often the designated repositories for these projects. Over time local Siberian museums came to possess important research collections.

As progressive as this structure was compared to the United States Government's seemingly dedicated aversion to cultural education, Soviet Native people were rarely appointed to positions of authority in Soviet regional museums. During the Soviet era regional museums usually followed policies determined by the local Communist Party line. Even during the *Glasnost* times, the situation we observed was largely the same as that described for the previous Soviet period in the Russian Far East. Museums had opened exhibits on the atrocities of the old regime, but Native voices were almost non-existent, and exhibits of Native culture were exhibits *of* Native culture rather than exhibits *by* or *with* Native people. These observations of the 1990 tour may be now obsolete, as by the time Laurel Kendall and Alexia Bloch visited some of the same museums in 1998, local conditions had changed markedly (Kendall and Bloch n.d.). Budgets were cut significantly and money was scarce everywhere; but many programs were blooming with local support.

Overall, one might say that during the past century Native cultures maintained themselves at roughly comparable levels across the North Pacific Region. While North American Natives never experienced Stalin's murderous purges and police state repression, they suffered greatly from official neglect and from loss of lands and subsistence resources. They found their cultures and languages ridiculed and repressed by the dominant majority, and in many places they often occupied a comparable position with their Siberian counterparts at the bottom of the local economic and social ladder. Where Soviet Native peoples had their cultures artificially controlled and were forced into Soviet modes of behavior, American Natives had their cultures trampled by private industry and government, and lost much to disease, alcohol, and poverty, as also was the case in Siberia.

Thus, by 1990, Native cultures in the Russian Far East suffered both the continued repression of the Soviet past as well as the crushing weight of a struggling economy, in which local people were frequently impoverished outsiders. Unfortunately, Soviet museum policy did nothing to help Native people maintain their culture anymore than the government helped them maintain a voice in local affairs. By this time in Alaska, cultural programming and revitalization had surged forward during the twenty years since the Alaska Native Claims Settlement Act had opened the way toward more intensive resource development and Native "corporate" independence. Although Native Alaskan cultural life and its museum expressions then, as today, was far from being a "bed of roses," significant strides had been made in self-determination and economic independence. Fortunately, there are indications that the situation in Siberia is now also improving for its Native people, at least as far as the preservation and documentation of their cultures is concerned.

Heritage Anthropology: Past and Future

Over the past twenty-five years, since the Arctic Studies Center began producing museum-based outreach programs, the importance of reconnecting cultural heritage materials gathered and preserved in museums with ongoing living traditions has become a surprising new and revitalizing force in museum anthropology. Institutions whose *raison d'etre* since their founding more than one hundred years ago had been to collect vanishing cultures and educate or entertain the public have had their missions deeply transformed. Academic scholars and museum curators have discovered that the world [out there] has dimensions not conceived of by the founders who charted anthropological and museum research for the past century. The discovery that these collections could be useful for more than simply preserving the remains of cultures being absorbed into the mainstream of society or for scientific studies of human history has been a surprising revelation to a field that has prided itself on understanding and serving its constituents and its audience.

For years that audience has consisted of museum visitors and other scholars who used museum collections and archival materials for generally altruistic goals of entertainment, appreciation, research, and erudition. Now, within the span of little more than a decade, a new pulsing vein of culture and tradition has become evident, arising not in the sometimes dowdy halls of museums and curators' stalls but in the reconnection between museum objects and records and the people from whom they originated. Somehow, most of the societies and cultures that had become the targets of salvage anthropology—at least, in the North—have survived the twentieth century and have emerged with a passion to re-invigorate their heritage and to learn from or absorb parts of their past into their modern lives.

The history of anthropology and museum collecting in the North Pacific during the past century provides a striking panorama of the forces that have shaped cultural studies and the use of cultural materials. Unlike most other areas of the world where complex societies had already heavily impacted traditional life, cultures of the North Pacific in the late nineteenth century were still largely intact. Here the past 100 years of change has been paralleled by a remarkable record of anthropological and museum-based documentation. Few areas of the world are so well represented in terms of material cultural and historical records.

During the century since the Jesup Expedition teams surveyed the North Pacific, anthropology and museum studies have come full-circle, with Native peoples emerging to reclaim their stake in their heritage and in this process. This transition went through several stages: from the "salvage documentation" of the vestiges of traditional cultures for purely historical and academic reasons (as practiced by Boas); to the "pro-activist ethnography and cultural construction" by government-employed scholars of the early Soviet era (initiated by Bogoras); to the purely scientific investigations of cultural origins as practiced by scholars like Henry Collins, Frederica de Laguna, and Sergei Rudenko; to the more reflexive museum and publication projects of the late 1900s, like *Inua: Spirit World of the Bering Sea Eskimo, Crossroads of Continents* and its 'mini-Crossroads' versions, *Chiefly Feasts: The Enduring Kwakiutl Potlatch* (Jonaitis 1991), *The Living Tradition of Yup'ik Masks: Agayuliyararput — Our Way of Making Prayers* (Fienup-Riordan 1996), and *Looking Both Ways: Heritage and Identity of the Alutiiq People* (Crowell, Steffian, and Pullar 2001). Today the peoples of these regions, as elsewhere, are rediscovering their past and are finding materials that inspire their future. This is the real and lasting legacy of the Jesup Expedition. The re-establishment of the connection between culture-bearers and their museum and archival heritage is emerging as a powerful new force that re-purposes museums and opens new responsibilities for curators and their new local constituencies.

Facing a paradigm shift that also includes the politics of repatriation, museum workers need to reassess their goals and methods of operation. While the outcomes are not clear, new technologies, especially the Internet, imaging, and information technologies offer powerful new tools for bringing museum treasures out of the archives and back into the mainstream of Native life and to the many other audiences seeking enrichment with cultural heritage materials. Programs of this new era, like the evolving permutations of the "Crossroads of Continents" program, have helped re-chart the route and find new partners. The original Jesup Expedition was instrumental in this effort, and I imagine Boas might not have been displeased to see the results of this new kind of museum anthropology that brings collections and Native peoples together again across Bering Strait after having drifted so far apart during the intervening century.

Notes

1. As it turned out, AMNH support for Russian and Native Siberian researchers who were studying these collections was to extend many years into the future, culminating in efforts that lead to the Jesup Expedition Centennial conference of 1997 and this publication.

References

Arutiunov, Sergei A., and Dorian A. Sergeev

1969   *Drevnie kul'tury aziatskikh eskimosov. Uelenskii mogil'nik* (Ancient Cultures of the Bering Sea Eskimos. The Uelen Cemetery). Moscow: Nauka Publishers.

1975   *Problemy etnicheskoi istorii Beringomor'ia. Ekvenskii mogil'nik.* (Issues in Ethnic History of the Bering Sea Region. The Ekven Cemetery). Moscow: Nauka Publishers.

Boas, Franz

1903   The Jesup North Pacific Expedition. *American Museum Journal* 3(5):72–119.

1905   The Jesup North Pacific Expedition. In *International Congress of Americanists, 13th Session, Held in New York in 1902.* Pp. 91–100. Easton, PA: Eschenbach.

1933   Relationship between North-West America and North-East Asia. In *The American Aborigines: Their Origin and Antiquity.* Diamond Jenness, ed. Pp. 357–70. Toronto: University of Toronto Press.

Bogoras, Waldemar

1929   Elements of the Culture of the Circumpolar Zone. *American Anthropologist* 31(4):579–601.

Chaussonnet, Valérie, ed.

1995   *Crossroads Alaska. Native Cultures of Alaska and Siberia.* Washington, DC: Arctic Studies Center.

Cole, Douglas

1985   *Captured Heritage. The Scramble for Northwest Coast Artifacts.* Norman: University of Oklahoma Press.

Collins, Henry B.

1937   Archeology of St. Lawrence Island, Alaska. *Smithsonian Miscellaneous Collections* 96(1). Washington, DC.

1951   The Origin and the Antiquity of the Eskimo. *Annual Report of the Smithsonian Institution for 1950.* Pp. 423–67. Washington, DC.

Crowell, Aron, Amy Steffian, and Gordon Pullar, eds.

2001   *Looking Both Ways: Heritage and Identity of the Alutiiq People.* Fairbanks: University of Alaska Press.

De Laguna, Frederica

1932   A Comparison of Eskimo and Paleolithic Art. *American Journal of Archaeology* 36(4):477–511; 37(1):77–107.

1940   Eskimo Lamps and Pots. *Journal of the Royal Anthropological Institute of Great Britain and Ireland* 70(1):53–76.

Dzeniskevich, Galina I., and Lyudmila Pavlinskaya

1988   Treasures by the Neva: The Russian Collections. In *Crossroads of Continents. Cultures of Siberia and Alaska.* William W. Fitzhugh and Aron Crowell, eds. Pp. 83–8. Washington, DC: Smithsonian Institution Press.

Fienup-Riordan, Ann

1996   *The Living Tradition of Yup'ik Masks: Agayuliyararput — Our Way of Making Prayers.* Seattle: University of Washington Press.

Fitzhugh, William W.

1994   Crossroads of Continents: Review and Prospect. In *Anthropology of the North Pacific Rim.* William W. Fitzhugh and Valérie Chaussonnet, eds. Pp. 27–52. Washington, DC: Smithsonian Institution Press.

1995   Preface. In *Crossroads Alaska. Native Cultures of Alaska and Siberia.* Valérie Chaussonnet, ed. Pp. 6–7. Washington, DC: Arctic Studies Center.

1996   Jesup II: Anthropology of the North Pacific. *Northern Notes* 4:41–62. Hanover, NH.

1997   Ambassadors in Sealskins: Exhibiting Eskimos at the Smithsonian. In: *Exhibiting Dilemmas: Issues of Representation at the Smithsonian.* Amy Henderson and Adrienne Kaeppler, eds. Pp. 206–45. Washington, DC: Smithsonian Institution Press.

Fitzhugh, William W., and Aron Crowell, eds.

1988   *Crossroads of Continents: Cultures of Siberia and Alaska.* Washington, DC: Smithsonian Institution Press.

Fitzhugh, William W., and Chisato Dubreuil, eds.

1999   *Ainu: Spirit of a Northern People.* Washington, DC: Arctic Studies Center, National Museum of Natural History; Seattle: University of Washington Press.

Fitzhugh, William W., and Susan Kaplan, eds.

1982   *Inua: Spirit World of the Bering Sea Eskimo.* Washington, DC: Smithsonian Institution Press.

1983   *Inua: Spirit World of the Bering Sea Eskimo.* Exhibition catalog. Smithsonian Traveling Exhibition Service. Washington, DC: Smithsonian Institution.

Fitzhugh, William W., and Igor Krupnik

1993   Jesup II Research Initiative. *Arctic Studies Center Newsletter* 2:5–8. Washington, DC: Arctic Studies Center.

1994   The Jesup II Research Initiative: Anthropological Studies in the North Pacific. *Arctic Studies Center Newsletter* (Special Issue: Jesup II Newsbrief). Washington, DC: Arctic Studies Center.

2001   Introduction. In *Gateways. Exploring the Legacy of the Jesup North Pacific Expedition, 1897–1902.* Igor Krupnik and William W. Fitzhugh, eds. Pp. 1–16. *Contributions to Circumpolar Anthropology,* 1. Washington, DC: Arctic Studies Center.

Giddings, James L.

1967   *Ancient Man of the Arctic.* New York: Knopf.

Hallowell, A. Irving

1926   Bear Ceremonialism in the Northern Hemisphere. *American Anthropologist* 28(1):1–175.

Hatt, Gudmund

1914   *Artiske Skinddragter i Eurasien og Amerika. En Etnografisk Studie* (Arctic Skin Clothing in Eurasia and America. An Ethnographic Study). Copenhagen: J.H. Schultz.

1949 Asian Influences in American Folklore. *Det Kongelige Danske Videnskabernes Selskab, Historisk-filologiske Meddelelser* 31(6):1–122.

Heizer, Robert F.
1956 Archaeology of the Uyak Site, Kodiak Island, Alaska. *University of California Anthropological Records* 17(1). Berkeley.

Ivanov, Sergei V.
1954 Materialy po izobrazitel'nomu iskusstvu narodov Sibiri XIX–nachala XX v. (Materials on Traditional Graphic Art of the Native Peoples of Siberia, the 19th and the early 20th century). *Trudy Instituta etnografii AN SSSR* 22. Moscow and Leningrad.

Jochelson, Waldemar
1925 Archaeological Investigations in the Aleutian Islands. *Carnegie Institution of Washington Publication*, 367. Washington, DC.
1928 Archaeological Investigations in Kamchatka. *Carnegie Institution of Washington Publication*, 388. Washington, DC.
1933 History, Ethnology and Anthropology of the Aleuts. *Carnegie Institution of Washington Publication*, 432. Washington, DC.

Jonaitis, Aldona, ed.
1991 *Chiefly Feasts: The Enduring Kwakiutl Potlatch.* New York: American Museum of Natural History; Seattle: University of Washington Press.

Kendall, Laurel, and Alexia Bloch
n.d. *The Museum at the End of the World: Two Anthropologists on a Road Trip in the Russian Far East.* Philadelphia: University of Pennsylvania Press (forthcoming).

Kendall, Laurel, Barbara Mathé, and Thomas Ross Miller, eds.
1997 *Drawing Shadows to Stone: The Photography of the Jesup North Pacific Expedition, 1897–1902.* New York: American Museum of Natural History; Seattle: University of Washington Press.

Krupnik, Igor
1998 Jesup Genealogy: Intellectual Partnership and Russian-American Cooperation in Arctic/North Pacific Anthropology. Part 1. From the Jesup Expedition to the Cold War, 1897–1948. *Arctic Anthropology* 35(2):199–226.
2001 A Jesup Bibliography: Tracking the Published and Archival Legacy of the Jesup Expedition. In *Gateways. Exploring the Legacy of the Jesup North Pacific Expedition, 1897–1902.* Igor Krupnik and William W. Fitzhugh, eds. Pp. 257–78. *Contributions to Circumpolar Anthropology*, 1. Washington, DC: Arctic Studies Center.

Krupnik, Igor, ed.
1996 *Perekrestki kontinentov. Kul'tury korennykh narodov Dal'nego Vostoka i Aliaski* (Crossroads of Continets. Cultures of the Native Peoples of the (Russian) Far East and Alaska). Valérie Chaussonnet, comp. Washington, DC: Arctic Studies Center.

Krupnik, Igor, and William W. Fitzhugh, eds.
2001 Gateways. Exploring the Legacy of the Jesup North Pacific Expedition, 1897–1902. *Contributions to Circumpolar Anthropology*, 1. Washington, DC: Arctic Studies Center.

Larsen, Helge, and Froelich Rainey
1948 Ipiutak and the Arctic Whale Hunting Culture. *Anthropological Papers of the American Museum of Natural History*, 42. New York.

Laughlin, William, S.
1985 Russian-American Bering Sea Relations: Research and Reciprocity. *American Anthropologist* 87(4):775–92.

Leroi-Gurhan, André
1946 Archéologie du Pacifique-Nord. Materiaux pour l'étude des rélations entre lès peuples riverains d'Asie et d'Amérique. *Travaux et Mémoires de l'Institut d'Éthnologie*, 42. Paris.

Michael, Henry P., ed.
1979 A U.S.-U.S.S.R. Symposium on the Peopling of the New World. *Arctic Anthropology* 16(1).

Michael, Henry P., and James W. VanStone, eds.
1983 *Cultures of the Bering Sea Region: Papers from an International Symposium.* IREX: New York.

Mitlyanskaya, Tamara B.
1996 Native Carvers and Outsider Artists: Patterns of Interaction in Siberian Eskimo/Chukchi Ivory Carving. *Arctic Anthropology* 33(1):67–88.

Murdoch, John
1988 *Ethnological Results of the Point Barrow Expedition.* With Introduction and Appendices by William W. Fitzhugh. Classics in Smithsonian Anthropology. Washington, DC: Smithsonian Institution Press.

Nelson, Edward W.
1983 *Eskimo about Bering Strait.* With Introduction and Appendices by William W. Fitzhugh. Classics of Smithsoninan Anthropology. Washington, DC: Smithsonian Institution Press.

O'Neil, Daniel
1994 *The Firecracker Boys.* New York:St. Martin's Press.

Ousley, Steven, and Richard Jantz
2001 500 Year Old Questions, 100 Year Old Data, Brand New Computers: Biological Data from the Jesup Expedition and the Paradox of the "Americanoid Theory." In *Gateways. Exploring the Legacy of the Jesup North Pacific Expedition, 1897–1902.* Igor Krupnik and William W. Fitzhugh, eds. Pp. 257–78. *Contributions to Circumpolar Anthropology*, 1. Washington, DC: Arctic Studies Center.

Quimby, George
1947 The Sadiron Lamp of Kamchatka as a Clue to the Chronology of the Aleut. *American Antiquity* 11(3):202–3.

Rivinus, Edward F. and E. M. Youssef
1992   *Spencer Baird of the Smithsonian.* Washington, DC: Smithsonian Institution Press.

Rudenko, Sergei I.
1947   *Drevniaia kul'tura Beringova moria i eskimosskaia problema* (Ancient Culture of the Bering Sea Region and the Eskimo Problem). Moscow and Leningrad: Glavsevmorput'. (Translated English edition of 1961).

Slezkine, Yuri
1994   *Arctic Mirrors. Russia and the Small Peoples of the North.* Ithaca and London: Cornell University Press.

Sokolova, Zoia P.
1994   Recent Ethnic Processes among the People of the Russian Pacific Coast. In *Anthropology of the North Pacific Rim.* William W. Fitzhugh and Valérie Chaussonnet, eds. Pp. 347–55. Washington, DC: Smithsonian Institution Press.

Spaulding, Albert C.
1946   Northwestern Archaeology and General Trends in Northern Forest Zones. In *Man in Northeastern North America.* F. Johnson, ed. Pp.143–47. Robert S. Peabody Foundation for Archaeology, 3. Andover.

82/ Jim VanStone's "method" for selecting ethnographic objects for the Crossroads of Continents *exhibit—in this case, a Tlingit war helmet from the MAE collection. Museum of Anthropology and Ethnography (Kunstkammer), St. Petersburg, Russia. 1983. Photographer, Jean-Loup Rousselot (ASC Collection)*

83/ *Aleut laborers working for the Jochelsons excavate the whalebone walls of an ancient Aleut barabara at the Aglagax site on Umnak Island (NAA 2003-20969). From an album presented by Waldemar Jochelson to the Department of Anthropology of the National Museum (also Jochelson 1925:32)*

Aleut Archaeology and Cultural Heritage:

The Legacy of the Jesup North Pacific Expedition

STEPHEN LORING
AND DOUGLAS W. VELTRE

As the far-reaching goals of the Jesup North Pacific Expedition (JNPE) of 1897–1902 developed, their initial scope narrowed to the extent that the research venture had eventually only a marginal presence in southwestern Alaska. Nevertheless, subsequent research in this area owes a considerable intellectual debt to the foundations laid by JNPE researchers and to its overall scholarly paradigm. In particular, Waldemar Jochelson and Dina Jochelson-Brodsky, who have had extensive Siberian experience and had worked with the JNPE, brought the broad anthropological approach of the Jesup Expedition program to the Aleutians in 1909–10 (Fig. 83).

In this paper, we first examine archaeological research in the Aleut region preceding that of the Jochelsons. Next we discuss the specific efforts of the Jochelsons, whose Aleut-Kamchatka Expedition of 1909–11 addressed a number of themes that have figured significantly in subsequent Aleutian research. These include the nature and timing of human colonization of the region; the nature of human maritime adaptations; and the cultural, linguistic and biological relationships and continuities between the past and the present. Third, we look at archaeological research done between that of the Jochelsons and about 1970. Finally, we review work done since 1970, in particular exploring the significant ways in which the contributions of the Jochelsons and other early researchers have combined with recent legislative developments to influence contemporary archaeological and cultural

heritage efforts in the Aleut region and to help shape Aleut identity in the modern world.

The Aleut region is that area of southwestern Alaska that was the traditional home of the Aleut people (a name which is discussed below). It includes the tip of the Alaska Peninsula from Port Moller westward, the Shumagin Islands group south of the Alaska Peninsula, and the entire Aleutian Islands archipelago, some seventy islands extending 1,600 km from the end of the Alaska Peninsula westward towards the Kamchatka Peninsula (see map Fig. 5). This area comprises a dynamic landscape shaped by glacial and tectonic processes, including volcanism, earthquake activity, and sea-level changes (McCartney and Veltre 1999). At the junction of the North Pacific Ocean and the Bering Sea, where marine upwelling provides nutrient-rich water, the Aleutian Islands ecosystem hosts one of the world's most productive fisheries and highest concentrations of pelagic birds and marine mammals. The bountiful marine resources available to human hunters and gatherers figured significantly in the early colonization of the archipelago and continue to shape regional social, political, and economic agendas.

Archaeological, biological, and ethnographic data show a cultural continuity in this region for at least the last 4000 years (cf. Laughlin 1963, 1980; McCartney 1977, 1984). Aleut oral tradition also suggests that the Pribilof Islands, north of the Aleutian chain in the Bering Sea, were known to the Aleut people prior to the islands' discovery by the Russians in 1786 and

1787. However, the limited archaeological research to date there has found no evidence of utilization of these islands by anyone prior to the Russian period, when they were settled by the Aleut (Veltre and Veltre 1986; Veltre and McCartney 1994, 2002).

At the time of contact in the mid-1700s, the Aleut population likely numbered some 12–15,000 (Lantis 1984:163). The traditional economy was focused on the sea as the provider of nearly all food and raw materials, with marine mammals, ocean and anadromous fish, marine invertebrates, birds, and eggs providing at least ninety-five percent of the diet (Laughlin 1980:49). Larger winter settlements and smaller seasonal camps were along the coast. Extended families, possibly organized according to principles of matrilineal kinship (Lantis 1970), lived in semi-subterranean houses.

In contemplating the legacy of the JNPE as it pertains to the Aleut region, we focus our remarks on the history of archaeological research in the Aleutians, mentioning only briefly the wider sphere of anthropological issues embraced by the Boasian school. Archaeology in the Aleutians began in the 1870s with the pioneering work of William Dall and Alphonse Pinart. Their revelations on the antiquity of Aleut occupations stimulated interest in the Aleutians as a possible gateway for people entering the New World and greatly influenced Franz Boas' (1905:91) statement of the Jesup Expedition goals: "one of the great problems of ethnological science is the relation of the American race to the races of the other continents" to be revealed through the comparative study of contemporary Native people, physical anthropology, and archaeology. While in Boas' original conception of the Jesup Expedition research program the Aleutians were scheduled for attention in 1901 (see Fig. 4, p.17), that survey never materialized.

The Beginning of Archaeological Research in the Aleutians

Anthropology and geography were the pre-eminent intellectual bases of eighteenth and nineteenth centu-

ries' expanding Western colonial enterprises. The discipline of archaeology has, until recently, been a peculiar and exclusionary system of knowledge that has served to extend Western intellectual hegemony over the past and has, for the most part, failed to capture the imagination and interest of people in northern communities. Nevertheless, by extending perceptions of the viability and existence of social (tribal, ethnic) institutions into the past, archaeology can play an important role in the preservation, formation, and interpretation of social identities. The Boasian anthropologists were much closer in time to the pre-contact past with their notions of traditional, static culture, and they expected archaeology to confirm ancient land tenure and perceptions shaped by ethnography. While Aleut community members have always been involved in the interpretation of their past (as guides, interpreters, informants, field-workers), it is only recently, as anthropologists have begun to surrender their position of authority and control, that they have taken a more active role in the construction of their past.

Archaeology in the Aleutians arguably begins with the collecting activities of the French ethnologist Alphonse Pinart who carted off a collection of remarkable wooden masks and associated objects from a burial cave on Unga Island in the Shumagins in 1871 (Pinart 1875). Knowledge of the Unga discoveries quickly spread and piqued the interest of William Dall, captain of a U.S. Coast and Geodetic Survey vessel in charge of a Smithsonian-sponsored scientific survey of the Aleutians from 1871 to 1874 (Dall 1875a, 1875b, 1878).

Dall was the epitome of a systematic naturalist. Trained by Louis Agassiz, he first came to Alaska in 1865 (when he was twenty-one) to work with and eventually lead the Western Union International Telegraph Expedition (Merriam 1927; Dall 1870). Dall was a splendid exemplar of the intellectual eclecticism of nineteenth century naturalists. While primarily a specialist on shells, his Alaska research also included publications on birds, fish, mammals, cetacean parasites, and meteorology. Dall's archaeological investigations, conducted sporadically as bad weather and logistics constrained his official survey work, pioneered the systematic excavation of shell middens (Dall 1873, 1877). His deep cuts in stratified midden deposits suggested a significant antiquity of the region.

In the Aleutians the question of the origins of the Aleut people structured early research, with the possibility that the earliest colonizers crossed from Kamchatka Peninsula to the Aleutian Islands via the Commander Islands. While Dall did not believe in the Asian colonization of the Aleutians, the intense debate surrounding the issue of the origin of humans in the New World and their possible migration routes figured significantly in Aleutian research prior to World War II.

There is an interesting aside to Dall's research. In 1872 he arranged to adopt a fifteen-year old orphan from Iliuliuk (present-day Unalaska), George Tsaroff (Fig. 84), who returned with Dall from Alaska

Fig. 84/ George Tsaroff, soon after starting to work at the Smithsonian Institution, ca. 1878 (NAA-SI 80-13437)

in 1873. Impressed by Tsaroff's cleverness, Dall arranged for him to be educated at the University of Michigan. In 1878, Tsaroff came to Washington as an "assistant" where he was placed in charge of the Smithsonian's ethnological hall. There he served as a guide to the collections: "himself forming an extremely interesting exhibit—that of a native Indian, well educated and instructed, and able to explain the special objects and applications of many articles manufactured and used in his own country" (Baird 1881:69).

Tragically, Tsaroff contracted consumption and died in 1880. His tenure as a museum guide and living-link between ethnography and museum collections precedes by twenty-three years the celebrated case of

Ishi, the "last" of the Yahi Indians, who was befriended by Theodora and Alfred Kroeber and who performed a similar function at the University of California Museum of Anthropology at Berkeley (Kroeber 1961).

Initiated by Dall, anthropological interest by the Smithsonian in the Aleutians was furthered by the collecting activities of Lucien M. Turner, an employee of the U. S. Army Signal Service who was stationed in the Aleutians in 1874–5 and again in 1879–81. He established meteorological stations on Atka and Attu Islands. Continuing in the broad natural science collecting tradition of Dall, Turner made large important collections of birds, fish, mammals, insects, and plants for the Smithsonian. His anthropological contributions included the acquisition of large archaeological and ethnological collections and Aleut vocabularies (Baird 1883). While Turner's collections have never been systematically analyzed or even described, they form a very valuable legacy for the insight they provide on Aleut culture in the Western Aleutians.

Another component of the Smithsonian interest in the Aleutians was the work of the pioneering naturalist Leonhard Stejneger (1851–1943), whose research on the extinct fauna of the Aleutians, including Steller's sea-cow and Pallas' cormorant (Stejneger and Lucas 1889), presaged interest in the consequences of human hunting and foraging practices on Aleutian ecosystems.

The Fieldwork of Waldemar Jochelson and Dina Jochelson-Brodsky

In preparing for the work of the JNPE, Boas traveled to Europe in 1898, where he was introduced to Waldemar Jochelson (Vakhtin 2001:80–2). While somewhat of a political liability, Jochelson was an extraordinarily gifted and experienced Russian ethnographer. He had worked with northern peoples of Siberia while in exile (between 1886–95) and in residence in Yakutsk (1895–7) prior to joining the Jesup Expedition research program. While on his JNPE assignment, Jochelson was accompanied by his wife, Dina Jochelson-Brodsky who had trained in medicine at the University of Zurich and who took responsibility for the expedition's health as well as for the acquisition of anthropometric and biological data. Dina Jochelson-Brodsky also produced a portion of the photographic record of the expedition's travels in Siberia. The Jochelsons were in Siberia from the summer of 1900 through the summer of 1902 working among the Koryak, Even (Tungus), Yukagir, and Sakha (Yakut) peoples (Boas 1903:102–9; Jochelson 1908, 1926). Their collections were primarily ethnological but also included physical anthropology (plaster casts of faces and measurements), photography, folklore and musical recordings, human skeletal remains and archaeological materials acquired from graves and recently abandoned villages, zoological specimens (including a 220 lb mammoth tusk!), and meteorological observations (Jochelson, in Boas 1903:109).

The Jochelsons' experiences with the JNPE led directly to their involvement with the Ryabushinski Aleut-Kamchatka Expedition of 1909–11, modeled closely on the Jesup Expedition protocol (Jochelson 1912). The Ryabushinski Expedition was under the auspices of the Imperial Russian Geographical Society (Fig. 92) and was financed by the Russian banker Feodore P. Ryabushinski (Theodore Riabouschinsky). It sought to pick up where the JNPE had left off in resolving the historical, cultural, and biological relations among Aleut, Eskimo, and Asian peoples. Foremost in its research agenda was a determination of Aleut origins in which the role of archaeology featured prominently. The Jochelsons arrived in Unalaska in January 1909. They conducted archaeological investigations on Attu and Atka Islands during the following summer, and then spent the next winter at Nikolski village on Umnak Island conducting linguistic research and collecting phonographic recordings of traditional Aleut myths and stories (Jochelson 1912; Bergsland and Dirks 1990; Korsun et al. 2001). In the spring of 1910 they made a brief visit to the Pribilof Islands before returning to Unalaska and thence to Kamchatka, where they spent a year conducting archaeological excavations (Jochelson 1928).

During their Aleutian fieldwork the Jochelsons were assisted by Alexei M. Yachmenev, the "Aleut chief of Unalaska," and other Aleut elders (making them the first to acknowledge the role of elders in the production of knowledge). Two volumes based on the Aleutian fieldwork were forthcoming, one on the history, ethnology, and anthropology (Jochelson 1933), the other on the results of their archaeological research (Jochelson 1925). The Aleutian fieldwork, following the broad Boasian agenda established by the JNPE researchers, included archaeological excavations, ethnological observations and collections, anthropometric measurements, and the collection of Aleut mythology, oral traditions, language, and music (Figs. 93 and 94).

Smithsonian Redux

For a decade beginning in the late 1920s, the Smithsonian's indomitable Aleš Hrdlička made annual archaeological expeditions to Alaska. Hrdlička was interested in the problems of racial history and origins, especially as they were applicable to finding the origins of human occupation of the New World, the origin of Eskimo cultures in Alaska, and the nature of prehistoric exchange, interaction, and migration. Hrdlička worked in the central and western Aleutians during three successive field seasons in 1936, 1937, and 1938 (Hrdlička 1945). He dug at a number of ancient Aleut sites and conducted physical anthropological and biometrical observations in Aleut communities, especially those in the Near Islands group of the western Aleutian Islands and in the Commander Islands in Soviet territory.

Due to his zeal for recovering human skeletal remains, Hrdlička never had a very good reputation among Native Alaskans. This research, regardless of the valid scientific questions the "data" sought to address, was conducted with little regard for Native concerns (Loring and Prokopec 1994). His enthusiasm also resulted in archaeological procedures that were far from satisfactory, even by the standards of his day. To his credit, however, Hrdlička did retain much of the faunal material exposed during his midden excavations.

Research from World War II to 1970

The pioneering work of Dall, the broad-based JNPE-inspired investigations of the Jochelsons, and the expeditions of Hrdlička were mostly undertaken without substantial Aleut involvement, except for the significant role of local people in sharing their cultural expertise and providing oral recordings for the

Jochelsons (Bergsland and Dirks 1990:10–15). Likewise, the archaeological research methodologies of these early researchers often left much to be desired by modern standards. Nevertheless, the groundwork laid by these scholars set the stage for a wide range of anthropological research in the post-World War II years. It also left an important legacy for recently emergent efforts at perpetuating Aleut cultural heritage.

The World War II years and the years following have arguably witnessed more changes in Aleut culture than any period since the early Russian era (cf. Veltre 1990, 1999). In 1942, Aleuts from far-western Attu Island were taken as prisoners by the Japanese, and all other Aleuts from St. Paul and St. George in the Pribilof Islands and from villages west of the Alaska Peninsula—some 881 individuals—were taken by the U. S. military to internment camps in southeastern Alaska for the duration of the war (Kohlhoff 1990; Veltre 1992). This was a period of severe deprivation and hardship, keeping the Aleut people away from their homes for several years, even long after the Japanese threat had been eliminated. Following the war, several Aleut villages were never reoccupied, while many of those to which the Aleut did return saw substantial changes in communication, education, economy, and the ethnic makeup of their communities. Although the Aleut returned to villages where pursuit of traditional lifestyles was increasingly difficult and where, in some cases, they were on the verge of becoming ethnic minorities in their own communities, they nevertheless emerged from wartime internment with new knowledge and skills stemming from their contacts with the people, economy, and politics outside of the Aleut region.

For the first twenty-five years following World War II, Aleuts in many communities became more and more assimilated into the larger world. In the Pribilof Islands, the fur seal industry continued to be the mainstay of economic life, while in the villages along the Alaska Peninsula and the Aleutian Islands seasonal cash employment in the growing fishing industry mixed with traditional subsistence pursuits sustained the widely dispersed population. During this time before 1970, a few small archaeological research projects were undertaken throughout the region. In addition, two larger efforts were begun—a long-term and multidisciplinary series of investigations in and around the village of Nikolski on Umnak Island by William Laughlin and his colleagues beginning in 1948, (cf. Laughlin 1975), and a program of archaeological surveys and excavations on Amchitka Island conducted as part of the U.S. Atomic Energy Commission's underground nuclear testing program from 1964–72 (Sense and Turner 1970; Turner 1970; Desautels et al. 1971; Cook et al. 1972). Although undertaken with the knowledge and general support of the Aleut people, these projects were initiated and conducted almost entirely without direct Aleut consultation and involvement.

Research Since 1970

It was not until the 1970s that the Aleut people were able to exercise meaningful influence and control over archaeological research in their region, and it has been only in very recent years that they have begun to take a more proactive role in determining the direction of such research efforts. These changes have come about largely due to the passage of several pieces of federal legislation.

The Alaska Native Claims Settlement Act. The most significant of this recent legislation is the Alaska Native Claims Settlement Act (ANCSA) of 1971, a law having direct relevance to cultural heritage in at least two main areas. First, ANCSA established regional and local Native for-profit corporations. As elsewhere in the state, legal title to certain lands in the Aleut region was given to the regional for-profit Aleut Corporation, while title to other lands went to each of thirteen local Aleut village for-profit corporations. The Aleut Corporation's lands are distributed throughout much of the region, while each village corporation's lands are for the most part immediately surrounding that village. Because these regional and village lands included the archaeological sites on them, Aleuts for

the first time owned outright a significant portion of their cultural heritage. Thus, while prior to the passage of ANCSA archaeologists needed only to obtain a federal Antiquities Act permit to pursue their work in most of the Aleut region, now archaeologists wanting to conduct research on regional or village lands were required only to go to the Aleut landowners to obtain permission, the details and conditions of which would be up to the parties to negotiate.

While archaeological projects on Aleut lands have been undertaken with the explicit permission of local and regional Aleut entities since 1971, few have involved the Aleut people directly in the planning, field, or analytical stages of work. This is primarily because the Aleut have historically not had extensive participation in the educational and research traditions of the universities and government agencies that typically sponsor such efforts. Also, real-life practical difficulties faced by residents of the region, who might have to decide, for example, whether to forego summer employment or subsistence pursuits to spend weeks or months away from home at a remote archaeological field camp, have made participation difficult.

Over the last few decades, however, this situation has changed somewhat, as Aleut entities have begun to see how archaeology can be of service to them. The first regional Aleut Corporation-sponsored archaeological project (Frøhlich and Kopjanski 1975) occurred in 1974, shortly after passage of ANCSA, when archaeologists were funded to conduct site surveys in the central and western Aleutian Islands as part of efforts to apply for 14(h)(1) sites (see below). Since then, several additional—and mostly small-scale—archaeological and ethnohistorical projects have been initiated and underwritten by the regional corporation to address other questions it deemed significant. These included, for example, research into historical Aleut land use patterns on Attu Island, done as part of World War II restitution (Veltre 1988), and an archaeological survey to examine the condition of possibly vandalized archaeological properties on Adak Island (Veltre 1997a).

Likewise, some Aleut village non-profit and for-profit entities—like the St. Paul TDX Corporation, the Ounalashka in Unalaska Corporation, and the former Unalaska Aleut Development Corporation—have supported archaeological investigations in their communities as part of their emerging interests in local history. One example of this was a project in historical archaeology and ethnohistory on St. Paul Island (Fig. 96). An initial archaeological survey of Russian and American period settlements on the island in 1994 (Veltre and McCartney 1994, 2002) was followed by excavations at one former village in 2000 and 2001. Archaeological efforts were combined with recording oral histories from community residents (Veltre and McCartney 2000, 2001). Instigated and underwritten in large part by the people of that community, this project served their dual desires to understand better their island's history as well as to determine if archaeological resources could somehow be incorporated into their economically important tourism industry.

Other projects which have done a great deal to further the goals of Aleut-initiated archaeology have taken place at several sites in the City of Unalaska under the guidance of Richard Knecht, Director of the Museum of the Aleutians. Working with the cooperation of both the City and the Aleut village corporation, the Ounalashka Corporation, which owns the land on which many of the sites are located, professionals and volunteers are able to balance archaeological pursuits with their work and family commitments (Fig. 95). Such broad-based support, combined with logistical ease, has enabled Knecht to undertake large-scale excavations at a number of sites over the last seven years (Knecht and Davis 2001; Knecht 2003). Like the St. Paul survey and excavations described above for the Ounalashka Corporation, such research efforts further not only cultural heritage goals but strategic ones as well, since the sites have been located in prime areas for future economic development.

ANCSA Section 14(h)(1). The second way in which ANCSA has affected Aleut cultural heritage is in its provision that title to culturally important lands not otherwise included within village or regional land selections could be transferred to the regional Aleut Corporation. This was accomplished through the Act's Section 14(h)(1), a relatively minor feature of the overall legislation, but a major force in matters of contemporary cultural heritage throughout Alaska from the mid-1970s to today.

Section 14(h)(1) of ANCSA provides for the transfer of title to regional Native corporations of archaeological and other historical sites not otherwise selected by local or regional Native corporations. By the filing deadline in the late 1970s, the Aleut Corporation had submitted approximately 400 individual claims for archaeological sites, the vast majority of which had never been investigated archaeologically. Importantly, the work of the early archaeologists in the region was critical to the Aleut Corporation's efforts: had many site locations not been noted by Dall, Jochelson, or Hrdlička, they most likely never would have been applied for by the Aleut Corporation. Field investigations of Aleut site applications by BIA ANCSA archaeologists took place largely between 1983 and 1989 (although some work continued until 1998), with crews mapping surface features, photographing site localities, and plotting their locations on detailed maps of the area. The only excavations that took place as part of these surveys were very limited tests.

Reminiscent of Jochelson's earlier interest in oral traditions as well as archaeological remains, an integral and important part of the BIA ANCSA site investigations was gathering oral testimony from the present-day Aleut residents, usually elders, from communities close to the sites being investigated. This testimony was used to bolster claims of significance for particular sites. The audiotapes recorded in the Aleut region remain a valuable—and untapped—resource on Aleut culture and history.

An important consequence of the ANCSA 14(h)(1) surveys is that the sites conveyed under this provision will become the property of the Aleut Corporation, whose explicit permission will be a prerequisite for conducting archaeological research. To date, Aleut Corporation leaders have been very supportive of archaeological research, recognizing therein an opportunity to enhance understanding of Aleut heritage.

One current archaeological initiative undertaken with Aleut Corporation permission is the *Western Aleutian Human Paleoecology and Biodiversity Project*, an international and interdisciplinary research program initiated in 1992 to focus on the Near Islands, the westernmost group in the Aleutian chain (Loring 1994; Corbett et al. 1997). Building upon earlier Smithsonian scholarship in the region by Dall, Stejneger, and Hrdlička (which focused on the possibility that the Aleutians served as a pathway for human entry into the New World), this research collaborative seeks to understand the emergence of cultural complexity in this remote archipelago—one of the most geographically isolated landscapes ever colonized by maritime hunter-gatherers.

The research also seeks to utilize innovative data recovery techniques from deeply stratified, well-preserved village midden deposits to acquire detailed Holocene distributional and demographic data on biodiversity. The analysis of faunal remains, especially from avian and marine mammals species, provides an opportunity to examine paleoecological changes at both the local inter-island level as well as in the greater North Pacific region as a whole. The research challenges the assumption of ecological and cultural stasis in the archipelago and reexamines the cultural and biological relationships between the Aleutian Islands and the Asian continent in light of the research initiatives of the JNPE.

Repatriation Legislation. Two relatively recent pieces of federal legislation have also had an important impact on Aleut cultural heritage. These are the National Museum of the American Indian Act of 1989 and the Native American Graves Protection and Repatriation Act (NAGPRA) of 1990. These laws, which parallel one another in purpose, provide for the repatriation of human remains, associated funerary objects, and objects of cultural patrimony from the Smithsonian Institution and other repositories around the country to Native American groups.

As an initial result of this legislation, the Aleut (like many other Native groups) are learning for the first time about the existence of collections of materials from their region. Aleut entities ranging from the regional Aleut Corporation to the various village councils and corporations have been inundated with inventories of specimens sent by over one hundred institutions. However, because these two repatriation laws are complex and costly to deal with for institutions as well as for Native groups, their full effects have not yet been felt in the Aleut region. Further, since there is no statute of limitations for making repatriation requests, regional and local Aleut groups have so far taken a conservative and cautious approach to the entire issue, learning from the repatriation experiences of other Native groups. To date, a small number of National Park Service NAGPRA Documentation Awards have been made to local Aleut groups, one being the Aleut Repatriation Commission, an entity set up specifically to deal with repatriation matters for a coalition of villages.

Aleut Cultural Identity. Concomitant with the processes discussed above has been another change instigated by the empowerment engendered by ANCSA and other legislation. In recent years many Native groups in Alaska (as well as indigenous groups worldwide) have begun to dispense with use of the names given to them by outsiders—either other Native groups or westerners—and to return to more traditional autonyms. In the Aleut region, this has meant that the traditional names *Unangan* (in the eastern dialect) and *Unangas* (in the Atka, or central, dialect) have begun to be used (often in the form *Unangax*) by some Native residents, since "Aleut" was never used in pre-Russian times to designate the people of the region as a whole. It was only after the arrival of Russians that "Aleut" became broadly—and confusingly—employed to include not only the Aleut but also Native residents of Alutiiq-speaking areas of south-central Alaska.

Whether *Unangax* will gain widespread acceptance among the Aleut is unknown at this time, although a survey of elders in the region in the summer of 1997 showed support for use of the term, and one local group—the Qawalangin Tribe of Unalaska—fully backs its use (Barbara Svarny Carlson, pers. comm.). What is clear, however, is that for some Aleut people today the use of the term is a matter of substantial cultural—and political—significance.

Conclusions

Throughout Alaska today, Native people are reasserting their rights of self-determination and are working both to strengthen and to reestablish connections to their traditional pasts. This is certainly the case in the Aleut region, where land ownership and control of archaeological properties have provided the basis for the Aleut people to take a more active role participating in, and developing goals for, cultural heritage projects of many kinds. For the first three-quarters of this century, at the same time that federal assimilationist policies and outside economic interests were increasingly undermining traditional aspects of Aleut culture, anthropologists, archaeologists, and linguists were attempting to document both the distant past as well as traditional aspects of contemporary Aleut life. Thus, Aleuts today, in their pursuit of cultural heritage efforts, are building an understanding of their past in part upon the foundations laid by earlier researchers in the region. The oral tradition research of Barbara Svarny Carlson, for example, has made extensive use of the recently published stories recorded on wax cylinders by Waldemar Jochelson some 90 years ago (Bergsland and Dirks 1990).

One recent and important development for cultural heritage pursuits in the Aleut region was the decision in early 1998 by the regional non-profit Aleutian/Pribilof Islands Association (A/PIA) to establish a formal Cultural Heritage Department. This program is currently pursuing a broad and creative range of cultural heritage goals, including developing a comprehensive Aleut resources library, working to revitalize the Aleut language, and furthering repatriation issues. In 1999 the A/PIA co-curated the installation of a case study on Aleut history and culture in the Native North American Hall at the Smithsonian's National Museum of Natural History. The exhibit marked the return to the Smithsonian of Aleut scholarship and self determination in providing an Aleut perspective that followed, by 120 years, the insights furnished by George Tsaroff. It is worth noting that even the Cultural Heritage Department owes its existence to ANCSA, since a significant portion of its operating budget comes from BIA 14(h)(1) funds which were contracted to A/PIA (Veltre 1997b).

It is clear that the survival of the Aleut as a distinctive cultural group will involve two particular efforts. On the one hand, in a process that began perhaps two decades ago, the Aleut have become increasingly interested in learning about their pre-contact and post-contact cultural heritage. This has been done largely through archaeological efforts, but has also been pursued through other ethnohistorical endeavors, such as the study of museum collections of ethnographic specimens, recording of local oral histories, family heritage projects, stewardship programs, and the like. Moreover, the Aleut have relatively recently begun to view archaeological research as a means to investigate questions of specific interest to them, such as those dealing with historical land use.

On the other hand, the Aleut have begun to resurrect traditional cultural activities—traditional in spirit if not in actual content. Skin boat building and traditional house building projects—as have been undertaken in Atka, St. Paul, and Unalaska—and similar undertakings are examples of this. Perhaps nowhere is interest in past traditions more evident than in the rediscovery—and, largely, the *re-invention*—of Aleut dance that began in 1995. Since that time, dance groups have emerged in at least three Aleut communities, Atka, St. Paul, and St. George, the dancers combining the very limited ethnohistorical information regarding older Aleut dance forms with elements of contemporary Alaska Native dance (Fig. 97). This synthesis has generated enormous pride among the Aleut throughout the region.

Finally, the survival of Aleut culture seems predicated on Aleuts' abilities to maintain a distinct self-identity, rather than on the content of that identity. That is, while this identity may be rooted in part on specific cultural traditions having demonstrable roots in their pre-contact past, it may just as well be based on modified or newly emergent cultural forms. When understood in light of the historical and legislative processes by which the Aleut people have come to have more control over their own lives, the legacy of the Jesup Expedition and related early anthropological ventures in the Aleut region lies both in the foundations they provided for subsequent more formal inquiry as well as in the wealth and diversity of information they collected which is now forming an important basis of modern Aleut cultural heritage efforts.

Acknowledgments

There are many entities which deserve thanks for their help over the years with our individual research projects mentioned in this paper. These include the Aleut organizations which made our work possible through permission to work on their lands and in kind support: The Aleut Corporation, the Aleutian/Pribilof Islands Association, the Ounalashka Corporation, the TDX Corporation, and the St. Paul Tribal Government. In addition, the U.S. Fish and Wildlife Service, especially the Captain and crew of their research vessel *Tiglax*, have provided logistical support and permission for some of our field projects. For their generous in kind assistance, thanks go to all the folks at Reeve Aleutian Air, PenAir and Northern Air Cargo who have safely, and so efficiently, transported our equipment, crews, and specimens. Finally, we wish to acknowledge Allen McCartney for his inspiration and collaboration over the years.

References

Baird, Spencer Fullerton
1881   *Annual Report of the Board of Regents of the Smithsonian Institution, Showing the Operations, Expenditures, & Condition of the Institution for the Year 1880.* Washington, DC: Government Printing Office.
1883   *Annual Report of the Board of Regents of the Smithsonian Institution, Showing the Operations, Expenditures, & Condition of the Institution for the Year 1881.* Washington, DC: Government Printing Office.

Bergsland, Knut, and Moses Dirks, eds.
1990   *Unangam Ungiikangin kayux Tunusangin/ Unangam Uniikangis ama Tunuzangis/Aleut Tales and Narratives, Collected 1909-1910 by Waldemar Jochelson.* Fairbanks: Alaska Native Language Center, University of Alaska.

Boas, Franz
1903   The Jesup North Pacific Expedition. *The American Museum Journal* 3:73-119.
1905   The Jesup North Pacific Expedition. In *International Congress of Americanists, 13th Session, Held in New York in 1902.* Pp. 91-100. Easton, PA: Eschenbach.

Cook, John P., E. James Dixon, Jr., and Charles E. Holmes
1972   Archaeological Report, Site 49 Rat 32, Amchitka Island, Alaska. *USAEC Report HN-20-1045.* Las Vegas: Holmes and Narver.

Corbett, Debra, Christine Lefevre, and Douglas Siegel-Causey
1997   The Western Aleutians: Cultural Isolation and Environmental Change. *Human Ecology* 25(3):459-79.

Dall, William Healy
1870   *Alaska and Its Resources.* Boston: Lee and Shepard.
1873   Notes on the Pre-historic Remains in the Aleutian Islands. *Proceedings of the California Academy of Science* 4:283-7. San Francisco.
1875a   Alaskan Mummies. *American Naturalist* 9(8):433-40.
1875b   Notes on Some Aleut Mummies. *Proceedings of the California Academy of Science* 5:399-400. San Francisco.
1877   On Succession in the Shell-heaps of the Aleutian Islands. In *Tribes of the Extreme Northwest.* John W. Powell, ed. Pp. 41-91. Contributions to North American Ethnology, vol.1. Washington, DC: Government Printing Office.
1878   On the Remains of Later Pre-historic Man Obtained from Caves in the Catherina Archipelago, Alaska Territory, and Especially from the Caves of

the Aleutian Islands. *Smithsonian Contributions to Knowledge* 22(318). Washington, DC: Government Printing Office.

Desautels, Roger J., Albert J. McCurdy, James D. Flynn, and Robert R. Ellis

1971   Archaeological Report, Amchitka Island, Alaska, 1969-1970. *USAEC Report TID-25481.* Archaeological Research, Inc.

Frøhlich, Bruno, and David Kopjanski

1975   *Aleutian Site Survey, 1975, Preliminary Report.* Report submitted to the Aleut Corporation. Storrs: Laboratory of Biological Anthropology, University of Connecticut.

Hrdlička, Aleš

1945   *The Aleutian and Commander Islands and Their Inhabitants.* Philadelphia: The Wistar Institute of Anatomy and Biology.

Jochelson, Waldemar

1908   The Koryak. *The Jesup North Pacific Expedition,* vol. 6. *Memoirs of the American Museum of Natural History,* 10. Leiden: E.J. Brill; New York: G.E. Stechert.

1912   Scientific Results of the Ethnological Section of the Riabouschinsky Expedition of the Imperial Russian Geographical Society to the Aleutian Islands and Kamchatka. In *International Congress of Americanists. Proceedings of the 18th Session, London, 1912. Part 2.* Pp. 334-43. London: Harrison and Sons.

1925   Archaeological Investigations in the Aleutian Islands. *Carnegie Institution of Washington Publication,* 367. Washington.

1926   The Yukaghir and the Yukaghirized Tungus. *The Jesup North Pacific Expedition,* vol. 9, pts.1-3. *Memoirs of the American Museum of Natural History,* 13. Leiden: E.J. Brill; New York: G.E. Stechert.

1928   Archaeological Investigations in Kamchatka. *Carnegie Institution of Washington Publication,* 288. Washington.

1933   History, Ethnology and Anthropology of the Aleut. *Carnegie Institution of Washington Publication,* 432. Washington.

Knecht, Richard A.

2003   Tapping into a Sense of Wonder: Community Archaeology and Museum Building in the Aleutian Islands. In *SAA Community Partnership Handbook.* Linda Derry and Marlene Malloy, eds. Washington, DC: Society for American Archaeology.

Knecht, Richard A., and Richard S. Davis

2001   Prehistoric Sequence for the Eastern Aleutians. In *Recent Archaeology in the Aleut Zone of Alaska.* Don Dumond, ed. Pp. 269-88. University of Oregon Anthropological Papers, 58. Eugene, OR.

Kohlhoff, Dean

1990   *When the Wind Was a River: Aleut Evacuation in World War II.* Seattle: University of Washington Press.

Korsun, Sergei A., Natalia Ch. Taksami, and Nikita V. Ushakov, eds.

2001   *Sokrovishcha Kunstkamery. Aleuty: kakimi ikh uvidel V. Iokhelson/ Treasures of the Kunstkamera. Aleuts: How They Were Seen by V. Iokhel'son.* Bilingual catalog. St. Petersburg: Museum of Anthropology and Ethnography (Kunstkamera).

Kroeber, Theodora

1961   *Ishi in Two Worlds.* Berkeley: University of California Press.

Lantis, Margaret

1970   The Aleut Social System, 1750 to 1810, from Early Historical Sources. In *Ethnohistory in Southwestern Alaska and the Southern Yukon: Method and Content.* Margaret Lantis, ed. Pp. 139-311. Lexington: University of Kentucky Press.

1984   Aleut. In *Handbook of North American Indians,* vol.5. *Arctic.* David Damas ed. Pp. 161-84. Washington, DC: Smithsonian Institution.

Laughlin, William S.

1963   Eskimos and Aleuts: Their Origins and Evolution. *Science* 142(3593):633-45.

1975   Aleuts: Ecosystem, Holocene History, and Siberian Origin. *Science* 189(4902):507-15.

1980   *Aleuts: Survivors of the Bering Land Bridge.* New York: Holt, Rinehart, and Winston.

Loring, Stephen

1994   Archaeology of the Western Aleutians. *Arctic Research of the United States* 8:110-11. Washington, DC: Interagency Arctic Research Policy Committee and National Science Foundation.

Loring, Stephen, and Miroslav Prokepec

1994   A Most Peculiar Man: the Life and Times of Aleš Hrdlička. In *Reckoning with the Dead: The Larsen Bay Repatriation and the Smithsonian Institution.* Tamara Bray and Thomas Killion eds. Pp. 26-40. Washington, DC: Smithsonian Institution Press.

McCartney, Allen P.

1977   Prehistoric Human Occupation of the Rat Islands. In *The Environment of Amchitka Island, Alaska.* Melvin L. Merritt and R. Glen Fuller eds. Pp. 59-113. Technical Information Center, Energy Research and Development Administration.

1984   Prehistory of the Aleutian Region. In *Handbook of North American Indians,* vol. 5. *Arctic.* David Damas ed. Pp. 119-35. Washington, DC: Smithsonian Institution.

McCartney, Allen P., and Douglas W. Veltre

1999   Aleutian Island Prehistory: Living in Insular Extremes. *World Archaeology* 30(3):503-15.

Merriam, C. Hart

1927   William Healy Dall. *Science* 65(1684):345-7.

Pinart, Alphonse

1875   *La Caverne d'Aknanh, Isle d'Ounga (Archpel Shumagin, Alaska).* Paris: E. Leroux.

Sense, Richard, and Christy G. Turner, II

1970   *Catalog of Archaeological Site Survey Records, Amchitka Island, Alaska.* Holmes and Narver, Inc., on Continent Test Division. Report submitted to United States Atomic Energy Commission.

Stejneger, Leonhard, and Frederic A. Lucas

1889   Contributions to the Natural History of the Commander Islands: a Contribution to the History of Pallas' Cormorant. *Proceedings of the National Museum* 12:83-8.

Turner, Christy G., II

1970   Archaeological Reconnaissance of Amchitka Island, Alaska. *Arctic Anthropology* 7(2): 118-28.

Vakhtin, Nikolai B.

2001   Franz Boas and the Shaping of the Jesup Expedition Siberian Research, 1895-1900. In *Gateways. Exploring the Legacy of the Jesup North Pacific Expedition, 1897-1902.* Igor Krupnik and William W. Fitzhugh, eds. Pp. 71-89. Contributions to Circumpolar Anthropology, 1. Washington, DC: Arctic Studies Center.

Veltre, Douglas W.

1988   *Aleut Use of the Western Portion of Attu Island in the Decades prior to World War II.* Report submitted to the Aleut Corporation.

1990   Perspectives on Aleut Culture Change during the Russian Period. In *Russian America: the Forgotten Frontier.* B. S. Smith and R. J. Barnett, eds. Pp. 175-83. Tacoma: Washington State Historical Society.

1992   *Imprisonment and Internment: World War II and the Treatment of Alaska's Aleut Population.* Unpublished paper presented at the symposium "Indigenous People and Global Conflict: World War II Fifty Years later" at the 91st Annual Meeting of the American Anthropological Association, San Francisco.

1997a   *An Archaeological Survey of Selected Sites on Northern Adak Island, Aleutian Islands, Alaska.* Report submitted to the Aleut Corporation, Anchorage, Alaska.

1997b   *Cultural Heritage Program Opportunities in the Aleutian and Pribilof Islands Region.* Report submitted to the Aleutian/Pribilof Islands Association, Anchorage, Alaska.

1999   Environmental Perspectives on Historical Period Cultural Change Among the Aleuts of Southwestern Alaska. In *Development and Environment in the North. Proceedings of the 13th International Abashiri Symposium, The Hokkaido Museum of Northern Peoples.* Pp. 1-12. Abashiri, Japan: Association for the Promotion of Northern Cultures.

Veltre, Douglas W., and Allen P. McCartney

1994   *An Archaeological Survey of the early Russian and Aleut Settlements on St. Paul Island, Pribilof Islands, Alaska.* Report submitted to the TDX Corporation, St. Paul, Alaska.

2000   *The St. Paul History and Archaeology Project: Overview of 2000 Field Operations.* Report submitted to the TDX Corporation, St. Paul, Alaska.

2001   *The St. Paul History and Archaeology Project: Overview of 2001 Field Operations.* Report submitted to the TDX Corporation, St. Paul, Alaska.

2002   Russian Exploitation of Aleuts and Fur Seals: The Archaeology of Eighteenth- and Nineteenth-Century Settlements in the Pribilof Islands, Alaska. *Historical Archaeology* 36(3):8-17.

Veltre, Douglas W., and Mary J. Veltre

1986   *Early Settlements on St. George Island: an Archaeological Survey of Three Russian Period Sites in the Pribilof Islands, Alaska.* Report submitted to the Alaska Division of Parks and Outdoor Recreation, Anchorage.

85/ "Crossroads of Continents" exhibit on tour at the Anchorage Museum of History and Art, 1991

86/ A dear friend, Sergei Serov (1940-1992), Russian Crossroads *exhibit coordinator and Latin American culture expert, seen here helping mount archaeological specimens during one of the American museum venues. Photographer, William Fitzhugh*

87/ Reception for the North American Crossroads *team at the Museum of Anthropology and Ethnography (MAE) director's office in St. Petersburg, then Leningrad in 1983. MAE director, Rudolf Its, stands at his desk under the portrait of Vladimir Lenin. Other participants include (sitting left to right): Joan MacDonald, Bill Holm, William Sturtevant, Sergei Arutiunov (Institute of Ethnography, Moscow), James VanStone, George MacDonald. Photographer, William Fitzhugh*

88/ Andres Slapinsh, Latvian film producer, making ethnographic films among the Evenk people in East Siberia. Several Slapinsh's videos were used for the public programs accompanying "Crossroads of Continents" exhibits. Slapinsh was killed by Soviet troops in the winter of 1991 while filming an independence rally in his native Latvia

89/ The "Mini-Crossroads" team departing on its tour to Siberia. Nome, 1990. Left to right: Roger Powers, Darlene Orr, Valérie Chaussonnet, James Dixon, William Fitzhugh

90/ Mini-Crossroads exhibition being unloaded from a Russian Yak-40 transport plane. Vladivostok, Russia, August 1997. Photographer, Olga Shubina

91/ Mini-Crossroads in Russia: school tours at the exhibit, Yuzhno-Sakhalinsk, December 1997. Photographer, Olga Shubina

92/ Jochelson's display of the results of the Ryabushinski Expedition's archaeological work in the Aleutian Islands and Kamchatka at the Imperial Russian Geographical Society in St. Petersburg. Model of a section from the shell-midden at Aglagax on Umnak Island reveals the deep stratigraphy of many Aleut village sites (NAA 2003-20968)

93/ Informal photographs of Aleut are almost non-existent in Jochelson's photography making this picture of Aleut children most unusual. It appears as the very last image in a photograph album that he presented to the National Museum which suggests that he was cognizant of the continuity between the archaeological materials he excavated and the contemporary Aleut communities he visited (NAA 89-11741).

94/ Waldemar Jochelson with Aleut laborers in a deep midden cut, probably on Umnak Island, 1909 (NAA 89-11750)

95/ Excavations at the Margaret Bay archaeological site by Rick Knecht have revealed a stone-walled Aleut house dating to ca. 3100 B.P. A structure of more recent vintage stands in the distance. Photographer, Douglas Veltre.

96/ A portion of the village of St. Paul in the Pribilof Islands, with fur seals resting on the beach in the foreground. Photographer, Douglas Veltre.

97/ The Atka Dancers (Atxam Taliigisnikangis) at the Aleut Elders' Conference, Unalaska, 1996. Since their founding in 1995, the Atka Dancers have performed at numerous national and Alaskan venues. Photographer, Douglas Veltre

98/ Yakut artisan, Anna Nikolaeva dressed in a fur coat or buuktaakh son, which she produced following the photos from the AMNH collection. Front view.

99/ Same fur coat. Back view.

100/ Birch-bark container (woman's storage box). Made by Anna Nikolaeva based on samples from the AMNH collection.

101/ Woman's fur coat created by costume designer Lena Gogoleva for characters in the Yakut/Sakha opera Nyurgun Bootur, performed by the Yakut Theater of Ballet and Opera

102/ Musqueam house post purchased by Harlan Smith, 1898 (AMNH 42936)

103/ Susan Point, House Posts, 1997. University of British Columbia Museum of Anthropology, Vancouver, B.C. Nbz 838, 837. Photograph courtesy Susan Point and Bill McLennan.

104/ Masset village, Haida, 1879. Photograph by O. C. Hastings (RBCM, PN-10980)

105/ Alert Bay, Kwakwaka'wakw, 1910. Photographer unknown (RBCM, PN-10189)

106/ Ellen Neel (1916–1966) in 1950. Photograph courtesy Phil Nuytten.

107/ Mungo Martin (1880–1962). Photograph courtesy Jim Ryan (RBCM, PN-13492)

108/ Ellen Neel, Totemland Pole, 1950. Photograph courtesy Phil Nuytten

109/ Matthias Joe Capilano, Thunderbird Dynasty Pole, Stanley Park, Vancouver, British Columbia, 1936. Photograph courtesy of Vancouver Archives IN N103.1

110/ Susan Point (b. 1952) in 1997. Photograph courtesy of Susan Point and Bill McLennan.

111/ Susan Point, Common Thread, 2000. Spirit Wrestler Gallery, Vancouver, BC. Photograph courtesy Susan Point, Spirit Wrestler Gallery, and Kenji Nagai.

In Memory of Vladimir Ivanov-Unarov, 1937–2000

MARJORIE MANDELSTAM BALZER

Vladimir Kharlampovich Ivanov-Unarov, sixty-four, scholar of the art and spiritual culture of indigenous peoples of the North, died in Yakutsk, Sakha Republic (Yakutia), Russian Federation, December 29, 2000. His careful fieldwork and refined scholarship covered a range of peoples, from the Evenk, Even, Yukagir, Chukchi and Yakut (Sakha) of his native republic, to peoples of North America. Author of numerous monographs and articles, including *Yakut Bone Carving* and *Problems of Folk Ornamental Art*, his knowledge of the peoples of the Far North was deep as well as broad.

Continuing the tradition of meticulous ethnographers of the nineteenth century, he brought back to life the Jesup North Pacific Expedition's volume by Waldemar Jochelson *The Yukaghir and the Yukaghirzed Tungus* by translating it into Russian and having it translated into Yukagir for the remaining indigenous communities of the Sakha North. He was active, with his wife and colleague Zinaida Ivanova-Unarova, in the *Jesup 2* project that brought indigenous peoples and scholars together at the American Museum of Natural History in New York in 1997. Famously productive, he was one of the only people in the history of foundation grants to complete a MacArthur-funded project before his supporters expected.

Vladimir bridged multiple disciplines with his perceptive, boundary-crossing intelligence, and bridged multiple cultures with his contributions to international communication. A mentor and friend to many, he encouraged colleagues in the Sakha Republic to make

112/ *Vladimir Ivanov-Unarov (1937-2000). Photographer, Marjorie Mandelstam Balzer.*

the leap into collaborative work with American and European scholars. After several trips to the U.S., he was pivotal in returning the knowledge and wealth of spiritual and material culture kept in American museums back to his people through successful academic and public lectures and slide shows. He was a founder and mainstay of the department he headed in the Academy of Sciences Institute of the Problems of Minorities of the North, and was often asked to take on more administrative responsibility than he wanted. Originally trained as a geologist before gaining a degree in Art History, Vladimir's combined scientific and humanities focused approaches were fieldwork based, ethnographic, and flexible. One of his last projects included helping to adapt a cultural studies curriculum to the needs of the Sakha Republic.

Gentle and generous, Vladimir's great empathy and brilliant analysis of the symbols that make lives meaningful made him one of the most important mentors and examples of my life. At one breakfast he patiently explained the symbolism and history of the beautiful wooden Sakha challices (*choron*) that hold fermented mare's milk. That breakfast lasted for hours, going nearly until lunch.

I am deeply privileged to have been welcomed into the love of his multigenerational family. Each time I enthusiastically would come home with news of meeting a Sakha, Even, Evenk or Yukagir colleague in Yakutsk, Vladimir would provide wonderful background on the significance of their work and the kin networks and political backgrounds of their families. His perspective on life in the republic was invaluable. I recall him at his happiest playing with his grandchildren, and teaching them how to get onto the Internet. He is survived by his wife and colleague Zina, "son the doctor" Maxim, his daughter Marina the artist, and their partners and wonderful children.

113/ Sakha (Yakut) ysyakh *summer festival, May 1902. Local residents in the village of Churapcha held the festival two months prior to its normal timing, so that Jochelson's team could fully document it (AMNH 1803).*

The Revitalization of the Traditional Culture of Northeast Siberian Peoples
The Role of the Jesup Expedition

VLADIMIR IVANOV-UNAROV
AND ZINAIDA IVANOVA-UNAROVA

From papers published in Russian anthropological journals at the beginning of the twentieth century, it is apparent that teams of the Jesup North Pacific Expedition (JNPE) had operated in the Northeast of Russia in 1898–1902. Unfortunately, this expedition was hardly mentioned during the Soviet period of Russia's history. Data on and references to the expedition's materials were censored primarily for political reasons. The former leader of the Siberian portion of the JNPE, Waldemar (Vladimir) Jochelson, after being officially permitted to go the U.S. in the 1920s to complete his Jesup Expedition monograph about the Yukagir, failed to return to Soviet Russia. Until the middle of the 1980s the overall scope of the Jesup Expedition, the value of its Siberian collections as well as their present fate, remained all but unknown in the former Soviet Union, particularly in the regions where the JNPE teams once operated.

How We Became Acquainted with the Collections of the Jesup Expedition

During Soviet times, any thought of traveling from the authors' native city of Yakutsk to New York to study the JNPE Siberian collection would have been equivalent to thinking about flying to the moon. But the great transformation that occurred in Russia during the past decade changed everything, including our lives. On February 3, 1991, then-US Ambassador to Russia, Jack Matlock, and his wife Rebecca Matlock stopped for two days in Yakutsk on their way to Khabarovsk, a city in the Russian Far East. They came not as official visitors but as guests of the newly established local association, "*Sakha omyk*" (Sakha Nation). The Americans, who were interested in the culture and art of the Native peoples of Siberia, paid a visit to the Artists' Union of the Republic of Sakha (then, *Yakutskaya ASSR*). We, as art historians, quickly organized a small display of indigenous art and introduced the guests to local artists. During our conversations we asked Ambassador Matlock about the current location of the Jesup Expedition's Siberian collections. He promised to find out and let us know. But Mrs. Matlock suggested that we could visit New York and search for the JNPE Siberian treasures ourselves. For the first time this previously unthinkable venture seemed possible.

In 1992 few Russian curators and art historians had the opportunity to leave the country on work-related trips. But luck was with us and we received a grant from the Soros Foundation for travel and a two-month stay in the U.S. Thus, in November and December of 1992, we were able to work full time in the collections of the American Museum of Natural History in New York. The American Museum astounded us with its openness. Laurel Kendall, curator of the Asian and Siberian collections, did everything possible to ensure that our work with museum materials, including not only the ethnographic objects but also archival documents and historical photographs, would be productive. She encouraged us to take photographs and to make photocopies of many historical documents, such as personal letters and diaries of the Jesup Expedition participants that were stored at the AMNH archives. Only someone who has once worked in the museums and archives of the former Soviet Union can fully appreciate the level of friendliness and hospitality we encountered at the AMNH.

The Siberian Team of the Jesup Expedition

The work of the Jesup Expedition is sufficiently described in the literature (Boas 1903, 1905; Freed et al., 1988a, 1988b). We will focus here on a few details that have not been covered and also, but very briefly, on those aspects necessary for an understanding of the issues we deal with in this article.

The main goal of the Jesup Expedition, formulated by Franz Boas, was to look for the origin of American Indians and for their possible routes into the New World from Northeast Asia using ethnographic evidence as well as folklore and linguistic data, and to study the physical anthropology of the local people. In accordance with this basic goal, Boas assigned to expedition participants strictly defined tasks in the collection of field materials. In order to study the connections between the Native peoples of North America and Northeast Siberia it was necessary to find scholars who were both familiar with the culture of the studied peoples and willing to work with the expedition, often in rugged and remote areas. For the northeast Siberian part of the JNPE, these two requirements were met quite successfully. The then-director of the Russian Academy of Sciences' Museum of Anthropology and Ethnology in St. Petersburg, Prof. Vasily V. Radloff (Radlov), recommended Waldemar Jochelson (Vladimir I. Iochelson, 1855–1937) and Waldemar Bogoras (Vladimir G. Bogoraz, 1865–1936) to Boas as highly qualified specialists with excellent first-hand knowledge of the region (see more in Cole 2001:37–9; Vakhtin 2001:78–82).

Jochelson and Bogoras were former political dissidents, who had been sentenced by the Russian court to spend several years in exile in northern Yakutia for their participation in the revolutionary Populist movement. Their place of exile eventually became both the location for and the object of self-initiated scientific study. The innovative idea of "going to the people" turned into an active interest in research on the languages and culture(s) of the local populations. In 1894, Dimitri Klements, then the Chairman of the East Siberia Branch of the Russian Geographic Society encouraged them to join the Yakut (Sibiryakov) Expedition, organized with funds from the Russian gold-mining magnate, Alexander M. Sibiryakov. Klements' task for Bogoras was to collect data on the Chukchi, the Even (Lamut), and the local Russian-speaking (Creole) populations of northern Siberia. Jochelson lived more than two years among the Yukagir people (1895–1896), traveled with them on their annual migration routes, documented two Yukagir languages, and put together a dictionary of 9000 words and over 150 folklore texts (Shavrov 1935:49). One of Jochelson's field journals from 1896, when he lived among the Upper Kolyma River Yukagir, is now preserved in the AMNH archive (AMNH-DA, Box A). A small notebook, entitled "Travel notes No. 3," contains valuable information but is written in small, Russian handwriting that is hard to make out. We prepared a few passages from the journal for publication in a recent issue of the Yakut (Sakha) literary journal *Ilin* (Ivanov-Unarov and Ivanova 1998).

In addition to the Yukagir, Jochelson's interests included the Yakut (Sakha) people. During his years of exile in Yakutia he became acquainted with many of the Yakut cultural workers and representatives of the Yakut intelligentsia. He also knew the Yakut (Sakha) language. According to several reports, the Yakut (Sakha) language was then the primary mean of communication in many areas of Yakutia, even for the local Russian population.

In the fall of 1898 Jochelson received a letter from Boas, offering him a three-year contract with monthly pay of $100 and $4000 for field expenses during the time he served with the Jesup Expedition

(Vakhtin 2001:80–1).[1] Intense correspondence began at this time between Boas and Jochelson, giving a picture of both their relationship and the course of the proposed fieldwork (these letters are now kept in Jochelson's file in the AMNH-DA archives). According to the contract, all scientific data, ethnographic collections, and field journals were to become the property of the American Museum of Natural History in New York.

In his letter of reply, Jochelson agreed to the overall plan for the expedition. Judging by Boas' response, Jochelson also submitted a series of his own suggestions, broadening the tasks set by Boas in the collection of materials and in subsequent publications. Boas responded appropriately, though somewhat severely, insisting that Jochelson should fulfill the tasks as they were assigned to him. He reminded Jochelson that, according to the original contract, Jochelson's primary job for the American Museum was the survey of the Koryak; his visit to the Yukagir was only to collect artifacts. Boas did not have any objections to the collection of additional material as long as it did not interfere with the fulfillment of Jochelson's basic task. Boas also stated that the museum did not have any interest in publishing Jochelson's materials other than a monograph about the Koryak; but that if there were to be a publication about the Yukagir it should be quite short.[2]

During the preparation and actual fieldwork of the Jesup Expedition, Jochelson managed to convince Boas and, it seems, AMNH President Morris K. Jesup , of the necessity of broadening the study area, to include—in addition to the Koryak and Chukchi—other Siberian peoples, such as the Yukagir, the Even (Lamut), and the Yakut (Sakha).

In August of 1899, Jochelson and Bogoras met in St. Petersburg and worked out a plan for their cooperative field research. Jochelson notified Boas of this in a letter on October 30.[3] Given Bogoras's knowledge of the Chukchi language, they proposed that they would work together for one and a half years with the Koryak, whose language is close to Chukchi. Bogoras would concentrate on study of the Koryak language and the collection of folklore texts. Jochelson would make anthropometric measurements, take photographs, and collect ethnographic objects for the Museum. After the joint survey of the Koryak, they would set off separately—Jochelson to the land of the Yukagir to the west and Bogoras to the Siberian Eskimo (Yupik) country to the northeast, along the shores of the Bering Strait and the Arctic Ocean. Boas did not approve their plan to work together, and they ended up working separately.

In March 1900, Jochelson received a letter from Morris K. Jesup saying that Jochelson was to be in charge of the (North) Siberian section of the expedition and stipulated the pay Jochelson would receive.[4] In August of the same year, Jochelson, his wife Dina Jochelson-Brodsky, and two other members of his field team, Alexander Axelrod and Norman Buxton, arrived in the small town of Gizhiga on the coast of the Sea of Okhotsk to study the local Koryak (Fig. 7). A month earlier, Bogoras, accompanied by his wife Sofia, arrived at the mouth of the Anadyr River to begin his work with the Chukchi.

As a result, the two Siberian teams of the Jesup Expedition gathered a huge amount of information about not only the Chukchi and the Koryak but also the Yukagir, Even (Lamut), and Yakut (Sakha). Altogether, some 6400 items they had collected were delivered to the American Museum of Natural History in New York. According to Jochelson's final report, 917 of these were Yakut (Sakha) objects, 300 were Yukagir, and more than 5000 were from the Koryak, Even, Chukchi, and Siberian Eskimo. In addition, there were hundreds of photographs, phonograph recordings, and other research materials. Besides the two originally planned monographs on the Chukchi (Bogoras 1904–9) and Koryak (Jochelson 1908) for the JNPE series, two more monographs were eventually published on the Yukagir (Jochelson 1926) and the Yakut/Sakha (Jochelson 1933).

The Siberian Collection of the Jesup Expedition

The ethnographic objects collected by Jochelson and Bogoras some 100 years ago were quite significant for academic and museum researchers who were interested in Native Siberian peoples. They also seemed "exotic" and exciting to the general European and American public. But at the time they were collected, these were quite ordinary items, used routinely for both daily life and festivals. Today, after a hundred years that have seen profound changes in these cultures, the significance of the Jesup Expedition collections has changed dramatically, first and foremost for the bearers of these cultures.

The Sakha (Yakut) Collection

878 items from the JNPE collections are identified in the AMNH catalog as "Yakut." These are not only pieces of Native art but also many everyday objects, without artistic embellishment, as well as models and toys. The most complete samples represent Yakut/Sakha decorated clothing, silver decorations, wood carvings, ceramic objects with ornamentation, and traditional horse gear.

There are also several ivory carvings, which the AMNH records identify as "Russified" objects. Interestingly, there is a storage box made of mammoth ivory that is almost an exact copy of a box from 1799 that is in the State Historical Museum in Moscow. It differs in only a few minor details, namely, the subject matter depicted on the sides of the box. We believe this piece was made by a Yakut ivory carver, most probably by Leontii Popov. Though Yakut ivory objects from the eighteenth century were commonly copies of carvings by northern Russian carvers from the town of Kholmogory, there were already at that time certain features that clearly distinguished Yakut artists, especially in technique, ornamentation, and subject matter.

On the whole, objects from the Yakut (Sakha) collection at the AMNH are typical and quite familiar, and not significantly different from objects in other museums. This further substantiates the stability of the Native traditions. However, within the Yakut collection at the AMNH there are many unique objects that do not exist in museums in Russia.

The collection illustrates the variety of women's winter and summer/fall fur coats. Altogether there are thirty-two coats and fur robes in the American Museum. Six of these are so-called "*khotoidookh son*" ("fur coat with eagle") the likes of which do not exist in any museum in Yakutia (Sakha Republic). Local artists are very interested in this type of traditional women's dress, although they had never before seen them. Having only before heard about this type, they are now creating their own modern versions based on items in the AMNH collections. For example, in 1992 Anastasia E. Sivtseva, an acclaimed Yakut seamstress, sewed a fur coat for the exhibition "*Kudai Bakhsy*" with an eagle on the back showing head, claws, and wings. In this case, the Yakut fur robes from the American Museum collection provided her with an original example of this type of fur clothing. They were acquired in the Middle-Kolyma (*Srednekolymsk*) and Verkhoyansk districts in northern Yakutia. It is most likely that they are from the second half of the nineteenth century. There is therefore no doubt that they represent the old type of Yakut *sangyakh*. These have been mentioned in the literature, including a mention by the famous Yakut historian, Sehen Bolo.[5] Jochelson, who acquired these fur robes from the northern Yakut calls them "*kybytyylaakh son*," apparently the name his informants used for them. This means simply, "fur robe with an inset."

It is well known that the eagle is a sacred bird for many peoples, including the Yakut and many North American Indians. Among the Yakut, its name may not even be spoken aloud. The folklorist and founder of Yakut literature, A. Kulakovskii, wrote that the Yakut do not dare pronounce aloud the word "*khotoĭ*" (eagle), calling it instead "*toion*," that is, "master." As a result, in many Sakha/Yakut settlements the word "*khotoĭ*" has been completely forgotten (Kulakovskii 1979:79, 92). At the same time, the technique for making the robe is reflected in the name "*kybytyylaakh son*" recorded by

Jochelson, which is *kybytan tigii*, "sewn inset." The robes from his collection are made from a variety of materials. For example, one robe is made of quite expensive lynx fur (AMNH # 70/8525). On the back it has a slit typical of all Yakut fur robes and coats. However, the slit is absent in all the other "eagle robes" from the Jochelson AMNH collection; instead, it is replaced by a mock slit—an ornamental fur stripe. This is strongly reminiscent of the northern type of caftan. An inset of dark brown otter fur is sewn on the back of the "eagle robe" (AMNH # 70/8525), reminiscent of a bird's spread wings. The other robes are made of dark brown Siberian marmot fur, white reindeer fur, and calf and foal hides. All the robes have the same inset made of darker fur in the form of open wings; this is why they are called "*khotoidookh son*" (fur robe with eagle).

The *belepchi* (AMNH # 70/8826) that Jochelson acquired in the village of Churapcha is another rare item. *Belepchi* is an article of clothing no longer made. Sakha/Yakut men wore it over their trousers, both for warmth and as a component of festival wear. There is only one specimen preserved in the local museum. It was found in the late seventeenth or early eighteenth century grave of a man. Sakha ethnographer F. Zykov sees a parallel between Yakut men's *belepchi* and women's *belebshi* among the Buryat, Kirgiz, and Kazakh (Zykov 1993:268). At the same time, the Kirgiz epic "Manas" mentions *bel'demchi* as male armor. It should be noted that Jochelson acquired most of the items for his Yakut (Sakha) collection in the village of Churapcha on the left bank of the Lena River, 200 km north of the city of Yakutsk. He justifiably thought that ancient Yakut tradition would be best preserved here and argued this in his letter to Boas. The Jesup *belepchi* is particularly valuable because, unlike the single surviving archaic specimen recovered from the grave, this was a type that was actually worn in Jochelson's time.

There are also decorated "ribbons for the fiancée's room." They are two leather straps, almost four meters long, but only about two centimeters wide, decorated with beads and round metal plates and finished on the

end with a fringe of suede leather (*rovduga*). Their significance is now forgotten, even by the elders.

The AMNH collection also contains engraved silver jewelry with the engraving in good condition. Among the unique artifacts made of wood and birch bark, there is a complete set of summer birch-bark covering for a Yakut *urasa* (summer dwelling). Jochelson suggested to Boas in a letter that he would like to build a full-size *urasa* in the American Museum courtyard, using the precise model that he had acquired for his Yakut collection. If Jochelson had indeed built this, it would today be the only authentic, non-reconstructed Yakut *urasa* in the world.

The Even (Lamut) Collection

There are 481 artifacts in the AMNH Even catalog. Most of these objects were collected by Bogoras' wife, Sofia Bogoras, in the village of Markovo on the Anadyr River. She made several trips there from the fall of 1900 to April 1901, while her husband, along with a Cossack and a local guide, was on a long trip to Kamchatka in search of Chukchi and Koryak materials.[6]

In addition to these, there are also several Even items acquired by Jochelson. During a trip in two boats on the Sea of Okhotsk to the mouth of the Nayakhan River he discovered a sixty-one tent Tungus (Even) camp. There he succeeded in collecting ample ethnographic data about Even people who were living along the Sea of Okhotsk coast. He wrote Boas about this in his letter-report from Kushka.[7]

We made a detailed study of Jochelson's collection of Even clothing and have concluded that it is typical for reindeer Even in cut and style, though the character of the decorations shows a certain Koryak influence.

The Yukagir Collection

Comprised of 342 artifacts, it is unique in that it contains practically every type of clothing and daily use objects of a small Native nation that was in danger of cultural extinction. Jochelson was fully aware of this and he stated many times that he considered his JNPE volume, *The Yukaghirs and the Yukaghirized Tungus* (1926) a memorial for a vanishing people. Following his earlier work among the Yukagir on the Russian Sibiryakov Expedition he wrote: "In a few decades the Yukagir language could disappear and the tribe would under these conditions, cease to exist, a part dying and a part dissolving into other tribes" (Jochelson 1900:xv).

In our view, the most valuable items in the JNPE Yukagir collection are the numerous birch-bark objects, including maps and letters engraved on bark as well as wooden and birch-bark animal figures.

The Koryak and Chukchi Collections

The very rich Koryak and the somewhat smaller Chukchi collections were acquired by Jochelson and Bogoras. The collecting process was unbelievably difficult because of the climate, lack of roads, and attitude of the local people. Bogoras almost died of influenza on his return trip from Kamchatka in the winter of 1901. The Koryak, who were on friendly terms with Jochelson, made sure that none of their traditions would be violated or dishonored in the collecting process. Nevertheless, Jochelson's Koryak collection contains several shaman drums and also samples of burial clothing, acquired in the village of Kamenskoe in northern Kamchatka. According to Koryak beliefs, the latter must not be shown to anyone.

Jochelson was evidently charming and persuasive as a collector and field worker. For proof of this here is another example: When he arrived in the Yakut village of Churapcha at the beginning of May 1902, the local residents gave him not only a complete *urasa* (birch bark summer dwelling), but they also held a *ysyakh* festival especially for him. This festival was usually held two months later, at the end of June, before haying began (Fig. 113).

Berthold Laufer, another Jesup Expedition Siberian collector, on his earlier trip among the Amur River people (1898–9) assembled a small collection from the local Evenk people who lived along the Amgun River, a tributary to the Amur River. Altogether, eighty-five Evenk artifacts collected by Laufer are listed in the AMNH catalog along with many from Laufer's objects acquired among the Nivkh, the Nanay, the Orok, and the Ainu.

One Hundred Years after Jesup 1

Although the European takeover of the Arctic began long before the start of the twentieth century, it at first did not move particularly quickly nor did it have any decisive impact. Thus, despite several destructive events, the peoples who inhabited the arctic regions usually had time to adapt to this tempo and to preserve the integrity of their cultures, traditional economies, their beliefs, customs, and rituals, clothing and utensils, and decorative art. But in the twentieth century the social shocks and intensive exploitation of natural resources in the North brought irredeemable losses to the Native people at all levels.

A number of factors have brought on the current crisis for the traditional cultures of the Native people of the Russian Arctic. The Soviet government's declared program for northern indigenous people of "transition from primitive social structure to socialism, by-passing the stage of capitalism" meant that the specific characteristics of these small nations and their cultures were ignored. This caused a quickening in the destruction of their way of life; a way of life that had adapted over millennia and was ideally suited to the extreme conditions of the Arctic. Many aspects of Native legacies were lost and there was the distinct threat of complete assimilation and/or extinction for the smaller indigenous nations such as the Yukagir.

Beginning in the 1930s the destruction of the social and economic fabric was hastened by the seizure of property, the formation of collective farms (*kolkhozes*) and "state-farms" (*sovkhozes*), the enforced transition to a settled way of life and "villagization." This was accompanied by a process of banning and hounding out traditional beliefs, customs, and rituals that were seen as out-dated, archaic, and even savage. This censure of Native spiritual traditions delivered a heavy blow to the indigenous people and triggered the loss of a substantial component of their cultural legacy. The Eurocentric theory of cultural evolution was firmly established as an ideological paradigm in the former Soviet Union. According to this theory, with the appearance of professional art and literature, traditional folk art becomes merely historical atavism and ought to disappear. It was thought that this was a natural step in the progressive development of a people and their culture.

This stereotypical viewpoint has unfortunately proved very persistent and is still held by many scholars even today. Supporters of this theory advised Native artisans to replace their traditional ornaments with modern Soviet emblems. They embraced the so-called authored, creative approach to artistic production and demanded of folk art that it be innovative and modern. The vulgar, materialist approach to folk art focused on the external form of the artwork, completely ignoring the semiotic content that had been worked out over centuries. It is well known that in each specimen produced by a folk artist, in every motif and in the composition of ornaments there is a definite symbolic meaning. This is the essence of folk art. Even though the semantics of the many ornamentation motifs had already been forgotten in the nineteenth century, the folk artists intuitively did as their ancestors had done. In this way, the continuity of traditional artistry and artistic thought was preserved.

Unfortunately, many transitions introduced by the Soviet system and, particularly, the mandatory boarding schools (*internaty*) for Native students tore children from their parents and accustomed environment, and changed peoples' lives. The centuries-old system of aural-visual transmission of crafts and knowledge from generation to generation was destroyed. This break in the transmission of tradition led to the disappearance of some forms of folk art and to the artificial mutation of others. At the same time, as the continuity in trans-

mission of tradition was destroyed, the informational boom caused great harm to folk art. It facilitated the introduction of many foreign elements into Native art (such as materials, technology, ornamental motifs, etc.), which, in turn, undermined traditional culture from within. This is directly evident in the case of Even and Evenk culture, whereas the Yukagir are in danger of completely disappearing as a culturally distinctive group.

Here we cite the story of the Berezov group of Even who managed to maintain until very recently a special, unique oasis of traditional language and culture. This group of nomadic reindeer Even remained fully isolated until the mid-1950s, when they were discovered by the Soviet security services and re-incorporated into the highly regulated life of the Yakut Republic. Due to decades of deliberate isolation, the Berezov Even, unlike other groups of Even in Yakutia, had preserved their language and traditional culture. One of the authors (V. I-U.) visited the village of Berezovka —to which these people had been relocated—in the late 1980s. Communication with several elder women of the village had to be through an interpreter because they knew neither Russian nor Yakut. In this they differ from other indigenous people of northern Yakutia (Sakha Republic) who commonly prefer to speak Russian or Yakut rather than their own language.

The relation to language and culture today can be assessed from a survey conducted by the second co-author [Z.I.] in two northern districts (*ulus*) of the Sakha Republic, the Srednekolymskii (Middle Kolyma), and Nizhnekolymskii (Lower Kolyma), in March 1997. Seven adults who consider themselves Native artists completed the survey, as did fifty-three high-school students in grades 8 to 10. In Berezovka, the village visited by Vladimir Ivanov-Unarov ten years earlier, the older women still speak primarily their native Even language; but now they also know a little Russian and a little Yakut. They live sedentary lives and raise the children in the family. Sewing and decorative traditions have been handed down from the older generation, but some women think them outdated and therefore do not concern themselves with teaching the children these handicrafts. Thirteen- and fourteen-year old Even children speak Russian at school and Even at home. Only one of the girls in the survey reported that she is learning Native sewing skills from her grandmother.

Once again, it was the artificial isolation of the Berezov Even that helped them preserve their traditional decorative art. Unfortunately, a tendency toward innovation and a desire to satisfy the tastes of audiences at folk-art exhibits, who are delighted with abundant bright beads and color, will soon lead to the use of quantity decor in their work.

Tundra Yukagir made up the majority of the population in the Lower Kolyma area at Jochelson's time (1895–1902). Today, of the twenty-five thirteen to fifteen year-old students surveyed in local schools in the towns of Cherski, Andriushkino, and Kolymskoe, only four considered themselves Yukagir, and two of them have Russian fathers. They do not know their native language and speak only Russian. They all have negative attitudes toward the traditional culture of handicrafts.

Nevertheless, since the mid-1980s there has been an intensive growth in ethnic consciousness among many peoples of Russia, including the indigenous small nations of the Russian North. Native intellectuals, including professional writers and artists are among those leading the movement for the preservation and revival of ethnic culture.

During the Soviet period the loss of Native cultures did not proceed at the same rate among all the groups. Thus, the Sakha people, who were the majority population in Yakutia until the 1960s, were granted a certain limited level of administrative autonomy in the early 1930s. For the most part they preserved their language and some of the traditional features of their way of life. Today, in comparison with other Native nations of the Sakha Republic, the Sakha people have been quite successful in reviving their cultural legacy. The popular festival *ysyakh* was revived and has come to be a focus of ethnic cultural life, including songs, dances, games, clothing, ceremonial dinnerware and utensils, decorations and foods. Related forms of folk art are correspondingly beginning to be revived.

Traces of the old customs have been preserved somewhere deep in people's memory. For several decades it seemed as if shamanism had long been cut out of the lives of Siberian peoples. In recent years, however, shamans have reappeared in Yakutia as well as numerous psychic healers who fill the role that shamans once filled. Moreover, it appears that active shamans still practice among the isolated, migratory groups of the Evenk in southern Yakutia, continuing to fulfil their traditional functions as protectors of the clan, soothsayers, and healers.

Today, in the Republic of Sakha there is an officially recognized Association for Traditional Medicine, headed by the contemporary Sakha shaman, Vladimir Kondakov, and a Center for Traditional Medicine whose doctors have medical training and also know traditional folk methods of healing.

We cite another example. During the 1980s, many students in Yakut folklore were talking about the fading out of the storytelling tradition among the Sakha people. At that time there remained only a few elders who were accomplished at improvisational storytelling. In the past few years, however, as a result of the increased interest in folklore and the growth in ethnic consciousness, the situation has changed dramatically as if some hidden resources were emerging from deep in Native memory. There are young people and even children with the gift of performing traditional epic folk tales. Many people have stepped forward to perform various old rituals and half-forgotten practices that demand great improvisational competence.

In Yakutia today much effort is being put into the revival and preservation of the culture of the Native people. There is emphasis on the development of song and dance traditions and all forms of professional art. A special presidential program supports talented young people who tour all over the world winning honors and awards. The so-called Academy of Spirituality was established in 1997 by a decree issued by Mikhail Nikolaev, then the President of the Sakha Republic. Many professional artists, writers, performers, composers, and even the local bishop of the Russian Orthodox Church, have become members of the Academy. However, not one representative of the traditional folk culture or practitioner of the traditional religion is a member. Several Centers for Folk Art have been established, and there have been many conferences on Sakha religion; however, these have neither official acceptance nor adequate financial support. But at least they have not been banned.

All the same, the obstacles on the path to cultural revival are mounting. Alongside the economic hardships produced by the general social-economic breakdown in Russia, there are also the difficulties connected with the loss of cultural continuity. Efforts to revive Native decorative arts are stalled because many contemporary artisans no longer know the traditional skills and have lost cultural information related to the old practices. In 1996, at a seminar for Native folk artisans and seamstresses in the town of Srednekolymsk in northeastern Yakutia, we witnessed the tremendous interest that exists in the recovery of the lost traditions. It seemed that many modern artisans do not know the traditional techniques and technologies of working with fur and leather, of sewing and decorating ethnic dresses. They use eclectic, quirky decorative motifs. The seminar participants thus were very excited to see the slides we made at the American Museum in New York of traditional objects from the JNPE Jochelson's collection.

The Present-Day Value of the JNPE Siberian Collections

The Siberian collections of the Jesup Expedition are now the most priceless resource for the traditional art and crafts of the Native people of northeast Siberia who have suffered enormous cultural losses during the twentieth century. Since our research at the American Museum of Natural History, we have frequently had occasion to speak of the Jesup Expedition collection on the media and at the various meetings with folk artisans. These conversations strengthened our conviction that the knowledge of this collection is of critical importance today for the bearers of the cultures represented in the Jesup Expedition collection.

The case of the artisan mentioned above, Anastasia Sivtseva, is a good example. Several pieces of her artworks and fur clothing have been acquired recently by the AMNH. After seeing pictures of traditional eagle robes in the Jesup Expedition collection, she acknowledged that she neither visualized nor made the "fur robe with eagle" properly. Another artisan, Anna Nikolaeva, sewed a *buuktaakh son* coat following a copy of Jochelson's photograph, "Yakut Woman in Feast Dress" (AMNH, # 70/7314 and 70/7318, 1818–9; Figs. 98 and 99). She also made a beautiful birch bark container after Jochelson's "Birch Bark" (AMNH # 70/8862; Fig. 100).

In a recent performance of the Yakut national opera *Nyurgun Bootur*, the main characters were dressed in national clothing made by the costume designer Lena Gogoleva. The styles she used for coats and ornaments were based on the photos and drawings we had made of objects in Jochelson's collection at the AMNH (Fig. 101). Unfortunately, since there were no good quality slides and photographs available for the Yukagir and Even artifacts, we were unable to generate the same amount of interest in these objects or to make them as widely known.

It is to be hoped that Bogoras' and Jochelson's monumental monographs in the Jesup Expedition series, *The Chukchee*, *The Koryak*, and *The Yukaghir and the Yukaghirized Tungus* will become available in full translation for a Russian-speaking audience, including the Native peoples of Russia. Bogoras' *The Chukchi* and Jochelson's *The Koryak* were already reprinted in Russian (Bogoras 1991; Jochelson 1997), although not in their original JNPE format and in small print. In 1996 we were commissioned by the Institute on Problems of Northern Peoples in Yakutsk to translate another

Jochelson's JNPE monograph, *The Yukaghirs and the Yukaghirized Tungus* (Jochelson 1926). The translation was done with help from a grant from the MacArthur Foundation, but publication is still pending.[9] This is, indeed, a unique and so far the only major source on Yukagir traditional ethnography, social life, family relations, and spiritual and material culture. It is especially significant that this book was written on the basis of almost four years of personal observations among the Yukagir, at a time when their language and many of their traditions were still alive. Yukagir poet and philologist, Gavril Kurilov, wrote a special *Foreword* to this modern translation of Jochelson's famous book, and his brother, the artist Nikolai Kurilov, redrew the original drawings. Both of the Kurilov brothers are highly respected cultural leaders of the modern Yukagir nation. They believe they are descendants of the shaman Somon, whom Jochelson met on his trip and named Shomonov (Shamanov) in Russian transcription.

In our translation we maintained all of Jochelson's original text, only adding several contemporary notes and corrections in the Footnotes section. Unfortunately, because of the long time between the recording of his Yukagir field data (in 1895–6 and 1901–2) and the final preparation of his monograph for the JNPE series (published in 1926), Jochelson allowed a few errors in attribution of some artifacts to slip in. For example, a few Even objects were identified as Yukagir. Sergei Ivanov later used these incorrect attributions in generalizations about the special characteristics of Yukagir ornamentation in his monograph on the ornamentation styles of the Native people of Siberia (Ivanov 1963). These were recycled in the recently published monograph, *Odezhda yukagirov* (Clothing of the Yukagir) by L. Zhukova.

It would also be of great value to bring the copies of the original Jochelson's photographs and an excellent photo exhibit, *Drawing Shadows to Stone*, to Yakutia. This exhibit was produced by the AMNH curators for the opening of the conference dedicated to the Centenary of the Jesup North Pacific Expedition in New York (Kendall et al. 1997). In the winter of 1998 a conference was held in Yakutsk on the occasion of the national festival *Ysyakh*. At this conference, we showed Jochelson's photograph of the *Ysyakh* opening ceremony in May 1902 in the village of Churapcha (see Kendall et al. 1997:91–2, Fig. 113). This photo from the AMNH collection was kindly given to us by Thomas Miller, one of the organizers of the *Drawing Shadows to Stone* Exhibit. Jochelson's photo attracted great interest because it was taken 100 years ago when the *Ysyakh* festival was still a living tradition and not a yearly festival with invented and staged performances. This photo and several of Jochelson's other Jesup pictures, along with our comments and a brief story of the Jesup Expedition, were reproduced recently by the Yakutsk-based journal *Ilin* (Ivanov-Unarov and Ivanova 1998).

The importance of the Jesup Expedition's ethnographic collections is that it represents the classic legacy of the traditional cultures of the Sakha, Koryak, Chukchi, Even, Evenk, and Yukagir peoples. The Yakutsk-based Institute on Problems of Northern Peoples of the Russian Academy of Sciences recently initiated an international research and publication program entitled *Circumpolar Culture of the Peoples of the Arctic and North: Monuments of Culture of the Peoples of the Arctic*. The goal of this project is to lay the groundwork for a series of basic encyclopedia-style volumes on each of the Native peoples of the North and the Arctic. The AMNH Jesup Expedition collections can make an invaluable contribution to this project. For this reason, project outlines include the publication of summary catalogs of the JNPE collections on each nation of Siberia, with photographs and detailed description of the objects. Once published locally, in Yakutsk and in Russian, these catalogs would constitute a crucial contribution to the revival of the cultures of the indigenous peoples of Siberia once depicted by the Jesup Expedition.

Acknowledgments

We would like to express our gratitude to the Soros Foundation for enabling us to study the collection of the Jesup Expedition in New York in 1992. Special thanks go to the many people on the AMNH staff: Laurel Kendall, curator of the Asian Ethnographic Collections; Thomas Miller, former Scientific Assistant; Ann Wright-Parsons, Senior Scientific Assistant; Belinda Kay, former head of the American Museum's archives; Nina Root, former head of the AMNH Library; and Thomas Baione, who generously helped us with photographs for the Russian translation of Jochelson's monograph (1926). With their help we were able to study in depth the AMNH Siberian collection, to familiarize ourselves with the archives and photographic records, and to amass the necessary sources and illustrations for a Russian translation of Jochelson's monograph—all in two months. We are especially thankful to Marjorie Mandelstam Balzer and Harley Balzer from Georgetown University, whose friendship comforted us during our visit in America. We are also very grateful to the MacArthur Foundation for a grant to our home Institute on Problems of Northern Peoples in Yakutsk for the translation of Jochelson's JNPE monograph, *The Yukaghirs and the Yukaghirized Tungus* (1926). Igor Krupnik provided critical assistance in the final editing of this paper and in our often arduous communication with our colleagues and conference organizers in the U.S. David Koester who translated this paper deserves our final thanks.

Notes

1. Boas to Jochelson, 28 October 1898 (AMNH-DA, Jochelson's collection, Box A). In this letter Boas suggested to Jochelson that he arrived in New York by February 1, 1899, in order to receive fieldwork instructions. He was then to head for the northern shore of the Sea of Okhotsk in the spring of 1899 to study the Koryak. According to preliminary plans, he was to take the summer of 1899 to the end of winter 1900 for the survey of the Koryak, adding a short visit to the eastern Yukagir (see copy of the letter in Vakhtin 2001:81).

2. Boas to Jochelson, 5 December 1898, AMNH-DA. This correspondence is now published in Vakhtin 2001:80–2.

3. Bogoras and Jochelson to Boas, 30 October 1899, AMNH-DA. See Vakhtin 2001:84–5.

4. Jesup to Jochelson, March 24 1900, AMNH-DA.

5. In his description of ancient Yakut clothing, Bolo writes that "[I]n ancient times Yakut robes were '*tangalaidaakh son*', *onoolookh son*', *buuktaakh son*', and '*buurukteekh son*', but in addition to these, according to some legends, there was also '*khotoidookh son*.'" (Bolo 1994:94).

6. Jochelson to Boas, 27 November 1902, AMNH-DA, Jochelson collection, Box A.

7. "We also made a very successful trip by sea in two boats to the mouth of the Najachan river, where we found a Tungus camp of 61 tents. It was a great opportunity for ethnographic work, unfortunately I couldn't stay long. The ethnological collection is now 1440 artifacts (including 173 from the Tungus)." Jochelson to Boas, 21 July–3 August 1901. AMNH-DA, Jochelson collection, Box A.

8. As of winter 2003, this manuscript remained unpublished, due to the minuscule budgets of today's academic institutions and presses in the Sakha Republic and to the shortage of funds from potential sponsors.

References

Boas, Franz
1903   The Jesup North Pacific Expedition. *American Museum Journal* 3(5):72–119.
1905   The Jesup North Pacific Expedition. In *International Congress of Americanists, 13th Session, Held in New York in 1902*. Pp.91–100. Easton, PA: Eschenbach.

Bogoras, Waldemar
1904–9 The Chukchee. *The Jesup North Pacific Expedition*, vol. 7, pts. 1–3. *Memoirs of the American Museum of Natural History*, 11. Leiden: E.J. Brill; New York: G.E. Stechert.
1991   *Material'naia kul'tura chukchei* (The Chukchi. Material Culture). Moscow and Leningrad: Nauka Publishers [Translation of Bogoras 1904, pt.1].

Cole, Douglas
2001   The Greatest Thing Undertaken by Any Museum? Franz Boas, Morris Jesup, and the Jesup North

Pacific Expedition. In *Gateways. Exploring the Legacy of the Jesup North Pacific Expedition, 1897–1902.* Igor Krupnik and William W. Fitzhugh, eds. Pp. 29–70. *Contributions to Circumpolar Anthropology* 1. Washington, DC: Arctic Studies Center.

Freed, Stanley A., Ruth S. Freed, and Laila Williamson

1988a   Capitalist Philanthropy and Russian Revolutionaries: The Jesup North Pacific Expedition (1897–1902). *American Anthropologist* 90(1):7–24.

1988b   The American Museum's Jesup North Pacific Expedition. In *Crossroads of Continents. Cultures of Siberia and Alaska.* William W. Fitzhugh and Aron Crowell, eds. Pp.97–104. Washington, DC: Smithsonian Institution.

Ivanov, Sergei V.

1963   Ornament narodov Sibiri kak istoricheskii istochnik (po materialam XIX-nachala XX v.). Narody Sibiri i Dal'nego Vostoka (Ornamentation of the Peoples of Siberia as a Historical Resource (Based upon the Data from the 1800s and the Early 1900s). Peoples of Siberia and the Far East. *Trudy Instituta etnografii Akademii Nauk SSSR*, 81. Moscow and Leningrad.

Ivanov-Unarov, Vladimir Kh., and Zinaida I. Ivanova

1998   O predystorii snimkov Jochelsona (On the History of Jochelson's Photographs). *Ilin* 1(2): 53–4. Yakutsk.

Jochelson, Waldemar (Iokhel'son, Vladimir I.)

1900   *Materialy po izucheniiu yukagirskogo iazyka i fol'klora, sobrannye v Kolymskom okruge* (Materials to the Study of the Yukagir Language and Folklore Collected in the Kolyma District). St. Petersburg.

1908   The Koryak. *The Jesup North Pacific Expedition*, vol. 6, pts. 1–2. *Memoirs of the American Museum of Natural History*, 10. Leiden: E.J. Brill; New York: G.E. Stechert.

1926   The Yukaghir and the Yukaghirized Tungus. *The Jesup North Pacific Expedition*, vol. 9, pts. 1–3. *Memoirs of the American Museum of Natural History*, 13. Leiden: E.J. Brill; New York: G.E. Stechert.

1933   The Yakut. *Anthropological Papers of the American Museum of Natural History*, 32(2). New York

1997   *Koriaki. Material'naia kul'tura i sotsial'naia organizatsiia* (The Koryak. Material Culture and Social Organization). St. Petersburg: Nauka Publishers [Translation of Jochelson 1908, pt.2].

Kendall, Laurel, Barbara Mathé, and Thomas R. Miller, eds.

1997   *Drawing Shadows to Stone. The Photography of the Jesup North Pacific Expedition, 1897–1902.* New York: American Museum of Natural History; Seattle and London: University of Washington Press.

Kulakovskii, Alexei.E.

1979   *Nauchnye trudy* (Academic Writings). Yakutsk: Yakutskoe knizhnoe izdatel'stvo.

Sehen Bolo

1994   *The History of the Yakut Nation Before the Arrival of the Russians to the Lena River.* Yakutsk (in Sakha language).

Shavrov, K.B.

1935   V.I. Iokhelson (Waldemar Jochelson). *Sovetskaia etnografia* 2:3–13. Leningrad.

Vakhtin, Nikolai B.

2001   Franz Boas and the Shaping of the Jesup Expedition Siberian Research, 1895–1900. In *Gateways. Exploring the Legacy of the Jesup North Pacific Expedition, 1897-1902.* Igor Krupnik and William W. Fitzhugh, eds. Pp. 71–89. *Contributions to Circumpolar Anthropology* 1. Washington, DC: Arctic Studies Center.

Zykov, F.M.

1993   Yakutskii *belepchi* i ego etnograficheskie paralleli (The Yakut *Belepchi* and Its Ethnographic Parallels). In *Etnicheskaia istoria narodov iuzhnoi Sibiri i Tsentralnoi Azii.* Pp. 263–9. Novosibirsk: Nauka Publishers.

114/ Susan Point, Spindle Whorl, 1994. Vancouver International Airport, Vancouver, BC. Photograph courtesy Susan Point and Bill McLennan.

The Invention and Perpetuation of Culture
The Boasian Legacy and Two 20th Century Woman Totem Pole Carvers

ALDONA JONAITIS

In 1898 Harlan Smith collected house posts from the Musqueam reserve in Vancouver, British Columbia (Fig.102). Like other British Columbia artifacts from the Jesup North Pacific Expedition, they became part of the American Museum of Natural History's vast Northwest Coast collections.[1] In 1997, the University of British Columbia's Museum of Anthropology asked Salish artist Susan Point (born 1952) to carve two new Salish house posts based on those collected one hundred years earlier. In keeping with the secretive nature of specific family prerogatives to which she had no right, Point was careful not to copy the AMNH models exactly but instead drew inspiration from them to create two new Salish fourteen-foot house posts (Fig. 103) with their own unique original power (McLellan 2000:94–7). But unlike the originals, which had been once erected within the Musqueam house, these were exterior public sculptures that stood on the Museum ground, among totem poles from other Northwest Coast First Nations.[2]

Most monumental Northwest Coast art was, and continues to be, made by men. Women usually make baskets, textiles, leatherwork and beadwork. Point's creations, and those of another Native woman artist, Kwakwaka'wakw Ellen Neel (1916–66), challenge this gender-based labor division by carving the iconic Northwest Coast sculpture – the totem pole. And, beyond that, their artworks contest some basic principles that have governed aboriginal art studies since the time of Franz Boas.

As Boas's life-time project was to understand pre-contact Northwest Coast culture, he sought the most unacculturated artifacts. Only items that we might characterize as embodying timeless traditionalism were considered worthy of collecting and study. Those emerging from the colonial encounter were to be disregarded, as products of a new, polluted tradition. To analyze culture historically, Boas tried to identify inventors of a traditional element, like the totem pole, and reconstruct its historic diffusion over time and geography. In his view, certain creative groups such as the Kwakwaka'wakw and Haida stood at the center and others, like the "imitative" Coast Salish languished at the margin. The essentialist premise underlying this approach has characterized much discourse on Northwest Coast cultures and art, in which types are real, but variations on those types are judged peripheral, derivative and imperfect.[3] The "essential" totem pole is that which is fixed in the contemporary imagination as what a totem pole *should be*: a tall, freestanding column developed during the Golden Age of cultural purity. As abundant anthropological analyses have demonstrated, essentialism and timeless traditionalism disregards the dynamic nature of cultural interactions.

A typical sightseer who enjoys being photographed next to a totem pole in a Vancouver, Victoria or Seattle park likely believes the carving to be ancient, and, if clearly new, the representative of an ancient tradition widespread across the Northwest Coast.[4] In reality, few poles existed at first contact, and then, probably, only among the Haida. They became more numerous and larger as new wealth from the fur trade necessitated more impressive expressions of status and metal tools enabled taller poles to be carved more quickly. From the one or two poles observed in Haida Gwaii (Queen Charlotte Islands) communities in the 1790s, totem poles proliferated so, by the mid-nineteenth century, these villages became forests of totem poles (Fig. 104). During the nineteenth century, the totem pole concept spread to the mainland of British Columbia, inspiring first the Tsimshian and only at the end of the century the Kwakwa̱ka'wakw (Fig. 105). Totem poles were popular in the southernmost part of the Alaska panhandle, but the northern Tlingit disdainfully dismissed them as "foreign." And exterior poles never became part of the Coast Salish artistic repertoire at all. Totem pole carving ceased among the Haida, Tsimshian and Tlingit by the late nineteenth century, but a few communities among the Kwakwa̱ka'wakw, Nuu-chah-nulth and Gitksan continued making poles for their own purposes into the twentieth century (Jonaitis 1999:106–110).

Beginning in the late nineteenth century, the non-Native Euro-American public became familiar with totem poles at world's fairs like the Chicago World Columbian Exposition, in museums such as the American Museum of Natural History's North Pacific Indian Hall, and along the popular Alaska Inside Passage steamer routes.[5] Although many poles standing in museum galleries are nineteenth century carvings removed from their original villages, most poles seen today in parks, along roads and outside buildings are the results of programs conceptualized and managed by museums, governmental agencies and private organizations that hired carvers to restore, copy or carve original poles. Only during the past two decades have First Nation communities themselves raised new poles on their own lands.[6]

Boas had large quantities of Northwest Coast material culture collected during the Jesup North Pacific Expedition, including totem poles. Many objects from the Jesup Expedition collections appear as illustrations in his various art publications, including his major *Primitive Art*, first published in 1927.[7] Better known for his paradigm-shifting anthropological writings and impressive competence in ethnology, linguistics, folklore and physical anthropology, Boas made significant contributions to scholarship on aboriginal art including his groundbreaking study of the formal and iconographic components of Northwest Coast art and speculations on the history of the Northwest Coast totem pole.

Boas found totem poles interesting as objects which could be subjected to historic analysis. In 1888, shortly after this first visit to Vancouver Island, Boas suggested that:

> I am inclined to believe that another custom of the North West Americans besides their dances originated among the Kwakiutl. I mean the use of heraldic columns. This view may seem unjustified, considering the fact that such columns are made nowhere with greater care than in the northern regions, among the Tsimshian and Haida, and farther north and south they are less frequent and less elaborately carved. The Haida, however, frequently took up foreign ideas with great energy, and developed them independently... It appears that the tribe has a remarkable faculty of adaptation (Boas 1888:195).

Boas ascribed to the Kwakwa̱ka'wakw, then as now clinging tenaciously to their traditions, the honor of inventing the totem pole, and suggested that the Haida, who by that time appeared thoroughly acculturated, had simply adopted the idea and elaborated upon it. Later, as a result of a far more careful historical reconstruction of the region, Boas modified his thesis of Northwest Coast cultural development in *Primitive Art* (Boas1955; first published1927) and gave the Haida, Tlingit and Tsimshian credit for originating the elaborate symbolic style which diffused north and south. Despite Boas' early inaccurate reading of history, his premise that one group invented poles that then spread to other groups signaled a new historical consciousness that would pervade subsequent studies of the totem pole. Of course, this history did *not* cease at contact, and late eighteenth century Haida carvings, early twentieth century Kwakwa̲-ka'wakw monuments, innovative creations by modern artists like Ellen Neel and Susan Point, and the totem poles of future generations all represent products of intellectual and material exchange that contribute to the ongoing "invention" of culture. Those exchanges, moreover, were not only among First Nations people but also between the original Northwest Coast residents and their colonizers.

Ellen Neel

In *Primitive Art*, Boas asserted that "It is not safe to base our arguments [on Northwest Coast art history] on models or on objects made for the trade," of which abundant examples were at that time in circulation. "I shall use, therefore, exclusively, older specimens which have been in use" (Boas 1955:209). Such disinterest in the modernization of First Nations people precluded Boas from understanding the wealth of meaning embodied in commodified art such as model totem poles made expressly for the tourist market.[8] These are not bastardizations of authenticity, nor the pathetic works of a shattered people completely dominated by their colonizers. Chris Gosden and Chantal Knowles state in the introduction to their study on colonialism in New Guinea:

> Chemists make a distinction between a mixture and a reaction. A mixture is a solution in which different chemicals combine, but retain their original form, whereas a reaction creates something new out of its original constituent parts. Colonial New Guinea was a reaction to which all parties contributed, so that there can be no question that all had influence and agency. (Gosden and Knowles 2001:xix).

An important concept here is agency, the power of an individual or group to affect its own destiny. Going on to criticize those who insist on an essentialist concept of culture, Gosden and Knowles assert that "Anthropologists have tried to undo or ignore the reaction and focus upon one part, New Guineans, creating a partial and static picture in the process." The model totem pole that Boas rejected as an unacceptable cultural "mixture" was in reality a "reaction" replete with agency.

One of the most well regarded mid-twentieth century model totem pole maker was Ellen Neel (1916–1966), a Kwakwa̲ka'wakw carver from northern Vancouver Island (Fig. 106). Neel's well-known artist grandfather, Charlie James (1867–1938) taught the young girl how to carve and by her teenage years, she was selling model poles to visitors in her native Alert Bay. In 1943, Neel married, moved from Alert Bay to Vancouver, and in 1946, began carving and selling model poles to help support her family. With the assistance of her six children, Neel produced numerous small, modestly priced models to sell to department stores and souvenir shops. In 1948, the City of Vancouver Board of Parks Commissioners permitted her to carve, display, and sell her works in an abandoned military building in Stanley Park. She gradually became more and more well known for both her model poles and full-size carvings, including a sixteen foot pole which Neel and her husband donated to the Alma Mater Society of the University of British Columbia (UBC) and a large pole for the Pacific National Exhibition, an annual fair.[9]

Tourism is deeply implicated in the history of totem poles, for as early as the 1880s, steamship companies beckoned prospective clients with descriptions of the abundant poles they would see on their Inside Passage cruise. Recognizing the value of poles for tourism, a group of British Columbians along with the-then Vancouver Mayor Charles Thompson formed an association and formally adopted the name "Totemland" to trademark the province, promote tourism, and encourage the use of totem poles on license plates, stamps and, especially, advertisements. So receptive was the community that a local newspaper wrote optimistically, "The BC totem may become as famous as the Idaho potato" (K. Phillips 2000:1). The goals of this group were published as follows:

To collect in writing and disseminate the legendary history, customs and philosophy of our native Indians; also to encourage and preserve their ancient weaving, painting and sculptural arts; to promote the use of a Thunderbird Totem and the slogan Totemland as the symbol of the colour and romantic interest of the British Columbia Indian together with their singular totemology and unique wood-carving art; to advise, encourage and support the British Columbia Indians in overcoming obstacles that may stand in the way of their attainment to the enjoyment of full citizenship (K. Phillips 2000:25).

The Totemland Society asked Ellen Neel to design the model pole which would become its official emblem (Fig. 108).

Neel created a unique two foot pole for that organization. A thunderbird sits on atop an egg-shaped globe prominently depicting western British Columbia with Vancouver Island, and a human figure kneels underneath. In creating this pole, Neel integrated symbols and sculptural forms from her own heritage with a distinctly western geographical representation. Understanding the non-Native desire to know the "story" of any pole, Neel explained its iconography as a narrative of the thunderbird giving British Columbia to the first man. Neel herself reproduced this vividly painted, highly original pole a number of times as gifts, while her popular image of Totemland appeared on society letterhead, scarves, T-shirts, ties, and a Royal Albert china dinner service.

One could judge this pole as a "degradation" of a treasured aboriginal artistic tradition appropriated by the colonialist class — but that would be wrong. As her friend Phil Nuytten (1982:47) commented, Neel, who never took herself too seriously anyway, "laughed a lot about the Totemland Poles." According to Nuytten (personal communication 2003) Neel's artist uncle Mungo Martin half-seriously, half-jestingly referred to it as a "white man's pole" but then agreed with his niece that "a white person wouldn't know the difference anyway," and they both laughed.

Perhaps Neel recognized the underlying fatuousness of this commission — or at the very least its silliness. But a serious message underlies this artwork as well, for the globe on the Totemland Society's pole depicts *only* Vancouver Island and the nearby mainland, not even the entire totem pole region of British Columbia. In the middle is Kwakwa̲ka'wakw territory, situating Neel's own tribal land at the center of the world (Phillips 2000:69–70). Nuytten (personal communication 2003) also points out that the human underneath the globe has a uncanny resemblance to the European concept of Atlas with the world on his shoulders; Neel seems to have appropriated a non-Native concept and transformed it into a very Kwakwa̲ka'wakw-like image. Every official who proudly displayed this pole, every T-shirt emblazoned with its image, every piece of Totemland china declared, to a largely white audience who may very well not have understood, the fundamental centrality of the Kwakwa̲ka'wakw, their traditional ownership of this land, and their new ownership of a European symbol.

Ellen Neel was certainly a major mid-century Native artist, admired by her contemporaries. However, since her death in 1966, she has effectively vanished from the discourse on Northwest Coast art. An episode in totem pole history may provide insights into why that might be. Two versions exist of the story of University of British Columbia's efforts to have several of their Northwest Coast totem poles restored. According to Phil Nuytten (1982:9-10, 52-53), the UBC's Totem Pole Committee approached Neel first, asking her to restore fifteen poles. This collection had special meaning for Neel, as one had been carved by her grandfather Charlie James, and another by her relative Mungo Martin. During that summer Neel restored four poles from Fort Rupert, including James'. Because her business had suffered during her absence and as a creative artist, she found replication uninspiring, Neel suggested that the next summer the Museum of Anthropology hire her uncle, Mungo Martin, for this job—which they did (Fig.107). Audrey Hawthorn, wife of

Harry Hawthorn, Director of the Museum of Anthropology from 1947–1974, offers an somewhat different account of Martin's hire, stating that he had been selected from the very beginning, and that the Museum had also approached Neel to be his assistant; "she was not, however, in a position to assist Mr. Martin on restoration work at that time" (Hawthorn 1993:9–10). With those words, Hawthorn effectively erases Neel's contributions to the Museum of Anthropology totem pole restoration project.

The museum, with a clear vision of its general role in cultural preservation as well as this project's historic significance, played a major role in overseeing the actual restorations. Such conscious attempt to recreate the past provided opportunities for museum anthropologists to appear as "cultural saviors." Harry Hawthorn directed Martin "to return to the style of the first phase of contact, using steel tools but painting sparingly," so, Martin abandoned his customary covering of bright paint (which his Kwakwa̱ka'wakw customers apparently liked) and colored only certain features. In a pamphlet explaining Martin's work in 1952 replicating poles in Victoria's Thunderbird Park, anthropologist Wilson Duff asserted that by remaining outside in the park, the old poles would have soon decayed:

> It was decided to obtain skilled Indian carvers to carve exact copies of the best old poles, and some new ones, to replace the old exhibits and produce a permanent and representative outdoor display of this unique art for the benefit of future generations. By employing native craftsmen and having them work in public view in the park, he programme accomplished the added aims of keeping alive native art and providing a public educational attraction (Duff n.d.:29).

It was thus the museum, not Natives, who "kept the culture alive" by hiring an authentic Indian, Mungo Martin, "one of the few surviving authorities in the old ways of life" (Duff n.d.:29). Despite his rudimentary English the highly personable Martin, along with his equally charming wife Abayah, became extremely popular with visitors to both the Museum of Anthropology and the British Columbia Provincial Museum, now known as the Royal British Columbia Museum. Mungo Martin, conforming beautifully to the "Vanishing Indian" myth which harmonized nicely with the myth of the totem pole as an ancient tradition on the verge of disappearance, became the most well known and highly regarded Northwest Coast Native of his time (Glass 2000).

Ellen Neel never became a significant player in the official history of British Columbia's totem pole projects, perhaps because, unlike Martin, she did not adhere to the timeless traditionalist stereotype favored by anthropologists and the public. Indeed, Neel was one of the first Natives to actually challenge the disappearing Indian trope to which Duff so compellingly refers. At a 1948 conference on Native art and culture, Neel dismissed the concept that Native art is dead, calling it "one of the great fallacies where the art of my people is concerned." She continued "For if our art is dead, then it is fit only to be mummified, packed into mortuary boxes and tucked away into museums... Whereas to me, it is a living symbol of gaiety, the laughter and love of color of my people." Innovation and change had always been aspects of her artistic tradition. It is striking that, in contrast to Harry Hawthorn's instruction to reduce the amount of color for historical verisimilitude, Neel and the contemporary Kwakwa̱ka'wakw "love" color. She pointed to the national identity inherent in her work: "Our art continues to live, for not only is it part and parcel of us, but can be a powerful factor in combining the best part of Indian culture into the fabric of a truly Canadian art form" (Nuytten 1982:50).

Neel spoke good English and instead of wearing ceremonial regalia, even at events, dressed in clothes more appropriate for a 1950s housewife. Moreover, by marrying a white man, she lost her Indian status according to Canadian law. Instead of purporting herself like Martin as a high status aboriginal, she presented herself as Mother, supervising her six half-Native cildren as totem pole apprentices. Her art, while capable of being quite traditional, also at times ventured into the unexpected, as in the Totemland pole. Ellen Neel did not make poles that alluded to the golden age of authenticity, did not fit nicely into the category of "disappearing Indian" so favored by the museums, and despite her lineage, did not go down in history as a truly "authentic" Native.

Today Neel is rarely mentioned in the literature, and the biography offered in Nuytten's *The Totem Pole Carvers* (1982) remains still her only significant source.[10] The most important catalogue of contemporary Northwest Coast art, *The Legacy* (1980) praises Charlie James and Mungo Martin, but fails to even mention Ellen Neel. Steven Brown, in his survey of Northwest Coast art history to the present includes Neel along with eight other male carvers in a list of Kwakwaka'wakw artists of her generation, but illustrates none of her work (Brown 1998:155). Just as Hawthorn excluded her from the history of the Museum of Anthropology's pole carving projects, the literature has, in effect, erased her from the history of Northwest Coast art. In contrast, her uncle Mungo Martin has been transformed into its super-star.

Susan Point

A very different reception was given a contemporary woman artist, Susan Point (born 1952) member of the Musqueam band of Salish (Fig. 110). In 1981, she took a jewelry-making course at Vancouver Community College, where she learned to make northern-style silver bracelets and rings. Courses were not offered in Salish art which was not greatly valued at that time. Because she recognized the impressive artistic tradition of her people, Point visited museums and began making prints based upon traditional Salish images. In 1991, she crafted the first Salish-style monumental carving in decades, a twelve-foot house post for the First Nations' House of Learning on the University of British Columbia campus. Then she embarked upon adventures into new media including glass and produced *Common Thread*, a remarkable seven foot house post of glass depicting

the moon, stars, our planet earth and an assortment of animals—wolf, raven, wolverine and sturgeon (Fig. 111).

Unlike Neel, Point has received many accolades. She has had solo exhibits at the Museum of Anthropology in Vancouver, Steilacoom Tribal Museum in Washington, and the Canadian Museum of Civilization in Hull, and has participated in numerous group exhibits in Canada, the United States, Japan, and Europe. She was one of three contemporary Northwest Coast Native artists featured in *Indianer Künstler der Westküste Kanadas* (*Native Artists from the Northwest Coast),* a major exhibition in Zurich in 1989 (Gerber and Katz-Lahaigue 1989).[11] And she is the subject of a beautiful coffee table book published in 2000, thus being one of the few Northwest Coast artists validated by a personal art monograph (Wyatt 2000). In that catalogue Peter Macnair writes, "more than any other contemporary Northwest Coast artist . . . Point has been successful . . . due to her desire for new challenges, her willingness to explore new mediums." As a truly brilliant artist, Point deserves every honor bestowed upon her. But as she herself says, "Coast Salish art is relatively unknown to most people today . . . much of the Native art associated with the Pacific Northwest Coast is from principle tribes of northern British Columbia" (Point 1996:132–3).

Why was then Salish art unrecognized as a major art tradition before Susan Point revealed its excellence? Why was so much more such attention paid to more northerly Northwest Coast art from the Kwakwaka'wakw to Salish? As Wayne Suttles has indicated on numerous occasions, Franz Boas and his successors created the stereotype of "imitative and passive" Salish as "a pale reflection of the 'real Northwest Coast' to the north" (Suttles 1987:xii; 257).[12]

Boas wrote the art section of Teit's Jesup Expedition publication, and in that asserted that the Salish were "a receptive race, quick to adopt foreign modes of thought," perhaps due to "a low stage of development of their early culture, or to social conditions unfavorable to the continued growth of their own culture"

(Boas 1900:390,387). He also characterized Coast Salish art as "cruder" than that of the Northern tribes (1900:389). This art became stigmatized as less complex, less interesting, and less aesthetically valuable than either "baroque" Wakashan or elegant northern Northwest Coast art.[13]

Perhaps because family-owned images were considered more private than they were farther north, the Salish carved only interior house posts, never exterior totem poles.[14] But, since tourists to Vancouver—a true capital of "Totemland"—wanted totem poles, throughout the twentieth century, poles made farther north filled the city's museums and parks. The art of local Salish was ignored. Before Susan Point began carving Salish-style monumental art, only one totem pole by a Salish carver, the Thunderbird Dynasty pole stood in Vancouver's Stanley Park. In 1936, Squamish Chief Matthias Joe Capilano made this pole for a group of Vancouver citizens who were planning to erect Haida and Kwakwaka'wakw poles in Stanley Park, and wanted one made by a local artist. Matthias Joe chose as his model not the minimalist carvings of Salish house posts, but instead created a Kwakwaka'wakw type of pole with assertively carved and vividly painted images surmounted by an open-winged thunderbird (Fig.109). Most poles publicly declare the crest privileges of an extended family; but this one depicted mythic beings associated with the Salish creation story – thunderbird, its wife, son and daughter, and the sea monster. It also commemorates not a major tribal event such as a potlatch, a wedding, or the death of a chief, but instead the first meeting of Captain Vancouver and the Salish people on June 13, 1792. S.W.A. Gunn, author of the 1965 booklet on Stanley Park poles approvingly appraised this pole, which, with thunderbird imagery communicating the story of the Creation, "commemorates the meeting of the Indians and the white man [which] opened up an entirely new world for both" (Gunn 1965:22–3).

In reality, the Capilano monument represented one of the first poles that embodied an explicitly political

statement, for what appeared to be celebrating an historic event was actually a subtle assertion of aboriginal land rights. During the early 1900's, Coastal First Nations people had been exceptionally active attempting to obtain sovereignty over their land; in 1906, a delegation of Salish chiefs made an unsuccessful trip to London to petition King Edward II to change governmental policy. In 1912, the Coast Salish, along with the Nishga, Haida and Interior Salish, joined together to form the Allied Tribes of British Columbia to contest the province's land allocation policies. Squamish chief Andrew Paul, along with Haida Peter Kelly, labored especially diligently for this, but ultimately to no avail. In 1927 the Allied Tribes disbanded, in part due to their failure to achieve their goals, and in part due to a new section of the Indian Act making it illegal to solicit funds to pursue land claims (Kew 1990:166). In this context of continual rebuffs to their appeals, the 1936 Matthias Joe pole served as a quiet, legal mechanism to proclaim Salish rights to the Vancouver region. This statement, like the position of Kwakwaka'wakw territory on Neel's Totemland totem pole, probably went over the heads of most observers.

In recent years, aboriginal people worldwide have been more vociferously defending ownership of their lands and insisting on more voice in government, education, and the arts. Australian aborigines, New Zealand Maoris, Scandinavian Saami, Canadian Inuit have all become significant forces within their countries. Concomitant with these actions of empowerment, Native people have used their artistic traditions to express identity, celebrate heritage, and, at times, make political statements. This was certainly the case on the Northwest Coast, where the totem pole has assumed yet new meanings as Native Americans and Canadians join in this worldwide movement.

The British North American Act (1867) and the Indian Act (1876) denied First Nations their sovereignty and defined them as wards of the state. In keeping with the national and international aboriginal sovereignty movements, British Columbia Natives, along with other Canadian First Nations sought to win back their independence as autonomous units with self-determination in political, social and economic affairs. This was slow in coming, as only in 1982 did First Nations appear as a category of citizens in the Canadian constitution. Its Article 35 now explicitly states, "The existing aboriginal and treaty rights of the aboriginal peoples of Canada are hereby recognized and confirmed... In this Act, 'aboriginal peoples of Canada' includes the Indian, Inuit and Métis peoples of Canada" (quoted in Gerber 1988:122). Ownership of the land and the right to control its resources, remain to this day highly contentious, as British Columbia Natives never signed treaties with the federal or provincial governments for their land, and have brought their land claims to court.[15]

In this contentious political atmosphere, Susan Point received a major commission in the early 1990s to create artworks for the International Terminal at Vancouver International Airport in Vancouver, BC. At the top of the escalator arriving international passengers must descend is a monumental, 16-foot diameter spindle whorl of red cedar (1994) hanging suspended over a waterfall symbolizing Salish rivers (Fig. 114).[16] Several messages — greetings, flight, subsistence — are conveyed by two large eagles constrained within the circle enveloping in their wings images of the Coast Salish people who hold salmon within them. At the base of the escalator, two welcome figures (1996, see title page), the male and female ancestors of the Musqueam, stand facing the spindle whorl and cascade to greet arriving passengers. On the backs of each figure a panel, *Flight*, depicts eagles of glass, and humans with upraised arms.

Point's images embody several messages intended for the new visitors. Ever gracious, the Musqueam welcome them to their land. The eagle, a motif found in earlier Salish art straddles the ancient with the modern by alluding to natural and man-made flight. The salmon and water signify not only the traditional economic basis of the Salish, but the contemporary struggles for

fishing rights. The very position of these images as the first monumental carvings that greet newcomers, communicates clearly and vividly that they have arrived on *Musqueam* land; with this welcome, the Salish are placing claim on ownership of the land. Point has taken the motifs of her ancestors and created a work that not only stands as an exceptional work of art but also makes some very contemporary politically charged statements. It is likely that the public, sensitized to aboriginal land claims issues, finally grasp this message that has been conveyed by various Northwest Coast art works.

The "Essential" Totem Pole

While the Northwest Coast Indians were carving and raising poles, Europeans, Canadians and Americans were creating an abstraction – *the* [essential] *totem pole.* Early on these carvings became signifiers of tradition, embodiments of authentic Nativeness, compelling presentations of the mythic world. Tourist literature for well over 100 years has represented the totem pole's antiquity and connection to nature; the more romanticizing passages in the literature project upon the pole a kind of aura that transforms them from ordinary to extra-ordinary.

In their Boasian quest for ethnographic purity, past scholars have sought a neat encapsulation of clearly defined types, and rejected or, at least, placed a lesser value on, hybridized forms. Adhering to a preconceived model of cultural purity discredits most, if not all, cultural hybridities, and disregards the dynamic nature of cultural interactions. In the popular imagination, the "essential" totem pole *should be* a tall, freestanding column of great antiquity, carved by Indians for Indians. In the quest for this totem pole, and the genuine Indian who makes it, Ellen Neel has been ignored and Salish art degraded. Neel's poles, made strictly as commodities, were judged not authentic and, for that matter, neither was the modern Ellen Neel herself. However, the more recent dismantling of such stereotypes and acceptance of creativity, originality, and challenges to the status quo have allowed space for Susan Point's innovative artistic expressions.

Let us address the issue of Neel and Point's gender. Because men are traditional carvers on the Northwest Coast, any woman carver is not traditional – and thus in the eyes of some, not "authentic." In addition, perhaps, as Nuytten argues, Neel was erased from the discourse on Kwakwaka'wakw art because she was female working at a time before feminism applauded endeavors such as hers (Nuytten, personal communication, May 2002). Some thirty years later, Point's gender did not negatively influence the public's reception of her works. However, one must ask whether the appreciation of her work has something to do with her being Musqueam. Her work emerges from the tradition of a marginalized group whose art has been underappreciated. In contrast to the canonical traditions to which many contemporary Northwest Coast Native artists adhere, Point enjoys enormous freedom to experiment. This lack of constraints imposed by a canon, coupled with the absence of Salish male artists measuring up to her brilliance, creates a place for her to be accepted and admired. It would be interesting to speculate on whether, if Point were from a more northern Northwest Coast group, she could successfully compete with recognized male masters of art styles long admired and valued. I personally hope that, with the enhanced consciousness of the contemporary era, any great artist, regardless of tradition or gender, would be recognized as such.

I have selected Neel and Point to discuss their roles not only as women artists, but also their importance in a revitalized history of Northwest Coast art. Fred Myers introduces a volume on contemporary perspectives about material culture by asserting:

> Movement, destablization, and dynamics are highly visible processes in the social life of things. ... changes in the intersections of different levels of circulation cannot be studied simply as "breakdowns" – either from art into commodity of from "culturally authentic" to inauthentic – or as simple appropriations.... The relocation of material culture demands understanding that value is never simply defined but is always involved in global as well as local circuits of exchange, display and storage. This is especially important as objects move through space and time with greater rapidly than ever before, breaking down the analytical categories that for so long have been used to contain and define them theoretically (Myers 2001:11–12.).

Both Neel and Point contributed to disassembling still-prevalent stereotypes of "authentic Indians" and genuine traditional Indian art, revealing as fictional the very concept of ethnic purity. In the Boasian paradigm, authentic Native artists would probably not have communicated political statements in their work. Neither would they be innovative in terms of integrating western and non-western concepts. And they certainly would not have made authentic art for commercial purposes. But, in the globalized world of today, Native artists like Neel and Point express resistance with art. Neel makes her homeland the center of the universe, whereas Point presents Vancouver as Musqueam territory. Both are innovative, creating new works of "reactions" between Native and non-Native concepts, with Neel transforming a common item of tourist art into a uniquely hybrid image of the Native and non-Native worlds, and Point creating a Salish masterpiece from a very untraditional medium, like glass. And both make excellent art for non-Native sponsors; Neel for visitors to Stanley Park and the Totemland organization, Point for the Vancouver Airport Commission. What Boas thought about the totem pole models as commodities, about the originality of the Salish, and, indeed, about the timeless traditionalism of Native art itself, has been turned on its head, opening the way for even more innovative Northwest Coast totem pole carvers—including women.

Acknowledgments.

This paper derives from talks given at the University of Rochester in April, 2002 and Stanford University, May

2002. The development of the totem pole will be the subject of a book in progress that I am writing with Aaron Glass, the working title of which is *Monumental Myths of the Northwest Coast Totem Pole*. I thank him for his impeccable research and compelling ideas on this subject. I also thank the Susan B. Anthony, Institute of Gender Studies and Janet Catherine Berlo, past Susan. B. Anthony Professor of Gender Studies at the University of Rochester as well as the Art Department at Stanford University where I was Visiting Distinguished Professor of American Art for providing the opportunity to research, write and give these talks. I want to express my appreciation for the generosity of Phil Nuytten in sharing his recollections of his friend Ellen Neel, Bill McLennan and Dan Savard for their assistance with the photographs, Laurel Kendall and Igor Krupnik for their editing of the manuscript and, especially, Susan Point for her permission to reproduce images of herself and her works.

Notes

1. See Jonaitis (1988) for an extended review of the American Museum of Natural History's Northwest Coast art collection, including its section originating from the Jesup North Pacific Expedition (Jonaitis 1988:154-213).

2. It is because they stand in public and visually resemble other carvings on the property that I categorize Point's monumental columnar carvings as totem poles.

3. I am indebted to Wayne Suttles who gave a talk "Northwest Coast Art and Essentialism" at the Otsego Institute for Native American Art Studies in 1999 and introduced this concept of Boas and essentialism, especially from the perspective of his life long research on the Salish. See also Michael Harkin's concept of Boas' "Kwakiutlism" (Harkin 2001:100-102).

4. During his 1996 interviews of visitors to the stand of totem poles at Stanley Park, Aaron Glass verified these stereotypes.

5. The literature on impact of fairs, collecting and tourism upon Native art is extensive. See in particular Cole (1985), Rydell (1984) and Lee (1999).

6. The most outstanding recent totem pole project at Qay'llnagaay, or Sea Lion Town, is the six new poles erected at Skidegate on Haida Gwaii (Queen Charlotte Islands) as part of a large-scale cultural tourism project. Each pole represents one of the main historic village sites of the southern Haida - Skidegate, T'aanuu, SGaang Gwaii Ninstints, Ts'aahl (Chaatl), K'uuna (Skedans), and Cumshewa.

7. See Jonaitis (1995) for reprints of all Boas' essays on art, selections from Primitive Art, and articles on his art history and his influences on twentieth century studies of Northwest Coast art.

8. The literature on tourist art is extensive, but the two most important books on the subject are Graburn's groundbreaking volume (1976) and Phillips and Steiner's recent edited volume of the current state of scholarship (1999).

9. As a result of winning an award for this pole at that fair, Neel began to receive orders for small poles. By this time, her model poles were not inexpensive, with a 14 inch piece selling for $30, a 36 inch one for $150 (Nuytten 1982:57). When the business was good, Neel, helped by her children, filled an order from the Hudson's Bay Company for 5,000 poles.

10. Kimberly Phillip's unpublished master's thesis written at the University of British Columbia Department of Fine Arts (K. Phillips 2000) is another excellent source on Ellen Neel.

11. The other two artists were Joe Davis and Lawrence Paul.

12. In *Coast Salish Essays* (1987:256, 266), Suttles suggests that the results of the Jesup North Pacific Expedition had a lot to do with the perpetuation of these stereotypes.

13. I have always thought that if the Salish did not live just south of the other Northwest Coast people who produce such incredible art that they would be thought of as an important North American art-producing people. In their publications, Bill Holm (1991) and Steve Brown (1998) have made significant contributions to the reassessment of Salish art.

14. See Suttles 1987:100-33, for further development of this idea.

15. There has been a wealth of material on British Columbia land claims. For a good source, First Nations Land Claims and Treaties in BC by the Vancouver Public Library (2002), on line at

www.vpl.vancouver.bc.ca.

16. This was done with the assistance of two other carvers, John Livingston and Jeff Cannell.

References

Barbeau, Marius
1929   Totem Poles of the Gitksan, Upper Skeena River, British Columbia. *Anthropological Series* 12, *National Museum of Canada Bulletin* 61. Ottawa.
1950   Totem Poles. *Anthropological Series* 30, *National Museum of Canada Bulletin* 119. Ottawa.

Boas, Franz
1888   The Development of Culture in Northwest America. *Science* 12:194–96.
1900   Art. In *The Thompson Indians of British Columbia*, by James Teit. Pp. 376–90. *The Jesup North Pacific Expedition*, vol. 1, pt. 4. *Memoirs of American Museum of Natural History Memoirs*, 2. New York: G.E. Stechert.
1955   *Primitive Art.* New York: Dover Press. 1st edition, 1927. Cambridge MA: Harvard University Press.

Brown, Steven
1998   *Native Visions: Evolution in Northwest Coast Art from the Eighteenth through the Twentieth Century.* Seattle: Seattle Art Museum and University of Washington Press.

Clifford, James
1997   *Routes: Travel and Translation in the Late Twentieth Century.* Cambridge, MA: Harvard University Press.

Cole, Douglas
1985   *Captured Heritage. The Scramble for Northwest Coast Artifacts.* Seattle: University of Washington Press.

Drucker, Philip
1948   The Antiquity of the Northwest Coast Totem Pole. *Journal of the Washington Academy of Sciences* 38(12):389–97.

Duff, Wilson
1981   Mungo Martin, Carver of the Century. In *The World is as Sharp as a Knife*. Donald N. Abbott, ed. Pp. 3–70. Victoria: British Columbia Provincial Museum.
n.d.   *Thunderbird Park.* Victoria: B.C. Government Travel Bureau.

Gerber, Peter, and Vanina Katz-Lahaigue
1989   *Susan A. Point; Joe David; Lawrence Paul: Indianische Künstler der Westküste Kanadas/Native Artists from the Northwest Coast.* Zürich: Völkerkundemuseum der Universität Zürich.

Glass, Aaron
2000   Cultural Salvage or Brokerage: The Emergence of Northwest Coast 'Art' and the Mythologization of Mungo Martin. Unpublished paper.

Gosden, Chris, and Chantel Knowles
2001   *Collecting Colonialism: Material Culture and Colonial Change.* Oxford: Berg.

Graburn, Nelson H.H., ed.
1976   *Ethnic and Tourist Art: Cultural Expressions from the Fourth World.* Berkeley: University of California Press.

Gunn, S. W. A.
1965   *Totem Poles of Stanley Park.* Vancouver: Whiterocks Publications.

Harkin, Michael
2000   (Dis)pleasures of the Text:Boasian Ethnology on the Central Northwest Coast. In *Gateways: Exploring the Legacy of the Jesup North Pacific Expedition, 1897–1902.* Igor Krupnik and William Fitzhugh, eds. Pp. 93–105, Contributions to Circumpolar Anthropology, 1. Washington, DC: Arctic Studies Center.

Hawthorn, Audrey
1993   *A Labour of Love: The Making of the Museum of Anthropology, UBC The First Three Decades 1947–1976.* Vancouver: University of British Columbia Press.

Holm, Bill
1990   Art. In *Northwest Coast. Handbook of North American Indians*, vol. 7. Wayne Suttles, ed. Pp. 602–32. Washington, DC: Smithsonian Institution.

Jonaitis, Aldona
1988   *From the Land of the Totem Poles: The Northwest Coast Indian Art Collection at the American Museum of Natural History.* New York: American Museum of Natural History; Seattle: University of Washington Press.
1995   *A Wealth of Thought: Franz Boas on Native American Art.* Seattle: University of Washington Press.
1999   Northwest Coast Totem Poles. In *Unpacking Culture: Art and Commodity in Colonial and Postcolonial Worlds*. Ruth Phillips and Christopher Steiner, eds. Pp. 104–20. Berkeley: University of California Press.

Kew, Michael
1990   History of Coastal British Columbia Since 1849. In *Handbook of North American Indians*, vol. 7. *Northwest Coast.* Wayne Suttles, ed. Pp. 159–68. Washington, DC: Smithsonian Institution.

Lee, Molly
1999   Tourism and Taste Cultures: Collecting Native Art in Alaska at the Turn of the Twentieth Century. In *Unpacking Culture: Art and Commodity in Colonial and Postcolonial Worlds*. Ruth Phillips and Christopher Steiner, eds. Pp. 267–80. Berkeley: University of California Press.

Macnair, Peter
2000   Susan Point: Her Place by the River. In *Susan Point: Coast Salish Artist*. G. Wyatt, ed. Pp. 25–44. Vancouver: Douglas & McIntyre.

Macnair, Peter, Alan Hoover, and Kevin Nearly
1980   *The Legacy: Continuing Traditions of Canadian Northwest Coast Indian Art.* Victoria: Royal British Columbia Museum.

Malin, Edward
1986   *Totem Poles of the Pacific Northwest Coast.* Portland: Timber Press.

McLennan, Bill
2000   Contemporary Architectural Carvings. In *Susan Point: Coast Salish Artist.* G. Wyatt, ed. Pp. 94–7. Vancouver: Douglas & McIntyre.

Myers, Fred, ed.
2001   *The Empire of Things: Regimes of Value and Material Culture.* Santa Fe: School for American Research.

Nuytten, Phil
1982   *The Totem Carvers: Charlie James, Ellen Neel, Mungo Martin.* Vancouver: Panorama Publications.

Phillips, Kimberly
2000   Ellen Neel. Unpublished paper (quoted with author's permission).

Phillips, Ruth, and Christopher Steiner, eds.
1999   *Unpacking Culture: Art and Commodity in Colonial and Postcolonial Worlds.* Berkeley: University of California Press.

Point, Susan
1996   Artist's statement in *Topographies: Aspects of Recent B.C. Art.* G. Arnold, M. Gagnon, D. Jensen, eds. Pp. 132–33. Vancouver: Vancouver Art Gallery.

Rydell, Robert
1984   *All the World's a Fair: Visions of Empire at American International Expositions, 1876–1916.* Chicago: University of Chicago Press.

Suttles, Wayne
1987   Coast Salish Essays. Compiled and edited with the assistance of Ralph Maud. Seattle: University of Washington Press.

Teit, James
1900   *The Thompson Indians of British Columbia; The Jesup North Pacific Expedition,* vol.1, pt. 4. *Memoirs of American Museum of Natural History Memoirs,* 2. New York: G.E. Stechert.

Wyatt, Gary, ed.
2000   *Susan Point: Coast Salish Artist.* Vancouver: Douglas & McIntyre.

Consumers, Then and Now

GLORIA CRANMER WEBSTER

In the early 1970s, I worked as an assistant curator at the Museum of Anthropology at the University of British Columbia in Vancouver BC. One day, when I was very busy, the late Wilson Duff came in and showed me a raven rattle, saying, "Isn't it beautiful?" I agreed that it was. Then he asked, "But how do you read it?" I replied impatiently, "Wilson, I don't read those things, I shake them." The title of this chapter could have been "Shakers and Readers," because that is how the world is divided for me. There are us and there are those who write about or "read" us. Readers have very little relevance in the world of Shakers, primarily because their statements are so often wrong.

Franz Boas' arrival on the Northwest Coast of British Columbia marked the beginning of a long relationship with our people, the Kwakwaka'wakw, more commonly known to the outside world as the "Kwakiutl," a term that is as inaccurate as calling the indigenous people of this continent "Indians". Kwakwaka'wakw is not a new word, as some Readers have suggested; it has always meant all of the people who speak the language, Kwakwala. I am a present-day Kwakwala speaker and the word is certainly known to me and other speakers with my level of fluency.

Boas collaborated with George Hunt in gathering material relating to nearly all aspects of Kwakwaka'wakw culture at a time when that culture was losing its center. His dependence on Hunt's knowledge of the Kwakwala language is repeatedly acknowledged throughout their long collaboration. George

Hunt was my great-grandfather. His oldest son, David, was my mother's father. We have always known that George was the half-breed son of an English father and a high-ranking £anget [Tlingit—ed.] woman from Tangas, Alaska. Counter to some modern Readers of our history who see this pedigree as an indication that George Hunt was not a legitimate participant in Kwakwaka'wakw culture, we take pride in our Alaskan connection. These ties give us the right, as Hunt's descendants, to treasures brought to Fort Rupert by *Anisalaga*, as my great-great-grandmother was known to us. Hunt's marriage to *Tlali³i'lakw* (Lucy) was a *Kwagu'³* ceremony, with her family bringing *kis'u*, including names, dances, and songs, to him, thus establishing his position in the society. Hunt's position became stronger each time one of his sons married into families rich in *kis'u*. Each of his daughters gave her husband's family *kis'u* coming from Lucy's family as well as from Anisalaga's family.

On March 20, 1905, Hunt wrote to Boas saying that, "The Indian Agent is trying to get my three boys to leave the Indians and turn to be white men, but the Indians don't want for my boys to leave them." The "boys" were my grandfather and his brothers Samuel and Jonathan, all of whom had married chief's daughters from different tribes of the Kwakwaka'wakw. That the "Indians" did not want them to leave seems a clear indication of acceptance, in my view. Furthermore, when George Hunt was dying, he called together the *Kwag'u³* chiefs and asked that one of them marry *fʰatʰaʰaʰ'widzamga* (Francine), his second wife, so that she would remain in Fort Rupert rather than return to her home village. George feared that she would not be well taken care of by her own people. Soon after Hunt's death, Charlie Wilson, a chief of the Kwagu'ʰ, married Francine. It seems highly unlikely that such a high-ranking person would honor the dying wish of one who was not accepted.

Boas entered our world when people were experiencing drastic changes in their lives, including rapid population decline due to introduced diseases, and loss of land and access to traditional resource sites. Missionaries and government agents added to the upheaval by attempting to "civilize" us in their residential schools, and, in time, succeeded in pressuring the Canadian government to enact legislation prohibiting the potlatch. In 1921, the federal government took many of our treasures from us, following a large potlatch that had been held in violation of the law prohibiting such ceremonies. In 1980, we opened our cultural center, in which is housed part of this Potlatch Collection, returned to us by the Canadian Museum of Civilization. We asked our old people what an appropriate name would be for our center. It was at their suggestion that we decided to call it the U'mista Cultural Centre. They saw the repatriation of our treasures as a kind of *u'mista*, that is, the return of people who, in earlier times, were taken captive by other tribes and returned to their homes, either through payment of ransom or by a retaliatory raid. Fluent Kwakwala speakers are familiar with the expression *u'mis'wist'as* that is used when one is angry with or frustrated by another person. It means, "may you go back to where you come from."

Other Readers have made the U'mista Cultural Center the subject of their reading in ways that have nothing to do with what we did. We did not even think about Readers when we designed the exhibit. Very simply, the exhibit turned out the way it did for two reasons: firstly, the only designer I wanted to work with was not available; secondly, I did not feel that I could tell the story of potlatch prohibition better than those people who actually experienced those terrible times. So, the exhibit texts are copies of letters, petitions, and reports, both for and against the potlatch. We did not need individual labels for the masks because we know what they are. Then, came the Readers who read all kinds of things that were not there. We certainly were not trying to confuse white visitors, or forcing any questions on them. As for the Readers' claims that we left off the labels for poetic impact, our Board of Directors, mostly fishermen, would have laughed.

In terms of Kwakwaka'wakw society, Boas and those who followed him were the consumers of our culture. They took away knowledge and treasures to distant places that had no connection to our world. Today, we have become consumers of a different kind. We are reclaiming what was lost during the "dark years," as our old people say. In recent years, on the Northwest coast, there has been a renewed interest in building canoes, an activity that had almost died out as our people adapted to motorized vessels. The detailed description of canoe construction recorded by Hunt and Boas has been invaluable to novice canoe builders. The missionaries almost succeeded in their efforts to wipe out our language, so that we utilize the Boas/Hunt texts in developing language material to teach Kwakwala to both adults and children.

Another example of the value of the Boas/Hunt material has to do with the construction of *kerfed* boxes. When one of our carvers bent his first box, he sewed it together with a twisted cedar withe. The next day, he looked at his work and found that the withe had unraveled. It was only when he referred to the Boas/Hunt volume on technology that he discovered the correct way to twist the withe.

Although Boas and Hunt did not work extensively with the *Hiʰdzakw* of Bella Bella, their work is valued there as well. A *Hiʰdzakw* friend said, "Boas certainly paved the way for doing business with our people in a more inclusive way when one considers the way the

CURATORS, COLLECTORS, AND CONSUMERS

anthros [anthropologists—ed.] of today are doing business." (P. Waterfall, personal communication, 1996). Her use of the material relates primarily to names, and she told me that her grandfather had given her son his name. Both her grandparents had very sketchy information about the history of the name. She then turned to the Boas/Hunt material and read it to the old people, who became very excited, because hearing it triggered additional information. She was then able to combine their version with the information from Boas and ended up with a complete history, which her son memorized. He wrote it out in a book form, completed with his own illustrations. She also uses the Boas/Hunt material to cross-reference names, which are still remembered while their histories are almost forgotten. These few examples of the way we "consume" the material produced by Boas and Hunt give some idea of the distance between us, the Shakers, and them, the Readers.

Following George Hunt's death in 1933, my father Dan Cranmer worked with Boas and his daughter, Helene Yampolsky, on the *Kwakiutl Grammar,* published in 1947. Franz Boas died in 1942, and I quote from a letter of condolence my father wrote to Mrs. Yampolsky, dated January 9, 1943: "The sorrowful tidings of your deep affliction reached me today and, oh my dear Helene, if only sympathy were like waves of light, how the rays would pour from my heart to illumine the gloomy veil of grief which wraps you in its somber folds." In the letter, my father refers to Boas as "my master," for whom he would sing mourning songs at an upcoming potlatch. He also mentioned that the Kwagu'[3] of Fort Rupert had sung mourning songs for Boas. I wonder how many people whom other anthropologists have studied have the same feelings of respect and affections that our people had and still have for Franz Boas?

In 1986, the descendents of Franz Boas and George Hunt gathered in Alert Bay and Fort Rupert to celebrate the centenary of the first meeting of these two remarkable men. Although the Hunts outnumbered the Boas family by several hundred, we had a great time getting to know each other. The Boas family presented us with copies of one thousand pages of the correspondence between Franz Boas and George Hunt, which has been of great value to us. Other anthropologists followed Boas into our territory, but I cannot imagine such a gathering happening with their families.

1990 marked the 10th anniversary of the opening of the U'mista Cultural Centre. At that time, my youngest brother gave a potlatch during which Dr. Norman Boas received his grandfather's name, originally given to Franz Boas in 1896. The name means, "speaking well from the beginning." Norman's wife, Doris, received the name Xwani, meaning, "swaying from side to side." The name had been given to (a young Russian anthropologist) Julia Averkieva when she accompanied Boas on his last trip of 1930-31. The decision to give these names was made by three of George Hunt's granddaughters, Agnes Cranmer nee Hunt, Helen Know, and her sister Margaret Frank, both of whom were daughters of Emily, George's oldest daughter.

George Hunt traveled to New York in 1903, to work with Franz Boas on the collections they had accumulated for the American Museum of Natural History. He kept a journal of his trip, beginning with his departure from Fort Rupert on January 24th. He named each place at which the train stopped, often adding the number of miles he had traveled, the population at each stop, and the elevation. Under one of the entries headed, "1807 miles from Fort Rupert," he wrote:

> ...and came to Keewatin and 1852 and we passed Normen and now feel like if I was in the world unknown for I did feel like I was daid man from all my relations or something like wounded duck with one wing broken. No friend near to me. O I thought how foolish I was to leave my near relations to go and pleas other man and that I only got a very short time to live in this world oh I felt sorry. But I at last made up my mind to go through with my trip.

Unfortunately, the entries stop before his arrival in New York, but there are no further regrets expressed about making the journey.

The exhibit «Chiefly Feasts», which opened at the American Museum of Natural History in 1991, was another chapter in the Boas/Hunt story. A year earlier, the curator of the exhibit, Aldona Jonaitis, invited a group of our old people to come to New York to look at the treasures that had been selected for the exhibit. Three of Hunt's grandchildren and two great-grandchildren were part of the group. So, 87 years after Hunt's lonely visit to this museum, some of his descendents came to do much the same work as he had done with Boas. This was the first time most of our group has seen the masks since they had been bought for the museum by Boas and Hunt. It was also the first time that George Hunt's detailed information on the collection was connected to individual masks, revealing that many of them belonged to the same story. Translating my great-grandfather's notes was one of the highlights of my involvement with the exhibit. Many of Hunt's descendants attended the official exhibit opening, and the Boas family was there as well. Norman Boas spoke on behalf of his family and my brother spoke on behalf of ours. Chiefly Feasts was our exhibit; I had worked on other exhibits in large museums, but Chiefly Feasts stands out as the one project to which I really felt that our people had made a significant contribution. My feeling has a lot to do with the legacy of Franz Boas and George Hunt. The exhibit was the beginning of a new relationship between Shakers and a few Readers that I hope will become widespread in the larger museum community. It brought together two different kinds of consumers, each of whom benefited from the experience in a very positive way.

In the last hundred years, the world of the Kwakwaka'wakw has changed irrevocably. Today, in common with most Native communities, we struggle with many social economic and other problems. We see the fishing industry that was the main source of income on our reserves becoming more uncertain each season, our environment being destroyed by industry and development, while the issue of land claims remains unsettled. At the same time, we strengthen what was left of our culture after the white people did their best to destroy it. In that task we are more fortunate than most indigenous groups, because we have a strong foundation to build on and for that we owe much to Hi³dzakwal's (Franz Boas) and Kixitasu' (George Hunt). *Gilakas'la, ninigad 'wi'ump* —thank you, wise forefathers.

OTHER TITLES IN THE SERIES

Contributions to Circumpolar Anthropology

Vol.1: *Gateways: Exploring the Legacy of the Jesup North Pacific Expedition, 1897–1902.* Edited by Igor Krupnik and William W. Fitzhugh. Arctic Studies Center, National Museum of Natural History, Smithsonian Institution. Washington, DC. 2001. xvi+335 pp.

Vol. 2: *Honoring Our Elders. A History of Eastern Arctic Anthropology.* Edited by William W. Fitzhugh, Stephen Loring, and Daniel Odess. Arctic Studies Center, National Museum of Natural History, Smithsonian Institution. Washington, DC. 2002. xvi+319 pp.

Vol. 3: *Akuzilleput Igaqullghet. Our Words Put to Paper. Sourcebook in St. Lawrence Island Yupik Heritage and History.* Edited by Igor Krupnik, Willis Walunga, and Vera Metcalf. Compiled by Igor Krupnik and Lars Krutak. Arctic Studies Center, National Museum of Natural History, Smithsonian Institution. Washington, DC. 2002. 464 pp.